BUSINESS PROCESS CHANGE:
Concepts, Methods and Technologies

By

Varun Grover
William J. Kettinger

Center for Information Management and Technology Research
College of Business Administration
University of South Carolina

IDEA GROUP PUBLISHING
Harrisburg, USA • London, UK

Senior Editor: Mehdi Khosrowpour
Managing Editor: Jan Travers
Printed at: Rose Printing

Published in the United States of America by
    Idea Group Publishing
    Olde Liberty Square
    4811 Jonestown Road, Suite 230
    Harrisburg, PA 17109
    Tel: 717-541-9150
    Fax: 717-541-9159

and in the United Kingdom by
    Idea Group Publishing
    3 Henrietta Street
    Covent Garden
    London WC2E 8LU
    Tel: 071-240 0856
    Fax: 071-379 0609

This publication is designed to provide accurate and authoritative information in regard to the subject matter covered. It is sold with the understanding that the publisher is not engaged in rendering legal, accounting, or other professional services. If legal advice or other expert assistance is required, the services of a competent professional person should be sought. *From A Declaration of Principles jointly adopted by a committee of the American Bar Association and a committee of publishers.*

Printed in the United States of America

Library of Congress Cataloging-in-Publication Data

Grover, Varun, 1959-
    Business process change: reengineering concepts, methods, and technologies /
Varun Grover, William J. Kettinger.
        p. 704 cm.
        Includes bibliographical references and index
        ISBN 1-878289-29-2 : $84.95
        1. Organizational change--Management. 2. Information technology--Management. 3. Strategic planning. I. Kettinger, William J. II. Title.
        HD58.8.G77 1995
        658.4'063--dc20   95-37
                                                               CIP

To Anita and Lynda who've settled for only incremental change in each of us,

and,

to Ankit, Arjun, Lindsey and David who have wonderfully begun the process of life-long change.

BUSINESS PROCESS CHANGE

...a business process is a set of logically related tasks that use the resources of an organization to achieve a defined business outcome.

Business Process Reengineering (BPR), Process Improvement, Business Transformation, Process Innovation and Business Process Redesign are terms frequently used interchangeably to represent the phenomenon of "Business Process Change."

Popular competing definitions of Business Process Change propose that it is:

"the fundamental rethinking and radical redesign of business processes to achieve dramatic improvements in critical, contemporary measures of performance"

"the analysis and design of team-based work flows and processes within and between organizations"

"a methodological process that uses information technology to radically overhaul business process and thereby attain major business goals"

"the reconfiguration of the business using IT as a central lever'

"the overhauling of business processes and organization structures that limit the competitiveness effectiveness and efficiency of the organization"

"the design of a company's core processes to yield breakthrough levels of improvement, laying the basis for continuous improvement"

"a strategy driven organizational initiative to (re)design business processes to achieve competitive breakthroughs in performance; differing in scope from process improvement to radical new process design, contingent upon the degree of socio-technical change required"

This phenomenon is typically known to:

involve **CROSS FUNCTIONAL CORE PROCESSES**
but
many improvement initiatives within narrower functional areas have also proved successful.

focus on **RADICAL/ONE TIME** process changes
but
continuous improvement through stewardship of processes may be more beneficial in the long term.

This phenomenon is typically known to:

takes a **CLEAN SLATE** approach
but
most process change methodologies advocate documentation and
analysis of existing "as is" processes and many firms are unwilling
to commit resources for clean slate "revolutionary" implementation.

be **STRATEGY LED** with initiatives from senior management
but
some bottom-up process change initiatives, with strong inputs from
line workers and middle mangers, have proven successful.

strive for **BREAKTHROUGH PERFORMANCE GAINS**
but
benchmarking and measurement of these gains can prove elusive
and in many cases moderate gains more consistent with organizational culture and orientation define success.

be **INFORMATION TECHNOLOGY ENABLED**
but
numerous organizational innovations involving people, jobs, skills
and structures can also facilitate new process oriented behaviors.

be **CUSTOMER DRIVEN** with value defined as satisfaction
but
some scholars and practitioners advocate a longer-term and more
strategic perspective to overcome the possible myopia of immediate
customer demands in order to discover new ways to benefit future as
well as present stakeholders.

enhance individual capacities through **EMPOWERMENT AND
TEAMS**
but
many process change projects are defended based on cost objectives
achieved through downsizing and outsourcing with few opportunities for retraining, team work or reallocation of decision rights.

adapt a number of **METHODS** touted by armies of consultants
but
few standardized and structured approaches exist.

This phenomenon is typically known to:

minimize redundancy, maximize concurrency toward a
VIRTUAL SYSTEM
but
many successful process change efforts have benefited from simple efficiency improvements without fully exploiting or optimizing the best utilization of a virtual enterprise's resources and knowledge.

be run by **OUTSIDERS** such as consultants
but
the lack of concern for maintaining new business processes once reengineered has caused process management responsibilities to shift toward internal managers closer to the processes and more vested in the business.

> Thus, the (r)evolution of reengineering, the requirement to sustain and integrate process change, the need to reconcile alternative process improvement and management approaches, and the recognition of organizational constraints to implementation, all serve to broaden the concept of BUSINESS PROCESS CHANGE, recognizing the need for the radical, the incremental, the continuous and the contingent.

FOREWORD

This book was conceived during a period of tumultuous change in the global business environment. Corporations were undergoing massive restructuring. Global competition, sluggish economies and the potential offered by emerging technologies were pushing firms to fundamentally rethink their business processes.

Prominent consultants seeking to provide solutions to these problems prescribed Business Process Reengineering (BPR) as a means to restructure aging bureaucratized processes in an attempt to achieve the strategic objectives of increased efficiency, reduced costs, improved quality, and greater customer satisfaction. These consultants typically repackaged existing change theories and techniques of organizational structure, technology, operations, quality, and human resources in a new and exciting synthesis directed at dramatic improvements in business performance.

BPR soon became the rage! Endless magazine articles heralded claims or tremendous payoffs resulting from process change. The popularity of BPR was in part fueled by claims of high pay-offs from early BPR projects. For example, Ford Motor Co. and AT&T reported major increases in productivity and decreases in staff after process reengineering and DEC was able to consolidate 55 accounting groups into five. Kodak reengineered its 1,500-employee black and white film operations by focusing on customer satisfaction and cut costs 15% below budget; cut response time in half; and dramatically reduced defects. Other early reengineering success stories include: Hallmark's product development process, Bell Atlantic's system billing process, an similar examples at GE, IBM's Credit Corp., Capitol Holdings, Taco Bell, Wal-Mart, CIGNA RE, XEROX and Banc One.

Ironically, while much has been discussed about BPR, most companies are still searching for theories and methods to better manage business process change. Academics are also now beginning to recognize the need to study this phenomenon, but precious little has been published. Basic questions lack consistent answers:

- What does process change entail?
- What are key enablers of process change?
- Is there a process change methodology?
- What techniques and tools have been found to successfully model and redesign business processes?
- What is the role of information technology in this change?
- What is the role of Information Systems personnel in changing business processes?
- What is the role of people empowerment and team-based manage-

ment in process change?
- How do we best plan, organize and control process change efforts?
- Under what conditions will BPR be most effective?

Answers to these questions are not easy, nor direct. Pondering these same questions from our "steamy southern" vantage point in the Summer of 1993, we recognized there was little impartial and scholarly analysis of this compelling management trend. A book idea was born! But where should we look for quality contributions on this topic?

Managers from firms that had actually undergone BPR? —These seasoned process "changees" certainly could provide important hands-on insights. But cursory descriptions of their experiences had been covered by the popular press. The time was right for moving beyond simple "lessons learned" to understanding models and attributes of successful BPR.

Management consultants and vendors? Many had been "doing" BPR for more than five years. They had a lot to add! But we, like many, were leery that books prepared exclusively by consultants may be motivated more by the desire to sell proprietary theories and methods, than to uncover the "truths" of BPR. Some balance was needed!

Management and Information Systems Academics? Well, we knew that they were interested in this topic — it involves addressing fundamental organizational and technological paradigms upon which much of their research is based. But up to that point, little real scholarly contributions had been set forth in the literature.

Ultimately, we were resolved that if a presentation was structured and balanced, each group had great potential as distinguished contributors. A decision was made — "Design a book and they will Come!" We are happy to report that they came! In this refereed book we have assembled enlightening contributions from the most eminent academics and practitioners in the field of Process Change. Their caliber is reflected in the enclosed chapters. Given the embryonic stage of the research on this topic, reading and discussing the chapter submissions has been a wonderful learning experience for the editors. And the diversity of perspectives provided opens up avenues for fresh thinking on this phenomenon. The authors represent both North American and European viewpoints, private and public sector perspectives, academic, consultant and managerial frames of reference and material is presented using case studies, empirical studies, conceptual frameworks and tutorials. We are deeply indebted to the authors for their contributions, their responsiveness to suggestions for changes and their overall enthusiasm in producing this quality endeavor.

On a final note, we have observed an evolution of the process reegineering concept through the development cycle of this book. This evolution is noted by Thomas Davenport in his insightful opening chapter and other prominent authors in this book. The radical tone of the concept while initially "hyped" has been somewhat tempered after a degree of contextual realism has set in. Further, reconciliation with other (more incremental) process change programs has resulted in the evolution toward a broader, yet more powerful process management concept.

V.G.
W.J.K.

BOOK ORGANIZATION

We recognize that senior managers are still familiarizing themselves with this concept and want to move beyond consultant and vendor recommendations to become in-house experts on BPR. At the same time academics desire information for both pedagogical and research purposes. Throughout this book we have made a concerted effort to offer a significant body of fresh knowledge on which future work can be grounded, provide a diversity of perspectives and treatments, maintain a healthy balance between academic scholarship and relevance, and include chapters that are visually stimulating and eminently readable.

The twenty-five chapters compiled in this book offer such variety in their treatment of this topic that functionalizing them by imposing a rigid structure on their organization might undermine the integrated nature of the phenomenon being examined. Nevertheless, we offer a general structure for this book that will guide the organization of articles and the flow of the book, while preserving its integrity in stimulating debate. The diagram below illustrates the transformation over time of the business process from a state of dynamic equilibrium with individuals and roles, strategy, structure, and technology to another point of relative equilibrium. This "business process change" is facilitated by multiple diverse entities. These are represented under the categories of information technology, meth-

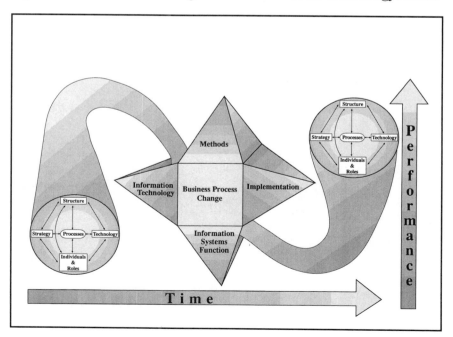

ods, implementation and the information systems function. Each of these entities can be comprised of a number of ideas, frameworks, theories, concepts and perspectives.

As shown in the figure below, the book can be divided into 5 major parts:

- Part I (Overview) examines the concept of process change, its major technological and organizational enablers, the importance of information management and some theoretical foundations.

- Part II (Information Technology) evaluates the centrality of information technology in process change, lessons from an information technology planning paradigm, and specific hardware and software initiatives.

- Part III (Methods) provides a generic methodology and a powerful repertoire of tools and techniques for modeling and evaluating process change.

- Part IV (Implementation) deals with the organizational problems in conducting process change, including issues related to individual attitudes, politics, teams and management of change.

- Part V (The Information Systems Function) examines the role of IS professionals in process change and the impact of process change on the systems development process and the IS function in general.

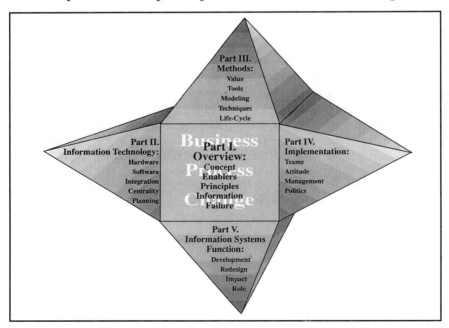

ACKNOWLEDGMENTS

The process we followed for creating this refereed manuscript included a number of steps. First, we requested proposals for chapters in an open solicitation. These proposals were evaluated with respect to the goals of the book and feedback was provided to the authors. In some cases proposals were rejected outright if they did not match the intent of the book. Next, completed manuscripts were received and put through an anonymous review process. Each manuscript was reviewed by two reviewers, one internal and one external. Detailed guidelines were provided to each reviewer regarding the purpose of the book and the types of papers desired. If the manuscript was acceptable to both reviewers (subject to minor revisions), the author(s) was invited to revise the manuscript. Manuscripts that were unacceptable to both reviewers were rejected. If there was disagreement among the reviewers, the editors extracted the major concerns and sent a letter to the author(s) providing them the option of resubmission with a major revision. In some cases these manuscripts were eventually rejected or went through additional rounds of review.

Clearly, in the above process the reviewers played a critical role. We wish to express our gratitude to the reviewers who critiqued the original manuscripts and in all cases provided detailed written feedback. Their sincerity and dedication to the work they undertook is highly appreciated. The following individuals through their review of chapters, advice and support deserve special thanks. These are Tom Davenport, Kirk Fiedler, Bob Galliers, Kirk Karwan, Al Lederer, Don Marchand, Lynne Markus, Manoj Malhotra, Nancy Melone, James McKeen, Vicki Mitchell, Arun Rai, Rajiv Sabherwal, James Teng and Al Segars.

We would also like to express appreciation for the support provided us by the Center for Information Management and Technology Research at the University of South Carolina. In particular, we owe a special round of applause to Midge Burgess who was instrumental in keeping our house in order. Through her patience, care and attention to organization, we were able to complete this project successfully. A final note of thanks goes to our families for their patience, support, and a modicum of food stains, allowing us to complete this project within an ambitious time frame.

February 23, 1995   **V.G.**
                                              W.J.K.

BUSINESS PROCESS CHANGE:
Concepts, Methods and Technologies

Table of Contents

INTRODUCTION
Business Process Reengineering: Where It's Been,
Where It's Going
> Thomas H. Davenport, University of Texas, Austin

Chapter 1
Technological and Organizational Enablers of
Business Process Reengineering
> Varun Grover, University of South Carolina
> James T.C. Teng, University of South Carolina
> Kirk D. Fiedler, University of South Carolina

Chapter 2
Business Process Redesign : A Framework for
Harmonizing People, Information and Technology
> Donald A. Marchand, International Institute for
> Management Development (IMD), Switzerland
> Michael J. Stanford, IMD, Switzerland

Chapter 3
Business Process Reengineering: Theory and
Practice — Views from the Field
> Paul E. Cule, Georgia State University

Chapter 4
Understanding Business Process Reengineering:
A Sociocognitive Contingency Model
> Matthew J. Klempa, Klempa & Associates

INTRODUCTION

Business Process Reengineering:
Where It's Been, Where It's Going

Thomas H. Davenport
University of Texas, Austin

Business process reengineering is the most popular business concept of the 1990's. Celebrated in best-selling books (in the U.S., Japan, Brazil, and many countries in Europe), articles in every major business publication, conferences, and even several videotapes, reengineering has penetrated into every continent except Antarctica. Thousands of companies and public sector organizations have initiated reengineering initiatives. Internal and external consultants on the topic have proliferated dramatically. Many universities have created courses on the topic for business school students.

Perhaps the greatest testimony to the concept of reengineering is the number of people who have adopted the term to describe what they do. Within organizations there are many different types of activities that are described as "reengineering," ranging from incremental process streamlining to headcount reductions and even new information systems.

Within the reengineering literature, however, which is quite voluminous, there is a much higher level of consistency about the meaning of the term.[1] Reengineering generally means the radical redesign of broad, cross-functional business processes with the objective of order-of-magnitude performance gains, often with the aid of information technology. The most common variation from this definition views reengineering not as change in processes alone, but as a general organizational transformation—though in my view this is an inappropriate extension of the term (Davenport and Stoddard, 1994).

One can only speculate as to why reengineering is so popular. When it was initially adopted in the United States (and in Europe and Japan), a recession was underway, which may have stimulated managers to search for new ways to reduce operating costs. However, the U.S. recession is over, and reengineering's popularity endures. Strassman (1994) speculates that reengineering's popularity relates to its focus on white-collar processes at a time when the proportion of white-collar employees in organizations has increased. Another possible explanation is that companies have spent vast amounts of money on information technology, and wanted to make better use of the resource by tying it to process changes. Finally, it is possible that reengineering's popularity is purely a matter of promotion by some of its creators. The concept offers so much potential benefit to consultants, IT vendors, and systems integrators that their publicity itself was an important causal factor.

Origins of Reengineering

Some argue that reengineering is new; others that there is nothing new about reengineering. They are both right. The "components" of reengineering all existed prior to 1990, when the first articles on the topic were published. However, these components had not previously been assembled in one management concept. Reengineering is new, therefore, only as a new synthesis of previously existing ideas.

The component ideas themselves came from multiple sources that cut across academic disciplines and business functions. The idea of managing and improving business processes comes primarily from the quality or continuous process improvement literature, which itself modified the process concept from industrial engineering concepts extending back to the turn of the century and Frederick Taylor. The notion of working on broad, cross-functional processes is somewhat more recent, but is certainly at least implicit in the value chain concept popularized by Michael Porter, and the concurrent engineering and design-for-manufacturing concepts employed in the manufacturing industry (Vogt, 1988; Schonberger, 1990).

Another key aspect of reengineering is the "clean slate" design of processes. Although firms often disregard existing constraints in designing a new business process, the constraints must be taken into account during implementation unless a new organizational unit is created. In any case, this idea is not new to reengineering. It was used prior to the reengineering concept at General Motors (in the Saturn project), at the Topeka pet food factory of General Foods in the early 1970s (Walton, 1977), and in the First Direct subsidiary of Midland Bank. The idea of such a greenfield site has been explored in the work design literature (Lawler, 1978).

Reengineering typically involves the use of information technology to enable new ways of working. This idea has been discussed since the initial application of information technology to business, though often not executed. It is present in the concept of the business analyst function, and was also frequently expressed in the context of the strategic or competitive system.

Each of the component concepts of reengineering, however, had some "flaw"—at least from the perspective of someone desiring reengineering-oriented change. Quality-oriented business processes were too narrow, and relied too heavily on bottom-up change, to yield radical new work designs. The idea of broader, cross-functional processes was limited to certain domains and to manufacturing industries. Greenfield change before reengineering often involved an entire organization at a single site, with no smaller, exportable unit like a process. Finally, while the notion that IT could change work was powerful, the business analysts or other purveyors of IT could not by themselves create a context in which radical organizational change could occur. Reengineering appeared to "solve" all of these shortcomings.

In terms of how the reengineering synthesis was created, IT-oriented management consultants (most of whom were also or formerly academics) deserve most of the blame or credit. The idea of redesigning business processes with the aid of IT was "kicking around" various consulting firms in the mid-to-late 1980's. I was working at Index Group (now a unit of Computer Sciences), and the term was mentioned frequently by some consultants, particularly those working to change management processes.[2] The concept was also mentioned in internally-published articles or presentations I have seen from Nolan, Norton & Company (now a unit of KPMG Peat Marwick) and McKinsey & Company. However, in none of these cases was there any evidence of deep understanding of the phenomenon at this time.

Index Group and Michael Hammer had a multi-client research program at this time called "Partnership for Research in Information Systems Management;" I directed this program. In 1987 we researched the topic of "Cross-Functional Systems." In this research we discovered that several firms (including Mutual Benefit Life and Ford) had adopted many of the components of reengineering, particularly using IT to make dramatic improvements in cross-functional processes. Michael Hammer learned more about these firms when he asked managers from them to speak at a conference on the subject.

I left Index in 1988, and Michael Hammer and I (in my case with Jim Short, then at MIT and now at London Business School) independently began writing articles on the topic. Short and John Rockart, also at MIT, had just completed an article suggesting IT's greatest use was in enabling change in cross-functional processes (Rockart and Short, 1989). Short and I viewed our article as a much more detailed elaboration of what that idea meant. We collected several examples of firms that had done what we viewed as reengineering (though we didn't like the term then, and I still don't), and tried to abstract from the examples some maxims and general steps to follow. Our article was published in June of 1990; Michael Hammer's more popular and exhortatory version emerged a few weeks later.

The reaction to these articles was very positive, and many companies began reengineering projects or brought previous efforts under the reengineering banner. Some early and particularly aggressive adopters included Mutual Benefit Life Insurance, IBM, Cigna, Xerox, and Bell Atlantic. Many consulting firms began to repackage their existing expertise (in continuous improvement, systems analysis, industrial engineering, cycle time reduction, etc.) to claim that they knew all about reengineering.[3] In the summer of 1991 one analyst of the consulting industry told me he had counted more than 100 firms offering reengineering services.[4]

Firms also began to reinterpret their previous experiences in reengineering terms. For example, of the oft-described reengineering projects at Ford (accounts payable process), IBM Credit (financing quotation process) and Mutual Benefit Life (new policy issue process), none were undertaken as "reengineering" initiatives. Another common reengineering success story, the food preparation process at Taco Bell, was not undertaken in a reengineering context. After it was successful and widely described as reengineering, Taco Bell executives decided that they would undertake another project—this time using formal reengineering methods and a well-known reengineering consulting firm. This time the project failed, primarily because of insufficient senior management sponsorship.[5]

Beginning around 1992, academics began to publish research on reengineering. Like the consultants, most of them came from the information technology field. Some wrote on reengineering in general (Short and Venkatraman, 1992; Grover, Fiedler and Teng, 1993; Earl, 1994), others on the specific relationship to IT (Grover, Fiedler, and Teng, 1994). Some of the most useful academic projects focused on empirical analysis of results and trends across multiple reengineering engagements (Jarvenpaa and Stoddard, 1993), and on the course of reengineering over time in a single company (Caron,

Jarvenpaa, and Stoddard, 1994). The collection in this volume is, however, by far the greatest concentration of academic work on the subject published thus far.

As I write in late 1994, it would appear that a backlash to reengineering is beginning to occur. There have been for some time articles in the trade and consulting press suggesting that reengineering projects have a high "failure" rate, though it is not exactly clear what this term means. The figure of a 70% failure rate was originally mentioned by Hammer and Champy, though both have since recanted this statement. Success and failure in reengineering is a complex phenomenon, and might be equated to success and failure in strategic planning. Many plans are created that never get fully implemented (Mintzberg, 1993). If we view a reengineering initiative as creating a strategic plan for how work will be done in the future, we should expect that many such plans will not be implemented as designed. We should also be aware that there are other benefits to planning that may accrue even if the plan is not implemented; these include learning, providing motivation for change, and communicating intentions.

Critics of reengineering generally focus on narrow aspects of the concept. One book by popular business strategists, for example, equates reengineering with cost reduction, and argues that firms cannot thrive unless they focus on the future rather than reducing costs of existing processes (Hamel and Prahalad, 1994). Given the rapid rise of the reengineering concept and the level of publicity and hype surrounding it, it is inevitable that some deflation of the concept will occur. But there are some valid concerns about reengineering. If IT-enabled radical process change is to avoid becoming just another (though a particularly prominent) management fad, I believe the movement must change in ways detailed below.

Reengineering Rhetoric vs. Reality

A critical factor in the understanding of reengineering is the difference between what it is supposed to be and what it is. This difference is most pronounced with respect to the radicalness of process change. As described above, reengineering espouses radical, order-of-magnitude change; its advocates urge taking a "clean sheet of paper" approach to work design. I argued, for example, in a relatively moderate form of this rhetoric, that:

> Process innovation initiatives start with a relatively clean slate, rather than from the existing process. The fundamental business objectives for the process may be determined, but the means of accomplishing them is not. Designers of the new process must ask themselves, "Regardless of how we have

accomplished this objective in the past, what is the best possible way to do it now?" (Davenport, 1993, p. 11)

In practice, many companies do take a clean sheet approach to *designing* a process. Design teams attempt to imagine "the best of all processes" without regard to constraints of existing information systems or organizational factors. Not surprisingly, the new process designs that many firms have shared with me are quite radical, with ambitious plans for new technologies, new skills, and new organizational structures.

The problem, of course, comes at implementation time. Few firms can afford to "obliterate" their existing business environments and start from scratch. Assuming that the organization is not disillusioned by this realization (and many are, contributing to the "failure" rate mentioned above), it proceeds to implement the new process incrementally. Thus the general rule for reengineering is "revolutionary design, evolutionary implementation." I have observed this pattern many times in my research and consulting work, and it has been confirmed in a more rigorous study of 35 reengineering projects (Jarvenpaa and Stoddard, 1993).

Where Reengineering is Going

There are several possible futures for reengineering. One is the ultimate fate of all management enthusiasms, as described by Richard Pascale (Pascale, 1990). He describes the rise and eventual fall of such movements as "one minute managing," "Theory Z," and more academically respectable topics like the use of decision trees. Reengineering has many features of such fads, including a prominent guru, a best-selling book, and extravagant claims of effectiveness. It may be impossible to prevent the decline of reengineering in terms of managerial and press attention.

Another possible future for reengineering is that it will become embedded, either in whole or in part, in other, more traditional approaches to business change. I know of several companies, for example, in which the strategic planning process has been modified to address issues of which processes should be reengineered. Reengineering is also being embedded in information systems development approaches and methods; the idea is to identify needed process changes before building a system to support the process. Reengineering might also be embedded in quality programs, which is an important topic unto itself.

Integrated Process Management

Despite the likelihood of reduced management attention for

reengineering and its embeddedness in other activities, there are some obvious means of extending its useful life. In the early days of the movement, for example, it was important to distinguish reengineering from less radical continuous improvement approaches. In practice, however, firms often seek to combine radical and incremental process changes within the same initiative. They may design a radically different process, but implement incremental improvements in the short term. Further, some methods and techniques found in more traditional process improvement programs, e.g., process value analysis and root cause analysis, are frequently useful in reengineering initiatives, particularly for diagnosing existing processes. Finally, the groups that support quality and reengineering programs in organizations are becoming more closely affiliated, and even merging in some cases (including DuPont, IBM, Ford, American Express, and Eastman Chemical).

Therefore, one obvious direction for reengineering is better integration with other approaches to process management. Some firms, for example, are beginning to construct a "portfolio" of process change programs, just as they might have a portfolio of financial investments. The portfolio includes some high-risk, high-reward reengineering programs, and some that are more incrementally-oriented and thus more likely to be implemented. In some such firms the senior management team has a sufficient understanding of alternative process change approaches to decide on appropriate uses of continuous improvement, traditional industrial engineering-oriented approaches (Rummler and Brache 1990), and reengineering. This requires not only a good knowledge of process improvement techniques, but also a high-level understanding of the current processes of the organization.

An even more integrated approach to process management would be to pull tools from a variety of process change approaches to construct a hybrid process design and implementation technique (e.g., to combine process value analysis with IT enablement and quality function deployment, each of which comes from a different process change tradition). This already happens to some degree within many reengineering initiatives in firms, but it has not been formalized.

The institutionalization of process management involves not only the redesign of business processes, but also changes in other management domains to create a process orientation. These include process-based measurement and information systems, process-based organizational structures, process-based management approaches (e.g., budgeting and resource allocation), etc. At present firms may undertake these after redesigning a business process, but changing them may offer more rapid benefit than the process design/ pilot/implementation cycle firms typically employ.

At one high-technology manufacturing firm, for example, two processes were selected for change. In the order management process a highly aggressive, exemplary approach to reengineering was adopted. A radical new work design was created that would employ significant new IT and human process enablers. After a year of design and pilot work, however, managers decided that the design was too expensive to implement and required too much change in organizational structure. An entirely new effort to reengineer the process was undertaken.

The other initiative was a logistics or supply chain management process. Instead of a typical design and implementation project, the management team for the process decided to focus on other levers of change. They created for the first time worldwide visibility of inventory levels across the company. They put managers in charge of the entire supply chain process for large geographical regions, and based much of their compensation on meeting inventory goals. Within a year, inventory levels had declined 30%. In summary, the fastest and most effective route to improvement may not be through traditional reengineering projects.

Process management may extend the useful life of reengineering in companies, particularly if a backlash against overly aggressive reengineering approaches develops. However, this idea may be too moderate and rational a message to inspire much frenzy in the marketplace. It is much more exciting to adopt a "new and different" approach to change than to realize that it is related to previous approaches.

Reengineering Knowledge Work

Most reengineering projects have involved relatively adminstrative processes such as order management or customer service. There exists a large opportunity for reengineering or improving knowledge work processes, e.g., new product development, management, system development, and professional service processes. For many companies these processes are significant sources of new revenue.

Knowledge work processes are difficult to reengineer because of the autonomy of knowledge workers, but they may be well-suited to improvement-oriented approaches. In some preliminary research on the knowledge work processes of ten companies, several stated that reengineering was too top-down and too structured a process for the kind of workers involved in their processes. They had adopted more incremental and participative process change techniques, and had focused more on process outputs and organizational structure (creating teams or co-locating workers) than on detailed work flows.

A non-traditional approach to reengineering that may be particularly appropriate for knowledge work is the use of ethnographic techniques to understand in detail the nature and context of the process under analysis. The assumption behind this approach, which as been most prominently advocated by the Institute for Research on Learning, is that the flow and activities of work processes are highly contingent and contextually based (Brown and Duguid, 1991). Unless the situational variables determining how work gets done are fully understood, it will be impossible to make changes that will be adopted by workers. This approach to reengineering has been adopted for knowledge work processes by such firms as Nynex, Hoffman-LaRoche, and Sun Microsystems.

Rapid Reengineering

A problem for existing approaches to reengineering is the cycle time for delivering results. Even the fastest project involves roughly six months to assemble a team, decide what to do, and then to create a new design. Implementation takes much longer; a year to implement a radical new process design is quite aggressive. This timeframe is not consistent with the short-term cultures of American and Western businesses, and the consequent impatience of senior executives for measureable results.

Therefore, a third future direction for reengineering might involve simply speeding up the cycle time for reengineering. Some firms have already adopted a "dual path implementation" approach in their reengineering initiatives, which emphasizes rapid implementation of improvements in the context of longer-term and more radical process change. Rapid reengineering might also involve the use of information systems packages as enablers of processes, and a "design for implementability" orientation. The use of rapid design and implementation approaches has been explored recently by researchers within the sociotechnical systems tradition (Pasmore, 1994).

Reengineering for Value and Growth

Most firms have had headcount and cost reduction as their primary benefit objectives for reengineering, but it is equally possible to use the approach to make products and services more attractive in the marketplace. This has already been the case in firms that have attempted to use reengineering to, for example, reduce the cycle time for new product development, or to improve the effectiveness of customer service processes.

This would seem to be a reengineering approach that is better-suited to the growing U.S. economy than cost-oriented reengineering. It would also be more appealing to employees, and could be tied to empowerment programs and design approaches that let employees who do the work do some design. Because growth-oriented processes are more likely to involve knowledge work, this emphasis might be combined with the focus on knowledge work processes described above.

A related aspect of this future direction for reengineering is a focus on changes in the business network for an organization or its overall business scope, rather than simply on internal business processes. As noted by several researchers (Davidson, 1993; Venkatraman, 1994), the same notions of radical process change used to address internal processes can be applied to the basic products and services offered by a firm, and the relationships a firm has with its business partners. Some examples of this type of change include the work of Federal Express' Business Logistics Service with its customers, Baxter Healthcare's inventory management services for hospitals, and relationships between automotive component suppliers and automobile manufacturers such as Ford and Toyota. With awareness of these examples, the term "reengineering" should not now be taken to mean only the redesign of internal business processes.

Summary

Reengineering may have aspects of faddishness or management myth, but there are timeless aspects to it as well. It will always be important for firms to improve how they do work, sometimes incrementally and sometimes radically. It will always be necessary to use information technology not to automate existing modes of work, but to enable new work processes. Even when attention inevitably shifts to the next management nostrum, the factors that made reengineering popular will still be present, and its approaches will still be useful.

But reengineering will also always be complex and difficult. As indicated by the wide variety of chapters and issues addressed in this volume, it has many different facets and success factors. Successful redesign and implementation of a cross-functional business process amounts to major organizational change, not unlike massive restructuring, major product line changes, or a merger or acquisition. As such, the percentage of organizations that fail to fully implement their new process designs will always be high.

One might even argue that the best organizations are those that never or rarely have to resort to reengineering. If a company's processes are continually being refined and improved through less dramatic and risky change approaches, there might never be a need for a step-function change. Some companies, such as Motorola and General Electric, seem to have internalized this notion. They have created broad "umbrellas" for process change (called "Six Sigma" and "WorkOut", respectively) that encourage managers and workers to continually seek better ways to do work. Judging by these firms' financial performance over the period of the change programs, their change approaches are well-suited to their business environments. Interestingly, both firms now refer to their change programs as combinations of reengineering and quality.

What these companies have really done is to go beyond the faddism of reengineering and address issues of process management. They have embraced techniques from a variety of different change approaches, including reengineering, and have employed aspects of top-down and bottom-up change. They have, on occasion, designed radically different new process visions, and have implemented those visions in an incremental fashion. They have focused their improvement efforts not on eliminating jobs, but on eliminating needless work so that employees can focus on activities that add value for customers. In short, these firms have anticipated the future direction for reengineering.

Endnotes

[1] In chronological order, the earliest articles and books on reengineering have been Davenport and Short, 1990; Hammer, 1990; Davenport, 1993; Hammer and Champy, 1993.

[2] This early interest in management process reengineering is somewhat ironic given that few such processes have been the subject of reengineering initiatives. The most frequent advocate of this sort of work at Index has been Gary Gulden.

[3] Indeed, I read one consulting proposal—from Andersen Consulting, though I am sure it might easily have been from other firms—saying boldly, "We invented reengineering." One wonders what invention means in this context, particularly when nothing on the subject was published by this organization.

[4] Conversation with Bruce Rogow, then of Gartner Group.

[5] The Taco Bell "success story" is described in Hammer and Champy, 1990, pp. 171-181, and in Schlesinger, 1992. The subsequent failure was described to me in conversation by a Taco Bell senior manager.

References

Brown, J.S. and Duguid, P. "Organizational Learning and Communities of Practice: Toward a Unified View of Working, Learning, and Innovation," *Organization Science* (2:1), 1991, pp. 40-57.

Caron, J.R., Jarvenpaa, S.L., and Stoddard, D.B., "Business Reengineering at CIGNA Corporation: Experiences and Lessons From the First Five Years," *MIS Quarterly* (18:3), September 1994, pp. 233-250.

Davenport, T.H. *Process Innovation,* Harvard Business School Press, Boston, 1993.

Davenport, T.H. and Short, J.E. "The New Industrial Engineering: Information Technology and Business Process Redesign," *Sloan Management Review*, Summer 1990, pp. 11-27.

Davenport, T.H. and Stoddard, D.B., "Reengineering: Business Change of Mythic Proportions?" *MIS Quarterly* (18:2), June 1994, pp. 121-128.

Davidson, W.H. "Beyond reengineering: the three phases of business transformation," *IBM Systems Journal* 32:1 (1993), pp. 65-79.

Earl, M.J., "The New and the Old of Business Process Redesign," *Journal of Strategic Information Systems* (3:1), 1994, pp. 5-22.

Grover, V., Fiedler, K.D., and Teng, J.T.C., "Business Process Redesign: An Integrated Planning Framework," *Omega: The International Journal of Management Science* (21:4), 1993, pp. 433-447.

Grover, V., Fiedler, K.D., and Teng, J.T.C., "Exploring the Success of Information Technology Enabled Business Process Reengineering," *IEEE Transactions on Engineering Management* (41:3), August, 1994, pp. 276-284.

Hamel, G. and Prahalad, C.K., *Competing for the Future*, Harvard Business School Press, Boston, 1994.

Jarvenpaa, S.L. and Stoddard, D.B., "Managing IT-Enabled Radical Change," research proposal, University of Texas at Austin/Harvard Business School, 1993.

Lawler, E.E., "The New Plant Revolution," *Organizational Dynamics*, Winter 1978, pp. 2-12.

Hammer, M., "Reengineering Work: Don't Automate, Obliterate," *Harvard Business Review*, Summer 1990, pp. 104-112.

Hammer, M. and Champy, J.A., *Reengineering the Corporation*, Harper Business, New York, 1993.

Mintzberg, H., *The Rise and Fall of Strategic Planning*, The Free Press, New York, 1993.

Pascale, R., *Managing on the Edge*, Simon & Schuster, New York, 1990.

Pasmore, W.A. *Creating Strategic Change: Designing the flexible, high-performing organization*, Wiley, New York, 1994.

Rockart, J.F. and Short, J.E., "IT in the 1990s: Managing Organizational Interdependence," *Sloan Management Review*, Winter 1989, pp. 7-16.

Rummler, G.A. and Brache, A.P., *Improving Performance: How to Manage the White Space on the Organization Chart*, Jossey-Bass, San Francisco, 1990.

Schlesinger, L., "Taco Bell," Harvard Business School case study, case # 692-058, 1992.

Schonberger, R. *Building a Chain of Customers*, Free Press, New York, 1990.

Short, J.E. and Venkatraman, N., "Beyond Business Process Redesign: Redefining Baxter's Business Network," *Sloan Management Review*, Fall, 1992, pp. 7-21.

Strassman, P. *The Politics of Information Management*, Information Economics Press, New Canaan, CT, 1994.

Venkatraman, N. "IT-Enabled Business Transformation: From Automation to Business Scope Redefinition," *Sloan Management Review*, Winter 1994, pp. 73-87.

Vogt, C.F., "Beyond CAD and CAM: Design for Manufacturability," *Design News*, March 7, 1988, pp. 18-19.

Walton, R.E., "Work Innovations at Topeka: After Six Years," *Journal of Applied Behavioral Science* (13), 1977, pp. 422-433.

Part I

Overview

Chapter 1
Technological and Organizational Enablers of Business Process Reengineering
Grover, Teng, and Fiedler

Many organizations are undergoing major changes in structure and management practice in order to be viable in today's competitive environment. Business process reengineering (BPR) efforts have been undertaken by numerous firms to redesign age old business processes. This chapter develops a framework for process change. The model shows how various functional activities involved in a business process may be fundamentally reconfigured, through the reduction of physical coupling and the enhancement of information coupling, to achieve breakthrough performance gains. Based on this model of process change, a suitable path for process reconfiguration may then be selected. Information technology and organizational catalysts for such reconfiguration are then identified and discussed.   In conclusion, the model is extended to derive implications for organizational transformation.

Chapter 2
Business Process Redesign: A Framework for Harmonizing People, Information and Technology
Marchand and Stanford

This chapter evaluates the role of information management in business process reengineering (BPR). The chapter addresses issues in information management in the context of a business restructuring or transformation framework through which business process reengineering can be channeled so that a company's BPR efforts are linked closely with other critical dimensions of change management such as the way a company is configured, the culture and behavior of its people as well as its processes of coordination. The chapter then focuses on the role of information management as a key dimension of BPR. As companies develop their BPR efforts, explicit consideration must be given to improving the ways information is or is not deployed and used within business processes. Based on the experience of global manufacturing companies with BPR in the 1980's and early 1990's, the authors highlight nine information management principles that are central to successful reengineering efforts in manufacturing companies and which can also be useful for managers involved in BPR in white collar and service companies. This chapter describes each of these principles and how information issues should be addressed in BPR. The chapter suggests that information management should be harmonized with the ways people and technology are deployed in transforming business processes and viewed as a critical factor influencing the success or failure of BPR efforts.

Chapter 3
Business Process Reengineering: Theory and Practice—Views from the Field
Cule

Increasingly, companies are turning to business process reengineering as a means of increasing their competitiveness in an ever more challenging global environment. Many of these efforts at reengineering are marred by failure. In this chapter a context is provided for reengineering and a model proposed that may provide an explicative capability in understanding why some reengineering efforts fail and thus may lead to better prescriptions for success. A range of approaches to business process reengineering is discussed and a categorization of companies based on the range is suggested. The results of a small study are discussed within the context of the proposed model to further explore the model. The roles of consultants, as perceived by study respondents, are discussed. Implications of this model and the study findings to practitioners and managers are suggested.

Chapter 4
Understanding Business Process Reengineering:
A Sociocognitive Contingency Model
Klempa

This chapter conceptualizes BPR innovation as a multiplicative interaction among three innovation metaforces—organization culture, organization learning, and knowledge sharing.   These three innovation metaforces determine the organization's positioning on a homeostatic (BPR improvement) / morphogenetic (BPR innovation) organization change continuum. The innovation metaforces establish the organization's BPR propensity, BPR capability, and BPR implementation effectiveness. Drawing upon structuration theory, the metaforces are both an antecedent to, and consequence of, organization actions. This BPR innovation dynamic involves interactions among the formal organization, informal organization, the organization's frame of reference, and information technology. The recursive dynamic occurs at three levels -CEO and top management team, BPR team, and the individual.   The chapter explicates resistance to change cybernetically, suggesting customization of individual interventions, according to placement on the individual change curve. The chapter discusses managerial application of the model, including organization culture, organization learning, and knowledge sharing interventions. The chapter synopsizes future research venues, including positivist research, as well as four interpretive research modalities—ethnography, hermeneutics, hermeneutic ethnography, and action research.

Technological and Organizational Enablers of Business Process Reengineering

Varun Grover
James T.C. Teng
Kirk D. Fiedler
University of South Carolina

Many contemporary organizations are undertaking the critical analysis and redesign of their business processes to achieve breakthrough improvements in performance. Commonly referred to as Business Process Reengineering (BPR), a 1993 CSC/Index survey of 224 IS executives found that 72% had a process improvement initiative underway (Champy, 1993). Another study by Deloitte & Touche revealed that 85% of the 532 IS executives surveyed had been involved in process redesign projects (Hayley, Plewa and Watts, 1993). Reports of successful results from many reengineering efforts have been reported recently. AT&T, Pacific Bell, Cigna RE, Hallmark, and among others, report significant improvement in productivity and reduction in staff after business reengineering. With the accelerated acceptance of the reengineering concept, however, comes the 'bandwagon' effect which is enticing some firms to seek a 'quick fix' to their problems through BPR (Davenport and Stoddard, 1994). BPR must be a well orchestrated effort involving the careful evaluation of the nature of desired process change prior to any application of IT or change in organizational structures (Grover, Teng and

Fiedler, 1993). Neglecting a careful process evaluation and arbitrarily throwing IT at an apparent problem could be a recipe for
disaster. Not surprisingly, BPR failures are reportedly on the rise
(Caldwell, 1994) and the concept itself is being brought under
scrutiny (Davenport and Stoddard, 1994). To better understand
factors contributing to reengineering success, researchers and
consultants are beginning to study methods for process analysis and
organizational contingencies related to BPR implementation (e.g.,
Bashein, Markus and Riley, 1994).

In an attempt to facilitate understanding of BPR, this chapter
presents a model of process change. The model describes various
processes in terms of the relationships between their constituent
functional activities. A change from one configuration to another
provides fundamental insight into the reconfiguration of business
processes to achieve breakthrough performance gains. Two major
sets of catalysts that can enable process change as depicted by the
model are then discussed. The first set includes information technologies that can accelerate changes in process structures. The
second set includes organizational structure innovations that can
support different process configurations. Such a model provides a
broad perspective on business process change and the "match"
between the nature of such change and its technological and
organizational enablers. Based on this change model, senior executives involved in process reengineering may be better able to plan and
implement the complex process of organizational change and possibly the evolving transformation into the information age.

BPR: A Process Change Model

While it is possible to reengineer business processes within
limits of a particular functional department, maximum performance
gains are typically achieved with processes that cross functional
boundaries where the required activities are performed by personnel
from several different functional units. In a recent study involving 20
reengineering cases, it was reported that projects targeted at single-
function processes yielded an average of less than 5% reduction in
business unit cost as compared to 17% for cross-functional projects
(Hall et al., 1993). To succeed in reengineering, therefore, it is vital
that we develop a proper understanding on how various functions of
the organization are coordinated while participating in the same
business process.

Functional Coupling of Business Processes

The way various functions are orchestrated while participating
in a particular business process will be referred to as the *functional*

coupling pattern of the process (Teng, Grover and Fiedler, 1994). This pattern can be differentiated along two dimensions: degree of physical coupling and degree of information coupling. When a function is included in a business process, it typically develops tangible input-output relationships with other participating functions involving either transfer of physical objects or hand-off of documents from one function to another. The extent of this *flow of input and output* among the participating functions is referred to as the *degree of physical coupling* dimension of a business process. At one extreme of this dimension, referred to as the serial pattern, the process consists of a large number of sequential steps performed by different functions. An example of this pattern often can be found in business expense processing which requires many layers of management approvals, auditor evaluation, and filing of receipts, etc. At the other extreme of the physical coupling dimension is the parallel pattern where several functions contribute directly to the process outcome without intermediate steps. For example, both production function and advertising function are involved in the process of launching a new product, but the advertising function need not possess the product inventory or obtain authorization from the production function in order to advertise the product. Between the serial and parallel patterns, there are different degrees of physical coupling corresponding to processes with less number of serial steps and a mixture of both serial and parallel patterns.

In addition to, and sometimes instead of relying on tangible input-output to orchestrate their activities, various functions involved in a process may collaborate with each other through "intangible" information exchange to make mutual adjustments. This informational coupling between functions constitute the second dimension of our functional coupling model of business processes. The frequency and intensity of information exchange between two functions can range from none (completely insulated) to extensive (highly collaborative).

Based on the two dimensions discussed above: degree of physical coupling and degree of information coupling, a functional coupling framework for business processes is presented in Figure 1 showing, for simplicity of presentation, the four extreme coupling patterns: serial-insulated (Region I), serial-collaborative (Region II), parallel-insulated (Region III), and parallel-collaborative (Region IV). These patterns are illustrated with two functions, X and Y, as they participate in a business process in producing a process outcome, labeled as Z. Collaborations between functions are represented by 2-way dotted arrows, and tangible input-output relationships by solid one-way arrows.

Interestingly, the relationships between various units in an organization were studied more than twenty years ago by manage-

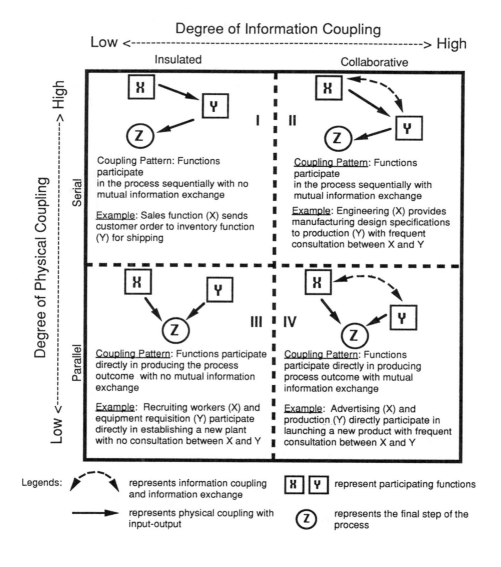

Figure 1 A Functional Coupling Framework of Business Processes

ment theorist James. D. Thompson, as detailed in the book entitled, "Organization in Action" (Thompson, 1967). The "sequential inter-dependence" relationship described by him corresponds to the serial end of the physical coupling dimension of the framework. Thompson also discussed the "pooled interdependence" relationship where a unit can perform its activities without regard to the other units. Such a relationship corresponds to the parallel end of the physical coupling dimension in the framework.

Changing Functional Coupling Patterns of Processes through BPR

Many organizations have reengineered their business pro-cesses to reduce degrees of physical coupling. At Bell Atlantic Corp., for example, a customer order for hooking up to a long-distance carrier took 15 to 25 days and passed through 25 hands before it was filled. Through BPR, many "irrelevant" serial steps were eliminated and the order can be filled in just a few hours (Stewart, 1993). At Bank One, the serial flow of paper documents has been drastically changed through the use of imaging technology which enables many functions to perform different steps for the mortgage approval process on the same document in a parallel pattern. As one bank officer examines the document to verify the applicant's employment status, another can do credit scoring, and yet another one can perform credit inquiry (McDonell and Somerville, 1991). Thus, the high degrees of physical coupling for processes currently in Region I and Region II (see Figure 1) may be significantly reduced through BPR and, as a result, shifted toward Region III and IV.

In addition to physical coupling, the information coupling pattern of a business process may also be changed through BPR. At Deere and Company, for example, the new product development process before reengineering consisted of insulated functions who always blamed each other whenever something went wrong. Failure to make a one-dollar change during product design would cost $100,000 to fix later in manufacturing. After many years of reengineering efforts, new product development at the giant farm equipment manufacturer now involves a number of functions that collaborate in every phases of the process. This process change was brought about mainly through the creation of cross-functional teams with specialists from marketing, design, engineering, manu-facturing, accounting, sales, and service functions (Davis, 1993). According to experts, around 60% to 70% of manufacturing quality problems start with the engineering function (Magnet, 1992). In recent years, many organizations have attempted to improve the collaboration between various functions related to new product development to shorten the development cycle. The development of

Jeep Cherokee at Chrysler, for example, took only a total of 39 months, rather than the usual 5 or more years, from the initial product conception to actual production. By enhancing collaboration between participating functions, this type of BPR would lead to process changes and move the process from Regions I and III (see Figure 1) to Regions II and IV.

In addition to vertical and horizontal movements in the grid, it is also possible to move diagonally to change both the physical and information coupling levels of a process, thus relocating the process from Region I to Region IV. At Texas Instruments (TI), for example, new product developments are now conducted at locations in a number of different countries: India, Malaysia, Japan, and the U.S. (Magnet, 1992). The company's global computer network enables design teams in different countries to achieve a high level of collaboration, while permitting them to work on different parts of the design in parallel fashion without the time-consuming flow of documents.

Strategic Paths for Process Reconfiguration

The lateral, vertical and diagonal movements in the functional coupling grid, as described above, provide a strategic perspective on BPR at the process level. These alternative directions for changing the functional coupling pattern of a process may be evaluated by following the decision tree as outlined in Figure 2. Based on an assessment of the process with regard to its potential for information coupling enhancement and the potential for physical coupling reduction, alternative directions for process change can be identified and represented by the four leaves in the tree. The environments for the various process coupling patterns are noteworthy. As indicated in the column labeled, 'typical condition,' the environment of the process in terms of uncertainty and other attributes should be evaluated in selecting a reconfiguration path. Many traditional business processes evolved in an environment with limited uncertainty, where the output of function X can be specified in advance to meet the input requirements of function Y, and the two functions can participate in the process without contacting each other and making adjustments. However, today's increasingly uncertain environment has rendered standardized rules and procedures too inflexible, and the penalty for an isolated function is the possibility that its output would be unsatisfactory or even useless to other functions in the process. To meet this challenge, functional coupling patterns of many traditional business processes are being modified or even radically altered to reduce physical coupling and enhance information coupling among the participating functions. It is important to note that not all processes can and should be reengineered. As indicated in the first leaf in the decision tree, the reengineering potential of some processes are restricted by mandate. Before marketing a new drug, for example, FDA approval is necessary which may take many years. Also, many processes with physical I/O flows are inherently sequential. If such processes operate in a stable environment without great need for collaboration, they can remain in Region I.

Such physical I/O flows in a process, as in a factory assembly line, can be contrasted to informational I/O flows, as in the issuance of a document from one function to another. As exemplified by the Bank One example, these types of processes may be reengineered by storing the information being transferred in a common information resource, such as digitized images or data bases, to facilitate parallel operations of the various functions in the process. Such processes, as indicated by the third leaf in Figure 2, are often operational processes (Davenport and Short, 1990) which typically have complicated mazes of serial steps accumulated over the years making them good candidates for vertical movement in the grid. For relatively unstructured managerial processes, lateral movement to improve collaboration (see leaf 2) may be necessary to absorb the higher level of uncertainty.

For *managerial processes* with limited processing steps, or operational processes with little or no uncertainty, straight lateral or vertical movements in the grid may be sufficient. Otherwise, as indicated in the last leaf in Figure 2, a diagonal path should be considered for those managerial processes with complicated serial steps, or operational processes that operate in a highly uncertain environment. Consider the new product development process. The process is undoubtedly a knowledge-intensive managerial process, and yet there are also many sequential input-output flows: product specification from R&D to engineering, design blueprint from engineering to production, etc. For this process, therefore, great reengineering potential can be realized along the diagonal path. A case in point is the new car design process at Ford (Davenport and Short, 1990). Relying on computer-aided design systems, members of the design team can simultaneously access a common design data base across the Atlantic, removing the need for serial input-output of design documents circulating among the designers. In the meantime, exchange of criticism and opinions can be fully supported through the network among members who have never met face to face.

Enablers of Process Change

In the process change model, two major catalysts can facilitate the vertical and horizontal movement in the grid. One of these

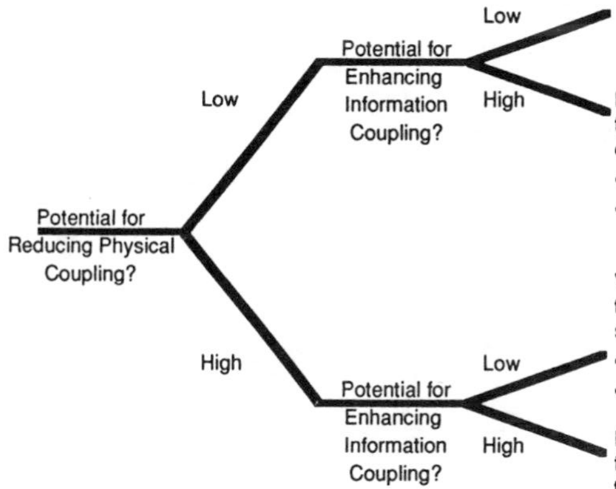

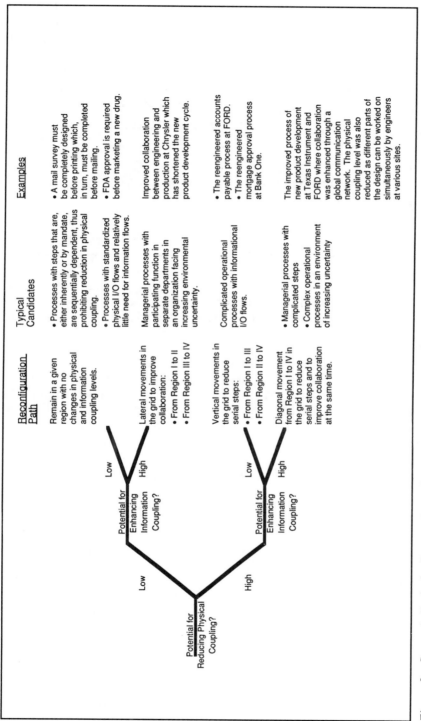

Reconfiguration Path	Typical Candidates	Examples
Remain in a given region with no changes in physical and information coupling levels.	• Processes with steps that are, either inherently or by mandate, are sequentially dependent, thus prohibiting reduction in physical coupling. • Processes with standardized physical I/O flows and relatively little need for information flows.	• A mail survey must be completely designed before printing which, in turn, must be completed before mailing. • FDA approval is required before marketing a new drug.
Lateral movements in the grid to improve collaboration: • From Region I to II • From Region III to IV	Managerial processes with participating function in separate departments in an organization facing increasing environmental uncertainty.	Improved collaboration between engineering and production at Chrysler which has shortened the new product development cycle.
Vertical movements in the grid to reduce serial steps: • From Region I to III • From Region II to IV	Complicated operational processes with informational I/O flows.	• The reengineered accounts payable process at FORD. • The reengineered mortgage approval process at Bank One.
Diagonal movement from Region I to IV in the grid to reduce serial steps and to improve collaboration at the same time.	• Managerial processes with complicated steps • Complex operational processes in an environment of increasing uncertainty	The improved process of new product development at Texas Instrument and FORD where collaboration was enhanced through a global communication network. The physical coupling level was also reduced as different parts of the design can be worked on simultaneously by engineers at various sites.

Figure 2 Strategic Paths for Process Reconfiguration

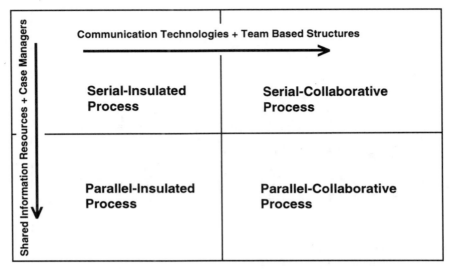

Figure 3   BPR: Enablers of Process Change

includes information technologies as can be seen from many of the examples discussed above. These technologies can be classified into (a) "communication" technologies that can better coordinate functional components of a process and enable lateral movement in the grid, and (b) "shared resource" technologies that can form a common repository to allow parallel operation of functions and enable vertical movement in the grid. The second catalyst includes changes in organizational structure, such as institution of cross functional teams, case managers and process generalists. These catalysts and their primary impetus for process change are illustrated in Figure 3.

Information Technology Enablers

Conceptually, an organization should be able to redesign a business process without the aid of IT. However, many recent successes in BPR would be difficult to consummate without the enabling IT. However, appropriate application of IT should stem from an understanding of the nature of the business change desired.

As indicated in Figure 3, the reduction of physical coupling in process reconfiguration may be enabled through the application of shared computing resources such as data base and imaging technology. Many firms have successfully capitalized on the enabling role of IT in re configuring their business processes from a highly serial pattern with many intermediate steps to a parallel pattern permitting several functions to proceed independently. In the well-publicized case at Ford Motor Corp. for example, the old accounts payable process involved three functions: purchasing, inventory and account payable, which participated in the process serially with many intermediate steps and a sequential flow of paper documents. With direct access to a shared data base, the three functions now participate in the reengineered process in a parallel fashion. The reengineered process achieved a 75% reduction in the workforce required, from 500 to only 125 (Hammer, 1990).

In addition to shared data bases, the application of imaging technology has also turned many serial processes into parallel ones. As illustrated by the Bank One example cited earlier, the processing of loan applications can be performed using the digitized image of the application which may be accessed by several officers directly in a parallel fashion. When one officer attempts to verify the applicant's employment status, another will do credit scoring at the same time, while a third officer can perform credit inquiry. Thus, innovative application of shared computing resources such as imaging and common data bases can be a powerful enabler for process change leading to the reduction of physical coupling for processes. In terms of the functional coupling framework portrayed in Figure 1, this means that processes currently in Region I and Region II may be moved vertically to Region III and IV.

While shared computing resources can enable process change through reducing physical coupling, the enhancement of information coupling is primarily enabled by the application of telecommunication technologies such as local area networks and a variety of office systems products under the rubric of "groupware." Application of these technologies may greatly improve communication and collaboration between different functions involved in a business process and enable horizontal movement in the grid (Figure 3). At Hewlett-Packard Co., for example, the sales process underwent significant change as 135 sales representatives began to use laptop computers to retrieve up-to-date inventory information from corporate data base during customer meetings (Berger, et. al., 1987). In addition, they can now use the portable computers to communicate with their peers and superiors, enabling frequent exchange of sales intelligence among the salespersons as well as timely dissemination of corporate directives pertaining to promotion, pricing, and discounting. The results showed that time spent in meetings decreased by 46%, and travel time was cut by 13%. Meanwhile, time spent with customers increased 27% and sales rose by 10%.

We have discussed the role of shared computing resources in enabling process change related to reduction of physical coupling, and the possibility of using telecommunication in enabling changes leading to enhancement of information coupling. With the convergence of computing and communication technologies, however, it may be impossible to have one without the other. Thus, it is important to realize that the major enabler for vertical movement in

Figure 1 is shared computing resources, even though utilization of these resources may require communications technology. Similarly, the primary enabler for lateral movement in the grid is communication technology but its effective application often depends on shared computing resources.

Increasingly, many business processes can benefit from a combination of shared computing resources and telecommunication technologies. These processes, as can be seen in Figure 2, are candidates for diagonal movement in the functional coupling grid. In an uncertain environment, collaboration is central to group activities, and telecommunication-based IT support can greatly improve team work. Without such support, the usefulness of shared computing resources may diminish. A team of engineers, for example, can share a common design data base. In the absence of telecommunication, however, they can not simultaneously modify different parts of the same object, nor are they aware of each others' changes. By combining both telecommunication and shared computing resources, a shared environment for team work may be developed. Approaches to provide such an environment have received attention from many researchers (Ellis, Gibbs & Rein, 1991). Currently, a number of emerging IT, including workflow software and the popular CAD/CAM systems, hold great promise in providing this shared environment for effective team work. With the application of workflow systems, not only can different processing steps be performed in parallel on the same document, but many 'unnecessary' steps can also be detected and eliminated in the attempt to analyzing and automating a process (thus reducing physical coupling). In addition, collaboration among those involved in the workflow may be significantly enhanced. When the popular CAD/CAM systems is tied to a global communication network, the creation of this environment can be a powerful enabler of process change following the 'diagonal' path. The new product development process at Texas Instruments cited earlier illustrates the benefits of this change. The company's global network and advanced computing resources enable design teams in different countries to sustain a high level of collaboration, while permitting them to work on different parts of the design directly without sequential flow of documents. As a result, the development cycle time for various products decreased substantially. The time needed to develop a calculator, for example, declined 20% soon after design drawings began to be sent electronically in 1989, and a further decrease of 17% has been achieved since then (Magnet, 1992).

Organizational Structure Enablers

Many business processes cross functional boundaries and significantly better performance can be attained through cross-functional BPR efforts than projects confined within traditional functions, according to a recent empirical study (Hall, et al., 1993). Merely automating or augmenting existing procedures, however, do not hold much promise since these procedures involve many 'vertical' movements of information and approvals within various functional areas which tend to slow down the process significantly. To facilitate cross-functional cooperation, traditional organization structure based on functional specialization can be modified through such structural enablers as cross-functional teams, case managers and process generalists. In many cases, these structural enablers provide a powerful means of complementing the IT enablers discussed above to successfully institute process change (See Figure 3).

The use of cross-functional teams has played a central role in many reengineering efforts. These teams enable functional interfaces and parallel design activities. At Modicon, Inc., a maker of automation-control equipment in Massachusetts, product development is no longer the sole responsibility of the engineering function. In the past, manufacturing wouldn't get involved in this process until the design was brought into the factory when their suggestions on the design changes become very costly. Now, a team of 15 managers from engineering, manufacturing, marketing, sales and finance routinely work together on the process. What was traditionally a serial process in both task and structure now involves cross-functional collaboration which has eliminated many unnecessary delays and costly changes, helping to bring six products to market in one-third of the time it would normally take (Byrne, 1993). The benefits of cross-functional teams can also be illustrated by attempts to reengineer the black-and-white film operation at Kodak. In 1989 when the reengineered process, called Zebras, began to operate, the operation was running 15% over budgeted cost, took up to 42 days to fill an order, and was late a third of the time. The reengineered process, which is centered around cross-functional teams, has over a period of two years turned the situation around completely: 15% under budgeted cost, cut response time by half, and being late only one out of 20 times (Stewart, 1992). Such team based structures can facilitate lateral movement in the process change model by improving coordination between functional components of a process. Coupled with telecommunication technologies, these teams can collaborate in remote locations, and asynchronously.

Another structural enabler for reengineering is the establishment of a case manager for a cross-functional process who has access to the latest status information on a given transaction and serves as the single contact point for customers. At Pacific Bell, for example, the use of case managers has been central to its BPR approach. Prior to reengineering, providing a customer with a Centrex telephone service took eleven jobs and more than five business days. Service representatives had to update 9 or more computer systems, making frequent errors and rework, and consulting customers several times. Now, Centrex service coordinators handle all interface with customers. Using a computer workstation that interfaces with all nine systems, they can now provide the service usually in the same day (Davenport and Nohria, 1994).

While case managers coordinate work performed by many functional specialists, a process generalist actually perform their work and eliminates the need for the specialists altogether. Given proper safeguards against frauds, this may mean the ultimate in efficient 'cross-functional' coordination, as there is no longer separate functions to coordinate. At IBM Credit, the financing service division within IBM, a single generalist is now performing credit checking, pricing and other activities previously done by four different specialists in processing a customer's loan request. This arrangement has reduced the application turnaround time from six days to just four hours. With no additional workforce, the redesigned process is able to handle 100 times as many applications as before (Hammer and Champy, 1993).

Both case managers and process generalists are powerful organizational innovations that can support vertical movement in the process change model. These structures can prove particularly useful in organizations with complex processes for bringing products and services to the customer. The inefficient interfaces between functions in these processes and the lack of an overall process perspective can result in poor responsiveness to customers. If the information requirements of the diverse functional components of these processes can be effectively integrated through shared computing resources, then with a powerful front end interface, case managers can be supported.

It should be noted that these structural (and technological) enablers must be consistent with the organizational orientation, design and culture. As indicated by sociotechnical research, all enablers must be aligned and in balance with other key aspects of the organization. Failure to actively consider these aspects (e.g., incentive systems, training, existing structures) could greatly constrain process innovation and its success (Davenport, 1993).

BPR and Organizational Change

Is it possible to manage a sales force of 10,000 in a traditional hierarchical organization? Undoubtedly, this would take a colossal amount of communication and coordination, which typically require many layers of middle management to absorb. At Frito-Lay, however, a coordination-intensive structure was developed to replace the traditional hierarchy with the aid of IT. A hand-held computer is given to each of the 10,000 salespersons to record sales data on 200 grocery products. Each night, the data is transmitted to a central computer which will send instructions back to the hand-held computers on changes in pricing and product promotions the next morning. In addition, weekly summaries and analysis are available to senior executives through an Executive Information System (EIS) (Malone and Rockart, 1991). In terms of the model presented (Figure 1), the Frito-Lay case corresponds to Region IV, the parallel-collaborative cell. The shared data base and hand-held computers facilitate the physical decoupling of serial procedures. The EIS and the electronic transmission of sales data and management directives intensify the information coupling among the participating functions - marketing and sales.

The steady progress of IT in the last four decades has now reached a critical point where the combined power of shared computing resources and telecommunication enable many organizations to coordinate their activities in ways that are not possible before. According to the recent research results (Malone and Rockart, 1991), these advanced IT applications would initially allow organizations to increase the amount and effectiveness of coordination with existing structures. Innovative use of advanced IT, however, would inevitably lead many firms to develop new, coordination-intensive network structures, as in the Frito-Lay case described above.

Networked organizations, according to Rockart and Short, "are usually conceived of as communication-rich environments, with information flows blurring traditional intracompany boundaries," which can be thought of "more as interrelationships within or between firms to accomplish work than as 'formal' organizational design per se (Rockart and Short, 1991). Thus, as an organization reengineers and improves its cross-functional processes, it will take on certain characteristics of a networked organization. For example, Chrysler Corp. has instigated a series of reforms since the late 80's to improve collaboration between functional departments. The product design function is now working closely with the engineering function and they no longer fight turf wars with each other (McWhirter, 1991). Thus, one may say that Chrysler is evolving toward a networked organization.

A number of prominent firms, including IBM, Xerox and Hallmark, have adopted a reorganization approach centered around core business processes. At Hallmark, the traditional functional structure is undergoing an interesting transformation. Before process reengineering efforts, the development of a new greeting card took two years because of a long list of serial steps in sketches, approvals, cost estimates, and proofs, which traverse many different departments. After reengineering, specialists such as writers, artists, and designers from various departments work side by side in teams. As a result, the cycle time for new card development was cut by half. The company still has functional departments, but the departmental headquarters now serve mainly as "centers of excellence" to which workers can return for training between projects. As such, they can be likened to the homerooms in high schools (Stewart, 1992).

Further indications on movements toward process-based organizations have surfaced recently. At Modicon, Inc., for instance, many of its 900 employees are involved in up to 30 teams that span several functions and departments. According to its president, "In five years, we will still have some formal functional structure, but people probably feel free enough to spend the majority of their time outside their functions." As a result of this cross-functional collaboration, the company is now able to bring products to market in one-third of the time it would normally take (Byrne, 1993). At Eastman Chemical Co., a unit of Eastman Kodak Co., several senior vice presidents have been replaced by self-directed work teams. There is no more VP for manufacturing. Instead, there is now a team of all plant managers (Byrne, 1993).

In general, functional hierarchies depend heavily on rules, procedures and upward referral which invariably increase the tendency for them to become rigid bureaucracies. This tendency may be avoided when functional specialists participate in a variety of teams attempting to accomplish different business processes at different times. These teams are given the "ownership" of the process and do not need to await several levels of approvals before making important decisions. This inherent flexibility is one of the most striking characteristics of an organizational form called "adhocracy" which has the ability to readily create and disband ad hoc teams on an on-demand basis. If the reengineering movement continues to gather momentum, organizations would be inevitably gravitate toward adhocracy.

Since most traditional hierarchies are organized around specialized functional departments, it is almost against their nature to conduct "cross-functional" endeavors. The hierarchical structure itself must be mobilized to ensure integration between functions, as these functions fulfill their assigned duties according to "cross-functional" plans set by higher levels, without sometimes even knowing the objectives of the assigned duties. While most information flows vertically to facilitate task assignments, lateral sharing and exchange of information related to common processes between functions are difficult in a hierarchy, and must be arranged through special efforts such as task forces and matrix structures (Lawrence and Lorsch, 1977). Furthermore, territorial battles are often waged between functions at the detriment of the overall organization. Such familiar patterns of organizational life would subside in a networked organization where cross-functional teams determine their own responsibilities and proceed to execute these duties with full access to necessary information.

Conclusion

Is BPR a management fad of the 90's or the start of something very big? Are we beginning to alter the very structure of organizations based on business processes rather than functional specialization? While the reengineering model guides more and more business processes, as shown on the top of Figure 1, from the serial-insulated cell to the parallel-collaborative cell, the organization will in the meantime undergo significant changes from an industrial age organization to an information age organization. This might involve extrapolation of the trends discussed to the extreme. Organizations would have widely accessible shared information resources that "informate" multiple logically distinct processes. Case managers, process generalists, and teams responsible for these processes interact and access information through ad-hoc networks which facilitate their existence and support their function.

The process change model shows how various functional activities involved in a business process may be fundamentally reconfigured, through the reduction of physical coupling and the enhancement of information coupling, to achieve breakthrough performance gains. Based on this model of process change, a suitable path for process reconfiguration may then be selected. As process reengineering takes place in the context of people and organization, risk of failure would be great if it proceeds without appropriate plans for organizational change.   While the process change model can provide guidelines for process reconfiguration with respect to patterns of functional coupling, the eventual success of process reengineering requires a high-level perspective of the complex, unprecedented organizational changes engendered by process reengineering. In developing these macro perspectives, it is important to realize that patterns of change will vary in speed and scope for individual organizations. Different industries may involve different facilitating and inhibiting factors. Also, it is important not to equate process reengineering with organizational transformation. As aptly observed by Davenport and Stoddard (1994), "reengineering is a process that can contribute to transformation, but it is not synonymous with transformation." In this chapter, we take a similar stand and point to the important dimensions of the organization changes that may be spawned by process reengineering. Senior business leaders should be keenly aware of these potential developments in order to effectively manage the difficult process of change.

References

Bashien, B. J., Markus, M. L. and Riley, P. "Preconditions for BPR Success," *Journal of Information Systems Management*, Spring 1994, pp. 7-13.

Berger, J., Angiolillo, P., and Mason, T. "Office Automation: Making it Pay Off", *Business Week*, October 12, 1987, pp. 134-146.

Byrne, J. A. "The Horizontal Corporation: it's About Managing Across, not Up and Down," *Business Week*, October 20, 1993, pp.76-81.

Caldwell, "Missteps, Miscues," *Information Week*, June 29, 1994, p.480.

Champy,J. A. "Grand Design," *CIO*, 6, 6 (1993), pp. 26-32.

Davenport, T.H., *Process Innovation: Reengineering Work through Information Technology*, HBS Press, Boston, MA, 1993.

Davenport, T.H. and Short, J. "The New Industrial Engineering: Information Technology and Business Process Redesign", *Sloan Management Review*, Summer 1990, pp. 11-27.

Davenport, T. H. and Nohria, N. "Case Management and the Integration of Labor," *Sloan Management Review*, Winter 1994, pp. 11-23.

Davenport, T.H. and Stoddard, D.B., "Reengineering Business Change of Mythic Proportions?" *MIS Quarterly*, June 1994, pp. 121-127.

Davis, T. R. V., "Reengineering in Action," *Planning Review*, July-August, 1993, pp. 49-54.

Ellis, C. A.,Gibbs, S. J. and Rein, G. L."Groupware: Some Issues and Experiences", *Communications of the ACM*, 34, 1, 1991, pp.38-58.

Grover, V., Teng, J. T. C. and Fiedler, K. D. "Information Technology Enabled Business Process Redesign: An Integrated Planning Framework," *OMEGA*, 21, 4, 1993, pp. 433-447.

Hall, G., Rosenthal J. and Wade, J. "How to Reengineering Really Work,"*Harvard Business Review*, 71, 6 1993, pp. 119-131.

Hammer, M. "Reengineering Work: Don't Automate, Obliterate", *Harvard Business Review*, July-August, 1990, pp. 104-112.

Hammer, M. and Champy, J. *Reengineering the Corporation: A Manifesto for Business Revolution*, Harper Collins Publishers, Inc., 1993.

Hayley, K., Plewa, J. and Watts, J. "Reengineering Tops CIO's Menu," *Datamation*, Vol. 39, No.8, 1993, pp. 73-74.

Lawrence, P. R. and Lorsch, J. W. *Organization and Environment: Managing Differentiation and Integration* (Richard D. Irwin, 1967) and J. L. Galbraith, Organization Design, (Addison-Wesley, 1977).

Magnet, M."Who is Winning the Information Revolution?", *Fortune*, November 1992, pp. 110-117.

Malone, T. W. and Rockart, J. F. "Computers, Networks and the Corporation", *Scientific American*, September, 1991, pp. 128-136.

McDonell, E. D. and Somerville, G. E. "Corporate Reengineering That Follows the Design of Document Imaging", *Information Strategy: the Executive 's Journal*, Fall 1991, pp. 5-10.

McWhirter, W. "Chrysler's Second Amazing Comeback", *Business Week*, November 9, 1992, p. 51.

Rockart, J. F. and Short, J. E. "The Networked Organization and the Management of Interdependence", in *The Corporation of the 1990s: Informa-*

tion Technology and Organizational Transformation, M. S. Scott Morton (Editor), Oxford University Press, 1991, pp. 191-192.

Stewart, T. "The Search for the Organization of Tomorrow", *Fortune,* 125, 10, May, 1992, pp. 92-98.

Stewart, T. A. "Reengineering; the Hot New Managing Tool," *Fortune,* August 1993, pp. 41-48.

Teng, J. T. C., Grover, V. and Fiedler, K. D. "Business Process Reengineering: Charting a Strategic Path for the Information Age," *California Management Review,* 36, 3, Spring 1994, pp. 9-31.

Thompson, J. D., *Organization in Action,* McGraw-Hill Book Company, 1967.

Chapter
2

Business Process Redesign:
A Framework for Harmonizing People, Information and Technology

Donald A. Marchand
Michael J. Stanford
International Institute for Management Development, Switzerland

I am enthusiastic over humanity's extraordinary and sometimes very timely ingenuities. If you are in a shipwreck and all the boats are gone, a piano top buoyant enough to keep you afloat may come along and make a fortuitous life preserver. This is not to say, though, that the best way to design a life preserver is in the form of a piano top. I think that we are clinging to a great many piano tops in accepting yesterday's fortuitous contrivings as constituting the only means for solving a given problem.
-R. Buckminster Fuller

After you've done a thing the same way for two years, look it over carefully. After five years, regard it with suspicion. And after ten years, throw it away and start all over.
- Alfred Edward Perlman

These quotations aptly describe the theoretical underpinnings of business process reengineering, a management philosophy that is enjoying new-found popularity in the business world. While manufacturing managers might tell us that as a philosophy for process improvement, reengineering has been around for a long time, for the first time process redesign is no longer exclusive to the manufacturing function. Recently, it has been reshaped and embraced by the ranks of white-collar managers and service companies seeking new ways to gain an advantage over their competitors by redesigning *non-manufacturing* processes. As a management philosophy for transforming parts of the firm to meet new competitive challenges, process reengineering is rightly considered by many companies to be an exceptionally powerful: both logical and irrefutable in its simplicity.

The theory, paraphrased by Messrs. Fuller and Perlman, is this: many of our current business processes were designed for a world which required a different set of competencies than those that are needed today, and are based on management techniques and technologies that under the BPR microscope seem outmoded or inefficient by modern standards. Manufacturing managers especially have long realized the dangers of relying on history when it comes to process efficiency, and have always sought new ways to improve their manufacturing practices. To most of them, it is not surprising that old processes no longer fit with the today's competitive requirements. To them - and now to white-collar workers and non-manufacturing enterprises - reviewing and redesigning existing processes to cut out inefficiencies is necessary in a time when companies are constantly searching for new ways to jump ahead of the competition.

Well-documented business process reengineering success stories have prompted managers from all backgrounds to explore the possibilities of the philosophy (Hammer, 1990). The resulting landslide of companies who have initiated their own process improvement efforts with little payback has made it apparent that a successful outcome to BPR may be the exception rather than the rule. Confusion contributes to the failure rate: the term reengineering has taken a dozen different meanings, from redesigning discrete work tasks to forcing radical change throughout the organization. A meaningful definition of the practice is difficult to find, and an accepted clear methodology has escaped the grasp of business managers. The reasons for failure are many: insufficient understanding of redesign techniques, weak management support, unwillingness to dedicate the effort necessary to deconstruct and rebuild old and inefficient processes. In this sense, process reengineering is like many other management philosophies that gain popularity in the business press. The idea is good, but implementation is difficult. Perhaps the greatest contributor to the inability of

BPR to deliver in practice what it promises in theory is the failure of managers to anticipate and address the "soft" side of BPR implementation. Too often, BPR efforts are confined strictly to processes and ignore process owners. In most cases, practitioners give little thought to the impact process reengineering has on people and corporate culture. Therein lies a great weakness in the way managers are currently applying BPR: they use it as a quick fix to attack isolated process-related problems, rather than as a part of organizational transformation that sends ripples of change throughout the firm.

This chapter describes a framework for understanding and managing business process redesign in a way that acknowledges its impact throughout the firm. It begins with the perspective of a broad restructuring or transformation framework through which BPR can be channeled so that it effectively addresses all the issues surrounding any type of significant organizational change. The restructuring framework guides managers through the critical corporate dimensions and resources which most strongly influence the success of their redesign efforts. The chapter then concentrates on information management, a subject that is critical to the success of BPR efforts. One of the key dimensions of the restructuring framework is information. In our experience, improving information management is a critical part of any process reengineering effort. As companies think about their BPR efforts, they need to give consideration to redesigning the way information is used within the process. Information is also a resource that is often mismanaged in such a way that it contributes more often to the failure than to the success of reengineering. Manufacturing companies who have been applying business process reengineering for many years have evolved certain information management principles that are incorporated into their BPR efforts. The balance of the chapter seeks to describe these principles explicitly. They define how information management should be approached in BPR to help business process reengineers manage information in a way that harmonizes their information resources with the other dimensions and resources described in the restructuring framework.

The Restructuring Framework

Like most popular management philosophies, business process engineering has captured the imagination of many an executive searching for ways to bolster the strength of his or her firm. Also, in common with most popular management philosophies, BPR has attracted the attention of many who are unsure of what to do with it. Some give it no more than lip service—in this sense, BPR shares notoriety with TQM, JIT, and a long list of other acronyms that have promised radical performance improvements. The link goes further; like these other philosophies, BPR in practice has managers baffled, confused and frustrated when it runs against corporate resistance, fails to provide the required outcomes, and spins off in unforeseen directions under the influence of misguided leaders. When BPR implementation stalls or dies a slow death from neglect, managers are left asking where it went wrong and why it failed to deliver what it promised.

Like any management philosophy that drives significant change in the enterprise, business process reengineering cannot be treated in isolation. To be successful, it must be integrated in a way that addresses its impacts throughout the firm. It cannot deliver sustainable performance improvements unless it is part of a program that acknowledges and addresses the changes reengineering requires of corporate culture, configuration and coordination, and in the way a company deploys its human, technological and information resources. These six dimensions—culture, configuration and coordination, people, information and technology—are the principal dimensions of the firm, and provide a dynamic framework (Collins, Oliff, Vollmann, 1991) in which the far-reaching effects of business process reengineering can be managed for success (see Figure 1). If a firm wishes to transform itself, changes in any one dimension must be balanced with changes in every other dimension. In any change

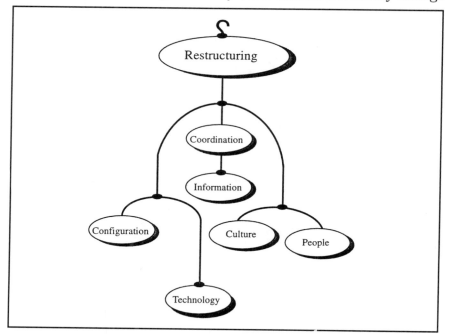

Figure 1: The Restructuring Framework—Processes of Dynamic Adaptation

program, all six corporate dimensions must be integrated, directing the firm along a common path so that it can quickly, efficiently and flexibly adapt to the environment. Reengineering managers who focus on only one dimension of the framework — for example, the role of information technology —while ignoring the others allow the firm to become unbalanced and unfocused. Changes in one dimension— like pulling the strings on a child's mobile—send ripples of change through the other dimensions that must be anticipated and managed to keep the firm consistently directed and properly targeted. Concentrating business process redesign efforts only on physical changes in existing processes, for example, without taking into consideration the resultant implications for the firm's processes of communication and information transfer, will doom any business process reengineering efforts to failure. Firm's who believe information technology is the dominant answer to their process redesign efforts are destined to run against barriers to change that prevent the integration of technology into the company. Managers who think they can change processes while ignoring process owners are likewise bound to find their change programs at best ineffective and at worst disastrous.

The first three dimensions in the restructuring framework - culture, configuration and coordination—represent the firm's dynamics. On these three dimensions rests the firm's strategic direction, objectives, and the way it manages itself to reach these objectives. The success of business process reengineering rests in part on the ability of managers to balance these dimensions—to anticipate and shape the changes that are likely to occur in each of these areas as a result of the reengineering program. The final three dimensions—people, technology and information—are the resources which the firm must redeploy in reengineering programs.

Culture

Culture consists of the shared values and beliefs which underlie and define corporate behaviors and objectives. It is often founded on a corporate vision, and in companies whose cultures are strong, it trails a consistent set of values through the corporate mission, strategies, objectives and employee behaviors. The importance of corporate culture on business process reengineering cannot be overstated. If existing corporate attitudes and values run against reengineering attempts in all or parts of the firm, either the reengineering program or the culture will have to change. Consider the case of a company in which the engineering department has historically been the political powerhouse. The firm depended on the creativity and technical genius of its engineers to develop products for the marketplace. Over time, however, and with the emergence of more technically astute competitors, relatively greater importance has been given to the marketing department's ability to sense, collect, interpret and distribute customer feedback regarding their product needs. Reengineering the product development process in this case is not just a matter of shifting the onus for product design from engineering to marketing: it also requires a fundamental shift in the values and behaviors of the firm from one that is internally focused to one which has a strong connection with the marketplace.

Likewise, culture provides the mental filters that influence the way in which information is used in a company. It is corporate culture that dictates who gets what information, how the information is used, what the formal and informal channels of communication are, and whether or not information is a political weapon or a business asset. Culture also dictates whether or not information is an active or static force in supporting the firm's strategy, whether it is enthusiastically shared throughout the firm as a competitive weapon or whether it remains in weighty data bases whose only exposure to the firm is under the occasional glance of disinterested IS professionals.

Configuration

If culture is the "soft" side of the firm, configuration is the firm's physical side. A company's configuration refers to the physical and organizational structures that exist internally and externally to the firm. Configuration includes the way in which the firm has developed and located its factories, marketing sites, and distribution channels. It also includes the corporate hierarchy, the network of suppliers and business partners, and the web of customer relationships on which the company depends. In many cases, business process reengineering efforts are aimed at breaking out of old, functionally structured configurations to ones that are cross-functional, flexible, and more responsive to changing customer demands. Some companies, particularly a few notable Japanese firms, have reconfigured their operations in a way that reflects a growing emphasis on customer satisfaction. Lexus, for example, has configured its dealerships in the United States to support their relationship-building capabilities and the service needs of their customers.

Coordination

Coordination includes the fundamental activities of process management and the flows of materials and information throughout the firm. Coordination is intent on creating synergies in the firm by directing activities in a logical and efficient way, with a minimum of waste or delay. Most business process reengineering efforts are aimed at coordination in different parts of the firm to improve information and material movement. One example of business process reengineering which has had profound impact on the coordination of a company is in the way Procter & Gamble redesigned the process of product replenishment to its largest customer, Wal-Mart. In response to Wal-Mart's request for daily replenishment of its goods, the two companies established a system of information transfer and distribution which allows P&G to gather sales information from Wal-Mart, distribute the information to the appropriate parts of the firm, and replenish goods within 24 hours. In a world in which speed and flexibility are paramount, this seamless, cross-functional coordination has become a distinct advantage for both companies.

People

"People" refers to the human resources that support the firm's activities. This resource includes all the decision-makers, managers, operators and support staff that impact in any way the operations of the firm. In many reengineering programs, people are an invisible resource; they are expected to adapt quickly to new ways of doing business regardless of the changes it requires in their behaviors, practices or work styles. Many BPR efforts are aimed not at making processes quicker or more flexible, but at making them less expensive, an objective that is most easily reached by taking people out of the process. As a result, people are often the first casualty of process reengineering. Further limiting the effectiveness of many reengineered processes is the tendency of the process owners to stick to their old ways of doing business, despite the process changes around them. Part of this tendency toward inertia is found in the way people use information. People are filters - the information they collect and share is subject to their cognitive styles, languages, and personal biases, all of which influence the way information is used in the processes the people are supposed to support.

Technology

Technology includes any enabling technology that the firm uses to support its business: its systems for manufacturing, information management, control, measurement, design and engineering. It is the resource often at the heart of process reengineering (Davenport & Short, 1990). Many managers start reengineering by deploying information technology and then adapting the uses of information and the skills of their people to the technology. This approach unfolds in three steps: first, rethink the business processes; second, select and implement new IT driven systems; and third, adapt the organization to the subsequent changes. While this linear process may sound logical, it masks an inherent bias toward emphasizing technology over people and information in process reengineering efforts.

Information

A firm's information resources includes its knowledge, expertise, databases, intellectual property - all the information it collects and distributes throughout the business that enables it to create, develop and distribute a product or service. Whereas technology refers to the machines that enable the firm, information refers to the substance of communication that the machines often deliver. Information is content and capability, not just hardware or technology. Information use in the firm, as has been mentioned, is subject to a wide assortment of outside influences, including the culture of the firm, individual styles and preferences, and the firm's prevailing communication and coordination strategies. Depending on the nature of these influences, information can be either an internal political weapon or an externally-focused competitive asset (Oliff, Marchand, 1991).

Harmonizing Resources in Business Process Reengineering

While the restructuring framework emphasizes that all six corporate dimensions must be balanced in business process reengineering, one of the strongest influencers of BPR is information management. Information management has become a strategy for companies seeking a means to regain their competitive advantage, a goal they increasingly turn to BPR to achieve. New technology, faster machines and more flexible networks have all promised vastly improved information management, inside and outside the context of BPR. But as a cure for competitive ills, new information technologies disappoint many who blindly embrace them, primarily because many managers confuse their *information* assets with their *information technology* resources. Those who buy the newest and most complex technology, install it on the factory floor or the office, and wait for it to change their red ink to black are universally dissatisfied (Naj, 1993).

To implement change successfully, the three corporate dimensions (culture, configuration and coordination) and the key resources (people, information and technology) of business process reengineering must be perceived as inextricably interdependent, like the objects on a mobile. Maintaining synergy in the firm while redefining its dimensions and redeploying its critical resources during the reengineering process is critical to successful organizational change. Successful business process reengineering does not confine itself to only one of the corporate resources but rather tries to harmonize all three in support of rebuilt processes. Many of the best redesign practitioners use the word "to harmonize" when they describe the necessary balance a company must achieve between the values and capabilities of people, the uses of information and the appropriate deployment of IT. In the view of these managers, it is more effective when redesigning processes to begin with people and information practices and use technology as an enabler as process redesign evolves.

Information Management Principles in Business Process Reengineering

Our ongoing study of strategic information management in leading American, European and Japanese firms (see accompanying study description)has uncovered some important insights into how the most successful business process engineers best harmonize information resources with human and technology resources in their reengineering programs. We have summarized our findings in nine information management principles which guide the use of information in support of business process reengineering efforts. The principles lie at the heart of BPR, whether or not it is approached from an information management perspective. Most of the principles show that technology is NOT an appropriate driver for BPR, but rather plays a supporting role as the firm's people and information management capabilities are balanced and redeployed in support of new processes (Davenport, 1994).

Principle 1: Eliminating the Problem Eliminates Information About the Problem

Most business processes reflect old and out-dated ideas about operations, such as the belief that defects are inevitable. The existence of defects and the inability to reduce their rate of occurrence prompted many manufacturing managers to develop complex information systems that identified poor quality products at the end of the production run. To identify and repair defective products, it was necessary to build information systems that monitored and controlled imperfections within production. The first principle of managing information in business process reengineering reflects a growing belief that production lines can be virtually problem-free.

The principle is this: eliminating unnecessary and problematic work processes eliminates the need for information to control those processes. The benefits here are two-fold: abolishing the problem eliminates both the information embedded in the problem (for example, procedural or instructional material) and the need for information to monitor and control the process.

A group of Japanese manufacturing companies are the world leaders in eliminating problem work steps in their business process reengineering efforts. In these firms, the task of identifying and doing away with process problems is reinforced strongly by a culture of continuous improvement. By focusing their production systems on defect-free manufacturing, the best Japanese firms have succeeded in creating problem-free manufacturing processes. At the same time, they have eliminated the need for complex quality control systems to monitor the production line. Since control is built into the system, complex quality control information is unnecessary. At its manufacturing facilities in Japan, for example, Nissan Motor has minimized its use of control systems. Its production line has no areas for re-work or repair, since the firm is eliminating defects during the manufacturing process rather than repairing defects after. By having every car come down the line in perfect condition, Nissan has no need for complex information systems to coordinate repair activities, no print-outs detailing the repairs needed, and makes no adjustments to component scheduling.

SONY Corporation runs its Bridgend television assembly plant in the United Kingdom in a similar fashion. By continuously eliminating unnecessary work-steps in the production line, Bridgend is able to employ a simple system to monitor production and quality status despite the plant's need to adjust to 150 design changes every year (Huycke, Oliff, Marchand, 1993). In keeping with the restructuring framework, SONY has clearly balanced its technological and information capabilities with the information needs of its people. This approach to process reengineering contrasts sharply with prevailing practices throughout the world. Most firms, assuming that imperfections are inevitable, develop sophisticated and information-intensive systems to monitor and control problems. The resulting output of exhaustive reports and documented data contribute significantly to information overload by inundating line workers and managers alike with control-oriented information.

Principle 2: Simplify the Process and Simplify the Information Embedded in the Process

In many cases, process simplification is at the heart of the firm's business process reengineering efforts. Business systems represent an accumulation of dated policies, procedures and practices that often outlive both the people who designed them and the purpose for which they were originally created. It is not surprising, then, that many procedures and work steps are out-dated, redundant, and misunderstood by those who perform them. While both the processes and the information that supports them may have been relevant in the past, the current business environment may require far different capabilities. Twenty years ago, when manufacturing strategy focused on cost reduction and economies of scale and most firms were constrained by capacity, systems were based on production and inventory control. Two decades later, global competition demands flexibility, speed, responsiveness, and new organizational forms geared toward globalization.

While the environment has changed dramatically, the business systems that support the firm's competitive thrusts haven't adapted. Many companies find themselves performing work steps not out of necessity but out of habit. IS departments collect, produce and distribute information related to those work steps in the mistaken belief that they are supporting value-adding activities. Companies continue to rely on old, complicated systems and out-dated procedures, and IS departments continue to produce volumes of data and printed reports based on past assumptions regarding the operation of business processes.

Process simplification and information management simplification go hand in hand in business process reengineering. More efficient processes dramatically reduce the quantity and complexity of information collected, stored, and distributed to support them. After eliminating from the production process any unnecessary or problem-causing steps, for example, SONY manually simplifies the process to its most basic levels. At its Bridgend plant in the United Kingdom, systems are continuously reviewed and up-dated to purge any redundant or superfluous activities. Likewise, as part of its restructuring strategies, Nissan Motor focuses on simplifying the processes and information flows inside each manufacturing facility, across factories and with suppliers. Key to the success of these information systems is that process reengineering focuses on developing the simplest possible information systems.

In the United States, one leading retailer reflects the same perspective on information systems. In its 1993 Annual Report, Wal-Mart states that it uses the newest equipment, software and communications to reduce costs and improve productivity. Its goals are the *simplification* of what it does, the *elimination* of waste, and access to more *meaningful information.* When the French division of Otis Elevator decided to redesign its procedures for processing customer orders, its goal was to simplify processes and make them clearer, and then to support the reengineered processes with the appropriate information systems. By doing so, Otis reviewed all aspects of the business process reengineering framework, from the firm's existing coordinating systems and physical configuration to its information management and technology needs. After completing a four-phase sequence of organizational and information systems reengineering, it developed SALVE, a contract negotiation support system that has cut order processing lead time from 1 month to 48 hours, a clear and distinct advantage Otis holds over its competition (Tawfik, 1993). Each of these companies has been careful to not let technology drive their process reengineering efforts. Rather, they harmonize the use of technology with the information needs of their people when redesigning processes.

Principle 3: Focus on the Appropriate Use of Information Technology

Many managers make the dangerous assumption that information technology is useful only if it is deployed in advance of the competition. To stay ahead of the pack, they quickly embrace new technologies with an imperfect understanding of their relevance to the firm's competitive needs or their impact on the people who must use them. They introduce new technologies and then shape the firm's process reengineering efforts, workforce and competitive strategy accordingly.

Such firms clearly favor focusing on technology rather than on balancing all the dimensions in the business process reengineering framework. Successful users of IT do just the opposite. The best firms fit technology according to the needs of the firm and the capabilities of the workforce, taking into account the firm's existing culture, coordinating systems and configuration. As a result, they use information systems that are *appropriate* to the requirements of their work processes. Using information tailored to the process, the people and the level of technology required allows these companies to deploy information technology that is only as powerful as it needs to be. These companies avoid new and expensive technology when it is not needed to support their business processes. Nissan, for example, deploys its best technology on the production line, where it feels advanced technology can most strongly support its manufacturing competencies. To monitor its pipeline flow, it uses simple computers that are only powerful enough to manage relatively straight-forward information requirements. Nissan also carefully targets its use of information technology, developing systems to collect more accurate information on customer attitudes and linking its American dealerships via a satellite network to give the company greater responsiveness to the needs of the market (King, 1991).

Similarly, the philosophy of the SONY Bridgend plant in the United Kingdom is to use whatever information technology is appropriate for the people who use the information. The company avoids using computer technology for its own sake, particularly when it is unnecessary or distracts people from using the information. The walls of the Bridgend plant are covered with highly visible but manually constructed charts that follow the daily status of production and quality. In many companies, similar information might be confined to high-tech but less visible computer displays. SONY also has the discipline to stop IS projects that lose their relevance or that misalign its corporate dimensions and resources. Among the projects considered no longer appropriate are sophisticated and automated quality feedback systems, bar-coding of all subassembly processes, and the creation of an automated warehouse. Following the guidelines of the restructuring framework, both SONY and Nissan harmonize their use of information systems with the needs of their redesigned business processes rather than shape their processes around the technology they employ. Each of these companies believes that technology is self-defeating unless the people information, and technology within the work system are harmonized. By confining their use of technology to only what is appropriate, they avoid using systems that produce and distribute more information than is needed. Likewise, they avoid favoring information and technology resources over their human resources.

Principle 4: Making Information Available Doesn't Make It Useful: in Business Process Reengineering, Concentrate on Targeted Information Use

While the attention span of managers and workers has not changed significantly over the past decade, the amount of information they are exposed to has grown exponentially. Well-intentioned executives excited by the promises of strategic information systems and information technology call for more sharing of information across functions, departments and work groups. At the same time, much of the information available in organizations is unfocused and unreliable. Predictably, productivity suffers as a result. Employees spend more time sifting through files, faxes, e-mails, reports and printouts in search of useful information.

The challenge of information management in business process reengineering is not to make information available, or to share as much information throughout the organization as possible; rather, it is to focus the attention of the firm's managers and workers on information which contributes value to their business processes. This perception of information value is key to leading business process reengineers, reflected throughout their organizations in their use of quality circles, the relatively high levels of information - and trust - shared between line workers and management, and the placement of responsibility for quality and customer responsiveness at the lowest levels of the organization, where relevant information is often most accessible. For successful process reengineers, information management moves information up, down and throughout the organization to support performance improvements. Because it believes that a greater focus on customer service is necessary in the highly competitive automobile industry, Nissan has developed AN-SWER, an information system linking sales and production activities so that Nissan can inform customers of delivery dates when they place an order (Anonymous, 1991). Communications systems within SONY's Barcelona & Bridgend TV assembly plants focus on producing high quality products. Managers at both plants say they have no time to analyze unimportant information: they are too busy trying to meet their production and quality targets. In both SONY and Nissan, information use is focused on competitive necessities, and is confined to the people to whom it is essential.

In contrast, many companies distribute so much information that it is difficult for both managers and workers to discern what information is useful. While meaningful information may be available, it might not be used by those for whom it is intended. Other companies control their information flows to stimulate competition inside the company rather than as a tool for improving processes and products. They use information as an internal weapon, to monitor workers and to promote competitiveness among managers and plants. In these companies, it is not surprising that calls for more information sharing often result in making more useless information available on the one hand, while increasing mistrust and conflict among functions, managers and workers on the other.

Principle 5: Use Lead Time Reduction In Your Process Reengineering Efforts to Drive Out Useless Information and Drive In Value Added Information

In the age of speed and flexibility, lead time reduction and greater responsiveness to customer needs are the two dominant requirements for success. To reduce lead time, companies are reengineering old work processes *and* the rigid information systems that support them. IS systems often contribute to long lead times through their cumbersome input and output procedures and through the control mechanisms embedded in inflexible applications programs and databases. In many cases, movement in the supply chain is delayed because information flows lag behind material flows; inventory sits idle while the production line awaits information regarding its use.

Lead time reduction drives out unnecessary information processing, paper flows and repetitive information collection, and focuses information systems only on work processes that add value.

Toyota's JIT system, a management process founded on the principle of lead time reduction, allows it to produce a car significantly faster than even its strongest competitors (Taylor, 1990). Toshiba Electronics, which operates in an industry in which products can be outdated before they reach the marketplace, uses portable computers to decrease lead time. Laptops help the company determine the difficulty of producing products while they are still in the early design stage. Similarly, Hitachi designers use computer-aided design technology to generate die specifications in only a few hours. By faxing the specifications to die manufacturers, the company can often design and receive new dies in the same day (Clark, 1989).

Toyota follows a similar path by targeting its information technology around its need for speed and responsiveness. Because it is in an industry that demands quick production and short lead times, Toyota has automated its die manufacturing processes—it now has a die-cutting system that can run for ten days without human interference (Taylor, 1990). Many of these companies also practice concurrent engineering, in which product and manufacturing engineers work closely together so that factory machinery is developed in tandem with product design. By sharing information among functions rather than confining them to their areas of expertise, practitioners of concurrent engineering avoid a long and tedious step-by-step process in product development. In each of these cases, lead time reduction and the process reengineering that supports it have changed the nature of information management. As companies strive to become more responsive to the needs of their customers, they produce and share focused and value adding information.

Principle 6: Use Reengineering to Tightly Link Work Processes and Information Management Responsibilities

Firms reengineering their processes to better fit today's competitive requirements are forced to rethink the role of the information systems function. By moving toward distributed client-server architectures, the IS function is enabling companies to integrate work activities and their related information management processes. As firms push decision-making responsibilities farther down the organizational hierarchy, they are obligated to support decision-makers with information that is relevant to their work processes. Accordingly, the separation of work processes and their supporting information processes is narrowing; line employees and executives alike are becoming "information managers" (Drucker, 1989, p.214). Tightly linking work processes and information management significantly reduces the amount of extraneous information circulating in the organization: information users are unlikely to demand more information than is of use to them, and will not ask for information systems that fail to add value to their reengineered work processes.

To handle their expanding mandates, newly-empowered employees require a significant increase in their information processing skills. IS is moving away from data processing toward supporting knowledge workers, usually through training, education, and designing IT architectures tailored to the needs of information users. The Information Services Department (ISD) at SONY Bridgend reflects this need for greater support of knowledge workers. ISD encourages, develops and supports the use of information systems throughout the organization. Since information management is considered the responsibility of all managers, supervisors and line workers, ISD lets the users set the company's IS mandate. Similarly, to improve the technical proficiency of its workforce, Nissan follows a job rotation program that exposes workers to a variety of different software and hardware (Bozman, 1991). Alps Electronics has shifted authority to the shop floor, and given workers operational decision-making powers. Since they have been given the responsibility to produce high quality products within strictly-imposed delivery dates, line workers at Alps have also been provided with the training and discretion they need to achieve their mandates. Each worker is inherently a process engineer, and is trained to diagnose operations, define improvements and design new approaches to production processes.

Principle 7: Flexible Business Practices Require Flexible Information Systems

Faced with the competitive imperative of flexibility, companies are looking to flexible information systems to empower their organizations. As flexibility and speed become critical in the design of business processes, they are also becoming the drivers of IS strategy. New principles of action for IS organizations are emerging which promote information elimination, simplicity, flexibility and speed. To respond to the emerging environment, information managers must find quicker and more efficient methods for collecting, processing and distributing information. Modular information systems, standard software platforms, networking and new IT architectures that can accommodate radical shifts in business processes are all reshaping the nature of information management by giving it an active role in implementing the results of business process reengineering efforts (Huycke, Oliff, Marchand, 1993).

Many examples of organizational flexibility occur on the production line. Hitachi is embracing a major effort in automation and robotics to give their manufacturing facilities the ability to respond quickly to change. Ultimately, Hitachi hopes to have a fully programmable manufacturing system. At Alps, computer-aided manufacturing includes activities both upstream and downstream from the production line. In the manufacturing process, the company includes other functional areas within the company, major suppliers and customers, all to give the company more flexibility and shorter product introduction times. In both Hitachi and Alps, information is used as a critical resource to help the firms respond more quickly to changes in the environment.

Principle 8: Manageable Works Groups Make Information Needs More Manageable

A team focus in manufacturing companies results in more active employee participation, greater trust and learning, and more effective information management. Many successful manufacturing enterprises allocate responsibilities on the basis of team efforts rather than according to functional alignments or individual duties. With a greater team focus in business process management, information management becomes more focused on the business requirements of the team and less dependent on individual needs or the desires of the IS function. Combining the analytical and information processing skills of team members results in information use that is directed at solving problems, responding to market needs and making operational decisions. In addition, using a team approach to improve processes and outputs at the operational level of the firm encourages the design of information systems that support team-based production and service processes rather than for monitoring and control. Accordingly, the firm's IS function is more likely to depend on a close, collaborative partnership with team users, and to develop information systems that result in direct performance improvements.

The same spirit of teamwork can be found in small firms and global manufacturers alike. Large scale manufacturing activities need not be supported by equally large and inflexible information systems. Likewise, complex operations do not necessarily require complex automated information systems designs. In fact, it is in large companies that the team-based approach to business process redesign and information management is most needed. By breaking down businesses into small groups, large companies can assign teams to manageable work processes and information flows. It is easier, then, for the company to focus its efforts on activities that address its competitive needs. CarnaudMetalbox S.A., Europe's largest and the world's third largest packaging company, has organized its operations into more than 85 widely-dispersed business units to better concentrate its efforts on the customer needs. Because its culture stresses a focus on local markets, CarnaudMetalbox encourages its business units to develop individual strategies in response to the specific needs of their customers. To cater to the needs of its multinational customers, networking systems connect the business units, thereby laying the foundation for a pan-European business. By organizing itself into small, focused units, CarnaudMetalbox is able to concentrate its business processes and information flows according to the unique competitive requirements of each of its many markets. The PC division of Hewlett-Packard chose a similar organization structure when it decided to attack a market dominated by low cost competitors by reorganizing into small teams focused on specific market segments (Anonymous, 1993).

Principle 9: Use Business Process Reengineering and Information Management to Balance Information and Material Flows

Federal Express Corporation has become famous as a company that strives to reach total customer satisfaction through the timely delivery of its customers' packages world-wide. In working toward that objective, Federal Express is creating information systems with complete accuracy in the identification, tracking and accounting of its customers' packages. Fed Ex executives claim that to clients, information about the package is as important as the package itself. After dealing with millions of customers who have received on-time delivery - and the minority whose packages were delayed or lost - the company has learned that its ability to tell customers where the package is or why it has been delayed is essential to clients who believe an honest answer is better than no answer at all. Fed Ex has been so successful in pleasing customers with its package tracking systems that competitors have been forced to build and promote similar capabilities.

Similarly, in manufacturing companies the movement of information concerning materials has become as important as the movement of the materials themselves. In the best companies, information management in the supply chain supports the movement of materials only when there is a clear reason for doing so. Accordingly, managers identify and remove all unnecessary and wasteful movement, storage and distribution of materials at any stage in the supply chain. Over the last eight years, leading Japanese industrial firms have evolved this concept of pipeline management beyond the introduction of JIT and lead-time reduction in manufacturing and distribution toward the regional coordination of sales orders, manufacturing, and distribution. While other companies have considered pipeline management on a national or country by country basis, the best multinational companies are implementing their global vision of market dominance by balancing information and material flows through pipeline management on a regional scale.

For them, pipeline management is an ambitious long term effort at improving information flows between sales and manufacturing to facilitate product design and production planning, to reduce inventory, and to shorten delivery lead times. They seek to improve order processing, design quality and lead time reduction on a regional scale without losing flexibility and customer responsiveness in local markets. Following this principle, global companies are able to combine the advantages of simultaneous centralization and decentralization of their business processes on a regional scale without sacrificing either their global vision or their local responsiveness.

Leveraging the Power of Information in Business Process Reengineering

Alive and well in corporate circles is the belief that effective information technology is necessary for most process reengineering programs. While this perception may be correct, it represents only a small part of the business reengineering picture. When reengineering their outdated business processes, companies must examine the basic managerial assumptions and beliefs that shape their current views of information management. Many of these assumptions are barriers to creating value for the business. One of the first mistaken beliefs that executives must reassess is the notion, as Thomas Davenport has concluded, that information "technology in and of itself can solve a company's information problems" (Davenport, 1994, p. 131). Rather, we believe that business process reengineering should emphasize not only how people use information, but, more importantly, how information management can be enhanced by eliminating, simplify and targeting information use more carefully within redesigned business processes. As Figure 2 suggests, at the center of process improvement is a focus on information issues which, if properly addressed, can significantly enhance the business payoffs of reengineering.

A second concern which arises from our analysis is that we have only just begun to understand the factors that contribute to reengineering successes and failures. In this context, we believe that more careful understanding of the lessons learned from process reengineering in manufacturing companies within Japanese, European as well as North American contexts can enhance the practice of reengineering as applied to white-collar and service processes. While perhaps it is understandable that executives in white-collar and service companies are caught up in the enthusiasm for reengineering worldwide in the context of the competitive crises and challenges they face, we believe that the lessons learned from

1. Eliminating the Problem Eliminates Information About the Problem.

2. Simplify the Process and Simplify the Information Embedded in the Process.

3. Focus on the Appropriate Use of Information Technology.

4. Making Information Available Doesn't Make It Useful in Business Process Reengineering, Concentrate on Targeted Information Use.

5. Use Lead Time Reduction in Your Business Process Reengineering Efforts to Drive Out Useless Information and Drive In Value Added Information.

6. Use Reengineering to Tightly Link Work Processes and Information Management Responsibilities.

7. Flexible Business Practices Require Flexible Information Systems.

8. Manageable Work Groups Make Information Needs More Manageable.

9. Use Business Process Reengineering and Information Management to Balance Information and Material Flows.

Figure 2: Information Management Principles in Business Process Reengineering

reengineering in global manufacturing in the 1980's and 1990's are directly applicable to the reengineering of white collar and service companies. In this regard, the central role of information in white collar and service enterprises makes even more meaningful the thoughtful application of the information management principles developed in this chapter.

A third important concern which this article addresses is the need to view business reengineering as part of a broader change management program in any organization in which reengineering is applied. It is not enough for there to be a close linkage between business strategy and reengineering efforts. In our view, for reengineering to succeed the changes in the ways people, information and technology are deployed as well as the impacts of reengineering on the ways a company is configured and on its culture, values and behaviors must be viewed wholistically and managed in an integrated manner. Thus, we have used the word "harmonize" to signify the managerial attitude which must all be adopted to manage the dimensions of strategic restructuring. Reengineering should not be viewed as simply a way of "rationalizing" business processes after downsizings have occurred or as just another "management fad" which will blow over in time. For reengineering to work, the reengineering philosophy and principles will have to be accepted and owned by people who understand both benefits and limitations in the context of their culture and business. This is a tall order for executives bent on realizing reengineering's "quick hits" or "radical change" potential and ignoring the longer term leadership challenges embedded in harmonizing the business to its competitive environment and the manner in which its key resources are deployed.

Finally, we have focused attention on the management of information in this chapter not because we feel that information management is the only key to successful reengineering, but because for too long the information management dimension of business process redesign has been overshadowed by concerns with the role of information technology. We believe that, if reengineering of white collar and service processes is to succeed, attention to how information is used in business processes and what information really adds business value will increasingly become critical if reengineering is to realize its promise. What we have learned in the context of examining information management's role in reengineering in global manufacturing companies is equally, if not more applicable, to reengineering service and knowledge-based enterprises.

The MANUFACTURING 2000 Project

In 1990, the MANUFACTURING 2000 (M2000) was launched at IMD as an action-based research initiative to examine the transformation of the manufacturing companies during the 1990's. This 10-year research project is the most comprehensive, pragmatic research project operating in any business school in the world. The project involves collaboration between a team of IMD faculty and senior executives representing the following sponsoring companies: Andersen Consulting, Bally, BP Chemicals, Dupont De Nemours International, GKN Automotive, Heineken, Johnson & Johnson, KNP BT, Nestle, Nokia Mobile Phones, Omega, Siemens, SONY Europa and Volkswagen/ Audi. There are six key areas of research within M2000 including Enterprise Transformation, Change Management and Culture, Benchmarking and Performance Measurement, Strategic Information Management, Marketing and Manufacturing Convergence and New Product Development.

The Strategic Information Management Project has four objectives: (1) to improve the capabilities of companies to sense and gather quality market intelligence on customers, markets, competitors, products and new technologies; (2) to understand how information is used in business and manufacturing processes and which factors are key to creating business value, particularly when firms are engaged in business process redesign and enterprise transformation; (3) to develop new ways of configuring organizations to enhance a company's ability to use and share critical information; and (4) to examine the ways information and technology can be used as core and distinctive competencies as companies seek to be more market-driven.

The M2000 project methods involve a combination of longitudinal case studies, cross-industry company surveys, interactive learning workshops, and benchmarking of best practices between IMD faculty and the sponsoring companies. The scope of the projects are global as well as regional. Although centered in Europe, there are M2000 companies located or doing business in North America and the Asia/Pacific region. The manufacturing sectors represented cover a broad spectrum of industries—food processing, packaging, telecommunications, automotive, electronics, chemicals, consumer goods and pharmaceuticals. Research findings are communicated through books, articles, executive reports, case studies as well as through executive education programs, seminars, benchmarking workshops and professional networks.

For more information on M2000 and the Strategic Information Management Project, contact the M2000 Project Coordinator, IMD, Chemin de Bellerive 23, P.O. Box 915, CH-1001 Lausanne, Switzerland. Tel: (O) 41 21 618 0111, (Fax) 41 21 618 0380.

References

Anonymous. (1991, September). Nissan Motor-New Information System Gives Customers Firm Delivery Dates. *Business Japan*, 22-23.

Anonymous. (1993, June 19) The Metamorphasis of Hewlett-Packard. *The Economist*, 63-65.

Bozman, J.S. (1991, March 11). Carmaker Turns Over Career Tracks. *Computerworld*, 47,50.

Clark, K.B. (1989, November-December) What Strategy Can Do For Technology. *Harvard Business Review*, 94-98.

Collins, R.S., Oliff, M.D., & Vollmann, T.E. (1991, August), Manufacturing Restructuring:Lessons for Management. *MANUFACTURING 2000*, Lausanne, IMD, Executive Report, Number 2, 1-20.

Davenport, T.H. (1994, March-April). Saving IT's Soul: Human-Centered Information Management. *Harvard Business Review*, 119-131.

Davenport, T.H. & Short, J.E. (1990, Summer). The New Industrial Engineering: Information Technology and Business Process Redesign. *Sloan Management Review*, 11-27.

Drucker, P.F. (1989). The New Realities, New York: Harper & Row.

Hammer, M. (1990, July-August). Reengineering Work: Don't Automate, Obliterate. *Harvard Business Review*, 104-112.

Huycke, C.B., Oliff, M.D. & Marchand, D.A. (1993, February 18). *Digital Equipment Corporation International, Fitting Information Technology Architecture to Competitive Restructuring*, IMD, Lausanne, Switzerland, POM 158

A, 1-11, B, 1-11.

_____ (1993, February 25). SONY Manufacturing Company, UK, *Appropriate Use of Information and Information Technology.* IMD, Lausanne, Switzerland, POM 151, 1-23.

King, J. (1991, September 2). Automakers Emphasize Service Enhancements. *Computerworld,* 84.

Naj, A.K., (1993, May 7). Some Manufacturers Drop Efforts to Adopt Japanese Techniques. *Wall Street Journal,* A1, 6.

Oliff, M.D. & Marchand, D.A. (1991, December). Strategic Information Management in Global Manufacturing. *European Management Journal,* 361-372.

Tawfik, J. (1993, March). Gaining Business From Information Technology: The Case of Otis Elevator, France. *European Management Journal,* 62-73.

Taylor, A. (1990, November 19). Why Toyota Keeps Getting Better and Better and Better. *Fortune,* 40.

**Chapter
3**

Business Process Reengineering:
Theory and Practice—
Views from the Field

Paul E. Cule
Georgia State University

Why has business process reengineering become such a hot topic in companies and in the press? What is driving this interest? In order to address these questions we need to put them into a context. The proposed context is that of a general restructuring of industrial economies. Business process reengineering may be viewed as one mechanism in achieving this restructuring.

Toffler (1990) suggests that the source of power is moving from wealth in the Industrial Age to knowledge in the Information Age. Thus, it has been suggested, we have moved from the Industrial Age to the Information Age. Whilst it is true we are no longer in the Industrial Age, we have not yet reached the Information Age. We are in a period of revolution, the Information Revolution. The Information Revolution has a parallel in the Industrial Revolution, except for an order of magnitude reduction in length. Revolutions of any form are typically accompanied by chaos and uncertainty, and the Information Revolution is no exception. The transition from age to age represents a paradigm shift. This shift is not instantaneous, and although the old paradigm no longer holds true the new paradigm may, as yet, be undefined. It is this lack of definition that leads to the chaos and uncertainty. There will be many new paradigms proposed whose adherents will avow that theirs is the only true way. These transient paradigms will come and go until a consensus is reached on some combination of the more successful ones. The decade of the 90's will be noted for uncertainty and chaos, paradigm shift in extremis.

In the Industrial Age, wealth was created by manufacturing, and the process of making things was changed by technology, steam driven machines. The industrial organization grew around manufacturing operations and had owners, managers and workers. Information was needed on what to make, how much to make, how to make it, and the financial status of the company. Information technology was word of mouth and pen on paper. The industrial organization evolved through most of the twentieth century, building on the process work of Frederick Taylor and Henry Ford, and the organizational work of Alfred Sloan. The underlying information technology was still pen and paper. The pinnacle of the Industrial Age organization occurred from the 1960's through the early 1980's. A new information technology, the computer, enabled organizations to store and process vast amounts of data. With computers, corporations were able to speed up the execution of their processes manyfold. Information became an additional source of power. However the processes and their attendant procedures did not change significantly.

In the late 1980's it became apparent that the environment was undergoing massive change. Change in corporations is being driven by change in all aspects of the environment in which corporations operate. Bennis succinctly describes these environmental changes.

> Everything's in motion. Mergers and acquisitions, deregulation, information technologies, and international competition alter the shape and thrust of American business. Changing demographics, escalating consumer sophistication, and new needs alter the marketplace. Changing industry structures, new strategic alliances, new technologies and modes, and stock market volatility alter the way we do business. Increasing competition, the shrinking of the world into one large global village, the move toward freer markets in communist countries, and the coming reality of the European Common Market alter the way we deal with the world and it deals with us (Bennis, 1989).

As a result, all companies are feeling the pressures of heightened competition. The globalization of markets has increased both the numbers of competitors and the quality of those competitors. Technology is changing at an increasing rate. At the same time, the natures of both work and the work force are changing. Companies must be increasingly *customer driven* or *market driven* just to survive.

How are companies addressing this changing environment? In the past, most companies looked to gradual change to get ahead of, or keep up with, changes around them. Change is now occurring at such a speed that most companies can no longer effect necessary changes in a gradual manner. Many are looking to more radical ways of achieving competitive advantage, or at least competitive parity. Some of these new approaches come under headings such as *re-engineering* the corporation, time-based competition, learning organizations. Any corporation proposing these approaches is facing radical surgery. Typically, such surgery carries the sobriquet business process reengineering.

In the next section we provide a general exploration of business process reengineering and its environment. We then introduce a model that we suggest may offer some explanation for why some companies meet their reengineering goals whilst others do not. We briefly present the results of a study in the context of the model. Finally we consider some implications for practitioners and researchers and draw some conclusions.

Background

Business process reengineering has become a much overused and abused term. When first promulgated by Hammer (1990a), it represented a radical departure from the usual methods of process rationalization and automation. Business reengineering has become the method of choice for achieving strategic goals (Bashein, Markus and Riley, 1994). Although it has become the program of choice, many of the programs are a far cry from the obliterate approach recommended by Hammer (1990a). Executives who are simply *downsizing* by layoffs call it business process reengineering. Incremental improvements, which we would classify as the Japanese approach of *kaizen*, long with similar approaches under the umbrella of Total Quality Management (TQM), are called by companies performing them, business process reengineering. In this chapter we use the term generically to represent a continuum of activity from incremental improvement, to major surgery of existing processes, to the obliterate model of Hammer (1990a). At one end of the continuum we have kaizen, or incremental improvement to existing processes. At the other, end we have the existing processes discarded and the corporation restructured. TQM lies in between and represents major surgery to existing processes in pursuit of improved product quality and reduced cycle times. It is a formal methodology. There are also those who are undertaking major surgery on their existing processes without using the TQM methodology. Both groups fall in the same range on our reengineering continuum so, for brevity, we have used

TQM to represent the general case of change at this level. This classification is a function of the degree of change exercised in one change effort. As a general rule, we see target improvements in the 5-10% range for kaizen versus 20-30% for TQM versus 50-80% for reengineering. Kaizen and TQM improve existing processes whereas the Hammer (1990a) approach starts from scratch.

Some call business process reengineering essential for success in the future, others call it a fad, still others regard it as a rehash of old ideas given a new name by consultants seeking business. A few, for example, Hammer and Champy (1993), see it as one element in "Reengineering the Corporation," a more holistic view of the changes through which their companies are going. Business process reengineering activities are driven by the need to reduce costs and increase competitiveness. However, as Drucker (1993) notes in an article in the *Wall Street Journal*: "A company beset by malaise and steady deterioration suffers from something far more serious than inefficiencies. Its 'Business Theory' is obsolete." No amount of reengineering will put a company on the right track without the right business theory.

Hammer (1990b), takes the position that companies are driven to reinventing the corporation by one of three forces; desperation or crisis (60% of cases); foresight (30%); ambition (10%). Those driven by desperation must do something radical in order to survive; they have little to lose by leaping to a new, and untried, paradigm. Those with foresight anticipate that they will reach the desperation state unless they do something to avert it. The ambitious will move to a new paradigm to create crises for their competition.

Reengineering offers tremendous opportunities to any corporation undertaking it. It offers the opportunities to increase revenue and broaden the scope of the business while reducing costs and utilizing fewer resources. However, the problem is that most reengineering efforts "fail," some say as many as 70% (Hammer and Champy 1993), some say more (Bashein et al., 1994). Clearly, such a failure rate is intolerable. CSC Index (1994) argue in the "Executive Summary" of their latest study that the failure rate is not this high. However, success seems to have been redefined. In the past, reengineering success has been seen as a binary condition, a project was either successful, or it was not. In this latest study, success is measured by degree; for example, "High achievers looked for an average 47% reduction in cycle times .... [and] reported nearly hitting their goal with a 45% average cut in cycle time"(CSC Index, 1994).

The current project failure rate represents a significant exposure to all practitioners and consultants in the field. Given the level of investment that a company must make if it is to reengineer, and the risk to its business if reengineering fails, many companies are likely to conclude that the risk of pursuing reengineering is too high.

If reengineering were seen by the corporate sector to be a fad, or just too risky to try, then reengineering would be limited to a few hardy souls willing to gamble all, or to those who have no choice. With such companies the chance of failure is increased because of the parlous situation from which they start. It is, therefore, in the interests of ensuring the continued productivity increase in corporate America to see a reduction in the failure rate. We need to understand why failures occur in order to foresee them in the first place, and prevent them in the second.

There is an emerging body of work aimed at prescriptions for success, for example, (Hammer and Champy, 1993; Barrett, 1994; Hall, Rosenthal, and Wade, 1993; Klein, 1994). Others have looked at preconditions for success (Bashein et al. 1994). The role of Information Technology has been explored, for example, Davenport and Short (1990). This body of work is found in journals that are directed to the practitioner, albeit some are academic journals of considerable standing. Many of the authors come from the practitioner community.

To shed some additional light on why failures occur, we propose an explanatory model we call the "Architectural Triad." The new environment for markets, economies, and business, is fundamentally different in structure and behavior. The depth and breadth of these changes in the environment require a corresponding degree of change within a corporation. The changes to the corporation will be fundamental, structural in form, and impact all aspects of the architectural triad.

A Reengineering Model: The Architectural Triad

We propose that all organizations are supported by what we will call The Architectural Triad. The members of this triad are "Process Architecture," "Organization Architecture" and "Information Architecture." We clarify these architectures in the following sections.

Process Architecture

The Process Architecture represents the "way things get done," i.e., "a series of actions or operations conducing to an end." It includes all processes and procedures, from human resource practices to manufacturing processes. It also includes the process measurement schema.

All human activities have a process, whether it be to set a table for dinner or to construct an aircraft. A process is that set of activities that must be completed for a given goal to be achieved. Using our dinner table example, the process might be: put the cloth on the table; get and set the cutlery; get and set the plates; get and set the glasses, etc. Note that this process has only one sequence requirement, the tablecloth must be on the table before other items can be placed on the table, beyond that, dishes, cutlery and glasses can be fetched and set in any sequence. Typically, a sequence is set when the process is operationalized and documented as a procedure.

All processes have an intended outcome and a targeted customer for that outcome. Davenport and Short (1990) define business processes as "a set of logically related tasks performed to achieve a defined business outcome." This definition is consistent with the above example. Measurement of business processes is task measurement. Business processes, in the context of the process architecture, are the fundamental, cross-functional processes rather than that within the function processes. For example, a fundamental business process would be the order fulfillment process which starts with the sale and includes order entry, manufacturing, warehousing, packing, shipping and accounts receivable processes. The functional processes, such as order entry, are sub-processes within the order fulfillment process. We call order fulfillment a fundamental process because the customer who placed the order is only interested in its fulfillment and therefore perceives it as a single process with a single outcome, satisfying the order. Other examples of fundamental business processes are product development, claims processing and supply fulfillment.

Organization Architecture

The process architecture represents the operation of the company, it contains the operational processes. The Organization Architecture represents the governance of the company, its values and beliefs and contains its management processes. The organization architecture is human-centered. It represents how a company organizes itself to get things done and with whom. It appertains to people, the way they are organized, the skills inventory, skills requirements, the way they are measured, promoted, paid. Measurement is oriented towards the performance of people rather than tasks. This architecture includes the internal relationships between people and between functions and the external relationships of the corporation. It also includes company policies and human resource practices. It covers the behavioral aspects of the company, its culture and its values.

For example, the recruiting process would be situated in the organization architecture and would include identifying sources of supply, evaluation and selection of candidates, the actual hiring sub-process and also introduction and initial training. Another example might be the promotion process which includes the characteristics, attributes and values of the job which will be compared with the characteristics, attributes and values of the candidates.

Information Architecture

The process architecture is operation process-centered. The organization architecture is human-centered, The Information Architecture is information-centered. Information architecture, information technology architecture, information systems architecture, are frequently defined in the information systems context as information engineering, or database design and management, or data repositories. This context, typically, refers to coded data held in data bases. Studies have shown that very little of the data executives use to make decisions is in this coded form; most comes from conversation or reading and is non-coded. In our terms, information architecture covers all information, whatever its source, whatever its form, that is required to effectively execute the business of the company. It requires a human-centered approach to information (Davenport, 1994), in which a category of data has different meanings to different people. For example, customer might have different attributes, meaning and be perceived differently across different functions in a company. Increasingly, the focus will be on the information architecture as a means to bring the system in balance. There are two major dimensions that must be considered in the information architecture. The first is the information itself and the second is the information technology infrastructure used to capture, maintain and disseminate the information.

In the information dimension we have the operational data, typically coded data held in data bases, along with all the other information used to support the process and organization architectures. This other information is generally acquired from purposeful reading and conversation. For example, this book becomes part of a company's information architecture when read purposefully by managers in that company who are planning, or undertaking, a reengineering effort. This category of information is frequently unstructured, non-coded and multimedia. Some may be acquired through information technology, such as on-line data base services, bulletin boards, or CD-ROM's and some will be acquired in the traditional methods of reading books and academic or business publications and by talking to others knowledgeable in a particular problem domain. This dimension also contains the rules of information. These rules cover the roles and responsibilities of individuals relative to information including conditions of access. The second dimension covers the information technology infrastructure. This infrastructure consists of all the communications networks, both voice and data, desk-top workstations, servers, mini-computers and mainframes. It includes all the software needed to capture and manage the information and to make it accessible under the rules of information.

The information systems function within a corporation should be the key group in establishing and implementing the information architecture and in providing the information technology support for the improved business processes. In so doing, it has critical business processes of its own, for example, the set of processes for application development, modification and maintenance.

Discussion

We can think of the triad as analogous to a tripod. Clearly, if we alter one of the legs of the tripod a state of imbalance will exist; the tripod and that which it supports will fall. The legs must be changed synchronously to maintain balance. So it is with the architectural triad. Change in one architectural "leg" must be balanced with corresponding changes in the other legs, that is, all three legs must stay aligned.

As an example of the effects of triad imbalance, let us consider one activity corporations are currently undertaking, downsizing. This is where the initial change focus is on the organization architecture. Many companies have reduced their staffing levels and flattened their organizations. However, many of these companies have changed neither their process nor their information architectures to parallel their organizational change activities. As a result the work has not changed and the people left behind have ever increasing workloads with attendant declines in morale and performance. The declining performance of the employees leads to declining performance of the corporation thus leading to further downsizing. The downward spiral continues until the corporation recognizes that it must change the other architectures in the triad. This example shows how the organization architecture cannot be addressed in isolation, neither should it be the primary driving force. However, any major changes to existing processes, or the creation of new, or greenfield, processes, inevitably impact the organizational architecture. The starting assumption for a greenfield approach is that no structure exists, that is, there is only a green field.

Different companies will approach reengineering in different ways depending on attributes of the company. We have categorized companies into two categories as a convenient way for describing their attributes. However the categories represent a continuum. In the first category, at one end of the continuum, will be found the

	Category 1: Industrial Age	Category 2: Information Age
Focus	-Cost driven -Cost Reduction -Efficiency	-Vision driven -Alignment (strategy, people, processes, technology) -Opportunity exploitation -Effectiveness

Process Architecture	-Rework existing processes
	  -TQM
	  -Incremental Improvement
		-New 'clean slate' processes
		-Transforming

Organization Architecture	-Restructuring -Downsizing/rightsizing -Outsourcing -Functional/Flattened -Alliances	-Cross-functional -Team based -'Virtual corporation' -Partnering
Information Architecture	-New technology for cost reduction and control -Workflow computing -Cooperative processing -Intra-organizational networks -Corporate database	-New infrastructure and architecture to exploit new processes. -Client/server -Inter-organizational networks -'Human-centered' Informtion

Table 1: Characteristics of Corporations by Category

companies whose management persists with its innate abhorrence of uncertainty and its desire to retain imperative control. Many of these companies will have been extremely successful and will have great difficulty in changing the cultural experience that generated that success. At the other end of the continuum, in the second category, we find those who are reinventing the corporation. These, of course, represent the extremes of the continuum. Category 1 companies will tend to view change within the existing Industrial Age model. Category 2 companies will tend to view change as a means of achieving the Information Age model. A summary, and comparison, of the two categories, in terms of their positions on business process reengineering and the architectural triad, is shown in Table 1.

Category 1: Industrial Age Model. Companies in this category will have, predominantly, a functional organization structure. Such a corporation may well be a leading edge adopter of new technology and hold information systems as critical to the success of the corporation. Downsizing will be used for cost reduction. Processes will be streamlined for increased efficiency. Downsizing will also occur as a result of the improvements in these processes. Technology will also be used for cost reduction and controls. Workflow computing will be very attractive. Outsourcing will be looked upon as additional opportunities for cost reduction. Sometimes, outsourcing will be viewed as enabling management to focus on the core business without having to concern themselves with the large investments in information systems. Reengineering will mean reworking existing systems in order to be able to take advantage of new tools and technologies and further enhance those applications. This category is, of course, a continuum.

Category 2: Information Age Model. In this category are the companies that are, or will be, undergoing a complete transformation. The focus will be on such things as; getting close to the customer, time compression or reducing the cycle for product development, manufacture and service, flexible cellular manufacturing, niche marketing, 24 hour a day availability and learning organizations.

The effect of this will be to create a new style of organization. The organization will be vision driven with strategies, people, processes, technology and measurements that line up with the vision. The new processes will create new classes of worker, new intra-company relations, and new inter-company relationships. Functional barriers will be broken down. Information will be commonly available and shared by all functions. Synergistic relationships among companies will arise to share information and tap into each other's value chains. These relationships are sometimes referred to as the virtual corporation. Although companies in this category will still have some functional structure, they will be predominantly organized around process. Projects will be formed as multi-function, multi-disciplinary teams who will have access to any and all information they need to achieve success. Team members will, in fact, be knowledge workers, (Drucker 1988). Reengineering the business processes also means that the technology systems and infrastructure that supported the old processes will no longer be useful. A new technology infrastructure will be built with new applications and systems to support the new processes. Process reengineering is not a one time effort. Companies in this category will be adaptive and learning organizations. Processes will undergo continuous improvement until they need to be reengineered again, possibly within 4-5 years. The technology infrastructure, applications and systems supporting these processes must be able to keep pace with process improvements and subsequent *n'th* time reengineering.

Reengineering in Practice: A Brief Study

In order to further explore the validity of the triad model we turn to the results of an exploratory study. The issues being addressed by this study have to do with the practical reengineering approaches being taken by companies, the role of information technology, the role of consultants and some of the human aspects of this level of change.

Study Methodology

A set of companies was requested, by letter, to participate in a survey on their activities in business process reengineering. Fourteen of those requested agreed to do so. Of these respondents, four were interviewed on their premises and the remainder were interviewed by telephone. All interviewees were at an executive level and well able to speak to the activities in their organizations. Respondent organizations were from a wide variety of industries.

Since this was an exploratory study, the interviews were semi-structured to allow interviewees to home in on what they felt were the most important aspects of their particular reengineering efforts. The interviews sought primarily to elicit the level(s) of reengineering, the roles of information technology and the information systems function, and the role(s) of consultants.

There is a significant bias in the study since a certain amount of self selection appears to have taken place. On the basis of the initial contacts we had in setting up the interviews we got the impression that those willing to be interviewed were active in business process reengineering and were confident that their activities were making a significant contribution to the corporate good. In addition, the number of companies surveyed was insufficient to form a statistically valid sample so any findings relate purely to the sample and should not be extended to the population at large.

Study Findings

General. The companies interviewed were all active to some degree in business process reengineering, albeit under different nomenclatures. We noted above that business process reengineering is a methodological continuum. Although the continuum runs from kaizen to obliterate, most respondents were in the middle of the range for the majority of their activities. There were a number of attributes, or characteristics of reengineering, that were highlighted by three or more respondents. We have classified these into five areas, namely, focus, process architecture, organization architecture, information architecture and the role of consultants. For example, focus relates to the primary forces driving the reengineering,

	Characteristics	Respondents
Focus	Cost reduction	7
	Quality	4
	Improved Customer Service	6
Process Architecture		
- Level of reengineering	Obliterate, any or all, processes	7
	TQM	5
	Change existing process, non-TQM	8
Organization Architecture		
- Issues	Company policies	3
	Leadership, any level	6
	Team skills	5
	Education	5
Information Architecture		
- Issues with IS function	Capabilities	5
	Involvement	3
- Role of IS function	Enabler	7
	Disabler	5
Role of consultants	External	13
	Internal	4
	Customized methodology	6

Table 2: Study Respondent Characteristics Related to the Architectural Triad

e.g., cost reduction. These are summarized in Table 2 showing each of these characteristics and its relationship to the classifications, along with the number of respondents highlighting the characteristic. Each classification and its associated characteristics and attributes are explored in more detail in the following sections.

Focus. The majority of reengineering activities were oriented toward reducing cost and cycle time. These were also seen as a method for improving customer service, particularly amongst respondents in the Insurance Industry. Improved product quality was also a focus item, particularly among those who were using formal TQM methods. Of those respondents who gave figures, the anticipated effects of reengineering would be to squeeze 20-50% out of the existing processes. Hammer (1990b) targets 70-80% improvement from the obliterate approach, but several respondents commented that the costs of taking his approach are too high and the impacts too destructive.

Downsizing should not be confused with reengineering, it should go hand in hand with reengineering. There are a number of ways of achieving downsizing. One way is the straight cost cutting approach of laying off employees without changing anything else. The problem with this is that the work to be done is still the same, simply fewer people to do it. On the other hand, one respondent company preceded reengineering with downsizing through attrition, forcing redeployment and creating the change environment to support the full reengineering effort. Outsourcing activities beyond a company's core competencies, for example, legal, information systems, was another method used for downsizing.

Process Architecture. By a strict definition, business process reengineering addresses only the process architecture. On the basis of our interviews and on other published material, business process reengineering can take many forms, from kaizen to the obliterate, greenfield or *clean slate* approach. Between the two is major change to existing processes. Two of the respondents were close to the obliterate end of the end of the continuum, while a further five used obliterate for the occasional process. Formal TQM processes were the preferred reengineering environment for five of the respondents. For example, several companies are reviewing their processes in the context of their overall TQM environment. One is eliminating what it calls the "re-'s" e.g., re-work, re-process, re-submit. It looks for the root cause and changes the process to eliminate the "re." Others use process flow diagrams to eliminate redundant activities. A further eight respondents were exercising major change to their existing processes without using formal TQM methods. Thus, by far the majority of all reengineering activities were oriented toward surgery on existing processes. When they start to look at a process most of these companies ask the question "Do I need this process at all?"

Kaizen, because of its incremental nature, will only bring incremental benefits in cost and cycle time reduction. Larger changes to existing processes bring larger, but still incremental, benefits. The risk of taking the process reengineering approach is that we are focusing on one member of the architectural triad and an out of balance situation will slowly arise. The legs on our tripod will become of different lengths and it will fall. Major change will bring greater incremental benefits than kaizen, however, the out of balance condition will also occur faster. These are, typically, category 1 companies. The majority of our respondents fell into this category. However, for some, surgery on their existing processes was radical enough to put their activities towards the category 2 end of the spectrum. Some of the companies that were, as a whole, in category 1 were, nevertheless, rebuilding some processes from scratch and, within the limits of those processes, were category 2. The greater the degree of change, the closer they get to category 2.

The greenfield or clean slate approach goes even further. These are the category 2 companies who are seeking to transform, as opposed to improve, themselves. Starting with the goal, they work back to develop the most effective process to meet that goal. This approach will almost always lead to a different organization, new skills and new job requirements. This in turn will lead to new measurement and reward systems. The organization becomes flatter and the definitions of management, and a manager, change. In many cases the organization is fluid and made up of multi-disciplinary teams of self-managed knowledge workers (Drucker 1988). Finally, the information systems that supported the original processes must be discarded and brand new ones built to enable the new process. Too often, reengineering activities display the same linearity as the above sequence. Again, this linear approach creates imbalances in the architectural triad, our tripod tips. The process leg is changed followed by the organization leg followed by the information leg. This drags out the timetable for effecting change and often requires rework or retrofitting of prior elements in the change effort.

Organization Architecture. In many cases, employees working on reengineering projects were working themselves out of a job. For other respondents, when people were freed up they went into talent pools for retraining and redeployment. These respondents noted that this puts tremendous pressure on the human resource aspects of the company. Leadership was seen as key to getting employee participation. Getting employee participation was key to success. This leadership, and commitment, must come from the top. Most respondents had a corporate organization with reengineering responsibility. In most cases these organizations acted as change agents and internal consultants. The leaders of the implementation teams came from line management. Various respondents noted that project management skills were essential for the team leaders and that the teams needed up front training in such things as team skills and change management. Some respondents also noted that the activities needed to be very carefully managed to prevent backlash.

A number of our respondents discovered that when they attempted to reengineer their processes their actions were inhibited by corporate policies which we would classify as part of the organization architecture. To quote one respondent: "We often find the reward systems at cross purposes with process improvements." For another company, some corporate policies were addressed by reducing the numbers of job classifications by an order of magnitude to enable change and redeployment.

Information Architecture. Respondents addressed two aspects of the information architecture, the role of the technology and the role of the information systems function in the organization. The role of information technology varied from "enabler" to "disabler," sometimes being both in the same company. The reasons for information technology being seen as a disabler were investment in legacy systems, and dissatisfaction with prior dealings with the information systems function. Older existing systems often lacked the data and infrastructure to support the modified processes. Significant investment and time were needed to upgrade, or replace, applications to support the new processes. For some, these legacy systems were an inhibitor to the degree of reengineering because they worked and companies were reluctant to discard the high investment they represented. On the other hand, technology became an enabler when it could drive business process redesign faster and further than initially envisaged.

As expected, the respondent companies viewed their information systems functions from being key participants, even drivers, to non-participants. In some cases the senior information systems function executive was an active member of the executive team driving the reengineering process. In others, the information systems function involvement was an afterthought. In the latter cases, the function was perceived as either avoiding participation, or less than competent to be involved. The role of the information systems group depended to a great extent on their attitudes and capabilities coupled with the level of confidence held in them by the other executives. Several of our respondents had concerns about the inability of the information systems function to participate in any reengineering due to various factors such as history, attitude, and lack of skills. These respondents were in the course of, or had completed, a considerable investment in bringing the information systems function to a point where it could participate in a meaningful way. These respondents deemed this to be a prerequisite to embarking on any major reengineering effort. However, in most cases someone from the information systems organization was a team member of the reengineering team. They were seen as valuable for their experience in systematic thinking as well as advising on new technology capabilities. In four of the cases, the Information Systems organization was taking a leadership role some, or all, of the time, though for the most part unofficially.

It was clear that many information systems organizations had undergone rapid changes themselves. The respondent companies ranged across the whole gamut of approaches to their information systems from obliterate by outsourcing all information technology, including application development, to change within the aegis of company wide TQM, to individual kaizen efforts, to very little, if any, focus. For one company the information systems service improved when everything was outsourced, for another it improved when everything was brought in house. In both cases, service was improved when a major change occurred. A number saw their own information systems processes as business processes that needed reengineering as much as did any others. In one case, the information systems organization had virtually become a TQM showcase. In three of the cases, the thrust was to acquire as many applications as possible from outside, either through outsourcing, or commercially available off-the-shelf systems. The latter would need to be easy to customize. Some respondents were building information architectures and information models to support business process reengineering.

The Role of Consultants. Our respondents made it clear that there is no "cook book" for business process reengineering methodology. The respondent set was just about unanimous that the methodologies must be tailored to the individual company. For several respondents, the methodology was further tailored to meet the needs of specific sets of activities. Although all respondents have used, or are using, consultants, some were averse to using those, such as Hammer, Duran, Demming, whom they described as "demagogues." Seminars and writing from such consultants were used to help create the atmosphere for change and to stimulate creativity. Several respondents commented that a number of consulting companies insisted on doing things by their own book and were not willing to work with the company to establish a customized methodology. Typically, consulting companies with this attitude were not hired. Another key element in choosing a consultant was fit. A clear compatibility with the company was a requirement; so much so that a number of respondents insisted on interviewing the individuals they would be working with and reserved the right to subsequently remove them.

Thirteen of the respondents were using external consultants to some extent. Four had developed their own internal consulting capability. Whilst all of our respondents used consultants to a greater or lesser degree, most used them at the early stages of problem identification and analysis. The majority used them in specific areas where their companies lacked a particular expertise. They were also used as a way of "getting management's attention" and to "take the heat" for things like headcount studies.

At the time of the interviews, respondents felt that there were few consultants who covered the full breadth of reengineering the corporation; still fewer who could cover it in depth as well. One interviewee referred to there being three groups of consultants, each of which had a different bias. The first group was in the business of selling software and used process reengineering as a vehicle to achieve this. The second group used formal analysis techniques such as flow diagrams and analysis charts. The third group has an organizational design background and focus. The interviewee noted that each of these biases was needed. We can relate these to our architectural triad. Group 1 is oriented toward the information architecture, group 2 toward the process architecture, and group 3 toward the organization architecture.

Implications

From our sample certain common threads appear. Business process reengineering cannot be undertaken casually; it requires intense planning and high commitment at all levels. The soft issues are the hardest to deal with and require constant attention. For most respondents a great deal of focus was placed on training, particularly for implementation teams. Information technology is perceived as an enabler, however some respondents were not able to capitalize on the enabling opportunity as much as they would have liked. Consultants were seen to be important to success but needed to be selected and used judiciously.

Companies were spread across the continuum from kaizen to obliterate. There was more activity towards the obliterate end of the scale than at the kaizen end. However, the obliterate approach was, in many cases, viewed as too expensive and too destructive. One respondent, who was in the obliterate mode, referred to it as "using differential equations when most people can only add and subtract; a great deal of education is required."

A corporation undertaking a reengineering of the corporation, or some significant part, as per Hammer and Champy (1993), would give equal, and simultaneous, weight to each architecture. Investment would be balanced and can be represented by the illustrative pie chart in Figure 1. This investment can be thought of terms of management focus, dollars, resources applied, people or some combination of these or other measures.

Most of our respondents, however, were looking at change to their existing processes, and thus starting with the process architec-

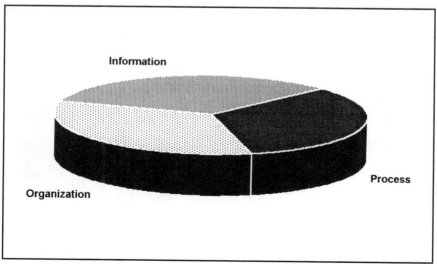

Figure 1: Reengineering the Corporation—Illustrative Investment Pattern

ture. A similarly illustrative representation of this pattern of investment is shown in Figure 2. Actual proportions are not important for this discussion, imbalance is.

A corporation can gain considerable advantage from the kaizen, or incremental change, approach to its business processes. This does not represent a large investment and the investment pattern will approximate Figure 1. However, as the level of process change increases, that is the more radical the surgery, the more the investment in the process architecture increases. This creates a proportionately lower level of investment on the information, and organization architectures, as illustrated in Figure 2, that can slow down the effectiveness of the process change activity. Our tripod is unbalanced. The requirement, then, lies in strengthening the investment in information and organization activities to bring the system into balance.

For the practitioner, the effect of this type of imbalance is that the expected return on an investment in changing one architecture will not be realized. Furthermore, unanticipated problems and costs will be incurred by the distortion in the other two architectures. To some degree, this may explain why we have not realized the anticipated productivity gains from investments in information technology. These distortions can often lead to problems associated with a dysfunctional organization, such as low morale, high employee turnover, "turf battles." Major changes to processes have organizational impacts; company policies often stand in the way of change; reward systems are often at cross-purposes with the change.

Process reengineering will result in downsizing. According to Ehrbar (1993) by some estimates as many as 25 million jobs could disappear out of a private sector job base of 90 million. As work is removed from a process fewer people are required to perform it. Often

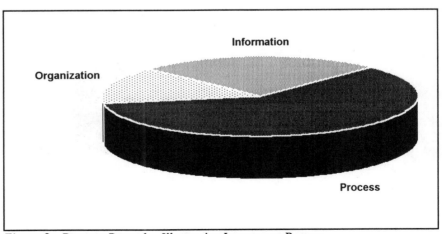

Figure 2: Process Rework—Illustrative Investment Pattern

whole departments disappear. Staff cuts can be as high as 75% in the obliterate approach (Hammer, 1990b). This does lead to flatter organizations and fewer people, the original downsizing objective. However, the new processes are parallel rather than serial. They are often executed by multi-disciplinary teams of self managed knowledge workers. The skills required are quite different from the old set. Changes in measurement and reward systems are necessary. This not only leaves organizations with a skills challenge, but also an attitude challenge. Champy notes:

> Curiously, we find that most resistance to reengineering comes not from the very top with senior management, or the very bottom from the people on the factory floor, answering customer calls, or out in the market selling. These people recognize that the business processes under which they labor are broken and must change. Some of them, in fact, believe that if they don't change, their organization may have no future. The real resistance comes from the middle to upper-middle level managers. They have the most vested in the old ways and old rules of the organization (Champy, 1992).

Many employees were quite comfortable with the old command and control structure. They did what they were told to do, management made decisions and worried how everything fitted together. In self managed teams they have to take responsibility for the success of the team; there is no traditional manager to hide behind. Many people who were thought of as excellent employees in the old model may be unable to make the change and become effective in the new model. Even those that want the change face new, and continuing, education. This is even more true with management. Many mid-level managers will become redundant. The responsibilities, functions and skills of managers will change radically. It is possible that no more than 30% of the existing management team will be able to make the transformation successfully. The new manager will be a leader, coach, and facilitator rather than one who assigns and measures tasks. It is quite likely that those who will be successful in the new environment would have had problems fitting comfortably in the old structure. This level of change demands extensive retraining across all levels of the organization.

Conclusions

The move to reengineer the corporation, or the parallel addressing of all three architectures in the architectural triad, has just begun. Companies can only go so far with the kaizen approach to improving their existing processes. At some point they will have to face reengineering along the Hammer (1990a) model of obliterate. After reengineering, kaizen will be used for improvement up to the point when the company has to reengineer again. This will be the paradigm for the Information Age company; reengineer, continuous process improvement, reengineer, continuous process improvement, the cycle being continued ad infinitum.

As competitive forces increase, more and more companies will start to rethink their fundamental business processes for one of Hammer's three reasons (Hammer, 1990b). The rate of reengineering by companies will be non-linear. IDC estimates that the market for business process reengineering will grow from $250M in 1991 to $2.2B by 1996. Another indication of this increase is the number of people attending Hammer's three-day executive seminar. In 1991 enrollment was 300, in 1992 it was 1500, and for 1993 Hammer estimated 3,000 executives would attend (Ehrbar, 1993).

However, the changes wrought by reengineering a corporation can have a major impact on the corporate culture. A certain level of trauma must be felt by a corporation before it is willing to reengineer itself to this level. For some companies, particularly those with strong cultures and a long history of success, the level of trauma needed to support rapid, culturally impacting change may not be reached before the destruction of the company.

As we have seen from our respondents, some are reengineering the corporation. These are the experimenters. The balance are performing surgery, sometimes radical, on their existing processes. As the pressures increase we posit that more companies will take the plunge until by the end of the decade those that have not reengineered at least once will be in the throes of their first, or will have ceased to be significant entities in the marketplace.

In order to avoid excessive disruption, companies may focus on changing their processes but try to hold their organization architecture constant. Furthermore, they may ignore the impacts on their information architecture. Frequently, the development and deployment of the required information systems and their attendant technology are deferred until late in the process redevelopment cycle thus delaying, if not negating, the new process. Alternatively, the introduction and deployment of a new technology can cause a change to all three architectures. Each of these approaches will lead to an imbalance in the triad and thus increase the possibility of failure.

We propose that the architectural triad offers a model for explaining why many reengineering efforts fail. It also offers a model, a context, for assessing reengineering plans and ongoing reengineering efforts. The triad forces are fundamental and apply to all organizations. We suggest that it is imperative that companies maintain the triad in balance if they wish to be successful in their reengineering efforts.

References

Barrett, J. L. (1994, Spring). Process visualization: Getting the vision right is key. *Information Systems Management,* 10, 14-23.

Bashein, B. J., Markus, M. L., & Riley, P. (1994, Spring). Preconditions for BPR success, and how to prevent failures. *Information Systems Management,* 10, 7-13.

Bennis, W. (1989). *On Becoming a Leader.* Reading, MA: Addison-Wellesley.

Champy, J. (1992, Spring). In reengineering, organizational change must start day 1. *CSCInsights,* 4, pp 2-3.

CSC Index, (1994). *State of reengineering report, executive summary.* Cambridge, MA: Author.

Davenport, T. H. (1994, March-April). Saving IT's soul: Human centered information management. *Harvard Business Review,* 72, 119-131.

Davenport, T. H. & Short, J. E. (1990, Summer). The new industrial engineering: Information technology and business process redesign. *Sloan Management Review,* 31(4), 11-27.

Drucker, P. (1988, January-February). The coming of the new organization. *Harvard Business Review,* 66, 45-53.

Drucker, P. (1993, February 2). A turnaround primer. *The Wall Street Journal.*

Ehrbar, A. (1993, March 16). 'Re-engineering' gives firms new efficiency, workers the pink slip. *The Wall Street Journal,* pp 1,11.

Hall, G., Rosenthal, J., & Wade, J. (1993, November-December). How to make reengineering really work. *Harvard Business Review,* 71, 119-131.

Hammer, M. (1990a, July-August). Reengineering work: Don't automate, obliterate. *Harvard Business Review,* 68, 104-112.

Hammer, M. (1990b, October). *The reengineering challenge: Implementing major change.* Presented at The Hammer Forum 90, Cambridge, MA.

Hammer, M. & Champy, J. (1993). *Reengineering the Corporation: A Manifesto for Business Revolution.* New York: HarperCollins.

Klein, M. M. (1994, Spring). Reengineering Methodologies and Tools: A Prescription for Enhancing Success. *Information Systems Management,* 10, 30-35.

Toffler, A. (1990). *Power Shift.* New York: Bantam Books.

Chapter 4

Understanding Business Process Reengineering:
A Sociocognitive Contingency Model

Mathew J. Klempa
Klempa & Associates

*All the clever thoughts have long since been thought.
What matters is to think them anew.*

*But few have comprehension and are at once capable
of action. Comprehension expands but paralyzes,
action inspires but delimits.*

Johann Wolfgang Goethe (1749-1832)

Private sector investments in information technology (IT) as a percentage of revenues range between 1.5-4% (Strassman, 1985), (Weill and Olson, 1989), (Gurbaxani and Mendelson, 1990). Further, IT as a percent of capital stock is rising—threefold from 1970 to 1988 in service industries; sixfold in manufacturing (Roach, 1989). At a macro level, IT has not effected predicted business transformations, not raised productivity (Morton, 1991), nor improved other measures of business performance (Venkatraman, 1994). For the most part, new IT has been superimposed on organizations designed according to Taylorian scientific management principles, focusing on control of variance. The result, as reflected in one CIO's comment from the research of Stoddard and Jarvenpaa (cited in Davenport and Stoddard, 1994) "we were investing a lot, but not getting the desired productivity...we did not change the processes that were being automated" (p. 123). For the most part, IT exceeded the organization's ability to use it because of lack of organization change (Kanter, 1984).

Earlier cross-functional process redesign conceptualizations include Porter's (1985) value chain analysis and Gibson and Jackson's (1987) business transformation via information technology. Both Davenport and Short (1990) and Hammer (1990) triggered intense interest from both academia and practitioners in business process reengineering (BPR). BPR is generally advocated as universally applicable to organizations and organization activities. The literature includes many normative examples of BPR innovation successes, e.g., Hallmark, Bell Atlantic, Taco Bell (Hammer and Champy, 1993), AT&T (Hall, Rosenthal, and Wade, 1993), Kodak (Stewart, 1992), Texas Instruments (Musser, 1992), (Shore, 1993), Bank of Nova Scotia (Russell, 1994), Mutual Benefit Life (Clarke, 1991), Shell Oil (Pope, 1993), and Merck, Cigna (Shore, 1993). A five year analysis of Cigna's reengineering efforts is found in Caron, Jarvenpaa, and Stoddard (1994). Descriptive literature typifies new research areas. Few conceptual models of BPR have emerged. Hammer and Champy's (1993) Business System Diamond model—business processes, values and beliefs, management and measurement systems, and jobs and structures focuses on the primacy of the linkages among these four organization elements. However, such normative conceptualizations do not readily help the practitioner understand the design and implementation of BPR.

An integrative understanding of BPR innovation as an organization dynamic requires a robust paradigm for understanding the systemic forces underlying BPR outcomes—BPR innovation versus BPR improvement. The paradigm should be well grounded in extant organization theory, thus enabling integration and understanding of existing information, as well as channeling future research directions which permit comparison of results and generalizability. This chapter presents a sociocognitive innovation metaforce contingency model well grounded in innovation research and literature themes. The innovation metaforce contingency paradigm[1] (Huber and McDaniel, 1986), integrates three major streams of innovation research: organization culture, organization learning and knowledge sharing. In addition, the model synthesizes research literatures on individual creativity, and innovation in organizations. The holistic approach of the innovation metaforce contingency model reflects a perspective on innovation called for by theorists such as Lewin and Minton (1986). Previous application of the innovation metaforce contingency model to the domain of IT diffusion, is explicated in

Klempa (1994a, 1994b, 1993).

The model serves both academic and practitioner needs. For the practitioner, the three innovation metaforces, organization culture, organization learning, and knowledge sharing, are dynamically linked to the organization's

- BPR propensity
- BPR capability
- BPR implementation effectiveness.

BPR propensity includes the organization's environmental awareness, information gathering, and conceptualizing antecedent to BPR decision making. BPR capability encompasses decision analysis of the situation and solutions, as well as implementation analysis and considerations. BPR implementation effectiveness includes all technical and organization operational implementation aspects.

Understanding each of the three innovation metaforces and their multiplicative interaction, addresses:

•*why* certain BPR innovations succeed where others fail
•*what* enhances or promotes BPR innovation
•*which* systemic organization properties enhance or inhibit organization change

The innovation contingency model serves both diagnosis and intervention purposes. Placement of the organization along a BPR continuum defined by the model enables the organization to assess the likely extent of BPR innovation. Placement along the BPR continuum also enables customization of organization intervention modalities in order to overcome resistance to BPR and accomplish desired organization change.

As a paradigm, the innovation contingency model is meant to influence the academic research domain of inquiry, by focusing on both the contingent aspects of BPR innovation and its interactionist perspective. Thus, research foci should be multilevel within the organization and account for interactions.

The objectives of this chapter are:

- to explicate the sociocognitive foundations of organization culture, organization learning, and knowledge sharing as multiplicatively interacting metaforces determining a continuum of BPR innovativeness, BPR improvement
- to synthesize the role of enhancing, orthogonal, and counterculture organization subcultures in the BPR dynamic
- to explicate the nonlinear, interactive, recursive nature of the BPR dynamic

- to explicate the formal organization, informal organization, organization's frame of reference[2] (OFOR) / decision making, and IT interactions within the BPR recursive dynamic
- to explicate resistance to organization change cybernetically, as an autopoetic[3] (automatic, equilibrium seeking) system response
- to address organization culture, organization learning, and knowledge sharing pathways to organization change

Sociocognitive Foundations of the Innovation Metaforces

This chapter utilizes a sociocognitively (Ginsberg, 1990) based paradigm, i.e., innovation is an antecedent to, as well as a consequence of, cognitive, social, and organizational events.   A sociocognitively based paradigm grounds the role of managerial cognition in the systemic properties of innovation, as well as in the behavioral dynamics of innovation. Organizations must have mechanisms and processes to interpret ambiguous events and provide meaning and direction to organization members. The organization must generate, develop, and implement innovations, i.e., new ideas or behaviors, which, in turn, change individuals, groups, and the organization itself.

Three innovation metaforces, organization culture, organization learning, and knowledge sharing, as depicted by the three dichotomous axes of the cube in the innovation metaforce contingency model (Figure 1), delineate the homeostatic (stability oriented) / morphogenetic (change oriented) organization change continuum, shown in Figure 2.   Homeostatic organizations (homogeneous, adaptive, hierarchical) will likely experience BPR improvement, i.e., beta[4] organization change. Morphogenetic organizations (heterogeneous, innovative, networked) will likely experience BPR innovation, i.e., gamma[5] organization change (Terborg, Howard, and Maxwell, 1980) and (Van de Vliert, Huismans, and Stok, 1985).   An organization's positioning on the homeostatic / morphogenetic (Wilkins and Dyer, 1988), (Lundberg, 1985) organization change continuum is a summative index of the organization's BPR propensity, BPR capability, and BPR implementation effectiveness.

The three innovation metaforces represent a parsimonious model, well grounded in theoretical underpinnings. Organization culture theory stems from the Tavistock Institute's sociotechnical system (Emery and Trist, 1972) approach to understanding technology and organization change, as well as Pettigrew's (1973, 1979) research. Daft and Huber (1987) ground organization learning in organization adaptation research (Lawrence and Lorsch, 1967), and experiential organization interpretation research (Argyris and Schoen,

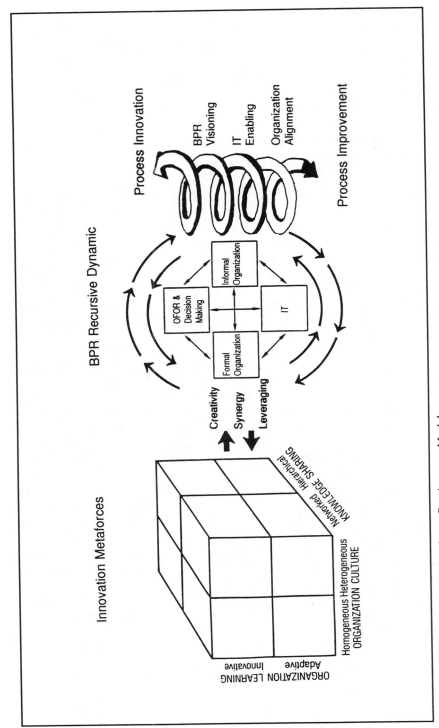

Figure 1: BPR—Innovation Metaforce Contingency Model

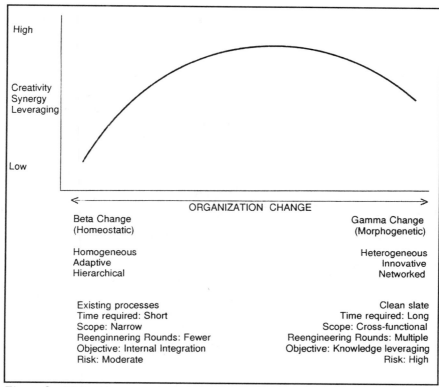

Figure 2: BPR—Homeostatic/Morphogenetic Change Continuum

1978). Huber (1984) grounds knowledge sharing theory in contingency theory, strategic management theory, and systems theory. Each of the three innovation metaforces is discussed in turn below.

Organization Culture

This chapter utilizes an interpretive view (Riley, 1983) of organization culture, i.e, something the organization is (Table 1), as expressed through socially constructed systems of shared meaning. Organization culture is both a macro and micro concept, serving to integrate the individual, group, and organization. Thus, organization culture both impacts, and is impacted by: the formal organization, informal organization, the OFOR / decision making, and IT. In terms of the formal organization, organizations are instruments for task accomplishment through organization forms and practices which are manifestations of both conscious and unconscious processes (Smircich, 1983). Organizations are systems of knowledge shared by organization members through a variety of channels (informal organization). Kilman, Saxton, and Serpa (1986) identify

Researcher(s)	Culture:
Tunstall, 1986	is a company's ways of conducting business that differentiate it from all other companies
Sproull, 1981	differentiates an organization, engenders commitment to it's purposes, promotes or impedes innovation
Duncan, 1989	is learned, shared, transmitted
Kilmann, Saxton, Serpa, 1986	is the social energy that drives or fails to drive the organization
Kerr & Slocum, 1987	is both the shaper of human interaction and the outcome of it, i.e., culture simultaneously determines and reflects beliefs, values, norms
Wiener, 1988	expresses the values that organization members come to share
Beyer, 1981	is the shared ideologies, beliefs, and norms that influence actions taken by the organization
Wilkins & Dyer, 1988	is socially acquired and shared knowledge that is embodied in specific and general organization OFORs
Tichy, 1982	is the most complex and pervasive influence on organization effectiveness

Table 1: Interpretive View of Organization Culture

the role of organization culture in undergirding the collection and interpretation of information and decision making modalities (OFOR / decision making). IT provides social and managerial systems the means to accomplish organization transformations, with implications for both individuals and groups. The social and technical systems simultaneously influence one another (Hulin and Roznowski, 1985).

The saliency of organization culture to BPR propensity, BPR capability, and BPR implementation effectiveness is better understood with reference to the three levels of depth of culture — ideologies and beliefs, values, and norms (Kilman, Saxton, and Serpa (1986), Beyer (1981), Schein (1984), and Sproull (1981). At the highest level, ideologies are coherent set of beliefs that bind individuals in organizations together and explain cause-and-effect relationships. Beliefs are understandings that represent credible relationships between objects, properties, and ideas. Ideologies/beliefs shape the collection and interpretation of information, undergird all decisions and actions, and reveal how the organization approaches decisions and problems, e.g., BPR. Ideologies and beliefs constitute the underpinnings of the OFOR (see later section in this chapter).

An individual's attitude is composed of beliefs (Calder and Schurr, 1981). Attitudes are dispositional, i.e., composed of the individual's perceptual interpretation of information through cognitive processing, as well as situational. Desired organization change, i.e., BPR innovation, must therefore deal with underlying ideologies and beliefs, and require both individual and organization attitudinal shifts.

Ideologies and beliefs explain the how and why of events; values influence choices of which courses of action to take. At an intermediate level of depth of culture, values are defined as an internalized, normative system of beliefs that are antecedents to behavior (Wiener, 1988). Functional values are explicit guides for member's behaviors, e.g., innovativeness of the organization. In the heterogeneous culture, for example, values foster entrepreneurship, avoiding being defensive, and a high tolerance for differences in values. In the homogeneous culture, values encourage conformity, defending oneself, and a low tolerance for differences in values.

An organization's value system provides pivotal values concerning organization related behaviors across units and levels of the organization. Thus, values may be shared by the organization as a whole and/or distinct subunits within it. Values exhibit a tenacity to resist change (Shore, 1993) because of their shared nature, as well as their verisimilitude. The value dynamic exhibits both reciprocity and synergies (Fitzgerald, 1988). Both the organization's and each subunit's values can be described by intensity[6] and breadth[7]. The importance of intensity and breadth of values emerges at significant organization breakpoints (Sheldon, 1980), e.g., BPR innovations with multidimensional organization impacts.

At the lowest level of depth of culture, norms are the unwritten and socially transmitted guides to behavior. Norms that promote innovation are of two types: those that promote creativity and those that promote implementation of the creative output. Creativity promoting norms include: risk taking, rewards valuing change, and openness. Norms promoting the implementational aspects of creativity output include: shared vision, respect and trust; autonomy coupled with expectation for action; and empowered people with focus on quality (O'Reilly, 1989). In the homogeneous organization, norms that discourage innovation include, for example, risk avoidance, skirting difficult issues, agreeing with other people, and competition with others.

The multidimensional organization change associated with cross-functional BPR innovation must address the three levels of depth of culture. The organization must develop and implement a comprehensive organization change program that addresses ideology/belief, value, and norm shifts required. Gamma organization change programs that address all three levels may require two to five year implementation programs (Davenport, 1993) and (Skinner, 1994). Such organization change programs may require successive rounds of reengineering (Shore, 1993).

Looked at as an integrated whole, the three levels of depth of culture constitute the organization's cultural potency (Saffold, 1988). Cultural potency is a summative index of the power of the organization's culture paradigm to act as an influence on behavior. Evaluation of the organization's cultural potency is relevant to the design of an effective BPR organization change program. In addition to cultural potency, organization culture diagnoses also must assess cultural dispersion (Saffold, 1988). Cultural dispersion includes the degree to which culture manifestations are shared across different groups or subcultures, as well as the degree to which beliefs, values, and norms are deeply internalized by subcultures, groups, and individuals.

Organization Subcultures. For purposes of exposition, the innovation metaforce contingency model conceptualizes organization culture at the level of the firm. Organization culture is not monolithic, i.e., subcultures within an organization can occur, for example, along gender, education, occupational specialty, task exigency, functional, product, or geographical lines. Several subcultures can coexist without one becoming dominant and with little friction. The innovative organization recognizes and manages organization subcultures (Wilkins, 1983). Subculture understanding is an integral part of organization culture analysis, assuming particular importance within BPR because of BPR's cross-functional nature.

Subcultures use structured perceptions to make sense of their own behavior and that of other organization units. Subcultures enter into negotiations in order to maintain and adapt their respective behaviors and activities in relation to the organization culture (Lucas, 1987). Three types of subcultures are identified—enhancing, orthogonal, and counterculture (Duncan, 1989). The enhancing subculture more fervently accepts the dominant culture's values than the dominant culture does. The orthogonal subculture accepts the values of the dominant culture, as well as a nonconforming set of values that it considers its own. A counterculture challenges the values of the dominant culture. Countercultures that are innovative within a latitude of tolerance by the dominant culture can be beneficial to the organization. Homogeneous orthogonal as well as homogeneous countercultures in a dominant heterogeneous culture organization will require an extensive organization subunit change program, if BPR innovation is undertaken. Conversely, heterogeneous subcultures in a dominant homogeneous culture organization, can be utilized to take on substantive roles in BPR change efforts.

Table 2 synthesizes the impact of culture characteristic differences on BPR propensity, BPR capability, and BPR implementation effectiveness. The heterogeneous culture is risk seeking and innovative; the homogeneous culture is risk averse with minimal innovativeness.

Researcher(s)	Heterogeneous	Homogeneous
BPR PROPENSITY		
Tushman & Nadler, 1986	Culture proactively managed; provides innovative energy	Culture passively managed; non-energizing
Delbecq & Mills, 1985	Open communication encouraged; quality stressed; distinctions in rank reduced	Reduced communication, e.g., ideas from below; power associated with distinctions in rank
Tushman & Nadler, 1986	Top management understands and manages the duality of stability and change	Top management focus on stability becomes a source of cultural inertia
Beyer, 1981	Organization's ideologies / beliefs encourage innovation, change	Organization's ideologies / beliefs maintain reliability, stability
BPR CAPABILITY		
Hammer & Champy, 1993	Inductive thinking -application of IT enables organization to do things it is not now doing	Deductive thinking - application of IT increases efficiency/reduces costs
Davenport, 1993; Weick, 1987	Mutual trust, support enlarges pool of inputs to organization's collective requisite variety	Multidimensional decision making at all levels suffers from lack of requisite variety
Lord & Maher, 1990	Cybernetically adjusted organization frame of reference; multidimensional feedback	Limited capacity information processing; narrow frame of reference
Cherns, 1976	Multi-functionally skilled individuals enable wider range of responses	Highly specialized individuals limit range of responses
BPR IMPLEMENTATION EFFECTIVENESS		
Lorsch, 1986	Organization linkages treated as systemic with interpersonal imperfections	Organizational linkages treated as mechanistic and static
Allaire & Firsirotu, 1985; Lucas, 1987	Inter-subculture behavior recognized and proactively managed	Culture treated as monolithic; sub-cultures ill defined and not understood
Saffold, 1989	Cultural dispersion, potency promote both sharing, internalization of values, assumptions	Minimal cultural dispersion, potency limits sharing, internalization of values, assumptions

Table 2: Organization Culture Dichotomy

Organization Learning

Organization learning takes place in systems of interrelated roles (Simon, 1991), both formal and informal. Learning is both individual and conducted in the social fabric of the organization, involving both cognitive and social communication bases (March, 1991) and (Simon, 1991). Individuals are socialized to organizational ideologies and beliefs, values, and norms. These organization culture elements impact both the formal organization, informal organization mechanisms, OFOR and decision making, and application of IT in the organization. Ideologies/beliefs, values, and norms are antecedent to, as well as a consequence of, higher level and lower level organization learning (Figure 3).

Higher level learning is double loop (Argyris, 1991), and Argyris and Schoen (1978, 1982). Double loop learning seeks out contradictions, in order to resolve them. The detection of contradictions produces learning, resulting in changes in both the individual and organization's underlying ideologies/beliefs, values, norms. Thus, higher level learning impacts the entire organization, develops understandings of causation and complex associations involving new actions, and is characterized by change in the OFOR and decision making (Fiol and Lyles, 1985). Higher level learning significantly impacts the organization's BPR propensity, BPR capability, and BPR implementation effectiveness. In contrast, lower level learning (single loop) occurs through repetition, in a well-understood context, focuses on behavioral outcomes, and institutionalizes formal rules. Single loop learning maintains the organizations' ideologies/beliefs, values, and norms, seeking to detect and correct error within that system of rules.

Higher level learning organizations are characterized by their absorptive capacity, diversity of knowledge, creative redundant knowledge (Cohen and Levinthal, 1990), regenerative learning, and creative tension (Senge, 1990). These five properties facilitate application of new knowledge to innovation, knowledge transfer, shared understanding, an ability to assess systemic sources of problems, and commitment, thus enabling organization movement to a future vision such as embodied in cross-functional BPR innovation.

Several higher level organization learning mechanisms permit organization exploration, thus testing of new understandings of causation and complex associations. These higher level learning mechanisms include: rich learning (March, Sproull, and Tamuz, 1991), action learning (Morgan and Ramirez, 1984), vicarious learning, unlearning, and experimental learning (Huber, 1991). Exploration through higher level learning permits discovery of contrary experience, i.e., exploring new validates. Exploitation contributes to

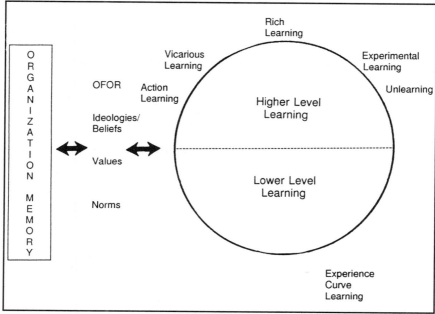

Figure 3 Organization Learning

organization reliability. Rapid socialization reduces creative organization exploration (March, Sproull, and Tamuz 1991). March (1991) explored the effects of socialization rate and employee turnover rate on aggregate organization knowledge. March found that a moderate level of employee turnover, with relatively slow socialization serves to increase exploration, thus improving aggregate organization knowledge. Innovative learning organizations balance reliability and validity[8].

Both the individual and organization are able to employ nonmonotonic reasoning through several mechanisms. Learning takes place through previous actions, not just by examining consequences. March, Sproull, and Tamuz (1991) refer to this as rich learning. Such methods as critical incidents in the organization's past, and hypothetical histories through simulation allow the organization to examine preferences and explore values and aspirations. Through unlearning (Huber, 1991), Hedberg (1981), and Klein (1989), organizations can discard obsolete and misleading knowledge. Such discarding of obsolescent processes and knowledge is central to BPR propensity, BPR capability, and BPR implementation effectiveness.

Innovative learning organizations develop and utilize informal networks, both for knowledge acquisition and learning processes. Such innovative learning organizations utilize informal communal noncanonical knowledge, rather than bounded and canonical knowledge associated with formal groups sanctioned by the organization

Researcher(s)	Innovative	Adaptive
BPR PROPENSITY		
Huber, 1991; Gioia & Manz, 1985	Vicarious learning characterized by dynamic, continuous organization benchmarking	Vicarious learning characterized by intermittent corporate intelligence
Huber, 1991; Nystrom & Starbuck, 1984; Klein, 1989	Top management unlearning process listens to dissent; converts events into learning opportunities	Minimal or no unlearning; top management does not listen carefully to subordinates
Huber, 1991; Lyles, 1988; Nystrom & Starbuck, 1984	Experimental learning enables dynamic adjustments; failure is a source of learning	Minimal or no experimental learning decreases receptivity to the unfamiliar; failure does not lead to learning
Fiol & Lyles, 1985	Organization effectively balances higher level, lower level learning	Ineffective balancing of higher level, lower level learning
BPR CAPABILITY		
Lyles, 1988; Fiol & Lyles, 1985; Klein, 1989	Higher level learning develops new cognitive frames of reference and interpretive schemes	Lower level learning focus on immediate behavior outcomes or performance
Senge, 1990	Generative learning focuses on systemic source of problems	Event orientation produces reactive stance toward change
Argyris, 1982, 1991	Double loop learning provides flexibility, insights	Single loop learning contributes to rigidity, inflexibility
Damanpour, 1991	Cross functional learning; balanced inward/outward	Compartmentalized learning; not balanced inward / outward
March, Sproull, & Tamuz, 1991	Rich learning facilitates multiple perspectives	Non-rich learning delimits organization frame of reference
BPR IMPLEMENTATION EFFECTIVENESS		
Brown & Duguid, 1991	Collaboratively robust noncanonical* learning contributes to informal communal knowledge	Individual learning focuses on interpretation of canonical* descriptions

*Canonical - simplistic, basic form or meaning

Table 3: Organization Learning Dichotomy

(Brown and Duguid, 1991). Organization assumptions are surfaced and challenged (Senge, 1990). Innovative learning organizations understand dynamic complexity, characterized by equivocality of information and uncertainty in cause-and-effect relationships. Decision making is typified by many cycles, few rules (Daft and Weick, 1984).

Fiol and Lyles (1985) found that as higher level organization cognitive learning increased, the organization's behavioral development, i.e., organization change, began to diminish. Thus,in terms of BPR, the organization must find an effective balance between the organization change targeted, BPR innovation versus BPR improvement, and the higher level cognitive learning development intervention necessary to be undertaken within the organization.

The contingency model classifies organization learning as innovative/adaptive. Table 3 summarizes BPR propensity, BPR capability, and BPR implementation effectiveness characteristics of this dichotomy.

Knowledge Sharing

This dimension of the innovation metaforce contingency model incorporates an information processing perspective, as well as knowledge sharing perspective, of the organization (Daft and Huber, 1987). All the information in the organization, i.e., meta-information (DeJong, 1994) consists of know-how, know-where, know-why, know-when, know-whom (Ackoff, 1989). The information processing perspective of the organization focuses on information as a resource and its acquisition and distribution, i.e., the organization as a system for capturing data and routing it to departments. Under this rational perspective of information processing in the organization, organizations apply expectancies to hard data, utilizing analytic, statistical judgement in decision making (Lord and Maher, 1990). IT may expand both the quantity of information flows and characteristics of such information. In the information processing perspective, information can be a source of power, justify ideologically based decisions, as well as symbolize adherence to norms (Daft and Huber, 1987). Information is seen as an organization resource, embodied in specific roles and relationships (Davenport, Eccles, Prusak, 1992). Information distortion occurs in the form of power struggles and coalition bargaining.

Smircich (1983) provides a contrasting perspective to the organization information processing perspective, i.e., an organization cognition framework. This framework considers organizations as systems of knowledge. Thus, organizations are interpretive systems (Walsh and Ungson, 1991) focusing on knowledge interpretation and sharing. In this framework, knowledge has a dynamic quality, defined by individuals' shared, coordinated interaction. Such organization knowledge sharing, rather than rational, analytical processes, constitutes organization decision making. Thus, organization interdependencies give rise to knowledge sharing.

Although impacted by Huber's (1984) C^2, computing and computer technologies, knowledge sharing is gestalt, i.e., flows through a social network. Strength and characteristics of individuals' ties impact knowledge transmission (Rockart and Short, 1989), (Stevenson and Gilly, 1991).

Knowledge sharing organizations can be characterized by the degree of differentiation and degree of equivocality (Daft and Weick, 1984), (Daft and Lengel, 1986). Knowledge sharing mechanisms bridge both disagreement and diversity among knowledge specialists. IT can be decision enabling with transparent data access, thus empowering individuals. Knowledge creating companies effectively process both tacit and explicit knowledge, and conversions of each type to the other (Nonaka, 1991). Such conversions enable an innovative approach to be shared with others, as well as leveraging of such knowledge by the organization as a whole (Charam, 1991), (Nonaka, 1991), (Nonaka and Johansson, 1985).

Innovation processes such as BPR, are both intensive and extensive (Kanter, 1988). The creative process within the BPR team

Researcher(s)	Networked	Hierarchical
BPR PROPENSITY		
Nonaka, 1991	Expanded knowledge base; regenerative spiral of knowledge, enables innovation sharing	Limited knowledge base, limiting innovation sharing
Daft & Huber, 1987	Organization scanning: high vigilance, personal, equivocality reduction, many cycles	Organization scanning: routine, impersonal, uncertainty reduction, many rules, few cycles
Weick, 1991	Cognitive operators enable rich patterns to be preserved in memory	Minimal patterned information stored in organization memory
BPR CAPABILITY		
Shrivastava & Mitroff, 1984	Alternative frames of reference and reflexivity in inquiry	Limited frame of reference reduces reflexivity of inquiry
Howe, 1992	Decision enabling IT; transparent data access; virtual organization	Transaction oriented IT; local data management
Ibarra, 1993	Individual: cognitive operators are personalized, informal with linkages to informal network	Individual: cognitive operators are not personalized; formal, tied to organization units
Nonaka, 1988	Middle management facilitates creative information generation and serves as agent for change	Information flow is to top management; focus is on reduction in "noise" and minimal variety of information
BPR IMPLEMENTATION EFFECTIVENESS		
Nonaka, 1991	Knowledge valued for usefulness; multi-directional knowledge flows	Knowledge valued for source; associated with power; vertical knowledge flows
Gupta & Govindarajan, 1991	Individual: High tolerance for ambiguity; internal locus of control facilitates homogeneous knowledge throughout organization	Individual: Low tolerance for ambiguity; external locus of control; knowledge isolation by position, function
Nonaka, 1988	Inarticulate (tacit) knowledge & individual autonomy leads to new points of view	Explicit knowledge & norms restrict new points of view

Table 4: Knowledge Sharing Dichotomy

generates knowledge intensity, relying on the collective individuals' human intelligence and creativity. The proposed BPR innovation is simultaneously extensive, i.e., uncertain, competing with alternative courses of action, and affecting multiple units requiring both change and cooperation. Organizations with multiple linkages, intersecting territories, collective pride in peoples' talents, and collaboration, are likely to achieve BPR innovation (networked organization). Organizations with limited linkages, separated territories, vertical flows, and hierarchical control of outcomes, are likely to achieve BPR improvement (hierarchical organization).

The contingency model explicates BPR propensity, BPR capability, and BPR effectiveness characteristics associated with a networked / hierarchical knowledge sharing dichotomy (Table 4).

Interaction of the Metaforces

Creativity, Synergy, Leveraging in BPR

The model's interaction of the three innovation metaforces (Figure 1) is consonant with research directions called for by Saffold (1988), Walsh and Ungson (1991), Nonaka and Johansson (1985), Fiol and Lyles (1985), Tushman and Nadler (1986), Hatch (1993), Senge (1990), and Adler and Schenbar (1990). For example, Saffold (1988) advocates a contingency approach, focusing on the dynamic interactions of organization culture interwoven with organization processes such as organization learning, and knowledge sharing. Research, including that of Saffold (1988), Dixon and John (1989), and Frost and Egri (1991) propounds innovation as a multiplicative model of sociocognitive dynamics, i.e., organization culture, organization learning, and knowledge sharing. Such multiplicative interactions establish the organization's creativity, synergy, and leveraging, or lack thereof, in terms of BPR propensity, BPR capability, and BPR implementation effectiveness. The multiplicative metaforce interactions determine placement of the organization on the BPR improvement (homeostatic organization) / BPR innovation (morphogenetic organization) change continuum (Figure 2).

BPR as a Recursive Dynamic

BPR propensity, BPR capability, and BPR implementation effectiveness are not phased processes, but rather are conceptualized as a nonlinear, complex dynamic (Pelz, 1983), (Quinn, 1985). The recursive dynamic of BPR, shown in Figure 1, is antecedent to, as well as a consequence of, the formal organization, informal organization, OFOR/decision making, and IT. The foundation for the recursive dynamic stems from Gidden's (1984) theory of structuration, embodied in the research of Lewis and Seibold (1993), Orlikowski and Robey (1991), Orlikowski and Baroudi (1991), and Pettigrew (1985). Tables 5, 6, and 7 explicate organization culture, organization learning, and knowledge sharing metaforce characteristics, expressed in terms of the formal organization, informal organization, OFOR and decision making, and IT characteristics.

Interactionist Perspective - BPR

The research of Amabile (1983, 1988) synthesizes the effectiveness of examining innovation of individuals and groups within their relevant social setting, thus providing a more comprehensive innovation paradigm than proposed previously. Woodman, Sawyer, and Griffin (1993) and Terborg (1981) suggest integration of the interac-

Heterogeneous	Homogeneous
Formal Organization	
Bonding of people involved in organization events	Impartiality and removal from the human side of organization events
Communication structure: personal networks, decentralization, many boundary departments	Communication structure: formal organization units, centralized, few boundary departments
Open communication encouraged, distinctions in rank reduced	Reduced communication, especially ideas from below, distinctions in rank associated with power
Multilevel, multidimensional feedback, locus of feedback loop at lower organization levels	Compartmentalized and single dimensional feedback, locus of feedback loop at higher organization levels
Informal Organization	
Champion presents dialectic ideology/value set through intellectual stimulation	Champion constrained by lack of reflexivity which limits exploration of the dialectic viewpoint
Informal organization highly developed and with a diverse membership	Informal organization limited in scope and membership diversity
Informal organization values conflict and provides constructive ways to solve it	Informal information less skilled in dealing with conflict and conflict resolution
O.F.O.R. & Decision Making	
High collective requisite variety of inputs to decision making, enlarged by mutual trust, support	Low requisite variety, parochial husbanding of potential inputs
Clinical judgement used in decision making	Statistical judgement used in decision making
Understanding events and processes that cause performance	Focus on results and performance
IT	
Gestalt impact of technology	Economic impact of technology
High conversion effectiveness	Low conversion effectiveness
IT: Inductive thinking - application of IT to enable organization to do things not now done	IT: deductive thinking - application of IT to increase efficiency / reduce costs

Table 5: Organization Culture Dichotomy

tional psychology perspective of individual creativity and organization research on innovation. Utilizing the gestalt of innovation explicated by Woodman, Sawyer, and Griffin (1993), innovative BPR arises from individual, group, and organization characteristics occurring within situational influences at each level of the social organization (Figure 4). Innovation among organization members is a person-situation interaction (Terborg, 1981), influenced by antecedent conditions as well as the current situation.

As shown in Figure 4, in the formal organization, BPR interactions occur among three levels: CEO and the top management team, BPR design team, and the individual. Salient characteristics associated with each formal organization level, that impact BPR propensity, BPR capability, and BPR implementation effectiveness are discussed in turn below.

Innovative	Adaptive
Formal Organization	
Top management encourages experimental learning; failure is a source of learning	Top management focus on stability limits experimental learning; failure becomes dysfunctional
Robust organization benchmarking facilitates vicarious learning (learning from other organizations)	Minimal/ineffective organization benchmarking severely limits vicarious learning
Middle management creatively employs constructive conflict, dialectics to foster innovation	Directive, top-down management inhibits action learning by middle and lower level management
Cross-functional learning; balanced inward / outward	Compartmentalized learning; not balanced inward / outward
Informal Organization	
Action learning enhances multi-functional capabilities* of individuals in informal network	Minimal action learning limits individuals' multi-functional capabilities in informal network
Champion helps the individual in a situation, doesn't just explain	Champion functions in a more impersonal mode
Gatekeeper characteristics and knowledge being transmitted characteristics facilitate unlearning	Both gatekeeper and information being transmitted characteristics impede unlearning
O.F.O.R & Decision Making	
Higher level learning develops new cognitive frames of reference and interpretive schemes	Lower level learning focuses on immediate behavior outcomes or performance
Perceptual, cognitive operators enable rich patterns of information and uncertainty to be preserved in organization memory	Limited cognitive processing results in less non-patterned information stored in organization memory
Informal sense making; insights; collective consciousness	Rational / analytical sense-making
IT	
IT enables discovery of knowledge by facilitating higher level learning	IT limits discovery of knowledge by primarily supporting lower level learning processes
IT becomes "competence building" in situ, enabling rich learning	IT becomes competence destroying in situ, limiting higher level learning

* Increasing individuals' multi-functional capabilities is an example of a holographic organization design

Table 6: Organization Learning Dichotomy

Formal Organization

CEO and Top Management Team. Both CEO and top management team characteristics are important in establishing and implementing innovation (Tushman and Nadler, 1986) and (Sitkin and Pablo, 1992). Transformational leaders create a vision for the organization that generates commitment and utilizes involvement-oriented management (Hambrick, 1994) and (Nadler and Tushman, 1990). Top management must "walk the talk"

Networked	Hierarchical
Formal Organization	
Organization uses inductive, synthetic, and holistic methodologies	Organization uses deductive, analytic, and reductionist methodologies
Empowered individuals with centrality in knowledge sharing network	Individual performance monitored using outcome control modalities
Group processes characterized by trust, enabling creative dialogue, open exchange	Group processes foster "groupthink"
High tolerance for ambiguity; individuals' locus of control is internal	Low tolerance for ambiguity; individuals' locus of control is external
Informal Organization	
Champions receive informational, resource, and political support	Champions receive inadequate information, resource, and political support
Strong linkages between idea generators and mentors (sponsors)	Weak linkages between idea generators and mentors (sponsors)
Gatekeeper characteristics and network centrality foster innovation and knowledge sharing	Gatekeeper characteristics and coalition connections impede innovation and information sharing
O.F.O.R. & Decision Making	
Alternative frames of reference; reflexivity in inquiry	Limited set of alternative frames of reference; reduced reflexivity of inquiry
Cognitive operators are highly personalized, non-standard, informal, with strong linkages to informal networks	Cognitive operators are formal, standard, not personalized, tied to formal organization units
Equivocality reduction: many cycles in decision making	Uncertainty reduction: Many rules, few cycles in decision making
Cybernetic information processing models	Rational or limited capacity information processing models
IT	
Decision enabling IT	Transaction oriented IT
Virtual organization, transparent data access	Local data access
IT enables decreasing knowledge costs	IT contributes to non-decreasing knowledge costs
Flexible, multimedia, on demand outputs	Limited, periodic, calendar driven outputs

Table 7: Knowledge Sharing Dichotomy

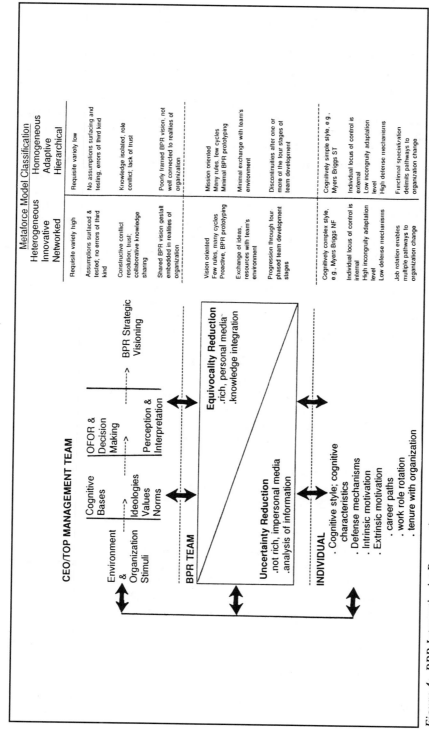

Figure 4: BPR Interactionist Perspective

(DeFiore, 1994). Visioning is a gestalt concept, enabling an innovative esprit de corps of mutual respect, feelings of trust, and individual empowerment.

CEO and top managements' cognitive characteristics, leadership, risk values and risk preferences, and demographics such as age, organization tenure, team tenure, and education level influence problem framing and changeability of the top management team's frame of reference (Hambrick and Mason, 1984), (Pfeffer, 1985), and (Wiersema and Bantel, 1992). Top management team composition, e.g., cohort characteristics, impacts degree of conflict, conflict resolution, and decision making. Top management team heterogeneity contributes to requisite variety[9] (Ashby, 1956), linked to innovativeness and characteristic of trust relationships (Weick, 1987) and (Nonaka and Johansson, 1985). Through simulations, critical incident techniques, near histories, and benchmarking, the senior team can function as a learning system, ultimately serving to create norms that promote innovation and problem solving (Nadler and Tushman, 1990). BPR begins with visioning, commitment, and enabling from the CEO and top management team.

BPR Design Team. Team innovativeness is influenced by team composition (heterogeneity), team characteristics (e.g., cohesiveness), and team processes, e.g., problem solving approaches and social information processes. Team heterogeneity and diversity has been generally found linked to performance (Erez, Earley, and Hulin, 1985), (Watson, Kumar, and Michaelson, 1993) and (Cox, Lobel, and McLeod, 1991). Innovative teams attain convergence to their goals by moving through both evolutionary and revolutionary periods (Gersick, 1991). Other researchers (Howe, 1992) and (Gersick, 1988) identify four distinct phases in a team's developmental process: forming, storming, norming, and performing. Principle team foci in these phases are, respectively, affiliation, conflict resolution, cohesion, and cooperative problem solving.

Innovative teams dynamically interact with their environment as necessary. In the BPR context, such interaction would include prototype development and testing of proposed BPR designs (Davenport, 1993) and (Shore, 1993). Individual members of innovative teams are empowered and energized through a shared commitment to the BPR vision of the organization. As shown in Figure 4, BPR teams may utilize both deductive, analytic as well as inductive, synthetic decision making modalities. In homogeneous, adaptive, hierarchical organizations, BPR team decision making will be characterized by uncertainty reduction. In heterogeneous, innovative, networked organizations, BPR team decision making will be characterized by equivocality reduction.

Individual. Woodman, Sawyer, and Griffin (1993) identify cognitive factors, intrinsic motivation, and knowledge and technical skills as antecedent conditions for individual innovation. Nonaka and Johansson (1985), Reichers (1985), and Locke, Latham, and Erez (1988) include extrinsic motivation factors as well. Innovative individuals' locus of control is internal (Rotter, 1966), i.e., they are self-directed and proactive. In addition, such innovative individuals have a high incongruity adaptation level (Budner, 1962), (Driver, 1978), as well as low defense mechanisms (Ihilevich and Gleser, 1993). Individuals whose response to BPR innovation is morphogenetic will utilize coping responses based on trust and realism. Coping responses based on trust and realism typify individuals with low defense mechanisms. In contrast, individuals whose response to BPR innovation is homeostatic will likely have high defense mechanisms, thus contributing to that individual's diminished problem solving efforts (Ihilevich and Gleser, 1993) and (Klempa, 1983). Prior research (Klempa, 1983) examining decision maker's cognitive style, incongruity adaptation level, and defense mechanisms found both incongruity adaptation level and defense mechanisms to be moderators of cognitive style. Individuals with cognitively complex styles, but with either low incongruity adaptation levels or high defense mechanisms were found to use an information system less, and be less accepting of an information system. In terms of the individual's placement on the individual change curve (see subsequent organization culture change section in this chapter), the individual's cognitive style, locus of control, incongruity adaptation level, and defense mechanisms impact such placement.

Informal Organization

Idea Generators and Champions. The research of Tushman and Nadler (1986), Delbecq and Mills (1985), and Frost and Egri (1991) identifies critical organization roles necessary for innovation, including idea generators and champions. Idea generators creatively link diverse ideas, enabling, for example, linking of both new technologies and promised new technologies to new business processes (Tushman and Nadler, 1986).

Champions seek out creative ideas and make them tangible (Tushman and Nadler, 1986). Champions are aggressive, risk-taking, nonconforming, and value creativity. Champions want opportunities to test their ideas, hence actively pursue through informal networks, bringing a surfaced idea to fruition (Howell and Higgins, 1990) and (Madique, 1980). Champions, via the informal organization network, are transformational leaders. Champions engage in coalition building in an information intensive process of knowledge sharing and persuasion (Beath, 1991). As such, they assist in bringing about gamma organization change by espousing ideologies and beliefs different than the established order, thus contributing to ideological and belief reorientation of individuals in the organization.

Mentors (Sponsors). Mentors serve important informational roles as well as sponsors of change in organizations (Rogers, 1983). Kram and Isabella (1985) and Wilson and Elman (1990) identify informational mentors, who constitute important linkages in an information transmission network. Such informational mentors increase individuals' awareness of significant management, organization, and technical matters, e.g., BPR. Senior organization level mentors also provide authority, protection, and resources, thus sponsoring innovation, i.e., organization change (Tushman and Nadler, 1986), (Evans, 1984), (Galbraith, 1982), and (Kanter, 1988). In this capacity, mentors help prevent innovations from getting smothered by organization constraints (Davenport, 1993). Certain senior level mentors also serve in the dual capacity of external gatekeepers, i.e., boundary spanners, who serve to transmit knowledge about innovations into the organization (Evans, 1984) and (Wilson and Elman, 1990). These types of mentor roles can significantly impact the organization's BPR propensity and BPR capability.

Gatekeepers. In contrast to the champion who seeks out creative ideas, the gatekeeper acquires, translates, and distributes knowledge to colleagues (Howell and Higgins, 1990). The gatekeeper can be an individual or team, receiving and processing (translating) both external and internal information and distributing it effectively to other components in a network (Delehanty, Sullo, and Wallace, 1982).

Information processing in a homogeneous, adaptive, hierarchical organization is driven by routing of information flows between information sources and information sinks, i.e., recipients. With multi-source/multi-sink networks, system reliability is impacted by path length, as well as number of nodes connected and frequencies of contact with gatekeepers (Delehanty, Sullo, and Wallace, 1982). Nodes in the network may assume intermediary, translational, or amplificational roles. Gatekeepers are more effective than other types of nodes. Although an informal organization network including gatekeepers exists in a homogeneous, adaptive, hierarchical organization, much of the information processing is through the formal organization where it is subject to political issues of power among coalitions.

By contrast, knowledge sharing in heterogeneous, innovative, networked organizations is achieved through shared definition and enactment. Knowledge sharing takes place through discussion and interpretation of events. Thus, gatekeeper characteristics, and intensity of linkages among gatekeepers become important (Cotter, 1977). The organization's absorptive capacity, i.e., the ability to recognize the value of, assimilate, and apply knowledge is a function of both the gatekeeper's capabilities and individuals to whom the gatekeeper is transmitting the information (Cohen and Levinthal, 1990). Knowledge characteristics being transmitted also become relevant. Some gatekeepers may be more effective than others in receiving/transmitting external information; other gatekeepers may be more effective in receiving/transmitting internal information. Specialized gatekeepers, i.e., technology gatekeepers may play significant roles (Huff and Munro, 1985) and (Nelson, 1990). Gatekeepers' relationships within the informal organization network are important. Evans (1984) concludes that gatekeepers who are mentored (sponsored), are better integrated into the organization's knowledge network. Gatekeepers can provide useful roles in increasing the organization's BPR propensity, strengthening its BPR capability, and facilitating BPR implementation effectiveness.

Organization Frame of Reference & Decision Making

The sociocognitive perspective of BPR innovation explicated in this chapter is synthesized in the concept of OFOR (Shrivastava and Mitroff, 1984), (Shrivastava and Schneider, 1984), and (Wilkins and Dyer, 1988). OFORs refer to the core of conceptual schemes, models and cognitive maps that individuals or groups of individuals employ to order information and make sense of it (Weick, 1979), Kuhn (1970), Beyer (1981), and Sproull (1981). The OFOR is a set of beliefs about the organization and the way it is or should be (Dutton, 1992). The OFOR serves to bracket, interpret, and legitimize issues (Weick, 1979).

Such interpretive schemata (Giddens, 1979) map the individuals' experience of the world, identify its relevant aspects, and enable understanding of them through assumptions about event happenings and individuals' situational responses (Bartunek, 1984). Such interpretive schemata are not simply individual predispositions, but rather social cognitive schema, i.e., intersubjective and reflecting a common knowledge and mutual understanding of the organization's members (Leblebici, Marlow, and Rowland, 1983). Both structure and content of the OFOR influence organization innovation. A diverse OFOR characterized by a shared, extensive organization knowledge base enhances identification of innovation opportunities. When the content of the OFOR, i.e., ideologies/beliefs and values, reflect a commitment to entrepreneurship, innovation, and change, identification of innovation opportunities is increased (Dutton, 1992).

As identified by Shrivastava and Schneider (1984), salient characteristics of frames of reference include: cognitive elements, cognitive operators, reality tests, domain of inquiry, and degree of articulation. Cognitive elements refers to the organization's preference for experiential bases that constitute sourcing of information.

OFOR Component	BPR Innovation	BPR Improvement
Cognitive elements	Subjective, personal experiences; data from personal sources	Objective, quantifiable data from formalized systems
Cognitive operators	Ability to shift perspectives; choice is through feedback guided by recognition	Problem formulation institutionalized in formal systems; limited perspective
Reality tests	Personal experience through shared definition and enactment of environment	Data acquisition and analysis of environment viewed as objective
Domain of inquiry	Organization self-image is innovative and change is valued; mutual support and trust	Organization self-image is stability; coalitions determine power distribution in organization
Degree of articulation	High degree of articulation and sharing of OFOR is through personal example, visibility to others	Low degree of articulation is formal through policies and procedures

Table 8: OFOR Dichotomy BPR Innovation/Improvement

Cognitive operators are methods by which information is ordered and rearranged to arrive at meaning and understanding. Reality tests provide the basis for legitimizing processes of inquiry through connection with past organization experiences and practices. Domain of inquiry is defined in terms of the organization's definition of itself, definition of individual-organization relationships, and organization-environment relationships. Degree of articulation refers to the modalities by which the OFOR is made known and codified to the organization's members. As shown in Table 8, these components of the organization's frame of reference differ significantly in organizations characterized as BPR innovative from those typified by BPR improvement.

BPR innovation requires multidimensional shifts in the OFOR. Yet simultaneously, the organization must retain some stability, serving to anchor the organization (Sheldon, 1980). As in shown in Figure 2, lack of creativity, synergy, and leveraging contributes to stability, e.g., only modest BPR improvement. Conversely, high levels of creativity, synergy, and leveraging may prove to be an overload for organization members, thus organization change begins to diminish as shown in Figure 2. As previously delineated, assessment of the organization's culture, learning, and knowledge sharing characteristics determines the organization's positioning on the homeostatic / morphogenetic change continuum. Over the time line of a given BPR effort, the organization may attempt moderate adjustment in either direction along the change continuum in order to find an appropriate and effective balancing point. Tushman and Nadler (1986) refer to this balancing as management of the duality of stability and change. In a given organization, effective balancing of the duality of stability and change impacts the organization's BPR propensity, BPR capability, and BPR implementation effectiveness.

IT

IT - Value Chain Management. IT serves as a nexus, providing the organization's individual, group, and managerial systems the necessary means to accomplish required organization transforma-

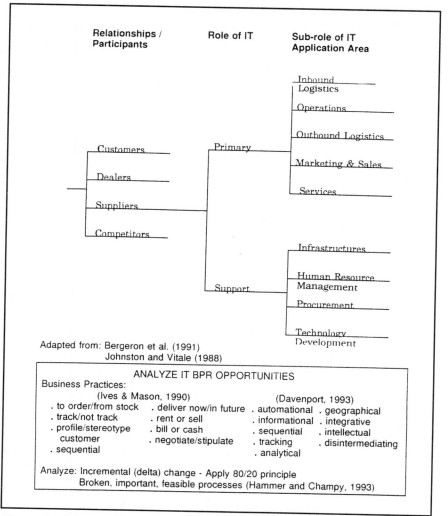

Figure 5: Value Chain Search Process—Decision Tree Exemplar

tions (Hulin and Roznowski, 1985). De Jong (1994) refers to the process of organization change caused by IT as *informatization*. Informatization includes changes in information flows, knowledge, culture, people, and activities. Such a recursive dynamic and IT induced change is illustrated by the application of IT to foster inductive thinking (Hammer and Champy, 1993), i.e., the organization's ability to creatively synthesize the business potential associated with IT. Johnston and Carrico (1988) found both organization culture and organization learning which translated into action, established innovation processes that continued to generate performance improvements in the value chain. Organizations who accomplish BPR innovation creatively reengineer the value chain by proactively leveraging boundaries and relationships within the value chain (Hopland, 1994). Both Ives and Mason (1990) and Davenport (1993) utilize an assumptions surfacing and testing, i.e., dialectic approach to challenge existing business processes on multidimensional fronts. Davenport's (1993) examination of IT as BPR enabling, dialectically explores IT impacts in terms of organization streamlining / simplification, capturing and distributing, coordination, monitoring, analysis and decision making, and parallelism enabling BPR innovations. An example of such a dialectically driven BPR value chain analysis, depicted as a decision tree, is shown in Figure 5. Pareto's Law, i.e., 80/20 concept is utilized to identify potentially significant candidate processes for BPR.

IT - Conversion Effectiveness. As conceptualized by Weill and Olson (1989) and Weill (1992), IT investments in organizations with a high level of conversion effectiveness will realize higher productive outputs, i.e., greater payoff, from such investments. Conversion effectiveness is defined by Weill as the quality of the firm-wide management and commitment to IT. Weill's conversion effectiveness construct includes four factors: top management commitment to IT, the firm's previous experience with IT, user satisfaction with IT systems, and political turbulence (Weill, 1992).

Prior research has consistently found top management commitment to IT linked to successful use of IT (Kwon and Zmud, 1987). The firm's previous experiences with IT leads to greater organization learning (Argyris, 1982). Prior experience with IT increases the firm's IT absorptive capacity, i.e., the firm's ability to recognize the value of, assimilate, and apply new information pertaining to IT (Cohen and Levinthal, 1990). User satisfaction measures users' perceived satisfaction with the IT portfolio as a whole. Dissatisfaction with IT hinders IT conversion effectiveness. Political turbulence, i.e., conflict which hinders organization change, decreases conversion effectiveness by wasting resources and misdirecting innovation associated with IT. The innovation metaforce contingency model subsumes Weill's (1992) four factors - organization culture (top management commitment); organization learning (previous experience with IT); knowledge sharing (user satisfaction with systems and political turbulence). Thus, a heterogeneous, innovative, networked organization is associated with high conversion effectiveness; a homogeneous, adaptive, hierarchical organization with low conversion effectiveness.

Application of the Innovation Metaforce Contingency Model

Organization Change

The extent of creativity, synergy, and leveraging associated with the multiplicative interaction among organization culture, organization learning, and knowledge sharing determines the organization's positioning on the homeostatic / morphogenetic organization change continuum (Figure 2). Undertaking an organization change program necessitates understanding of both the general and specific OFORs, i.e., their organization culture, organization learning, and knowledge sharing components. Gamma organization change associated with BPR innovation requires both individuals' and work groups' internalizing of a new OFOR. Both individuals' and work groups' ideologies/beliefs, values, and norms must be transitioned into the organization's new ideology/beliefs, values, and norms. Such transitions to the new OFOR occur at both a rational and emotional level (Sheldon, 1980). Overcoming resistance, whether at the level of the individual, work group, or organization is inevitable and should be prepared for (Leonard, 1994). For example, in a recent survey of CIO's (Profit Oriented Systems Planning Program, 1994), 82% found significant resistance to change in BPR projects undertaken, including resistance from individuals executing the new process, individuals and organization subunits outside the scope of the process, and individuals managing the process.

Resistance to change is often thought of as willful, i.e., overt, a negative model of resistance. However, when viewed cybernetically, resistance is a homeostatic response, i.e., an autopoetic response by the system (individual, group, or organization) to maintain equilibrium by carrying out established patterns of behavior in order to survive in a stressful and difficult situation (Goldstein, 1988). Thus, an autopoetic organization, group, or individual will resist changes that are perceived as a threat to that individual's, group's, or organization's frame of reference.

Direct confrontation will probably only increase resistance capacities. New tasks need to be found, employing the homeostatic resistances, but placing them within a new context so that new

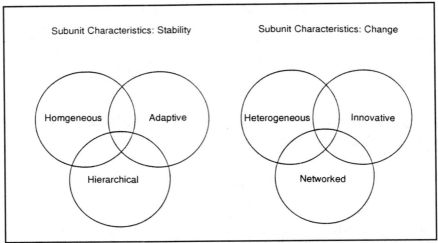

Figure 6: Subunit Stability Versus Change Orientation

experiences can emerge. Such tasks allow change from within the individual, work group, or organization, Such internal change provides the individual, work group, or organization the ability to express responses within new contexts that consequently change the responses' communicational meaning and impact, thus reframing the individuals', work groups', and the organization's frame of reference (Hirschhorn and Gilmore, 1980). Such change from within can utilize difference questioning, i.e., contrasting the individual, work group, or organization's autopoetic identity and the targeted identity desired. Difference questioning from within surfaces information about alternative ways of achieving the targeted identity (Goldstein, 1988). Looking at BPR as an opportunity contributes to the individual's sense of control, facilitates search and use of external information, contributes to internalized values of progressiveness, and focuses on the future (Dutton, 1992).

Audit and Gap Analysis

The innovation metaforce contingency model is used to conduct an audit at the level of the firm, as well as the organization subunit level, for all subunits involved with/impacted by a proposed BPR project. The Venn diagrams shown in Figure 6 depict the conditions of organization subunit stability versus change orientation.

A subunit classified as homogeneous culture, or adaptive learning, or hierarchical knowledge sharing is stability oriented, thus requiring varying degrees of organization change intervention. A subunit whose culture is homogeneous, learning is adaptive, and with hierarchical knowledge sharing will require maximum change intervention. Conversely, the Venn union of heterogeneous culture,

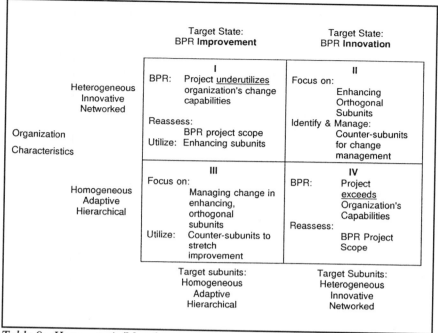

Table 9: Homeostatic/Morphogenetic Organization/Organization Subunit Analysis

innovative learning, and networked knowledge sharing defines vary-ing degrees of increasing potential subunit change, with maximum change potential occurring in the heterogeneous and innovative and networked knowledge sharing subunit.

Having undertaken both organization and subunit culture, learning, and knowledge sharing diagnoses, a summative assess-ment of the organization's overall potential extent of change, i.e., placement on the homeostatic / morphogenetic change continuum (Figure 2) can be done. Table 9 synopsizes analysis of targeted outcome (BPR process improvement versus BPR innovation), domi-nant organization characteristics, and subunits' characteristics.

In quadrant IV, the organization is predominantly homoge-neous, adaptive, and hierarchical, i.e., capable of beta (moderate) organization change. However, the organization is attempting BPR process innovation. The organization should assess and prioritize each affected counter-subunit's criticality to the proposed BPR innovation. If there are insufficient counter-subunits (heteroge-neous, innovative, and networked) impacted by the proposed BPR project, the undertaking of the BPR project should be reassessed. If the organization elects to undertake the BPR project, homeostatic / morphogenetic analysis dictates a major organizational subunit change effort, carefully planned, with longer lead times. This situation is a high risk situation. Quadrant I, targeting process

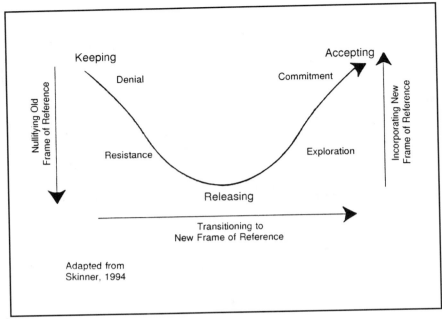

Figure 7: Individual's Change Curve

improvement, in an organization dominantly heterogeneous, innovative, and networked, represents underutilization of the
organization's change capabilities. Such a BPR undertaking is low
risk, and should require a lower level of organization change intervention. Quadrant II represents a match, i.e., a dominantly heterogeneous, innovative, networked organization undertaking BPR innovation. Organization subunits with matching characteristics can
energize the BPR effort. Organization subunits with homogeneous,
adaptive, hierarchical characteristics, impacted by the proposed
BPR project will require substantive change intervention programs.
Quadrant III also represents a match, i.e., BPR process improvement
undertaken in homogeneous, adaptive, hierarchical organizations.
Even though the proposed BPR undertaking is process improvement, a solid and widely based change management program needs
to be undertaken, since homogeneous, adaptive, and hierarchical
subunits are more stability oriented, rather than change oriented.
Counter-subunits, i.e., those heterogeneous, innovative, and networked, can be utilized to try to achieve as much as possible within
the scope of the BPR project, albeit a BPR improvement undertaking.

Organization / Organization Subunit Culture Change

Organization metamorphosis directed at changes in individuals' behavior patterns, but which does not pay attention to their

shared ideologies/beliefs, values, and norms is not going to accomplish lasting, longer term change. Innovation is about ambiguity. Individuals have varying degrees of response to the ambiguity associated with organization change. The individual's response is dispositional, i.e., situational, as well as impacted by the individual's cognitive style, locus of control, incongruity adaptation level, and defense mechanisms (see previous section in this chapter). For each individual impacted by the proposed BPR, a diagnosis and assessment of that individual's location on the individual change curve (Skinner, 1994), shown in Figure 7, needs to be undertaken.

Both stakeholder mapping and assumption force-field analyses (Mason and Mitroff, 1981), can be performed for each affected individual.   Utilizing such stakeholder mapping and force-field analyses at Bell Atlantic (Skinner, 1994) enabled customization of Bell Atlantic's change program, according to the individual's placement on the change curve . At Bell Atlantic, this proactive change program utilizes multiple tools including open door management practices, feedback, one-on-one handholding, a change agent network (the Jonahs), newsletters, rap sessions, and electronic surveys of opinions.

A successful program of change incorporates transformational leadership (Bass, 1985) principles —charisma, inspiration, intellectual stimulation, and individualized consideration. Nadler and Tushman (1990) delineate a three-faceted organization change program incorporating such principles: envisioning, energizing, and enabling; managing reward and control processes; and broadening and institutionalizing the change. Such institutionalizing includes a significant role for middle management as agents of change. Such pivotal roles for middle management in Japanese companies are described by (Nonaka, 1988). For many organizations, the most difficult group to get to buy into BPR change programs is middle management (DeFiore, 1994), yet many companies devote inadequate attention to this group. Nadler and Tushman (1990) broaden the institutionalizing of the change program to include individuals one or two levels down from the executive team. In most larger companies, this set of individuals constitutes the senior operating management. This group may be more embedded in the current system and less prepared for change.

Changing Organization Learning

Higher Level Learning Processes. Consistent with the organization's initial positioning on the homeostatic / morphogenetic organization change continuum, the organization should customize development of appropriate higher level learning mechanisms (Figure 3). Higher level learning mechanisms increase the organization's reflexivity of inquiry (Shrivastava and Schneider, 1984), build requisite variety (Ashby, 1956), and should incorporate minimum critical specification (Morgan and Ramirez, 1984) principles into the organization's operating modalities. Thus, in terms of requisite variety, the range of knowledge, beliefs, values, ideas which pertain to the problem domain, e.g., BPR innovation, must be represented within the BPR inquiry process itself. Minimal critical specification suggests that there be no more predesign of the BPR innovation than is necessary for learning to occur. The more advanced the predesign, the less opportunity for collaborative insights to emerge. By additional application of the higher level learning mechanisms (Figure 3) appropriate to its circumstances, and by doing so under conditions of both minimal critical specification and requisite variety, the organization will build reflexivity of inquiry into the OFOR. Continued application of these concepts, to the organization's BPR undertakings over time, will build organization learning.

Changing Knowledge Sharing

As adapted from (Kanter, 1988) and (Tichy, 1981), the following highlights fundamental organization change efforts which can be undertaken in order to accomplish a metamorphosis of knowledge sharing modalities within the organization.

- Environmental Interfacing
- Build external gatekeeper (boundary spanner) capabilities and linkages
- Establish multiple information gatherers, each utilizing multiple sources
- Establish tight linkage of boundary spanners to internal organization subunits
- Network Redesign
- In homogeneous cultures, focus on lateral integration, slack resources, rewards
- In heterogeneous cultures, focus on increasing communication density, i.e., multiple communication links, and network density, i.e., smaller interdisciplinary business units
- Individuals
- Build in frequent mobility, include lateral career moves, job rotations, incorporate extensive use of team mechanisms, focus on educating, not just training the individual
- Technical / Political Systems
- Technical —severing old, and creating new information linkages
- Political —severing old, and creating new influence linkages

Future Research Directions

This chapter presents a framework within which the practitioner can more readily understand the systemic forces underlying BPR innovation within the organization, as well as the dynamic of business process change. In addition, the innovation metaforce contingency model enables researchers to address a more complete picture of BPR innovation and organization change than is currently addressed in the literature. Such a framework adopts the perspective of BPR innovation as an integrated system of both technological and organization change, with attention to both the organization's and individuals' roles in BPR innovation at multiple organization levels. This complex dynamic suggests *in situ* research, utilizing three research modalities: positivist, interpretive, and combined positivist-interpretive. Each is discussed in turn.

Interpretive Research Category	Researcher(s)	Nature of Research
Hermeneutic*	Boland & Day, 1989	Systems design project
	Lee, 1994	E-mail as a communication medium
Ethnography*	Orlikowski, 1991	Systems development project, software consulting firm
	Gregory, 1983	Management of technical professionals' careers intracompany and intercompany
Hermeneutic Ethnography*	Baskerville & Davies, 1992	Operations of an information technology center
	Morey & Luthans, 1984	Emic perspective and ethnoscience methods for organization research
Action Research*	Baskerville & Davies, 1992	Development of a budgeting system for a government agency

* Hermeneutic - Makes explicit the meaning of experience.

Ethnography - Observation of everyday practices and interpretation in terms of socially constructed meaning

Hermeneutic - Understanding the reality of others (emic); adoption
Ethnography   of a defensive knowledge framework (etic)

Action   - Complex social process best studied by introducing
Research   change and observing effect of change

Table 10: Exemplars—Proposed Interpretive Research Modalities

Positivist Research

Nomothetic[11], i.e., positivist based research would employ diachronic (longitudinal) studies. Research studies are needed that address the time dimension of BPR innovation and include use of qualitative methods as well. Cross-sectional positivist research cannot adequate address the interactive, recursive innovation dynamic. The complex, recursive dynamic of the three innovation metaforces requires diachronic research, in order to explore a given BPR undertaking through its life cycle. Longitudinal studies should be multilevel within the organization - CEO/top management team, BPR design team, and the individual. Longitudinal research provides opportunity for improved measurement validity. First, contemporaneous data collection as events occur, contributes to validity. In addition, triangulation, i.e., multiple data collection modalities can enhance validity.

Interpretive Research

In contrast to nomothetic research, idiographic research is conducted through the researcher's immersion in the social system under study, e.g., the organization's culture, learning, and knowledge sharing milieu. Table 10 identifies the four principle interpretive research modalities. Additional use of interpretive research is highly appropriate, given the innovation metaforce dynamic.

Integration of Positivist and Interpretive Research Modalities

Lee's (1991) research framework bridges the positivist and interpretive research constructs. Lee's proposed research modality moves beyond the simpler, confirmatory purposes of triangulation, by explicating a proactive, cyclical relationship, utilizing both positivist and interpretive constructs, in order to dynamically develop three mutually reinforcing levels of understanding of the phenomenon being researched.

Concluding Remarks

An epistemology of BPR is at the stage of infancy. The extant literature, generally descriptive and normative, offers few conceptual models of BPR. Future cross-sectional positivist research is likely to yield fragmented results, characterized by operational conflicts, contradictions, and exceptions. Future research needs to employ richer, more complex, and multifaceted models. Such research would attempt to identify common patterns among variables which may exist in different organization contexts.

For example, future research would strive to identify BPR

organization configurations or innovation patterns that are richly described by the dynamic interaction of formal organization, informal organization, OFOR / decision making and IT within the context of the organization's culture, learning, and knowledge sharing characteristics. Such configurations will have highly interdependent and mutually supportive components whose significance is understood within the context of the organization's culture, learning, and knowledge sharing characteristics. Such a research approach would attempt to identify typologies of organizations along the BPR innovation / improvement continuum, such as the eight position conceptual typology[12] defined by the three dichotomous axes of the innovation metaforce contingency model. Such configurations along an organization culture, organization learning, and knowledge sharing typology would seek to understand how relationships among the formal organization, informal organization, OFOR / decision making, and IT vary systematically according to the particular typology ideal type.

Acknowledgments

The author wishes to thank an anonymous reviewer for very helpful comments on an earlier draft of this manuscript.

The Goethe quotations are from: Goethe's World View Presented in His Reflections and Maxims, translated by Heinz Norden, Frederick Ungar Publishing, 1963.

Endnotes

[1] A paradigm is a set of major concepts and assumptions in a substantive area, serving to orient research and theorizing in that area.

[2] An organization frame of reference is a cultural "map" that enables the organization to understand a situation and develop a response. Other terminology, with similar constructs, includes "weltanschauung" (world view), master script, and organization paradigm. See section in this chapter, Organization Frame of Reference.

[3] The term autopoiesis is from biology. An living system is equilibrium seeking, or homeostatic, given that it faces a constantly changing environment.

[4] Beta change - moderate level of organization change. Organization or organization subunit norms (evaluation criteria) shift. Minimal change in ideologies/beliefs and values.

[5] Gamma change - highest order organization change. Requires radical shift in the organization's frame of reference, e.g., ideologies/beliefs and values. Other essentially synonymous terminology - second order change.

[6] Intensity of values refers to the degree to which members agree with the value system as a whole

[7] Breadth refers to the relative number of members who do not actually hold central values, i.e., the extent to which values are shared.

[8] Also referred to as stability and change.

[9] Requisite variety dictates that for a system to cope with the problems

and demands of its environment, variety equal to that found in the environment must be included within the system.

[10] Also referred to in the literature as the balancing of reliability and validity.

[11] The nomothetic perspective uses quantitative methods to establish general laws.

[12] The ideal types described within a typology represent organization forms that might exist, rather than existing organizations. Actual organizations may be more or less similar to an ideal type.

References

Ackoff, R.L. (1989). From data to wisdom: Presidential address to ISGSR. *Journal of Applied Systems Analysis,* 16, 3-9.

Adler, P.S. & Shenbar, A. (1990). Adapting your technological base: The organizational challenge. *Sloan Management Review,* 32, 25-37.

Allaire, Y. & Firsirotu, M. (1985). How to implement radical strategies in large organizations. *Sloan Management Review,* 27,19-34.

Amabile, T.M. (1983). *The social psychology of creativity.* New York: Springer-Verlag.

Amabile, T.M. (1988). A model of creativity and innovation in organizations. *Research in Organizational Behavior,* 10, 123-167.

Argyris, C. (1982). Organizational learning and management information systems. *DataBase,* 13(2&3), 3-11.

Argyris, C. (1991). Teaching smart people to learn. *Harvard Business Review,* 69, 99-109.

Argyris, C. & Schoen, D.A. (1978). *Organization learning: A theory of action research.* Reading, MA: Addison-Wesley.

Argyris, C. & Schoen, D.A. (1982). *Theory in practice: Increasing professional effectiveness.* San Francisco: Jossey-Bass.

Ashby, W.R. (1956). *An introduction to cybernetics.* London: Chapman and Hall.

Bartunek, J. (1984). Changing interpretive schemes and organizational restructuring: The example of a religious order. *Administrative Science Quarterly,* 29, 355-372.

Baskerville, R.L. & Davies, L. (1992, December). A workshop on two techniques for qualitative data analysis: Action research and ethnography (a workshop). Thirteenth International Conference on Information Systems, Dallas.

Bass, B. (1985). *Leadership and performance beyond expectations.* New York: Free Press.

Beath, C.M. (1991). Supporting the information technology champion. *MIS Quarterly,* 15(3), 355-372.

Beyer, J.M. (1981). Ideologies, values, and decision making in organizations. In P. Nystrom & W. Starbuck (Eds.) *Handbook of Organizational Design,* Volume 2. England: Oxford University Press.

Boland, R. & Day, W. (1989). The experience of systems design: A hermeneutic of organizational action. *Scandinavian Journal of Management,* 5(2), 87-104.

Brown, J. & Duguid, P. (1991). Organizational learning and communities-of-practice: Toward a unified view of working, learning, and innovation. *Organization Science*, 2(1), 40-57.

Budner, S. (1962). Intolerance of ambiguity as a personality variable. *Journal of Personality*, 30, 29-50.

Calder, B. & Schurr, P. (1981). Attitudinal processes in organizations. *Research in Organizational Behavior*, 3, 283-302.

Caron, J.R., Jarvenpaa, S.L. & Stoddard, D. (1994). Business reengineering at CIGNA corporation: Experiences and lessons from the first five years. *MIS Quarterly*, 18(3), 233-250.

Charam, R. (1991). How networks reshape organizations - for results. *Harvard Business Review*, 69, 104-115.

Cherns, A. (1976). The principles of sociotechnical design. *Human Relations*, 29(8), 783-792.

Clarke, T. (1991). *Theory and practice: Reengineering practices at Mutual Benefit Life* (POSPP Report P-72-1). Atlanta: Chantico Publishing.

Cohen, W.M. & Leventhal, D.A. (1990). Absorptive capacity: A new perspective on learning and innovation. *Administrative Science Quarterly*, 35, 128-152.

Cotter, L. (1977). Information flow into research and development projects: An exploratory study of the flow of important information. Unpublished doctoral dissertation, University of California, Los Angeles.

Cox, T., Lobel, S., & McLeod, P. (1991). Effects of ethnic group cultural differences on cooperative and competitive behavior on a group task. *Academy of Management Journal*, 34(4), 827-847.

Daft, R.L. & Huber, G.P. (1987). How organizations learn: A communications framework. *Research in the Sociology of Organizations*, 5, 1-36.

Daft, R.L. & Lengel, R.H. (1986). Organizational information requirements, media richness, and structural design. *Management Science*, 32, 554-571.

Daft, R.L. & Weick, K.E. (1984). Toward a model of organizations as interpretation systems. *Academy of Management Review*, 9(2), 284-295.

Damanpour, F. (1991). Organizational innovation: A meta-analysis of effects of determinants and moderators. *Academy of Management Journal*, 34(3), 555-590.

Davenport, T. (1993). *Process innovation: Reengineering work through information technology*. Boston: Harvard Business School Press.

Davenport, T. & Short, J. (1990). The new industrial engineering: Information technology and business process redesign. *Sloan Management Review*, 32, 11-27.

Davenport, T. & Stoddard, D. (1994). Reengineering: Business change of mythic proportions? *MIS Quarterly*, 18(2), 121-127.

Davenport, T.H., Eccles, R.G. & Prusak, L. (1992). Information politics. *Sloan Management Review*, 33, 53-65.

DeFiore, R. (1994, May). Managing the shock and aftershock of organizational change. In DeFiore (panel moderator). *Preparing for 21st century: Reshaping business, enterprise-wide IT, and the IT professional*. POSPP Spring General Meeting, Montreal, Canada.

Delbecq, A. & Mills, P. (1985). Managerial practices that enhance innovation. *Organizational Dynamics*, 13, 24-34.

Delehanty, T., Sullo, P., & Wallace, W.A. (1982). A method for prescriptive assessment of the flow of information within organizations. *Manage-

ment Science, 28(8), 910-924.

DeJong, W.M. (1994). The management of informatization: A theoretical and empirical analysis of IT implementation strategies. Published doctoral dissertation. Groningen, Netherlands: Wolters-Noordhoff.

Dixon, P.J. & John, D.A. (1989). Technology issues facing corporate management in the 1990s. *MIS Quarterly,* 13(3), 247-255.

Driver, M. (1978). Individual decision making and creativity. In S. Kerr (Ed.) *Organization Behavior.* Columbus: Grid Publishing

Duncan, W.J. (1989). Organizational culture: 'Getting a fix' on an elusive concept. *Academy of Management Executive,* 3(3), 229-236.

Dutton, J.E. (1992). The making of organizational opportunities: An interpretive pathway to organizational change. *Research in Organizational Behavior,* 15, 195-226.

Emery, F.E. & Trist, E.L. (1972). *Towards a social ecology.* London: Plenum Press.

Erez, M., Earley, P., & Hulin, C. (1985). The impact of participation on goal acceptance and performance: A two-step model. *Academy of Management Journal,* 28(1), 50-66.

Evans, M.G. (1984). Reducing control loss in organizations: The implications of dual hierarchies, mentoring and strengthening vertical dyadic linkages. *Management Science,* 30(2), 156-168.

Fiol, C.M. & Lyles, M.A. (1985). Organizational learning. *Academy of Management Review,* 10(4), 803-813.

Fitzgerald, T.H. (1988). Can change in organizational culture really be managed?. *Organizational Dynamics,* 17, 5-15.

Frost, P. & Egri, C. (1991). The political process of innovation. *Research in Organization Behavior,* 13, 229-295.

Galbraith, J.R. (1982). Designing the innovating organization. *Organizational Dynamics,* 10, 5-25.

Gersick, J.G. (1988). Time and transition in work teams: Toward a new model of group development. *Academy of Management Journal,* 31, 9-41.

Gersick, J.G. (1991). Revolutionary change theories: A multilevel exploration of the punctuated equilibrium paradigm. *Academy of Management Review,* 16(1), 10-36.

Gibson, C.F. & Jackson, B.B. (1987). *The information imperative.* New York: Lexington Books.

Giddens, A. (1979). *Central problems in social theory.* Berkeley: University of California Press.

Giddens, A. (1984). *The constitution of society: Outli..e of the theory of structure.* Berkeley, CA: University of California Press.

Ginsberg, A. (1990). Connecting diversification to performance: A sociocognitive approach. *Academy of Management Review,* 15(3), 514-535.

Gioia, D. & Manz, C. (1985). Linking cognition and behavior: A script processing interpretation of vicarious learning. *Academy of Management Review,* 10(3), 527-539.

Goldstein, J. (1988). A far-from-equilibrium systems approach to resistance to change. *Organizational Dynamics,* 17, 16-26.

Gregory, K. (1983). Native-view paradigms: Multiple cultures and culture conflicts in organizations. *Administrative Science Quarterly,* 28, 359-376.

Gupta, A.K. & Govindarajan, V. (1991). Knowledge flows and the structure of control within multinational corporations. *Academy of Management Review*, 16(4), 768-792.

Gurbaxani, V. & Mendelson, H. (1990). An integrated model of information systems spending growth. *Information Systems Research*, 1(1), 23-46.

Hall, G., Rosenthal, J. & Wade, J. (1993). How to make reengineering really work. *Harvard Business Review*, 72, 119-131.

Hambrick, D. (1994). Top management groups: A conceptual integration and reconsideration of the "team" label. *Research in Organizational Behavior*, 16, 171-213.

Hambrick, D. & Mason, P. (1984). Upper echelons: The organization as a reflection of its top managers. *Academy of Management Review*, 9(2), 193-206.

Hammer, M. (1990). Reengineering work: Don't automate, obliterate. *Harvard Business Review*, 68, 104-112.

Hammer, M. & Champy, J. (1993). *Reengineering the corporation*. New York: Harper Collins.

Hatch, M.J. (1993). The dynamics of organization culture. *Academy of Management Review*, 18(4), 657-693.

Hedberg, B.L. (1981). How organizations learn and unlearn. In P.C. Nystrom & W.H. Starbuck (Eds.) *Handbook of organizational design*. New York: Oxford University Press.

Hirschhorn, L. & Gilmore, T. (1980). The application of family therapy concepts influencing organizational behavior. *Administrative Science Quarterly*, 25, 18-37.

Hopland, J. (1994, May). Dynamic business structures and the virtual corporation. (A presentation). *Preparing for 21st century: Reshaping business, enterprise-wide IT, and the IT professional*. POSPP Spring General Meeting, Montreal, Canada.

Howe, J.C. (1992). *Teams, teamwork, and team building*. UCLA Graduate School of Management, Office of Executive Education.

Howell, J. & Higgins, C. (1990). Champions of technological innovation. *Administrative Science Quarterly*, 35(2), 3117-341.

Huber, G.P. (1984). The nature and design of post industrial organizations. *Management Science*, 30(8), 928-951.

Huber, G.P. (1991). Organizational learning: The contributing processes and the literatures. *Organization Science*, 2(1), 88-115.

Huber, G.P. & McDaniel, R.R. (1986). The decision-making paradigm of organizational design. *Management Science*, 32(5), 572-589.

Huff, S.L. & Munro, M.C. (1985). Information technology assessment and adoption: A field study. *MIS Quarterly*, 10(4), 327-339.

Hulin, C. & Roznowski, M. (1985). Organizational technologies: Effects on organizations' characteristics and individuals' responses. *Research in Organizational Behavior*, 7, 39-85.

Ibarra, H. (1993). Network centrality, power, and innovation involvement: Determinants of technical and administrative roles. *Academy of Management Journal*, 36(3), 471-501.

Ihilevich, D. & Gleser, G. (1993). *Defense mechanisms: Their classification, correlates, and measurement with the defense mechanisms inventory*. Odessa, Florida: Psychological Assessment Resources.

Ives, B. & Mason, R. (1990). Can information technology revitalize your customer service? *Academy of Management Executive*, 4(4), 52-69.

Johnston, H.R. & Carrico, S.R. (1988). Developing capabilities to use information strategically. *MIS Quarterly*, 12(1), 37-50.

Kanter, R.M. (1984). Innovation - the only hope for times ahead. *Sloan Management Review*, 25(4), 51-56.

Kanter, R.M. (1988). When a thousand flowers bloom: Structural, collective, and social conditions for innovation in organization. *Research in Organizational Behavior*, 10, 169-211.

Kerr, J. & Slocum, J.W., Jr. (1987). Managing corporate culture through reward systems. *Academy of Management Executive*, 1(2), 99-108.

Kilmann, R., Saxton, M., & Serpa, R. (1986). Issues in understanding and changing culture. *California Management Review*, 28(2), 87-94.

Klein, J.I. (1989). Parenthetic learning in organizations: Toward the unlearning of the unlearning model. *Journal of Management Studies*, 26, 291-308.

Klempa, M.J. (1983). Decision support systems: A field investigation integrating cognitive style, incongruity adaptation level, defense mechanism and organizational characteristics. Unpublished doctoral dissertation, University of Southern California, (University Microfilms No. 83-25646).

Klempa, M.J. (1993). Management of IT innovation: A heuristic paradigm research perspective. In M. Tanniru (Ed.) *Proceedings of the 1993 ACM SIGCPR Conference*, St. Louis.

Klempa, M.J. (1994a). Managing information technology: An integrative acquisition/diffusion contingency model. In M. Khosrowpour (Ed.) *Information technology and organizations: Challenges of new technologies*. Harrisburg, PA: Idea Group Publishing.

Klempa, M.J. (1994b). Management of information technology diffusion: A meta-force integrative contingency diffusion model. In L. Levine (Ed.) *Diffusion, transfer, and implementation of information technology (A-45)*. Amsterdam: North-Holland.

Kram, K.E. & Isabella, L.A. (1985). Alternatives to mentoring: The role of peer relationships in career development. *Academy of Management Journal*, 28(1), 110-132.

Kuhn, T.S. (1970). *The structure of scientific revolutions*. Chicago: University of Chicago Press.

Kwon, T.H. & Zmud, R.W. (1987). Unifying the fragmented models of information systems implementation. In R.J. Boland & R. Hirschheim (Eds.), *Critical Issues in Information Systems Research*. New York: Wiley, (pp. 227-251).

Lawrence, P. & Lorsch, J. (1967). Differentiation and integration in complex organizations. *Administrative Science Quarterly*, 12, 1-47.

Leblebici, H., Marlow, E., & Rowland, K. (1983). Research note: A longitudinal study of the stability of interpretive schemes, organizational structure, and their contextual correlates. *Organization Studies*, 4(2), 165-184.

Lee, A.S. (1991). Integrating positivist and interpretive approaches to organizational research. *Organization Science*, 2(4), 342-365.

Lee, A.S. (1994). Electronic mail as a medium for rich communication: An empirical investigation using hermeneutic interpretation. *MIS Quarterly*, 18(2), 143-158.

Leonard, J. (1994, May). Managing the shock and aftershock of organizational change. In DeFiore (panel moderator). *Preparing for 21st century: Reshaping business, enterprise-wide IT, and the IT professional.* POSPP Spring General Meeting, Montreal, Canada.

Lewin, A. & Minton, J. (1986). Determining organizational effectiveness: another look, and an agenda for research. *Management Science*, 32(5), 514-538.

Lewis, L. & Seibold, D. (1993). Innovation modification during intraorganizational adoption. *Academy of Management Review*, 18(2), 322-354.

Locke, E., Latham, G., & Erez, M. (1988). The determinants of goal commitment. *Academy of Management Review*, 13(1), 23-39.

Lord, R. & Maher, K. (1990). Alternative information processing models and their implications for theory, research, and practice. *Academy of Management Review*, 15(1), 9-28.

Lorsch, J. (1986). Managing culture: The invisible barrier to strategic change. *California Management Review*, 28(2), 95-109

Lucas, R. (1987). Political-cultural analysis of organizations. *Academy of Management Review*, 12(1), 144-156.

Lundberg, C. (1985). On the feasibility of cultural intervention in organizations. In P.J. Frost, L.F. Moore, M.R. Louis, C.C. Lundberg, & J. Martin (Eds.) *Organization Culture*. Beverly Hills, CA: Sage Publications.

Lyles, M.A. (1988). Learning among joint venture sophisticated firms. *Management International Review*, 28, 85-98.

Madique, M.A. (1980). Entrepreneurs, champions, and technological innovation. *Sloan Management Review*, 21(2), 59-76.

March, J.G. (1991). Exploration and exploitation in organizational learning. *Organization Science*, 2(1), 71-87.

March, J.G., Sproull, L., & Tamuz, M.(1991). Learning from samples of one or fewer. *Organization Science*, 2(1), 1-13.

Mason, R.O. & Mitroff, I. (1981). *Challenging strategic planning assumptions*. New York: Wiley.

Morgan, G. & Ramirez, R. (1984). Action learning: A holographic metaphor for guiding social change. *Human Relations*, 37(1), 1-28.

Morey, M. & Luthans, F. (1984). An emic perspective and ethnoscience methods for organizational research. *Academy of Management Review*, 9(1), 27-36.

Morton, M.S. (Ed.). (1991). *The corporation of the '90s: Information technology and the organizational transformation.* New York: Oxford University Press.

Musser, C. (1992). *Implementing the I/T vision: Business process reengineering* (POSPP Report P-12-2). Atlanta: Chantico Publishing.

Nadler, D. & Tushman, M. (1990). Beyond the charismatic leader: Leadership and organizational change. *California Management Review*, 32(2), 77-97.

Nelson, D.L. (1990). Individual adjustment to information-driven technologies: A critical review. *MIS Quarterly*, 14(1), 79-98.

Nonaka, I. (1988). Toward middle-up-down management: Accelerating information creation. *Sloan Management Review*, 29(3), 9-18.

Nonaka, I. (1991). The knowledge-creating company. *Harvard Business Review*, 69, 96-104.

Nonaka, I. & Johansson, J. (1985). Japanese management: What about the "hard" skills? *Academy of Management Review*, 10(2), 181-191.

Nystrom, P. & Starbuck, W. (1984). To avoid organizational crises, unlearn. *Organizational Dynamics,* 13, 53-65.

O'Reilly, C. (1989). Corporations, culture, and commitment: Motivation and social control in organizations. *California Management Review,* 31(3), 9-25.

Orlikowski, W.J. (1991). Integrated information environment or matrix of control? The contradictory implications of information technology. *Accounting, Management, and Information Technology,* 1(1), 9-42.

Orlikowski, W.J. & Baroudi, J.J. (1991). Studying information technology and the structuring of organizations. *Information Systems Research,* 2(1), 1-28.

Orlikowski, W.J. & Robey, D. (1991). Information technology and the structuring of organizations. *Information Systems Research,* 2(2), 143-169.

Pelz, D.C. (1983). Quantitative case histories of urban innovations: Are there innovating stages. *IEEE Transactions on Engineering Management,* EM-30(2), 60-67.

Pettigrew, A. (1973). *The politics of organizational decision-making.* London: Tavistock.

Pettigrew, A. (1979). On studying organizational cultures. *Administrative Science Quarterly,* 24, 570-581.

Pettigrew, A. (1985). *The awakening giant.* Oxford:Basil Blackwell.

Pfeffer, J. (1985). Organizational demography: Implications for management. *California Management Review,* 28(1), 67-81.

Pope, D. (1993). *Reengineering the application delivery process* (POSPP Report P-11- 3). Atlanta: Chantico Publishing.

Porter, M. (1985). *Competitive Advantage.* New York: The Free Press.

Profit Oriented Systems Planning Program (1994, July). *Business process reengineering survey.* (Available from POSPP Information Management Institute, 4380 Georgetown Square, Suite 1002, Atlanta, Georgia 30338)

Quinn, J.B. (1985). Managing innovation: Controlled chaos. *Harvard Business Review,* 63(3), 73-84.

Reichers, A. (1985). A review and reconceptualization of organizational commitment. *Academy of Management Review,* 10(3), 465-476.

Riley, P. (1983). A structurationist account of political culture. *Administrative Science Quarterly,* 28(3), 414-437.

Roach, S.S. (1989). *Pitfalls on the 'new' assembly line: Can services learn from manufacturing.* Morgan Stanley & Company: New York.

Rockart, J.F. & Short, J.E. (1989). I/T in the 1990s: Managing organization interdependence. *Sloan Management Review,* 30, 7-17.

Rogers, E. (1983). *Diffusion of innovations* (3rd ed.). New York: Free Press.

Rotter, J.B. (1966). Generalized expectancies for internal versus external control of reinforcement. *Psychological Monographs,* 80, No.609.

Russell, T. (1994). *IS at the bank of Nova Scotia: The engine of change* (POSPP Report P-31-4). Atlanta:Chantico Publishing.

Saffold, G.S., III. (1988). Culture traits, strength, and organizational performance: Moving beyond "strong" culture. *Academy of Management Review,* 13(4), 546-558.

Schein, E.H. (1984). Coming to a new awareness of organizational culture. *Sloan Management Review,* 25, 3-16.

Senge, P.M. (1990). The leader's new work: Building learning organizations. *Sloan Management Review*, 32, 7-23.

Sheldon, A. (1980). Organizational paradigms: A theory of organizational change. *Organizational Dynamics*, 8(3), 61-80.

Shore, E.B. (1993). *Business reengineering: Fast track to operational excellence*. (Critical Technology Report C-4-3). Atlanta: Chantico Publishing.

Shrivastava, P. & Mitroff, I. (1984). Enhancing organizational research utilizations: The role of decision maker's assumptions. *Academy of Management Review*, 9, 18-26.

Shrivastava, P. & Schneider, S. (1984). Organizational frames of reference. *Human Relations*, 37(10), 795-809.

Simon, H.A. (1991). Bounded rationality and organizational learning. *Organization Science*, 2(1), 125-134.

Sitkin, S.B. & Pablo, A.L. (1992). Reconceptualizing the determinants of risk behavior. *Academy of Management Review*, 17(1), 9-38.

Skinner, L. (1994, May). Engineering for competitive advantage. (A presentation). *Preparing for 21st century: Reshaping business, enterprise-wide IT, and the IT professional*. POSPP Spring General Meeting, Montreal, Canada.

Smircich, L. (1983). Concepts of culture and organizational analysis. *Administrative Science Quarterly*, 28(3), 339-358.

Sproull, L.S. (1981). Beliefs in organizations. In P. Nystrom & W. Starbuck (Eds.) *Handbook of Organizational Design*, Volume 2. England: Oxford University Press.

Stevenson, W.B. and Gilly, M.C. (1991). Information processing and problem solving: The migration of problems through formal positions and networks of ties. *Academy of Management Journal*, 34(4), 918-928.

Stewart, T. (1992). The search for the organization of tomorrow. *Fortune*, (May), 93-98.

Strassman, P. (1985). *Information payoff*. New York: Free Press.

Terborg, J.R. (1981). Interactional psychology and research on human behavior in organizations. *Academy of Management Review*, 6(4), 569-576.

Terborg, J.R., Howard, G.S., & Maxwell, S.E. (1980). Evaluating planned organizational change: A method for assessing alpha, beta, and gamma change. *Academy of Management Review*, 5(1), 109-121.

Tichy, N. (1981). Networks in organizations. In Nystrom, P. & Starbuck, W. (Eds.) *Handbook of Organizational Design*, Volume 2. England: Oxford University Press.

Tichy, N. (1982). Managing change strategically: The technical, political, and cultural keys. *Organizational Dynamics*, 11, 59-80.

Tunstall, W.B. (1986). The breakup of the bell system: A case study in cultural transformation. *California Management Review*, 28(2), 110-124.

Tushman, M. & Nadler, D. (1986). Organizing for innovation. *California Management Review*, 28(3), 74-92.

Van de Vliert, E., Huismans, S.E., & Stok, J.J.L. (1985). The criterion approach to unraveling beta and alpha change. *Academy of Management Review*, 10(2), 269-275.

Venkatraman, N. (1994). IT-Enabled business transformation: From automation to business scope redefinition. *Sloan Management Review*, 35(2), 74-88.

Walsh, J.P. & Ungson, G.R. (1991). Organizational memory. *Academy of Management Review*, 16(1), 57-91.

Watson, W., Kumar, K., & Michaelsen, L. (1993). Cultural diversity's impact on interaction process and performance comparing homogeneous and diverse task groups. *Academy of Management Journal,* 36(3), 590-602.

Weick, K.E. (1979). *The social psychology of organizing.* Reading, MA: Addison-Wesley.

Weick, K.E. (1987). Organizational culture as a source of high reliability. *California Management Review,* 24(2), 112-127.

Weick, K.E. (1991). The nontraditional quality of organizational learning. *Organization Science,* 2(1), 116-123.

Weill, P. (1992). The relationship between investment in information technology and firm performance: A study of the valve manufacturing sector. *Information Systems Research,* 3(4), 307-333.

Weill, P. & Olson, M.H. (1989). Managing investment in information technology: Mini-case examples and implications. *MIS Quarterly,* 13(1), 3-17.

Wiener, J. (1988). Forms of value systems: A focus on organizational effectiveness and cultural change and maintenance. *Academy of Management Review,* 13(4), 534-545.

Wiersema, M. & Bantel, K. (1992). Top management team demography and corporate strategic change. *Academy of Management Journal,* 35(1), 91-121.

Wilkins, A.L. (1983). The culture audit: A tool for understanding organizations. *Organizational Dynamics,* 12, 24-38.

Wilkins, A. & Dyer, W. (1988). Toward culturally sensitive theories of culture change. *Academy of Management Review,* 13(4), 522-533.

Wilson, J.A. & Elman, N. (1990). Organizational benefits of mentoring. *Academy of Management Executive,* 4(4), 88-94.

Woodman, R., Sawyer, J., & Griffin, R. (1993). Toward a theory of organizational creativity. *Academy of Management Review,* 18(2), 293-321.

Part II

Information Technology

Chapter 5
The Place of Information Technology and Radical/Incremental Organizational Change in Business Process Redesign
Galliers

This chapter provides an approach to business strategy formulation and implementation which enables the integration of Information and Information Technology (IT) issues into the process and helps to ensure that the necessary change — whether it be radical or incremental —can and does take place. While the approach incorporates Information and IT into the process, this chapter questions some of the more trite statements that are often heard about the centrality of IT in Business Process Redesign (BPR). In addition, it questions a central tenet of BPR, namely the need for one-off radical change. In so doing, it stresses the need for organizational learning and feasible as well as desirable strategies. It achieves this by utilizing extant theory, and in doing so, also questions the extent to which BPR is entirely new.

Chapter 6
Automation, Business Process Reengineering and Client Server Technology: A Three-Stage Model of Organizational Change
O'Hara and Watson

While the concept of business process reengineering (BPR) is being touted as revolutionary, the idea of reinventing one's business to remain competitive or cope with environmental changes is not really novel. Reengineering efforts earlier this century resulted in new organizational forms and current efforts may also result in radical changes—not just to business processes but to the manner in which work is managed and the very fiber of the organization. In this chapter, the sweeping changes taking place in what has been labeled the information era are discussed, and how BPR fits into this change process. Also discussed is client/server technology and how it may facilitate both BPR and the move to new organizational forms. Data from three case studies are presented and linked back to a Stage Model of Organizational Transformation.

Chapter 7

The Search for Processes to Reengineer: Avoiding the Pitfalls of Strategic Information Systems Planning

Lederer and Sethi

Managers increasingly use strategic information systems planning methodologies to identify business processes to reengineer. This chapter first defines strategic information systems planning. It then identifies the problems that arise during it. It discusses a survey of practicing strategic information systems planners who had encountered the problems and it shows the severity of each problem. The chapter concludes with some potential prescriptions for managers who are involved in using strategic information systems planning for business process reengineering. The prescriptions are intended to help these managers better identify and reengineer the processes.

Chapter 8

Alternative IT Strategies: Organizational Scope and Application Delivery

Ponce-de-Leon, Rai, and Melcher

This chapter presents a framework with nine alternative reengineering strategies as determined by their organizational scope and the application delivery strategy. Organizational scope of the business reengineering project could include a single function, several functions, or several business units. Application delivery strategy refers to how software is delivered for the reengineering project—adoption of off-the-shelf software, adaptation of commercially available software, or complete customization. A particular reengineering strategy has important implications for how the reengineering projects should be managed and the organizational issues that should be considered.

Chapter
5

The Place of Information Technology and Radical/ Incremental Organizational Change in Business Process Redesign

Robert D. Galliers
University of Warwick, U.K.

In much of the earlier literature on Business Process Redesign (BPR) it was almost always the case that Information Technology (IT) was given a central role. Indeed, IT was seen as the catalyst for radical change. "Don't automate, obliterate", opined Hammer (1990). Look for opportunities not only to reengineer business processes but redefine the very scope of the business itself, was the message given by Venkatraman (1991) in his contribution to MIT's Management in the 1990s research program (Scott Morton, 1991).

This followed a decade in which there was the much-heralded era of strategic information systems. IT for competitive advantage was a key issue for management in the mid-1980s (Brancheau & Wetherbe, 1987). Arising from the work of Michael Porter (Porter, 1980, 1985; Porter & Millar, 1985), we were given a vision of IT being used in a proactive way in changing the very nature of competition (eg., McFarlan, 1984).

As the decade wore on, however, questions began to be asked about the sustainability of any advantage that might have been achieved through the judicious utilization of IT (Clemons, 1986), and interest in the topic waned (Niederman, et al., 1991). In much the same way, although still a key component of the process, we now see the centrality of IT in BPR being questioned (Davenport, 1993)[1]. Furthermore, the need for radical innovation to achieve strategic success with IT has also been called into question (Senn, 1992).

As a result of this experience, this chapter attempts to provide a more balanced view of the role of IT in BPR. Indeed, following Quinn (1980), it questions what seems to be the received wisdom of many a proponent of BPR, namely that radical change will always be required and that IT is the key to this change. The chapter's major focus is to provide a means by which managements can identify:

(i) the extent of change required, and
(ii) the role that IT may or may not play in achieving necessary change.

Existing tools are applied (based, eg., on the work of Leavitt, 1965; Lewin, 1951 and Checkland, 1981) with a view to demonstrating an approach to BPR which takes into account the range of change that may be necessary (for example, with respect to the skills, roles and attitudes of key personnel, and procedures and organizational boundaries, as well as IT). In doing so, both the old and the new of BPR (cf., Earl, 1994) are identified.

The chapter is organized as follows. Consideration is first given to the topics of business strategy and the management of change, and integrating information systems strategy with both business strategy and the change process. This provides a means of setting the scene for the remainder of the chapter. An approach to the management of change which takes account of the multi-faceted nature of business change is then described, with illustrations as to how this might be implemented in practice. In this way, some of the more limited views that have been expressed concerning the role that IT might play in business change are challenged, and the topic is located within the broader management systems literature than is often the case.

Business Strategy and the Management of Change

Egelhoff (1993) reminds us that there has been a tendency in the West to attempt to compete by developing unique business strategies, while many Japanese companies tend to compete by implementing not-so-unique strategies better than their competitors. In many respects, BPR echoes this call given its focus on the way we go about our business, as opposed to the 1980s' concentration on the competitive environment (Porter, 1980; 1985). The focus of BPR is not entirely internal, however: a key component is the identification of the requirements of one's customers. Once these have been identified, however, the focus shifts to ways in which these can be met more efficiently and effectively.

Where both the BPR and the strategic management literature tend to let us down —to some degree at least—is on how we go about implementing the change their analysis suggests should occur. While there is much useful advice to be had in terms of identifying strategic opportunities and while the BPR literature has developed from early exhortations simply to "think discontinuously" - to recognize and break away "from the outmoded rules and fundamental assumptions that underlie [current] operations" (Hammer, 1990, p.107), there remains the problem of how we might go about implementing that change and deciding whether radical change is indeed feasible and approporiate.

Hammer warns us that "unless we change [outdated] rules, we are merely rearranging deck chairs on the Titanic" (ibid.). To continue with this analogy, and while it is recognized that many have already suggested that the mere computerization of an ineffective operation will lead to an automated mess (see, eg., Lundeburg, et al., 1981; Galliers, 1985), there is always the danger that BPR and IT may actually turn out to be the iceberg! Clearly, we need to ensure that we have the wherewithal to effect the required change in a way that is beneficial rather than actually harmful.

Quinn (1980) propounds the theory of logical incrementalism as a means of effecting major change while minimizing its negative impacts. He argues for a step-by-step approach towards clearly defined goals. This would seem to be at variance with the philosophy of BPR. An aim of this chapter is to see if we can have our cake and eat it too - whether it is in fact feasible to achieve the kind of radical change called for by the proponents of BPR while achieving feasible, as well as desirable change (cf., Checkland, 1981), thereby minimizing negative impacts and easing implementation.

Integrating Information Systems Strategy and Business Strategy

A starting point to a consideration of the place of IT in BPR is the view that IS strategy should be but one aspect of business strategy, both in terms of strategy formulation and implementation. This view is illustrated by Figure 1 which presents IS strategy in broader terms than is often the case. For example, Lederer and Sethi (1992) perceive IS strategy as being concerned with the identification of required IS applications and the necessary resources to develop these. All too often, when considering IS strategy, our thinking has been confined to outcomes associated with required applications and necessary

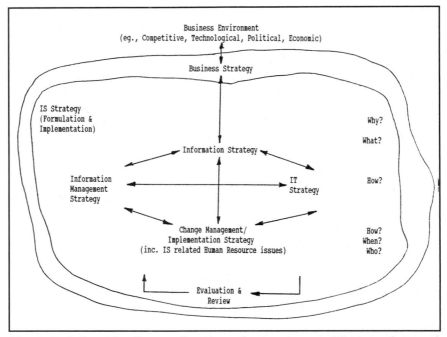

Figure 1: Information Systems Strategy as but one Aspect of Business Strategy (amended from Galliers, 1991, 1994)

resources. In the same way that, until quite recently, business strategy has focussed on strategy formulation at the expense of implementation, so has IS strategy. This is why Figure 1 extends the earlier model developed by Earl (1989) by overtly including an implementation/change management component. Figure 1 is slightly unusual in that, at first sight at least, it appears to mix together strategy content (e.g., information strategy) and strategy process (eg., implementation). The point is that strategy formulation (formation) and implementation are meant to be considered contemporaneously. In addition, Figure 1 attempts to show that IS strategy both feeds off and feeds into business strategy and can usefully be perceived as a continuous process, requiring on-going assessment, review and feedback.

Earl (1989) talks also of a three-pronged approach to IS strategy, illustrated in Figure 2. Here we are not solely reliant on the 'top-down' approach of the formative years of IS strategy (i.e., feeding off an existing business plan) or the 'bottom-up' approach which was the hallmark of the very earliest attempts to plan for IS (i.e., being reliant on an audit of existing systems and the demands of users). In addition, Earl's so-called 'multiple' methodology incorporates the thinking of the mid-1980s in reviewing the Business Environment (e.g., Competitive, Technological, Political, Economic) in an attempt to identify, as a result of a creative process, the strategic opportuni-

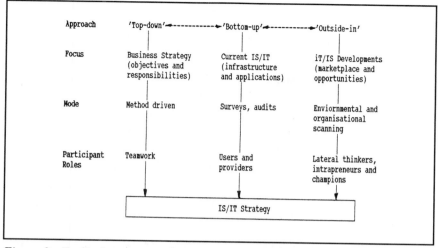

Figure 2: Earl's three-pronged, 'multiple' approach to IS strategy (amended from Earl, 1989, p.71)

ties that IT might provide. He labels this the 'inside-out' leg of the methodology. In many ways, however, a more appropriate label might be 'outside-in', given that this orientation is often dependent on a review of the market forces affecting the competitive environment of the company concerned (cf., Porter, 1980; 1985).

Such a three-pronged approach is a step toward the more balanced perspective we are seeking. It takes account of the company's current IS/IT status, attempts to identify IS/IT requirements in line with existing business objectives, but also takes a more proactive stance with respect to the opportunities offered by IT to alter business strategy and refocus the business. It also takes note of the developments in our thinking regarding the changing nature of the desired outcomes of the IS strategy process.

Figure 3 illustrates the point. From simple beginnings, when IS strategy was viewed simply as a means of identifying required IS developments, our attention moved to a concern to identify the required portfolio of IS applications across the spectrum of business functions and not just those in the traditional application areas such as finance and accounting. With the advent of powerful database technology, in the latter half of the 1970s and into the 1980s, our attention was turned to the creation of corporate databases, and IS strategy refocussed on what might be termed datacentric approaches such as that advocated by Martin (1982). Indeed, there is still a school of thought which favors this approach, including today's adherents to the BPR philosophy such as Davenport (1993). As we have seen, however, there then followed an era when IT for competitive advantage was in the limelight, with IS strategy focusing on

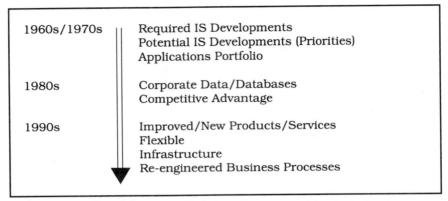

Figure 3: Trends in IS strategy: the changing nature of the desired outcomes from the process (amended from Galliers, 1994, p.2)

strategic IS (Porter & Millar, 1985). The view here was that IS/IT could improve and actually create new products and services, leading to a refocussing of the business (Venkatraman, 1991), and acting as a catalyst in radically reengineering business processes (Davenport & Short, 1990; Hammer, 1990). Figure 3 is also meant to illustrate the rapidity with which proposed outcomes from the IS strategy process have changed during the current decade, especially when compared to the 1960s and 1970s, and even the 1980s.

A central argument of this chapter is that while each of these views has validity, they each present but one aspect only of the totality of the issues confronting us in IS strategy. We should not forget the lessons provided thirty years ago by Leavitt (1965) when he identified the interactions and interdependence of task, technology, structure and people in his famous 'diamond' (Figure 4).

In the same way that we cannot assume a purely technological solution, neither should we assume a purely processual solution either: BPR and radical change are unlikely always to be the answer. We need to take into account each component (and their interrelationships) of each individual situation we face.

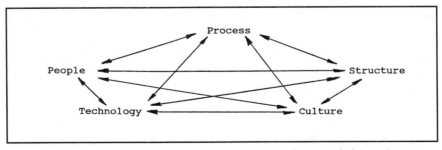

Figure 4: An amended version of Leavitt's 'Diamond' (amended from Leavitt, 1965 and Davis & Olsen, 1984, p.355).

A Multi-Faceted Approach to Business Change

The approach advocated herein attempts to take account of the above arguments and does not assume that required change will always take the form of a technological or processual solution, nor that it will always be radical, as opposed to incremental change that is the answer. Based on the work of Checkland (1981), the approach described below takes into account Lewin's (1951) analysis that a period of change requires creation of a favorable climate in which change can take place ('unfreezing'), followed by a period in which the required change is set in place ('freezing'). The approach is outlined in Figure 5.

A number of feedback loops have been incorporated into the process in order to indicate that it is essentially an iterative one which builds upon past experiences and an evaluation of both intended and unintended consequences of the changes that are being implemented, and the changing nature of the business (and technological) environment in which the organization is operating. In other words, the process aids organizational learning of the kind advocated by Argyris and Schön (1978). In this respect, it argues against the somewhat facile concept of one-time, radical change propounded by many a BPR proponent.

The approach has been divided into three sections (i.e., Organizational Environment, Business Strategies & Processes, and Information Infrastructure) for ease of reference, but it is important to stress the point that it is essentially an iterative, on-going process. That is why I have resisted the temptation of numbering the boxes in Figure 5.

Organizational Environment

Key stakeholders have to be favorably disposed to change for change strategies to have any real chance of success. There is a tendancy in much of the BPR literature to view BPR as a process instigated by senior executives and often orchestrated by external consultants. This is not the only mode of operation, nor is it always likely to lead to a motivated workforce should the change include - as it often does—downsizing and forced redundancy. Indeed, we should be aware that in many firms, the anticipated economic and organizational benefits of downsizing have failed to materialize and that any "reductions in headcount need to be viewed as part of a process of continuous improvement that includes organizational redesign, along with broad, systemic changes designed to eliminate [redundant processes], waste, and inefficiency" (Cascio, 1993, p.95).

Downsizing as a sole objective of BPR is likely to be unsuccessful.

A climate in which change is eagerly anticipated is likely to be achieved by a realization that all is not well, for example, that competitors are making inroads into one's markets, that key customers are becoming increasingly discontented with one's products and/or services, and that personnel are becoming increasingly frustrated with the way business is conducted.[2] This perceived need for action can be reinforced and harnessed by the process advocated herein. The very analysis of organizational strengths and weaknesses and environmental opportunities and threats, when undertaken by key executives and the involvement of personnel who are responsible for key day-to-day operational activities, can often lead to concerted action and, properly handled, an enthusiastic response to ways and means of dealing with the problems and opportunities that have thereby been uncovered.

The benefits to be gained from workshops of this kind are well documented (see, for example, Hardaker & Ward, 1987 and Galliers, et al., 1994), but it is as well to prepare for these in terms of clarifying the nature of such roles as project champion, project manager and facilitator; carefully selecting a team from a range of functional backgrounds and/or business units, and deciding on the membership of a steering committee (see, for example, Ward, 1990).

The analysis of the internal and external environments can usefully utilize such tried and tested techniques as SWOT (analysis of strengths, weaknesses, opportunities and threats), PEST (analysis of political, economic, social and technological environments), Porter's (1980; 1985) five forces and value chain analysis, and the like. In addition, however, it is worthwhile, especially in the context of understanding the nature of the IS/IT agenda in all of this, to take stock of the quality of IS provision and the full range of issues associated with the management of IS services.

For the purposes of this chapter, I shall deal with the information (systems) aspects of the organizational environment under the Information Infrastructure section below. First, though, we now turn to the Business Strategies & Processes aspects of the approach.

Business Strategies & Processes

Having taken stock of the current (and recent past) situation, it is useful then to consider possible future scenarios (Schnaars, 1987; de Gues, 1988) for the organization as a precursor to considering alternative business strategies that appear to be appropriate in these different contexts. A helpful technique in this aspect of the process is one developed by the SEMA Group. This considers the future in terms of "facts" (those elements that are considered to be relatively stable within the planning period); "heavy trends" (those trends that

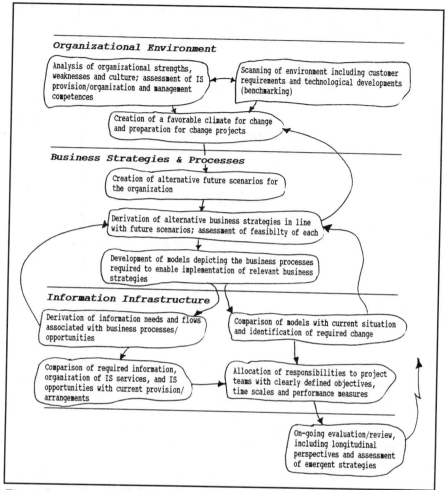

Figure 5: A Socio-Technical approach to business and IS strategy formation and the management of organizational transformation (source: amended from Galliers, 1993, p.206; 1994, p.6)

are thought very likely to continue during the planning period), and "issues" (those elements over which there is disagreement or considerable doubt). By building up alternative scenarios by altering the "issues" while keeping the "facts" constant and making minor alterations to the "trends", it is possible to consider alternative strategies in the light of the differing "futures" thus constructed. It also proves useful to include a counter-intuitive "future" (ie., altering key "facts"), to identify what the firm might do in such unforeseen circumstances.

Having agreed on a small number of scenarios following discussion of a range of alternatives (three or four is fairly normal), one can begin to consider an appropriate business strategy and the potential role of IS/IT in each. Questioning the key assumptions on which these strategies are based is an important route to the identification of strategic information.

The statement of strategy should comprise the following (after Checkland, 1981):

Viewpoint	(taken for granted view that makes the notional system of activity meaningful)
Owner	(the person or persons who could destroy the system or change it beyond recognition)
Customer	(the beneficiaries or victims of the system)
Actors	(those involved in carrying out the tasks implied by the system objectives)
Transformation	(the means by which defined inputs are transformed into defined outputs; the central point of the system)
Environment	(the constraints or givens within which the system has to operate),

to enable the development of a sufficiently rich process model which should itself comprise the minimum set of processes that are required to fulfil the strategic objectives associated with each scenario.

An illustration of these two steps in the process, taken from Checkland and Scholes (1991, p. 188) is given below in Figure 6. The definition of the notional system in this illustration relates to the perceived need for change in role and reduced conflicts between different parts of the Product Marketing Division (PMD) of ICL. It is included here to demonstrate the point that the approach is a general one that can be used in a range of quite different circumstances. In this instance, the focus was on organizational change within a particular sector of a company. In different circumstances, the approach can be used, for example, to deal with organizational change company-wide; to consider alternative strategies, or to incorporate IS/IT considerations into the equation.

A comparison of the processes that go to make up the kind of models illustrated in Figure 9, and their interrelationships, especially when the potential of IS/IT is being considered at the same time, often leads to the realization that some of the current business processes, which until this time were considered to be key to business success, can actually be streamlined or even omitted altogether. Conversely, processess that are crucial may not be in place or may be undertaken poorly.

It is important to remember that the models are based on required processes and do not relate to existing organizational arrangements nor to current functional boundaries. An information architecture based on key information needs and flows as these

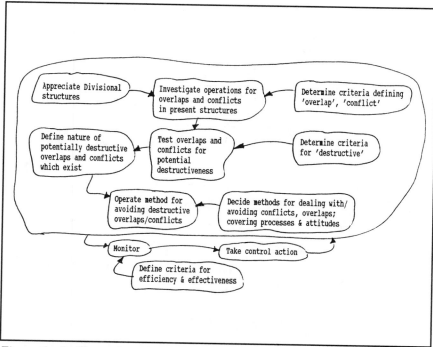

Figure 6: An illustration of aspects of Checkland's (1981) Soft Systems Methodology

relate to required, not existing, processes, is a natural outcome of this kind of thinking. Key information can be identified by using such techniques as the critical success factor (CSF) approach (Rockart, 1979), augmented by its corollary, critical failure factors and the critical assumptions upon which the strategies are based (Galliers, 1993). On-going assessment of the impact of change projects is assisted by the collection of information of this kind.

Information Infrastucture

The extent to which an organization is dependent on IS can be estimated by the application of McFarlan's (1984) so-called strategic grid, as depicted in Figure 7. In addition, an assessment of the appropriateness of an aggressive competitive strategy with respect to the utilization of IS/IT can be made using a similar grid developed by McLaughlin, et al. (1983), as shown in Figure 8.

Referring to Figure 7, having undertaken the kind of analysis advocated by Porter & Millar (1985), for example, it is possible to estimate the value adding potential to the firm of IS/IT. An assessment of the quality of IS resources (cf., Figures 8 and 9) also needs to be undertaken and this will be discussed below.

As shown in Figure 8, organizations with sound IS resources

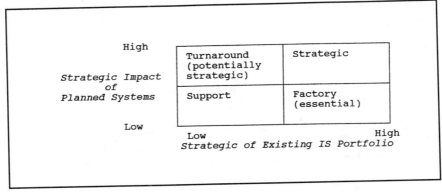

Figure 7: The IT Strategic Grid (amended from McFarlan, 1984)

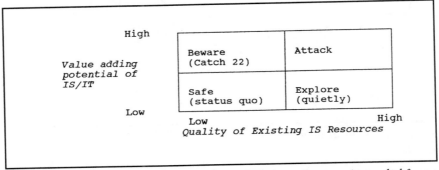

Figure 8: Choosing an Appropriate IT-Based Business Strategy (amended from McLaughlin, et al., 1983)

and good business opportunities from the application of IS/IT are clearly in a position to adopt an aggressive stance. Those that have identified only limited opportunities are likely to be relatively safe from attack by competitors even if their IS resources are weak. Conversely, those in a similar position but with sound IS resources may wish quietly to explore the situation further as the business/technological environment changes and/or they uncover a previously hidden opportunity. Should a firm identify considerable value adding potential from IS/IT, but have relatively poor resources, there is a requirement to act with due urgency. Such an enterprise is currently in a "Catch 22" situation. In other words, the enterprise may be "damned if they do and damned if they don't"! An aggressive strategy is likely to become unstuck since they are likely to lack the capacity - both in technological and human terms - to see it through to a successful conclusion. Inaction is likely to lead to the firm coming under attack from the competition.

How then can a firm make an assessment of the quality of its IS resources and decide what urgent action it should take? This is not simply an assessment of the strategic impact of IS as in McFarlan's (1984) analysis. A broader evaluation is required and this can be achieved by a development on the well known "stages of growth" concept (Gibson & Nolan, 1984; Nolan, 1979) which incorporates the so-called "7S" analysis pioneered by McKinsey & Co. (see, eg., Pascale & Athos, 1981). This broader stages of growth model is described in detail in Galliers and Sutherland (1991) and lessons from its application are recounted in Galliers (1991). It is illustrated in outline in Figure 9.

We have found that the revised model is best used in a workshop environment where key stakeholders can debate their different perceptions about the current state of affairs—and there almost certainly will be different perceptions expressed! It is often the case that certain elements of the 7S framework will be at different stages of growth and a profile will emerge that will indicate where particular urgent action is required.[3] In addition, it is almost bound to be the case that different parts of the organization (eg., functions, SBUs, sites) will find themselves at different stages of growth.

Placing the current company profile in relation to the profile of, say, five years, three years and one year ago can be particularly insightful, as this gives an indication of the rate of progress, if any: there is no God-given right for firms to move toward the later stages of growth as implied by earlier models. Indeed, it can often be the case that firms may revert to earlier stages. Discussion on the reasons for lack of progress or reversion to earlier stages is particularly enlightening.

The outcomes from all this assessment can be compared against the information identified as being required from an analysis of the business strategy and associated model(s) of the kind depicted in Figure 6. Bear in mind, however, that we should not simply focus our attention on IS and assocated IT requirements. Consideration should also be given to the impact of IT on business processes and strategy, and on the alternative ways we might organize our information services—the information management strategy, in other words (cf., Figure 1).

Concluding Remarks

This chapter has attempted to provide a means by which the kind of discontinuous thinking advocated by Hammer (1990) can be achieved, without dismissing organizational learning. The comparison of what is needed in the context of alternative future scenarios may lead to a decision that radical change is required —and, just as likely, it may not! Incremental change may well be more appropriate during a period following rapid change (cf., 'freezing') or where the

ELEMENT* \ STAGE	I	II	III	IV	V	VI
STRATEGY	ACQUISITION OF IT (SERVICES)	AUDIT OF IT PROVISION	TOP-DOWN ANALYSIS	INTEGRATION, COORDINATION	COMPETITIVE ADVANTAGE	INTERACTIVE PLANNING; COLLABORATION
STRUCTURE	INFORMAL	FINANCE CONTROLLED	CENTRALISED DP DEPT	INFORMATION CENTRE(S)	SBU COALITIONS	COORDINATED COALITIONS
SYSTEMS	AD HOC, OPERATIONAL, ACCOUNTING	GAPS/ DUPLICATION; LARGE BACK-LOG; HEAVY MAINTENANCE	UNCONTROLLED END-USER COMPUTING VERSUS CENTRALISED SYSTEMS	DECENTRALISED APPROACH, SOME EXECUTIVE INFORMATION SYSTEMS	COORDINATED CENTRALISED AND DECENTRALISED IS; SOME STRATEGIC IS	INTER-ORGANISATIONAL SYSTEMS; IS/IT-BASED PRODUCTS & SERVICES
STAFF	PROGRAMMERS, CONTRACTORS	SYSTEMS ANALYSTS, DP MANAGER	IS PLANNERS, IS MANAGER, DATABASE SPECIALISTS	BUSINESS ANALYSTS, INFORMATION RESOURCE MANAGER	BUSINESS & IS PLANNERS INTEGRATED	IS/IT DIRECTOR (BOARD LEVEL)
STYLE	UNAWARE	"DON'T BOTHER ME (I'M TOO BUSY)"	ABROGATION, DELEGATION	PARTNERSHIP; BENEFITS MANAGEMENT	INDIVIDUALISTIC (PRODUCT CHAMPIONS)	MULTIDISCIPLINARY TEAMS (KEY THEMES)
SKILLS	INDIVIDUAL; TECHNICAL LOW LEVEL	SYSTEMS DEVELOPMENT METHODOLOGY; COST-BENEFIT ANALYSIS	IS AWARENESS, PROJECT MANAGEMENT	IS/BUSINESS AWARENESS	ENTREPRENEURIAL, MARKETING	LATERAL THINKING (IT/IS POTENTIAL)
SHARED VALUES	OBFUSCATION	CONFUSION	SENIOR MANAGEMENT CONCERN, DP DEFENCE	COOPERATION	OPPORTUNISTIC	STRATEGY MAKING & IMPLEMENTATION

Amended from Galliers & Sutherland, 1991

* Note: Elements are taken from Pascale & Athos, 1981

Figure 9: Assessing the Quality of an Organization's Information Systems Management: A Revised 'Stages of Growth' Model (amended from Galliers & Sutherland, 1981, p.111)

analysis suggests that this change is either unnecessary or fool-hardy. IT can often be a catalyst in this process and IT opportunities for new or enhanced products and services should certainly not be overlooked. Having said that, an aggressive competitive strategy with IT at its heart is only likely to yield benefits when the firm's IS resources (human as well as infological and technological) are sound. Organizations should be wary of the hyperbole surrounding the topic of competitive advantage arising from IT, especially those without a sound IT and IS management track record.

The approach that has been described above gives equal weight to internal as well as external concerns. Customer - potential as well as current - requirements are highlighted, as is the changing competitive, political, economic and technological environment. A fresh review of what might otherwise be seen as essential internal business processes is also at the heart of the analysis. Above all, however, concern needs to be focussed - as part of the process itself - on the propensity of key stakeholders for change and on the implementation issues.

One final word on the process is that it is meant to be applied flexibly and on an on-going basis so that it contributes to organizational learning. The techniques that have been incorporated into it in this chapter are meant to be illustrative rather than prescriptive. They are included for the purposes of ensuring greater understanding. While they have been found to be extremely helpful in a range of BPR projects, it is more than likely that other techniques can be applied as successfully. The approach described in this chapter should not be applied rigidly - rigid application leads to rigid thinking and that is certainly not what is required!

Endnotes

[1] Despite constant references to a more holistic perspective on BPR, the subtitle of Davenport's book on the topic—Reengineering Work Through Information Technology —and the constant references to IT's enabling role in radical change, tend to suggest that perhaps "he doth protest too much"!

[2] But change can also be welcomed in successful, innovative enterprises: 1. such change is part of the ethos anyway, and 2. in such organizations, it will be readily appreciated that one doesn't keep ahead of the competition by staying still.

[3] For example, in one company, it was apparent that its current situation could be best described as passing between stages 3 and 4 of the model - except for the fact that a Board level IT Director had just been appointed. In the discussion which ensued, it became clear that his Board colleagues had assumed that his appointment was practically all that was needed to move the company rapidly ahead in terms of the strategic use of IT, and to deal with the residual relationship problems between the IS function and the business units typical of stage 3. As a result of this workshop, expectations regarding what the new IT Director could be expected to achieve were revised downwards, and a joint approach, with other members of the Board taking responsibility for a number of intitiatives, was agreed. The CEO indicated that had the model not been applied, it was highly likely that expectations would have remained high, little would have been achieved and the IT Director's career would have been in jeopardy within a matter of months!

References

Argyris, C & Shôn, D (1978). *Organizational Learning*, Addison-Wesley, Reading, MA.

Brancheau, J C & Wetherbe, J C (1987). Key Issues in Information Systems Management, *MIS Quarterly*, 11(1), pp.23-45.

Cascio, W (1993). Downsizing: What Do We Know? What Have We Learned? *Academy of Management Executive*, 7(1), pp.95-104.

Checkland, P B (1981). *Systems Thinking. Systems Practice*, Wiley, Chichester.

Checkland, P & Scholes, J (1990). *Soft Systems Methodology in Action*, Wiley, Chichester.

Clemons, E K (1986). Information Systems for Sustainable Competitive Advantage, *Information & Management*, November, pp.131-136.

Davenport, T H & Short, J E (1990). The New Industrial Engineering: Information Technology and Business Process Redesign, *Sloan Management Review*, Summer, pp.11-27.

Davenport, T H (1993). *Process Innovation. Reengineering Work through Information Technology*, Harvard Business School Press, Boston, MA.

Davis, G B & Olson, M H (1984). *Management Information Systems: Conceptual Foundations, Structure and Development* (2nd edition), McGraw Hill, New York, NY.

de Gues, A (1988). Planning as Learning, *Harvard Business Review*, 66(2), March-April, pp.70-74.

Earl, M J (1989). *Management Strategies for Information Technology*, Prentice-Hall, New York, NY.

Earl, M J (1994). The New and the Old of Business Process Redesign, *Journal of Strategic Information Systems*, 3(1), March, pp. 5-27.

Egelhoff, W G (1993). Great Strategy or Great Strategy Implementation? - Two Ways of Competing in Global Markets, *Sloan Management Review*, Winter, pp.37-50.

Galliers, R D (1985). An Approach to Information Needs Analysis. In B Shackel (ed.), Human-Computer Interaction - *INTERACT '84, Proceedings of the IFIP Conference*, London, 4-7 September, 1984, North-Holland, Amsterdam, pp. 619-628. Reprinted in R D Galliers (ed.) (1987), op cit., pp.291-304.

Galliers, R D (ed.) (1987). *Information Analysis: Selected Readings*, Addison-Wesley, Sydney.

Galliers, R D (1991). Strategic Information Systems Planning: Myths, Reality and Guidelines for Successful Implementation, *European Journal of Information Systems*, 1(1), pp.55-64.

Galliers, R D (1993). Towards a Flexible Information Architecture: Integrating Business Strategies, Information Systems Strategies and Business Process Redesign, *Journal of Information Systems*, 3(3), pp.199-213.

Galliers, R D (1994). Information Systems, Operational Research and Business Reengineering, *International Transactions on Operational Research*, 1(2), pp.1-9.

Galliers, R D, Pattison, E M & Reponen, T (1994). Strategic Information Ssytems Planning Workshops: Lessons from Three Cases, *International Journal of Information Management*, 14(1), February, pp.51-66.

Galliers, R D & Sutherland, A R (1991). Information Systems Management and Strategy Formulation: The 'Stages of Growth' Model Revisited, *Journal of Information Systems*, 1(2), pp.89-114.

Gibson, C & Nolan, R L (1974). Managing the Four Stages of EDP Growth, Harvard Business Review, 52(1), January-February, pp.76-88.

Hammer, M (1990). Reengineering Work: Don't Automate, Obliterate, *Harvard Business Review*, 68(4), July-August, pp.104-112.

Hardaker, M & Ward, B K (1987). How to Make a Team Work, *Harvard Business Review*, 65(6), November-December, pp.112-120.

Leavitt, H J (1965). Applying Organizational Change in Industry: Structural, Technological and Humanistic Approaches, in J G March (ed.), *Handbook of Organizations*, Rand McNally, Chicago, IL.

Lederer, A L & Sethi, V (1992). Meeting the Challenges of Information Systems Planning, *Long Range Planning*, 25(2), pp.69-80.

Lewin, K (1951). *Field Theory in Social Science*, Harper & Row, New York, NY.

Lundeburg, M, Goldkuhl, C & Nilsson, A (1981). *Information Systems Development: A Systematic Approach*, Prentice-Hall, Englewood Cliffs, NJ.

McFarlan, F W (1984). Information Technology Changes the Way You Compete, *Harvard Business Review*, 62(3), May-June, pp.98-103.

McLaughlin, M, Howe, R & Cash, Jr., J I (1983). Changing Competitive Ground Rules —The Impact of Computers and Communications in the 1980s. Unpublished working paper, Graduate School of Business Administration, Harvard University, Boston, MA.

Martin, J (1982). *Strategic Data Planning Methodologies*, Prentice-Hall, Englewood Cliffs, NJ.

Niederman, F, Brancheau, J C & Wetherbe, J C (1991). Information Systems Management Issues in the 1990s, *MIS Quarterly*, 16(4), pp.474-500.

Nolan, R L (1979). Managing the Crises in Data Processing, *Harvard Business Review*, 57(2), March-April, pp.115-126.

Pascale, R T & Athos, A G (1981). *The Art of Japanese Management*, Penguin, Harmondsworth.

Porter, M E (1980). *Competitive Strategy: Techniques for Analyzing Industries and Competitors*, The Free Press, New York, NY.

Porter, M E (1985). *Competitive Advantage: Creating and Sustaining Superior Performance*, The Free Press, New York, NY.

Porter, M E & Millar, V E (1985). How Information Gives You Competitive Advantage, *Harvard Business Review*, 63(2), March-April, pp.149-160.

Quinn, J B (1980). *Strategies for Change. Logical Incrementalism*, Richard D Irwin, Homewood, IL.

Rockart, J F (1979). Chief Executives Define Their Own Data Needs, *Harvard Business Review*, 57(2), March-April, pp.81-93. Reprinted in R D Galliers (ed.) (1987), op cit., pp.267-289.

Schnaars, S P (1987). How to Develop and Use Scenarios, *Long Range Planning*, 20(1), pp.105-114. Reprinted in R G Dyson (ed.), *Strategic Planning: Models and Analytical Techniques*, Wiley, Chichester, 1990., pp.153-167.

Scott Morton, M S (ed.) (1991). *The Corporation of the 1990s: Information Technology and Organizational Transformation*, Oxford University Press, Oxford.

Senn, J A (1992). The Myths of Strategic Information Systems: What Defines True Competitive Advantage? *Journal of Information Systems Management*, Summer, pp.7-12.

Venkatraman (1991). IT-Induced Business Reconfiguration. In M S Scott Morton (ed.) (1991), op cit.

Ward, B K (1990). Planning for Profit. In T Lincoln (ed.), *Managing Information Systems for Profit,* Wiley, Chichester, 1990.

Watts, J (1993). The Future of Business Process Re-engineering, *Business Change & Re-engineering,* 1(3), Winter, pp.4-5.

Automation, Business Process Reengineering and Client Server Technology:
A Three Stage Model of Organizational Change

Margaret T. O'Hara
University of Georgia

Richard T. Watson
University of Georgia

The idea of reengineering a business is not new. Although the current focus is on reengineering business *processes*, the concept of reinventing the business has been around at least since the turn of the century. Reengineering is critical to a firm's survival during certain periods when there are major upheavals in the economy that threaten the firm's existence. In today's chaotic business environment, many firms that do not reinvent themselves are doomed to become part of business history.

In this chapter, we have two themes. First, we present a three-stage model that illustrates the role of business process reengineering (BPR) in organizational transformation. Then, we discuss why client/server technology can have a significant impact on reengineering management. We demonstrate how client/server technology can be used both to reengineer work processes and to redesign work management. We argue that client/ server computing has a unique capability to change how work is managed and, as such, is an important agent in restructuring organizations to a form appropriate to an information era.

BPR—An Historical Perspective

Background

The current emphasis on business process reengineering began in 1990, with Hammer's article in *Harvard Business Review*. Hammer defined BPR as using "the power of modern information technology to radically redesign our business processes in order to achieve dramatic improvements in their performance" (Hammer 1990, p. 104). This definition has evolved to the one in vogue now:

> "the fundamental rethinking and radical redesign of business processes to achieve dramatic improvement in critical, contemporary measures of performance, such as cost, quality, service, and speed." (Hammer and Champy, 1993, p. 32).

The more recent definition downplays information technology's role in reengineering and adds a measurement dimension. Basic to these and other definitions (Hunt 1993, Davenport 1993, Morris and Brandon 1993), are the concepts of radical redesign and dramatic improvement. If either of these concepts is missing, the effort falls short of reengineering.

Recent interest in BPR represents the resurgence of a concept that seems to swing in and out of fashion. There is evidence of widespread reengineering efforts to increase blue–collar productivity early this century. Interestingly, this earlier reengineering effort began approximately fifty years after the start of the industrial era, and today's reengineering efforts are occurring approximately fifty years after the start of the information era.

We see some clear parallels between the industrial and information eras (Table 1). Our analysis of the industrial era indicates the existence of three stages, each of which represents a different focus for the organization. While some organizations may be firmly within a single stage, it is much more likely that a firm will straddle two stages at once. As our case data will indicate, an organization often continues to automate some processes concurrently with a search for ways to revolutionize other processes.

The Industrial Era

During stage one of the industrial era, machines such as the steam engine and the internal combustion motor had simple appli-

	HISTORICAL SETTING	INDUSTRIAL ERA	INFORMATION ERA
STAGE / FOCUS			
STAGE ONE: *AUTOMATING* REPLACING WORKERS		Steam engine, internal combustion engine, electric motor	Computer, word processor, calculator, spreadsheets, data bases
STAGE TWO: *INFORMATING* REDESIGNING WORK		Scientific management, time and motion studies, the assembly line	Total Quality Management, Business Process Reengineering
STAGE THREE: *TRANSFORMING* REDESIGNING ORGANIZATIONS AND THE MANAGEMENT OF WORK		Functional organizations, multi-divisional organizations	Learning organizations, collaborative work teams, empowered workforce

Table 1: Stages of the Industrial and Information Eras

cations: replace human or animal energy sources. Attention was not given to radical improvement of work; there was no need. Large productivity gains were easily reaped through the straightforward substitution of machine for human. For instance, the horse–drawn carriage was replaced by a truck. The truck was faster, required less attention, and was not subject to the vagaries of the animal mind.

After replacing workers, firms searched for ways to redesign work processes that existed before machines were used. This search signaled the entrance of firms into Stage Two of the industrial era, and sparked the concept of scientific management.   Scientific management, concerned with managing work and workers, offered a radical departure from past practices, and Frederick Taylor played a dominant role in this departure. We suspect that,were Taylor reincarnated today, he would sound much like Hammer and Champy in their preaching for radical departures from existing mindsets.

Taylor believed that productivity improvements would result from following certain basic principles. One principle was to develop a science of management to identify the best method for performing a task (Stoner and Freeman 1989). To succeed, Taylor felt that labor and management must undergo a "complete mental revolution." He carefully examined work methods, and redesigned them to achieve radical results. For example, Bethlehem Steel increased the loading and unloading of steel from 12.5 tons to 47.5 tons per day (a radical, 380% improvement) by following Taylor's methods. At another firm, the work force was reduced to 35 from 120 while accuracy improved over 60% (Daft 1991). Thus, many firms changed the way in which work was accomplished because of Taylor's concept of scientific management.

After changing their work methods, firms still needed to develop a way to manage the new organizations that evolved from the industrial revolution. In effect, firms needed to learn how to manage industrial work. For many organizations, the pattern was similar. Chandler (1962) presents this progression in his classic study of organizational histories. First, firms vertically integrated. Vertical integration created the need for a different management structure, since each firm now performed several different functions. Thus, the functionalorganization emerged, and areas such as finance, production, and marketing were separately managed. Finally, as firms grew larger and diversified, the multidivisional (M–form) organizational structure emerged.

Moving to the M–form organization was not a trivial task. Chandler's work clearly depicts the struggle that corporations such as Sears, General Motors, and Du Pont endured as they tried to move into an M–form organization. Often it is only during times of crisis, when the organization is threatened, that it will overcome the barriers to change (Goss, Pascale, and Athos, 1993) and, in many cases, this was the compelling reason for the adoption of the M–form. Once adopted, however, the M–form proved an effective way for large firms to manage work in the industrial age. For large organizations, it has remained the dominant organizational form, and most large firms have adopted it. Firms that have not adopted the M–form have no need to —either because their core function is relatively simple (such as mining companies) or because they are in highly customized market niches (Hunt 1993).

The Information Era

The information era is also unfolding in three stages. Schein (1994) refers to these stages as automating, informating (Zuboff 1988), and transforming the organization. In Stage One, productivity gains were made by replacing clerical workers with data processing systems. The success of microcomputer word processing and spreadsheet software is a demonstration of how information–era technology, like industrial–era technology, was initially used to harvest obvious gains by replacing workers or highly leveraging existing work.

Technology, whether industrial– or information–based, enables an organization to take on new functions, enter new markets, and generally expand its operational scope. Given such expansion and change, existing management structures often become ineffective and even dysfunctional. Furthermore, the nature of work within the firm also changes. Just as the unskilled manual laborer of the early industrial era became a skilled blue–collar worker, so did the high school graduate, a clerical worker of the early information era, become a knowledge worker with an MBA in Stage Two. In Stage Two, the focus shifts to redesigning work to realize a further round of productivity gains. Thus, today's BPR and total quality management (TQM) efforts parallel the industrial era's scientific management.

In an era when 70% of workers were employed in manufacturing, Taylor's scientific management concepts worked to improve blue–collar productivity. Today, 70% of workers are in the service sector, so focusing attention on improving white–collar productivity makes sense (Ginzberg 1982). Additionally, we have achieved the obvious gains from replacing workers with computers; future productivity gains will come from radically redesigning work. Thus, the current interest in BPR represents a transition of focus from stage one to Stage Two of the information era.

In the 1990s, individuals and organizations must be given the tools to "work smarter" by better managing complexity (Schrage, 1993). To manage this complexity, firms must eventually enter the third stage of the information era. They must redesign not only their processes, but also themselves. In an intensely competitive and global world, leading edge companies are already confronting the third stage of the information era. These organizations are finding that they need a new way to manage work. Functional and multidivisional organizations are often not appropriate to the information age; they hinder rather than enhance the rapid exchange of information. Many enlightened organizations are already moving beyond reengineering business processes to total organizational transformation. These organizations are seeking new ways to organize work, new ways to communicate, and new authority relationships (Schein 1994).

There is no clear demarcation between the stages of the information era; many firms are in transition from one stage to the other. Specifically, Stages Two and Three may be intertwined: as businesses continue to reengineer selected processes they often begin to reengineer their basic structures, thus leading to organizational transformation — Stage Three of the information era.

Being in the midst of this revolution makes it extremely difficult to identify what the new organizational form will be. After all, Chandler's analysis was not completed until long after the M–form had emerged as a successful solution to managing industrial–era work. Nevertheless, current trends seem to indicate that managing work in an information era involves creating flatter organizations, autonomous work groups, and the devolution of power.

Scholars and early experience suggest that the M–form structure of the industrial era is giving way to a new design centered on creating learning organizations and collaborative work teams. The new organizational form is perhaps best encapsulated in the word *empowerment*. Empowerment occurs when employees who perform certain jobs are given the responsibility for determining how those jobs should be done. It assumes that the people doing the work are those most informed about how best to do the work and how best to improve it (Pine 1993).

There are four keys to empowerment: information, knowledge, skills, and control (Taylor and Felton 1993). First, employees must have the knowledge and skills to perform their jobs, or they must be able (authorized to *and* willingto) obtain what they need. Second, employees must have available the information needed to perform their jobs. This leads to less closely–guarded data within the organization and implies that information sharing is commonplace and encouraged. Finally, empowered workers have control over their jobs. They can make decisions regarding any aspect of the task and expect to be supported by upper management in those decisions.

Empowered workers are actively engaged in their jobs and in first developing and then fulfilling organizational goals. They have the authority to form autonomous teams with self–defined roles and structure. Empowering workers leads to radically different organizations.

In these new organizations, decision making and responsibility are diffused so that the organization can react rapidly to environmental change and customer demands. The new organization is highly responsive and adaptive. Intelligence and control are no longer concentrated in divisional offices; they exist in all the tentacles of the organization. Information technology (IT) can play a key role in forming and sustaining the transformed organization.

The Link Between BPR and Information Technology

General Information Technology Enablers

Most current literature on business process reengineering acknowledges the role that information technology (IT) must play in the procedure. Some view specific information technologies, such as work–group computing, as enabling organizations "to go beyond traditional time and motion studies to reengineer business processes and refocus organizations" (Tapscott and Caston, 1993a, p. 41). Davenport and Short (1990) note that:

> information technology should be viewed as more than an automating or mechanizing force; it can fundamentally reshape

the way business is done."(p. 12)

And, as previously noted, Hammer (1990), suggested that businesses use information technology to reengineer. Thus, it is clear that information technology and BPR are intricately linked in the redesign of work processes. It is also clear that BPR represents a transition from Stage One—automating work—to Stage Two — redesigning work.

Many of today's business processes were developed and institutionalized long before computers became the powerful tools they now are. The true challenge in Stage Two is to redesign work processes around existing and future information technologies to maximize their possibilities. Thus, IT is viewed as an enabler in business process reengineering rather than a solution in itself. For Hammer and Champy (1993), IT is an "essential enabler" of any reengineering effort. They caution, however, that "throwing computers" at existing business problems does not lead to a reengineered business.

There are numerous examples of information technology being used to enable BPR. In a current reengineering project, a firm chose to reengineer its business communications processes, including the mailroom. A survey of mailroom operations revealed that a large percentage of incoming mail being handled is actually comprised of inter–office memos. By implementing an electronic mail system to handle such communications, the firm will eliminate this particular mailroom process. Remaining mail will be scanned using an electronic imaging system and distributed to the addressee electronically, largely eliminating handling (Kelly and Daniel 1994).

Electronic data interchange has often been cited as a technology that redesigns work. Some organizations that conduct a large part of their business electronically have completely eliminated, or greatly reduced entire departments and functions. When the management at General Motors designed the operations for the new Saturn plant, they worked the concept of EDI directly into the design and eliminated the need for complex purchasing systems (Hammer and Champy 1993).

While electronic mail, imaging, and EDI are good examples of technologies that enable firms to reengineer by helping them redesign work, none of these technologies is able to radically change the manner in which work is managed. We maintain that the technology that does this is client/server computing. While client/server technology may be used simply to automate work or reduce costs (Stage One enabler), it may also be used to redesign business processes (Stage Two enabler). Furthermore, because this technology parallels the organizational goals of empowerment and cooperation by distributing information and processing power closer to the user (Tapscott and Caston 1993a), it may also be a Stage Three enabler.

Client/Server Computing

Client/server computing has been defined in a number of ways (Huff 1992, Tapscott and Caston 1993a). The typical client/server model is two–fold. Simply stated, the client makes requests; the server usually fulfills those requests. The model has three components: data management, application and presentation. These components can be distributed to the clients and servers in a variety of ways, however, the presentation software usually resides entirely on the client workstation. Application software may reside on either the client or the servers, or it may be split among them. The data management software usually resides only on the servers although

BENEFITS	DRAWBACKS
Lower processing costs (micro v. mainframe computer)	Higher start-up training costs; many IS professionals unskilled in client/server development tools
Graphical User Interfaces (GUI) are easier to use	Difficult to manage operating systems
Avoids reliance on a single vendor or mainframe system	Unreliable networks
Greater flexibility in configurations	"Plug and play" open systems not yet a reality
Decision-making authority at user level and therefore closer to customers	More difficult data security, backup and recovery, and data management
Empowered users have information to make decisions	More systems and links to manage and maintain
Faster development cycles because applications can be modularized more easily	Lack of sophisticated development tools

Table 2: Benefits and Costs of Client/Server Computing

client workstations may have some software for data management.

The client hardware is normally a workstation, equipped with a graphical user interface (GUI). In some cases, the client workstation may be equipped with enough software to handle certain requests without server involvement. This software usually includes a standard office automation package (word processor, spreadsheet, and graphics) and may also include a statistical analysis package. Application software and processing power are often distributed among many networked systems; thus, in theory, each computer system can be configured to perform its job most efficiently.

Anecdotal evidence suggests vast benefits possible from client/ server computing, as well as a number of significant drawbacks (Table 2). There has been much debate as to whether client/server reduces costs when compared to a mainframe–based system. The client workstation's GUI normally provides some cost savings from ease of use, reduced user training time, and productivity gains. Typically, client/server user interfaces, such as Windows, Presentation Manager, and Macintosh, overcome many problems associated with the less friendly, character–based interfaces of older operating systems. Yet, many firms report increased costs associated with managing the more complex networks and in training the information systems personnel.

For many firms that have moved to client/server technology, the primary benefits have come not from reduced costs, but in other areas. A move to client/server may mean escape from an undue reliance on the products of a single vendor. While true open systems have not yet arrived, client/server technology is moving in that direction more rapidly than its mainframe counterparts.

Another advantage of client/server is that it facilitates organizations getting closer to their customers. As more customers request information suited specifically to them, organizations must find a way to meet those demands. Decision making authority must be placed closer to the customer, and client/server computing is the way to do this (Dodge 1993).

Client/server technology is not without its drawbacks. Early movers experienced unreliable networks, difficult to manage operating systems, and a lack of the much–touted development tools. Tasks such as data security, backup and recovery, and database management are often more difficult in a client server environment, simply because there usually are more machines and links that can fail (Gillin 1993).

Client/server technology represents more of a "philosophy of operation" than a strictly defined architecture. The nature of client/ server is such that it can be configured differently for different firms, thus offering the flexibility needed in a rapidly changing business environment (Datamation 1994).

Case Studies

Data from three firms that are moving to or have moved to a client/server computing environment are presented. Two of the firms are banks; examining their move to client/server computing is especially interesting because the banking industry was largely responsible for the move to large mainframe systems twenty years ago (Radding 1992). The third is a large collection agency. Specifics about each firm are disguised so that confidentiality is maintained.

In two of the cases, the reasons for considering a move to client/server and the degree of senior level management involvement are similar. This suggests that the firms may be in the same stage of the information era. In the first case, client/server was initially thought of as a way to automate current practices and possibly eliminate the mainframe. In Cases Two and Three, client/server technology is redesigning work management and enabling the transformation of the organization.

Case One: Large Bank (LB)

Through recent acquisitions and mergers, LB has grown considerably during the last ten years. It now ranks among the ten largest banks in the United States. The computing environment is strictly mainframe, and the systems are totally outsourced. Billing for mainframe usage is based on a sliding scale per processing cycle used. At the branch offices, not every teller has a personal computer; deposit and withdrawal information is not on–line. Currently, there is a project underway to bring more technology to the branches, eliminating much of the batch processing. An IS staff is maintained at LB's corporate office to manage financial production and reporting. There are three primary components of the reporting system: the database management side, the development/ad hoc reporting section, and the consolidation reporting department. It was the ad hoc reporting group that first looked at a move to client/server technology.

Production reporting at LB currently takes place in a COBOL environment. The production system produces all standard reports used by the financial group. A 4GL is used to run the ad hoc reporting. The product is perceived as a resources hog, and the ad hoc group is often criticized for its consumption of mainframe processing cycles. Another difficulty with the current system is that it runs under an operating system that has not been supported for nearly ten years. LB cannot add any more users to the system; therefore, they must make some change to it.

The ad hoc group's original goal was to find a mainframe

replacement that would give identical functionality, use the same programs with minimal changes, provide all existing services at a substantially reduced cost and better performance level, and offer more control than the outsourced system. According to the manager for the ad hoc group, the current production system is "very bureaucratic; changes require an Act of Congress." Like many IS departments, the ad hoc group has a workaround for this situation. Ad hoc reports are not put into production, but are instead kept in the ad hoc group's own libraries.

Once the need for a new system was identified, the group asked three large vendors to present proposals. At this point, a client/server solution was not specifically requested. Somewhere during the proposal stage, however, the idea of client/server came to the forefront. As a manager recalls, "One of the vendors had a client/server product he wanted to sell."

When the first vendor was ready with a proposal, they presented it to the ad hoc group. Phase One of the project (for which the vendor assumed all costs) was scheduled to last five days. The first two days would be used to download data to the servers; a rehearsed script of tests were to be conducted on the last three days.

Loading the data onto the servers took two weeks. Problems occurred for several reasons: programs written to convert packed fields did not work correctly, some key players were not available during the scheduled cutover week, and the software did not perform as expected. The test results were not spectacular, as processing on the servers was not faster than on the mainframe. Nonetheless, the group believed that the move to Client/server was justified because mainframe savings were projected to be two million dollars per year.

The outsourcing contract, however, was not favorable to the change. Due to the sliding billing scale, the loss of the ad hoc group's mainframe cycles each month actually resulted in an overall cost increase for LB. The group then tried to justify the new system not as a savings but as a wise idea because it meant a move to newer technology. This attempt failed because the system would have solved only the ad hoc group's problems, and there was trouble in the production group as well. The COBOL–based system locked all files during any processing, and the production group often could not gain access to the data. Consequently, every general ledger account was stored in three files — in the general ledger itself, in the production system, and in the ad hoc system. Maintaining common, current versions on three systems was a nightmare.

Ultimately, upper management decided to invest the time and money needed to develop a new system that would solve the problems in both groups, and a development project is currently underway at LB. As to whether the new system will use client/server technology, the manager said, "People don't really care if it's client/

server or not. All they want is to have all the functions they need. No one cares about the technical architecture." Yet, the new system will most likely be a client/server system for several reasons. LB's information systems management staff believe that a client/server system would keep up with technology and provide a "cohesive, integrated platform." They also believe that a major advantage of a client/server system is its flexibility. Users will have more flexible tools to build applications that will do what needs to be done. These tools will be easier to use and information will be easier to obtain. Rekeying will be eliminated, and downloading will be simplified. Both functions are currently critical to the financial area. As the manager stated, "We ... produce all this data and about 80% of it is either downloaded or rekeyed into a spreadsheet so they (the users) can add a font, a shading and a bold, and that's all they care about." Although the official position is that the new system will provide a cost savings, no one really believes that is likely.

Vendors have been asked back to demonstrate products in three areas: data base management, consolidation reporting systems, and development and ad hoc reporting tools. Later this year, a single data base system, a specific hardware platform, and a variety of tools will be selected for testing. Managers and staff have six months to "play with the tools and see how they work and if they like using them." Although the senior management at LB is committed to this, managers in the three groups are currently managing their on–going projects while researching the new systems.

Changes in the information flow and decision making process are not expected at LB from the client/server system. Although the manager acknowledges that the new system will offer more on–line tools and reporting, no one really expects senior management to use them. The present culture of LB is such that upper management doesn't log on to computers; their staff runs reports for them.

Case Summary

It is clear that Large Bank's primary intention in developing the new system was to save money. While giving users more flexibility and information was important, the driving force behind the change was financial. Although the most recent look at client/server systems is motivated by more than money—replacing a legacy system and embracing new technology—the project retains a pre-dominantly Stage One focus.

There is some indication, however, that LB's senior management does recognize the need to change the manner is which work is accomplished, and is teetering at the brink of Stage Two. That is, they are positioning themselves to reengineer their business processes. While some work has begun in this area, it is largely unrelated to the client/server project, and the new technology is expected to have only a minimal effect on the BPR effort. In fact, the manager expressed little hope that even the BPR efforts would change the management structure and the way things are done at LB.

Case Two: Large Collection Agency (LCA)

The system in this case was originally developed in 1977, and evolved over time to suit the needs of the business. To understand the system, it is necessary to examine the organization at the time the legacy system was first developed and implemented. In the mid–70s, LCA maintained several hundred geographically dispersed collection offices, each of which followed its own collection procedures, most of which were manual. In general, the collection process began with a customer's request to collect an invoice. A manual file folder was created, and all transactions were recorded on the jacket. All collections took place in the office that received the request, irrespective of where the delinquent customer was located. This often resulted in large telephone costs and delays in mailings.

Each local manager decided the collection cycle. Some placed several direct phone calls before mailing any letters; others mailed letters first, then placed personal calls. In some cases, attorney involvement was threatened quickly; in others this was looked upon as a last resort. Thus, a customer with delinquent accounts in two different areas of the country could be treated differently by each collection office.

In the late 70s, LCA went through a major restructuring and merged many of its offices. The corporate office, in an effort to establish and enforce policy, —in the chief technology consultant's words "to homogenize service," developed the initial information system. As time passed, subsystems were added to the legacy system, until in 1985 the composite system consisted of seven different applications.

In 1985, the economy was such that revenues in the organization needed a boost. Previously, LCA had grown largely from efficiency (i.e., replacing manual work with computers), but it is difficult to repeat those gains from year to year. Instead of looking further at the bottom line for more efficiency gains, the focus shifted to the top line. As the technology consultant stated, "The bottom line gives only once; the top line gives many times." LCA developed a number of information–based products for the customers and acquired new firms that they promptly gathered under the same system, thus presenting a unique identity in the marketplace.

With the major downturn in the economy, however, the business went into a tailspin, prompting another major restructuring. In the consultant's words, "When business is slow, there are no sales;

consequently, there are no invoices, and ultimately, no overdue invoices for us to collect." The economy was not the only negative impact on the firm. Other smaller collection agencies, and the customers themselves, began using computers to improve their collection efforts. Thus, both the quality of the claim (i.e., the chances of collecting it) and the number of claims were lower.

The regional office personnel were instructed to get closer to the customer and provide them with what they needed, but that was extremely difficult with the information system in use. The earlier monolithic systems were fine at producing standard requests but when customers needed specialized information, the systems could not provide it. Changes to the system usually took one year; the competition, being smaller, could change much more rapidly. Management decided that what was really needed was a way to empower associates to respond to the customer's needs. A different tool set is needed when the objective is to push customer service to the point of customer contact. This according to the consultant, was "a real disconnect with a centralized system that enforces policy." Managers could not make more decisions without the tools to provide needed information.

Thus, LCA had come full circle in the way they view their information systems. At the start, field offices handled collections however they wanted. When LCA was first computerized, people in the field could only do what the system let them do. Now, the objective was to allow people in the field to do what they needed to do, and to decide for themselves what that was. The firm also needed a system that would support a rapidly changing business environment; thus, continuing in the tradition mainframe arena was ruled out because of the mainframe's lack of flexibility.

To determine what the new system would be, LCA first rightsized their operations over last three years. This process involved senior managers from all departments. Through close examination of the business processes (in effect, a reengineering of the processes), LCA realized they needed a decentralized management structure, but their highly centralized information system could not support such a structure. Tools that could be used to distribute information from the mainframe were either not available, or not practical. Client/server technology was selected based on the belief that it would enable the reengineered management recently put into place to work better. In effect, the firm wanted to distribute management, but then needed an information system to handle the redistributed authority. The conversion to client/server, currently underway, has a budget of nearly two million dollars and a time frame of one year.

Case Summary

The discussion above indicates that Large Collection Agency (LCA) has moved into Stage Three of the information era. They have reengineered their business processes; they have reengineered and restructured their management. Work has been organized in new ways and the lines of communication have been restructured. Now, they seek an information system to support and enable this new organizational form.

Case Three: Small Bank (SB)

When SB opened seven years ago, management made the decision to use service bureaus for all their data processing needs rather than purchasing their own mainframe systems. As a start-up company, this decision made sense because it represented a lower short–term investment in information processing power. SB continues to use these service bureaus today. Currently, one service bureau handles their credit card business, another handles their traditional banking business (commercial loans, savings accounts, equity loans, etc.), a third firm supplies processing for their non-banking trust accounts. The bank has only a single branch office; most business is conducted via phone, facsimile, or direct mail.

Initially, users had dumb terminals through which they could connect to the service bureau of their choice and obtain needed information.   For the most part, the service bureaus provided consistent service with very scaleable costs, but they were inflexible. Customized reporting, especially for a smaller customer such as SB, was too expensive. Yet, as SB began to grow, the need for such customization became obvious.

SB needed more management information, in a more usable format, than what was available from the service bureaus.   To accommodate management needs, analysts would receive a multi-tude of reports from the bureaus, take a few lines of data from each, and rekey the data into spreadsheet applications to produce the necessary information. This method was time consuming, tedious, and expensive, and it greatly under utilized the analysts' talent. The goal, therefore, was to provide flexible reporting without high costs in a way that would enhance, rather than ignore SB's analytical resources. The general ledger was the area first targeted.

The bank selected a client/server technology for several rea-sons. As a start up company, they didn't want to make a huge investment in mainframe computers. They also wanted to empower their employees, giving them all the information they needed to make decisions. The decision was made to start out with small machines that could grow as the firm (and its profits) did. The decision to move horizontally to multiple servers instead of one large server reflects these considerations since failure of a single system does not mean that every user is off–line.

The solution was to install a database server to which general ledger data were downloaded each morning from the mainframe. As the data were written to the server, they were processed to obtain information not available directly from the mainframe, such as account average balances. Users (clients) were given access to the data on the local server via intelligent workstations equipped with sufficient software so that they could manipulate and massage the data as they needed. The users build queries to see what they need to see. Queries are ad hoc; users can ask any questions using a point and click scheme for ease of use.

There are presently six file servers in use at SB. Once general ledger data were made available, users quickly asked for trust account, commercial loan, savings account, credit card, and home equity data. The Information Systems personnel at SB believe that several more servers will be added in the next few years. One manager stated that either the users or the IS department always finds a need for another server. The most recent addition is a server dedicated to tracking telecommunications costs. The data switch talks directly to the server for every connection made.

The information systems department at SB consists of twenty–two people, and services three separate floors of users on three distinct LANs. Many of the staff are systems and financial analysts who are working together to develop new client/server applications in the financial reporting area.

The advent of client/server computing has changed the manner in which many of SB's employees perform their jobs; it has reengineered the work processes. In the past, month–end closing would take up to eight working days; it can now be done in two. If, for some reason, the database servers aren't working, there is no need for some employees to report to work. The IS manager's comments on this are interesting:

"Organizations tend to structure themselves to fit the main-frame. The mainframe spits out report A or B, someone gets them, then rekeys lines 10 and 30, and then an army of analysts replays the information into something the mainframe didn't provide. In the old world, that's what things looked like... The value of the client/server structure became so valuable that they (the users) ended up, without prompting from us, reengineering their work around its capabilities."

A systems analyst also had some telling comments:

"We don't give our users a hole; we give them a shovel. We no longer build systems for them; we build tools for them to use. We have become toolmakers. The organization has moved decision making further and further down, in data processing we have moved it to the end user."

Another process that has been completely reengineered is closing an account. What once took several days of processing through numerous approval channels now takes about twenty seconds. This has happened through a combination of three factors. First, the process itself has been reengineered; unnecessary steps are gone. Next, client/server enabled the new process to take place. Finally, customer service representatives (CSRs) were empowered to make account–level decisions.

IS management at the bank believes that client/server technology is no more expensive for them than buying and maintaining mainframe systems would have been; in fact, they feel it may be less expensive. The focus of client/server for SB, however, is not on costs. It is on user satisfaction with the performance and information availability. As the Data Base Administrator said:

> "When it comes right down to it are the costs (for client/server) going to be significantly cheaper, I don't know. Is it going to be cheaper, I believe so. But better than any of that, it's (client/server) going to be better. If you get better for the same price, you've still got a better deal. You have a better front–end for the users, you've got a better implementation of everything. But we're not doing client/server because it's cheaper or because the users like the GUIs. We're doing it because it solves business problems."

No one in the IS department at SB sees the mainframe going away completely. All agree that for number crunching and transaction processing, the mainframes and service bureaus will remain. Yet, they continue to develop new client/server applications to replace mainframe functions they find unacceptable. Thus, while SB never faced the legacy system problems that the large bank and large collection agency face, they do have systems that no longer work well for them.

The focus at SB has always been on empowering their users. When perspective programmer/analysts are interviewed, they are asked by the COO how they feel about empowering users — writing tools and not systems for them. Thus, the idea of empowering users filters down from the top. Indeed, senior management is intimately involved with the IS projects at the bank, and IT plays a central role in the strategic plan.

SB's president has always focused on two issues: the quality of the customer service representatives and the quality of the information systems that support the bank. Since customers don't walk into the bank to make transactions, the person on the phone becomes all–

important to them. The voice, attitude, and demeanor of the CSR are critical, but also important is the information the CSR can offer the customer. Thus, the corporate culture doesn't see IT as an expense but rather as a "keeper of the business."

Client/server technology has changed several things within SB. First, the flow of information has been streamlined. Formerly, several different processes updated the mainframe sequentially and long delays resulted from an overnight wait for each update. The general ledger system processing has been reduced from more than 3 days to less than 1 day.

The sources of information for many bank employees have also changed. Managers just below the senior vice–president level once called on analysts to run reports; now, they can get the information themselves very easily. Information is also more readily available to clerical employees. Thus, the client/server systems have distributed information up and down the organization.

Decision making has moved down the organization so that now CSRs and clerical employees are given the information and authority to make decisions. There are fewer layers of management for each decision to travel through; thus, the organizational structure has flattened.

Case Summary
Work is organized in new ways, communication paths are simplified and redefined, and authority relationships have changed. These are all indicative that an organizational transformation has occurred. Thus, SB seems to be in Stage Three of the information era.

The New Organizational Structure

References to the new organization, the organization of the future and new organizational forms and structures abound throughout this paper, and in much of the current literature. What do all these catchphrases mean?

One vision of the organization of the future is a move away from the hierarchical structure to a flatter one comprised of small business units focused by product or market segment. In these firms, reengineered for quick response to a changing environment, information flows freely and processes are streamlined (Ligus 1993). Autonomous business teams are critical in these new information–based organizations (Tapscott and Caston 1993b). Employees are empowered and encouraged to participate in the decision making process (Davenport 1993).

The organization of the future will be knowledge based, and have fewer levels of management (Drucker 1988). It will be a learning organization —one that is constantly enhancing its capacity to create

(Senge 1990). By building a shared vision of an organization's future, the organization will become learning rather than controlling and the behavior of people within the organization will be fundamentally different. The new organization will also be better able to respond to opportunities – whether they be in new technologies, new revenue sources, or new market segments (Berquist, 1993). Another term often used to characterize the new organization is "boundarylessness" (Tichy 1993). As used by Jack Welch, the CEO of General Electric, the term connotes an organization that de–emphasizes hierarchical and functional boundaries and focuses instead on partnerships, alliances and teams. Critical to this new organization is the free flow of information among its employees.

There are several influences compelling organizations to become "more flexible, far–sighted, and able to learn continuously" (Watkins and Marsick, 1993, p. 5) These include global turmoil and competition, the rise of self–directed teams, participatory management, and time compression. Managers, however, may find it difficult to respond to these influences because the infrastructure of their firms does not support such response (Rummler and Brache 1990).

Thus, the organization of the future will be characterized by empowered associates who have the responsibility, knowledge, and authority to make decisions. Information Technology (IT) will play a key role in enabling this organizational form.

Conclusion

We have put forth a three–stage model to explain the changes in the automation and the management of work that occurred during the industrial era and are occurring during the information era. Our model suggests that BPR is primarily a second stage phenomenon that initiates new organizational forms based on collaborative teams and empowered employees. Indeed, there is evidence that some firms are already abandoning the constraints of the M–form for less rigid structures. Thus, while in 1985, Williamson could maintain that the M–form organization was "the most significant organizational innovation of the twentieth century;" six years later Bettis was calling it an "organizational fossil" (Hosskisson, Hill, and Kim, 1993). In a world of increasing complexity, rapid change, virtual corporations, and global competition, Bettis may indeed be correct.

We propose that client/server technology is a major enabling technology for every stage of the information era. It has this capability because it can be used to automate existing processes, simplifying an interface or providing information more easily. It may also enable informating the organization as it reengineers its business processes because it provides users with a friendly interface, tools for extracting and manipulating data, and access to a range of servers.

As a Stage Three enabler, client/server technology deregulates information access. The monopoly era of the mainframe as the sole provider of information is replaced by a free market of multi-servers and user self-service. Users are empowered because they have choice, tools, and personal processing resources. Users can choose what data they want from what is available.

As marketing discovered decades ago, customers like to serve themselves. Users want to have the tools to manipulate data and change its format to meet their personal preferences and decision style. Customers want customized products, even if they have to do the tailoring themselves. Users have desktop computers with sufficient processing power to quickly and easily process data without being reliant on the IS custodians of processor cycles. Customers want independence and control over their destinies. A marketing perspective on client/server illustrates that it results in satisfied users who can better serve their customers.

The three case studies illustrate how some firms are using client/server technology as a means of empowerment. The small bank and the large collection agency both perceive client/server technology as a medium for transferring power from the IS department to the users. Furthermore, it is clear that this movement is a deliberate response to a competitive business environment that requires a more agile and maneuverable organization. Clearly, these organizations are in the third stage of the information revolution.

In contrast, the large bank seems to be teetering between phases one and two. Client/server is initially seen as a way of rearranging processing to reduce costs; it is just a cheaper way of automating work. This is not surprising because the impetus for change is not external market forces but internal cost saving measures. Competition is not promoting the change; rather, some cost accountant is tallying the score. There is some indication, however, that the bank also sees client/server as a way of redesigning work since it is now looking into a large–scale cutover to a client/server environment.

The cases support our argument that client/server technology enables organizations to empower employees to create a new organizational form. While two cases directly support this contention, one supports it indirectly. The large bank has no compelling reason to undertake the massive organizational upheaval and realignment of power that is necessary for a new organizational form. It is far easier to stay in the automation phase than endure the rigors of transition to another phase.

There is little doubt that organizations must change to survive into the 21st century. Hammer and Champy argue that simple gains from automation are no longer enough and that radical advances must be made. Evidence suggests that even these radical gains from reengineering business processes are not enough. What is needed for survival is a totally transformed organization, one that is able to learn and grow continually. We believe that client/server technology can enable this new organizational form.

References

Berquist, W. (1993). *The postmodern organization: Mastering the art of irreversible change.* San Francisco: Jossey-Bass.

Chandler ndler, A. Jr., (1962). *Strategy and structure: Chapters in the history of the American industrial enterprise.* Cambridge MA: MIT Press.

Daft, R. (1991). *Management* (2nd ed.). Fort Worth: Dryden.

Davenport, T., (1993). *Process innovation: Reengineering work through information technology.* Boston: Harvard Business School Press.

Davenport, T. and Short J. (1990, Summer). The new industrial engineering: Information technology and business process redesign. *Sloan Management Review*, 31(4), 11–27.

Dodge, M. (1993, November 15). Client server may be ragged, but it's not on the ropes. *Computerworld*, p. 37.

Drucker, P. (1988, January–February). The coming of the new organization. *Harvard Business Review*, 66(1), 45–53.

From Client to Server and Back Again. (1994, April). Datamation, p. S–19.

Gillin, P. (1993, September 27). Valley of dearth. *Computerworld*, p. 36.

Ginzberg, E. (1982, September). The mechanization of work. Scientific American, 247(3), 67–75.

Goss, T., Pascale, R., and Athos, A. (1993, November–December). Risking the present for a powerful future. *Harvard Business Review*, 71(6), 97–108.

Hammer, M. (1990, July–August). Reengineering work: Don't automate, obliterate. *Harvard Business Review*, 68(4), 104–112.

Hammer, M. and Champy, J. (1993). *Reengineering the corporation: A manifesto for business revolution.* New York: HarperCollins.

Hosskisson, R., Hill, C., and Kim, H. (1993). The multidivisional structure: Organizational fossil or source of value? *Journal of Management*, 19(2), 269–298.

Huff, S. (1992, Summer). Client–server computing. *Business Quarterly*, pp. 30–35.

Hunt, V. (1993). *Reengineering.* Essex Junction, VT: Oliver Wright Publications.

Kelly, G. and Daniel, L. (1994). Applying electronic meeting systems to the strategic planning process. University of Georgia Working Paper.

Ligus, R. (1993, January). Methods to help reengineer your company for improved agility. *Industrial Engineering*, 25(1), 58–59.

Morris, D., and Brandon, J., (1993). *Reengineering Your Business.* New York: McGraw–Hill.

Pine, B. (1993). *Mass Customization.* Boston: Harvard Business School Press.

Radding, A. (1992, December). Banking's new technology revolution: From mainframes to PC power. *Bank Management,* pp. 35–40.

Rummler, G., and Brache, A. (1990). *How to manage the white space on the organization chart.* San Francisco: Jossey–Bass.

Schein, E. (1994) Innovative cultures and organizations. In T.J. Allen and M.S. Scott Morton, (Eds.), *Information Technology and the Corporation of the 1990s,* New York: Oxford University Press, 125–146.

Schrage, M. (1993, September 27). No frills, fewer tangles. *Computerworld,* p. 37.

Senge, P. (1990). The Fifth Discipline. New York: Doubleday.

Stoner, J., and Freeman, R. (1989). *Management* (4th ed.). Englewood Cliffs, NJ: Prentice Hall.

Tapscott, D., and Caston, A. (1993a). *Paradigm Shift.* New York:McGraw–Hill.

Tapscott, D., and Caston, A. (1993b, Summer). The new promise of information technology. *Business Quarterly,* pp. 51–60.

Taylor, J., and Felton, D. (1993). *Performance by Design.* Englewood Cliffs, NJ:Prentice Hall.

Tichy, N. (1993, December). Revolutionize your company. *Fortune,* pp. 114–118.

Watkins, K. and Marsick, V. (1993). *Sculpting the learning organization.* San Francisco: Jossey–Bass.

Zuboff, S. (1988). *In the age of the smart machine.* New York: Basic Books.

The Search for Processes to Reengineer:
Avoiding the Pitfalls of Strategic Information Systems Planning

Albert L. Lederer
University of Kentucky

Vijay Sethi
University of Oklahoma

Improved strategic information systems planning has been a key issue facing both corporate general managers and information systems executives (Brancheau and Wetherbe, 1987). Because it has been used to identify the best applications to computerize, it has been recognized for its ability to contribute substantially to an organization (Henderson and Sifonis, 1988). Besides identifying applications, it can help an organization use its information systems to carry out its existing strategies (Hartog and Herbert, 1986) and it can help it define new strategies (Porter, 1985).

Strategic information systems planning is also used to identify business processes. Thus, it is suggested as a tool for reengineering especially during the process enumeration stage, one of the key activities in business reengineering (Davenport, 1993). This was validated by our recent empirical study of 105 companies who have performed strategic information systems planning in which we found that 63% of the respondents used strategic information systems planning specifically to identify such processes for reengineering. On average, those who had used it for that purpose had recommended nearly ten business processes for that purpose.

The linkage between strategic information systems planning

and reengineering may, in fact, be intricate. According to Errico, Goll, Mabey, Marsteller, and Sullivan (1993), "there is a lot of commonality" between reengineering and strategic information systems planning. In addition to the common emphasis on process, both are concerned with data sharing. While data sharing is one of the main objectives of strategic information systems planning, it plays a central role in reengineering because cross–functional activities can only work together if they have access to the same data. Another similarity arises because of both strategic information systems planning and reengineering have "information technology components in their solution" (p. 30). In fact, a recent study notes that the percepts of reengineering are becoming more and more absorbed into strategic planning and systems development methodologies (Davenport and Stoddard, 1994).

To perform effective strategic information systems planning, organizations usually follow a well–defined and documented methodology during an extended process requiring top management, user management, and information systems management participation (Martin and Leben, 1989; Arthur Andersen and Co., 1986; Moskowitz, 1986). However, research has shown that doing so is a top challenge to many information systems executives (Lederer and Mendelow, 1986; Sinclair, 1986). For example, many recommendations of a strategic information systems planning study are often disregarded while many other ideas, ignored by the study, are implemented (Earl, 1990; Lederer and Sethi, 1988). Hence, the failure to execute the plan is a serious problem. Given the importance of strategic information systems planning to both general and information systems management (Brancheau and Wetherbe, 1987), researchers should try to understand this perplexing situation and identify actions to avoid it.

The purpose of the research reported here was to understand strategic information systems planning better by identifying the problems that prevent its success. A second purpose was to identify possible actions for strategic information systems planning planners to enable them to perform it more effectively. These actions assume an even greater significance given that strategic information systems planning is linked with reengineering, a concept which is generating an ever increasing interest in both IS and senior management both in the U.S. and abroad (Alter, 1994; Maglitta, 1994). In fact, the chapter specifically discusses how the lessons learned from strategic planning apply to reengineering.

The chapter first defines strategic information systems planning. It then identifies the problems that arise during it. It then discusses a survey of practicing strategic information systems planning planners who had encountered the problems and shows the severity of each. The chapter concludes with some potential prescriptions for managers who are involved in strategic information systems planning or reengineering.

What is Strategic Information Systems Planning?

Information systems planning has evolved over the last 15 years. In the late 1970s, its primary objectives were to improve communication between computer users and MIS departments, increase top management support for computing, better forecast and allocate information system resource requirements, determine opportunities for improving the MIS department, and identify new and higher payback computer applications (McLean and Soden, 1977).

More recently, new objectives have emerged. One is the identification of strategic information systems applications - those that can give the organization a competitive edge (Vitale, Ives, and Beath, 1986). However, because applications have too often focused on limited functional areas, it is becoming increasingly important to think in terms of corporate–wide process to reengineer rather than individual applications. Another objective is the development of an organization-wide information architecture (Moskowitz, 1986).

While the importance of identifying strategic information systems and corporate–wide processes is obvious, the importance of the organization-wide information architecture may not be. However, such an architecture of information systems that share common data and communicate easily with each other is highly desirable. Just as new business ventures must mesh with the organization's existing endeavors, new systems must fit with the existing information architecture.

Thus, this chapter embraces two distinct yet usually simultaneously performed approaches to using strategic information systems planning to identify processes to re–engineer. On one hand, strategic information systems planning entails the search for high-impact opportunities with the ability to create an advantage over competitors (Clemons, 1986; Ives and Learmonth, 1984; McFarlan, 1984; Parsons, 1983; and Wiseman, 1985). On the other hand, strategic information systems planning is the process of identifying a portfolio of computer-based systems to assist an organization in executing its current business plans and thus realizing its existing business goals. The distinction between the two approaches results in the former being referred to as attempting to *impact* organizational strategies and the latter as attempting to *align* MIS objectives with organizational goals.

Carrying Out Strategic Information Systems Planning

To carry out strategic information systems planning, an organization usually selects an existing methodology and then embarks on a major, intensive study. The organization forms teams of business planners and computer users with MIS specialists as members or as advisors. It likely uses the strategic information systems planning vendor's educational support to train the teams and consulting support to guide and audit the study. It carries out a multi-step procedure over several weeks or months. The duration depends on the scope of the study. In addition to identifying the portfolio of applications, it prioritizes them. It defines databases, data elements, and a network of computers and communications equipment to support the applications. It also prepares a schedule for developing and installing them.

One of the central elements in carrying out strategic information systems planning is the identification of business processes. This is done by first identifying business functions which are defined as "a group of activities that together support one aspect of furthering the mission of the enterprise" (Martin and Leben, 1989; p. 144). A function is ongoing and continuous, it is not based on organizational structure, and categorizes what is done and not how. Functions are then examined for their component processes. Some characteristics of a process are they can be described in terms of inputs and outputs, they are not based on organizational structure, and they too identify what is done and not how.

These functions and processes then form the basis for the identification of databases and information systems applications (as described below). They can also form the basis for reengineering. In addition, the hierarchical decomposition approach of subdividing functions into processes is particularly relevant for reengineering which first identifies broad processes and then breaks them into subprocesses (Davenport, 1993).

Organizations usually apply one of several methodologies to carry out this process. Four popular ones are Business Systems Planning (IBM Corporation, 1975), *PROplanner* (Holland, 1989)), Information Engineering (Martin and Leben, 1989), and Method/1 (Andersen, 1987). These will be described briefly as contemporary, illustrative methodologies although all four undergo continuous change and improvement. They were selected because, together, they accounted for over half the responses to the survey described later.

Business Systems Planning (BSP), developed by IBM, involves *top-down* planning with *bottom-up* implementation. From the top-down, the study team first recognizes its firm's business mission, objectives and functions, and how these determine the business processes. It analyzes the processes for their data needs. From the bottom-up, it then identifies the data currently required to perform the processes. The final BSP plan describes an overall information systems architecture comprised of databases and applications as well as the installation schedule of individual systems. Table 1 details the steps in a BSP study.

BSP places heavy emphasis on top management commitment and involvement. Top executive sponsorship is seen as critical. MIS analysts might serve primarily in an advisory capacity.

PROplanner, from by Holland Systems Corp. in Ann Arbor, Michigan, helps planners analyze major functional areas within the organization. They then define a Business Function Model. They derive a Data Architecture from the Business Function Model by combining the organization's information requirements into generic data entities and broad databases. They then identify an Information Systems Architecture of specific new applications and an implementation schedule.

PROplanner offers automated storage, manipulation, and presentation of the data collected during strategic information systems planning. *PROplanner* software produces reports in various formats and levels of detail. *Affinity* reports show the frequencies of accesses to data. *Clustering* reports guide database design. Menus direct the planner through on-line data collection during the process. A data dictionary (a computerized list of all data in the database) permits planners to share PROplanner data with an existing data dictionary or other automated design tools.

Information Engineering (IE), by KnowledgeWare in Atlanta, provides techniques for building Enterprise Models, Data Models, and Process Models. These make up a comprehensive knowledge base that developers later use to create and maintains information systems.

In conjunction with IE, every general manager may participate in a critical success factors (CSF) inquiry, the popular technique for identifying issues that business executives view as the most vital for their organization's success. The resulting factors will then guide the strategic information systems planning endeavor by helping identify future management control systems.

IE provides several software packages for facilitating the strategic information systems planning effort. However, IE differs from some other methodologies by providing automated tools to link its output to subsequent systems development efforts. For example, integrated with IE is an application generator to produce computer programs written in the COBOL programming language without hand-coding.

Method/1, the methodology of Andersen Consulting (a division of Arthur Andersen & Co.), consists of ten phases or work segments

Enterprise Analysis The team documents the strategic business planning process and how the organization carries it out. It presents this information in a matrix for the executive sponsor to validate.

Enterprise Modelling The team identifies the organization's business processes, using a technique known as value chain analysis, and then presents them in a matrix showing each's relationship to each business strategy (from the Enterprise Analysis). The team identifies the organization's entities (such as product, customer, vendor, order, part) and presents them in a matrix showing how each is tied to each process.

Executive Interviews The team asks key executives about potential information opportunities needed to support their enterprise strategy (from the Enterprise Analysis), the processes (from they Enterprise Modelling) they are responsible for, and the entities (from the Enterprise Modelling) they manage. Each executive identifies a value and priority ranking for each information opportunity.

Information Opportunity Analysis The team groups the opportunities by processes and entities to separate "quick fix" opportunities. It then analyzes the remaining information opportunities, develops support recommendations, and prioritizes them.

I/S Strategies and Recommendations The team assesses the organization's information management in terms of its information systems/enterprise alignment, ongoing information planning, tactical information planning, data management, and application development. It then defines new strategies and recommends them to executive management.

Data Architecture Design The team prepares a high level design of proposed databases by diagramming how the organization uses its entities in support of its processes (entities and processes were defined during Enterprise Modelling) and identifying critical pieces of information describing the entities.

Process Architecture Design The team prepares a plan for developing high priority applications and for integrating all proposed applications. It does this by tying business processes to their proposed applications.

Existing Systems Review The team reviews existing applications to evaluate their technical and functional quality by interviewing users and information systems specialists.

Implementation Planning The team considers the quality of existing systems (from the Existing Systems Review) and the proposed applications (from the Process Architecture Design) and develops a plan identifying those to discard, keep, enhance, or re-develop.

Information Management Recommendations The team develops and presents a series of recommendations to help it carry out the plans that it prepared in Implementation Planning.

Table 1: Description of BSP Study Steps

that an organization completes to create its strategic plan. The first five formulate information strategy. The final five further formulate the information strategy but also develop action plans. A break between the first and final five provides a top management checkpoint and an opportunity to adjust and revise. By design however, a typical organization using Method/1 need not complete all the work segments at the same level of detail. Instead, planners evaluate each work segment in terms of the organization's objectives.

Method/1 focuses heavily on the assessment of the current business organization, its objectives, and its competitive environment. It also stresses the tactics required for changing the organization when it implements the plan.

Method/1 follows a layered approach. The top layer is the methodology itself. A middle layer of techniques supports the methodology and a bottom layer of tools supports the techniques. Examples of the many techniques are focus groups, Delphi studies, matrix analysis, dataflow diagramming, and functional decomposition. FOUNDATION, Andersen Consulting's computer-aided software engineering tool set, includes computer programs that support Method/1.

Besides BSP, *PROplanner*, IE and Method/1, firms might choose a variety of older methodologies including Information Quality Analysis (Vacca, 1984), Business Information Analysis and Integration Technique (Carlson, 1979), Business Information Characterization Study (Kerner, 1979), CSF, Ends/Means Analysis (Wetherbe and Davis, 1982), Nolan Norton Methodology (Moskowitz, 1986), Portfolio Management (McFarlan, 1981), Strategy Set Transformation (King, 1978), Value Chain Analysis, or the Customer Resource Life Cycle. More recently, many large consulting firms (e.g., CSC Index, Booz Allen, DeLoitte & Touche) have begun to offer strategic information systems planning methodologies. Also, firms often select features of these methodologies and then, possibly with outside assistance, tailor their own in-house approach (Sullivan, 1986).

The Problems of Strategic Information Systems Planning

Despite strategic information systems planning's methodical approach, it has long been recognized as an intricate and complex process with numerous problems that plague planners and can prevent its success (McFarlan, 1971). Several authors have described these problems based on field surveys, cases, observations, and personal reflection on their experiences. An extensive review of their work resulted in the first 46 of the 49 items in Table 2. The source of the last three items in the Table was a pilot study described below.

A Survey of Planners

After summarizing the problems into the items in Table 2, the authors created a survey instrument asking respondents to rate the extent to which they had encountered each problem on a scale of 1 to 5 where 1 represented "not a problem;" 2, an insignificant

1. The methodology fails to assess the current information systems applications portfolio (Schwartz, 1970).
2. Strategic information systems planning output fails to provide a statement of organizational objectives for the IS Department (McLean and Soden, 1977).
3. Strategic information systems planning output fails to identify specific new projects (McLean and Soden, 1977).
4. Strategic information systems planning output fails to include an overall financial plan for the IS Department (McLean and Soden, 1977).
5. Strategic information systems planning output fails to include an overall personnel and training plan for the IS Department (McLean and Soden, 1977).
6. Strategic information systems planning output fails to include an overall organizational hardware plan (McLean and Soden, 1977).
7. The output plans are not flexible enough to take into account unanticipated changes in the organization and its environment (McLean and Soden, 1977).
8. The planning horizon considered by the methodology is inappropriate (McLean and Soden, 1977).
9. The methodology fails to take into account organizational goals and strategies (King, 1978).
10. Strategic information systems planning output fails to determine a uniform basis for prioritizing projects (King, 1978).
11. Many support personnel are required for data gathering and analysis during the study (Rockart, 1979).
12. The methodology does not sufficiently involve top management (Kay, Szypenski, Horing and Bartz, 1980).
13. The methodology does not sufficiently involve users (Kay et al., 1980).
14. The strategic information systems planning output does not capture all the information that was developed during the study (Gill, 1981).
15. The output is not in accordance with the expectations of top management (Gill, 1981).
16. It is difficult to secure top management commitment for implementing the plan (Gill, 1981).
17. The success of the methodology is greatly dependent on the team leader (Zachman, 1982).
18. The experiences from implementing the methodology are not sufficiently transferable across divisions (Zachman, 1982).
19. Implementing the projects and the data architecture identified in the strategic information systems planning output requires substantial further analysis (Zachman, 1982).
20. The methodology fails to take into account issues related to plan implementation (Zachman, 1982).
21. The methodology is not based on any theoretical framework (Zachman, 1982).
22. The planning procedure is rigid (Zachman, 1982).
23. The documentation does not adequately describe the steps that should be followed for implementing the methodology (Zachman, 1982).
24. Adequate external consultant support is not available for implementing the methodology (Zachman, 1982).

Table 2: Strategic Information Systems Planning Problems

25. Strategic information systems planning output fails to determine an overall data architecture for the organization (Zachman, 1982).

26. Strategic information systems planning output fails to provide priorities for developing specific databases (Zachman, 1982).

27. The methodology lacks sufficient computer support (Zachman, 1982).

28. The size of the planning team is very large (Vacca, 1983).

29. It is difficult to find team members who meet the criteria specified by the methodology (Vacca, 1983).

30. It is difficult to find a team leader who meets the criteria specified by the methodology (Vacca, 1983).

31. It is difficult to convince top management to approve the methodology (Vacca, 1983).

32. The planning exercise takes very long (Bowman, Davis and Wetherbe, 1983).

33. The methodology requires too much top management involvement (Bowman, Davis and Wetherbe, 1983).

34. The methodology makes inappropriate assumptions about organization structure (Yadav, 1983).

35. The methodology makes inappropriate assumptions about organization size (Yadav, 1983).

36. The methodology fails to analyze the current strengths and weaknesses of the IS Department (King, 1988).

37. The methodology fails to assess the external technological environment (King, 1988).

38. The methodology fails to take into account legal and environmental issues (King, 1988).

39. The methodology fails to assess the organization's competitive environment (King, 1988).

40. Strategic information systems planning output fails to sufficiently address the role of a permanent IS planning group (King, 1988).

41. The final output document is not very useful (King, 1988).

42. Managers find it difficult to answer questions specified by the methodology (Boynton and Zmud, 1984).

43. The methodology requires too much user involvement (Boynton and Zmud, 1984).

44. Strategic information systems planning output fails to sufficiently address the need for Data Administration in the organization (Sullivan, 1985).

45. Strategic information systems planning output fails to include an overall organizational data communications plan (Sullivan, 1985).

46. The planning exercise is very expensive (Moskowitz, 1986).

47. The methodology fails to take into account changes in the organization during strategic information systems planning.

48. Strategic information systems planning output fails to designate specific new steering committees.

49. Strategic information systems planning output fails to outline changes in the reporting relationships in the IS Department

Table 2: (continued)

problem; 3, a minor problem; 4, a major problem; and 5, an extreme problem of the strategic information systems planning methodology.

To operationalize the construct, strategic information systems planning methodology, and ensure that the data are reliable and valid indicators of it, the authors followed the procedures suggested by construct measurement research (Churchill, 1979). Thus in accordance with Churchill's (1979) construct operationalization procedure, they developed a definition of the construct. A strategic information systems planning methodology is "the application of a formal process for identifying a portfolio of computer-based applications that will assist an organization in executing its business goals." Then, as recommended, a sample of items (i.e., the problems listed in Table 1) that belong to the construct was generated. The focus of problems was motivated by McLean and Soden's (1977) survey of strategic information systems planning pitfalls as well as by similar research in other areas such as Steiner and Schollhammer's (1975) study of pitfalls in multinational long-range planning.

In addition to these and demographic questions, the instrument asked four questions using a Likert scale from extremely satisfied to extremely dissatisfied. The first dealt with their overall satisfaction with the strategic information systems planning methodology and the others concerned their satisfaction with the strategic information systems planning resources, process, and output.

The choice of respondents and the scheme for data elicitation were based upon guidelines suggested by the key informant approach for obtaining retrospective reports from managers (Huber and Power, 1985). The decision to use single informants rather than multiple respondents was made because the latter strategy depresses the response rate and may also lead to data being withheld (Glick, Huber, Miller, Doty, and Sutcliffe, 1990). To choose respondents knowledgeable about the issue of interest, only those who had participated in a completed strategic information systems planning study were selected. "To motivate the informants to cooperate with the researcher (Huber and Power, 1985, p. 176)," respondents were offered a summary of the results. To explain "how the research results can be useful to the manager [and] the organization (p. 176)," the cover letter outlined in detail the benefits from the study.

To "use questions that are pretested (p. 177)," two experienced strategic information systems planners pilot tested the questionnaire. This resulted in three more problems, the final items in Table 2.

To "minimize the elapsed time between the events of interest and the collection of data (p. 177)," respondents were asked to answer the questions with respect to their most recently completed strategic information systems planning study. Respondents were specifically asked to indicate the methodology used in their last strategic information systems planning study from a comprehensive list of twelve commonly recognized methodologies and their variations. They then evaluated the problems of this particular methodology. (According to Goodhue, Quillard, and Rockart ,1988, the strategic information systems planning methodologies are very similar in their objectives, underlying assumptions, and limitations. Thus combining the responses is quite reasonable).

The questionnaire was mailed to the members of the Strategic Data Planning Institute (a nationwide users group, under the auspices of Barnett Data Systems in Rockville, Maryland, comprised of systems planners participating in seminars, conferences and educational courses) and to the firms who had attended IBM–sponsored planning seminars (Vacca, 1982 and 1983). A total of 251 organizations received the questionnaire. Three weeks after a first mailing, reminders were sent.

Of the 163 returning completed surveys (a response rate of 65%), 83 had begun but not yet completed an strategic information systems planning study. Eighty others (or 32%) had completed at least one strategic information systems planning study and thus provided the data used in the following analysis. The overall response rate of 65% is high and suggests the respondents found this topic interesting and important.

The respondents came from diverse industries with manufacturers representing 26%, utilities 13%, insurance 10%, and the remainder from many other backgrounds. They currently worked for firms with an average of 18,300 employees and 273 information systems professionals. Generally, they were highly experienced professionals with an average of 16 years in the information systems field and exposure to more than one employer. Fourteen percent were president or vice president of their firm while 56% held the title of director, manager, or supervisor. All had taken part in at least one completed strategic information systems planning study and their responses pertained to their most recently completed strategic information systems planning study. Table 3 provides detailed demographic information.

Although their titles differed, statistical analysis showed the sample to be homogeneous. Analysis of variance tested for differences across titles in respondents' ratings of the 49 strategic information systems planning problems and showed that the ratings for 46 of the problems were not significantly different (at the .05 level). Only three items differed at the .05 level, approximately the number that might be expected by chance.

In addition to the respondents' perceptions about strategic information systems planning, their employment and information systems experience were similar. Analysis of variance found no significant differences across titles in respondents' work experience in the current organization or in the information systems field. Hence, although the respondents had a variety of titles, the analysis suggests that the sample was homogeneous.

Job Titles of Respondents		Number of Employees	
President	6%	Fewer than 1000	23%
Vice President	8%	1,000 to 10,000	42%
Director	14%	More than 10,000	32%
Manager	36%	Not available	3%
Supervisor/Group Leader	6%		
Analyst/Data Administrator	9%	**Number of IS Employees**	
Consultant	6%	Fewer than 100	36%
Other	15%	100 to 500	55%
		More than 500	9%
IS Experience of Respondents			
Less than 10 years	17%	**Methodology**	
10 to 20 years	63%	Business Systems Planning	21%
Over 20 years	20%	Strategic Systems Planning	15%
		Information Engineering	14%
Industries of Respondents		Method/1	9%
Manufacturers	26%	Critical Success Factors	4%
Utilities	13%	Nolan Norton	3%
Insurance	10%	In-house	14%
Government	8%	Others	16%
Retailers	5%	Not available	5%
Other/Not available	38%		
Scope of Studies			
Entire Enterprise	44%		
Division	40%		
Functional Area	10%		
Not available	6%		

Table 3: Characteristics of Respondents

Actions for Strategic Information Systems Planners

Table 4 shows the percentage of the respondents who felt each problem was extreme or major and minor. The problems are ordered by severity.

On the basis of each problem, we developed recommendations for both information planners and top management considering a planning study for the purpose of identifying processes to re-engineer. Each recommendation corresponds to a problem in Table 4 which at least 25% of the subjects rated as extreme or major. Both the problems and our recommended actions provide checklists for improved strategic information systems planning.

1. Planners should assess in advance the likelihood that top management will fund the implementation of its final plan.

Over half the respondents were concerned about securing top management commitment to implement the plan. Once their study was done, they struggled to convince top management to authorize their recommendations. This suggests that top management may not understand the plan or may lack confidence in the organization's ability to carry it out. It implies that those planning a study assess in advance the chances top management will actually fund their proposals. They may also want to improve the chances of funding by touting to top management the potential for information technology to influence their firm's success. They can do this by telling top management about the information technology successes of competitors and other firms.

It is equally important for reengineering to gain top management commitment for implementation. Top management support is ranked as the most important key success factor in reengineering (Furey, Garlitz, and Kelleher, 1993). By explicit attention to implementation of redesigned processes, reengineering projects are less likely to fail at least due to a lack of resources (it is estimated by Stewart (1993) that 50–70% of the projects do not achieve their goals).

2. *Planners should choose a planning methodology that links the development of the plan to its implementation.*

Nearly half the respondents were concerned that implementing the plan requires substantial further analysis. Strategic information systems planning might not provide the analysis needed to start the design and programming needed to re–engineer the processes. This suggests that strategic information systems planners seek a methodology in which the documentation produced in the planning effort is easily reusable in the implementation effort. Otherwise, they can expect the frustrations of delays and duplicated effort before seeing their plans reach fruition.

Reengineered projects must also pay continual attention to implementation. As noted by Furey (1993), even though the most resources are spent in the formal implementation stage "if careful attention has been paid to completing the first five steps (planning and design), some aspects of the reengineered process will already be underway before the final redesign (implementation) stage." (p. 23, explanation added). This considerably reduces the time and resources spent in the formal implementation stage.

3. *Management should choose a dynamic, respected, technology–savvy veteran in the organization's business as team leader.*

Because the success of the methodology is greatly dependent on the team leader, the choice of this person is especially important. If the team leader is unable to convince top management to support the study or cannot obtain a top management mandate that functional area management and information management cooperate, the study may be doomed. The team leader motivates team members and pulls the project along. The team leader should be one of the organization's top movers and shakers.

Reengineering efforts must also be led by a respected and

Abbreviated problem statement	Extreme/ Major	Minor
Difficult to secure top management commitment	52%	16%
Requires further analysis	46%	31%
Success dependent on team leader	41%	30%
Difficult to find team leader meeting criteria	37%	17%
Methodology lacks sufficient computer support	36%	27%
Planning exercise takes long time	33%	30%
Ignores plan implementation issues	33%	18%
Difficult to obtain top management approval	32%	36%
No training plan for IS department	30%	29%
Difficult to find team members meeting criteria	30%	24%
No financial plan for IS department	29%	28%
Documentation is inadequate	28%	33%
No priorities for developing databases	27%	26%
No overall data architecture is determined	27%	22%
Very expensive	26%	29%
No permanent IS planning group	26%	24%
Many support personnel required	26%	23%
No data administration need addressed	26%	16%
Experiences not sufficiently transferable	24%	19%
No organizational data communications plan	22%	38%
No changes in IS reporting relationships	22%	31%
No prioritization scheme provided	22%	19%
Output belies top management expectations	22%	15%
No analysis of IS department strengths/weaknesses	21%	32%
No hardware plan	20%	36%
Heavy top management involvement	20%	21%
Resulting plans are inflexible	20%	18%
No analysis of technological environment	19%	20%
Too much user involvement	18%	28%
Final output document not very useful	18%	20%
Questions difficult for managers to answer	17%	39%
Information during study not captured	17%	25%
Methodology ignores legal/environmental issues	14%	16%
Bad assumptions about organization structure	14%	14%
Ignores organization changes during planning	13%	25%
No objectives for IS department are provided	13%	21%
Insufficient user involvement	13%	5%
Very large planning team required	12%	21%
Methodology ignores competitive environment	12%	19%
No new projects identified in final plans	12%	13%
Output fails to designate new steering committees	11%	18%
Rigidity of planning procedure	9%	17%
No assessment of current applications portfolio	9%	16%
Lack of top management involvement	9%	13%
Ignores organizational goals and strategies	8%	10%
Inappropriate planning horizon	6%	7%
Inadequate consultant support	5%	11%
Inappropriate size assumptions	4%	8%
No theoretical framework	3%	5%

Table 4: Extent of Problems

influential team leader. This is important because it will ensure that reengineering is being led "from the top" (Hammer and Champy, 1993).

4. *Planners should choose a well structured and defined methodology.*

   Because it is difficult to find a team leader who meets the

criteria, organizations should reduce their dependency on this person. One way to do so is to use a well structured and defined methodology to simplify the team leader's job. Thus, strategic information systems planners must examine the methodology carefully before choosing it. Likewise, by obtaining as much visible, top management support as possible, the organization will depend less on the team leader's personal ties to top management.

Reengineering would also be served well through the use of well-defined tools and approaches. Davenport and Stoddard (1994) caution that it is a myth that reengineering is so novel that it requires only a clean-slate approach and totally new methods and techniques. It is therefore suggested that organizations "combine tools from various traditional approaches, e.g., root cause analysis from quality, process value analysis from focused improvement approaches, and IT enablement from reengineering." (p. 124). Thus, structured tools, though traditional, should be a part of the inventory of techniques for reengineering.

5. *Planners should choose a methodology with adequate computer support.*

Strategic information systems planning produces reams of reports, charts, matrices, and diagrams. Planners cannot manage that volume of data efficiently and effectively without automated support. Thus when planners buy a methodology, they should carefully scrutinize the vendor's computer support. They should examine the screens and reports. On the other hand, if they customize their own methodology, they must be certain not to underestimate the need for such support.

Information technology support for reengineering is also critical. Management systems are necessary to control progress of reengineering projects (Talwar, 1993). They include systems for risk assessment, scheduling, communication, and progress reporting.

6. *Planners should keep the planning exercise short in duration.*

The planning study often takes weeks or months. This may exceed attention span of many organizations. Many managers feel they need results almost immediately and lose interest if a study drags on. Also, many organizations undergo major changes even during the planning period. Likewise, an overrun during the planning study will probably reduce top management's confidence in the organization's ability to carry out the final plan. Hence planners should strive to keep the duration of the planning study as short as possible while still producing a worthy plan.

Similarly, keeping a reengineering project short can generate a "sense of urgency" (Stewart, 1993) so important in reengineering.

7. *Planners should consider issues related to plan implementation.*

The study may produce an excellent plan with a list of high-impact processes. However, as said above, the study may fail to recommend actions that will bring the plan to fruition. For example, the study may fail to address the resistance of those managers who oppose the plan. Thus strategic information systems planners should pay careful attention to ensure that the plan is actually followed and not prematurely discarded.

The management of organizational impact is particularly important in reengineering because "Reengineering can tear apart working relationships, collaboration patterns, and cultural habits, which can lead to organizational paralysis." (p. 27, Rigby, 1993). Thus, every effort must be made to anticipate and to reduce the trauma to the organization.

8. *Planners should prepare convincing arguments to authorize the study.*

It is not only difficult to convince top management to implement the final plan but also difficult to convince top management to even fund the initial strategic information systems planning study. Strategic information systems planning is slow and costly. Meanwhile, many top managers want working systems immediately, not plans for an uncertain and distant future.

Thus advocates of strategic information systems planning should prepare convincing arguments to authorize the funding of the study. They should be ready to discuss the successful strategic information systems planning experiences of competitors and other firms. Typically, vendors of the methodologies can supply the names of clients who have had such successful experiences and are willing to discuss them.

Top management approval is currently not a problem for reengineering projects because of the tremendous hype surrounding the concept. However, the problem is unrealistic expectations and a misunderstanding of the concept (Davenport and Stoddard, 1994). Through a more rigorous assessment of reengineering projects, especially comparing them with those of other firms, there is likely to be a better understanding of process redesign issues and their real impact on the organization.

9. *The plan should include an overall personnel and training plan.*

Many information services departments lack the necessary skills to carry out the innovative and complex projects recommended by a strategic information systems planning study. A strategic information systems plan thus must consider new personnel. The study will probably recommend additions to existing positions, permanent information planners, and such new positions as expert systems and network specialists. A study also often recommends training current information services staff in today's personal computer, network, and database technologies. Thus, planners will need to be sure that their study accurately assesses current skills and staffing and suggests appropriate hiring and training.

This guideline is particularly relevant for reengineering which leads to multi–dimensional jobs and worker empowerment. These dramatic changes must be accurately assessed in terms of the needs for training and education, new performance and compensation measures, advancement criteria, and shifts in organizational values (Hammer and Champy, 1993). Only through such a detailed assessment can the impacts on personnel be managed.

10. Management should choose team members carefully.

Qualified team members, in addition to team leaders (as in item #4 discussed above), are scarce. Team members from functional area departments must feel comfortable with information technology while computer specialists must understand the business processes. Both need excellent communication skills and must have time to participate. Thus management should check the credentials of team members carefully and be sure that their schedules allow them to participate fully in the study.

The role of team members is similarly critical in reengineering. There is, in fact, universal emphasis on the requirement that the team be cross–functional in nature, drawing resources from several different functional areas (Furey, 1993; Talwar, 1993).

11. Planners should include an financial plan for proposed projects.

Responsible top management demands financial justification for new projects. Because computer projects might appear different from other capital projects, strategic information systems planners might treat them differently. After all, the costs and benefits of computer projects can be very difficult to quantify accurately. However, the information plan must contain projections for costs and benefits. Because top management will scrutinize and probably challenge them, planners must be sure that they are not only present but also defensible.

In reengineering, it is often the case that redesigned processes are implemented gradually because of resource constraints. According to Davenport and Stoddard (1994), clean slate implementation – throwing out the existing process in favor of a totally new environment – is a myth. A more realistic description is a "firm breaks implementation into several projects, beginning with those that offer the most immediate benefit (p. 123)." Under this perspective, it may be important to undertake an assessment of the costs and benefits of the various projects, just like in strategic information systems planning.

12. Planners should carefully examine the methodology's documenta-

tion.

The documentation describing some proprietary strategic information systems planning methodologies may not adequately describe the steps that should be followed for implementing the methodology. Strategic information systems planners might feel it gives them insufficient guidance or it may be erroneous, ambiguous, or contradictory. Thus, strategic information systems planners who purchase a proprietary methodology should read its documentation carefully before buying. Those who develop their own methodology should be ready to devote great effort to its documentation.

Similarly, because reengineering is a part of almost every consultant's tool box, it is important to critically evaluate various approaches and their validity. A close scrutiny of their documentation can help identify whether the emphasis in really on business process redesign or on other management nostrums (Davenport and Stoddard, 1994).

13. *Planners should ensure that their plan provides priorities for specific processes.*

Both top management and functional area management must agree with the plan's priorities. They must agree on what to do first and what to delay. Without top management agreement on the priorities of the targeted processes, the plan will never be executed. Without functional area management agreement, battles to change the priorities will rage. Such changes can halt ongoing projects. One risk is unequaled: Everything is started but nothing is finished. Planners should be sure that the plan stipulates priorities that top and functional area management sincerely accept.

As discussed above, reengineering implementation occurs through several projects and thus it is important to prioritize them according to benefit and maximum impact.

14. *Planners should include an overall data architecture for the organization in the plan.*

Although a major objective of many strategic information systems planning studies is to determine an overall data architecture, some studies don't identify the specific databases and the linkages between them. Thus, the portfolio of applications may appear piecemeal and disjointed. Although these may appear to be technical issues, strategic information systems planners should still understand major data architecture issues and be sure that their strategic information systems planning will provide such an overall, integrated architecture, and not just a list of processes to re–engineer.

Data architecture is also an important issue for reengineering because a stable architecture helps support and improve existing processes (Teng, Kettinger, and Guha, 1992). In fact, one of the reasons for failure of change efforts has been the lack of cohesiveness and comprehensive in information services and technology (Morris and Brandon, 1993).

15. Planners should carefully monitor and control the study's cost.
The planning study can demand considerable time from top, functional area, and information services department management. These are often the organization's busiest, most productive, and best paid managers, precisely the people without the time to spend on the study.   Hence, strategic information systems planners should carefully plan the study and control the amount of time these executives spend on it.

Reengineering is also extremely demanding in terms of the time of team members, some of the best people in the organization. Thus, every effort must be made to expedite such projects.

16. Planners should recommend a permanent information planning group.
Like general business planning, strategic information systems planning is not a one-time endeavor. It is an ongoing process where planners periodically review the plan and the issues behind it. Thus, as with many other planning endeavors, planners should view the strategic information systems planning exercise as an initial effort in an ongoing process.   They should also consider the need for a permanent planning function devoted to strategic information systems planning.

There is growing realization that reengineering too must be considered an on–going activity and not a one–time event (Davenport and Stoddard, 1994). To make reengineering the means and not the end (Rigby, 1993), the concept can be institutionalized by integrating it with on–going improvement approaches such as quality and by creating an environment in which employees are constantly thinking of quality (Harrison and Pratt, 1993).

17. Planners should budget staff and computer support during the study.
Strategic information systems planning can require many support personnel to collect and collate data. Thus planners should budget for support staff to carry out many data collection tasks. They should also budget for computer assistance for the manipulation and presentation of the data.

Reengineering is also a data intensive exercise because existing processes that span multiple functional areas must be documented. Thus, adequate support personnel must be allocated for such projects.

18. Planners should address data administration needs.

Because long-range plans usually call for new databases, the need for more data administration personnel - people who ensure that databases are up and working - is often necessary. In many firms, new databases continue to force the data administration function to grow dramatically.

Reengineering must also recognize that more administration personnel would enable greater access to data and thus better process redesign (Teng, Kettinger, and Guha, 1992).

Conclusion

Strategic information systems planning is a complex and challenging endeavor. It is time–consuming, expensive, and often requires major changes in the organization. This description fits reengineering equally well which is described as a high–stakes, risky, and disruptive activity (Hammer and Champy, 1993). Just as strategic information systems planning is fraught with problems, so is reengineering facing issues such as justifying the concept, top management commitment, reengineering team characteristics, and organizational resistance during implementation (Hammer and Champy, 1993). Given these similarities, it should not be a surprise that many of the lessons learned in strategic information systems planning can be applied to reengineering as discussed in this chapter.

Overall, not only is strategic information systems planning important as a tool for reengineering, it is also valuable because it shares common problems and thus similar solution with reengineering.

References

Alter, A.E. (1994, March 7). "Japan, Inc. embraces change" *Computerworld*, 28(10), pp. 24–25.

Andersen Consulting (1987). *Foundation-Method/1: Information Planning*, Version 8.0, Chicago, IL.

Arthur Andersen and Co. (1986). *The Changing Shape of MIS*, #86-6230.

Bowman, B., Davis, G., and Wetherbe, J. (1983). "Three Stage Model of MIS Planning," *Information and Management*, 6, 1, pp. 11-25.

Boynton, A.C. and Zmud, R.W. (1984, Summer). "An Assessment of Critical Success Factors," *Sloan Management Review*, pp. 17-27.

Boynton, A.C. and Zmud, R.W. (1987, March). "Information Technology Planning in the 1990's: Directions for Practice and Research," *MIS Quarterly*, 11, 1, pp. 59-71.

Brancheau, J.C. and Wetherbe, J.C. (1987, March). "Key Issues in Information Systems Management," *MIS Quarterly*, pp. 23-45.

Carlson, W.M. (1979, Spring). "Business Information Analysis and Integration Technique (BIAIT): A New Horizon," *Data Base*, pp. 3-9.

Churchill, G. (1979, February). "A Paradigm for Developing Better Measures of Marketing Constructs," *Journal of Marketing Research*, XVI, pp. 64-73.

Clemons, E.K. (1986, October). "Information Systems for Sustainable Competitive Advantage," *Information and Management*, 11(3), pp. 131-136.

Davenport, T.H. (1993). *Process Innovation: Reengineering Work through*

Information Technology, Harvard Business School Press, Boston, MA.

Davenport, T.H. and Stoddard, D.B. (1994, June). "Reengineering: Business change of mythic proportions?" *MIS Quarterly,* 18(2), pp. 121–127.

Earl, M.J. (1990, December 16–19). "Approaches to Strategic Information Systems Planning Experience in Twenty–One United Kingdom Companies," *Proceedings of the Eleventh International Conference on Information Systems,* Copenhagen, pp. 271–277.

Errico, S., Goll, E., Mabey, C., Marsteller, F., and Sullivan, T. (1993). *Reengineering the Business: Advanced Methodologies and Tools,* Critical Technology Report #C–6–3, CHANTICO Publishing Co., Inc., Atlanta, GA.

Furey, T.R., Garlitz, J.L., and Kelleher, M.L. (1993, November/December). "Applying information technology to reengineering" *Planning Review,* pp.22–25,55.

Furey, T.R. (1993, March/April). "A six–step guide to process reengineering" *Planning Review,* pp. 20–23.

Gill, S. (1981). "Information Systems Planning: A Case Review," *Information and Management,* 4, 5, pp. 233-238.

Glick, W.H., Huber, G.P., Miller, C.C., Doty, D.H. and Sutcliffe, K.M. (1990). "Studying Changes in Organizational Design and Effectiveness: Retrospective Event and Histories and Periodic Assessments," *Organization Science,* 1, 3, pp. 293-312.

Goodhue, D.L., Quillard, J.A., and Rockart, J.F. (1988, September). "Managing the Data Resource: A Contingency Perspective," *MIS Quarterly,* pp. 372-392.

Hammer, M.H. and Champy, J. (1993). *Reengineering the Corporation,* Harper Collins Publishers, Inc., New York, NY.

Harrison, D.B. and Maurice, P.D. (1993, March/April). "A methodology for reengineering businesses" *Planning Review,* pp. 6–11.

Hartog, C. and Herbert, M. (1986, December). "1985 Opinion Survey of MIS Managers: Key Issues," *MIS Quarterly,* pp. 350-361.

Henderson, J.C. and Sifonis, J.G. (1988). "The Value of Strategic IS Planning: Understanding Consistency, Validity, and IS Markets," *MIS Quarterly,* 12, 2, 1988, pp. 187-200.

Holland Systems Corporation (1989). *4FRONTstrategy Method Guide,* Ann Arbor, MI.

Huber, G.P. and Power, D.J. (1985). "Retrospective Reports of Strategic-Level Managers: Guidelines for Increasing their Accuracy," *Strategic Management Journal,* 6, pp. 171-180.

IBM Corporation (1975). Business Systems Planning - Information Systems Planning Guide, Publication # GE20-0527-4.

Ives, B. and Learmonth, G. (1984, December). "The Information System as a Competitive Weapon," Communications of the ACM, 27, 12, pp. 1193-1201.

Kay, R.M., Szypenski, N., Horing, K., and Bartz, G. (1980). "Strategic Planning of Information Systems at the Corporate Level," Information and Management, 3, 5, pp. 175-186.

Kerner, D. V. (1979, Spring). "Business Information Characterization Study," *Data Base,* pp. 10-17.

King, W.R. (1978, March). "Strategic Planning for Management Information Systems," *MIS Quarterly,* pp. 27-37.

King, W.R. (1988). "How Effective is Your Information Systems Planning?," *Long Range Planning,* 21, 5, pp. 103-112.

Lederer, A.L. and Mendelow, A.L. (1986, May). "Issues in Information Systems Planning," *Information and Management,* pp. 245-254.

Lederer, A.L. and Sethi, V. (1988, September). "The Implementation of Strategic Information Systems Planning Methodologies," *MIS Quarterly,* 12, 3, pp. 444-461.

Maglitta, J. (1994, January 12). "In Depth: Michael Hammer", Computerworld, 28(4), pp. 84–86.

Martin, J. and Leben, J. (1989). *Strategic Information Planning Methodologies,* 2nd edition, Prentice-Hall Inc., Englewood Cliffs, N.J.

McFarlan, F.W. (1971, March-April). "Problems in Planning the Information System," *Harvard Business Review,* 49, 2, pp. 75-89.

McFarlan, F.W. (1981, September-October). "Portfolio Approach to Information Systems", *Harvard Business Review,* 59(5), pp. 142-150.

McFarlan, F.W. (1984, May-June). "Information Technology Changes the Way You Compete," *Harvard Business Review,* 62, 3, pp. 98-103.

McLean, E.R. and Soden, J.V. (1977). *Strategic Planning for MIS,* John Wiley and Sons, Inc.

Morris, D. and Brandon, J. (1993). *Re-engineering Your Business,* McGraw-Hill,Inc..

Moskowitz, R. (1986, May 12). "Strategic Systems Planning Shifts to Data-oriented Approach," *Computerworld,* pp. 109-119.

Parsons, G.L. (1983, Fall). "Information Technology: A New Competitive Weapon," *Sloan Management Review,* 25(1), pp. 3-14.

Porter, M.E. (1985). *Competitive Advantage: Creating and Sustaining Superior Performance,* New York: Free Press.

Rigby, D. (1993, March/April). "The secret history of process reengineering" *Planning Review,* pp. 24–27.

Rockart, J.F. (1979). "Chief Executives Define Their Own Data Needs," *Harvard Business Review,* March-April, pp. 215-229.

Schwartz, M.H. (1970, Sept. 1). "MIS Planning," *Datamation,* pp.18-31.

Sinclair, S.W. (1986, Spring). "The Three Domains of Information Systems Planning," *Journal of Information Systems Management,* 3, 2, pp. 8-16.

Steiner, G.A. and Schollhammer, H. (1975). "Pitfalls in Multi-National Long-Range Planning," *Long Range Planning,* April, pp. 2-12.

Stewart, T.A. (August 23, 1993). "Reengineering: The Hot New Managing Tool" *Fortune,* pp. 41–48.

Sullivan, C.H. Jr. (1985). "Systems Planning in the Information Age," *Sloan Management Review,* 26, 2, Winter, pp. 3-13.

Talwar, R. (1993). "Business re-engineering – a strategy–driven approach" *Long Range Planning,* 26(6), pp. 22–40.

Teng, J.T.C., Kettinger, W.J., Guha, S. (1992). "Business process redesign and information architecture: Establishing the missing link," *Proceedings of the Thirteenth International Conference on Information Systems,* pp. 81–89.

Vacca, J.R. (1982). *Business Systems Planning: An Implementation Approach,* M.S. thesis, Kansas State University.

Vacca, J.R. (1983, March). "BSP: How is it working," *Computerworld.*

Vacca, J.R. (1984, December 10). "IBM's Information Quality Analysis," *Computerworld.*

Vitale, M., Ives, B., and Beath, C. (1986, December 15-17). "Identifying Strategic Information Systems: Finding a Process or Building an Organization," *Proceedings of the Seventh International Conference on Information Systems,* San Diego, CA, pp. 265-276.

Wetherbe, J.C. and Davis, G.B. (1982). "Strategic Planning through Ends/Means Analysis", MISRC Working Paper, University of Minnesota.

Wiseman, C.(1985). *Strategy and Computers: Information Systems as Competitive Weapons* Dow Jones-Irwin, Homewood, IL.

Yadav, S.B. (1983, Spring). "Determining an Organization's Information Requirements: A State of the Art Survey," *Data Base,* pp. 3-20.

Zachman, J.A. (1982). "Business Systems Planning and Business Information Control Study: A comparison," *IBM Systems Journal,* 21, 1, pp. 31-53.

Chapter
8

Alternative IT Strategies:
Organizational Scope and
Application Delivery

Jesus A. Ponce-de-Leon
Arun Rai
Arlyn J. Melcher
Southern Illinois University

Substantial attention has been paid to reengineering as a means to enhance the competitive posture of contemporary organizations. Business process innovation (Davenport, 1993), reengineering (Hammer and Champy, 1993), and business process redesign (Grover et al. 1993), have one central theme—a fundamental change to the business processes. The expected results of such efforts are dramatic changes in costs, cycle time, and profitability. Generally, it is expected that such redesign efforts will lead to a radical new way of carrying out processes that are central to the operation of the business. Terms such as 'nimble', 'flexible', 'adaptive', and 'responsive' have been used as metaphors to highlight the transformed organization. Consider the following examples:

C.F. England Trucking Co., a transportation company located in Salt Lake City saw information technology (IT) as a strategic investment to "carry more freight and satisfy the customer." Initially, England invested in automating the backoffice paperwork. But its latest investments in IT were more strategic oriented. They equipped 1,200 semi tractor-trailer rigs with mobile communication technology linked to a satellite. The drivers now can transmit data, do their daily reporting, and receive directions wherever they are (Bartholomew, 1992).

Reebok installed a real time sales, order-entry, and production tracking network linking all of the U.S. offices and manufacturing plants with a custom developed software. The internally developed IT gives Reebok a competitive advantage in the market by gaining access to manufacturing capabilities around the world and by shortening the cycle time of order to production dramatically (Pepper, 1990).

Reengineering projects can produce substantial improvements but critics report that only a few are successful (Moad, 1993a). Embarking on a program demands an understanding of reengineering, the customer's requirements, the capabilities of available information technology (IT), and of the key business processes of the firm. Reengineering projects differ in two respects: (1) the organizational scope (single function, to several functions, to a whole business unit, to several units being involved), and (2) in how IT application is delivered. (adoption, adaptation, or in-house development; see table 1). The scope of the project largely determines the organizational and economic impact of the reengineering effort. Whether a software technology is customized or bought as a package to enable a reengineering implementation may further influence its impact.

We examine the likely impact and organizational implications that breadth of reengineering projects and IT delivery approaches have upon reengineering efforts. While IT enables and serves as catalyst in reengineering projects (Davenport, 1993; Hammer and Champy, 1993; Grover et. al. 1993; Johansson, Mchugh, Pendlebury & Wheeler III, 1993), little has been said about the interaction between the breadth of the business process reengineering (BPR) application and IT delivery strategy (adoption, adaptation, or customization).

The organizational scope of reengineering projects may be restricted to changing activities within a function such as the accounts receivable function. Broader projects transform entire sets of activities that cross functions, departments and units within a business unit, for example, from order entry all the way to shipping and billing customers. At a higher level of complexity, reengineering projects encompass the redesign of business processes that affect an entire corporation and in some instances customers and suppliers (Cash and Robinson, 1992; Hall, Rosenthal and Wade, 1993).

From an IT delivery standpoint, Rockart and Hoffman (1992)

IT applications delivery strategy

		Vendor driven <--> User driven		
BPR scope		Vendor developed application solution	Application adaptation	Customized application
Narrow focus	Intrafunctional (localized teams)	Functional localized vendor constrained work-flow BPR C_{11}	Functional semi-customized localized work flow BPR C_{12}	Functional customized localized work-flow BPR C_{13}
	Interfunctional (cross functional teams)	Cross functional vendor constrained BPR C_{21}	Cross functional semi-customized BPR C_{22}	Cross functional customized BPR C_{23}
Broad focus	Interorganizational (Cross business teams)	Strategic business network vendor constrained BPR C_{31}	Strategic business network semi customized BPR C_{32}	Strategic business network redefinition customized BPR C_{33}

Table 1: Business Process Reengineering Strategies

observe that firms can employ a variety of approaches. Organizations may rely on off-the-shelf software solutions, use customization approach, or a balance of both strategies to implementing the IT to enable the business process redesign. We propose a framework to classify BPR strategies according to the combinations of IT delivery strategy and BPR organizational scope strategy. This framework results in nine BPR strategies (see Table 1) ranging from outright adoption of a vendor developed solution with an intrafunctional scope of the BPR project to a fully internally developed solution with an interorganizational BPR project scope.

The reminder of the chapter is organized as follows: First, we present our proposed model and a brief review of definitions that relate reengineering and IT; second, we then review the practitioner literature to classify reported reengineering projects into this framework; based on this classification, we derive implications for choosing a reengineering strategy. Finally, we conclude with recommendations for managerial and research studies.

Definitions

Business process reengineering (BPR), business process redesign, reengineering and process innovation are used interchangeably in the literature to refer to a fundamental change in how core business processes are carried out (see for example Hammer and Champy, 1993; Davenport, 1993; Grover et al., 1993). Whereas Total Quality Management (TQM) seeks slow but continuous improvements, business process reengineering seeks radical departures from the old way of doing business. BPR is oriented to achieve quantum leaps of change rather than incremental ones. However, our discussion clarifies that the scope of projects varies widely in firms.

Cooper and Zmud (1990) define an IT as "any artifacts whose underlying technological base is comprised of computer or communications hardware and software." A similar definition was used by Geisler and Husain (1993) in a survey of IT acquisition. They broadly defined IT "to include all equipment, systems, components, firmware and software utilized throughout the organization." Both definitions agree on hardware and software as two major components of IT. The hardware component of the IT application is generally limited to buying from vendors, whereas software applications actually range from make to buy (Geisler & Husain, 1993; Greenbaum, 1993). We have focused on software applications to operationalize IT delivery strategy to be consistent with the studies and definitions just mentioned.

We use the following terms to differentiate and classify BPR projects based on their organizational scope:

- **intrafunctional:** business process redesign projects that are aimed at single and isolated tasks, activities, or single functions.
- **interfunctional:** projects that target cross functional business processes but are contained within a business unit.
- **interorganizational:** projects that bridge between two or more business units, or two or more organizations such as the firm and its customers and suppliers. Figure 1 depicts these levels of organizational scope.

The application delivery strategy parallels the buy or make decisions. At one extreme the organization finds it more economical to buy a prepackaged software application. On the other hand, the organization may decide to internally develop a fully customized software application. A middle of the road is also possible where the organization buys software applications and customizes them to better meet its requirements. Thus, we use the following classifications of strategies used to deliver applications systems:

- software application adoption: the purchase of an off-the-shelf or standardized prepackaged software that requires little or no modifications when applied to the BPR project.
- software application adaptation: the purchase of a software pack-

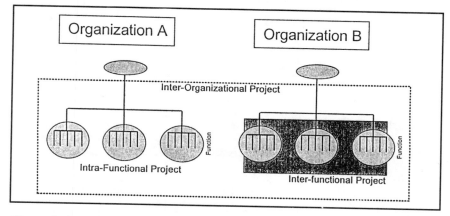

Figure 1: Scope of Reengineering Projects

age that serves as the backbone or shell of the application requiring partial customization to make the BPR project operational.
• software application customization: the organization undertakes a development effort to build the necessary applications software for the BPR project.

BPR Strategies

Table 1 enables us to map the various approaches firms are taking to reengineer their operations. Table 2 classifies some firms that have undertaken reengineering projects. The cases were identified through a search of trade journals, books, business newspapers, and academic journals. A little more than sixty projects were reported by these public sources as reengineering projects between 1990 and 1993. Only those reengineering projects that were detailed enough were included in this classification. These are discussed below.

Intrafunctional BPR and Alternative Applications Delivery Strategies

BPR projects with a narrow scope focus efforts at the intrafunctional level (Cells C11 to C13). The BPR project is focused on work flow within a department or function. There is a functional focus insofar as the business activity selected is contained within a specialized area. Work flow denotes routine processes that are performed within a business (for example, archiving, credit verification, and mailing).

At Chase Manhattan Bank, work flow reengineering began in 1991. The project was initiated with the need for streamlining

	Software Application Adoption	Software Application Adaptation	Software Application Development
Intrafunctional	**Functional Localized BPR** • Chase Manhattan Bank's work flow reengineering. • Connecticut Life Insurance's paperwork reduction and work flow compression. • Con Edison's paper trail simplification to improve customer service.	**Functional semi-customized BPR** • Delta's integrated data base adapted from Arthur Andersen.	**Functional customized BPR** • Nestle's internal development of software for local units.
Interfunctional	**Cross functional vendor constrained** • Corning Asahi's reengineering of order-fulfillment process using DCS Logistics. • CN North America's rail operations management software bought from Santa Fe.	**Cross functional semi-customized BPR** • Schwab's reengineering project of cashiering. • Brach's quality and manufacturing software application.	**Cross functional customized software application** • CSX Transportation's EDI based software development for shipping, inventories and faster order processing.
Interorganizational	**Strategic business network vendor driven BPR** • Sears's credit and cash register system. • Eastman Chemical's software from SAP-AG for sales, order processing, materials management and more.	**Strategic business network semi-customized BPR** • Levi Strauss's $400 million reengineering to deliver faster to retail stores. • Spartan Stores bought commercially available software from vendor and adapted it to reengineer its logistics and warehouse management.	**Strategic business network customized software application** • Reebok's linking plants and order entry to production. • Banc One's MIS system that integrates acquisitions and runs quality and banks performance.

Table 2: Cases of Reengineering Strategies

archiving, mailing and credit verification. Today Chase has one business unit and several divisions with work flow projects. The challenge today is to tie these disparate projects to produce cross-divisional, cross-business information sharing (Klein, 1994).

According to International Data Corp., IT work flow application software can be divided into three major groups: software oriented to routine, structured work flow; administrative systems for white collar less structured work flow; and ad-hoc software that requires substantial modifications of unstructured tasks. Typical applications are electronic mail, document imaging, forms management, document processing, and transaction oriented tasks such as order entry and record keeping (Fischer, 1994).

The narrow BPR approach is useful when the organization is cautious, prefers minor disruption of operations or feels it is not ready for massive business process reengineering. It is estimated that this type of reengineering, "via the backdoor" reached $390 million in 1993, and is expected to grow to $700 million by 1994.[1] Among the most popular software applications reported in the popular press include Lotus Notes, FileNet, RemoteWare, WorkMAN, Omindesk, Workbench, and FlowMark.

According to the BIS Strategic Decisions research group about 60% of work flow intrafunctional BPR projects prefer desktop and LAN platforms. This finding reflects reengineering projects at the intrafunctional level. Experts suggest that this type of BPR should bring about productivity gains for individuals in a given function, but is not designed to change the basic building blocks of the organization.

In this intrafunctional BPR, the IT application is vendor driven requiring minor programming for its adoption, as illustrated by Connecticut Life Insurance Co.:

Connecticut Life Insurance Co. launched its BPR effort focusing on reducing paperwork, compressing workflow, and worker productivity. The goals were an increase of 35% in worker productivity and boosting service for its policy holders. Their approach was to launch localized workflow projects in an incremental way. Today, they report "Work flow, reengineering, and imaging are all interconnected" reporting a 20 to 25% productivity gain.[2]

Intrafunctional BPR projects are manned by local teams. The local team (users) is led by the expertise of vendors and IS personnel to select and implement the software application. At this end of the spectrum of the IT delivery strategy, the projects are vendor constrained in that the BPR solution will be limited by the extent of the flexibility of the prepackaged software solution.

The piecemeal, localized strategy of intrafunctional BPR projects, is less risky and disruptive than a major BPR undertaking. However, in the long run it may cause major headaches if the projects aren't planned and coordinated. The multiplicity of localized BPRs may end up in a potpourri of hardware platforms, and softwares that do not talk to each other. The alternative IT strategy is an ad-hoc work flow BPR (Cell13). Here a localized work flow BPR project is aimed at unstructured tasks. Customization is necessary in these projects. The IS personnel take a supporting and advisory role and the vendor takes a back seat to the implementation process. The users become empowered because they are the most knowledgeable of the rules, processes and exceptions of the business process. Consider the following case:

> Nestle's local teams developed the core applications with the assistance of corporate experts in hardware and software technologies. Once the applications were developed, they were sent to local offices for further adaptation. The applications aren't operational until they meet the specific requirements of the local users (Greenbaum, 1994).

Interfunctional BPR projects and Alternative Applications Delivery Strategies

The most publicized BPR projects appear to fall within this category (C21-C23). In the interfunctional BPR project, the team is composed of members representing all of the functions and support areas affected by a core business process. A typical example of this kind is a process initiated by a customer's order to design, and associated manufacturing, shipping, inventory management, and billing.

> At Corning Asahi Video products unit, a division of Corning Inc. the glass maker, a cross functional team co-led by an IS manager and a division's manager, were assigned to reengineer the order-fulfillment process. The new process reduced the number of steps from 123 to nine and produced annual savings of $400,000 in personnel costs alone (Caldwell, 1994). The total cost for 30 months was $985,000. The Corning Asahi team decided to buy DCS Logistics software application from Andersen Consulting to reduce the technology risk, and be able to meet the deadline for testing and maintain the cost of the project as low

as possible (Maglitta, 1994).

The coordination of these BPR projects is more demanding because the teams are larger, members come from diverse organizational backgrounds, diverse interests are represented, and broader authority is needed for the team to initiate and implement change. Deciding who is the "owner" of the project is in itself a difficult task. Businesses with some experience in forming and managing multifunctional teams effectively stand a better chance to succeed on BPR projects of this nature. Others may prefer to start the change process with smaller projects such as the ones outlined in the intrafunctional BPR projects.

Even market leaders with visionary and supportive management falter in their attempts of reengineering core business processes. Charles Schwab provides a recent example of a major reengineering project that failed to materialize in spite of having a multifunctional team, a named process leader, management support, and had originally focused on customer satisfaction. The reasons reported for the failure include the team's focus on internal shortcomings of the existing IT rather than on the business process itself, design being carried out with incomplete and superficial information about customer's requirements, inadequate intervention by management, and team members did not perceive themselves as real agents of change. All together these factors produced an incremental improvement as opposed to a radical change (Moad, 1994).

"Ultimately, however, a reengineering project, like any major change program, can produce lasting results only if senior executives invest their time and energy. .. Inevitably, managers and employees may feel that their turf, jobs, and organizational equilibrium are under attack" (Hall, Rosenthal, Wade, 1993).

As the examples show, at this level of organizational scope the success of the BPR project begins to be sensitive not only on the selection of the business process, the selection of IT strategy, but also on organizational factors of team composition, assigned leader(s), authority granted, and expert support provided. These BPR projects are aimed at radical changes that will affect all of the involved parties and most importantly affect the overall performance of the business unit.

As with the intrafunctional BPR projects, the IT delivery strategy ranges from buying the software application outright from the vendors to customization. At one end we find the vendor driven IT strategy where the business process is redesigned around the software application package (Cell C21). We call it a "vendor constrained BPR project". In this type of BPR project, the business process is not unique to the firm and IT solutions are available in the market, such as in priority and capacity planning integrated with purchasing and inventory management. Several software packages are available in the market with these capabilities, such as Four Shift, Platinum, and MCS-3. In this type of project, the IT strategy is virtually an outright adoption with little or no modification. A case in point:

> CN North America, a $4 billion railroad owned by the Canadian government, bought a software application developed by Santa Fe Railway Co. of Atchison, Topeka. The software program will help CN North America to increase flexibility in billing, track customer's request, scheduling shipments, tracking freight, revenue and accounting and controlling freight yard traffic (Caldwell, 1993).

IS personnel are in a position to lead these projects because the selection decision is largely responsible for ensuring the compatibility between task and the requirements of the business process redesign. At this end of the spectrum of software delivery strategy the vendor's application becomes the solution but also the constraint. This is because a vendor's software application tends to be specific to the task or focused on an industry (called vertical market application) as was the case with CN North America's software.

BPR projects that require adaptation of the vendor's software (C22), can be served with horizontal software applications such as manufacturing, human resources and customer support. For example, in the manufacturing horizontal software the ASK Group, Datalogix International, Dun Bradstreet, Oracle Corporation and SAP America, offer software packages that are well developed and take advantage of the similarities of manufacturing processes (Greenbaum, 1993). Consider for example:

> In 1988, J. Brach Corp. got underway a $4 million, six-year modernization plan of its candy manufacturing plants. Brach evaluated several vendors and decided for Prism MRP horizontal software application. The application provided what Brach found as necessary to improving quality and manufacturing flexibility. A committee working with IBM's consulting group analyzed, designed, and implemented the new process in cooperation with end users (Bartholomew, 1991).

The other end of the software delivery strategy is customized applications (Cell C23). As with the intrafunctional BPR projects, the more unstructured and complex the business process and/or the more unique the business, the more it will require adaptation and customization.

CSX Transportation Inc. developed an in-house software application to improve customer service. It started back in 1985 when CSX began investing in building an IT infrastructure to reduce costs and improve control and communications. The software application developed by CSX was built upon an EDI initiative originally aimed at cost reduction only. The reengineered business process now allows customers to track their products and get a fast response from CSX as to shipping, information, inventories, location and faster order processing and billing (Pepper, 1991).

IS personnel and end-users alike take an active leadership in such BPR projects. In these cases the cross-functional team is empowered to design, suggest and implement the necessary modifications to make it operational. These teams are more complex because they require a good balance between end-users, those affected by the redesign, experts in the fields to which the redesign relates, and IS hardware and software personnel.[3] The issue of BPR project leadership remains a difficult one. Some BPR projects are co-managed by the line manager and the IS manager, some by the Chief Information Officer (CIO) or head of the Management Information Systems function, and in some others the line manager leads the effort. A recent survey at 350 companies conducted by Deloitte & Touche revealed that 35% of BPR projects are being led by IS managers, 42% by business-line managers and 20% by the president or CEO.[4]

Customization is a preferred alternative when the software available in the market does not meet the requirements of the BPR project and the skills for its development can be found in the IS group. The effectiveness of the IS team in developing the software application largely determines the technical success of the reengineering effort. The team of users, who are the most knowledgeable of the business process, will determine, however, how radical the departure from the old process should be. At this end of the IT delivery strategy the IS personnel take on the role of advisor in at least two ways: as an expert in IT available technologies and as an expert software developer. An advantage of the internal software development strategy is that both teams (users and IS) constantly interact during the redesign and implementation process to enrich and enhance the redesign. Perhaps the greatest advantage of this approach is that the redesigning team is free of the constraints inherent in commercially available software. The downside are the difficulties of making a complex team work effectively, the costs associated with assigning a group of programmers and analysts full time to the development of the application, and the likelihood of running over allowed time and budget.

Interorganizational BPR and Alternative Applications Delivery Strategies

Interorganizational BPR projects reach out beyond the boundaries of the business unit and link with other organizations to form a business network (C31-C33). A business network can be thought of as organizations that become more interdependent through core business processes. These common objectives are to improve customer satisfaction, reduce costs, become more efficient, and be more competitive and flexible in the market place. These business networks can involve customers (for example Eastman Chemical), suppliers (for example Wal Mart), logistically tightly coordinated units (for example Sporting Goods, Inc., Reebok), and acquisitions being merged into the mainstream business (for example Banc One, Elf Atochem).

Interorganizational BPR projects, target business processes that affect the entire organization by cutting across several business units. More complex and ambitious BPR projects also involve outside organizations such as customers and suppliers. Venkatraman (1991) has labeled IT's role at this stage as that of enabling a business network redesign.

> Spartan Stores Inc. of Grand Rapids, Michigan, is a wholesaler that wants to become a "just-in-time" linch pin for other companies. Its strategy is to become the most efficient wholesale distributor between manufacturers and retailers. A committee of eight people, together with an IBM team, identified 104 business processes that had an impact on this strategy. At present four divisions are involved in nine BPR projects that tie together finance, order management, warehouse management, retailers, suppliers and customer support. Sophisticated neural network software is being tested in one of these projects to speed up decision making, reduce errors, cut costs and improve customer service (Wilson, 1993).

BPR initiatives should be consistent with the strategic direction of the firm, its IT strategy, and customer's needs (Grover et. al., 1993). Thus the selection and targeting of business processes for reengineering should be guided by the strategy of the business. As it has been discussed in this chapter, the scope and organizational resources required by the BPR project will in turn influence the decision for adoption, adaptation or customization of the software application (Bartholomew, 1992; Grover et al.; Henderson & Venkatraman, 1992).

Interorganizational BPR projects can also be undertaken by buying outright the software application (C31), adapting it (C32), or developing it internally (C33). At this level of BPR scope, the strategy of the business, the market (customers), and other related organizations (for example suppliers) are an integral part of the BPR project. Thus, it is to be expected that the projected benefits from these projects should impact in a significant way the bottom line of the business. Hall et al. (1993) report that the broader the scope of the reengineering project the higher the impact on the bottom line of the business. In their in-depth study of 20 cases they found that the broadest scope produced 17% cost reductions versus less than 1% for the narrowest focused projects.

> At Sears Roebuck and Co. a project was launched in early 1992 that affects 868 of its retail stores. The project will link the backoffice, the cash registers, credit verification, and automated service kiosks. This move is expected to increase face-to-face service by liberating employees time, eliminating paperwork, speed up service to customers, simplify sales, and cut costs. Sears contracted with CompuAdd for the hardware and software applications (McCormick, 1992).

> Eastman Chemical Co., the 10th largest chemicals producer, has undertaken a complete overhaul of its way of integrating the operations of offices and plants around the globe. Their BPR project is dubbed the Global Business Integrated Information System. Eastman bought the software application from SAP AG of Germany because the vendor will install it in half the time than if developed internally. The business processes to be reengineered are not considered unique to Eastman. The applications involve sales and distribution, order-taking and invoicing, materials management, inventory controls, assets management, and financial reporting. The new system replaces more than 40 disparate applications that had difficulty communicating with each other (Appleby, 1993).

It is widely recognized that the role of IT has changed from backoffice support (automation of clerical work) to a more strategic and market opportunity oriented one (Allen & Scott Morton, 1994; Henderson & Venkatraman, 1992; Porter and Millar, 1985; Zuboff, 1988). Thus, the interaction between BPR, IT, and business strategy is a crucial one. IT plays a key role in these interactions as an enabler of BPR implementation and BPR effectiveness (Davenport, 1993;

Grover et al.,1993). Consider Banc One's experience:

> Banc One is an example of an organization that in the last ten years has managed through acquisitions to increase its size fivefold but not its complexity. This has been achieved by integrating its acquisitions while reducing complexity through an internally developed IT. It is so effective that in just a few months each newly acquired unit reduces costs dramatically, its service capability is enhanced, and operations get fully integrated to headquarters on a real time basis. IT has redefined the coordinating capabilities of the organization and dramatically reduced the complexity of managing and integrating a rapidly growing business (Teitelman, 1991).

Assigning ownership of the project at the interorganizational level is more difficult than at any other organizational scope. Because these BPR projects cut across several business units, representatives from several business units, with different backgrounds, different experiences and areas of expertise, and most likely from various organizational levels (both internal and external to the reengineering organization) must work together. Designating a leader and owner of the project may become more politicized and sensitive to power positions especially when the project involves several equals at the top. Hall et. al. (1993) recommend that in addition to getting the CEO involved, a second top executive be designated for its implementation.

The typical role of the IS function is one of business wide expert advisor in IT matters, implementer and provider of support for the IT systems. As a common advisor to all units involved, the IS function can take a technical position and play a co-leading or leading role in the reengineering team. The solution by some organizations has been to create a full time position for reengineering managers (for example Schwab).

In the vendor driven BPR projects (C_{31}), the IS function is charged with the responsibility for the evaluation and selection of the software application that best fit the BPR requirements. Thus, the IS personnel become a key resource to the reengineering team.

At the other extreme of the continuum of the software application strategy are the internally developed software applications (Cell C_{33}). These are complex BPR projects that require detailed planning and a careful assessment of the magnitude of change, the resources needed, the timeline, and coordination. Industry experts suggest that careful consideration be given to the strategy of customization through development. Greenbaum (1993) recommends consideration of:

- the business needs.
- the programming skills of the IS organization.
- if sufficient resources are available to fund the BPR project.
- the cost of maintaining the technology.
- the need for added functionality and flexibility of the software.
- the workload involved.
- the risk of failure.
- the required training and flexibility of the IS organization.
- the time that it will take to develop, test and implement.
- the total cost and degree of portability between hardware platforms.
- who will manage the application?

In these projects the reengineering team should be empowered to radically change the business process. Because of the nature of the interdependencies between the various business units involved, a large scale organizational transformation potentially can occur. Thus, a high level executive has to be actively involved to provide the authority and top managerial support before the reengineering team can become a real change agent. The popular press reports that these projects take anywhere between 18 months and 6 years, between initiation and implementation. In addition, some unexpected situations often arise as the projects move from design to software writing. For example take the case of Texas Instruments:

> TI initiated its BPR projects in 1988. Although originally TI wanted to reengineer core processes in less than a year, it soon found out that analysts and developers could not make the change to a reengineering mentality. Projects got delayed, early software applications were aimed at automating rather than reengineering the process, and IS personnel had difficulty broadening their vision from a narrowly focused application to one that encompassed several functions and business units. TI reorganized its IS staff into centers of excellence (each center focused on a business process), spent heavily in retraining them, and changed the reward system to emphasize breadth of knowledge and performance (Moad, 1993a).

TI reports that its success rate for BPR projects jumped to 80%. Experts say that it is not only the speed of development that matters but also the ability of the IS team to create applications in a different way (Moad, 1993a). Put in another way, IS personnel have to reengineer themselves if a project of this nature is to succeed. Consider the following:

> "Many in IS expect requirements to be defined and things to be predictable before they start coding... But reengineering is

anything but predictable." (Ed Goll , partner of Price Waterhouse in New York, as cited in Moad, 1993a).

"The idea that you don't leave the room or start developing an application until you've got 100% of the requirements defined up front just won't work in reengineering." (David Sutherland consultant with CSC Index, as cited in Moad, 1993a).

Implications and Conclusions

BPR projects may grow from a single-function-vendor-driven solutions (C11) to an interorganizational-customized solution (C_{33}). As their scope enlarges and IT delivery strategy changes the organizational and technological complexity of the BPR projects mount. Table 3 highlights some of the major points addressed in the discussion of reengineering strategies. The organizational scope of the BPR project in conjunction with the software application delivery strategy generate a nine cell framework suggesting important implications for selecting a reengineering strategy. This framework also suggests that firms that are planning to reengineer their businesses should consider their business needs, their resources, the software applications available in the market, the time needed from design to implementation, the formation, organization and management of the reengineering teams, and the time and commitment the CEO can make.

The business trade journals report numerous companies are going through some form of reengineering. However, many BPR projects do not produce the dramatic results that its proponents anticipate. Although the successful cases are frequently cited, the failures are often not publicized. Some critics report that is likely that only 20 to 25 percent of reengineering projects actually result in real dramatic results, while the other 70% produce only minor improvements, or none at all (Hall, Rosenthal and Wade, 1993; Moad, 1993a). Faltering and weak support from top management, lack of organizational changes to support business process redesign (lack of depth), and lack of breadth or scope as referred in this chapter (not cutting across functional areas or business units) are cited as the most frequent causes of failed business process redesign efforts (Hall et al., 1993; Moad, 1994).

Subscribing to a vendor solution implies that knowledge barriers associated with requirements definition and product development are addressed by drawing upon external competencies. The redefinition of the process occurs largely within the confines of the product capability. Such redefinition, no doubt, is a temporal

	Software Application Adoption	Software Application Adaptation	Software Application Development
Intrafunctional	**Functional Localized BPR** • Vendor's software adopted. • Small BPR projects. • Work Flow oriented. • IS organization evaluates and selects application. • Single tasks, isolated functions targeted. • Local teams. • Routine tasks.	**Functional semi-customized BPR** • Functional focus retained. • IS personnel empowered to adapt vendor's software. • IS evaluates and selects software. • Tasks or functions being reengineered are less routine. • Local teams.	**Functional customized BPR** • IS empowered to develop the software application. • Users empowered to lead redesign. • Local teams. • Business processes are less structured. • Functional focus is retained.
Interfunctional	**Cross functional vendor constrained** • Vendor's software adopted. • Cross functional team. • IS evaluates and selects software. • Business processes cut across several functions or departments. • Project starts to get bigger.	**Cross functional semi-customized BPR** • Vendor's software adapted to business requirements. • IS evaluates and selects software application. • Cross functional teams. • Business process is less structured. • Business process cuts across several functions.	**Cross functional customized software application** • IS organization empowered to develop software application. • Cross functional teams. • Business needs are not met by commercial software. • Business process cuts across several functions. • Projects are complex.
Interorganizational	**Strategic business network vendor driven BPR** • Business process interfaces with other business units. • Vendor's software is adopted. • Vendor's alternative is perceived as cheaper, less risky, and faster in implementation. • BPR focused on linking with external markets and organizations. • Cross business teams.	**Strategic business network semi-customized BPR** • Interfaces with external organizations, interfaces with markets. • IS personnel empowered to adapt the software application to business needs. • Cross business teams. • Business process cuts across several business units. • Issues of team leadership, control and implementation are important.	**Strategic business network customized software application** • Users empowered to redefine the business processes. • IS empowered to redesign the software applications. • Business needs not met by commercial software. • Business process affects the entire organization and external linkages • IS organization has the skills and resources and management support. • Cross business teams.

Table 3: Reengineering Strategies

phenomena and depends on the capability of organizational members to learn as to how the product can enable obliteration of existing business processes. It also depends on the ability of the vendor community to realize the shortcomings of products and their willingness to address such gaps in an expedient fashion.

As the firm moves the scope of its BPR projects from a single function, to the enterprise, to the interorganizational level, the composition of the teams change and organizational issues such as leadership, control, coordination, management of the team and who is in charge of implementation become more salient.

The framework also highlights the need for tightly linking the strategy of the firm with its IT strategy and the reengineering strategy. BPR projects focused on single tasks and isolated functions will tend to be less disruptive of the operation of the firm. Even these small projects are strategic in nature when they improve customer service and enhance the bottom line through cost reductions. The strategy requires the accumulation of many small hits of this nature to amount to a significant bottom line impact. The risk here is ending up with disparate software applications that do not talk to each other.

At the other end of the spectrum, we find the interorganizational BPR projects where software applications are customized. The risks taken here are of a different kind. The organization has to carefully assess its systems development capabilities and specific business needs. The projects are large in scale, have time pressures, and the issue of leadership and project ownership is difficult to resolve. These BPR projects are more critically linked to the strategy of the firm because the investments in time, money and people are of a significant magnitude and tend to be irreversible (for example Brach's $4 million investment, Corning Glass's Asahi group $1 million and more than 2 years into its reengineering effort, CSX's $250 million in IT reengineering, and CN North America's $50 million paid price for its purchased software application). Table 3 highlights some of the examples that represent each one of the cells of the proposed framework.

Being a customized approach, the redefinition of the process and information technology applications occur concurrently here. Because of the large scope of these projects, it is useful to recognize that frequent concurrent redefinitions can involve significant costs. In essence, while the general theme of concurrent redefinition is laudable, with increases in scope of the BPR project, the costs necessitate careful reassessment of the frequency of such redefinitions.

The choice between making or buying software applications is a difficult one. An industry expert estimates that if "You can find a product that satisfies about 70% or 80% of what you need to do, you should buy it." (Judith Hurwitz of the Hurtwitz Consulting Group in Watertown Mass.; as cited in Greenbaum, 1993). Outsourcing is becoming a viable economic alternative and appropriate skills needed from external sources can now be purchased to facilitate implementation of any of the nine enumerated strategies. For example, consultants and vendors can be used to implement a prepackaged application and provide requisite training. Alternatively, consultant organizations may be charged with requirements determination and development of a customized application. Our point here is that IS organizations need to carefully evaluate the mix of human resources deployed (internal IS personnel versus outsourcing agents) for the implementation of a particular reenginering strategy.

Our chapter develops a classification framework for BPR projects. In general, classification frameworks order emergent fields and provide a basis for future theoretical work in the area. We have clarified here that it is useful to differentiate between BPR strategies along the two dimensions considered here. Rest assured, our classification framework needs to be debated and elaborated. Within the confines of the present framework a number of interesting questions emerge. What are the critical success factors associated with a particular strategy? Is it advisable for a firm to migrate from simpler, low-risk BPR strategy (C_{11}) to a complex, high-risk BPR strategy (C33)? What paths are more likely to build success along the way? What paths are riskier and why? What paths are easier and cheaper? What is the nature of organizational learning that firms should try to strive to achieve and manage for each of the strategies? Needless to say, the research challenge is to understand the dynamics of BPR strategies, selection, implementation, migration paths, entry points, costs and likelihood of success.

We have discussed some of the requirements that a particular BPR strategy create. Organizations may opt for a BPR learning curve by starting with a small and focused isolated function and work their way up to larger and complex interorganizational BPR projects. It is clear from this proposed classification that the decision to buy, adapt, or internally develop an IT application hinges not only on the capabilities of the organization but also on the available time, costs, the organization's risk preferences, and the ability of the firm to form, manage, support, and control a BPR team. We hope that we have provided managers and researchers with a classification system that reduces the confusion by the apparent diversity of reported BPR projects.

Endnotes

[1]Klein, Paula. (1993). Reengineering via the backdoor. *Information Week*. July 5. 39-42.

[2] Klein, Paula. (1993). They are 'Wacky', but they are no fools.

Information Week. July 5, 39-42.

[3] For more in depth views of teams see for example on measuring team performance: Meyer, Christopher. How the right measures help teams excel, Harvard Business Review, May-June 1994, pp 95-103. On types of teams, their management, composition and rules of thumb for better team effectiveness see Jon R. Katzenbach and D.K. Smith *The Wisdom of Teams,* New York: Harper Collins Publishers, 1993. For examples of how cross functional teams have been organized and structured in various industries see Kenji Kurogane (ed.) *Cross-Functional Management.* New York: Quality Resources, 1993 (Originally published by the Asian Productivity Organization).

[4] Caldwell, Bruce. (1994). Leading the Charge. Information Week. February 7. 38-44.

References

Allen, Thomas J. & Scott Morton, M. (1994). *Information Technology and the Corporation of the 1990s.* New York: Oxford University Press.

Appleby, Chuck. (1993, December 13). A case of chemical reengineering. *Information Week.* p 48.

Bartholomew, Doug. (1991, November 18). Sweet Dreams for Brach IS. *Information Week,* p. 24.

Bartholomew, Doug. (1992, October 26). Business Alignment: The CEO's view. *Information Week.* pp 12-18.

Caldwell, Bruce. (1993, June 28). Casey Jones is a reengineer. *Information Week.* pp 36-40.

Caldwell, Bruce. (1994, February 7). Corning IS makes room for reengineering. *Information Week.* p 41.

Cash, James, & Robinson, J.E.. (1992, September 21). IT gets the line. *Information Week.* pp 38-44.

Cooper, R.B. & R.W. Zmud (1990). Information technology implementation research: A technology diffusion approach. Management Science. 36:2, 123-139.

Davenport, Thomas H. (1993). *Process Innovation.* Boston MA: Harvard Business School Press.

Davenport, T.H., & Short, J.E. (1990, Summer). The new industrial engineering: Information technology and business process redesign. *Sloan Management Review.* 11-27.

Fischer Lent, Anne. (1994, March 28). Documenting change. *Information Week.* pp 46-50.

Geisler, Eliezer, & Husain, J. (1993, October). Selection and acquisition of information technology in service companies. Paper presented at the meeting of the Midwest Division of the Academy of Management. Chicago, IL.

Greenbaum, Joshua. (1993, December 20). Build or buy? *Information Week.* pp 36-44.

Greenbaum, Joshua. (1994, April 25). Nestle's global mix. *Information Week.* , pp 44-46.

Grover, V., Teng, J.T.C., & Fiedler, K.D.. (1993). Information technology enabled business process redesign: An integrated framework. *OMEGA.* 21(4), 433-447.

Hall, G., J. Rosenthal, & J. Wade. (1993, November-December). How to Make Reengineering Really Work. *Harvard Business Review*, 1919-131.

Hammer, M . (1990, July-August). Reengineering work: Don't automate, obliterate. *Harvard Business Review*. , 18-25.

Hammer, M. & J. Champy (1993). *Reengineering the Corporation: A Manifesto for Business Revolution*. New York: Harper Business.

Henderson, John C. & Venkatraman, N. (1992). Strategic alignment: A model for organizational transformation through information technology. In T. A. Kochan & M. Useem (Eds.), *Transforming Organizations*. (pp 97-117). New York: Oxford University Press.

The human factor. (1991, June 10). *Information Week*. pp 27-36.

Johansson, Henry J., Mchugh, P., Pendlebury, A.J., & W.A. Wheeler III. (1993). *Business Process Reengineering*. New York: John Wiley & Sons.

Jonscher, Charles. (1994). An economic study of the information technology revolution, in Allen, Thomas J. & Scott Morton (Eds.), *Information Technology and the Corporation of the 1990s*. (pp 5-42). New York: Oxford University press.

Klein, Paula. (1994, March 28). Go with the flow. *Information Week*. pp 41-45.

Maglitta, Joseph. (1994, January 17). Glass act. *Computerworld*. pp 80-88.

McCormick, John. (1992, January 13). *Information Week*. pp 10-11.

Moad, Jeff. (1993a, August 1). Does reengineering really work? *Datamation*. pp 22-24.

Moad, Jeff. (1993b, November 1). New rules, new ratings as IS reengineers. *Datamation*. pp 85-87.

Moad, Jeff. (1994, March 15). Reengineering a report from the trenches. *Datamation*. pp 36-40

Pepper, Jon. (1990, December 17). Reebok Toes the production line. *Information Week*. pp 26-27.

Pepper, John, (1991, November 11). Getting service on track, *Information Week*. pp 20-22

Porter, M.E. & Millar, V.E. (1985, July-August). How information technology gives you competitive advantage. *Harvard Business Review*. pp 49-60.

Tapscott, Don & Caston, Art. (1993). *Paradigm Shift: The New Promise of Information Technology*. New York: McGraw Hill, Inc.

Teitelman, Robert. (1991, July). The magnificent McCoys: Running America's best bank. *Institutional Investor*. Reprint.

Wilson, Linda. (1993, November 15). A Spartan existence. *Information Week*. pp 40-42.

Zuboff, Shoshana. (1988). *In the Age of the Smart Machine: The Future of Work and Power*. New York: Basic Books.

Part III

Methods

Chapter 9
The Process Reengineering Life Cycle Methodology: A Case Study
Kettinger, Guha, and Teng

Properly constructed, a BPR methodology, is designed to steer the reengineering of business processes toward success. As a road map, methodology, should act as a guide rather than a rigid set of rules that must be followed in an inflexible order. In this way BPR methodology should guide analytic thinking without a built-in bias toward one "right" answer. This chapter introduces the Process Reengineering Life Cycle (PRLC). Based on analysis and synthesis of many of the leading BPR methodologies and techniques used in practice, the PRLC methodology presents the stages and activities of a typical business reengineering project. Using a life cycle as a metaphor for reengineering, its socio-technical design philosophy captures the process, human, communication, and technological dimensions of a reengineering project. Consistent with a process management life cycle view, the PRLC ties BPR's one-time/radical process change objectives with other process stewardship management activities including process improvement and TQM. This methodology is further illustrated by a corporate reengineering example.

Chapter 10
A Framework and a Suite of Methods for Business Process Reengineering
Mayer, Benjamin, Caraway, and Painter

As organizations seek to obtain strategic advantages by redesigning the way they do business, they are finding the process fraught with uncertainty. Put simply, change is difficult. In some instances, the prospect of change is so onerous that the only way to effect change is to liquidate the existing enterprise and start again. The technique for Business Process Re-engineering (BPR) has evolved as a powerful and practical tool enabling rapid enterprise restructuring and change management. This chapter describes a framework for BPR. An important component of this framework is a suite of methods and tools for BPR. Attention is focused on a subset of the IDEF suite of methods. The role of the IDEF methods in facilitating the BPR process is illustrated using simple examples. The chapter also shows how the IDEF methods can be combined with analysis methods such as simulation and ABC.

Chapter 11
Business Reengineering with Business Rules
Appleton

Businesses are complex systems, not machines. Like other complex systems, their apparently chaotic behavior, viewed as business processes, is controlled by a relatively simple set of internal rules. These internal rules, called "business rules," control how messages are formed within the business, between the business and its customers, and among the business and its suppliers, and they ultimately determine the information quality, productivity, adaptability, and process structure of the business. In this chapter, Dan Appleton introduces business rules as a powerful device for business reengineering. He explains why business rules are important, what they are, how they control business processes, how they dramatically effect business process change, how they can be modeled, and how business rule models can be employed to increase significantly the impact of information technology on business performance.

Chapter 12
Process Modelling—Who, What and How—Role Activity Diagramming
Huckvale and Ould

There are a number of situations when managers involved in Business Process Reengineering need to achieve and share a thorough understanding of the ways in which people work together to achieve business objectives. They need process models for describing, communicating, analysing and designing business processes. Traditional DP modelling techniques, with their emphasis on data, are not good at capturing the key elements of interest in modelling business processes. This chapter presents a view of what those key elements are, and compares several popular process modelling notations. That of Role Activity Diagrams (RADs) is described in some detail, as one which is particularly good at focusing on process rather than data features. Techniques for capturing the information necessary to build a process model, for handling complexity, and for using the model in analysing the process for improvement are described in the context of Praxis' own STRIM method, which has process modelling with RADs at its heart.

Chapter 13
Reengineering and REAL Business Process Modelling—Event Driven Modelling
Denna, Jasperson, and Perry

Recent reports about the low success rate of business process reengineering (BPR) have caused it to lose some of its luster. For every piece of good news there are typically three or more untold failures tucked conveniently out of sight. It is believed much of this is due to the lack of a theory about business processes and their relationship with an organization's strategy, stewardship and structures, measurements, and IT application architecture. The purpose of this chapter is to introduce both a theory of the essential nature of business processes and their relationship with an organization's structures and stewardships, strategy, measurements, and IT application architecture. The chapter also describes how to model the essential nature of business processes using REAL Business Process Modelling.

Chapter 14
Value-based Business Process Reengineering: An Objective Approach to Value-added
Kanevsky and Housel

The promise of business process reengineering (BPR) must be validated by its effect on the "bottom line." It will be taken seriously as a new process improvement framework only when executives can be assured, *a priori*, that it will produce the desired ROI in the reengineered processes, and after the BPR, whether there have been actual improvements. An objective way to measure the value added by component processes must be developed to make this kind of assessment possible. Using an extension of Kolomogorov's Complexity theory, this chapter provides a new methodology for calculating the return on investment in process (**ROP**). This new methodology offers a way to understand not only what company processes add value, but also allows objective calculation of how much value is added by various company processes. Armed with this new information, BPR analysts can estimate the value that will be added by reengineering processes.

Chapter 15
Lessons Learned from Business Engineering with the Amsterdam Police Force—Dynamic Modelling
van Meel, Bots, and Sol

A Business Engineering case study with dynamic modelling within the Amsterdam Municipal Police Force is described. Business Engineering (BE) is seen here as 'the integral design of both organizational structures and processes and information systems for the solving of actual business problems'. BE is not without risks, and must be carefully managed and planned. What is needed is in fact a design methodology for guiding and structuring actual BE-efforts. However until now, BE has achieved little methodological and theoretical support. In order to overcome this problem, an explorative case study with dynamic modelling was carried out. Dynamic modelling is a structured approach for the analysis and diagnosis of organizational problems by means of dynamic simulation models. The use of this approach within the Amsterdam Municipal Police Force is further described and evaluated. The result is an outline of an BE-approach consisting of: a SocioTechnical, engineering way of thinking, a problem solving way of working, an adaptive way of controlling and a dynamic way of modelling. The proper fit between these different approaches is examined in further detail, herewith showing the consistency and coherence of the described approach.

Chapter
9

The Process Reengineering Life Cycle Methodology:
A Case Study

William J. Kettinger
University of South Carolina

Subashish Guha
AT&T Global Information Solutions

James T.C. Teng
University of South Carolina

Most managers now recognize that they should concentrate as much on the flow of products and information between departments and customers, as on the activities within departments. Managing this "white space on the organization chart" calls for organizational design around networked business processes rather than functional hierarchies (Rummler & Brache, 1990). A business process is a group of logically related tasks that use the resources of an organization to provide defined results in support of the organization's objectives (Davenport & Short, 1990; Harrington, 1991). Typical business processes include proposal development, sales tracking, order processing, distribution, claims processing, quality assurance, etc. Many leading companies such as AT&T and Hewlett-Packard have recognized this process view and have long established programs and methodologies for continuous process improvement and total quality management (TQM).

Even given TQM's success, mounting competitive pressures have pushed many firms to look beyond incremental process improvement to more dramatic process change. Companies such as Xerox, Hallmark, and Ford have embarked on "radical" business process reengineering to realize dramatic improvements in quality, cost and cycle time. Some leading consultants, in fact, stress that radical process change is a periodic necessity for even those companies that have established TQM programs as a means to establish significant leaps in competitive advantage and business transformation (Davidson, 1993; Hammer, 1990). Most popular definitions require "Business Process Reengineering," (or "Business Process Redesign", "Business Process Innovation," "Process Transformation" as it is sometimes referred) to undertake a broad and fundamental analysis of the organization. In addition, to improvements in process efficiency, reengineering efforts typically impact organizational design, human resource architecture, communication architecture, reward systems, and information systems.

The majority of methodologies for conducting reengineering are the intellectual property of the leading reengineering consulting firms (for example, Andersen Consulting, Booz-Allen & Hamilton, Cooper and Lybrand, CSC/Index, D. Appleton Co., DMR Group, Gateway Management Consulting, Ernst & Young, International Systems Services, McKinsey Co., Nolan & Norton, Price-Waterhouse, SRI, and Symmetrix). Typically, consultants conduct reengineering by following a proprietary methodology which factors in their own philosophical assumptions concerning BPR while tailoring the methodology to fit each client's unique needs. These approaches usually share some high-level similarities in that they call for the articulation of a strategic vision, development of a BPR plan, establishment of appropriate performance measures, and implementation of improved process and organizational systems. In this way, these methodologies typically proceed through a project life cycle. However, there are several points on which these approaches often fundamentally differ. The first concerns the extent to which a BPR project focuses on redesigning an existing process as opposed to immediately focusing on designing a new process. Second, methodologies differ in the inclusion and sequence of steps. Third, the specific techniques applied will often differ depending on the two preceding factors. For example, BPR methodology may differ to the extent that they require an examination of the firm's "core" competencies, involve senior management, and to the degree of business transformation.

Many reengineering consultants, including Hammer & Associates and CSC/Index have adopted a more radical approach to reengineering. Sometimes referred to as a "Greenfield" approach, these consultants adhere to the belief that "the grass may be greener" by directly designing a new process rather than trying to rework an old "farmed-out" process. Such radical views advocate that there is little value in detailed study of existing processes and new design based on strategic visioning is the medicine required for American business. As Hammer states it, "if you automate a mess, what you get is an automated mess." An opposing school of thought views it necessary to properly diagnose an existing disease before devising a cure. While believing that linkage needs to be established between process redesign and strategic "stretch targets," many reengineering consultants such as Louis Fried of SRI, Del Langdon of ISS, and James Bair of Cooperative Systems believe that BPR involves a systematic examination of current process as well as strategy driven design.

Clearly, this philosophical difference in the definition and approach to reengineering reflects yet another sign of reengineering methodology's immaturity and that moving beyond the "hype" to proven successful approaches is now a much needed priority. While both schools of thought appear to have merit, these definitions and approaches to reengineering might be placed along a spectrum from process improvement, requiring an understanding of the existing business process prior to redesign, to radical reengineering which stresses the design of totally new processes based on a powerful "business vision" (Davenport, 1993).

The inclusion or exclusion of specific steps along the BPR life cycle tend to differ depending on where the project falls along this continuum. Based on this view, we define:

Business process reengineering as an organizational initiative to accomplish strategy-driven (re)design of business processes to achieve competitive breakthroughs in quality, responsiveness, cost, flexibility, and satisfaction. These initiatives may differ in scope from process improvement to radical new process design.[1]

This process management perspective assumes BPR employs a combination of management theory, system analysis, industrial engineering, operations research, quality management, communication analysis, and information systems techniques and tools. Although the degree of change may differ on a project by project basis, BPR typically lead to a (re)design of work flows, control processes, job definitions, reward structures, communication structure, organizational structure and boundaries, technological infrastructure, and, in some cases, organizational culture, philosophy and the nature of the business itself. For the purposes of this chapter, this definition of business process reengineering is adopted and the acronym BPR will be used synonymously with "reengineering."

The remainder of this chapter will introduces the Process Reengineering Life Cycle (PRLC). The PRLC methodology is comprised of stages and activities of a reengineering project. Consistent with a process management life cycle view, the PRLC ties BPR's one-time/radical process change objectives with other process steward-ship management activities including process improvement and TQM. During the course of this discussion, the PRLC methodology will be illustrated by a corporate reengineering case example.

The Process Reengineering Life Cycle

The Process Reengineering Life Cycle is based on the analysis and synthesis of stages, tasks, and techniques of many of the leading BPR methodologies in practice today. The compilation of these various methodological approaches was completed in a study using both primary and secondary research. Although this study did not uncover a standard BPR methodology, most approaches follow a sequence of steps that may be divided into three broad phases: conceptualization of a project, creation of a new process, and integration of that process into the organization. Using a life cycle as a metaphor for reengineering, these three phases may be further divided into the six stages of the Process Reengineering Life Cycle (PRLC). Figure 1 presents the PRLC methodology by stages and activities. Based on the priorities established in many of the methodologies studied, the PRLC attempts to capture the proce-dural, human, communication, technological, and socio-technical dimensions of a business process. In addition, the PRLC is based a contingent view that allows the adaptation of a comprehensive reengineering cycle to a firm's specific reengineering requirements. By tailoring the sequence of stages and activities, a BPR project's focus may range from business process improvement to radical design. By offering this non-proprietary, comprehensive and flexible approach, it is hoped that the PRLC provides a valuable reengineering framework. To help illustrate this proposed approach, an example based on the reengineering of a Quality Assurance process at a major computer and software manufacturer is provided in which they decided to study the existing process prior to redesign. Names in the example are altered for reasons of confidentiality. After each stage is discussed, the example will be presented in a boxed segment.

Envisioning Process Change

Due to the strategic nature of BPR and the extent of risk involved, some championship from the top is imperative. The envision stage emphasizes securing management commitment and the discovery of reengineering opportunities by matching corporate strategy with emerging IT levers. This stage requires the selection of

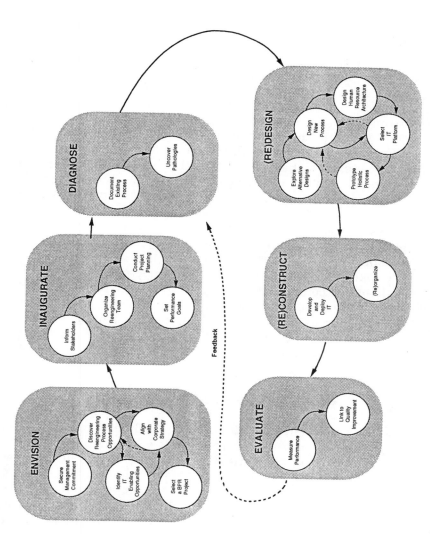

Figure 1. Process Reengineering Life Cycle

a business process to be reengineered and the definition of the project scope.

Securing Management Commitment

The first critical step of the PRLC is to persuade top management that a BPR project is strategically important. Ultimately, it is the corporate leaders who provide the legitimacy needed to initiate BPR and to ensure that recommendations are implemented. To spearhead the effort, a "reengineering champion" typically emerges or is identified (Guha, Kettinger & Teng, 1992). The champion should be a high-ranking manager with significant authority and influence to mobilize resources and stimulate enthusiasm for BPR. An external BPR consultant may also be employed to act as a catalyst and to provide insight gained from past successful BPR efforts. In either case, the role of these individuals must be to sell major reengineering opportunities. Such opportunity targets include cost cutting, decreased cycle time, or improved customer satisfaction.

The individuals responsible for introducing BPR often presents, in an introductory fashion, the potential benefits and costs to senior management. Topics to be discussed during this executive orientation may include: introduction to BPR and its techniques; a review of past reengineering successes and failures in other firms; a discussion of the company's business process problems; how BPR would enhance the company's strategic objectives; organizational implications; and, a consideration of a BPR plan-of-action. Based on a preliminary decision to move ahead, members of senior management, along with consultants (if used), form a high level reengineering task force responsible for conducting all the activities and tasks in the ENVISION and INAUGURATE stages until a project team is formally assigned. The task force then monitors the progress of the team and ensures the successful accomplishment of the BPR project.

Discovering Process Opportunities

As a prerequisite to identifying candidate processes for reengineering, the top management task force should conduct a high-level evaluation of existing business conditions and performance in the context of corporate strategy. Using such techniques as Competitive Analysis, Value Chain Analysis (Porter & Millar, 1985), and Critical Success Factors (CSF) (Rockart, 1979), a clear assessment of corporate goals, objectives and Key Performance Indicators (KPIs) should be outlined. Next, the major corporate processes that support these business objectives and goals should be identified. These may be product, service, or managerial processes, and in most cases are cross-functional in nature. The completed list of business processes will later be prioritized and one of them selected for the initial reengineering project.

Certain planning tools such as Information Systems Planning (ISP) (Martin, 1990), Business Systems Planning (BSP) (IBM, 1975), CSFs and Core Process Analysis (Kaplan & Murdock, 1991; Ostroff & Smith, 1992) may be used in the identification of business processes. Two approaches currently used for defining processes are the "comprehensive" and "targeted" methods (Davenport & Short, 1990). The targeted method defines those processes known to be most vital to the organization, as determined by discussions among top management or managerial interviews. The advantage of a targeted approach may be fast payoff and timeliness of project completion. The comprehensive approach, on the other hand, attempts to identify all the processes within an organization and then prioritize them. This comprehensive approach can be labor intensive and time consuming, however, it can offer a well thought out rationale for BPR in terms of project prioritization that is consistent with corporate strategic goals.

Davenport and Short (1990) categorize process dimensions as entities, objects and activities, each with unique types. Within this scheme there are three levels of processes dealing with entities. First, inter-organizational processes are the means by which companies along the same value chain interact. Second, inter-functional processes cross functional boundaries within one organization. Third, inter-personal processes involve people within one functional group. The objects with which a business process deals may be physical, informational, or contain elements of both. Activities involved in a process can be classified as operational or managerial, and such demarcation can simplify the redirection of responsibility and accountability across the entire process.

Methods for Information Architecture (IA) design can also be utilized for comprehensive identification of an organization's business processes (Teng, Kettinger, & Guha, 1992). For example, the first task in IA design calls for identifying business processes relative to the organization's products, services, and support resources as they pass through their life cycle: requirements, acquisition, stewardship, and disposition. By using an established IA, processes are identified in relation to data classes, data entities, functional departments, and application systems, etc. (Martin, 1990).

The Core Process Technique, as developed by Ostroff and Smith (1992) at McKinsey Co., captures cross-functional interdependencies and links improvement efforts to a shared set of strategic objectives. The Core Process Framework views a company as being made up of three to four core processes (e.g., new product development; order generation and fulfillment, integrated logistics). Vital firm processes consists of interrelated subprocesses and activities, decisions, information, and material flows, which together determine competitive success (Kettinger, et al., 1994). Core processes cut functional, geographical business units, and company boundaries and have outcome impacts affecting such things as throughput, total cost, and quality. Core process identification requires the firm's executive to rethink the value chains and re-evaluate the organizational structure. Several principles may assist in the "art" of core process definition: 1) a core process addresses strategic directions and key problems in competitiveness; 2) a core process should have identifiable owners and customers; 3) the definition of a core process should make as much sense to external customers or suppliers as to internal staff; and 4) dependencies across core processes should be discrete and minimized (Kaplan & Murdock, 1991).

Regardless of the technique used to identify processes, the top management task force should next complete a preliminary analysis of the "health" of each business process to identify processes that are candidates for process reengineering or process improvement. This preliminary effort need not be overly precise or detailed. Senior managers usually have considerable understanding of the various business processes and their performance level (Zmud, 1984). High-level criteria, both quantitative and qualitative, may be employed in this evaluation. Judgmental and subjective assessment may also be necessary, lest the task be delayed by time-consuming formal investigation. One technique that can assist in this assessment is the CSF/Process Matrix. Using this approach, CSFs are listed along the horizontal dimension and business processes are listed along the vertical dimension. Each entry in the matrix is marked as either E (Essential) or D (merely desirable). Since CSFs are based on corporate strategy, those processes in the matrix deemed "essential" for meeting corporate objectives may be viewed as potential candidates for BPR. The output of this step should be a list of candidate processes for consideration of BPR.

Identifying IT Enabling Opportunities

While reengineering can occur without computers or telecommunications, IT must be viewed as a major catalyst that has the potential for magnifying the effects of BPR (Huber, 1990; Keen, 1987; Venkatraman, 1991). Underlying most business reengineering efforts are technologies such as Local Area Networks (LANs), object-oriented systems, imaging, Electronic Data Interchange (EDI), Executive Information Systems (EIS), expert systems, client-server architecture, workgroup technologies and decision support systems. In particular, coordination technologies, groupware and workflow (Mora-Medina, Winograd, Flores, & Flores, 1992) are critical IT enablers that facilitate group cohesion, enterprise information sharing, and process workflow automation.

The BPR project should identify "IT enablers" that have the opportunity to improve internal efficiency, satisfy customers, and allow organizations to operate independent of geography. Senior IS staff, along with the task force members, should review the corporate IT plan to determine the extent to which the firm's overall Information System Architecture (ISA) (Zachman, 1987) meets identified strategic goals and objectives. The potential to use new IT should be examined for their compatibility with the firm's ISA, applicability for implementation, and enabling capabilities toward achieving performance breakthroughs. The IT/CSF Linkage Matrix is a technique that facilitates this analysis (Teng, Kettinger, & Guha, 1992). Based on information from the CSF/Process matrix, those business processes deemed essential to the organization's strategy are listed along a matrix's vertical axis and the list of IT (such as Client-Server, Imaging, Workflow Automation, etc.) are listed horizontally. In each cell of the Process/IT matrix, a letter "E" (essential) or "D" (desirable) is entered. In this way, IT most essential in supporting the CSF's of the various critical processes is determined. The output of this task is a list of IT that are enablers of candidate BPR processes.

Selecting a BPR Project

With an understanding of corporate strategic direction, candidate processes and IT enabling opportunities, the top level management task force should next make a high-level assessment of candidate processes and their relationships to products and services provided by the firm. This alignment analysis includes potential redesign impact on key performance measures, with major problems involved in each process identified and discussed. The results of the alignment assessment should indicate the level of ease/difficulty in reengineering each process. After this high-level analysis of each process is completed, the processes should be ranked with respect to conformance to corporate goals and objectives, availability of IT levers, and level of difficulty and risk in reengineering. With this prioritization the most critical process(es) may be selected. Upon determination of a process for reengineering, the definition and boundary of the process should be delineated to remove any ambiguity as to what constitutes the process. In addition, it is necessary to specify the level of effort required to conduct the selected reengineering project. This includes the evaluation of necessary resources and other high-level budgeting issues.

ARROW SYSTEMS INC.— ENVISION STAGE

Arrow Systems, a major software manufacturer with a global customer base and a goal to balance customer satisfaction with cost efficiency, was concerned with the delivery time and development costs of its new products. In particular, Mr. White, Senior V. P. of Marketing and Product Planning, was tired of customer complaints and especially about the time to get new software releases "out the door." He discussed the problem with Ms. Black, V. P. of Information Systems. Ms. Black, who had been reading about BPR, conveyed to Mr. White that reengineering may be an effective way to address these problems. Jointly they persuaded the CEO to call together a group of top managers to discuss BPR opportunities. It was decided to hire Mr. Bose, a highly regarded process redesign consultant, to conduct a BPR seminar that was attended by senior management representatives from departments including: Product Planning, Software Engineering, Quality Assurance, Customer Support, Technical Documentation, Information Systems, and Accounting. Based on positive feedback from the seminar participants, Mr. Bose was retained to further guide their BPR efforts.

Seminar members were invited back to begin to identify candidate processes for BPR. This group determined that a comprehensive study of all corporate processes should be undertaken. Mr. Bose advised the group that this could be a long and tedious undertaking, but it had the advantage of thoroughness. However, one month and eight meetings later, the group realized they had neither the time nor patience for a detailed examination of all the firm's processes. Mr. Bose, recognizing the group's ambivalence toward the level of work involved, recommended that a targeted process identification strategy be taken. After several brainstorming sessions, top management decided that given the risk involved, the Quality Assurance (QA) process offered the greatest possibility for achieving improved customer satisfaction, shorter cycle time, and cost-efficiency. This decision was partially supported by Ms. Black's discussion of opportunities for using client-server, groupware, and object-oriented technologies in a reengineered QA process.

Mr. Jones, the Vice President of Corporate QA, and a participant in these meetings, agreed that the quality assurance process was a good candidate for BPR. In particular, he stated that several QA related business units were "getting out of hand" and the time for product delivery was too long. He was also concerned that staffing levels and overhead costs were high and it appeared that there was duplication of effort. Upon Mr. Bose's recommendations, top management agreed upon the following overall project parameters:

Project Selected
- The Quality Assurance Process - the decision was made to study and pilot a process redesign project within one business unit (office and group/communication software). Based on the success of this pilot, the new process design might be implemented within other business units.

Alignment with Corporate Strategy
- The QA process should be reengineered to improve product delivery time, quality, and reduce cost.

Enabling IT Opportunities
- Client-server technology and distributed database.
- Workflow automation and forms processing technologies.

Inaugurating the Reengineering Project

The inaugurate stage ensures the careful launching of the reengineering project and encompasses the assignment of a BPR "working" team, the setting of performance goals, project planning, and stakeholder/employee communication.

Informing Stakeholders and Organizing the Reengineering Team

BPR represents significant organizational change and, as such, demands careful attention to both internal and external stakeholders interests. A message, typically from the CEO or president, addressing the need, scope, commitment, and leadership of the project should be communicated to stakeholders. Managing resistance to the BPR project typically involves a concerted in-house public relations campaign that may focus on the project's "challenges as opposed to threats," the "urgency or risk" of not proceeding, and clear definitions of project success and levels of involvement. This may be accomplished by stimulating themes of pride, innovation, achievement, and cooperation. Next, management should appoint a "process owner" responsible for the BPR project's conduct and accountable for its results. The first task of the process owner should be to assemble a BPR working team.

In developing a BPR team it is important to collect the right pool of personnel, including those knowledgeable in the functional areas of the selected process, but also who possess creative talents for process design. In determining the proper skill-requirement match, selection criteria may include past BPR and TQM expertise, industrial engineering, operation research and systems analysis skills and project and change management experience. At least one human resource specialist should be assigned to the team to assist in organizational structural changes. Three types of IS professionals should be included in a BPR team: staff application analysts, technology specialists, and system planners. One job of information technology specialist should be to educate fellow team members on the suitability of various IT platforms for alternative process designs (e.g., networking, client-server databases, imaging, multi-media). The system planner provides expertise concerning enterprise-wide system integration and compatibility. This individual should also possess some process modeling skills to assist in the selection of an appropriate process alternative. Working with the other IS team members, the application analyst should provide advice concerning system feasibility, development, and implementation issues.

While many companies assign one team to study a process from its first activity to its last node, an alternative approach is to use multiple teams of varying composition and specialization for different stages of BPR; however, common members typically include executives from the IS department and other major functional departments (finance, marketing, manufacturing, etc.) as well as key staff and line managers from the areas under study. While the appointment of a project leader may come from internal ranks, in the case of an initial BPR project, many companies enlist the help of consultants as either co-leaders or facilitators. Appointing a consultant who is experienced in aiding other companies in BPR can bring in an objective viewpoint and creativity.

Preparing the Project Schedule and Setting Performance Goals

Using such techniques as Gannt Charting, PERT or CPM, the team should complete a project schedule that outlines the project's resource requirements and budget, milestones, and deliverables. The next critical task involves the setting of high-level "stretch goals" and process attributes that will later provide the metric for judging project success. Based on the preliminary analysis of the process, which was performed in conjunction with process selection in the ENVISION stage, process performance targets may strive for very ambitious, but achievable, goals resulting from a newly designed process. These performance goals should be derived directly from market-based corporate objectives such as product quality, customer/supplier satisfaction, and delivery time. Many BPR experts such as CSC/Index Inc. suggest that lofty goals establish the organizational momentum necessary to affect "radical" change. Techniques that are used to assist in setting performance goals include: brainstorming, "Out-of-Box Thinking," Nominal Group and Delphi Techniques, "Visioning," and Affinity Diagramming (AT&T, 1991). Often these "stretch goals" are based on "world-class" standards or "best practice" as set by industry leaders and determined through formal benchmarking techniques. It is important to determine whether the performance measures of the existing process reflect the goals and missions of the firm.

To assist in process attribute setting, it may be prudent to conduct a Process Customer Requirement Analysis which involves the evaluation of requirements demanded by the final process customers to ensure that process objectives and attributes support determined customer requirements. Typical techniques used to undertake such analysis include: customer interviews, Focus Groups, Quality Function Deployment (QFD) (Akao, 1990), Transaction Analysis, Customer Analysis, and Customer-Supplier Protocol Modeling (Scherr, 1993).

ARROW SYSTEMS INC. — INAUGURATION STAGE

Mr. Jones, as the process owner, organized a BPR team with members knowledgeable in the QA procedures and policies. He tried to select those members who were highly creative and possessed strong analytic skills. Mr. Chang, a QA section manager, was chosen to be the senior project leader. Ms. Black, wanting to ensure that the first BPR project was a success, recommended five of her top IS employees for team membership. The team's initial assignment was to prepare a project plan and to formalize the performance goals that would be the basis of the BPR effort and subsequent evaluation.

BPR Team
- BPR Champion - Mr. White Senior V. P. Marketing and Product Planning
- Process Owner - Mr. Jones, V.P. QA
- BPR Consultant - Mr. Bose
- QA Staff and other functional area staff (e.g., Product Certification, Customer Support)
- BPR Project Leader - Mr. Chang, QA Section Manager
- IS Specialists: (1) System Planner, (1) Technology Specialist, (3) Application Analysts
- Human Resource Specialist

Performance Goals
- Reduce cycle time and defects by 40%.
- Reduce QA labor costs by 25%.
- Improve customer satisfaction of delivered products.
- Integrate processes with improved information access and report generation.

Diagnosing

In the case of "radical" or "Greenfield" reengineering (where the time, cost, or strategic objective does not warrant study of the existing process) the DIAGNOSE stage may be completed in a very cursory manner or completely skipped and the BPR team may move directly to the DESIGN stage. However, if the existing process is deemed worthy of detailed analysis, then the BPR project should document and critically analyze the pathologies of the existing process.

Documenting the Existing Process

Documenting the existing process, or "process capture" as it is often referred, involves the capture of activities, resources, controls, business rules and information flows. This includes the representation of relationships between activities, information and other relevant process characteristics. This task must develop high-level diagrams of the selected process and also decompose this into sub-processes. Several levels of decomposition may be necessary. In documenting an existing process, the following guidelines should be considered:

- Depict the process from its starting node to its end node, which may include several functions, departments, internal and external customers and external linkages.
- Identify components of the process such as information systems, human, controls, physical, and other process resources.
- Document the performance of the existing process in terms of customer satisfaction, inventory turnover, cycle time, waiting queues, defect rates, activity times, transfer rates, priority rules, and other relevant measures.
- Decompose a large process into a set of sub-processes and assign BPR team members to the appropriate sub-processes based on their expertise.

The participants in a process should be interviewed to reveal the flow of information and linkages. The added value may be determined by the nature of the information being processed, how it is processed, and the resources used during processing. The time required for information capture, processing, transport, and waiting should be recorded to indicate costs and to act as a benchmark against which improved processes will be measured. Many documentation techniques and tools may be used to support process capture including: Data Flow Diagramming (DFD), Block Diagramming, Process Flowcharting, and Process Data Flow Diagramming (PDF), and commercially available work flow design tools. IDEF (ICAM Definition), a process definition and design methodology developed by the U. S. Air Force in support of its Integrated Computer and Manufacturing (ICAM) program (Mayer, Keen, & Menzel, 1992) has exerted considerable influence on process reengineering practice and is increasingly popular as a structured technique for process capture. The IDEF 0 version is designed to capture process through a structured method using notations for inputs, outputs, controls and resources.[2] IDEF software that will facilitate the collaboration of BPR and IS analysts is now commercially available.[3]

In addition to process and data flows, other dimensions of a process may be captured. To develop a detailed measurement of the current process cost in both manpower and monetary terms, Activity Based Costing (ABC) is often used. To document the current process relative to jobs and IT, Job Analysis and Critical Incident Technique is frequently employed. And, to capture such dimensions as the nature, frequency and purpose of formal and informal communication patterns associated with the processes, such techniques as Information Control Network Modeling (ICN) (Cook, 1979), Communication Media Analysis, and Speech Interaction Modeling (Mora-Medina, 1992), Customer-Supplier Modeling (Scherr, 1993) can be used. The information from these analyses provides a baseline and may greatly facilitate the use of socio-technical methods to enhance the likelihood of implementation success of the newly designed process in a real organizational setting.

Uncovering Pathologies

Process pathologies may be defined as work flow activities, business policies, unchallenged bureaucracies, missed communication, and non-value added roles that hinder and fragment the overall effectiveness of a business process. To uncover such pathologies, a critique of the newly documented existing process should be undertaken. The following guidelines are suggested:

• Identify undesirable sequential activities, bottlenecks and unnec-

---

ARROW SYSTEMS INC.—DIAGNOSTIC STAGE

Mr. Chang and the BPR team conducted several task group meetings with the QA staff to document the work flows of existing activities. The team determined that the six sub-processes of QA were: version control and code compile; system test; module change requests; product certification; deployment to customers; and maintenance (See Figure 2). A detailed report with process flowcharts was developed by the IS team members that depicted all activities from the start points to the end node. The relationships between sub-processes and the roles and responsibilities of each QA worker were documented by the QA BPR team members.

Based on process modeling, the existing process was graphically depicted including inputs, outputs, controls, resources, and performance measures. It was found that each sub-process had its own stand-alone systems and performance standards which were not based on any process-wide criteria. This resulted in each sub-process having excessive paper work and duplicate information, and the two most critical sub-processes had high levels of authorization. Using techniques such as the Fishbone Analysis, the team identified one major problem as the time delay during the software certification prior to customer product release. It was found that information was being re-entered manually to complete many standardized forms that were mandated by the headquarters' standards committee. In fact, 90% of the information used in the product certification sub-process was duplicate (i.e., being re-keyed). Many simple problems that could have been solved by sharing sub-process information at lower levels were escalated to higher levels of management, causing additional delays. Two major authorization bottlenecks that caused time delay were identified. For example, one software developer complained "it only takes a half an hour to compile my software fix, but managers are always in meetings and it takes me half a day to finally get their approvals."

Pathologies:
• Disjointed sub-processes.
• Lack of shared information to support autonomous decisions.
• Long and rigid authorizations to certify forms.
• Excessive dependence on sequential and manual activities resulting in delays.
• Unnecessary signatures and form authorizations.
• Too much time spent in relaying information rather than creating value-adding activities.
• Lack of direct customer feedback vs. quality check.

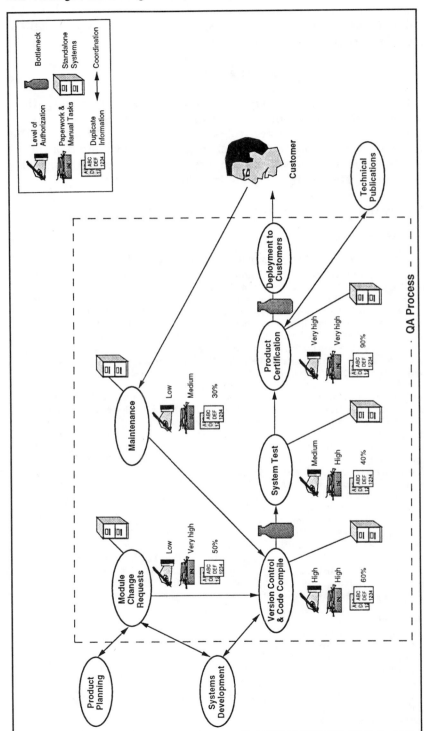

Figure 2. Existing QA Process

essary bureaucratic steps.
- Identify separate functional information systems and integrate into a single process-wide system.
- Identify all unnecessary paper work and question the need for forms, approvals, and reports.
- Identify formal and informal dysfunctional policies and rules which lead to non-value adding activities.

Each activity of the documented existing process should be related to performance measures set in the INAUGURATE stage. For example, if the goal is to reduce time and cost, it is beneficial to depict: the elapsed time, bottleneck delays, labor requirements, and incremental costs of each activity. Performance-based process flow charts may be used for comparison with the redesigned process in the next stage to allow the BPR team to select the optimal new process configuration. The performance of the existing process may also be compared to the requirements determined earlier for both internal and external customers, deviations may then analyzed and causes traced. Many commonly used TQM and industrial engineering techniques are particularly effective at determining the root causes of problems in the existing process, these include: Backward Chaining, Fishbone Analysis, Force Field Analysis, and Pareto Diagramming. Once identified, process pathologies may be rank ordered and prioritized in terms of criticality and their relative "contribution" to deviation from desired performance measures. This step would make it more likely that the new process ideas generated subsequently will indeed eliminate existing pathologies and meet performance goals.

(Re)designing

The (Re)design stage involves iterative design through the exploration of process alternatives that meet strategic objectives and integrate new human resource and IT architectures. This stage entails prototyping of alternatives and development of the selected IT platform. In pursuing such improvements, the BPR team should not be bound by existing concepts of organization or process designs. However, if the DIAGNOSE stage was undertaken, input from this stage should be used to eliminate pathologies identified. This (re)design becomes more than a system design and should strive to achieve a proper "fit" between people, work process, information management, and technology in a newly configured socio-technical system.

Exploring Alternative Designs

There is no universal recipe for designing an effective process. However, a key component of this task is to unbridle the creativity of the BPR team to explore alternatives that may at first seem "outrageous." This is typically accomplished through brainstorming sessions using such creativity techniques as word and thought variation, creativity barrier exploration, idea generation exercises and open-forum, non-critical discussion. These ideas should represent broad new approaches rather than detailed blueprints. Often referred to as "Visioning," this task requires asking the fundamental questions: "Where do we want this firm to be? and, How do we get there ?" Process visioning involves assessing the outlined strategy and external and internal inputs gathered, and then translating this information into specific process attributes with specific measurable objectives. This may be difficult given that strategy and attributes, as originally envisioned, rely more on estimation than exactness. Because of this difficulty, process visions should be based on what is necessary from a business standpoint, rather than what initially seems reasonable or accomplishable. Nominal group technique as well as Critical Analysis, Backward Chaining, and Affinity Diagramming may also be used to support this task.

To ensure that various process alternatives translate into customer requirements, a Customer Analysis Matrix may be used. This matrix lists critical customer needs and determines whether process activities and performance goals are in sync. The matrix is completed by comparing various internal and external customer requirements with alternative process designs, using a scale ranging from 1 to 5, with 5 being the optimum achievement of performance goals. Weightings may also be applied based on different priorities for different requirements. The inherently best design should be considered from a customer and business perspective before finally selecting a supporting technology. Based on the advice of the team's technology specialists and process modelers, the BPR team should carefully consider IT's enabling affect on various alternatives. For example, an imaging system for credit transactions and authorizations using expert systems and workflow automation may provide a better means of handling forms processing, routing, distribution, and approval. An alternative may be to consider a wide-area network application tied into the corporate SQL server to allow immediate approvals on-line by remote sales personnel. Each of these solutions entail different work flow activity, staffing, and cross-functional support. In this way the IS BPR team members should be continually communicating and educating fellow team members concerning the IT opportunities, and thus foster the iterative nature of the DESIGN stage.

Based on the new design ideas, the basic configuration of several alternative process designs may be generated and documented at a high-level using techniques like process flowcharting, block diagramming, DFD, PDF, IDEF-0, 1, 3, or workflow design. These alternative design "concepts" may be subject to high-level process prototyping using a variety of approaches including: dynamic process modeling, process simulation (e.g., Hierarchical Colored Petri-Nets), and investment analysis (Clemons, 1991). This high-level prototyping may also include feedback from customers and employees using such approaches as role-playing and paper process testing. As a result of these analyses, a selection of a specific process alternative should be made for subsequent detailed design.

Designing The New Process

Using similar documentation techniques as employed in the high-level design, the selected alternative may next be expanded into several levels of details. Depending on the technique used, various aspects of the process may be captured including inputs, outputs, job, resources, control procedures, timing, etc. The key to a successful design is to constantly question why a certain task is performed, who should be responsible for it, and which information technology will support the new process. Some fundamental elements of process design are summarized below:

- *Pattern breaking:* break age old principles and rules such as: "In this company, travel requests must be approved at the unit, departmental, and divisional levels."
- *Align with Performance Goals:* ensure that performance goals set earlier are truly aligned with process outcomes. Think of performance in terms of meeting customer requirements and not just short-term profits.
- *Job Assignment:* Design a person's job around the goals and objectives of the process, not a single task.
- *Eliminate Hierarchies:* Replace bureaucratic hierarchies with self-organized teams working in parallel.
- *Eliminate Identified Pathologies:* Question activities and roles that simply relay information, as these can be handled with information technology.
- *Improve Productivity:* Move focus from work fragmentation and task specialization towards task compression and integration.
- *Consider IT:* Consider the appropriate IT configuration that will support and enable the redesigned process.

One major focus in design is on leveraging time. Vast amounts of time can be saved by eliminating multiple approval levels and non-critical control checks, by integrating data processing into the work that produces the information, by eliminating wait buffers, and by integrating multiple tasks. An important redesign possibility involves the substitution of sequential activities for simultaneous ones. This will reduce the waiting time involved in processes and can be achieved by applying on-line databases and information networks across the process. This will allow information access to nodes without delay or waiting time. Separate tasks within processes should be integrated as much as possible into one job description to keep important information from being lost. Appropriate information, including immediate feedback on performance, should be provided to the line workers to ensure that problems are resolved immediately. The performance of the detailed design may be further simulated using many of techniques previously mentioned to determine its strengths and weaknesses. This simulation not only can facilitate the tuning of the overall performance such as cycle time, but can pinpoint bottlenecks that should be removed to smooth and balance the workflow.

Designing Human Resource Architecture

BPR may cause significant change in organizational structure. By reducing the "we versus they" mentality, a by-product of traditional functional boundaries, confrontations that consume time and money can be bypassed. Minimizing interdependencies between sub-units can be accomplished by increasing the alignment of objectives, tasks, and people within a single sub-unit. Where possible, a well designed human resource architecture should support a free exchange of information and a refocusing of decision-making and actions at the individual and work-group levels. The (RE)DESIGN stage should include a human resource component that incorporates the following:

- Redefinition of job titles and positions affected by changes in cross-functional processes.
- Team-based management techniques: self motivated teams assigned to specific business processes based on unique skills.
- Continual organizational learning assisted by on-the-job training.
- Performance evaluation based on team productivity, measured by group effectiveness.
- Incentives and reward structures based on group performance and an individual's team contribution.
- Modification of management structures that require managers to be equals as well as team leaders.
- Continuous BPR project progress updates to all employees.

Empowering workers means placing decision points where work is performed; in essence, allowing individual workers to control the process. This basic assumption contradicts traditional bureaucratic theory, namely, that people doing the work have neither the time nor the inclination to monitor and control their own work performance. Building control and accountability into the work process is accomplished by making those responsible for producing information also accountable for its processing. Properly reorganizing the process and related organizational structure should allow empowered employees to use discretion in judgment and significantly increase the outlook that their work is a rewarding experience.

The BPR team may begin this task with several brainstorming sessions to identify new ideas for human resource architecture. The focus of these sessions is job assignments, organizational structures, layers of management and authorizations, extent of team-based structures, reward structures and metrics. One or more human resource architecture idea should be refined to constitute a specific team or work-group structural design using such approaches as job design (Alic, 1990; Smith, 1989) or socio-technical systems technique (Mohramm & Cummings, 1989; Pasmore, 1988; Taylor & Felten, 1993) and team-based management (Katezenback & Smith, 1993). Based on Job Design Analysis the new sub-unit team structure may call for some existing jobs to be eliminated and others altered in terms of job skill requirements and responsibilities. In some cases, completely new jobs may be established. The content and responsibilities of all jobs should be documented in detail relative to the new process. This task also includes the development of new performance and satisfaction metrics that capture the qualitative and quantitative measures of individuals and teams consistent with new process performance goals.

Next, using the detailed process design and the new sub-unit human resource structure, associated communication structures should be designed to support and enhance the process effectiveness and human resource requirements such as team and individual satisfaction. This structure includes the identification of communication channels, classification of role-based communication, and message routing rules and protocol. Finally, a comprehensive training and education plan must be designed to allow employees to develop skills and knowledge required in their new job assignments. This should reflect the level of skill and knowledge necessary to perform effectively on an individual basis, as well as in collaboration with fellow team members.

Selecting an IT Platform

Several factors influence the selection of an IT platform to support the newly designed process. Often, the IT base requires support of communication between corporate systems and decentralized systems; and ties suppliers, vendors, and customers using wide-area networks. The need for greater flexibility and economy may call for down-sizing mainframe-based systems to LAN-based open systems using object-oriented technology. The need for information sharing may determine the extent of corporate vs. process database design requirements. In light of these concerns, the selected IT platform should be related to the enterprise-wide ISA architecture. A feasibility analysis by the IS professionals, along with other members of the BPR team, may be generated in terms of migration plans, interoperability, cost, availability of technology, and systems development efforts. The best IT alternative that supports the (re)designed process should be selected for implementation.

The IT platform selected should outline platform decisions such as choice of hardware, operating systems (e.g., OS/2, UNIX, MVS, DOS/Windows), and data architecture at all levels of systems implementation. Such selection must also detail the appropriate software systems to be implemented at every level, including the development of an Executive Information Systems (EIS) and/or Decision Support Systems (DSS) at the executive level and integrated workgroup applications for transaction processing. A conscious decision may also be made in the choice of the IT deployment of third-party software, in-house software development kits (SDKs) to support application development, software reengineering plans, documentation, and training plans.

Prototyping the Holistic Process

The "Holistic" process prototype may be undertaken at this step to depict the new process in an intuitive manner and to provide top management with a certain level of detail of the process characteristics, process flow, job assignments, IT infrastructure and system requirements. This is similar to the idea of prototyping in the traditional information systems sense, where the system behavior can be "tried out" to solicit users' feedback. Here, the entire process is to be "rehearsed" (possibly with a selected group of real customers) using such techniques as role playing, paper process tests, and workflow designs to identify further opportunities for refinements. Since IS professionals are quite familiar with prototyping because it is widely used in traditional systems development, they are well qualified to facilitate these prototyping tasks. Prototypes should be reviewed and evaluated by the BPR team and should provide management with a vehicle to make judgments toward a final process design. If the decision is to move ahead, the determination of the best phasing strategy should be made (e.g., Piloting, Phased, or "Burning Bridge") including phasing for human resource reorga-

ARROW SYSTEMS INC. — (RE)DESIGN STAGE

Mr. Chang called the BPR team together. Across the conference table, they placed the process flow charts, process models, and the listing of process pathologies. Mr. Bose challenged the team to "rethink the process from scratch, not just making minor modifications to the existing process, but achieving 'stretch' goals." The BPR team brainstormed on several alternative redesigns. Both the requirements of internal customers (between sub-processes) and external customers were evaluated for each process design. One of the options considered was developing self-managed QA product groups, with each responsible for a specific product from start to finish. Ms. Black and the technology specialist recommended using groupware to provide better information sharing and to automate manual activities. A second alternative would use interdependent groups and integrate sub-processes into a more integrated QA process. This approach would allow the elimination of several authorization levels and the reduction of clerical staff performing manual activities.

Based on discussion, the second alternative appeared to be the best solution because it would lead to the design of a tightly coupled process. The focus of this alternative was improved customer satisfaction and efficiency. Based on a recommendation from Mr. Bose, the BPR team used simulation techniques to analyze the two alternative process designs. Simulation seemed to confirm the team's previous analysis, demonstrating that the second alternative would lead to accelerated product delivery, reduced internal cycle time, fewer defects, and cost reduction.

A high-level diagram of the redesigned process can be seen in Figure 3. The external customers would be tied in with the Maintenance and Change Request sub-process by developing an on-line bulletin board system (BBS) controlled at headquarters. Thus, Maintenance and Change Request group team members would not only perform maintenance and new feature recommendations, but would also interact with customers for sales and customer service. Using a client-server architecture with an on-line database, this design would improve information sharing and increase simultaneous activities within each sub-process. This design allowed several sub-processes to be integrated. For example, the Version Control and Code Compile and Systems Test sub-processes would be consolidated into one sub-process and empowered group members would be responsible for authorizing tasks ranging from compiling modules to testing systems. This unified QA process design would allow information to be captured at the point of entry into the process. Forms processing would be totally on-line and distributed using workflow automation.

A prototype of the client-server based workflow system was tested using three clients linked to the workflow and database server. Mr. Bose and Mr. Chang interviewed the users to generate rules and graphic interfaces and also the routing and distribution of forms needed in the network. A demonstration of the prototype was given initially to Mr. Jones, Ms. Black, and other top management and then to the QA staff. Management was pleased with performance improvement figures and approved the new process design. Mr. Jones realized that in addition to technical skills, personal traits such as creativity, flexibility, and the capacity to make decisions were of paramount importance for selecting employees of the new integrated QA process. Based on these traits, Mr. Jones selected QA staff members for the new sub-processes (Code Compile & System Test, Maintenance & Change Request, and Certification).

Alternative Designs
- Alternative 1: Independent product-based sub-processes using self-managed teams.
- Alternative 2: Integrated Process using interdependent sub-processes and cross-functional groups.

New Process Design (Alternative 2 Chosen):
- Single process with interacting groups conducting simultaneous activities, integrates several sub-processes and uses cross-functional groups to handle the sub-processes.
- Eliminates manual forms entry and unnecessary approvals.

Human Resource Architecture
- Flattening of organization and reduced numbers of authorization levels.
- Less focus on task specialization and more on overall process objective of customer satisfaction.

IT Platform
- Use an on-line database in a client-server architecture to allow information sharing and eliminate data redundancy.
- Use workflow automation and forms generation software to route, distribute, and fill forms electronically and update information to a central server database.
- Use 4 GL packages to automate certification forms and use information that is available in the server database to automatically generate all necessary certification forms.

---

nization, IS development and implementation, and process procedure/policy cut-over. Some forms of piloting may also be conducted to help determine the best overall conversion strategy.

(Re)constructing

In accordance to the human resource architecture specified and IT platform selected, the (RE)CONSTRUCT stage uses information system development and change management techniques to implement the new process. As with any major organizational change, a methical approach should be adopted which takes advantage of user training and user feedback. When problems arise, those involved must retain their commitment to the major ideas of the process redesign, while also being amenable to changes required to facilitate the installation.

Developing and Deploying IT

A major effort undertaken during the (RE)CONSTRUCT stage is the development and deployment of new information systems and

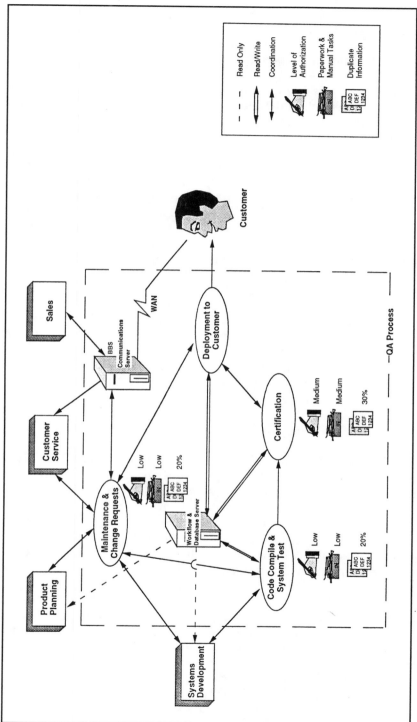

Figure 3. Redesigned QA Process: High Level Diagram

technology to support the new process. A primary task of the IS professional of the BPR team is to develop detailed systems analysis specifications in terms of information requirements, information/ data flows, logical and physical system design, database designs, systems configuration, distributed access, and security. This task may take place at a higher-level prior to final design selection, but must be completed in a detailed fashion before coding, testing, and other steps for actually implementing the information systems can be undertaken.

In the extreme case, the firm's existing systems and technology are replaced entirely with new hardware platforms and application programs. Migration to LAN-based platforms and groupware applications based on object oriented design and open systems may allow the firm to develop more easily integrated applications. Depending on the technology platform selected, various development options might be chosen including JAD/RAD, CASE tools or IDEF 1X, 4, 5, and 6. As opposed to developing new application systems from scratch, "software reengineering" may be employed to redesign and reuse existing system code for migration to improved hardware and software platforms. By reverse engineering object code to produce recyclable source code forward-engineering techniques, such as CASE tools, may be used to add functionality to current systems. The IS staff assigned to the BPR Team should oversee systems integration, testing and walk-through procedures. Next, shared databases and client interfaces are typically implemented, and coordination with existing systems operation is tested.

Reorganizing Human Resources

The Human Resource architecture outlined in the (RE)DESIGN stage must be thoughtfully executed with careful attention to minimize animosity and disruption to employee morale. This step focuses on a smooth transition to a new organizational design that incorporates improvements such as sub-unit reorganization, staff reduction, team and employee selection, job rotation, empowerment of remaining employees through training and educational programs, and improvement in the quality of work life. Based on the new process design, various job roles and descriptions may have been altered, eliminated or redefined. New organizational structures and detailed job assignments must be conveyed to the affected employees outlining their new responsibilities and performance expectations.

Training personnel in a newly installed process-based environment is critical. Awareness, enthusiasm, and expectations must be properly infused. A plan for developing knowledge and skills for the employees should be prepared and be directed at retraining employees to think in terms of process and customers. In addition to specific job and systems training, education may also be given in terms of the new organizational structure and cultural change philosophy. Incentives and reward structures must be redesigned based on group performance. In addition, individual reward structures need to be redefined based on the individual's contribution to the group. The dramatic changes during this step may cause anxiety that must be addressed by continual communication between top management, the BPR team and employees.

ARROW SYSTEMS INC.—(RE)CONSTRUCTION STAGE

The news of the approved process redesign and the impending reorganization spread quickly through the corporate "grapevine." Mr. Jones, anticipating staff's apprehension as well as their excitement, felt it was necessary to quell their fears and channel their energies into positive momentum. He called the 42 members of the QA department together (consisting of 30 system professionals and 12 clerical staff workers) and candidly explained the objectives, benefits, and impacts of the new process design on each of his staff members. Mr. Jones reassured those 10 employees (8 clerical and 2 professional) whose positions were to be eliminated that they would be given top priority in filling vacancies within the corporation. Due to the dramatic change that would occur with the redesign and the fact that customer satisfaction was at stake, the new process would be gradually phased-in.

Mr. Chang and Mr. Bose launched an extensive education program with the three new QA groups, covering their new roles and responsibilities. To support this effort, the human resource department developed a customized team building workshop that focused on orienting employees in "being their own boss" and "kicking old habits." This was done in the hope that employees would act more autonomously and reorient themselves toward accomplishing the common process objectives. In addition, the human resource department worked closely with Mr. Jones to design a group-based appraisal system that would reward employees based on individual, group, and process performance dimensions.

The IS application analysts assigned to the BPR team began to develop the graphical interfaces, database design, workflow applications, and the overall client-server architecture for the new QA process. This critical function was guided by a consultant, who had experience with workflow design. As IT was installed, users began to tinker with the graphical interface and tried to put in practice their recent training. Mr. Chang used the assistance of the IS Systems Integration Group (SIG) to install the Ethernet-based LAN and applications on servers and clients. SIG installed Windows 3.1™ platforms on each client and the UNIX™ server with the database and workflow applications. Each user had on his/her desktop a set of graphical icons which represented each system function of the redesigned process.

During the phase-in period, Mr. Jones met many times with his newly designed QA groups to keep them informed, to reinforce their enthusiasm, and to boost morale. During these meetings, Mr. Jones would allow his staff to discuss their resentments, problems, and concerns. Cross-group discussions were encouraged to facilitate coordination and collaboration. As groups were given total ownership of their sub-processes, they began to be held responsible for achieving performance goals and for taking corrective actions.

The phase-in period was not entirely smooth; however, after about a month, the operation of the new process began to stabilize. Figure 4. depicts the workflow of the redesigned QA process. The process begins when a developer submits code electronically to QA. A developer selects the Code Submission icons that bring up electronic forms. Upon forms completion, the workflow application updates the server database with code submission information (e.g., version number, code fixes, etc.) and routes the forms immediately to a QA staff person for verification and approval. Once all modules are submitted, and all versions are controlled and compiled successfully, the executable modules undergo system integration tests. Bugs or problems encountered during testing are entered into the problem tracking system on the workflow and database server. Developers, QA staff, and management constantly query this database to keep track of code fixes and outstanding problems that need to be removed prior to certification.

Once all system integration test criteria are met, certification forms are automatically generated. Mr. Jones, approves the certification forms and authorizes the software for customer release. The software is then duplicated for customer delivery. Simultaneously, the maintenance and change request staff monitors the bulletin board system for customer complaints, recommended new features, or maintenance work. Based on these comments, the Maintenance and Change Request group recommends new features and "patch" changes to the System Development group and the whole process starts anew. The marketing and sales group also posts new customer sales on the BBS, which stimulates morale. In addition, on-line surveys are periodically administered to customers over the BBS to ensure continuous feedback.

Reorganize
• Inform Employees.
• Phase-in.
• Education Programs and Workshops.
• Group-based Appraisal Systems.
• Group Meeting.

IT Deployed
• Application Development.
• Client/Server Architecture Implementation.
• Workflow and Database Installed.

Evaluating Process Performance

During the EVALUATION stage, the performance of the (re)designed process is measured and links to the firm's other process management activities such as process quality control are established.

Measuring Performance

After implementation, an ongoing task is monitoring and evaluating process performance. This may include the dynamic monitoring of qualitative and quantitative performance measures set in the INAUGURATE Stage. A rich spectrum of process measure should be

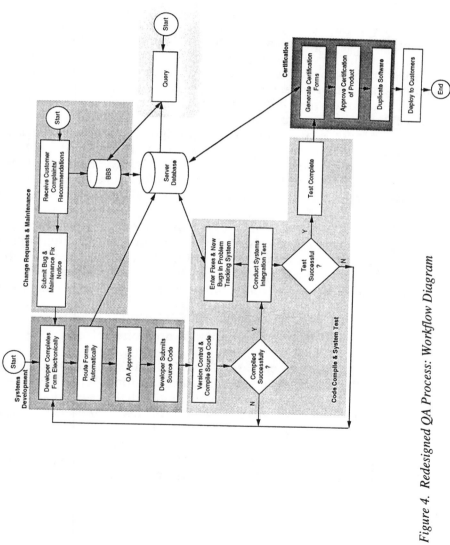

Figure 4. Redesigned QA Process: Workflow Diagram

implemented including:
- *Process Performance:* cycle time, cost, customer satisfaction, resources consumption, quality.
- *IT Performance:* downtime, system use, paper reduction.
- *Productivity Indices:* orders processed per hour, number of sales closed per week.

Such monitoring should not only be based on "hard" measures, but also "soft" measures such as morale and customer good will.

The communications flow between jobs, activities and sub-processes can also be measured for effectiveness and conformance to design specifications. A comparative analysis of customer requirements to process performance goals may be conducted to identify un-met expectations that demand further design improvement. Due to BPR's greater reliance on self-managed team structures and the use of generalists, a detailed audit of the redesigned process may be prudent to ensure process integrity. Individual and team satisfaction measures also should be analyzed. Results of these evaluation may be fed into the process simulation model for possible process improvement.

Continued evaluation of the (re)designed process is especially important in the early stages of deployment. An efficient feedback loop must exist between the EVALUATION stage and the DIAGNOSE stage as indicated in Figure 1. Such a loop provides an audit of the performance of the (re)designed process and identifies other needed modifications to adapt to change. It may be necessary to fine tune certain aspects of the new process and associated IT until acceptable performance gains are achieved. If thoughtfully and thoroughly completed, these evaluation and integration efforts may lay the foundation for the continuing success of the (re)designed process and may lead to further diffusion of the BPR to other areas of the business.

Linking to Quality Improvement

Process management and Total Quality Management (TQM) have been the subjects of major corporate attention. While BPR goals typically differ from process management activities aimed at incremental gains, the EVALUATION stage provides a fundamental link between the more radical/one time focus of BPR and the continuous incremental improvements of TQM (Kettinger and Lee, 1994). By using traditional TQM techniques on the newly designed process it may be anticipated that additional substantial process improvement will be made over time.

ARROW SYSTEMS INC.—EVALUATION STAGE

Evaluating the performance of the new process was given a high priority. The evaluation efforts centered on measuring overall cycle time, defect rates, customer satisfaction, and cost reduction. A baseline of cycle time was established by using the company's pre-reengineering estimation methods which were based on historical data. After six months, the average cycle time for the new process (new software development, order to delivery time, and maintenance) was calculated and compared with the old baseline figures. Mr. Jones found an average cycle time reduction of 27%. Defect rates were determined in terms of number of bugs, customer complaints, and patches. Again, using historical metrics, a 38% reduction in defects was found. Prior to BPR, no formal channels of collecting customer feedback existed. Using the BBS, the redesigned process collected periodic perceptual measures of service reliability, quality of customer interaction, and responsiveness. These measures showed a monthly upward trend. Labor productivity benefits were determined as a result of initial staff reductions and decreased cycle time. Weekly meetings in the QA department were conducted to evaluate group effectiveness, cross-functional training, and skill improvement. Group members gave priority rankings to issues of high concern. These issues were evaluated by the BPR team to determine whether further action on these issues was needed. In general, Mr. Jones saw visible improvements in staff motivation and esprit-de-corps.

The results of the BPR pilot project received high accolades from top management. The QA staff's BPR success was documented in the corporate newsletter and was circulated to serve as a paradigm for conducting further BPR within other business units of the firm. Shortly, thereafter a comprehensive corporate-wide study began to identify other candidate processes.

Measure Performance
- Reduced QA labor costs by 18%.
- Reduced cycle time by 27%.
- Reduced defects by 38%.
- Improved customer satisfaction trend line.

Conclusion

Many organizations are now faced with the daunting task of selecting a BPR approach that meets their unique objectives. In choosing between BPR consultants and/or methodologies, it would be prudent to fully understand the specific stages and activities of alternatives approaches. For example, some methodologies may not adequately make a connection between the BPR project's goals and the firm's overall business strategy, while other methodologies may not incorporate organizational change techniques, while still others may not link the newly designed process to corporate process management programs.

We found that while BPR methodologies do vary based on philosophical and situational differences, there is enough common-ality among the practiced approaches to generally describe a prototypical BPR effort. On the basis of these observations, this chapter offers a life-cycle methodology for conducting BPR with the intent to assist general and technical mangers in their transition to their new roles as process managers and engineers. Practitioner may use the PRLC Framework as a starting point in understanding high-level similarities descriptive of BPR projects. The PRLC may be tailored to various forms of BPR implementation, ranging from traditional process improvement initiatives to radical new process design depending on a firm's process management posture. As has been demonstrated in this chapter, BPR is not necessarily a new phenomenon but draws heavily upon techniques developed for other problem-solving disciplines such as strategic planning, human resources, information systems, operations research and quality. Therefore, managerial and organizational skills developed previously may be readily applied to BPR. Future research should provide more detailed and refined methods, techniques and tools, as well as be directed at identifying appropriate performance benchmarks, human resources impacts, IT enablers, and critical success factors for BPR.

Endnotes

[1] The brackets in (re)design reflect the contingent nature of the methodology and when a project includes the study of the existing process we would term this redesign. If the BPR project bypasses the existing process and move directly to design then the (re) would be dropped. This same logic for use of brackets follows in the description of various other stages and activities of the PRLC.

[2] The IDEF family of process and information architectural modeling methods also includes the IDEF 1 convention which provides tools for identifying information resources in the enterprise, the logical relationships among information, and the rules governing its management. IDEF 1X can be used to design relational data bases, IDEF 2 allows dynamic simulation of function, information and resources of the enterprise, and IDEF 4 supports information integration in object-oriented data modeling. This architectural evolution has led to enterprise integration approaches as depicted in the IDEF 6 concept, that attempts to model the knowledge and rationale for process design.

[3] Examples of IDEF based BPR design tools include: Design/IDEFTM from Meta Software Corporation, 125 Cambridge Park Drive, Cambridge MA, 02140, U.S.A.; KBS™ from Knowledge Based System, Inc. 2726 Longmire, College Station, TX, 77845, U.S.A.; BDF™ from Texas Instrument, 6550 Chase Oaks Blvd., Plano TX, 75023, U.S.A.

References

Akao, Y. (1990) Quality Function Deployment: Integrating Customer Requirements Into Product Design. Cambridge: Productivity Press.

Alic, J.A. (1990) Who Designs Work? Organizing Production In an Age of High Technology. *Technology In Society*, 4, 301-317.

AT&T Quality Steering Committee (1991). *Reengineering Handbook,* Technical Publications: AT&T Bell Laboratories.

Clemons E. K. (1991) Investment in Information Technology. *Communication Of The Acm,* 34(1), 22-36.

Cook, C. L. (1979) Streamlining Office Procedures: An Analysis Using the Information Control Net Model. Working Paper: Xerox, Palo Alto, CA: Palo Alto Research Center.

Davenport, T. H. (1993) *Process Innovation: Reengineering Work Through Information Technology.* Boston: Harvard Business School Press.

Davenport, T. H. & Short, J. E. (1990, Summer) The New Industrial Engineering: Information Technology and Business Process Redesign. *Sloan Management Review,* 11-27.

Davidson, W. H. (1993) Beyond Re-Engineering: The Three Phases of Business Transformation. *IBM Systems Journal,* 32(1), 65-80.

Guha, S., Kettinger, W. J. & Teng, T. C. (1992). The IS Manager's Enabling Role in Business Process Reengineering," In *Information Management,* NY: Auerbach Publishers.

Hammer, M. (1990, July-August) Reengineering Works: Don't Automate, Obliterate. *Harvard Business Review* 68(4), 104-112.

Harrington, H. J. (1991) Business Process Improvement. New York: McGraw-Hill.

Huber, G. (1990) A Theory of the Effect of Advanced Information Technologies on Organizational Design, Intelligence, and Decision Making. *Academy of Management Review,* 15(1), 47-71.

IBM Corp. (1975) *Business Systems Planning: Information Systems Planning Guide,* Fourth Edition. White Plains, NY: IBM Corp.

Kaplan, R. B. & Murdock, L. (1991) Rethinking the Organization: Core Process Redesign. *The McKinsey Quarterly,* 2, 27-43.

Katezenback, J. R. & Smith, D. K. (1993) *The Wisdom of Teams.* Boston: Harvard Business School Press.

Keen, P. (1987) Telecommunications and Organizational Choice. *Communications Research,* 14(5), 588-606.

Kettinger, W. J., Grover, V., Guha, S. & Segars A.H. (1994). Strategic Information Systems Revisited: A Study of Sustainability and Performance. *MIS Quarterly,* 18(1), 31-58.

Kettinger, W. J. & Lee, C. (1994, September-October). Perceived Service Quality and User Satisfaction with the Information Services Function. *Decision Sciences.*

Martin, J. M. (1990) *Information Engineering,* Englewood Cliffs: Prentice-Hall.

Mayer, R. J., Keen, A., & Menzel, C. P. (1992, May) *Information Integration for Concurrent Engineering (IICE) IDEF 4 Object-Oriented Design Method Report.* Report No. Alt-1992-0056. Air Force Systems Command, USA.

Mohramn, S. A. & Cummings, T. S. (1989) *Self-Designing Organizations.* Reading: Addison-Wesley.

Mora-Medina, R., Winograd, T., Flores, R., & Flores, F. (1992, November) The Action Workflow Approach of Workflow Management Technology. In *Proceedings of The ACM 1992 Conference on Computer-Supported Cooperative Work,* Toronto, Canada.

Ostroff, F. & Smith, D. (1992) Redesigning the Organization. The

Horizontal Organization. *The Mckinsey Quarterly*, 1, 148-169.

Pasmore, W. A. (1988) *Designing Effective Organizations: The Sociotechnical Systems Perspective.* New York: John Wiley.

Porter, M. E. & Millar, V. E. (1985, July-August) How Information Gives You A Competitive Advantage. *Harvard Business Review*, 63(4), 149-160.

Rockart, J. F. (1979, March/April) Chief Executives Define Their Own Data Needs. *Harvard Business Review*, 57(2), 81-91.

Rummler, G. & Brache, A. (1990) *Improving Performance: How To Manage The White Space on The Organizational Chart.* San Francisco: Jossey-Bass.

Scherr, A. L. (1993) A New Approach to Business Processes. *IBM Systems Journal*, 32, 1, 80-99.

Smith, M. & Carayon-Sainfort, P. (1989) A Balanced Theory of Job Design. *International Journal Of Industrial Ergonomics*, 4(6), 67-79.

Taylor, J. C. & Felten, D. F. (1993) *Performance by Design: Sociotechnical Systems In North America.* Englewood Cliff: Prentice Hall.

Teng, J. T. C., Kettinger, W. J. & Guha, S. (1992) Information Architecture and Business Process Redesign: Establishing the Missing Links. In *Proceedings Of the Thirteenth International Conference On Information Systems*, Miami, FL, December 20-27.

Venkatraman, N. (1991) *IT-Induced Business Reconfiguration. In The Corporation Of The 1990's, Information Technology and Organizational Transformation,* Oxford: Oxford University Press.

Zachman, J. A. (1987) A Framework for Information Architecture. *IBM Systems Journal*, 26(3), 272-292.

Zmud, R. (1984, June) An Examination of 'Push-Pull' Theory Applied to Process Innovation in Knowledge Work. *Management Science*, 30(6), 727-738.

Chapter
10

A Framework and a Suite of Methods for Business Process Reengineering

Richard J. Mayer
Texas A&M University

Perakath C. Benjamin
Bruce E. Caraway
Michael K. Painter
Knowledge Based Systems, Inc.

As organizations seek to obtain strategic advantages by redesigning the way they do business, they are finding the process fraught with uncertainty. Put simply, change is difficult. In some instances, the prospect of change is so onerous that the only way to effect change is to liquidate the existing enterprise and start again. A consensus is emerging that successful organizations of the next millennium will be those that embrace *continuous change* as a business paradigm. Such organizations will be able both to adapt to changes in the marketplace and to lead the market in directions optimal to the organization's goals by continually adapting their products, processes, and internal structures to changes in the business environment.

The technique for Business Process Re-engineering (BPR) has evolved as a powerful and practical tool enabling rapid enterprise restructuring and change management. The deluge of published literature on BPR and related techniques, such as Continuous Process Improvement (CPI), evidence the popularity of the reengineering paradigm in the industry and research community (for example, Hammer and Champy (1993) and Morris and Brandon (1993)). Conspicuous in their absence, (though not surprisingly, given the novelty of the technique), however, are scientific methods and theories focused on BPR. The purpose of this paper is to describe a *framework and a suite of methods* for BPR, and the role of these methods in realizing the practical benefits of BPR. We foresee this framework establishing the conceptual foundations for a more comprehensive *BPR theory* that we are developing.

Business Process Re-engineering

The term *Business Process Re-engineering* has, over the past couple of years, gained increasing circulation. As a result, many find themselves faced with the prospect of having to learn, plan, implement, and successfully conduct a real Business Process Re-engineering (BPR) endeavor, whatever that might entail, within their own business organization. Amid all the fervor over BPR, there has been an understandable amount of effort exerted in defining exactly what BPR is as well as how to best accomplish it. Although many definitions have been proposed, the majority provide only vague, high-level philosophical approaches. Even the term "re-engineering" is something of a misnomer. It suggests that the business process was initially engineered at its inception (Morris and Brandon, 1993). We will now make our own attempt at clarifying the terminology relevant to BPR.

Hammer and Champy (1993) define [Business Process] Re-engineering as "the fundamental rethinking and radical redesign of business processes to achieve dramatic improvements in critical, contemporary measures of performance, such as cost, quality, service, and speed." *Continuous Process Improvement* (CPI) is the collection of activities that are systematically and continuously performed to bring about enhancements in enterprise performance. The main difference between BPR and CPI is in the extent of improvements targeted by these two methodologies. BPR targets radical change while CPI is focused on incremental change. A related methodology, *Total Quality Management* (TQM) is "a means of operating a business that seeks to maximize a firm's value through maximizing customer satisfaction at the lowest possible cost" (Spitzer, 1993). Therefore, TQM is the systematic application of methods and tools to accomplish CPI.

One of the predominant distinguishing characteristics of *engineering* that separates it from other professions is the creation and use of models. Whether those be physical models, mathematical models, computer models, or structural models; engineers build and analyze models to predict the performance of designs or to understand the behavior of devices. In the context of BPR then, we use the term "engineering" in the broad sense to mean the creation of a process system with predictable behavior using some methodology that employs models as a basic tool. Whether that new system embodies an incremental refinement of an existing process or a paradigm shift, the engineering element must provide the modeling support required. Incremental improvement employs models that enable quantitative analysis of a proposed change to an element of a process. Continuous improvement using such models can achieve the lowest cost, highest performance implementation of a process. Breakthrough change of a process (paradigm shifts) generally is preceded by establishing a shared understanding of the fundamental nature of the situation at hand. This can be accomplished by teams building models that capture knowledge and experiences from which such an understanding evolves.

For this paper, we define BPR as the use of scientific methods, models, and tools to bring about the radical restructuring of an enterprise that results in significant improvements in performance. The phrase "the use of scientific methods, models, and tools" reiterates the importance of using methods and tools when initiating a BPR effort. This is important, for there has been a surprising abundance of sophisticated software supporting BPR, but there has been a noticeable lack of standard, robust methods for successfully engaging in BPR.

In general, scientific methods and tools may include any of those available to assist in a BPR effort. For the purposes of this paper, we are specifically concerned with the use of the IDEF (Integration Definition) Methods, Systems Simulation, and Activity-Based Costing. The purpose of this paper is to present a framework for Business Process Re-engineering that is centered around the use of *methods, models, and tools* that can provide the necessary guidance to successfully implement a BPR effort.

A Framework for BPR

Frameworks

The term *framework* has been defined in several different ways. In general a framework can be defined as a basic structure, arrangement or system. In this sense, it refers to a structure that serves to hold the parts of something together. From an information system development viewpoint, a framework is "an organization of characterized situation types that are known to occur commonly during a system life cycle" (Mayer, et al. 1992). In essence, a framework is an organizing structure for a system. Frameworks provide for expressions of the characteristics of the conceptual parts of a system and the interrelationship between these parts. We define a *BPR Frame-work* as a characterization of BPR in terms of 1) a set of guiding principles for BPR, 2) the BPR process (a set of BPR activities and their inter-relationships), and 3) a set of methods and tools for BPR and the role of these methods and tools in supporting the BPR process.

We will now outline a framework for BPR. The focus of the paper will be on describing the role of the IDEF methods in supporting the BPR activities in the framework and will focus attention on the relationship between the BPR process and the BPR enabling methods.

It is important that a BPR framework be comprehensible and that the underlying methods be easy to understand and apply to any given application scenario. This is especially true for those who are interested in making BPR an organic function of their enterprise. In such a case, the enterprise's own personnel would perform and manage the BPR effort themselves without having to rely on some outside source of expertise to guarantee success.

Proposed BPR Framework

The proposed BPR Framework is shown in Figure 1. The top half of the figure (enclosed within an ellipse) illustrates the fundamental structure of our BPR Framework. The BPR *process* is at the heart of the framework. The BPR process is a collection of activities that are performed in typical BPR projects, along with the relationships between these activities. The activities are performed opportunisti-

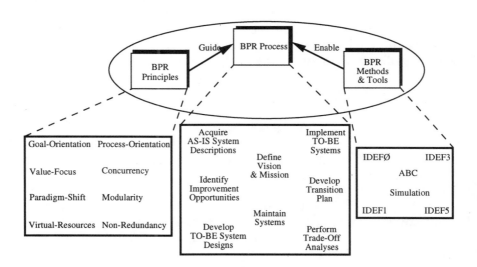

Figure 1: Preliminary Framework for BPR

cally; that is, there is no predefined temporal ordering that can be prescribed for the activities that are invoked as required by the BPR team members of the organization involved in the BPR effort. These activities and their interrelationships are described briefly in the section entitled "The BPR Process." The BPR *principles* provide the philosophical and conceptual underpinnings to structure and guide the BPR process. These guiding principles have been incorporated as part of our characterization of BPR in order to set the context for the BPR process description, and are briefly outlined in the section entitled "BPR Principles."

The focus of this paper, however, is on a set of BPR *Methods and Tools*. The BPR Methods and Tools facilitate the BPR process by providing support for the knowledge acquisition, design, and analysis activities of BPR. This paper describes a subset of the Air Force IDEF suite of methods (Painter, 1991b) and the role played by these methods in BPR projects. We also make reference to two other well known BPR-enabling techniques, Activity-Based Costing (ABC) (Kaplan, 1990) and Systems Simulation (Shannon, 1975).

BPR Principles

This section summarizes a few important principles of BPR. Some of these principles have been described in detail in (Hammer and Champy, 1993). This list is partial, and is presented here to both stimulate more work in the development of BPR theories and focus attention on the scientific aspects of BPR.

- **Institute-Leadership.** Among the principles of BPR, effective leadership is first on the list, and first in importance. Characteristics of an effective leader include competence, commitment, involvement, and genuine interest in people and their activities. A leader is found in front of his followers, *leading* the way. Leadership includes granting stewardship coupled with clear accountability. Good leaders encourage creativity, initiative, and trust.
- **Goal-Orientation.** The principle of goal-orientation states that the processes of an enterprise must be organized around goals (outcomes) and not tasks. This principle helps ensure that the activities of an organization are structured in a manner that emphasizes the accomplishment of business goals.
- **Responsiveness to customer needs.** BPR activities are ultimately devoted to increasing customer (the acquiring agent) and user (the actual operator of an end product) satisfaction. This devotion necessitates responsiveness to customer needs and priorities. Such responsiveness includes dedication to satisfying needs that are explicitly stated as well as those that are merely expected.
- **Process-Orientation.** The principle of process-orientation states that the users of process output must perform the process. A

secondary process orientation principle is to create and empower process owners, and make them responsible for process outputs. Process-orientation leads to greater accountability for process performance.

- **Value-Focus.** The value-focus principle states that non-value added activities must be identified and targeted for elimination. This principle ensures that business activities are focused on keeping customers satisfied, because "value" is defined in terms of perceived benefits to the customer. Techniques such as ABC and Simulation facilitate the realization of the value-focus principle.
- **Virtual-Resource.** The virtual-resource principle states that geographically distributed resources and agents must be treated as if they were centralized. This principle ensures the best utilization of organization assets, promotes sharing of enterprise knowledge, and minimizes chances of local performance optimization (thereby ensuring global optimization).
- **Concurrency.** The principle of concurrency states that activities must be performed concurrently to the greatest extent possible within the budget constraints of an organization. This principle is motivated in part by the success of the science and by the practice of Concurrent Engineering over the past decade.
- **Non-Redundancy.** The principle of non-redundancy (with reference to information capture) states that information must be captured only once, and at the source. This principle will enhance the cost-effectiveness of the information systems that support the business process.
- **Modularity.** The modularity principle states that the decision making agents must be placed (to the extent practical) where the work is performed. A direct implication of this principle is that control will be engineered into the business process.
- **Paradigm-Shift.** The paradigm-shift principle states that business engineers must not limit their thinking: that is, encourage "thinking out-of-the-box." Such "paradigm-shift" thinking leads to radical and fundamental changes that are the target of re-engineering initiatives.
- **Management Information and Knowledge Assets.** The basic principles represented here are that first, information and knowledge are resources (like manpower, materials, and machines) that can be leveraged to achieve competitive advantage, and second, that actual realization of the "Information Integrated Agile Enterprise" vision can only be accomplished by taking full advantage of those resources.

The BPR Process

This section provides a brief description of the BPR process. BPR is intrinsically complex and requires the concerted effort of personnel with many different kinds of skills and experience. Successful re-engineering requires a close-knit team that is committed to the accomplishment of the project objectives. However, the human and organizational aspects of the BPR process are beyond the scope of this paper. We focus on the task aspects of activities that we believe are important for the success of BPR projects, and the interrelationships between these activities. Given the complexity of BPR, it is important to note that BPR activities do not fit cleanly into a "cookbook" procedure. Rather, it is useful to conceptualize the BPR activities described in this section as "modes of thought" that humans use in an opportunistic and iterative fashion. Business re-engineering activities involve many different cognitive tasks such as conceptual design and analysis, detailed design and analysis, etc., as sketched in Figure 2. The description presented in this section is therefore a coarse-grained characterization of the BPR process that (hopefully) provides practitioners with insight into the nature of the underlying activities.

Define BPR Vision, Mission, and Goals

An essential and early step in a BPR project is to clearly understand the mission of the organization implementing and define a vision for the re-engineering effort that is consistent with this mission. An enterprise mission statement is a statement about an enterprise that summarizes the reasons for its very existence. For example, the mission statement of a Widget manufacturing company

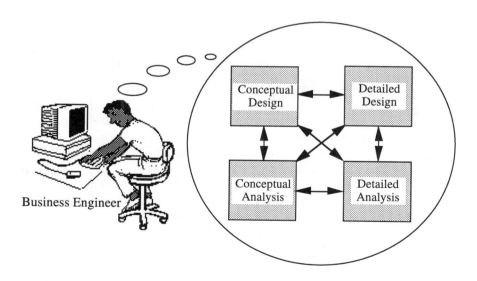

Figure 2. The Multi-Faceted Nature of BPR

may be "To be world-wide market leaders in the Widget business." It is important to be cognizant of the enterprise mission while developing the vision of a BPR effort. A statement of the vision of a BPR effort may be "To reduce the profit margin of the XYZ Company by 100% over the next two years." Vision definitions typically cover long periods in time and are at a coarse level of granularity (that is, they are not very detailed). BPR envisionment is usually done by top-management executives, and lead to the definition of BPR goals and objectives. The goal(s) describe the desired outcome(s) of a BPR project. The objectives are a more detailed description of the goals.

Other preliminary BPR activities include:

- Selecting a BPR project leader and assembling a BPR team,
- Establishing the scope and the level of detail of the BPR effort, and
- Developing a time and resource schedule for the BPR project.

Acquire AS-IS System Descriptions

An important initial activity for BPR projects is to acquire descriptions of the business systems.[1] Knowledge Acquisition (KA) has been the subject of much research over the past two decades, particularly in the Artificial Intelligence (AI) community. The research results have benefited industry significantly. The main AI application of KA techniques has been in the field of Expert Systems (Waterman, 1986). The use of KA for traditional information system design has been through information analysis methods such as the Nijssen Information Analysis Methodology (NIAM) (Nijssen, 1978), the Entity-Relationship (ER) method (Chen, 1976), the Object Modeling Technique (OMT) (Rumbaugh, et al., 1991), and the IDEF suite of methods (Painter, 1991). Each of these methods has been used with varying degrees of success in several application areas.

KA methods facilitate the acquisition and design of both *descriptions* and *models*. The differences between descriptions and models are important, and are summarized in the following. Descriptions reflect the state of the world as known or believed to be true by an agent. Models built from structured, accurate descriptions are used by decision makers to reason logically from observations to conclusions (e.g., regarding cause and effect relations in our organization). Unfortunately, what we know about the world is often incomplete and, hence, descriptions are often partial. To fill in the gaps, we employ models based upon idealizations. Idealizations are typically precise concepts that can be used to build models. Models built from these idealizations can be validated against a set of observations, but are not true or false. Models can be used in a valid context to predict characteristics that we cannot directly observe or easily measure. For example, while the concepts of points and lines from our grade-school geometry don't actually occur in the real world, we use them every day to compute a variety of useful data, from the amount of cloth in a shirt to the structural characteristics of a space craft. The ability to acquire and represent descriptions and idealizations is important for BPR. Descriptions provide factual evidence of what the organization does and how it performs its activities. Models are useful in predicting data (particularly economic and performance data) that otherwise would be expensive or even impossible to acquire. Together, descriptions and models provide the business engineer with the information needed to determine 1) what to change, 2) how to change, and 3) what will be the result of the change. The IDEFØ method (as described in the section entitled "Overview of the IDEFØ Function Modeling Method") was designed to support the development of models, and the IDEF3 and IDEF5 methods (as described in the sections entitled "Overview of the IDEF3 Process Description Capture Method" and "Overview of the IDEF5 Ontology Description Capture Method," respectively) were designed to facilitate the capture and analysis of descriptions.

An important requirement of KA methods is the ability to acquire and represent knowledge at multiple levels of abstraction and from multiple points of view. The ability to represent information taken from multiple perspectives is essential to manage complexity and facilitate communication in BPR projects. This is to 1) account for the difference in the cognitive skills of humans and 2) enhance the synergy between different views. Managing knowledge at multiple levels of detail is vital to managing complexity through information hiding.

Once a raw system description has been acquired, it needs to be refined to produce a more structured, knowledge-rich description, through a *validation* process. Validation is the process of ensuring that the description is an adequate representation of the real system with reference to the analysis goals. Description refinement involves two major activities: 1) consistency checking (semantic validation) and 2) syntactic validation. Consistency checking is the process of ensuring that the facts in the description are consistent with each other. This can be done incrementally during the knowledge acquisition process, or after an initial set of facts has been gathered. Syntactic validation ensures that the description is structured according to the syntax rules of the knowledge representation methods.

The results of applying the KA process are 1) functional models, 2) process descriptions (process maps), and 3) ontology descriptions (object-based descriptions). The role of the IDEF methods in KA is described in the section entitled "Capturing the AS-IS System Description."

Identify Improvement Opportunities

The identification of business process improvement opportunities is a vital, though complex activity in the BPR process.[1] In simple terms, identifying improvements is an activity (rather than an end state) directed toward finding ways to work smarter, not harder. Working smarter starts with examination of the basic business goals and customer needs. From a review of these items, a new business design can be conceived. In BPR, this design activity is often referred to as "out-of-the-box" thinking. However, approaching large organizations with out-of-the-box thinking and no methodology is dangerous (Jones, 1994). In the following sections, we present a methodology that involves several interrelated activities including 1) analysis of AS-IS processes, 2) evaluation of reference models and benchmarks, 3) cause and effect analysis, 4) constraint discovery and analysis, and 5) envisionment of TO-BE processes and the quantitative/qualitative evaluation of those designs. An understanding of the philosophy of this methodology can be acquired by considering the following excerpt from (Jones, 1994).

> In Jazz, there is a well established and accepted idea of "playing" outside. This means that an experienced Jazz musician will deviate from the original structure and the rest of the band will follow. The idea is to go outside enough to create tension and hence excitement. The problem here, however, is the same for out-of-the-box organizational thinkers. If you go too far outside and don't have a thorough understanding of the musical/organizational structure, you get chaos.

> We need to use innovation (dynamic quality) to make major changes to the company and its products. But, this needs to be tempered with continuous improvement of existing process, products, and structures (static quality) if a company wants to be successful in a competitive world market. To improve productivity and innovation, we must define and measure what we mean by improvement. We need to measure and report on productivity and innovation as often as we measure and report on profit and growth if we intend to increase the real wealth of the company.

> Many out-of-the-box and other "brilliant" ideas need to be verified before they are used to put companies out of business. The farther out-of-the-box, the more verification. This is not suggesting analysis to the point of paralysis. As is usual with thinking that is three-standard-deviations-from the mean (systems jargon for "out-of-the-box"), it can be true wisdom or utter

nonsense. A powerful systems view supported by business modeling (including cybernetic models) and simulation (with animation) with metrics for quality (Statistical Process Control and/or ISO 9000) and performance (Activity-Based Costing or Economic Value Added) is mandatory for reengineering any large organization.

AS-IS Process Analysis

Establish Analysis Goals

An important activity in the process analysis process is to identify and characterize system analysis goals. These analysis goals are often the same as, or are derivable from, the BPR goals and objectives (as described in the section entitled "Define BPR Vision, Mission, and Goals"). The BPR analysis goals are an important determinant of the analysis approach required. For example, the analysis goal "to estimate the approximate lead time for the procurement process" suggests a qualitative IDEFØ-based analysis approach (see the section entitled "The Role of IDEFØ in Activity Analysis"). On the other hand, the goal "to determine the effect of a 50% reduction in program budget on the system throughput" may require the use of a quantitative simulation-based analysis approach (see the section entitled "The Role of IDEF3 in Simulation-Based Process Analysis").

Classify Activities and Objects

This activity involves the selection of activities and objects in the model and classifying these based on the role they will play in the analysis. The nature of the classification performed, therefore, is influenced by the analysis goals. The analysis goals suggest the use of a particular analysis approach or technique(s). The selected analysis approach, in turn, determines the kinds of classification required to make the analysis meaningful. Note that the IDEFØ, IDEF3, and IDEF5 methods provide classification mechanisms that are useful for analysis. However, the techniques of Activity-Based Costing (ABC) (Kaplan, 1990) and Simulation Modeling (Shannon, 1975) suggest additional classification schemes that enrich the analysis process. To illustrate, for the purposes of ABC, it is useful to classify activities as follows (McDonald, 1993):

- Value-adding vs. Non Value-adding (often called "Value-added" and "Non Value-added" in the literature): activities that are perceived to generate valuable output(s) of value to the customer are value-adding and those that are not are non value-adding.

Value, according to (McDonald, 1993) is anything ". . . that directly increases the profitability, capability, or mission-readiness of the organization."

• Primary vs. Secondary: activities that directly support the primary goals (or mission) of a system. A secondary activity is an activity that supports a primary activity.

• Discretionary vs. Required: discretionary activities are those that may or may not be performed, at the discretion of the system personnel. Required activities are those that must be performed as required by external or internal policy or mandate.

Perform Quantitative Analysis

Quantitative analysis methods play an important role in business process analysis. Many of the quantitative analysis methods were developed as part of the field of study called Operations Research (OR). Quantitative OR techniques that are relevant for process analysis are Queuing Theory, Systems Simulation, Linear Programming, Dynamic Programming, and Network Techniques Phillips, et al., 1976). The cost accounting method, Activity-Based Costing (ABC) has gained popularity in recent years as an analysis tool for BPR (Kaplan, 1990). The main advantage of quantitative methods is that they facilitate the evaluation of performance in a quantitative way (with numbers). These methods have been successfully used for a number of applications over the past four decades. The main limitation of quantitative techniques, however, is that they often are constrained by restrictive assumptions.[2] The section entitled "The Role of IDEF3 in Simulation-Based Process Analysis" will show the utility of the IDEF3 method for performing simulation analysis.

Perform Causal Analysis

Causal Analysis is an important component of business system (and business process) analysis. The main goal of BPR causal analysis is to identify cause and effect chains that link aspects of the system (usually the "controllable" system factors) to the performance goals of the system. An important step in causal analysis is to identify causal associations between system factors.[3] These associations must be characterized in enough detail so that the effect of the factor change on the association can be accurately estimated. Influence diagrams (Richardson, 1981) and Ishikawa Diagrams (Gitlow, et al., 1989) have been shown to be useful helping identify qualitative causal relationships. An influence diagram showing the causal relationships between production rates and Work In Process (WIP) is shown in Figure 3. The '+' indicates direct proportionality

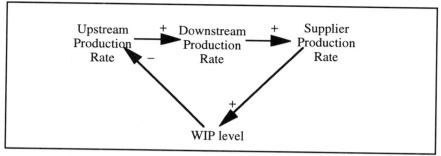

Figure 3. An Influence Diagram

and the '-' depicts inverse proportionality.

Discover and Analyze Constraints

The role of constraints in business analysis and re-engineering has gained much attention in recent years through the work of the physicist, Eliyahu Goldratt (Goldratt, 1985). Goldratt's Theory of Constraints (TOC) is an approach to discovering the constraints that limit the accomplishment of the organizations' goals. The TOC philosophy seeks continuous improvement by systematically breaking the identified constraints. Goldratt defines a constraint as anything that limits a system from achieving higher performance versus its goal. We define a constraint as a relationship that is maintained as true in a given context. Analysis of constraints is key to understanding relationships between the different components of a system and the whole of which they are a part. Constraints encapsulate the assumptions, policies, and procedures of an organization. From a BPR perspective, three kinds of constraints are important 1) constraints that improve an organization's throughput, 2) constraints that limit an organization's throughput, and 3) constraints that should be enforced to improve an organization's throughput (KBSI, 1994b). The knowledge structuring and analysis mechanisms provided by the IDEF methods facilitate the discovery and analysis of constraints.

Locate Reference Technologies and Models

A careful study of existing "best in class" processes, systems, and success stories is useful for the success of a BPR project. This may be done through a survey of industry, assessing published reference models (for example, by using the electronic World-Wide Web on the Internet) or reviewing published BPR "success stories." The organization performing the BPR project must then try to leverage the existing knowledge and technology to make the effort more cost-effective.

Envision TO-BE Processes

The capacity to envision solutions to a problem is a critical, though difficult aspect of any problem solving endeavor. In BPR, it is important to envision promising TO-BE processes as part of the re-engineering process. This envisionment of TO-BE processes is inductive and involves hypothesizing possible solutions to a given problem. Knowledge of state-of-the-art techniques and tools will facilitate this envisioning process. Ready access to reference technologies and models will also accelerate the identification of possible TO-BE process alternatives.

Develop TO-BE System Designs

System design is at the heart of BPR. Although it is often difficult to determine when analysis completes and when design begins (design and analysis are closely inter-locked in many practical situations), this section is focused on describing salient aspects of the system design activities. We will focus attention on the design of the processes that the system will support.

Currently, process design is often thought of more as an art than as a science. For this reason, the actual task of designing a TO-BE process can prove to be quite difficult. In actuality, it may be better to think of process design as an iterative process of refinement. Rather than being a set of clearly defined, sequential steps, the design process may be better represented by a set of successive, though less-precise stages that eventually lead to an ideal process design for a given scenario. The process engineer who undertakes the process design challenge does not follow a list of sequential design steps, but, rather, relies on a set of acquired process design skills that will be employed in any one of a variety of process design scenarios that might be encountered.

Initially, the process engineer has some set of desired outputs from which to design a process. It is these outputs, often realized in the form of either a product, system, or service, which give the process engineer a purpose. Along with this set of desired outputs, the process engineer will (hopefully) have some idea of the inputs that will be necessary in generating those outputs. Depending on the process to be designed, the inputs might be the raw materials used in a manufacturing process or the information used in a business process. At this point, the link between the inputs and the outputs is called a "process" and could be thought of as just a "black box" which takes in a given set of inputs and produces a set of desired outputs. It is this black box, though, that the process engineer must be willing to open. Upon opening the box, he or she must design the inner workings–the process which actually "makes the box work."

At this point, the process engineer must start with a generalized process that will "fit in the box." In other words, the engineer must provide a starting point at which to begin designing the process. This generalized process may be based on a process that exists in a similar scenario with outputs similar to those desired of the TO-BE process. If no reference process is known to exist, the process engineer must identify some experience or knowledge base from which the generalized process can be (organically) developed.

Once a generalized process has been identified, the next step involves decomposing it into a set of more specific activities or tasks that can be performed by assignable resources. As the tasks are identified an "extended process" will become apparent. That is, one task will take in a given set of inputs and will result in some set, intermediate outputs which will then, in turn, be used as a set of inputs for the next task until the desired set of outputs results.

In the following section, eight principles of process design have been compiled. These represent a set of basic tenets that one should consider when designing a process as in a TO-BE system design.

Principles of Process Design

The **first** principle of process design is that it is a design endeavor. That is, it is primarily inductive in nature. When faced with a design situation, the designer will generally start with a design that is already familiar and try to modify that design to address the new situation.

The **second** principle of process design is that it is not a process. Rather, it is a set of skills that are employed in an opportunistic fashion.

The **third** principle of process design is that it is object design; processes produce some output object(s) and consume or are triggered by some input object(s). One mode of thought for a process designer is the design of the input and output objects. The design of the structure of the input/output objects, their roles relative to a process (supply versus control for inputs, measurement versus product for outputs), and their frequency/rate of arrival are all considered as part of the design process. One of the key aspects of process design is determining which of the input/output objects specified in the requirements for the process are modifiable and which are fixed, which are controllable and which are uncontrollable, and which are independent and which are dependent. An experienced process designer is always looking for ways to design the input or output objects to both streamline the resulting process and also to optimize the upstream and downstream interfacing processes.

The **fourth** principle of process design is that it is decomposition and allocation; processes must be specified to a level of sub processes that can be allocated to specific resources available in the execution environment. One of the reasons for process re-design is that the resources available and their capabilities change over time. Thus, a process that was once acceptable because there was a highly capable resource available, becomes no longer acceptable due to the loss of that resource, the unavailability of a replacement, and vice versa. Process design involves decomposition of sub processes until a level is reached in which the sub processes can be allocated to an available resource.

The **fifth** principle of process design is that it is input/output contiguity; during the decomposition process, the input/output of each sub process must be specified and matched with the input available and the output required at the position of the sub process in the process flow. When there is not a match, additional processes may have to be added to make the interface or the sub process must be modified to perform the interface function itself. When neither occurs, another decomposition must be considered.

The **sixth** principle of process design is that it is failure management; the possible failure modes, those considered expected or reasonable, of the resulting system must be identified. For each possible failure modes (and for possible combinations of failure modes) the effects of failure must be predicted. Then, a design decision must be made to determine whether the sub processes will be added to detect and manage the effects of each possible failure mode.

The **seventh** principle of process design is that it is by-product (waste or scrap) management. During the execution of a process, products will be produced that are not useful as input to downstream processes or considered a part of the desired output of the overall process. These types of objects must be identified and sub processes put in place to collect and dispose of them properly.

The **eighth** principle of process design is that it is execution resource management. During the execution of a process, there are normally multiple activations of the process being attempted simultaneously. In normal situations there are limited resources available to perform the sub process instances. This naturally results in resource contention situations for which resource management sub processes must be added by the process designer.

Perform Trade-off Analysis

The purpose of trade-off analysis is to evaluate the relative merit of completing alternative process/system design alternatives. The system design will be carried forward up to a stage in which such analysis is possible. Often, trade-off analysis and system design are done incrementally, and iteratively; that is, trade-off analyses is performed initially with a partial system design, the analysis results are used to refine the design, the analysis is invoked again, and so on. Depending on the goals of the BPR effort, the nature of the analysis may vary from *Qualitative* (rough-cut, order of magnitude) to *Quantitative*. Trade-off analyses often focus on measures of system performance and include cost/benefit analyses. Trade-off analysis is difficult in practice because of the existence of multiple, competing criteria. Multiple-criteria decision support techniques may be applied to guide the analysis process. The IDEF methods can be used effectively in conjunction with analysis techniques such as ABC and simulation to perform trade-off analyses.

Of particular importance is the tradeoff between process streamlining and flexibility. Paradoxically, these two qualities are competing design goals. Greater efficiency, accomplished primarily through process streamlining, often results in less flexibility. Likewise, enhancement of flexibility levies constraints on attainable efficiency. The appropriate balance between these competing design goals is sought initially through accounting for known downstream concerns. For example, where demand for parallel products (e.g., automobile offerings with either standard or automatic transmissions) can be anticipated, manufacturing process flexibility becomes more important than it would be otherwise (Cook, 1990).

Develop Transition Plan

After the TO-BE process/system design has been determined, the next step is to develop a plan to transition to the re-designed process from the AS-IS process. the overall transition strategy must align the organizational structure, information systems, and business policies and procedures with the re-engineered processes/ systems. The transition plan often includes 1) a system integration strategy, 2) a technology strategy, and 3) an information system strategy. The IDEFØ and IDEF3 methods have been shown to be effective tools for representing and communicating the transition plans.

Implement TO-BE Systems

The purpose of this activity is to test, implement, and document the TO-BE process/system. This will typically start with a test and tryout phase. The test results will be used to refine and harden the requirements of the TO-BE process/system. The test procedures must, in addition to evaluating nominal functionality, analyze boundary cases and failure modes. The final implementation is often done in an incremental/phased manner. It will often involve purchase of technology, hiring of workers, training (of new and existing workers), restructuring the organization, and re-allocation of resources.

Maintain Systems

This activity refers to the continuous maintenance of the system over extended periods of time. Because the requirements of a system change over time, it is important that a system respond appropriately to these changes. Mechanisms must be in place to incorporate incremental changes in the system descriptions over extended periods of time.

A Suite of Methods for BPR

Overview of Methods

The use of methods is critical to the success of the framework for Business Process Re-engineering. Informally, a method is a procedure for doing something (i.e., an attempt to capture the best practice or experience). Moreover, the method may have a representational notation to communicate this procedure more effectively. More formally, a method consists of three components, as illustrated in Figure 4: definition, discipline, and use. The definition contains the concepts, motivation, and theory supporting the method. The discipline includes the syntax of the method, a computer-interpretable format (e.g., ISyCL (Mayer, 1991)), and the procedure governing its use. Many methods have multiple syntaxes that have either evolved or are used for aspects that are different from their original use. Perhaps the most visible component of a method is the language associated with the discipline. Many system analysis and engineering methods use a graphical syntax to display collected data so that key information is unambiguously displayed. The third component,

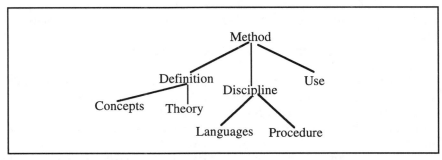

Figure 4. Components of a Method

the use, refers to the context-specific application of the method.

Formal methods provide the structure and guidelines for successfully defining the boundaries of reliable application. The graphical languages of methods highlight key information so that it may be easily identified and extracted. In other words, methods provide the practitioner with tools useful in dissecting the world into more manageable pieces while bringing the more important facts into focus (Painter, 1991a). As a result, the non-pertinent information is discarded while the useful pieces of information remain.

It is this capacity–assisting and motivating the intellectual activities of the human mind–that makes the use of methods so attractive. But, it is important to remember that methods neither make the decisions, create the insights, nor discover the problems. Just as shovels themselves do not dig holes but rather provide leverage for a human to dig, methods provide leverage for the human mind to more effectively accomplish a job.

As one might expect, multiple methods exist for various applications. Similarly, for the purposes of the BPR framework, several different methods are required to perform certain tasks in successfully employing the framework. Rather than attempting to analyze a given organization with a single super method, an attempt which would undoubtedly result in an overly complex and burdensome model, the use of the IDEF methods serves as a more useful, efficient, and effective means. A set of methods originally designed to be used in quick and efficient analysis, the IDEF methods represent a set of independent, self-standing methods that are still highly useful when employed in an integrated fashion; hence the meaning of their name, Integrated DEFinition (IDEF).

In summary, methods facilitate BPR by enhancing:

- the speed and accuracy with which you extract knowledge/ information from the members in the organization, and
- the effectiveness of presenting that information to other members for validation and consensus building.

Overview of the IDEFØ Function Modeling Method

Basic Concepts of IDEFØ

The IDEFØ Function Modeling method is designed to model the decisions, actions, and activities of an organization or system. IDEFØ was derived from a well-established graphical language known as the Structured Analysis and Design Technique (SADT). The Air Force commissioned SADT developers to develop a function modeling method for analyzing and communicating the functional perspective of a system. Effective IDEFØ models assist in organizing system analysis and promoting effective communication between the analyst and the customer. Furthermore, the IDEFØ modeling method establishes the scope of analysis either for a particular functional analysis or for future analyses from another system perspective. As a communication tool, IDEFØ enhances domain expert involvement and consensus decision-making through simplified graphical devices. As an analysis tool, IDEFØ assists the modeler in identifying the functions performed and what is needed to perform them. Thus, IDEFØ models are often created as one of the first tasks of a system development effort.

The IDEFØ model diagram displayed in Figure 5 is based on a simple syntax. Each activity is described by a verb based label placed in a box. Inputs are shown as arrows entering the left side of the activity box while the outputs are shown as exiting arrows on the right side of the box. Controls are displayed as arrows entering the top of the box and mechanisms are displayed as arrows entering from the bottom of the box. Inputs, Controls, Outputs, and Mechanisms (ICOMs) are all referred to as concepts.

An IDEFØ model diagram is then composed of several activity boxes and related concepts to capture the overall activity. IDEFØ not only captures the individual activities but also reveals the relationships between and among activities through the activities' related concepts. For example, the output of one activity may in turn become the input, control, or even a mechanism of another activity within the same model (Figure 6).

Modeling From an IDEFØ Perspective

IDEFØ includes both a procedure and a language for constructing a model of the decisions, actions, and activities in an organization. Applying the IDEFØ method results in an organized represen-

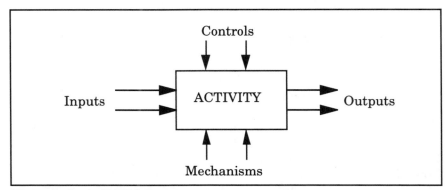

Figure 5. Basic IDEFØ Syntax

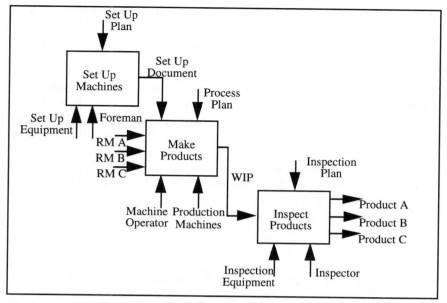

Figure 6. Basic Construction of an IDEFØ Model

tation in a non-temporal, non-departmentalized fashion of the activities and important relations between them. IDEFØ is designed to allow the user to tell the story of what an organization does; it does not support the specification of a recipe or process. Such detailed descriptions of the specific logic or the timing associated with the activities requires the IDEF3 Process Description Capture Method.

A strategy for organizing the development of IDEFØ models is the notion of *hierarchical decomposition* of activities. A *box* in an IDEFØ model, after all, represents the boundaries drawn around

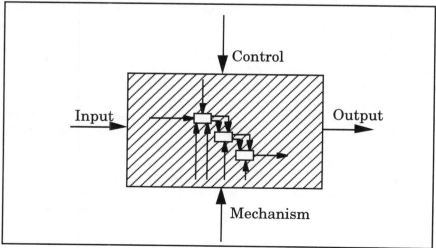

Figure 7. Looking Outside-In

some activity. Inside that box is the breakdown of that activity into smaller activities, which together comprise the box at the higher level. This hierarchical structure helps the practitioner keep the scope of the model within the boundaries represented by the decomposition of the activity. This organization strategy is also useful for hiding unnecessary complexity from view until a more in-depth understanding is required (Figure 7).

IDEFØ captures "what" the organization does and thus, more specifically, is very effective in identifying the core activities and secondary functions of the organization. The actual act of identifying what the organization does will often result in answering the more important question of "why" the organization does what it does. This represents the first step of many BPR efforts focused on identifying candidate organizational areas for BPR. An activity for which one cannot answer the question of "why do we perform this activity?" is a definite target for BPR.

Overview of the IDEF3 Process Description Capture Method

Basic Concepts of IDEF3

One of the most common communication mechanisms to describe a situation or process is a story told as an ordered sequence of events or activities. IDEF3 is a scenario-driven process flow modeling method created specifically for these types of descriptive activities. IDEF3 is based on the direct capture of descriptions, of the precedence and causality relations between situations and events, in a form that is natural to domain experts in an environment. The goal of IDEF3 is to provide a structured method for expressing the domain experts knowledge about how a particular system or organization works.

An IDEF3 Process Flow Description captures a network of relations between actions within the context of a specific scenario. The intent of this description is to show "how" things work in a particular organization in the context of a particular problem-solving (or recurring) situation. IDEF3 uses the "scenario" as the basic organizing structure for establishing the focus and boundary conditions for the process description. This feature is motivated by the tendency of humans to describe what they know in terms of an ordered sequence of observed activities experienced within the context of a given scenario or situation. The natural tendency toward organizing thoughts and expressions within the context of a process description has motivated widespread use of the scenario as an informal framework for proposing alternative "external views" of

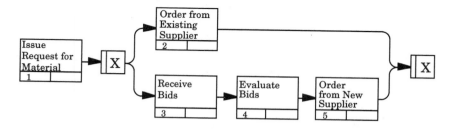

Figure 8. Example IDEF3 Process Flow Diagram

possible system designs, the roles of which will be to support the activities of the organization within the established context. Such development approaches have been referred to as "External Constraint-Driven Design" approaches, and have been repeatedly demonstrated in practice as an effective mechanism for the design of new systems. Figure 8 shows an IDEF3 Process Flow Diagram.

The basic syntactic unit of IDEF3 graphical descriptions within the context of a given scenario is the Unit of Behavior (UOB) represented by a box. The UOB may further be classified as a function, activity, action, act, process, operation, event, scenario, decision, or procedure, depending on its surrounding structure. Each UOB represents a specific view of the world in terms of a perceived state of affairs or state of change relative to the given scenario. Each UOB can have associated with it both "descriptions in terms of other UOBs," otherwise called decompositions, and a "description in terms of a set of participating objects and their relations," called elaborations (Figure 9).

UOBs are connected to one another via junctions and links (Figure 10). Junctions provide the semantic facilities for expressing synchronous and asynchronous behavior among a network of UOBs. Links are 1) temporal precedence, 2) object flow, or 3) relational. Relational links are provided to permit constraint capture not accommodated by the default semantics of the precedence and object flow links.

The IDEF3 Process Description Capture Method is used by system developers to capture domain-expert knowledge about the behavioral aspects of an existing or proposed system. Process knowledge that has been captured using IDEF3 is structured within the context of a scenario, making IDEF3 an intuitive knowledge acquisition device for describing a system. Unlike IDEF∅ models that adopt a single perspective of the system and explicitly remove all temporal logic to promote generality and simplification, IDEF3 serves to structure different user descriptions of the temporal precedence and causality relationships associated with enterprise

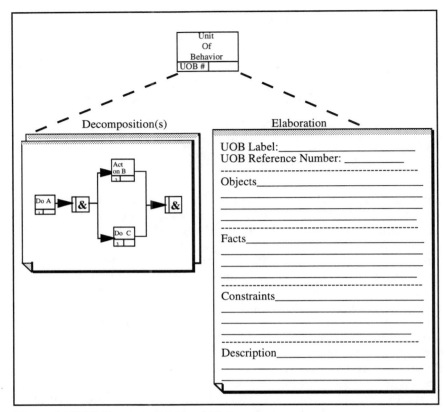

Figure 9. UOB Decomposition and Elaboration

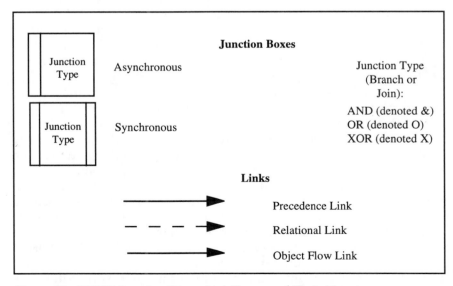

Figure 10. IDEF3 Junction Types, Link Types, and Their Meanings

processes. The resulting IDEF3 descriptions provide a structured knowledge base from which analysis and design models can be constructed.

Description Capture From an IDEF3 Perspective

Two modeling modes exist within IDEF3: process flow description and object state transition description. Process flow descriptions are intended to capture knowledge of how things work in an organization. The object state transition description summarizes the allowable transitions an object may undergo throughout a particular process. Both the Process Flow Description and Object State Transition Description contain units of information that make up the description. These models form the basic units of an IDEF3 description.

An IDEF3 Process Flow Description captures a network of relations between actions within the context of a specific scenario. The intent of this description is to show how things work in a particular organization in the context of a particular problem-solving (or recurring) situation. IDEF3 uses the scenario as the basic organizing structure for establishing the focus and boundary conditions for the process description. This feature is motivated by the tendency of humans to describe what they know in terms of an ordered sequence of activities which they have experienced or observed within the context of a given scenario or situation. The natural tendency toward organizing thoughts and expressions within the context of a process description has motivated widespread use of the scenario as an informal framework for proposing alternative external views of possible system designs, the roles of which will be to support the activities of the organization within the established context. Such development approaches have been referred to as External Constraint-Driven Design approaches, and have been repeatedly demonstrated in practice as an effective mechanism for the design of new systems.

Overview of the IDEF1 Information Modeling Method

Basic Concepts of IDEF1

IDEF1 was designed as a method for both analysis and communication in the establishment of requirements. IDEF1 is generally used to 1) identify what information is currently managed in the organization, 2) identify which of the problems identified during the needs analysis are caused by lack of management of appropriate information, and 3) specify what information will be managed in the TO-BE implementation.

IDEF1 captures what information exists or should be managed about objects within the scope of an enterprise. The IDEF1 perspective of an information system includes not only the automated system components, but also non-automated objects such as people, filing cabinets, telephones, etc. IDEF1 was designed as a method for organizations to analyze and clearly state their information resource management needs and requirements. Rather than a database design method, IDEF1 is an analysis method used to identify the following:

1. The information collected, stored, and managed by the enterprise,
2. The rules governing the management of information,
3. Logical relationships within the enterprise reflected in the information, and
4. Problems resulting from the lack of good information management.

The results of information analysis can be used by strategic and tactical planners within the enterprise to leverage their information assets and achieve competitive advantage. Their plans may include the design and implementation of automated systems which can more efficiently take advantage of the information available to the enterprise. IDEF1 models provide the basis for those design decisions, furnishing managers with the insight and knowledge required to establish good information management policy.

IDEF1 uses simple graphical conventions to express a powerful set of rules that help the modeler distinguish between 1) real-world objects, 2) physical or abstract associations maintained between real-world objects, 3) the information managed about a real-world object, and 4) the data structure used to represent that information for acquiring, applying, and managing that information. IDEF1 provides a set of rules and procedures for guiding the development of information models. One IDEF1 goal is to provide a structured and disciplined process for analyzing information managed by an organization. This goal is accomplished by the evolutionary process defined in the method and by the measurable results and specific products required by the method. IDEF1 enforces a modularity that eliminates the incompleteness, imprecision, inconsistencies, and inaccuracies found in the modeling process.

There are two important realms for modelers to consider in determining information requirements. The first realm is the real world as perceived by people in an organization. It is comprised of the physical and conceptual objects (e.g., people, places, things, ideas, etc.), the properties of those objects, and the relations associated with those objects. The second realm is the information realm. It includes information images of those objects found in the real-world. An information image is not the real-world object, but the information collected, stored, and managed about real-world objects. IDEF1 is designed to assist in discovering, organizing, and documenting this information image, and thus is restricted to the information realm.

An IDEF1 *entity* represents the information maintained in a specific organization about physical or conceptual objects. An IDEF1 *entity class* refers to a collection of entities or the class of information kept about objects in the real-world. There are two basic concepts that distinguish entities:

1. They are persistent. The organization expends resources to observe, encode, record, organize, and store the existence of individual entities.
2. They can be individuated. They can be identified uniquely from other entities.

Entities have characteristic *attributes* associated with them. Attributes record values of properties of the real-world objects. The term *attribute class* refers to the set of attribute-value pairs formed by grouping the name of the attribute and the values of that attribute for individual entity class members (entities). A collection of one or more attribute classes which distinguishes one member of an entity class from another is called a *key class*.

A *relation* in IDEF1 is an association between two individual information images. The existence of a relation is discovered or verified by noting that the attribute classes of one entity class contain the attribute classes of the key class of the referenced entity class member. A *relation class* can be thought of as the template for associations that exist between entity classes. An example of a relation in IDEF1 is the label "works for" on the link between the information entity called "Employee" and the information entity called "Department." If no information is kept about an association between two or more objects in the real-world, then, from an IDEF1 point of view, no relation exists. Relation classes are represented by links between the entity class boxes on an IDEF1 diagram. The diamonds on the end of the links and the half diamonds in the middle of the links encode additional information about the relation class (i.e., cardinality and dependency). Figure 11 illustrates the manner in which IDEF1 diagrams are drawn.

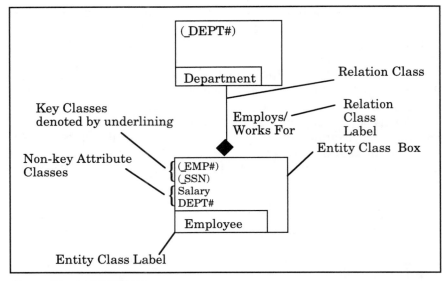

Figure 11. An IDEF1 Diagram

Overview of the IDEF5 Ontology Description Capture Method

Ontologies

Historically, ontology has chiefly been thought of as an attempt to "divide the world at its joints:" to discover those categories, or *kinds*, into which the world's denizens naturally fall. Natural science can be viewed as an example of ontology *par excellence.* Perhaps the chief goal of subatomic physics, for example, is to develop a taxonomy of the most basic kinds of objects that exist within the physical world–electrons, protons, muons, etc. This sort of inquiry is not limited to the natural sciences, however. The abstract sciences as well–mathematics, in particular–can be thought in part at least as an attempt to discover and categorize the domain of abstract objects such as prime numbers, abelian groups, and topological spaces.

The natural and abstract worlds, however, do not exhaust the applicable domains of ontology. For there are vast, human designed and engineered systems–manufacturing plants, businesses, military bases, etc.–in which the task is just as relevant, and just as pressing. Here, though, the ontological enterprise is motivated not so much by the search for knowledge for its own sake, as, ideally, in the natural and abstract sciences, but by the need to understand, design, engineer, and manage such systems effectively. This being the case, it is useful to adapt the traditional methods and tools of ontology to these domains as well.

IDEF5 Concepts

The notion of "kind" (as distinct from class or type) is a central concept of IDEF5. It is important to recognize the distinction between the usual meaning of "kind" and what it represents in IDEF5. In naturally occurring systems, all objects of the same kind often have a distinguishing set of properties which must be maintained to remain a member of that kind. That is, the properties for membership are essential properties of the member. Thus, the usual notion of a kind is a collection of objects, all of which share a common nature (i.e., a set of properties that belong essentially to all and only the members of the kind). However, in the manufacturing systems, objects frequently must have a certain set of properties to become part of a kind but are not required to keep those properties to remain part of the kind. Consider the semiconductor manufacturing domain.

A chemical has certain properties that identify it as an etchant, and all etchants have those properties. This is the traditional idea of a natural kind. Contrast this with the kind of object a manufacturing "rework" item represents. A rework item might be any wafer that has more than three defects. Therefore, a wafer with four defects becomes a rework item. However, after one or more of the defects on a wafer is repaired, it is still a rework item. In fact, it remains so until it is reclassified by an inspector as an acceptable wafer or it is discarded. This is an example of the "kinds" that typically arise in human-designed systems. IDEF5 supports the identification of both notions of kinds.

In other words, when an ontology is built for a certain human-designed system, the broader notion of a kind allows the objects within a system to be divided and categorized in useful and informative ways. An ontology categorization scheme is justified only insofar as it is useful for organizing, managing, and representing knowledge or information in the system so categorized. If objects of a certain kind, K, play a useful role in the system, that is all the justification necessary to admit them into the system ontology, irrespective of whether the defining properties of K are essential to its members.

There is more to characterizing objects in a system than merely listing their properties. In the context of a given system, it is equally important to detail the associations that objects in the system can and do bear to one another. Just as with properties, system-essential associations must be distinguished from system-accidental associations partially because associations occur that way and also because the association may be a defining property of a kind (e.g., the marriage association and the kind "married"). A system-essential association relative to two (or more) kinds, K_1 and K_2 is an association that must hold whenever there are instances of K_1 and K_2. A system-accidental association relative to K_1 and K_2, by contrast, is one that need not hold between *any* instance of those kinds. In addition, system-essential relations don't need to hold between *all* possible instances of the participating kinds.

The IDEF5 method has three main components:

1. A graphical language to support conceptual ontology analysis,
2. A structured text language for detailed ontology characterization, and
3. A systematic procedure that provides guidelines for effective ontology capture.

The IDEF5 Language

IDEF5 provides several schematic (diagram) types for the visualization of an ontology. These schematics are useful conceptual aids for both the construction and the validation of the ontology. *Classification Schematics* are used in IDEF5 to show "subkind-of" relations between kinds in an IDEF5 model. The classification relations selected for use in IDEF5 incorporates prominent AI research results ((Brachman, 1983) and (Gruber, 1992)). IDEF5 supports three types of classification mechanisms: 1) generalization/specialization, 2) AKO (a kind of), and 3) description subsumption (see Figure 12).

Generalization/specialization relations (also called superset/subset links) represent the specialization of a kind by another kind. For example, a **hex-headed bolt** kind is a specialization of a **fastener**

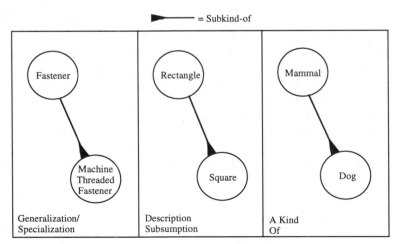

Figure 12. IDEF5 Classification Mechanisms

kind for bolts with hex heads. AKO relations are useful for classifying natural kinds. For example, a **dog** kind is a kind of a **mammal** kind. Description subsumption relations are useful for classifying abstract kinds. The fact *a square is a rectangle with four equal sides* would be captured in a description subsumption relation.

Composition Schematics are provided in IDEF5 to discover and characterize different uses of the part-whole relation. The part-whole, or meronymic relation (derived from the Greek *meros* = part) is very important in several application areas including the manufacturing, engineering, and business domains. For this reason, IDEF5 provides the structures needed to express several different interpretations of this relation.

A composition schematic is a special type of *Relation Schematic* in IDEF5. Relation schematics are used to represent the relations between kinds in an ontology. The capture of knowledge about relations is critical to knowledge acquisition, because relations specify the behavior governing interactions between the components of a complex system. For example, the relations between the electrical (distribution) system and the power system will determine how the engine starts. Figure 13 illustrates the use of a relation schematic used to describe a semiconductor manufacturing facility.

Figure 13 asserts the relation between a wafer and a conveyer. It also shows the relation between an instance of a kind (My-Wafer) and the kind (Wafer).

The IDEF5 Elaboration Language provides a structured text format for capturing complex relation knowledge at any level of complexity. The Elaboration Language can express everything that can be recorded using the Schematic Language; it can also express knowledge that is beyond the scope of the Schematic Language. For example, the five-place relation $z = a + b + c + d$, where z, a, b, c, and d are integers, can only be expressed in the Elaboration Language.

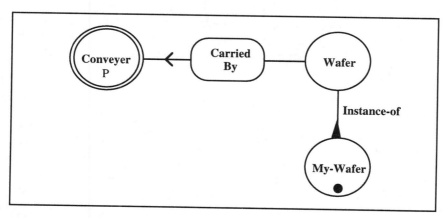

Figure 13. A Relation Schematic

The IDEF5 Procedure

The IDEF5 procedure is an important component of the ontology description method and consists of the following five activities:

1. Organize and Scope the Project: this activity will establish the purpose, viewpoint, and context for the ontology development project and assign roles to the team members.
2. Collect Data: this activity will acquire the raw data needed for ontology development.
3. Analyze Data: this activity will analyze the data to facilitate ontology extraction.
4. Develop Initial Ontology: this activity will develop a preliminary ontology from the acquired data.
5. Refine and Validate Ontology: this activity will refine and validate the ontology to complete the development process.

Although the above activities are listed sequentially, there is a significant amount of overlap and iteration between the activities. Thus, for instance, the initial ontology development (Activity # 4) often requires the capture of additional data (Activity #2) and further analysis (Activity #3). Each of the five activities will involve other activities and tasks. A more detailed description of the IDEF5 method is found in (KBSI, 1994a).

The Role of IDEF Methods in BPR

Initial Activity Modeling

As discussed in the section entitled "The BPR Process," the first step of the BPR process is to define the vision, mission, and goals of the BPR effort. It is at this point that the initial IDEF∅ modeling is to begin. Revisiting the enterprise mission statement during this step of the BPR process lends itself to using IDEF∅ to capture the top-level activities of the enterprise which begin to become apparent at this stage.

Capturing the AS-IS System Descriptions

The IDEF∅ models initiated in the first step will be further developed in capturing the AS-IS System Description. These models will be employed to identify those areas of the enterprise that are candidates for BPR. Again, the resulting activity model(s) will provide insight into "what" and "why" certain activities are performed. If the actual existence of a given activity is difficult to legitimize as a result of IDEF∅ modeling, this is a definite signal that the activity in question may be unnecessary and would be a legitimate candidate for BPR.

As the activity models become more detailed through decomposition, the practitioner may find the description moving away from the what and why toward a description that conveys "how" an activity is performed. This phenomena is often indicated when the practitioner starts capturing information about the activities in terms of timing and sequence as well as the decision logic information required to describe activities that may need to be performed in parallel.

IDEFØ and IDEF3 complement each other well and it is often the case that the practitioner will find that switching from IDEFØ to IDEF3 and vice versa is highly useful in capturing the AS-IS system descriptions. Each method provides a unique perspective through which to view the organization and the functions it performs. The knowledge organization and structuring mechanisms provided by IDEFØ and IDEF3 enhance the productivity of this process. Conceptually, the difference in the ability of the two methods to support analysis stems from inherent differences in the level of representation abstraction that these methods were designed to support. Thus, for example, an arrow between two activity boxes in IDEFØ carries no temporal semantics. In IDEF3, an arrow between two UOB boxes is used to represent a precedence relationship. The sophisticated detailing capabilities of IDEF3 therefore make it a suitable vehicle for launching quantitative analysis efforts such as discrete-event simulation. The more abstract representational apparatus provided in IDEFØ makes it a powerful tool for qualitative/conceptual design and analysis activities.

The main advantages of IDEFØ and IDEF3 for acquiring business process descriptions are summarized as follows:

- Ability to express function and process knowledge: facilitates representation of "what" a system does (IDEFØ) and "how" a system works (IDEF3). IDEFØ is designed to capture and organize information about the functions performed by an organization and their inter-relationships in terms of their inputs, outputs, controls, and mechanisms. IDEF3 facilitates the capture of process knowledge: the temporal and logical relationships between activities and the roles played by objects that participate in these activities.
- Ability to model at multiple levels of abstraction: the decomposition mechanisms in IDEFØ and IDEF3 are useful for both selective information hiding and for focusing attention on specific areas of concern. IDEF3 also supports the representation of alternative viewpoints through the use of multiple decompositions.
- Ability to capture and represent object knowledge: this capability is useful to show the role of objects in accomplishing system goals.

Object roles are restricted to inputs, outputs, controls, and mechanisms in IDEFØ. IDEF3 objects are categorized as agents, participants, affected, created, and destroyed.

• Ability to represent multiple perspectives: IDEF3 supports the representation of alternative viewpoints through the use of multiple decompositions. This capability is particularly useful for large systems analysis projects involving multi-disciplinary teams.

Identify Improvement Opportunities

The Role of IDEFØ in Activity Analysis

IDEFØ has been shown to be a valuable aid in process analysis studies (KBSI, 1993b). The following example illustrates the role of IDEFØ in supporting *Activity Analysis* (Activity Analysis is an important part of ABC[4]).

Consider a generic purchasing department that supports the various departments of the company by processing and, subsequently, filling any purchase request that is generated by those departments. Suppose that the purchasing department manager initiates a BPR effort. The manager uses the IDEFØ method to help identify process improvement opportunities relevant to the "Fill Purchase Request" function. An IDEFØ-based representation of this function is shown in Figure 14.

The Fill Purchase Request function results in "Delivered Items" as shown in Figure 14. The decomposition of Fill Purchase Request has four activities: 1) Approve Request, 2) Send Order, 3) Receive Order, and 4) Distribute Ordered Items, as shown. We have deliberately simplified the activity descriptions to illustrate the main concepts of activity analysis and qualitative cost analysis. The main objects in the model are the IDEFØ ICOMs. The Approved Request is produced and is used in the activity "Send Order." The resulting Purchase Order (P.O.) is then used to check that the correct items have been received in the "Receive Order" function. The Ordered Items are then distributed to the person(s) from whom the purchase request originated. The items are distributed using the P.O. as a guide in identifying and locating the order originators in the field.

An important activity to support ABC is to classify activities under the three ABC-based schemes as described in the section entitled "AS-IS Process Analysis." The categories selected are shown in parentheses next to the activity costs. (The coding scheme for the activity categories is given in the table shown in the lower left of Figure 14.) Notice that the only Value-Adding activity (coded 'V') is Distribute Ordered Items. It is interesting to note that some of these activity categorizations are viewpoint-dependent. For example, the Approve Request, Send Order, and Distribute Ordered Items activi-

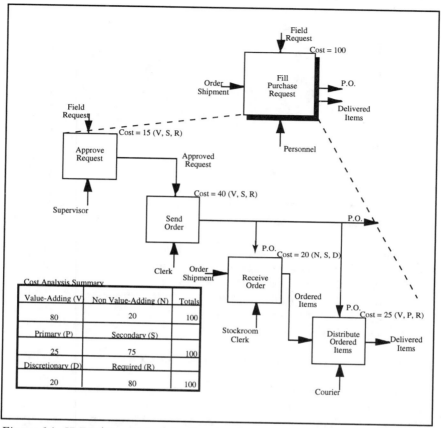

Figure 14. IDEFØ-based Activity Cost Analysis

ties are categorized as *Required*. That is, these activities are "Required" from the point of view of the purchasing department manager. Suppose that the activity Send Order is a requirement from the viewpoint of the purchasing department manager, but from the CEO's viewpoint, this activity is not always required because there is also the option of manufacturing the required item in house. Therefore, from the CEO's perspective, the Send Order activity is categorized as *Discretionary*. This illustrates the fact that the same activity can (conceivably) be categorized differently, when viewed from different perspectives.

After the activities have been categorized and the cost information specified, the next step is to summarize the cost information. Such "cost roll-up" computations provide valuable information for decision support. Example cost summaries that may be generated for this example are shown in Figure 15.

The advantages/benefits of IDEFØ-based activity analysis (illustrated through this example) are:

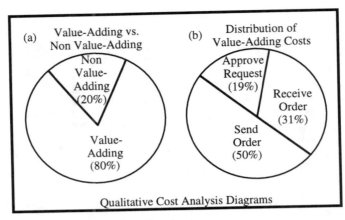

Figure 15. Example Cost Analysis Results

1. Helps focus attention on problem areas: for example, high cost non value-adding activities could be candidates for reorganization or elimination under the BPI initiative.
2. Suggests areas for more detailed analysis: by focusing attention on high cost activities, the analysis may lead to more detailed analysis efforts such as discrete-event simulation studies.

The Role of IDEF3 in Simulation-Based Process Analysis

Simulation analysis[5] has been shown to be useful for three important reasons: 1) to evaluate the effect of randomness, 2) to measure the effect of shared resources, and 3) to estimate the impact of alternative organization policies on system performance (KBSI, 1994a). We now describe a simple example to demonstrate the utility of IDEF3 in supporting simulation-based process analysis. Consider our previous IDEFØ model of Fill Purchase Request. This model captured the four basic sub-activities that are required to fill a purchase request independent of the sequence and timing of the related process steps. In order to describe the details of this activity, we have created an IDEF3 description of the process of Fill Purchase Request (Figure 16). Initially, a request for material is received, at which time the inventory is checked to see if the material is currently available. If the material is available, it is pulled from stock. If the material is not available, the stockroom personnel check the material catalog and submit a request for bid. Incoming bids are evaluated and a subsequent order is placed to the appropriate vendor. We will show the utility of IDEF3-based simulation analysis technique for re-engineering this process.

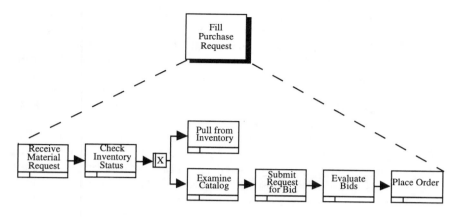

Figure 16. IDEF3 Process Description of Procure Material Activity

- **Effect of Randomness.** Suppose that in this example, the originating department of the incoming material requests is a major determinant of the proportion of requests that are filled by pulling from inventory. Suppose further that the distribution of this proportion is a random variable that varies from department to department. Therefore, we need to build a separate simulation model (for modeling this request for each department) that uses a different input proportion probability distribution. Because of the randomness in arrivals and the random decision logic that consequently results at the fan-out junction (see Figure 4), the cost of the scenario will also vary randomly. The need for a dynamic analysis method that accounts for random behavior is apparent from this example. Dynamic design and analysis software tools can be used to evaluate the effect of randomness on the cost of a system over time (for example, queuing analysis tools, simulation tools). These tools will generate data for analyzing the time varying behavior of costs.
- **Effect of Shared Resources.** Suppose that in this example, the Pull from Inventory process and the Evaluate Bid and subsequent processes process are performed by the same individual, say Storeroom Clerk. Storeroom Clerk is an example of a "shared resource:" that is, a resource that is shared by two different processes. When such shared resources are also scarce resources (that is, they have a finite capacity), their impact on the cost of a process can be significant. The IDEF3 method by itself does not provide sufficient information to accurately quantify the impact of shared resources on organization performance metrics such as cost. However, IDEF3 models can be used to rapidly generate discrete-event simulation model specifications (see Benjamin, et

al. (1993)). The analysis of simulation output data will help evaluate the impact of shared resources on the process cost.

- **Sensitivity Analysis.** Suppose that in this example, the material requests that are waiting for processing by Storeroom personnel wait in a "stack" inside the "in-box" located at the storeroom office. Suppose further that the Storeroom personnel pick up the waiting requests from the box on a "first-come-first-serve (fcfs)" basis. Now, suppose that the manager of the company decides that all waiting requests must be processed using a "priority rule" rather than the fcfs policy. That is, requests are given a priority according to originating department: claims with a higher priority number must be processed before claims with a lower priority number. Before implementing this new policy, the manager would like to evaluate the impact of this policy change on 1) resource utilization, 2) average request process time, and 3) average request process cost. A simulation-based sensitivity analysis can be used to quantitatively evaluate the policy change. As described earlier, the IDEF3 knowledge structures make the transition to a simulation model relatively straightforward.

This simple example illustrates the utility of IDEF3 for dynamic process analysis that leads to the identification of process improvement opportunities. We will now summarize the role of IDEF∅ and IDEF3 in BPR.

IDEF∅ and IDEF3 as BPR Enablers: A Summary

The role of IDEF∅ as a BPR enabler can be summarized as follows:

1. Helps focus attention on *what* happens in an organization: although IDEF∅ also allows for the modeling of *how* things are done in an organization to a limited degree, this is more naturally accomplished by the IDEF3 method. Focusing on what happens (rather than how) is very valuable for BPR projects that emphasize fundamental and radical improvement opportunities, rather than incremental gains.
2. Facilitates modeling at multiple levels of abstraction: IDEF∅ promotes a hierarchical or top-down analysis approach to model development. This is a powerful and valuable feature that manages complexity and facilitates communication.
3. Focuses functional relationships: the IDEF∅ ICOMs (Inputs, Outputs, Controls, and Mechanisms) provide a structured framework for performing functional analysis. The IDEF∅ diagramming mechanisms present an activity-centered view of the organization, and help establish how activities consume resources to deliver value to customers.

The role of IDEF3 as a BPR enabler can be summarized as follows:

1. Helps focus attention on *how things work* in an organization: descriptive and prescriptive knowledge of how organizations perform their work are important for BPR projects. Descriptions of how things work help acquire the AS-IS business scenarios. Prescriptions of how things should work are the subject of the TO-BE business scenarios.
2. Facilitates modeling from multiple perspectives and at multiple levels of abstraction: modeling at multiple levels of abstraction helps manage complexity. Allowing for multiple perspectives facilitates bottom-up modeling. Often the same function or activity can be detailed from different perspectives. IDEF3 allows for the recording of these multiple perspectives.
3. Facilitates both Top-Down and Bottom-Up modeling: this provides flexibility to the personnel performing the BPR work.
4. Facilitates both Process-Centered and Object-Centered Analysis: two modes of description exist within IDEF3: process flow description (PFD) and object state transition network (OSTN) description. The PFDs focus attention on the processes to describe how things work in an organization. The OSTNs provide an object-centered view of the organization by studying the allowable states of an object, and the rules governing the transitions between these states. Our experience indicates these two viewpoints can be used synergistically in BPR projects.
5. Facilitates modeling of temporal and logical relationships: IDEF3 mechanisms, such as temporal relation links and junctions, enable the modeling of complex, real world behavior. This gives domain experts the facility of describing in considerable detail how things work in their organizations. This feature is particularly useful in situations in which the IDEF3 models are used as the basis to quantitatively assess the performance of a business process. For example, IDEF3 models have been used to rapidly prototype quantitative simulation models (KBSI, 1992).

The Role of IDEF5 in BPR Constraint Analysis

The role of IDEF5 in BPR will be illustrated through a simple example. Consider the XYZ manufacturing company that makes widgets. Consider a hypothetical AS-IS scenario: widgets are assembled from manufactured component types A and B (Figure 17). Suppose that the analysis of the AS-IS process results in a redesign of the widget. The change in the design specification is that component type B is replaced by component type C (the TO-BE scenario). This denotes a structural change in the product specification of the widget. An ontology model of widget (Figure 17) may represent the two components B and C as *variants* of a more abstract part type, say X. Variants are varieties of a component or product that have similar overall functionality but have significantly different design specifications. For example, the automatic transmission and the manual transmission are variants of the transmission system. The IDEF5 Elaboration Language (see the section entitled "The IDEF5 Languages") can be used to record important characteristics of the Variant-of relation. For instance, the Elaboration Language may be used to make assertions such as "Different variants necessarily require different manufacturing processes." The nature of the manufacturing processes actually needed will need to be derived from the process planning knowledge base.

Knowledge of the ontological difference between the widget structures in the AS-IS and TO-BE situations facilitates the flow of information that is necessary for change impact prediction. Specifically, the impacts of the change in the product structure of the widget must be effectively propagated to all relevant decision-making units of the enterprise. For instance, the impact of the structural change in the widget may have a dramatic impact on the manufacturing process as shown in Figure 18. The XYZ company does not have the technology to make components of type C. Thus, it needs to outsource this item and assemble the purchased components with the type A components made in house, as shown in Figure 3. The ontological knowledge about the Widget (stored in the IDEF5 models) provides useful information needed to generate the TO-BE process model from the AS-IS process model. More specifically, a detailed characterization of the Variant-of relation provides clues that a fundamental change in the manufacturing process will be required;

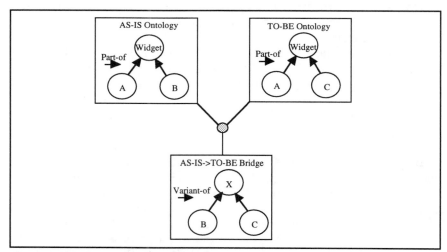

Figure 17. IDEF5 Relation Schematics of the Widget Product Structure

this ontological knowledge, along with knowledge about the technological constraints relevant to the XYZ company, are needed to design the new (or redesigned) manufacturing process shown in Figure 18. In the example XYZ company, ontological knowledge helped "discover" the *constraining relationship* between the structure of the AS-IS manufacturing process model and the structure of the TO-BE process model. Ontologies have been found to be useful in identifying underlying relationships (and constraints) between different domain areas and between different functional units of an enterprise. The discovery and analysis of constraints is an important BPR activity (see the section entitled "Discover and Analyze Constraints").

Develop TO-BE System Designs

After performing the AS-IS Process Analysis, evaluating just how the current system performs, discovering constraints, and identifying reference technologies and models, the next step involves conceptualizing the TO-BE system. The use of IDEFØ and IDEF3 will continue during the planning and design of the newly re-engineered activities and processes of the system. Once these are established, IDEF1 will provide the medium for modeling the information necessary to support the re-engineered system and will provide the roadmap for designing the necessary information systems. (For example, document management systems or enterprise information delivery systems.)

The Role of IDEF1 in BPR Information Requirements Analysis

The IDEF1 Information Modeling Method facilitates the identification and analysis information requirements. It is useful for the analysis of both AS-IS and TO-BE systems. Our experience indicates

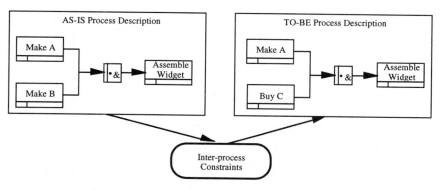

Figure 18: IDEF3 Process Descriptions of the Widget Making Processes

that IDEF1 is particularly useful in the AS-IS->TO-BE transition phase. Specifically, AS-IS information analysis is often performed toward the end of the AS-IS analysis step just prior to initiation of the TO-BE phase. The TO-BE information model will be used to identify and structure that information which is crucial to establishing and successfully performing the TO-BE activities and functions.

It is expected that the TO-BE information model will be much more streamlined and precise than the AS-IS model because non-critical, redundant, and often useless information will no longer need to be managed. At the same time, the TO-BE model will also capture newly discovered information that was not used in the AS-IS, but is now deemed to be critical to the success of the system organization. In other words, the core information that is vital to keeping the organization's competitive advantage, as well as transaction-based information and office automation-based information, needs to be managed. This information, therefore, must be identified and ana-lyzed.

To illustrate the utility of the IDEF1 method, consider the Widget example described in the section entitled "The Role of IDEF5 in BPR Constraint Analysis." The change from the AS-IS to the TO-BE production system had the following implications for the information systems:

1. New Information: the XYZ company requires a new information system to manage the procurement process from procured item "C." For example, a system to track and monitor the performance of the suppliers of "C" may need to be developed. IDEF1 will help analyze the information requirements leading to the design and implementation of the system.
2. Unnecessary Information: because item "B" is no longer required, the information relevant to this item (production reports, quality reports, inventory reports, etc.) will no longer need to be gener-ated. XYZ's production information systems will need to be redesigned to service the modified requirements.

Figure 19 shows a partial IDEF1 diagram that portrays the information managed by XYZ's procurement system.

Summary and Conclusions

This paper described a framework for BPR. An important component of this framework is a suite of methods and tools for BPR. Attention is focused on a subset of the IDEF suite of methods (Painter, 1991b). The role of the IDEF methods in facilitating the BPR process was illustrated using a simple example. The paper also

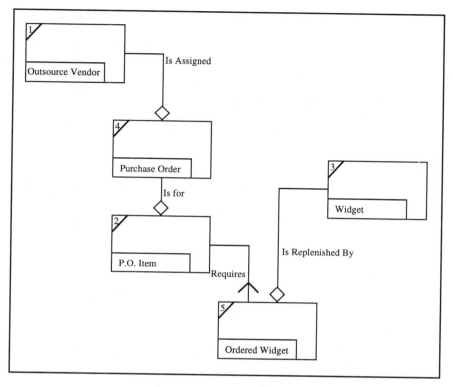

Figure 19. Partial IDEF1 Model of the XYZ Procurement System

shows how the IDEF methods can be combined with analysis methods such as simulation and ABC. The methods presented in this paper will likely benefit two groups of people:

1. BPR methodologists and scientists: by providing a framework that integrates the different components of BPR and clarifies the basic BPR concepts.
2. BPR Practitioners: by providing a set of well-researched and widely-used methods and demonstrating the utility of these methods for BPR projects.

Endnotes

[1]We use the term *system* in this paper to refer to ". . . a group or set of objects united by some form of regular interaction or interdependence to perform a specified function" [Shannon 75]. This (generic) definition allows us to talk about the activities that an organization performs, the objects

(such as agents and resources) that participate in these activities, and the constraints maintained by an organization performing these activities.

[2]Systems Simulation is a notable exception, though being fairly robust for analysis assumptions.

[3]System factors are relevant objects or properties of the system that are necessary to characterize the system and that have some influence on the structure or behavior of the system.

[4]ABC is a powerful cost accounting technique that has been the subject of intense interest in recent years. The technique is well documented in [Cooper 88], [Kaplan 88], [Brimson 91], and [O'Guin 91].

[5]Systems simulation is a powerful and well-established tool for the design and analysis of complex systems ((Forrestor, 1961), (Shannon, 1975), (Pritsker, 1979), (Pegden, et al., 1989)). The authors have succesfully used simulation for process analysis and design in a variety of applications ((Mayer, 1989), (Benjamin, 1991), (Benjamin, et al., 1993)).

References

Benjamin, P. C. (1991). Towards a New Method for the Design of Robust Systems using Computer Simulation Experiments. Ph.D Dissertation, Texas A&M University, College Station, TX.

Benjamin, P. C., Fillion, F., Mayer, R. J., and Blinn, T. M. (1993). Intelligent support for simulation modeling: a description-driven approach. *Proceedings of the 1993 Summer Simulation Conference*, Boston, MA.

Booch, G. (1991). *Object-Oriented Design with Application*, Redwood City, CA: Benjamin Cummings.

Brachman, R. J. (1983). What IS-A Is and Isn't: An Analysis of Taxonomic Links in Semantic Networks. *IEEE Computer*, 1, 6, 10, 30-36.

Brimson, J. (1991). *Activity Accounting*, New York, NY: John Wiley.

Chen, P. P. S. (1976). The Entity-Relationship Model–Toward a Unified View of Data. *ACM Transactions on Database Systems*, 1, 9-36.

Cook, W. J. (1990, October 22). Ringing in Saturn: GM's New Factory Heralds an American Manufacturing Revolution. *U.S. News & World Report*, 51-54.

Cooper, R. (1988). Elements of activity-based costing. *Journal of Cost Management*, 3-23.

Forrester, J. W. (1961). *Industrial Dynamics*, Cambridge, MA: MIT Press.

Gitlow, H., Gitlow, S., Oppenheim. A., and Oppenheim, R. (1989). *Tools and Methods for the Improvement of Quality*, Homewood, IL: Irwin.

Goldratt, E. (1985). *Theory of Constraints*, New York, NY: North River Press.

Gruber, T. R. (1992). Ontolingua: A Mechanism to Support Portable Ontologies, *Knowledge Systems Laboratory Technical Report KSL 91-66*, Final Version, Stanford University.

Hammer, M. and Champy, J. (1993). *Reengineering the Corporation: A Manifesto for Business Evolution*, New York, NY: HarperCollins Publishers.

Interleaf, Inc. (1994). *The Document Management Guide*, Waltham, MA: Interleaf.

Jones, J. I. (1994). *Organizational Metaphysics or Tavern Topics for*

Out-Of-The-Box Thinkers, Informal Working Paper, Priority Process Associates, Inc. Rochester Hills, MI.

Kaplan, R. S. (1988). One cost system isn't enough. *Harvard Business Review*, 61-66.

Kaplan, R. S. (1990, February). The Four-Stage Model of Cost Systems Design. *Management Accounting*, 22-26.

Knowledge Based Systems Inc. (1992). *Knowledge-Based Assistant for Simulation Model Generation from IDEF3 Descriptions*. National Science Foundation Phase II SBIR Grant No. III-9123380.

Knowledge Based Systems, Inc. (1993). *Cost Benefit Analysis Support Environment (CBASE) for C4 Applications*, Final Report. Air Force Phase I SBIR Contract No. F19628-93-C-0154.

Knowledge Based Systems, Inc. (KBSI). (1994a). *Ontology Description Capture Method*. KBSI Technical Report Number KBSI-IICE-94-TR-01-09-93-02. College Station, TX.

Knowledge Based Systems, Inc. (KBSI). (1994b). *A Method for Constraint Discovery*. KBSI Internal Report. College Station, TX.

Mayer, R. J. (1988). Cognitive Skills in Modeling and Simulation. Ph.D Dissertation, Texas A&M University, College Station, TX.

Mayer, R. J. and Decker, L. (1991). *ISyCL Technical Report*. KBSL Technical Report Number KBSL-89-1002. Knowledge Based Systems Laboratory — Texas A&M University, College Station, TX. Air Force Human Resources Laboratory, Wright-Patterson Air Force Base, OH.

Mayer, R. J., deWitte, P. S., and Blinn, T. M. (1992). *Framework of Frameworks*. Knowledge Based Systems, Inc. Internal Report. College Station, TX.

McDonald, K. K. (1993). The Use of IDEFØ in Activity-Based Costing: Evaluating the Costs of Doing Business in a Service Industry. *Proceedings of the May 1993 IDEF Users Group Conference*. College Park, MD.

Morris, D. and Brandon, J. (1993). *Re-engineering Your Business*, New York, NY: McGraw-Hill.

Nijssen, G. M. (1978). On conceptual schemata, databases, and information systems. Paper presented at: Data Bases — Improving Usability and Responsiveness Conference. Haifa, Israel.

O' Guin, M. (1991). *The Complete Guide to Activity-Based Costing*, Engelwood Cliffs, NJ: Prentice Hall.

Painter, M. P. (1991a). *Integrating Methods: Aftermath to the Tower of Babel Knowledge Based Systems, Inc., Internal Technical Report*. College Station, TX.

Painter, M. P. (1991b, May). Information Integration for Concurrent Engineering (IICE): Program Foundations and Philosophy. *Proceedings of the May 1993 IDEF Users Group Conference*. College Park, MD.

Painter, M., Mayer, R., and Menzel, C. (1992). Integrating Methods: Aftermath to the Tower of Babel, *Proceedings of the October 1992 IDEF Users' Group Conference*. Washington, D.C.

Pegden, C. D., Shannon R. E., and Sadowski R. P. (1991). *Introduction to Simulation Using SIMAN*, New York, NY: McGraw-Hill.

Phillips, D. T., Ravindran, A., and Solberg, J. (1976). *Operations Research: Principles and Practice*, New York, NY: Wiley.

Pritsker, A. B. and Pegden, C. D. (1979). *Introduction to Simulation and SLAM*, New York, NY: Halsted Press.

Richardson, G. P. and Pugh, A. L. (1981). *Introduction to Systems Dynamics Modeling With DYNAMO*, Cambridge, MA: MIT Press.

Rumbaugh, J., Blaha, M., Premerlani, W., Eddy, F., and Lorenson, W. (1991), *Object-Oriented Modeling and Design*, Englewood Cliffs, NJ: Prentice-Hall.

Shannon, R. E. (1975). *Systems Simulation*, Englewood Cliffs, NJ: Prentice-Hall.

SofTech. (1981, June). *Integrated Computer-Aided Manufacturing (CAM) Function Modeling Manual (IDEF₀)*, Technical Report UM 110231100.

Spitzer, R. E. (1993, June). TQM: The Only Source of Sustainable Competitive Advantage. *Quality Progress*, 59-64.

Waterman, D. A. (1986). *A Guide to Expert Systems*, Reading, MA: Addison Wesley.

Business Reengineering with Business Rules

Daniel S. Appleton
D. Appleton Company, Inc.

Business process reengineering has become a sobriquet for a widening variety of schemes designed to increase organizational performance. A conviction common among these schemes is that the best way to improve organizational performance is to think of the organization in terms of its "business processes," rather than its organizational hierarchy. Processes are viewed more or less as threads which transcend the vertical and horizontal boundaries inherent in the hierarchy, weave together behavior patterns based on predefined performance criteria, and ignore congenital hierarchical inefficiencies.

Business process reengineering schemes all employ a *reductionist* approach to changing organizational behavior: they fundamentally presume the total business is a single process; then they reduce that gross process down into sub-processes (such as "strategic processes"); then they further reduce each strategic process into its sub-processes, those sub-processes down into their sub sub-processes, and so on, until they achieve a level of process reduction at which meaningful change can be made *to a process*. The problem with this strategy is that it stubbornly focuses on processes and never penetrates those processes to discover their determinants.

In science, reductionist thinking is classically employed by scientists searching for natural laws. Typically, these scientists start with observed natural phenomenon and proceed down a reduction path until they arrive at what they believe to be the primitive cause of the phenomenon. In discovering gravity, for example, Sir Isaac Newton started with observations of Mars, Jupiter's satellites, and the wobbling of the earth and moon on their axes. He undertook a separate reduction path in analyzing each set of observations. At the end of these separate reduction paths, he found the same thing: inverse-square attraction. He subsequently decreed the "inverse-square law of universal gravitational attraction." Newton is by no means alone in using the reductionist approach to discover basic laws of nature. Francis Crick and Thomas Watson discovered the DNA Double Helix using a reductionist approach. Einstein discovered the theory of relativity using reductionist thinking. Each of these reductionist thinkers started by observing "effects," and used reductionist thinking to search out the primitive causes of those effects. Intuitively, they recognized that the cause, once uncovered, would not resemble the effect in form or function.

The primitive causes uncovered through scientific reductionism can be thought of as the "internal rules" of a system under observation. These internal rules preordain the observed behaviors of the system. Once understood, they can be used not only to explain observed behavior but to predict behaviors that have not yet occurred. Understanding the rules at play is no simple task in a complex system such as an organization. It is difficult even to believe that there are relatively few simple rules underlying the boggling complexity we observe as organizational behavior. But, not only does each organization behave in accordance with a set of internal rules, those rules are its own, and create its uniqueness.

The relatively new sciences of complex systems and chaos tell us that just a very few simple internal rules can cause incredibly complex effects, but the rules themselves represent an underlying order which not only causes certain behaviors, but it makes other behaviors impossible.[1] It stands to reason, therefore, that if we desire to make changes in the behavior of a complex system such as an organization, we should seek out the internal rules that underlie the observed behavior and effect changes directly to those rules.

It is the thesis of this chapter that business processes are *specific manifestations of organizational behavior* and as such *they are the result of a relatively simple set of internal organizational rules.* These rules, which I will call *business rules,* are not hostage to individual processes. They transcend *all* business processes, enabling some and eliminating many others. As we will learn, some rules may appear to be "owned" by a specific business process, but the appearance of ownership is an illusion. A single process does not *own* its business rules. It is better to think of business processes as *sharing* business rules, and of business rules as *enabling* business processes and *integrating* them.

To win the game of business performance improvement, so to speak, business engineers must gain the perspective and learn to use the tools necessary to penetrate business processes and discover the business rules which underlie and preordain them. Once this is accomplished, even minor changes to the internal rules can generate major changes in business processes and business performance.

What are these mysterious business rules? Very simply, they are the rules that control the *symbols* which can be used in constructing transactions among action agents in and around the business. The overwhelming majority of business transactions are messages. There are only two types of messages: information messages and noise messages. An information message is a message that resolves uncertainty or stimulates action. As Stafford Beer puts it, information is "that which changes us."[2] All other messages are noise. The ratio of information messages to all messages sent is called the "information quality ratio." As we shall see, information quality has a direct relationship to organizational productivity; and improving information quality has a direct effect on improving business performance.

One cannot address information quality without linking it to information technology (IT). This observation is not meant to imply that information technology is necessary to improve information quality. Indeed, improperly implemented, information technology can utterly destroy information quality (which is one of the underlying explanations of what has come to be known as the "productivity paradox" of information technology). What we shall discover is that not only should business rules be employed in reengineering business processes, but business rules—not business processes—should be employed for automation and reengineering the business information infrastructure.

Robert Frost wrote, "We dance round in a ring and suppose, But the secret sits in the middle and knows." In the world of business engineering, the secret is information quality. The purpose of this chapter is to give the business engineer a heat-seeking missile that will allow him or her to home in directly on information quality as a means of effecting business performance improvement. This missile is called *business rules.*

To achieve its purpose this chapter is divided into five parts. First, it addresses the question: "What is the relationship between information quality and organizational productivity?" Information quality and productivity are so intimately related that if reengineering were only to focus directly on information and improving information quality in the business, productivity improvement would automatically follow, regardless of whether information *technology* were ever applied. Second, it elaborates the concept of the business conceptual schema and its components, business rules. Third, the chapter examines the relationships between business rules and business processes and the effects that changing business rules have on changing business processes. Fourth, the chapter describes semantic modeling and develops exemplar business rule models using the IDEF1X semantic modeling technique. And, fifth, the chapter amplifies the concept of the business information infrastructure, explaining the relationship between information quality, business rules, and information technology.

Information Quality and Organizational Productivity

A business is a jungle of transactions. We invariably measure productivity in units related to transactions. A transaction is an output transmitted from a sender to a receiver. Every transaction has a cost. This cost is computed by prorating total cost (input) across the number of transactions (outputs) a sender generates. Productivity, itself, is a ratio developed by the sender of the cost assigned to an individual transaction to the total costs incurred by the sender for all transactions. If the ratio goes down, that is, if the cost per transaction unit goes down relative to total cost, then productivity goes up, and *visa versa*. Other ways to think of productivity are as the change in the number of transactions generated for a fixed cost, or as reductions in marginal transaction costs.

Besides the cost per transaction, there is one other significant variable in the productivity equation. This variable is called *value*. A corollary to value is *quality*. Clearly, if a transaction has no value (or quality) to a receiver, then it cannot be counted as an output by the sender. In such cases, the sender should reassign its costs only to transactions having value, thereby increasing the costs of those transactions and, sadly, reducing the sender's productivity ratio by that much. Obviously, neither value nor quality can be assigned by the sender. That would lead to an artificial productivity ratio. Value and quality can only be assigned by the receiver. (Note: If you prefer to interchange the words receiver and customer, please do.)

Information Is a Message

Businesses are 99% logical. They are created by human minds, and they operate entirely by means of the exchange of human thoughts and actions in the form of transactions. The vast majority of these transactions are *messages* sent from senders to receivers. The productivity ratio of message sending is usually computed by the sender who prorates its total cost across all of the messages it sends. However, from the standpoint of the receiver, each message it receives falls into one of two categories. If the message resolves some uncertainty in the receiver, or, if it adds to the receiver's knowledge or stimulates action, it is an *information message.* If it does none of these things, it is a *noise message.*[3] This logic commutes the idea of *information* from a passive concept somehow analogous to knowledge or wisdom, into a active agent and a direct measure of message value and quality (and cost). The concept that information is an active agent in business, as opposed to something that is passively stored in a file or database, is not generally considered by business engineers, but it is a pivotal concept.

From the receiver's viewpoint all messages are either information or noise messages. Information messages add value. Noise messages do not. By means of feedback from the receiver, then, the sender's original productivity calculations must be altered by reassigning its costs across *only* the information messages it sends, eliminating all noise messages from its productivity figuring. Further, a high proportion of noise messages detracts from the *receiver's* productivity, not just the sender's. From the receiver's viewpoint, its productivity is directly effected by the cost it incurs in filtering out noise messages from noisy senders. Since the costs of noise filtering are a component of its total costs, the receiver must reassign these noise filtering costs across its own messaging activities. The implication, of course, is that productivity draining noise filtering costs tend to accumulate at an astounding rate as noise messages build up along transaction chains. Noise messages are, therefore, extremely expensive to both senders and receivers, and should be excoriated with specifically targeted business reengineering tools and techniques.

Altering Information Quality

It is entirely presumptuous to assume that a sender can ever know for sure that a message it sends will be an information message or a noise message to a receiver. At best, the sender can only work to increase the *probability* that its messages will be information messages and not noise messages. And, this is where business reengineering must focus its attention. A primary ambition of business reengineering must be to increase information quality in the business by concentrating on increasing the probability that messages sent from its senders to its receivers will be information messages and not noise messages. The question then becomes, "How do we increase the probability of information messages?"

We don't have to travel long intellectual distances to discover the answer to this question. Simply, the answer lies in the symbols that are used to construct a message. More precisely, we are concerned that senders and receivers agree not just on the symbols that they will use in their messages, but that they agree on the *meanings* that are assigned to those symbols. Most noise messages occur for one of four reasons: (1) the receiver does not understand the sender's symbology, (2) the receiver *thinks* he understands the sender's symbology, but doesn't, (3) the same symbol means different things to the sender and the receiver, or (4) the message was constructed in such a way as to make the symbols confusing to the receiver.

These four problems point us to the conclusion that it is critical that senders and receivers *agree* to some convention regarding which symbols they will use, in what kinds of messages, how, and what these symbols mean, by themselves and in relationship to each other. The value of such a convention is obvious when we think of an isolated situation involving a single sender-receiver couplet. The complexity of the challenge of enacting such a convention increases by several orders of magnitude when we think of the entire messaging infrastructure of a business which includes hundreds (if not thousands) of sender/receiver couplets, some of which are predefined (in business processes) but *most of which are opportunistic and temporary.*

If the complexity of improving information quality increases so alarmingly, so does its importance. Clearly, the lack of effective conventions to control the messaging activity among thousands of permanent and temporary sender/receiver couplets has the potential to dramatically erode the productivity of any business. But, the reverse is also true. The existence of an effective convention controlling message content and structure will dramatically improve overall information quality and, coincidentally, business efficiency and productivity. Establishing this convention of business symbols—and using it to drive process improvements as well as information technology investments—is a basal challenge for business reengineering.

Information and Business Rules

Business rules are the elements of symbolic conventions intended to increase the probability that any message sent between senders and receivers subscribing to the same convention will be information and not noise. As in the game of bridge, a convention must be created and agreed to between partners before communications can effectively occur. The value of a bridge convention lies in the information quality of each bid message. Some conventions have higher information quality than others, which is why there is such a wide variety of conventions. On the other hand, if a convention is not agreed to by bridge partners, the information quality of their bids will be nil, and they will eventually lose the game.

Conceptual Schemas

In business, a symbolic convention constructed from a set of internally consistent business rules is called a *conceptual schema*.[4] To increase information quality, senders and receivers must agree to a common conceptual schema. Invariably, this common conceptual schema must be engineered—or in today's parlance, re-engineered— by objectively integrating the business rules that reside in the individual conceptual schemas of *potential* senders and receivers. This is a primary means of breaking down the traditional walls between organizational modules, between business processes, and between automated business systems, the so-called "silos" of business, and gaining the quality, temporal, and financial rewards of integrated organizational behavior.

The difficulty of engineering conceptual schemas is dramatically ameliorated by modeling techniques that can be used to articulate and evaluate the business rules in various parochial conceptual schema and determine whether these business rules are, in fact, consistent with one another. These same techniques can be employed to integrate the business rules from *diverse* conceptual schema into a single, *shared* conceptual schema, which is, itself, internally consistent. Inconsistency in a conceptual schema means that its symbols and business rules are conflicting, redundant, or unclear. Such inconsistency is equivalent to having no conceptual schema at all since messages constructed by senders from conflicting, redundant, or unclear symbols have a high probability of becoming noise messages, and a low probability of becoming information messages, to receivers.

Every business has a conceptual schema. Every individual person has a conceptual schema. Every department, team, system, center of excellence, strategic business unit, cost center, and business process has a conceptual schema. These entities can only communicate with one another and operate efficiently together if they are conceptually aligned. Otherwise, their messages to one another do not make sense. Entities in the same business can only communicate with each other if they share a common conceptual schema. For example, a production supervisor and an accountant in the same company may each have conflicting ideas as to what they mean when they say "standard cost." Each might have acquired his or her personal definitions from formal education or from experience in another business environment. Nevertheless, they will not be able to communicate until they agree on a single meaning for the symbol "standard cost." The *right* definition, the one they must agree on, is the definition in the business conceptual schema, the one that *makes sense to the business.* This means that the business must consciously *engineer* its definition of standard cost, and do so in the context of other symbols that it uses, symbols such as actual cost, standard operation, standard hour, variance, employee hourly rate, and so on.

Customers and suppliers can only communicate with each other if they share a common conceptual schema. Members of a value chain must likewise share a common conceptual schema. Indeed, each inconsistency from one conceptual schema to another exacts its own insidious penalties in quality, cost, timeliness, and efficiency, and these penalties take their toll in organizational cost, quality, flexibility, competitiveness, and, ultimately, survival. One is reminded of Senator Everett Dirksen's comment about federal spending: "A billion here, a billion there, pretty soon it adds up to a lot of money."

How Conceptual Schemas Get Built

People and businesses build their own conceptual schemas, from the inside out, using what we know as a "learning process." The learning process is controlled by internal meta rules that provide for the refinement and extension of a conceptual structure, ensuring that these refinements and extensions always make sense. If a human being observes something that doesn't make sense, his learning process will not integrate it into his conceptual structure. It will either discard that something, or it will put that something in "the back of his mind," with no guarantee that he or she will ever be able to find it again.

The business' learning process operates the same way, by altering and incrementing the business conceptual schema. As changes occur from reorganization, process reengineering, automation, downsizing, right sizing, total quality management, or whatever, each change must be evaluated for its impact on the business rules in the existing business conceptual schema. If existing business rules are not adjusted, there is a very high probability that the change will actually hurt performance—perhaps in a distantly related department or process—because the change will unwittingly cause noise messages to proliferate and productivity to suffer as it creates inconsistencies and contradictions in the business conceptual schema. Sustained change activity that ignores the need to reconcile new business rules with the business conceptual schema, while it may proclaim temporary parochial improvements, will ultimately erode information quality in the business, and the business' overall ability to effectively communicate internally as well as with its customers and suppliers will deteriorate.

All of the symbols used in a business have meanings which have evolved with the business, and these meanings are not easy to change. If they are ignored, if they are arbitrarily preempted by individual employees or departments, or if they are purposefully altered to meet the needs of individual business processes, the result is inevitably a promulgation of noise messages (and noise filtering costs) in the business. Thus, it is exceptionally crucial that the business soberly engineer its information infrastructure with its conceptual schema as the nerve center and nucleus. Any business that employs a reengineering approach which either ignores its conceptual schema or fabricates an information infrastructure with the unreconciled conceptual schemas of individual employees, individual departments, or individual business processes is sentenced to eventual defeat in its reengineering endeavors.

Business Rules

The ingredients of a conceptual schema are called business rules. A business rule is an explicit statement of a constraint that exists on what some symbol, such as customer, part, drawing, account, inventory item, etc., can mean. In a service business, the following are examples of viable business rules that might comprise a subset of its conceptual schema:

- "A customer is a business with which we have at least one but possibly more than one active or inactive contract."
- "There are three types of customers: long term customers, new customers, and prospective customers."
- "There are only two types of contracts: fixed price contracts and time and materials contracts."
- "Every contract has at least one and possibly more than one invoice."

If we take these business rules apart, we see that each has a subject, a verb phrase, and an object. The subject and the object are both symbolic names (nouns) for sets. "Customer," for example, is a symbolic name for the receiver of an external, margin bearing transaction. Since there are (hopefully) numerous instances of these customers, the symbol "customer" is the business rule's way of referring to all of them. In the information infrastructure, each individual instance of "customer" must be uniquely identifiable.

The subject and object of a business rule are symbols for sets of things that the business wants to know something about. The verb phrase in a business rule describes the relationship that exists between at least two sets. This relationship is a constraint because it describes the only allowable relationship between the two sets. (This makes it a rule.) For example, the rule: "There are only two types of contracts: fixed price contracts and time and materials contracts," says that there is no such thing as a contract that is both fixed price and time and materials. If there is a need for a third type of contract, then either the existing rule must be changed, or, as often happens, a new business rule must be constructed. This new rule would require the development of a new symbol, for example, "fixed-price-time-and-materials contract," and it would enable the information infrastructure to track individual instances of customers with "fixed-price-time-and-materials contracts." Until the rule is modified, no individual, department, or business process can accommodate "fixed-price-time-and-materials contracts." For example, even if the order booking process wanted to accept "fixed-price-time-and-materials contracts," the accounting process would be forced to object until the rule is changed. Further, simply changing a rule is not the end. All involved business processes must be modified to accommodate the rule change. Until this happens, these processes will be out of sync, and they will be unable to communicate or work together effectively.

A conceptual schema's business rules must be consistent. By examining the first two rules above, we can detect an inconsistency that will, inevitably, cause a proliferation of noise messages. That inconsistency stems from the business rule that identifies the idea of "prospective customers." Since the previous business rule specifies a condition of a customer requiring "at least one but possibly more than one active or inactive contract," these two rules, together, say that we must have an active or an inactive contract with any prospective customer. But, what do we call businesses with which we have never done business, but which occur on the prospect list? If we use the symbol prospective customer, we will create confusion.

Business Rules and Business Processes

Today, we drive reengineering with the objective of radically or continuously, quantumly or incrementally—take your pick—improving business processes. Given this viewpoint, we consider information only as something that *flows* through business, and we think of information flow as having some correlation to productivity: "The more efficiently information flows through a business, the more productive the business will be." Hence, business reengineering is driven by the faith that if we reengineer business processes so that information flows more efficiently through the business, increased productivity will be our reward. However, we have *no* direct evidence that this is actually the case. To the contrary, there are very strong telltales that much of the information that flows through a business is not information at all, it is noise, and regardless of how efficiently it flows, it adds no value, only cost. One of the primary failings of information technology has been that it tends to increase the volume and speed of noise flowing through our businesses, thereby actually reducing our productivity, or at least offsetting real productivity increases sufficiently enough to neutralize any overall improvement.

Despite the fact that information flow is an extremely popular concept, so popular that it has reached apotheosis in the business reengineering community, its value as the sovereign medium for improving productivity is highly suspect. "Flow" is a physical measure, generally associated with physical systems. Businesses are much more logical than they are physical. In fact, just as the human body comprises 99% water and 1% other elements, businesses are 99% information and 1% other elements. Little of the water in a human body actually flows through it—though, obviously some does. Most of the water in a human body *is* the human body. The same is true with information and business. Take the information away, and you essentially have nothing left. Erode its information quality, and the business begins to disintegrate.

Being able to objectively describe the processes of a business is an invaluable step toward understanding and eventually changing behavior. However, individual processes are arbitrarily defined. Not only that, but most processes that operate in businesses are temporary and constantly changing. A specific process exists only in the eye of its beholder. On the other hand, processes do not operate in a vacuum. In fact, business processes are constrained by business rules.

To find business rules controlling a business process, we need only look closely at the transactions that occur between activities in the process. These transactions describe the information environment within which each activity operates. For example, one activity in, say, the purchasing process, may take in "purchase requisitions" and produce "purchase orders." The business rules constraining this "create purchase order" activity are those that define what a "purchase requisition" is and what a "purchase order" is, and they establish a relationship between the two, for example, "a single purchase requisition cannot be transformed into more than one purchase order." This business rule not only constrains the create purchase order activity, but the purchasing process, and all of the other processes it touches.

A more complex business rule might be "a single purchase requirement cannot be transformed into more than one purchase requisition, nor can multiple purchase orders be generated for a single purchase requisition, nor can a single purchase order be generated for multiple vendors." The short form of the logic reflected in this business rule is that "a single purchase requirement can be satisfied only by a single vendor." However, since the process of "buy something" involves three different activities, each with its own inputs and outputs, this business rule must be decomposed into a transaction structure supportive of all three of the activities.

Business rules must be validated across activities and to the highest level of process possible. They may be subsequently refined into more specific rules, but without high-level validation, they may actually be destructive. For example, it would be unusual for a firm to have a business rule like the one in the last paragraph. Why? Because this rule creates an unnatural buying pattern, not to mention a lot of buying transactions (and probably paper). Every firm has requirements for multiple sourcing of individual purchase requirements. This business rule would only allow multiple sourcing if each buy for the same article were driven by a different purchase requirement.

Business rules describe the symbology of business transactions and, as a result, they control the ability of the business to communicate within and among employees, teams, work groups, departments, and business processes. Take, for example, the concepts of "account," "customer," and "client." Every business uses these symbols differently. One business may say that "an account can exist even if it is not a customer." Another may require that "an account comprises both customers and clients, where customers are people it has done business with in the past but clients are customers with whom it has active purchase orders." The meaning of these three symbols and the relationships that have been established among them directly affect numerous processes, including marketing, sales, invoicing, collections, planning, etc. Inconsistent business rules create intellectual chaos in a business, and they create numerous extraneous and redundant activities and transactions. And, who could even determine the excess (and unnecessary) costs?

On the other hand, since we can model business rules, we can render them objective and provide a basis for diagnosis, analysis, and manipulation of business processes. Such a business rule model is shown in Figure 1. Depicted are several of the symbols and business rules employed in the "purchasing" process. The symbols introduced in the model are "purchase order," "vendor," "purchase order line item," "part type," and "customer order." Some of the business rules that can be read from the model are:

"A **purchase order** may be issued to one and only one **vendor**."
"Each **purchase order** will have at least one **purchase order line item**, but it has a maximum of 30 **purchase order line items**."
"Each **purchase order line item** may order one and only one **part type**."
"No **purchase order** may be placed that orders **part types** for more than one **customer order**."

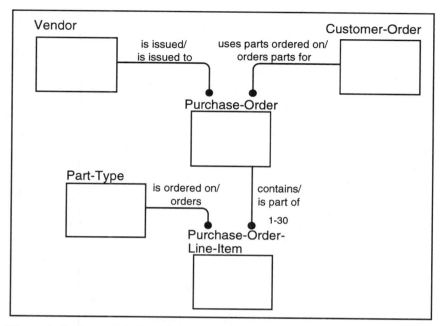

Figure 1: Business Rule Model for Purchasing Process

These rules explicitly constrain the "purchasing" business process, *and all other processes that relate to it,* such as the "order entry process," the "inventory control" process, and the "cost accounting" process. Take the last two rules. Combined they prohibit the "purchasing" process from issuing a single purchase order or purchase order line item to buy parts that *might* be used to satisfy multiple customer orders. This rule has a dramatic effect, not just on the "purchasing" process, but on numerous other processes such as inventory control and finance. One might wonder why such a rule would exist in a typical business, and the answer is that many manufacturers are saddled with this rule because they are constrained by specialized accounting regulations and/or legal statutes.

Measuring Process Performance

An important role of business rules comes from the fact that they are focused on identifying the symbols used in the business for "things that can be counted." Given the concept of "purchase order," for example, we know that we can count the number of purchase orders. Since we can count instances of the symbols represented in business rules, we can develop metrics around those symbols. We can ask, for example, how many purchase orders did we generate last month? If the answer is 100, we can ask, "What will it take to increase the number of purchase orders generated per month to 150?" (This example presumes that the number of purchase orders should increase, possibly because the number of sales orders is expected to increase.) The answer to this question is gained by referring to an activity model, "generate purchase order." Going back to such a model, we can examine costs and time.

Here we actually have a case where an inappropriate business rule would drive costs of numerous activities up if we tried to increase the transaction volume of a single activity. According to the business rules of the "buy something" business process, if we attempt to increase the number of purchase orders generated by the "generate purchase order" activity, we would cause the number of purchase requirements and purchase requisitions to increase proportionally.

Not only do business rules provide the basis for developing process metrics, setting goals, and measuring performance to those goals, they also provide the means for introducing new concepts into the business. Obviously, we cannot have a new concept unless we have a set of symbols and rules articulating the concept. Take the idea of *frequent flyers*. Prior to 1975, no airline had articulated the concept of a frequent flyer. Now, every airline employs the symbol, but each has a different meaning for the symbol. Some say frequent flyers must have flown more than 10,000 miles on the airline. Others say that frequent flyers must have flown more than 20,000 miles on a combination of designated airlines. Some say that all passengers are either frequent flyers or infrequent flyers. Some have levels of frequent flyers, for example, platinum frequent flyers, gold frequent flyers, and regular frequent flyers. Some say all of the above.

Despite the fact that all airlines now employ the symbol frequent flyer, and each has different business rules regarding frequent flyer symbols, all of them have defined processes based on frequent flyers, have metrics related to frequent flyers, have goals and strategies driven by those metrics, and so on. In short, all of them classify and count frequent flyers.

We can only manage things we can count. Business rules control the symbols used in the business that control the things that it can count. They are the natural linkage into the business's databases. Business rules, therefore, should be used to control these databases. Since databases provide the source for the vast majority of the information (and noise) created, consumed, and sold by the business, business rules are quite important indeed.

Confusion Among Processes

It is easy to see why noise is generated from inconsistent business rules, and why this noise can create major communications problems in a business. Inconsistency creeps into these business rules if they are developed to support only a single process, in effect setting up the database specifically for that process. Confusion arises when messages are transmitted from one process to another, each process having its own business rules, and the business rules among processes being inconsistent.

No business process should be performed if it is inconsistent with the business rules in the overall conceptual schema, even if its own business rules are internally consistent. For example, purchase orders should not be issued that cover several vendors or that supply parts to several customers. Also, no purchase order line item should order both nuts and bolts (two different instances of the entity "part type") even if from the same vendor.

If business rules are changed to facilitate or enable a business process that they had previously inhibited, the overall model is affected, and it too must be changed. For example, if it becomes desirable to allow several part types to be ordered by the same purchase order line item, then the business rules governing inventory management must be modified because there was undoubtedly a business rule aligning inventory account replenishment with single purchase order line items, which, in turn, affected standard costs.

It would be very difficult for a single person to know, much less enforce, the total set of business rules, the conceptual schema, employed by a business or a government agency. Most people (and organizations) see only subsets of the business rules—those that directly affect them and their activities. For this reason, it is normal to have many different subsets of business rules, each of which is internally consistent, but the sum of which is inconsistent. This explains why different information systems, each with their own business rules, have difficulty exchanging messages and often require very expensive translators. The only way to ensure communications efficiency among processes is to require that their parochial business rules be validated against an overall conceptual schema. In most cases, this means that business rule subsets cannot be independently developed. They must be developed as extensions to the overall conceptual schema. In other words, they must either reuse business rules already in the overall conceptual schema, or they must modify or extend the conceptual schema's existing rules.

Business Rules and Process Change

The problem is that business processes are constantly changing. As a result, business rule change management is very serious. If business processes need to be changed, and new business rules are required by the new processes, then proposed business rule changes must be evaluated with respect to how the current conceptual schema will be affected. (See Figure 2)

Changes to a company's conceptual schema can be extremely expensive and traumatic. Therefore, if they must be made, they should be made with careful planning. New business processes must be evaluated to determine if they can be performed within the existing set of business rules. If not, then the business processes should be challenged and a determination made as to whether the processes can be modified to be more compatible with existing business rules, or even whether the new process should be performed at all, given the cost and culture implications of business rule changes. Only if they are valid processes, should the business rules be changed to accommodate them.

Further, if a conceptual schema is changed to accommodate the new business rule requirements of a single process, the effects of the change will ripple out to other processes. Initially, these effects may be negative or problematic, but the effort to reconcile business rule changes are almost always rewarded by heading off future interprocess communications problems. (As an example of such an interprocess communications problem ask yourself whether or not you can enter one of your own sales orders into your own purchasing system.)

Businesses may not have a choice in either process or business rule change. For example, airline companies could not choose whether or not to be deregulated. But without the business rule concept, a business does not know the cost or culture implications

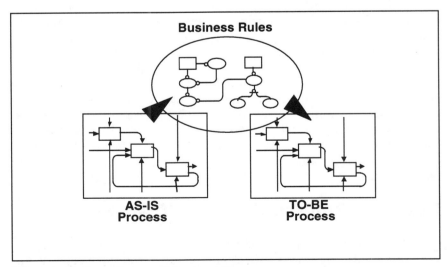

Figure 2: Business Rules and Business Processes

of making process changes, nor can it evaluate alternative process changes. If it is reengineering with business rules, it should follow a simple axiom:

Any process change that requires a change in a company's business rules will be more expensive and more difficult to implement than one that doesn't.

Business Rules and Quantum Change

A corollary to the above axiom is:

Quantum process changes are rarely possible without business rule changes.

Major changes to business rules lead to quantum changes in performance. These business rule changes are engendered by the introduction of a new conceptual frame of reference to the enterprise. Examples include the introduction of the notion of "frequent travelers" by American Airlines, or the notion of "six sigma quality" at Motorola. An enlightening example of quantum change from business rules is the introduction by Nike, Inc. of the concept of "Futures."

Futures

Futures, and the business rules that formed around it, was, in the mid-1970s, singularly responsible for catapulting Nike, Inc.— then called Blue Ribbon Sports—over its competitors in the sports shoe business. It was not only the primary catalyst to success, it was the panacea for a panoply of problems that had been plaguing the fledgling organization for years, and now threatened to drive it out of business. Futures:

"The idea behind Futures was to offer major customers like Nordstrom an opportunity to place large orders six months in advance, and have them commit to that noncancellable order in writing. In exchange, customers would get a 5 to 7 percent discount and guaranteed delivery on 90 percent of their order within a two-week window of time."[5]

With this single concept, Buck Knight, CEO of Blue Ribbon, got himself a unique forecasting tool, shoved the risk of late deliveries onto the shoulders of large retailers, and established a new, credit-supporting asset structure based on large noncancellable orders from customers with impeccable credit ratings. In exchange for

Futures contracts, he committed his firm to a level of on-time delivery it had never before even approached.

As soon as the first major customer, Foot Locker, signed a Futures contract, Blue Ribbon Sports began a massive readjustment of its internal processes from finance, to marketing, to sales, to forecasting, production control, purchasing, inventory control, transportation, costing, and pricing. Eventually, even engineering was affected. There was not an internal business process that remained untouched by Futures, and to be successful—and avoid destroying the whole company—these processes had to come into alignment with Futures, fast. Futures orders had to be uniquely identified, managed and controlled. The concept of "a Futures contract" had to be introduced and differentiated from other existing concepts, such as, traditional contracts "Futures customers" were different from traditional customers. So were "Futures orders," "Futures prices," Futures inventor items," "Futures deliveries," "Futures schedules," and so on. And, as the percentage of total orders began to shift in favor of Futures, the processes controlling Blue Ribbon's traditional business had to be readjusted and balanced with Futures business, adapting to the different requirements for behavior demanded by the new Futures business rules. In some cases, Futures demanded their own unique processes. In other cases, existing processes were adjusted to accommodate Futures.

There are hundreds of stories like Nike's. American Airlines and its Frequent Traveler concept. MBNA and Affinity Credit Cards. Wal-Mart and Cross Docking. Federal Express and Overnight Delivery. Motorola and Six Sigma Quality. John Deere and Computer Integrated Manufacturing. Toyota and Lean Production. Nissan and Just-In-Time inventory control. In each and every case, the introduction of new business concepts, and, subsequently, new business rules, catalyzed quantum changes in performance. These enterprises genetically reengineered themselves as management changed business rules, and this genetic reengineering caused major adjustments across business processes.

Successful genetic reengineering through business rules can create major performance change in a business. Other businesses look on with envy and some even attempt to map the successful new genes of competitors onto their own genetic structure through reengineering techniques such as benchmarking. Some are successful with the transplant. But, most fail just as Sears failed to effectively internalize Lowest Everyday Price and General Motors failed to effectively implement Lean Production from Toyota. These failures are just as eloquent as the successes. Most of these failures result from the inability to internalize new business rules into an existing conceptual schema and then to effect process changes based on the new conceptual schema.

Modeling Business Rules Using IDEF1X

In this section, I discuss how to model business rules. Business rule modeling is the most effective way of articulating business rules such that they can actually be operated upon, that is, engineered. As will be shown, business rule modeling is a mathematically based process, and, as a result, it provides a stable basis for engineering activities. It is noteworthy that because of their mathematical basis, business rule models are more precise than business process models. Actually from the business rule perspective, process models serve primarily as a discovery tool, an abstract device which provides a reduction path to the discovery of business rules.

In the first part of this section, I introduce the concept of semantic modeling. Subsequently, I proceed with the introduction of the IDEF1X modeling semantics and syntax, and finally I present the IDEF1X modeling process, itself.

Semantic Models

Business rules, and subsequently conceptual schemas, are constructed from what are called "semantic models." The semantic model is the only tool available to the business to discover the semantic rules of its conceptual schema and then to build an information infrastructure around that conceptual schema. A semantic model is constructed using a semantic modeling technique. This technique provides the process needed to construct, verify and validate business rules, integrate them into a conceptual schema, and subsequently transform them into data models and physical databases.

What is a semantic model? According to Michael L. Brodie in his book *On Conceptual Modeling*, *"A [semantic] model is a collection of mathematically well defined concepts that help one to consider and express the static and dynamic properties of [symbols] . . ."* [6]

Static symbol properties are "meanings." Dynamic properties are those properties required to assemble meanings into messages. In mathematics, we call these operands and operators. In programming languages like COBOL, we refer to data and procedures. In database management systems (DBMSs), we talk about data definition and data manipulation. In artificial intelligence, we talk about knowledge and inference. The basic trend in business rule modeling is toward creating richer and more static semantic structures, because these structures can be "reused" time and time again to create messages.

In *On Conceptual Modeling*, Brodie describes five subtypes of semantic models: (1) direct extensions of the classical models, (2) mathematical models, (3) irreducible models, (4) static semantic hierarchy models and (5) dynamic semantic hierarchy models. To Brodie's list, which he developed in 1984, we can probably add object-oriented models which have lately begun to come into vogue.

A critical difference between classical data models and semantic models is that semantic models provide for different types of symbol abstraction. Abstractions are mandatory if symbol models are to capture true symbol meanings. There are basically four forms of symbol abstraction that must be represented in the semantic modeling language:

1. **Classification**—Also called the instance-of relationship, classification describes the most fundamental relationship between facts and meanings, that meanings are represented in the schema and facts are represented as instances of meanings in the database. For example, the concept of drawing may be represented in the schema as having the attributes of author and release date, and in the database you would find John Jones and March 12, 1983, describing an instance of the entity *drawing*.

2. **Aggregation**—Also called the part-of relationship, aggregation describes how component entities represented in the schema are part of a higher level aggregate entity. For example: the aggregate entity *part* is composed of component entities *drawing, specification*, and *change order*.

3. **Generalization**—Also called the is-a relationship, generalization describes how category entities can be represented in a schema as higher level generic entities. For example: the generic entity *drawing* can be used to describe category entities like *schematic, detailed drawing*, and *machine drawing*.

4. **Association**—Also called the member-of relationship, association describes how member entities in a schema can be represented as higher level set entities. For example: the set entity *detailed design baseline* is an association of *part* member entities, and the set entity *bill of material* is an association of *part* member entities.

Because they explicitly describe generalization and association, static semantic hierarchy models have the ability to express "value added" symbol structures, which provide the unique capability to track the inter-dependencies of different applications from a common symbol perspective. For example, if the production planning process adds production symbol to part symbol originally created by the engineering organization, this value added chain will be explicitly described in the business rules of the static semantic hierarchy model.

Semantic modeling languages that *cannot* at least express the relational concepts of keys, entity (or object) integrity, referential integrity, consistent treatment of null values, roles, aggregation, and generalization relationships over classes (i.e., objects, entities or sets) are useless for conceptual schema representation. This assertion is supported by the "Assessment Guidelines for Conceptual Schema Language Proposals" developed by the International Standards Organization (ISO).[7]

IDEF1X

To construct individual business rules, and subsequently a conceptual schema, requires a semantic modeling technique. To demonstrate how business rule models are built, I have chosen to present them in the context of a specific modeling technique known as IDEF1X. The IEEE IDEF1X semantic modeling standard[8] includes a set of modeling semantics, graphics, language and machine syntax's for variously representing the semantic models, and modeling rules, procedures and documentation formats. In this discussion of IDEF1X semantic modeling, I will first address the semantics and syntax dimensions of the modeling technique, and then I will present the model-building process.

IDEF1X Semantics and Syntax

Before going into greater detail, here are some quick and easy definitions for some of the basic terms involved in business rule modeling.

- An entity is a concept that is important to a business and for which there are numerous, uniquely identifiable instances, e.g., customer, patient, purchase order, drawing, etc.
- A message is a transaction between two or more activities that is composed of two or more entity symbols.
- An attribute is a characteristic of an entity, e.g., age, weight, color, start date, etc.
- A relationship is the constraint on how two or more entities can be interrelated, for example, "a customer *is a* patient" within a given message.

IDEF1X Entities

The fundamental component of a rule model is an entity. An entity is a set of real or abstract objects such as people, places, ideas, things, or events that have common attributes or characteristics. An

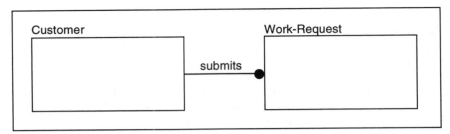

Figure 3: Entity-Relationship (ER) Model

individual member of the set is referred to as an entity instance. In other words, an entity instance is a specific occurrence of an entity. For instance, Rockwell could be an entity instance of the entity "Customer." Entity instances are not directly portrayed in a business rule model.

Entities are illustrated by boxes and are always named using a noun or a noun phrase. An entity name is placed outside the box, across the top as shown in Figure 3. Entities containing two or more words may be hyphenated.

Between the two entities shown in Figure 3 is a line with a dot at one end. It represents a relationship. The relationship name defines and restricts the relationship between the two entities. If the relationship involves two or more words, the words might be hyphenated as with the entity names. Figure 3 represents the simplest form of a business rule model. It is an example of what is called an entity-relationship (ER) model because it depicts only entities and their relationships to each other. ER models are discussed in greater detail below.

IDEF1X Attributes

The properties or characteristics that identify or describe entities are called attributes. Attributes are labeled with singular, generic nouns. A particular value of an attribute is an attribute instance, which equates to a particular characteristic of an individual member of the set. An attribute is identified by both the type of characteristic and its value. Each attribute in a business rule model is associated with a particular entity. An entity instance, therefore, must have a single specific value for each associated attribute.

IDEF1X Key and Non-Key Attributes

The attribute or set of attributes that uniquely identifies an entity instance is called a key attribute while the remaining attributes are referred to as non-key attributes. It is important to be able to identify each instance of an entity so an entity must have one or more key attributes that identify every instance of that entity. Within the model, each attribute is owned by only one entity and is said to be native to that entity.

Figure 4 shows placement of entity and attribute names in a generic model. The primary syntax of a business rule model includes square corner boxes representing self-contained entities, that is, entities that can exist without relying on another entity. Round-cornered boxes identify dependent entities. The entity name is placed outside the box. Inside the box, key attributes are placed above the line and non-key attributes below the line. Note that at the detail level of the example in Figure 4, key attributes serve primarily to logically distinguish one instance of an entity from another.

IDEF1X Relationships

One of the functions of IDEF1X diagrams is to illustrate the manner in which one entity is related to another entity. A relationship is named using a verb or verb phrase that describes the nature of the association. It is shown as a line that connects two entity boxes, the parent entity and the child entity. At one or both ends of the line, there may be a dot that represents the numerical instances of the relationship, its cardinality.

Cardinality expresses how many instances of one entity can be related to instances of another entity. The default, a plain black dot, in a relationship is interpreted as "zero, one, or many." When further definition is required, the dot will have a letter next to it. A "P" will indicate "one or more" a "Z" indicates a cardinality of "zero or one." Occasionally, other symbols may also appear. Later it will be explained that rule models are read in two directions. In reading the rule in reverse, the line, which now ends without a dot, is read as

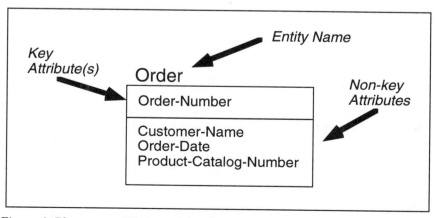

Figure 4: Placement of Entity and Attribute Names

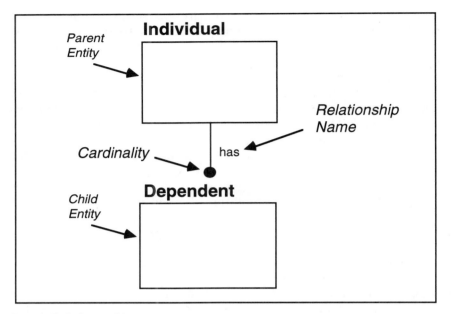

Figure 5: Relationships

"only one." As we go further into the IDEF1X modeling technique, other subtleties such as dashed lines and the round-cornered boxes come into play. Figure 5 is a generic model of the relationship components of an IDEF1X model.

Relationships are business rules. It is the relationships that constrain the way business is conducted. The complete entity-relationship diagram shows all the business rules needed to support the business process and the way these entities relate to one another to constrain the activities in the business process. For that reason, it is best to have functional users, those actually involved in the business process, construct the model because only they fully understand the importance of the business rules imposed by a business model.

IDEF1X Modeling Procedure

The result of applying the IDEF1X modeling technique is a specification of business rules typically represented by the following:

• A set of graphic models representing real or abstract objects, their characteristics or attributes, and their relationships to one another. IDEF1X diagrams are refined into three different levels of detail:

- Entity-relationship(ER), the least detailed level that merely identifies the entities and the relationships that exist among those entities
- Key-based (KB), the next level of detail that resolves the business rules into more specific relationships and identifies the primary keys of the entities
- Fully attributed (FA), the most detailed business rule model level that captures the additional non-key elements that describe each entity
• A glossary that defines the entities and attributes used in the models.
• Business rules, which are detailed, written descriptions about the business symbols and the manner in which they relate to other business symbols. These rules describe the constraints governing the use and creation of the organization's business rules. At the entity-relationship level, the rule model provides general business statements. Key-base and fully attributed models describe the enterprise business rules.

Business rule models, like business process models, are refined from the most general level to progressively more specific levels. Thus, the entity-relationship model is refined to the key-based level and then to the fully attributed model.

Three levels of rule models can be developed using the IDEF1X modeling technique as shown in Figure 6. Each level is essentially a refinement or more detailed version of the previously developed IDEF1X model. Each model is cumulative. If the same IDEF1X modeling technique is used and the same rules are followed, and if consensus is achieved for each model, then each model adds to the organization's knowledge base without changing what already exists. In other words, each model level adds more detail to discovered business rules. For some, it might help to visualize a pyramid with the entity relationship level at the tip and an ever widening base of discovered business rules as the rule model works its way down the pyramid through the key-based level to the fully attributed level. For others, looking at Figure 6, it will be evident that the entity-relationship level is larger in scope but more limited in depth than other levels. The key-based level is more focused in scope with a bit more depth while the fully-attributed level is even more limited in scope but has great depth.

Entity-Relationship Level

The most generalized level is an entity-relationship IDEF1X model. This model focuses on entities and their relationships. At this modeling level, it is impossible to draw precise conclusions about

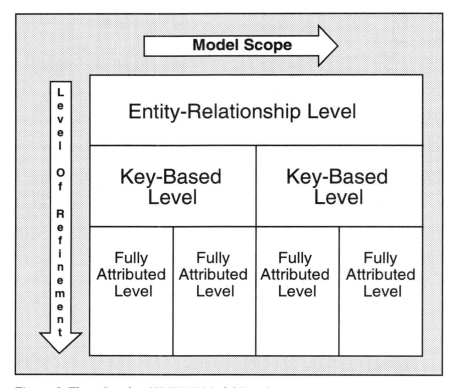

Figure 6: Three Levels of IDEF1X Model Development

how an organization operates. Entity-relationship level models reveal a bigger picture and are therefore useful to develop during the planning stages of a business process improvement project.

The entity-relationship IDEF1X model provides a first stepping stone to the final, fully attributed IDEF1X model. Since model-building takes a top-down, refinement approach, the entity-level is the broadest level to be considered. It is useful for planning because it helps define initial business statements that represent constraints in the environment.

The entity-relationship model focuses on just a few details at a time—in this case entities and their relationships—rather than having to deal with a large amount of detail (characteristics of the objects and relationships) at once. The result is a reasonably digestible amount of information that facilitates good rule modeling. Figure 7 shows a simple entity relationship model diagram. This E-R level model addresses three critical concepts: Requester, Order, and Part.

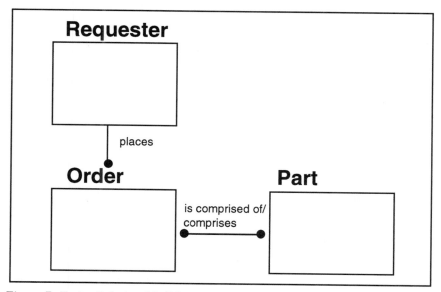

Figure 7: Entity-Relationship Diagram

At the entity-relationship level as well as subsequent levels, a special type of relationship between a parent entity and one or more category entities may be drawn. Looking at Figure 8, it is quickly apparent that a parent entity can have one or more subsets, each known as a category entity. Each category entity contains all data pertinent to the parent entity type. In addition, in the illustration in Figure 8, the category "Buy-Part" might contain an attribute name "Part-Price" and the category entity "Make-Part" might have the attribute "Part-Cost." Neither one of these attributes would be owned by the generic parent entity "Part," because each applies to only one category.

Key-Based Level

The second level is the key-based IDEF1X model, which adds the unique attributes (identifiers) to each entity, as well as other refinements to the model's structure. The key-based model usually takes a smaller scope of a subject area and represents greater depth. It is the next step to take in establishing business rules.

In this level of business rule modeling, the primary attributes that define each entity are shown. This level also indicates which of these attributes are unique identifiers of an entity so that particular instances of the entity can be accessed. For example, if a "Part" has a specific "Part Number," that would be a key identifying attribute since it is reasonable to expect that no other part would have the identical number. A fully developed key-based business rule model

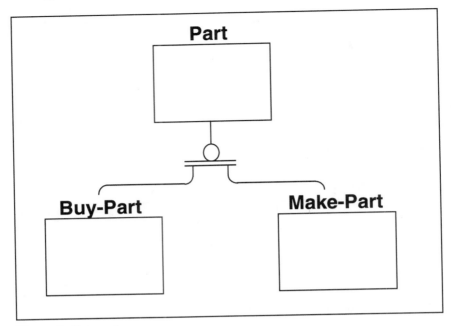

Figure 8: Categories

will show all of the entities together with their key attributes, plus the relationship between and among entities. The key-based model may also include a few non-key attributes, if needed for clarity.

Figure 9 shows a key-based diagram. In this diagram, the round-cornered box indicates an identification-dependent entity as mentioned earlier. The square box labeled "Order" is an existence-dependent entity. The (FK) attribute shown in each of these dependent entities means "foreign key," defined as a key in a child (dependent) entity that is inherited from its parent entity. Only primary keys may be inherited. The foreign key may or may not become part of the primary key of the child entity. If it should not become part of the primary key, the relationship line connecting the two entities will be dashed instead of solid.

Fully Attributed Level

The third level is the fully attributed IDEF1X model, which is a candidate for incorporation into the organization's common business rule pool, that is, its conceptual schema. While it may be limited in scope, it represents a subject area in the greatest amount of detail. All non-key attributes are added and precise mathematical normalization is applied as a quality control check on the model. Normalization is a set of tests that ensure stable groupings of attributes by housing them in the appropriate entities. This quality control test

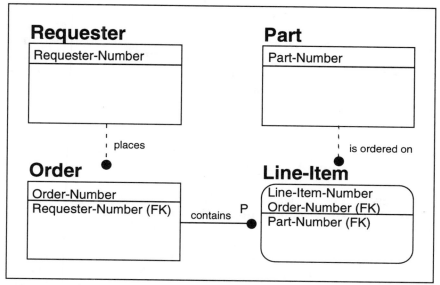

Figure 9: Key-Based Diagram

against a fully attributed rule model eliminates data redundancy and allows the model to be fully extensible as new business rules are discovered.

In Figure 10, the key-based example from Figure 9 is now shown as a fully-attributed model diagram.

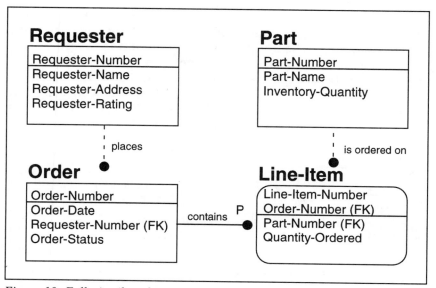

Figure 10: Fully Attributed Diagram

Business Rules

All of this discussion of semantic models has been leading up to the formation of business rules. Business rules are a translation of a conceptual schema expressed in an IDEF1X rule model, into English language statements. It may be said that IDEF1X models are business rules in graphic form.

Business rules identify and describe:

* The classification of an organization's people, places, things, ideas, and   events (entities), which need to be communicated and measured
* The descriptors of those entities (attributes)
* The relationships among the entities and their attributes

Business rules help to validate the entities, attributes, and relationships that are being modeled. They are tests of quality of the model. If the business rules are unreadable or if they have no meaning to the reviewers of the model, it is a clear indication that the model has not captured the correct structure of the business and the model should be adjusted accordingly.

Figure 11 demonstrates how business rules concerning attributes are read. Remember that the attribute above the line in the box representing the entity is the key attribute while those below the line are non-key. Non-key does not mean less important, but simply signifies that these attributes are not necessary to identify particular instances of an entity.

The syntax for a business rule is easy to keep in mind. Business rules that apply to relationships take the form of a sentence in which one entity name is the subject, the relationship is a verb or verb phrase, the cardinality is the adjective, and another entity is the object. These business rules must be identifiable and readable directly from the completed model in both directions between a pair of entities. Every business rule can be read forward and backward and needs to be correct in each direction.

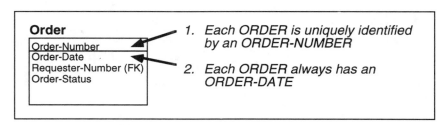

Figure 11: Reading Business Rules

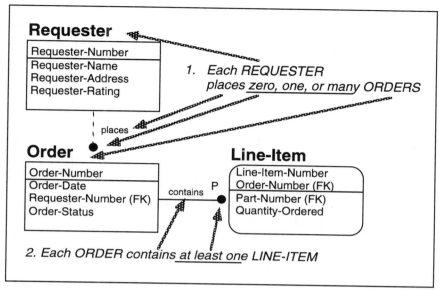

Figure 12: Business Rules Concerning Entity Relationships

Look back at Figure 10. In this example, it is possible to read two business rules very quickly reading the right side of the diagram in both directions.

(1) Each Part is ordered on zero, one, or many Line-Items
(2) Each Line-Item orders only one Part

Figure 12 shows how to read two business rules from the diagram but each in only one direction.

Constructing a Conceptual Schema

When we think about it from a distance, it seems self-evident that there would be more than one business process concerned about the concepts of Requester, Order, Line Item, and Part. It also seems self evident that messages exchanged within and among these processes would be much more information intensive if these processes and the activities within them shared the same business rules regarding these entities. Ergo, the business rules defined above should represent a subset of the conceptual schema shared by these processes and the activities within them. However, rarely do we have the luxury of setting off with business rules that are comfortably shared among diverse processes. Rather, we start with different processes, expose their business rules, and then embark on a process of negotiation in an attempt to converge their unique business rules into an internally consistent conceptual schema. This negotiating process is almost always adversarial with strong political undertones. But, the negotiation is not nefarious. It is healthy, because it quickly points out the inherent differences among processes; differences that induce severe productivity problems; differences that would, without the discerning lens of the semantic model, be nearly impossible to pin down and reconcile.

Business Rules and Information Technology

The final subject we need to address is: "What is the relationship between information quality, business rules, and information technology?" Given a traditional view of information technology, there is no clear answer to this question. Information quality, for example, is measured as a ratio of information messages to all messages sent, while the quality of information *technology* is measured in terms of thousands of lines of code (KLOCS), millions of instructions per second (MIPS), or response time. The correlation between these two is difficult to make, if not impossible. However, business rules and the notion of the conceptual schema demonstrate how the two concepts can be integrated within an information infrastructure through a logical device called the "three schema architecture."

Information Infrastructure

It seems reasonable to assume that if information technology is to play its expected role as a multiplier in the information equation, that it must be brought into synergistic alignment with the organizational sense of productivity and information quality. This correlation must be accomplished in what has come to be called the "information infrastructure" of the organization. Information infrastructure, contrary to popular belief, is not just some computers, some telecommunications software, and some applications code and databases. It is much more.

Figure 13 depicts the three critical elements of information infrastructure: (1) information demand, (2) business software, and (3) information technology platform.

I have already proposed that information demand, while reflected in business processes, is in large measure determined by business rules. I have also made the case for separating business behavior (processes) from business rules when reengineering a business to change its behavior. As we begin to implement information technology to support business behavior, it is mandatory that we maintain this separation and the interconnection between rules and processes at the level of business software design. This means

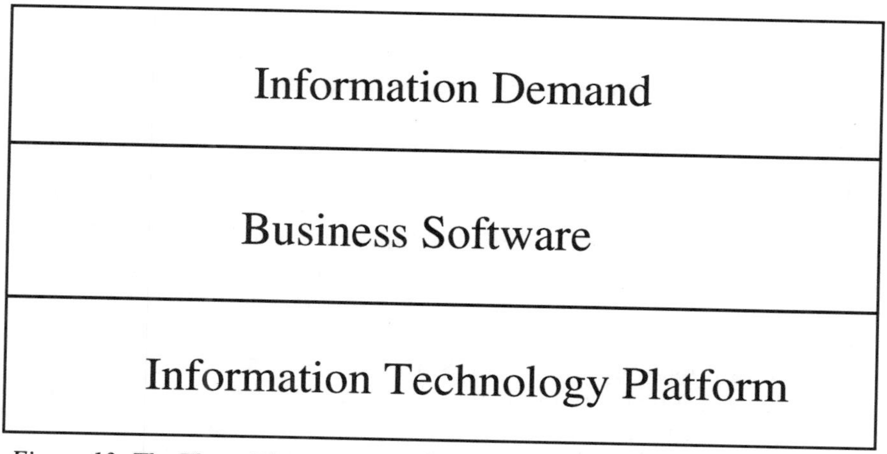

Information Demand
Business Software
Information Technology Platform

Figure 13: The Three Dimensions of Information Infrastructure

using business rule models to drive business software design.

The business software incarnation of business rules is called a "database." The route from information demand defined in terms of a conceptual schema to physical database *implementations* on a computer involves two critical steps: (1) transforming a business rule model into a data model (by adding dimensionality to the business rule model such as field type and size), and (2) designing the physical data base (which converts a data model into an optimum mix of data definition statements and procedural code, using the data definition and data manipulation languages of a specific database management system). By following these steps, we can neatly transform business rules into business software designs which can subsequently be implemented on an information technology platform, still maintaining the separation and interconnection between processes and rules.

Three Schema Architecture

There are a set of principles that have proven useful in effecting these transformations, first from information demand to business software design and then from business software design to implementation in the information technology platform. These principles are embodied in a concept called the "three schema architecture."

The importance of the three schema architecture is that it provides a notional framework that focuses attention on the business rules that comprise knowledge infrastructure of the business. In doing so, it provides a mechanism not only for visualizing (and directly managing) the business rules that govern the behavior of the business, but it also places those business rules in the proper perspective relative to business software (and hardware), on one hand, and the information messages demanded by business processes, on the other.

Originally developed in 1971 by the Data Base Task Group (DBTG) of the American National Standards Institute (ANSI/X3/SPARC), the three schema architecture was intended as a set of design guidelines for future database management systems (DBMS). Its primary objective was to specify a DBMS architecture that provided the maximum level of *data independence*. In those days, data independence was seen to be the primary purpose of database management systems. The concept was that if data (which are relatively stable) could be separated from processes (which are relatively dynamic), then programmer productivity would be increased. Programmers could make changes to databases without having to change the programs that operate on them, and, conversely, the programs could be changed without having to worry about changing the database on which they operated.

The basic concept of data independence has proven itself to be one of the major lasting improvements to programmer productivity. Database management systems are the largest selling class of systems software in the world, and hardly an IS organization exists that does not have at least one database management system. In fact, it is the database management system that initially gave rise to the data administration function, a precursor to what we know today as the data management function.

The eight members of the DBTG who developed the three schema architecture were reactionaries. The Committee On Data Systems and Languages (CODASYL), which had made its name by standardizing COBOL (the Common Business Oriented Language), which is still, today, the dominant programming language in business, had just established the CODASYL standard architecture for database management systems. This architecture was basically an extension of the COBOL language. However, the DBTG felt that the CODASYL architecture was not the optimum architecture for achieving data independence, and decided that yet another attempt should be made at defining the ideal architecture.

According to the DBTG, the problem with the CODASYL architecture, and with all other database management system architectures developed to that point, was that it focused on tight binding between what a user saw (a report) and the physical structure of the computer database. The reason for this requirement was that tight binding between output and storage structures was required to maximize machine efficiency. In the war between data independence and machine efficiency, machine efficiency won out.

In designing the three schema architecture, the DBTG did not concern itself with machine efficiency. It was committed to build an architecture that would maximize human efficiency through data independence from software. To accomplish this, the DBTG decided to separate data structure from file structure and from report structure. The basis for this tripartite separation was the observation that data structures represent the invariant part of a database and have nothing to do with efficiency issues, while file structures (which are important to efficiency) and report structures change constantly. Further, data structures, which are derived from data models, provide a mathematically sound representation of the semantic rules that control information potential within an organization. Because they are mathematically sound, data models can be validated by means of symbolic logic, and, as a result, the internal consistency of the knowledge infrastructure can be directly checked and controlled purely by means of models. These models can subsequently be employed for the development of computer databases.

The capability to mathematically describe data structures, and to ensure their internal consistency, meant that several independently developed data structures could be integrated into a single model, and that such a process would flush out inconsistencies among various independently developed data structures *before* they were committed to software. This capability gave rise to the notion that a single data structure that could support multiple software implementations could be developed, and that the same data structure could be used to support multiple report structures. Further, if the single composite data structure were interposed between the multiple file structures and the multiple report structures, it became unimportant, as far as the report structures were concerned, as to which of the multiple files were required to provide data required by a single report.

As a result of this thinking, the DBTG proposed a DBMS architecture comprised of three schemas, or structures. Ergo, the three schema architecture shown in Figure 14.

The three schema architecture defines three different, but integrated, views of business rules: external schemas, internal schemas, and conceptual schemas. Multiple   and multiple internal schemas are integrated by a single conceptual schema. Unlike the classical two schema approach, which directly maps external schemas onto internal schemas, the three schema approach, through the introduction of the conceptual schema, makes external and internal schemas independent of one other. Instead, they are both dependent on the conceptual schema.

The importance of buffering changes in business behavior (external schema) from changes in the information technology platform (internal schema) with software design based on business

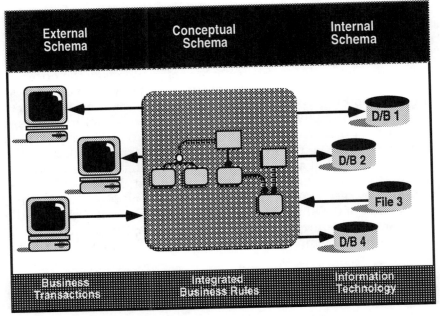

Figure 14: The ANSI/SPARC Three Schema Architecture

rules (conceptual schema) cannot be understated. Business behavior wants to change at its own pace, driven by all sorts of dynamic management imperatives, including business reengineering programs. However, the forces driving change in the information technology platform, for example, from traditional file structures to very modern client-server, multi-media, and object-oriented technologies, have little or nothing to do with fundamental changes in business behavior.

It is the clear purpose of business reengineering to change business behavior. Given the traditional view of what we call information engineering, each time a business process is redesigned, its supporting business software must be redesigned and, in all probability, the information technology platform must be changed. In the vast majority of cases, the time and expense involved with bringing information technology into alignment with new business processes creates a tremendous drag on the whole business reengineering process, in many cases rendering it impotent. In far too many situations, the information technology drag on business reengineering is so severe that business reengineering can only be accomplished within the constraints of the existing information technology legacy. The only way out of this dilemma is to employ the three schema architecture in driving information infrastructure reengineering. This means pivoting all three dimensions of information infrastructure around business rules.

Implications

Advice for Management

If you need further convincing as to the importance of business rules in reengineering your business, I challenge you to conduct the following test. Pick five symbols that you consider to be critical to your business. Examples might be symbols like "customer," "part," "account," "supplier," and "inventory." Write a brief definition for each of these symbols. Be as precise and as detailed as you possibly can, but do not use examples or metaphors (that's cheating). Write your definitions using the concepts of entity, attributes, and relationships as much as you can. Next, go to each of the managers reporting to you, to each of your peers, and to your Chief Information Officer. Ask them to give you a precise definition for each of the five symbols. Finally, compare these definitions. If they are all the same for a given symbol, you get ten on a scale of one to ten, and you can assume that your information quality ratio relative to that symbol is fairly high. If they are significantly different for a given symbol, you get one on a scale of one to ten, and your information quality ratio relative to that symbol is low. If you want a picture of your overall information quality ratio, you can rate each of the five symbols on a scale from one to ten (use your own judgment on the tweeners), and total up your score for each symbol, then divide by five. If your total score is less than eight, you had better plan to introduce business rules into the middle of your performance improvement program.

Implications for Future Research

While it is clear that there is tremendous power in using business rules to reengineer organizational behavior, it should also be understood that we have just scratched the surface. But, what lies below? It could be that by seizing on business rules, we have found the key to understanding organizations as chaotic or complex systems. This statement is not meant to be as glib as it may seem. Over the last decade, we have seen the emergence of new sciences called Chaos and Complex Systems. At the heart of these new sciences is a very powerful hypothesis: *a few simple rules can create incredibly complex behavior*. Given the concepts presented in this chapter, we could restate this hypothesis in organizational terms: *a few simple business rules can produce an incredible complex of business processes*. If, on the surface, a business appears to be a chaos of tasks, transactions, teams, departments, people, and what not, is it not conceivable that underneath this apparent chaos lies a relatively simple set of business rules, quietly orchestrating everything that goes on?

The problem with chaotic systems, of course, is that we immediately assume that they are so complex that we can never really understand how they work. We are blinded by the behavior we observe. The message of Chaos Theory, however, is that we must drive right through the observable manifestations of behavior, penetrating until we find the internal rules that govern that behavior, like a weather plane penetrates a hurricane until it arrives at the eye. What awaits us there, we can only guess, but if Chaos Theory is any indication, we will find some fascinating things. For example, Chaos scientists have learned that, while the internal rules of a system remain constant, the behavior patterns of the system change *as the level of excitement of the system increases or decreases*. Using our organizational vocabulary, this could be translated as follows: while business rules remain constant, business processes change as the level of activity in the business increases or decreases. While this may not appear to be a blinding revelation, it does tell us something we do not think much about: *if we are going to operate directly on business processes, we had better think about how those processes will operate at different levels of business activity*. We should also consider in our process designs how to make our reengineered processes self-adapting so that they can automatically adjust themselves as the level of activity of the business fluctuates.

At this point in time, I am not advocating that reengineering teams run out and study Chaos or Complex Systems. However, I am postulating that given the perspective that business rules provides us, the perspective that a business is a complex system whose processes behave in accordance with the possibilities and constraints of its business rules, it only makes sense to explore the potential relevance of Chaos Theory and the science of Complexity to organizational performance improvement.

Conclusion

If, after reading this chapter, you are giving second thoughts to the viability of approaching business reengineering strictly by a reductionist approach to reengineering business processes, I have accomplished my primary objective. Business processes are manifestations of business behavior, but business behavior, itself, is controlled by business rules. Think about it this way. A single game of chess is a process. Each game is played according to the same rules. These rules determine what the pieces are and how they are allowed to move. Given this single set of internally consistent business rules for chess, players can conjure up an infinite number of different games, some of them better than others. On the other hand, if *one* rule is changed, say we allow a pawn to move one space laterally, or we introduce a new piece, say a "jack" that is allowed to jump over other pieces on the board, the whole concept of the game is changed, and a new infinity of games immediately presents itself. We might even question whether this new game should be called Chess.

The essential challenge of business reengineering is to understand the rules of our business game, and once we have that understanding to change them to engender the types of behaviors that will generate more revenues and allow us to service those revenues with lower costs. These rules control our productivity; they control our ability to measure and reward desirable behavior; and they control our ability to communicate effectively internally and with our customers, suppliers, and service vendors. Effective control over business rules allows us to expedite organizational learning, and to empower and provide meaningful incentives to individuals, teams, centers of excellence, profit centers, and other organizational modules to effect process changes without threatening the entire business. Effective control of our business rules allows us to expedite change, create adaptive organizations, and increase the level of business activity without shaking the whole organization apart. Effective control over business rules allows us to bind information technology into the fabric of the business, rather than sustaining IT as an objectionable appendage. And, finally, effective control over business rules allows us to implement truly meaningful change with a minimum of cost, risk, and time.

References

[1] Cohen, Jack and Ian Stewart (1994). *The Collapse of Chaos.* New York: Viking.

[2] Beer, Stafford (1979). *The Heart of Enterprise.* Chichester: John Wiley & Sons.

[3] Shannon, Claude E. and Warren Weaver (1963). *The Mathematical Theory of Communication.* Urbana and Chicago: University of Illinois Press.

[4] Appleton, Daniel S. (October 1984). Business Rules, The Missing Link. *Datamation,* 19-27.

[5] Strasser, J.B., and Laurie Becklund (1991). *The Story of Nike and the Men who Played There.* New York: Harcourt, Brace, Jovanovich.

[6] Brodie, Michael L., John Mylopoulous and Joachim W. Schmidt (1984). *On Conceptual Modeling.* Springer-Verlag.

[7] International Standards Organization TC97/SC21/WG5-3 (August 1985). *Assessment Guidelines for Conceptual Schema Language Proposals.*

[8] IEEE (1994). *IDEF1X Modeling Standard.*

Chapter
12

Process Modelling—Who, What and How:

Role Activity Diagramming

Tim Huckvale and Martyn Ould
Praxis plc

People involved in Business Process Reengineering (BPR) are concerned with the way people work together to achieve business objectives, generally with a view to building a new organisation with new processes—an organisation that is more effective and more efficient. The approach that is chosen to seeking radical change, and the skills, experience and motivation of the BPR practitioners are central. Our concern in this chapter is to look in detail at an ancillary topic: the techniques available for modelling those ways that people work together. A process model can help the BPR practitioner in several ways:

1. As a focus for discussion. A good modelling technique, with sound syntax and semantics, and accompanied by a disciplined process for creating the model, will help us ask the right questions about the real world and bring to light the important points for discussion and agreement.
2. As a means for communicating a process to others. People not involved in developing the model may review it or use it as a basis for approving a new or changed process. A model of an approved process may serve as a guide to those who have to carry it out.

3. As a basis for analysis. Analysis of the model can reveal weak points in the process, for example actions that add little value or are potential bottlenecks. Given suitable animation and simulation tools, the model may be used to explore the effects of change.
4. For designing a new process. Comparison of models of the "same" process as performed by different parts of the same organisation can help arrive at a common "best" process. Comparison of the model of a current manual process with the process model that is assumed by a bought-in applications package can help to reveal activities where change in the manual process or customisation of the package is needed.
5. As a baseline for continuing process improvement. Suggestions for change can be expressed as changes to the model. For those interested in collecting metrics, a model is not only necessary for a clear understanding of what the metrics mean, but the model may itself suggest useful things to measure.
6. As a program for controlling the real world process. A sufficiently formal model may be used to drive an enaction system, such as a Workflow Management System. This executes the process within a computer system and can ensure that the process is carried out faithfully every time it is used, that deadlines are met, and that accurate metrics and audit trails are kept automatically.

In short, process models have a role to play in radical change programmes (BPR), incremental change programmes (TQM), quality management systems, and the use of process technology and IT. In the BPR context, process re-design, process comparison, and detailed process understanding, especially with regard to the relationship between process and organisation, can all be facilitated by a good process model. The question then becomes "what form should a process model take?". Early process-modellers tended to seize on the familiar data flow diagram (DFD) notation, but its limitations in meeting the needs of BPR are becoming generally recognised: DFDs have a limited vocabulary and are imprecise about the details of sequence and concurrency; they do not show who does what. More fundamentally, concentrating on the data objects used in a process diverts attention from the process features that are most relevant for BPR.

This chapter begins by identifying what are relevant process features. We then compare some popular process modelling notations to see how well they bring out these features. We conclude that the notation of Role Activity Diagrams (RADs) is especially well-suited to business process modelling. The main body of the chapter describes in outline the RAD notation, as used in Praxis' own approach to process modelling, STRIM [1]. (A full description of STRIM will be found in Ould (1995)).

Background

Models are a means of showing the essentials of complex problems. They allow us to abstract from the real world, highlighting those objects and relationships which are of interest and ignoring those that are not. What are the relevant abstractions for assisting BPR practitioners?

The paper Process Modeling, by Curtis et al (1992), although chiefly concerned with modelling the software development process, is useful for giving a conceptual framework of process modelling techniques and their uses. They represent the abstractions that may be useful as the sorts of questions that people want to ask about the process, classified into four perspectives:

- Functional, representing what activities are being performed and what dataflows connect them.
- Behavioural, representing when activities are performed, with sequencing, feedback loops, iteration, decision making, triggering conditions, etc.
- Organisational, representing where and by whom activities are performed, plus physical communication mechanisms and storage media.
- Informational, representing the entities (documents, data, artifacts, products) produced or manipulated by a process, including their structure and inter-relationships.

We might add to their list the Quantitative perspective, in which we wish to explore such features as cycle times and resource consumption. More on this later.

The key perspectives for BPR are the behavioural and organisational ones. The rules that govern sequencing and decision-making are at the very heart of the process, and the parts that people play in the process are exactly the components that are likely to be rearranged when it comes to improving the process.

Figure 1 indicates the strengths of several popular notations in representing these four main perspectives (none of the notations address the quantitative perspective).

- The familiar dataflow diagram (DFD) notation has already been mentioned. It is described in many books on structured analysis and design methods: one such is Dickinson (1980).
- IDEF0 (USAF, 1981) is widely used for process modelling but also suffers from being firmly rooted in a data-oriented view. It includes notation for some elements of the behavioural and organisational perspectives, such as decisions and mechanisms (the "resources" that carry out a function). On the whole, though, it captures only

	Funct- ional	Behav- ioural	Organis- ational	Inform- ational
DFD	■			
IDEF0	■	▪	▪	
Process Map	■	▪	■	
Action Workflow	▪	▪	▪	
RAD/RIN	▪	■	■	
ERA Modelling				■

The larger the box, the stronger the support of the notation for that perspective.

Figure 1: Notational Perspectives

a small variety of process features, as Earl (1994) has shown.

Revealing its roots in the hard, neat and tidy world of the information technologist, IDEF0 forces a strictly hierarchical view of human activity which is not realistic and may inhibit the mapping of a process "as is".

- The Process Map notation of Rummler & Brache (1990) is that of the traditional flow chart, with extensions to show organisational responsibility for process steps (by horizontal layering of the diagram) and performance constraints or goals. It covers a broader range of process features than IDEF0, and is easily understood by "ordinary" readers.

Although the Process Map does address organisational aspects, its limitation to unidirectional flow as the only relationship between activities means that other types of interaction between people, such as a meeting, have to be fudged.

- Action Workflow is a proprietary notation of Action Technologies, based on an interpretation of work as the making and fulfilling of commitments, as proposed by Winograd and Flores (1987). It is sufficiently formal to be used as the basis for an "Application Builder", ie for computer-supported enaction of the defined process. A concise introduction and case study is given by Denning and Medina-Mora (1994). Its single-minded strength is also its weakness: not all processes are easily mapped as commitments between two parties.

- Role Activity Diagrams (RADs) were developed by Anatol Holt (1983) for modelling coordination in the workplace. With a concise and rich notation that is easy to read, they offer good coverage of the functional, behavioural and organisational perspectives, particularly at the detailed level. They have a formal basis in Petri-net theory, and thus can be used as a basis for enaction. They do not assume the world is neatly structured and they allow multiple perspectives.

- Role Interaction Nets (RINs) (see Singh and Rein, 1992) are very similar to RADs, sharing the Holt pedigree. They have additional notation for showing dataflows (lack of which is a common criticism of RADs as used so far) and for distinguishing optional and manual actions (as opposed to automatic actions, carried out by a computer). They rely on relative positioning of symbols in the diagram to indicate sequential dependencies of actions. Some may find this harder to read than the corresponding explicit constructions in RADs (see below).
- Entity Relationship Attribute (ERA) modelling (see Chen, 1976) illustrates exactly the informational perspective. It is therefore of value in complementing any of the other notations.

Some modellers have found that a combination of notations is useful. Kawalek (1994), for example, has used IDEF0 for high level process views and RADs, with roles explicitly linked to IDEF0 activities, to fill in the detail.

What makes a good process modelling notation? We have already touched on some of the features that are important. To summarise Ould (1994):

- the concepts, objects and relationships represented in the model should be intuitively familiar, so that people can readily understand and talk about them,
- the notation should be easy for readers to grasp, after (say) a fifteen minute verbal introduction,
- the notation should be unambiguous (another way of saying that it should have formal syntax and semantics) so that it can be analysed and, possibly enacted,
- it should be possible for the notation to draw attention to the purposes of what people do rather than the detail of how they do it; this requires a concept for relationships between people (such as the RAD/RIN interaction or the Action Workflow commitment loop) that is at a higher level than simple document flow,
- it should be possible to handle complexity.

The choice of a good process modelling notation and supporting method can make all the difference between a model that is useful and revealing and one that is not. Further guidance on this choice is offered by Clough (1993), based on the sorts of process questions to which the modeller is seeking answers. Our own experience is that Role Activity Diagrams meet the criteria for a good process modelling

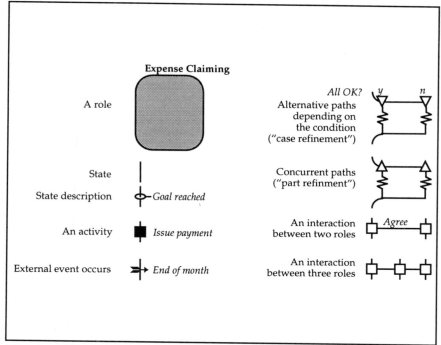

Figure 2: The RAD Notation

notation that we have listed above. In the rest of this chapter we hope
to convince the reader to share our view.

Process Modelling with Strim

STRIM has been developed at Praxis as an approach to process
modelling to support Business Process Reengineering. At its heart
is process modelling with RADs. In this section we introduce the
notation of RADs, illustrated with an everyday example process. The
reader will find it useful to refer to Figure 2, summarising the RAD
notation, and Figure 3, a RAD for Claiming Expenses [2].

As we shall discuss later (How will I know when my model is
complete?) it is very important, when modelling, to have a clear idea
of the purpose of our model: What point of view is being taken? Who
will use the model? What for? Our example is the process of claiming
expenses, from the point of view of the Expense Claimant, to be used
in documenting the process so that claimants understand what is
required of them and what to expect in return.

The STRIM Perspective

STRIM takes the view that there are five key concepts that need
to be modelled for a business process:

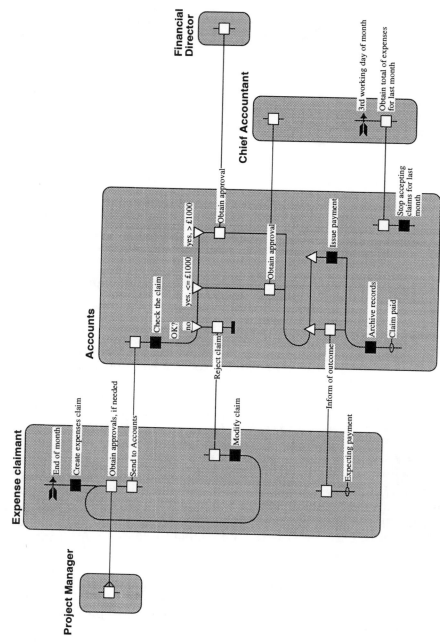

Figure 3: RAD for Claiming Expenses

1. How activities are divided amongst roles.
2. What the organisation is trying to achieve with the process: the process goals.
3. What people do to achieve the goals: activities.
4. How people within groups interact collaboratively to get the job done.
5. What constraints the organisation puts on what people can do and how they should operate: the business rules.

Let us look at each of these in turn.

Processes are divided over roles. A role is a set of activities that are generally carried out by an individual or group with some organisationally relevant responsibility. Associated with the role are the resources required for performing that role, such as files, desks, tools, and skills.

Each role in a process behaves independently, with its own set of resources (such as specific skills, files, reference material), and coordinates with other roles as necessary, via interactions.

Holding Figure 3 at arm's length, it is the roles and their interactions that are the most apparent features—each role is represented as a separate shaded area, and interactions are the horizontal lines joining them.

One role is that of Project Manager. This role is typically acted by one person at a time, and within the role there are many activities that that person would undertake: planning, reporting, monitoring, managing staff, liaising with suppliers, working with the client, and so on. The role of project managing project X could be acted by me today, and by another person tomorrow. The role is separate from the people who act it.

We are only concerned here with the part that the project manager plays in the Expense Claiming process, from the claimant's point of view, so most of the project managing activities listed above are not shown. We could have made this plainer by naming the role Project expense approving, which you may think of as a "sub-role" of Project Manager. Naming roles in this way, to cover the minimal set of activities necessary to the process, is a good way to focus on what needs to be done rather than who (which person or position) does it. This helps us to see roles independently of current organisational structure. Kawalek (1994) has used this feature of RADs to facilitate process redesign.

In Expense Claiming, we are content to use the title Project Manager, since it is more meaningful to the model reader (a person trying to get their expenses approved). In this organisation, the project expense approving role is always carried out by someone with the job-title of Project Manager.

Similar considerations apply to the example roles Chief Accountant and Financial Director.

The role of Expense claimant is a straightforward abstraction. No-one has this as a job-title; it is a role that anyone can assume, at the end of the month.

In the case of the Accounts role, we are naming the part played by a whole group of people. This is convenient, because although we are interested in showing several different types of activity within the Accounts department, we are not interested in how the Accounts department is internally organised; we want to portray them as a single group providing a service to the Expense claimant.

It is often useful in a RAD to represent computer systems as roles, in order to show at what points in a process they are used, without going into the detail of what they do.

The process goals. In STRIM, we define a process as a coordinated set of activities, carried out by a group of people, in order to achieve some corporate goal. It is important therefore to identify in our model the point in the process where the goal can be said to have been achieved.

The notion of goal is a special case of the more fundamental concept of state: a goal may be thought of as a state (or combination of states) that the process is trying to get to. People are not generally aware of the concept of state, yet they use it all the time; the cry "Where have you got to with my expense claim?" is a question about what state a process is in, and the question "Are we all agreed?", addressed to a meeting, is an attempt to confirm that a key state has been reached.

In a RAD, states are represented as vertical lines. "Interesting" states, such as those that are goals (or parts of goals), are suitably labelled, as for example Expecting payment in Figure 3.

Activities: what people do. An activity is shown on the RAD as a black box, with a state line above it (the pre-state that the role must reach for the activity to start) and a second state line below it (the post-state that is reached on completion of the activity). The symbolism of the "black box" is intentional, carrying the implication that we are not concerned with how an activity, such as Create expense claim or Issue payment is carried out. The role is empowered (and has the responsibility) to act on its own, without (at the level of detail we are interested in) involving other roles.

It is the notions of pre-state and post-state that allow us to define a sequence of activities, by identifying the post-state of one activity with the pre-state of another (done on the diagram by joining the respective statelines together). "Time proceeds downwards in a RAD."

Interactions between roles. People (acting in some role) do not only operate as independent individuals. Processes almost invariably involve the collaboration of a number of individuals or groups, and that collaboration takes place through many sorts of interaction, such as

- I pass you some information
- I delegate a task to you
- we agree on an action
- you pass me the results of your work
- I wait for you to do something.

In the process of Claiming Expenses, the role Expense claimant interacts with the role Accounts in several ways. In the first interaction, Send to Accounts it presents the claim, approved by the Project Manager, to Accounts for payment. This is shown on the diagram by a white box in each role, connected by a horizontal line. Each box has pre-state and post-state lines attached, just like a black-box activity. The interaction takes place when both roles are in their respective pre-states, and finishes with both roles simultaneously entering their post-states. At its simplest, therefore, an interaction is simply a point of synchronisation between roles.

In Send to Accounts, Accounts' pre-state is not tied to any other state. This means that Accounts is always ready to participate in this interaction; in other words it will accept an expenses claim at any time. Expense claimant, on the other hand, may only send in their claim after obtaining necessary Project Manager approvals.

An interaction often involves, as in this case, a transfer of some object (here an expenses claim) from one role to another. In some cases there may be an exchange of objects: I give you money in return for goods. But an interaction need not involve the transfer of anything: for instance, you and I might meet (interact) to agree on something; nothing changes hands, but our respective states are certainly altered by the interaction.

On the RAD, we usually label the interaction from the point of view of the role that is responsible for initiating it, and position the label at that end of the interaction. If, in our organisation, expenses claims were collected by a representative of the Accounts department each month, we would have labelled the interaction Collect claim at the Accounts end, showing where the responsibility lies.

Our RAD does not indicate the physical form of each interaction; we have concentrated on the significance of each interaction. The expenses claim could be a piece of paper, or an electronic document; the RAD has abstracted away this physical detail. Similarly, the interaction Obtain approval between Accounts and Financial Director could be implemented by physically sending the expenses claim (post or email), and waiting for them to come back "approved", or by taking them into the Financial Director's office and waiting while they are approved (with the advantage of being available to answer any queries the Financial Director may have), or (in a less bureaucratic organisation), by making a phone call. The RAD does not say how it's done, but it does tell the intended reader (the Expense claimant) all they need to be aware of in order to participate in the process.

If we are interested in the physical form of interactions, we can add more detail. We could label the interaction more precisely, e.g., Obtain approval via phone, or we could break it up into two interactions: Send claim via Red Box and (in Financial Director) Return approved claims by post, separated by an additional activity in Financial Director of Approve claim.

Interactions may be two-role, as are all those in our example, or multi-role, with the horizontal line linking white boxes in all participating roles. All the participating roles must be ready for the interaction to take place before it can start, it starts at the same moment for each role, and it completes at the same moment for each role.

In some cases an interaction might physically take a few seconds (I give you an expenses claim), in others months (a vendor and purchaser agree on the contractual terms of a sale).

The business rules. As we have seen, the concepts of role, goal (as a state to be reached), activity and interaction are represented directly in a RAD. The business rules show up as the pattern of sequencing, decision-making and concurrent activity that binds them all together. The additional notation that makes this possible is that of case refinement and part refinement.

Case refinement is exemplified following the activity Check the claim in the Accounts role. The three upturned triangles (reminiscent of logical "or" symbols) indicate that the state following Check the claim may be refined, case-wise, into three alternatives, only one of which is true in a particular instance of the process. The choice of alternative is made by querying the attributes of some object available to the role, in this case the checked expense claim. If it fails the check, Accounts engages in an interaction with the claimant to reject the claim (who has to modify it and return to the state of seeking Project Manager approval); this ends the involvement of Accounts in the claim.

Alternatively, Accounts seeks approval from either the Chief Accountant or the Financial Director, depending on the total amount of the claim.

Having completed whichever approval interaction pertains, Accounts then enters a state which has been part-refined into two concurrent (sub-)states, headed by triangles (reminiscent of logical "and" symbols). In other words, Accounts carries out two actions in parallel: informing the claimant that their claim has been accepted, and issuing the payment (perhaps via the banking system). When both these actions are complete, Accounts archives the records; the goal Claim paid has been reached.

Part refinement does not require that the relevant actions be carried out in parallel; rather it says that we do not know, or it is up to the role actor, which is done first: as far as this process model is concerned, it doesn't matter.

Other RAD notation. Processes have to start somewhere. The event that kicks off the process at End of month is indicated on the RAD with an arrow. It is often useful to think of an event as an interaction with a role not shown on the RAD (in this case a calendar, or clock).

The "crows foot" on the Project Manager interaction is a useful shorthand to indicate that this interaction is replicated, concurrently, with many Project Managers, each of whom approves the expenses related to their project.

Other RAD notation, not exemplified here, is available to show an activity in which one role starts up another role.

STRIM in fact includes two languages for modelling processes: the RAD "language" described above and a textual language, SPML (Strim Process Modelling Language). SPML is derived from RML (Greenspan, 1984). The interested reader may refer to Ould and Roberts (1988) for a demonstration of the use of both RAD and SPML to model a simple process.

How to Capture a Process

So far we have discussed the concepts and the notation of process modelling with STRIM. But we also need a way of going about creating the model. We will not go into this in great detail, but will make some important general points, in the form of answers to the following questions:

1. How do I gather information to build my model?
2. How do I handle complexity?
3. How will I know when my model is complete?

How do I gather information to build my model?

Let us assume that we wish to model an existing process. The modeller gathers facts principally by interviewing those who carry out the process, ideally as a group. The aim of the questioning is to flush out the roles, activities, entities, and interactions that form the organisation's process. At each stage, the business rules and goals that govern the process are also recorded. A series of questions can be asked under a number of general headings:

- What is the overall organisational structure and its business goals?
- What do people do in their separate roles?
- How do the roles interact?
- What entities (documents, forms, etc) are essential to the process?

As well as conducting interviews and group sessions to elicit this information, the analyst can use traditional techniques for finding out what is going on in an organisation. These include:

- Examining existing documents. For example, distribution lists represent potential interactions, whether or not they serve a useful purpose.
- Examining the contents of people's in- and out-trays. Again we are looking for interactions.
- Examining existing procedures manuals, work instructions, Quality Manuals, etc. These can be an important source for the analyst, but we need to be careful that the processes described therein are the ones that are actually carried out. Are we modelling how it is supposed to be done, or how it is actually done?

We have modelled processes on a whiteboard with the group of people who actually carry out the process and an expert modeller acting as facilitator. We have also done it by first carrying out interviews with individuals who have their own part to play in the process, and then going away to draw the models separately. Whenever possible, we like to start by getting an overall picture, no matter how coarse or inaccurate, and this can be done either by getting the group together for say half a day (this is often logistically difficult), or by interviewing someone who has a good grasp of the whole process even though they might only operate a part of it. This overall model usually has "large" roles each containing several disconnected threads of activity that, at a more detailed level, will turn out to be roles in their own right.

It is important to get representative views of all participants in the process. It is dangerous, for example, to rely solely on a supervisor's view of the process carried out by their juniors.

RAD notation is intuitively straightforward and we find that people readily model in it, provided that the expert modeller does the actual drafting.

People find it much easier to describe what they do in terms of RAD interactions rather than (for example) the artificial "dataflows" that DFD modelling demands: the user is more likely to say "I Obtain the total of expenses for last month from Accounts" rather than "I send Accounts a total-of-expenses request".

How do I handle complexity?

The traditional systems analyst's tools like DFDs, Entity Life Histories (ELH) and Jackson structure charts are the products of software engineering minds, and software engineers (and the vendors of software engineering tools) are very fond of hierarchically structured things they are amenable to elegant, simple and well understood handling. As a result, the models themselves take the form of hierarchies ("levelling" in DFDs), which is a good way of dealing with complexity.

Unfortunately, organisational processes do not necessarily fit into a neat structured decomposition. In fact, rather than being hierarchical, processes tend to be multi-dimensional networks. (Looking at business processes in software engineering terms, we observe that this is because they include notions of concurrency and interrupts—always difficult to model in the standard notations.)

What, then, happens if we "open" a black box on a RAD? Rather than seeing a "decomposition" of that activity, we prefer to say that we are looking through a window and seeing part of the process from another perspective. What we see and what we model depends again on why we are modelling. For instance, take the activity Issue payment in Figure 3. Suppose we open this black box. When we look through it we may find a whole world of process there involving, in particular, new roles such as Bank, and Post Room. These do not appear on the first RAD, nor are they "part of" any of the roles therein. In taking Issue payment as a process in its own right, we are starting to look at new parts of the world, parts that we were not interested in when drawing up the original RAD.

The same applies to interactions. As an example, take a simplification of this interaction: "two parties, A and B, meet to discuss, negotiate and agree the price of a piece of work, drawing up the agreement as legal document and obtaining financial securities from a bank". On a RAD we might choose to represent this as an atomic interaction between roles A and B because we are not interested in that model in any further "detail" —we simply want to say that A and B have that interaction with that result, and we do not mind how they do it.

Suppose we now choose to "open up" this interaction. Rather than showing just more detail of what happens between A and B, we will find other roles involved, roles which perhaps did not appear on the first RAD: Bank Manager, Giving legal advice, Auditor for example. We have not decomposed the atomic interaction in the DFD sense: we have opened it up and looked at the process from a new angle, an angle which introduces new roles and perhaps new entities, all of which were of no interest to the first RAD.

The right way to handle complexity in a RAD, therefore, is by exploding an activity or interaction into a new RAD, but we do not expect the roles and entities referred to in the new RAD to tie up in some formal way to those in the "higher-level" RAD.

How will I know when my model is complete?

Suppose we want to measure the length of the coastline of an island. If there is a road around the island we could drive round it and use the vehicle's odometer. We could get a "more accurate" (and larger, and more time-consuming) answer by walking around the coastline with a pedometer, dipping into each inlet and around each promontory along the coastal path.

This is a good metaphor for process modelling. There is always more detail if you want to look for it. Whether the detail is useful and justifies the expense of collection, only the process modeller can determine—there is no simple rule that can tell you "you have finished!". Completeness is in the eye of the modeller.

In fact, things are more complicated than this. There is no single viewpoint of a process. It will vary as our motives vary. If we are interested in why a process seems to have a bottleneck around certain activities we will want to model the process from the point of view of how work is allocated to individuals. If we are interested in how the functional subdivisions of the organisation impede or facilitate the flow of a transaction through a process that crosses functional boundaries we will want to view the process in terms of those boundaries. There are as many models of a single process as there are viewpoints that we might want to take.

In our work for a pharmaceutical company, we initially prepared two models of the same process, seeing it from two viewpoints: one from that of the scientists doing the science necessary to take a new compound to market, another from that of the management pushing the development of the compound through the various stages of process scale-up and trials whilst weeding out those compounds that do not offer future success. Both models were useful. In *Soft Systems* terms (Checkland and Scholes, 1992) the models were holons which we "put against the world" in order to learn about it. Each corresponded to a different idea of the "purposeful activity" of the process.

We conclude that it is essential that the modeller have in mind some clear purpose for drawing the model, and some idea of the boundaries of the model.

How to Analyze a Process

It is our experience that much is learnt about a process, to the benefit of the business, simply by going through the exercise of creating a RAD. Concentrated thinking about the process in a disciplined way combined with the bringing together of different perceptions often brings out obvious improvements.

Common sense plays a large part in analysing a process for improvement, but we also need techniques for analysing the model in a systematic way. These fall into the two broad categories of qualitative and quantitative analysis.

Qualitative Analysis

We should ask these questions about the objects and relationships represented on the RAD:

- Goals: Are they all identified? Are they met?
- Roles: Are there roles that have few activities of their own, seeming to be only third-parties in other roles' interactions? They may be redundant, adding no value, and slowing the process.
- Interactions: Is the interaction necessary? Is is a bottleneck? We can borrow ideas from speech act theory (Winograd and Flores, 1987) and check the commitments that are being made when an interaction occurs. We will be looking, for example, for delegation without feedback, implicit promises that are not kept, or information that is transferred but not used.

Quantitative Analysis

Some simple metrics of the efficiency of the process may be derived by counting the numbers of actions and interactions. A process (or role) with fewer interactions or a lower ratio of interactions to actions is likely to be better: each interaction is a potential bottleneck while waiting for synchronisation.

By adding numerical properties such as duration and effort to actions and interactions, we can calculate total process time. Techniques based on traditional network planning or Monte Carlo simulation can be applied.

Having said that, it is as well to add that RADs are not really aimed at quantitative analysis. In order to answer questions about costs, use of resources, bottlenecks, and the profiling of these over time, it is generally better to take a completely different approach, based on something like Systems Dynamics (Forrester, 1961), preferably using a software tool such as *ithink* [3].

Examples of Use

At Praxis we have been using the STRIM techniques described here on various client assignments.

- It was used to assist managers in a major computer manufacturer to model the process they used for planning their product portfolio and for monitoring the progress of development of each individual product. The objectives were to understand the process and to agree how it should run, with particular emphasis on who had the responsibility for key activities. Starting with an outline textual description of a proposed new version of the process, the group of managers were brought together for a couple of days with a STRIM facilitator. The discipline of modelling the process in detail ensured that the end result was a complete description of the process that everyone had signed up to. The RADs themselves became the reference material for the process.
- As part of the development of a Quality Management System for the IT department of a large service provider, we modelled all Information Systems processes, including service development, service maintenance, service operation, and those at the top management level. The resulting RADs were used as a basis for:

  - documenting the processes
  - assigning quality controls and authorisation levels
  - disseminating via a Quality Manual
  - subsequent improvement.

- We modelled a decision-making process related to the granting of credit by a client, to identify those parts of the process where Knowledge Based Systems techniques could be applied.

    Additionally, within Praxis, we have used RADs to illustrate our own key business processes including project planning and reporting, purchasing, change control, and bid management in our Quality Manual. Figure 4 is a fragment of the RAD used to describe the company's Purchasing process.

Conclusion

In the "classical" BPR context, radical change means radical thinking and an emphasis on vision and change management. Within this broad canvas there is an important place for powerful ways for practitioners and "end-users" of BPR to understand proposed or current business processes. Process modelling is, we believe, an important tool which can provide insights to both radical change and incremental change programmes. Process modelling can only add value to a BPR programme if the notation used to represent the process is itself revealing. Our experience with RADs is that their concentration on roles and interactions and their flexibility in allowing the modeller to take different perspectives and deal with the untidiness of the real-world gives them that revealing power.

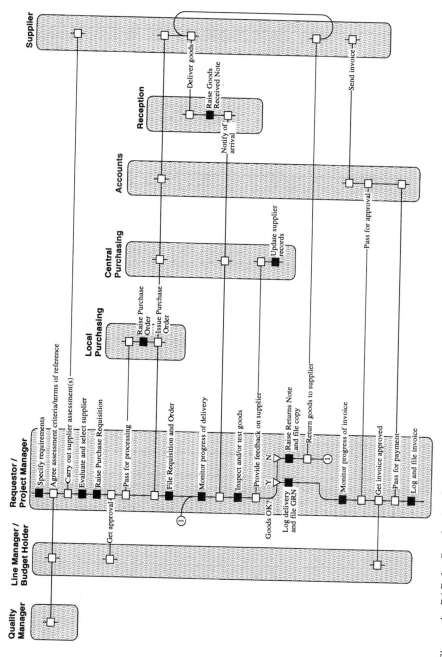

Figure 4: RAD for Purchasing Process

We always remember though that, in the words of Don Dwiggins of Mark V Systems, "all models are false, but some are useful".

Endnotes

[1] STRIM is a registered mark of Praxis plc.

[2] Figure 3 was drawn with MacDraw. Tools with support for drawing RADs are commercially available:

RADitor from Co-Ordination Systems Ltd, 3a Cornbrash Park, Bumpers Way, Chippenham, Wiltshire, SN14 6RA, United Kingdom. Tel +44 1249 448 870, fax +44 1249 448 200.

ProcessMaker from Mark V Systems Ltd, 1501 Elm Street, Ft Collins, CO 80521-1624. Tel +1 818 995 7671, fax +1 818 995 4267.

[3] *ithink* is available from High Performance Systems Inc, 45 Lyme Road, Hanover, NH. Tel +1 603 643 9636, fax +1 603 643 9502, or Cognitus Systems Ltd, 1 Park View, Harrogate, HG1 5LY, United Kingdom. Tel +44 1423 562 622, fax +44 1423 567 916.

References

Checkland, P and Scholes, J. 1992. *Soft Systems Methodology in Action.* Wiley, Chichester, United Kingdom. ISBN 0-471-92768-6.

Chen, P P. 1976. The Entity-Relationship Model: Towards a Unified View of Data. *ACM Transactions on Database Systems,* Vol 1 No 1, March 1976, pp 9-35.

Clough, Anne J. 1993. Choosing an Appropriate Process Modeling Technology. *CASE Outlook,* Vol 7 No 1.

Curtis, W; Kellner, M I and Over, J. 1992. Process Modeling. *Communications of the ACM,* Vol 35 No 9, September 1992, pp 75-90.

Denning, Peter J and Medina-Mora, Raùl. 1994. Case Study: George Mason University. *New Tools for New Times: The Workflow Paradigm.* Edited by Thomas E White and Layna Fischer. Future Strategies Inc, Alameda, CA. ISBN 0-9640233-0-X.

Dickinson, Brian. 1980. *Developing Structured Systems.* Yourdon Press, New York. ISBN 0-917972-24-3.

Earl, Anthony. 1994. *A Study of the Concepts Found in Graphical Process Design Notations.* Mark V Systems, Ft Collins, CO. Tel +1 303 484 4101.

Forrester, Jay W. 1961. *Industrial Dynamics.* MIT Press, Cambridge, Mass.

Greenspan, Sol. 1984. *Requirements Modeling: A Knowledge Representation Approach to Software Requirements Definition.* Technical Report CSRG-155, Computer Systems Research Group, University of Toronto.

Holt, A W; Ramsey, H R and Grimes, J D. 1983. Coordination System Technology as the Basis for a Programming Environment. *ITT Technical Journal* (Electrical Communication), Vol 57 No 4, pp 307-314.

Kawalek, Peter. 1994. Comments on the Use of RADs in Case Studies. *IOPener* Vol 2 No 4, July 1994, pp 6-9. Praxis plc, Bath, United Kingdom. Tel +44 1225 444 700.

Ould, Martyn A and Roberts, Clive. 1988. Defining formal models of the software development process. In: Brereton P (Ed) *Software Engineering Environments* 1987, Ellis Horwood, Chichester, United Kingdom. ISBN 0-7458-0291-5.

Ould, Martyn A. 1994. Eight Laws for Process Modelling. *IOPener* Vol 2 No 4, July 1994, pp 9-12. Praxis plc, Bath, United Kingdom. Tel +44 1225 444 700.

Ould, Martyn A. 1995 (in preparation). *Modelling business processes.* John Wiley & Sons, London.

Rummler, Geary A and Brache, Alan P. 1990. *Improving performance: how to manage the white space on the organization chart.* Jossey-Bass, San Francisco. ISBN 1-55542-214-4.

Singh, Baldev and Rein, Gail L. 1992. *Role Interaction Nets (RINs): a process definition formalism.* MCC Technical Report No CT-083-92.

USAF ICAM Office. 1981. *Integrated computer aided manufacturing (ICAM) architecture part II, Volume IV function modeling manual* (IDEF0). Report number AFWAL-TR-81-4023 V.4.

Winograd, Terry and Flores, Ferdinand. 1987. *Understanding Computers and Cognition.* Addison-Wesley. ISBN 0-201-11297-3.

Chapter
13

Reengineering and REAL Business Process Modeling

Eric L. Denna
Lee Tom Perry
Brigham Young University

'Jon (Sean) Jasperson
Florida State University

Recent reports about the low success rate of business process reengineering (BPR) have caused it to lose some of its luster (see King, 1994; Moad, 1993; Stewart, 1993; McPartlin, 1993). For every piece of good news there are typically three or more untold failures tucked conveniently out of sight. These failures range from multi-million dollar enterprise-wide fiascos that result in sponsoring executives getting the ax, to the too-good-to-believe "low hanging fruit" projects that turn out to be anything but cherry picking.

While we are certainly among the many who believe that the promise of BPR has been oversold and underdelivered, we are not ready to give up on it simply because its image is tarnished. Why this enduring interest in BPR? When BPR wins, it wins big, either saving businesses from certain ruin or launching them to new heights of competitiveness. Given BPR's significant promise, it is important to determine whether its problems are superficial or deep. Perhaps BPR's luster can be restored by applying a little polish.

In our experience, the primary reason reengineering projects fail is the lack of alignment among an organization's business processes, structures and stewardships, strategy, measurements, and IT (information technology) application architecture. We call these five factors: business solution components. We believe the reason for the lack of solution component alignment is the lack of a theory about the nature of business processes and their relationship with the other solution components.

The purpose of this chapter is to introduce both a theory of the essential nature of business processes and their relationship with an organization's structures and stewardships, strategy, measurements, and IT application architecture. We also describe how to model the essential nature of business processes using *REAL* Business Process Modelling (see McCarthy, 1982; Denna, Cherrington, Andros, and Sawyer-Hollander, 1993; and Denna, Jasperson, Fong, and Middleman, 1994). The importance of this chapter is it describes a conceptual foundation for both defining and doing reengineering that significantly increases the likelihood of reengineering success.

The chapter begins with a brief review of the objectives of BPR. We conclude that what BPR needs most is a precise definition of a business process. We then introduce the notion of an event-driven theory of business processes distinguishing business processes from information views, business artifacts, as well as information and decision processes. We introduce a modelling tool called REAL Business Process Modelling that uses E-R diagram notation to model the essential nature of business processes. We conclude the chapter by showing how a precise definition of business processes provides a way for organizations to define, clarify, and align stewardships and structures, strategy, measurements, and IT application architecture.

One More Time: What is Business Process Reengineering?

Michael Hammer (1990) defines reengineering as:

The fundamental rethinking and radical redesign of business processes to achieve dramatic improvements in critical measures of performance (e.g. cost, quality, capital, service, speed).

Hammer, in his *Harvard Business Review* article, shouts: "Don't automate, obliterate!" His recent book with James Champy (1993) adds: "Forget everything you have known about how business should work—most of it is wrong."

Reengineering, therefore, means industrial strength change that breaks eggs, dishes, rules, and concepts. It is a radical departure, not an incremental improvement in the way we organize businesses. The logic behind BPR is similar to Albert Einstein's when he observed, "The world will not evolve past its current state of crisis by using the same thinking that created the situation." More importantly, the world will not evolve past its current state without a fight. Because BPR rewrites established business rules, resistance to change is an inevitable by-product.

BPR is also a list of principles to guide the fundamental rethinking and radical redesign of business processes. Michael Hammer (1990) identifies seven principles of reengineering that can help jump start BPR projects. These principles are:

- Organize around outcomes, not tasks.
- Have those who use the output of the process perform the process.
- Subsume information-processing work into the real work that produces the information.
- Treat geographically dispersed resources as though they were centralized.
- Link parallel activities instead of integrating their results.
- Put the decision point where the work is performed, and build control into the process.
- Capture information once and at the source.

Also basic to BPR is cross-functional teaming and thinking. This explains why BPR projects typically fail when they set sail under the flag of a single business function. Because BPR is cross-functional in its scope, it requires top-down, enterprise-wide support. A group of McKinsey consultants (Hall, Rosenthal, and Wade, 1993) recommend: ". . . get as much time as you can from the CEO." Specifically, they argue that a minimum 20% to 50% of the CEOs time should be dedicated to BPR for it to be successful.

Obviously, the work done by McKinsey is at a different level than Hammer's list of principles. They have moved down to the level of offering BPR prescriptions. Like McKinsey, one of us (Denna, Cherrington, Andros, and Sawyer-Hollander, 1993) has argued for executive-level sponsorship as part of a longer list of prescriptions for successful BPR. These prescriptions include:

1. *Secure executive sponsorship at the outset of BPR projects.* Without executive sponsorship, any efforts to re-engineer will eventually be thwarted by the hordes of function-minded and tradition-bound individuals who resist any kind of change that redraws organizational boundaries.
2. *Business people should manage reengineering efforts.* Too often, IT professionals lead reengineering efforts. When this occurs, technology is the focus, not business solutions. Reengineering is not something IT professionals can do for, or to, an organization. Solving business problems requires the leadership of business people and those responsible for business processes.

3. *Get everyone in the organization involved.* The message that must be given to the entire organization is that reengineering will affect all processes, people, and systems. Key business people across the organization should be given the opportunity to provide ideas and input for modifying and improving the process. However, an organization's reengineering efforts must not be delayed or postponed by resistance to change. Everyone must be given the opportunity to lead, follow, or get out of the way. For this to be possible, everyone needs to develop an enterprise-wide, not a parochial, perspective.

4. *Survey large fields and cultivate small ones.* Everyone involved should understand the big picture, but focus reengineering efforts on smaller, more manageable business processes. When the big picture is missing, people tend to become parochial. When efforts are not focused on the manageable, people begin trying to "boil the ocean". Proper balance between perspectives and purposes requires the constant attention and involvement of management to the costs and benefits of collective and individual efforts.

5. *Assess costs and benefits.* Unless the costs and benefits of a proposed change can be clearly identified, and the benefits demonstrated to provide an adequate return on the cost of investment, there is little reason to proceed with change. Assessing costs and benefits should not focus solely on financially quantifiable aspects of the proposal. Many costs and benefits are not quantifiable in a traditional sense, but are equally worthy of consideration. Evaluation research should provide a set of measurements for assessing the results of change to determine whether the goals of the project were actually achieved.

6. *You can't change what you can't measure.* Any efforts to change business processes will require changes in measurements. Sometimes the measurements will include traditional parameters such as cost/profit ratios, reduced cost per unit of output, or increased revenues. However, alternative measures may often be more effective in assessing the impact of changes in process quality, customer satisfaction, or rework errors.

7. *Communicate or fail.* Because reengineering typically cuts across functional boundaries, everyone must be kept informed. Surprises generally cause resistance, if not open rebellion.

8. *Keep your eye out for "low hanging fruit."* Not all reengineering efforts are major projects that require convening a session of Congress to ratify a proposed change. Frequently, there will be opportunities to simplify processes that require minimal amounts of work. Taking advantage of these opportunities can provide momentum, encouragement, and credibility for further reengineering efforts.

So what is BPR? Typically, it is a list of principles and prescriptions to promote and guide the radical rethinking and redesign of organizations around business processes?

When introducing his list of reengineering principles, Michael Hammer (1990, p. 108) observed: "Creating new rules tailored to the modern environment ultimately requires a new conceptualization of the business process—which comes down to someone having a great idea." This raises an interesting question: Possibly, BPR projects frequently fail, not because of what BPR is, but because of what it is not? When individuals and teams are equipped only with principles and prescriptions, perhaps great ideas are harder to come by than they were led to believe. Moreover, are great ideas really enough? For successful implementation, don't organizations also need to think about how each BPR initiative fits into a larger whole?

While principles and prescriptions are enormously helpful, there is an incredibly huge gap between them. BPR advocates starting with a blank piece of paper. The $64,000 question is: How do we fill that blank piece of paper? Neither principles nor prescriptions really answer this question. If BPR's failure rate is ever going to be reduced significantly, it needs a methodology and tools because while principles and prescriptions are necessary, they are insufficient. A side-benefit of a well-defined BPR methodology is it enhances and refines both principles and prescriptions.

Building a BPR methodology, first requires a giant step backward. Methodologies are not simply pulled out of a hat. A primary benefit associated with building a BPR methodology is the discipline it brings to our thinking about business processes. Before we can build a BPR methodology, we must refine our definition of business processes.

So What is a Business Process?

To understand the nature of business processes let's take a look from a couple of different perspectives. First, the "organization as a system" perspective and then, second, the "events" perspective of business processes.

The "Organization as a System" Perspective
of Business Processes

Looking at the organization as a system (see Figure 1) suggests that there are three basic types of business processes:

The acquisition/maintenance/payment process consists of a series of business activities that result in the acquisition of

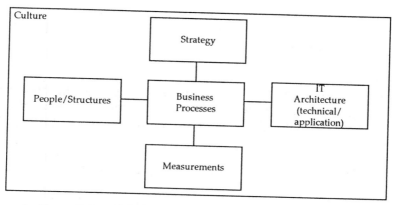

Figure 1: Event-Driven Solution Perspective

goods and services needed by the organization (e.g. supplies, inventories, human skills and availability, or financing). This process also includes maintaining and paying for goods and services acquired so the resources are available when needed by the organization. The acquisition/maintenance/payment process is rather generic across organizations in that there are only a few different ways to acquire, maintain, and pay for resources. Any differences are driven primarily by characteristics of the process (e.g. the type of resource being acquired, the means of communication between the buyer and supplier, and the means of payment).

The conversion process can actually involve a variety of processes that transform the goods and services acquired into goods and services for sale to customers. The nature of the conversion process varies widely across industries ranging from assembling and manufacturing enterprises to distribution and professional service firms. First, and foremost, the nature of conversion processes is largely a function of the variety of extant methods and technologies for transforming goods and services acquired into goods and services for customers (e.g. assembly, excavation, education and training, distribution). The nature of the conversion process is also shaped by other factors such as customer preferences, societal and regulatory requirements, and management policy.

The sales/collection process involves events that attract customers to acquire an organization's goods and services, deliver goods and services to customers, and collect payment for the goods and services delivered. As with the acquisition/maintenance/payment process, the sales/collection process has a fairly predictable nature across organizations. Therefore, any differences are driven primarily by the type of resource being sold and the type of payment method utilized by the customer.

The "organization as a system" perspective simply provides a framework for classifying any business process and understanding how the processes are interrelated. Furthermore, this perspective helps ensure completeness in identifying an organization's processes.

The "Events" Perspective of Business Processes

The building block of business processes is an individual business event. In a nutshell, business events are *any strategically significant business activity management wants to plan, control, and/or evaluate.* Why the "and/or"? It is because some events management can, and should, plan, control, and evaluate. Examples include Salesperson Calls on Customer, to Order Goods/Services From Vendor, to Ship Goods to Customer, to Receive Customer Payment. Other events, however, management can only plan for or evaluate. These events are typically outside the scope of an organization's business processes, and thereby, outside its control. Examples include Change Prime Interest Rate, Competitor Changes Prices, or Competitor Introduces New Product.

Although the concept of a business event is rather straightforward, identifying business events can be a bit challenging. The difficulty lies in seeing through that which can obscure our vision of business events. Instead of standing out in plain view, many times business events lie under a thick cover of views, business artifacts, and information and decision processes.

Views of Events

Imagine that a salesperson for a large computer manufacturer sells 2,000 computers to a wealthy retail magnate. How many different views are there of this one simple business event? That depends on who wants to know about new customer orders. Let's list just a few of the possibilities:

- Production personnel want to know about the order to plan production processes.
- Marketing wants to know about the order to possibly adjust prices, plan advertising, and target future sales efforts.
- Personnel want to know about the order to pay sales commissions.

- Executive management wants to know about the order to plan, control, and evaluate its impact on the organization.
- Investors and creditors want to know about orders to assess the profitability of their investments and the likelihood of returns on their investment.

Not only is there a variety of different information customers interested in knowing about the order, each view of the order is different.   Each class of information customers wants to know something a bit different from the others. Traditionally, we have addressed this diversity by building a different system for each view. Each system captures slightly different data about the same business event, each selecting its own subset of available data about the events and recording it in its own classification scheme. As Peter Drucker (1992, p. C1) points out, the variety of systems (both financial and nonfinancial):

> increasingly overlap. They also increasingly come up with what look like conflicting, or at least incompatible, data about the same event; for the two look at the same event quite differently. Till now this has created little confusion.

Anyone who has tried to reconcile the data that support the alternative views across an organization understands what we mean by conflicting views. Reconciling differences among the conflicting views is difficult at best and occasionally impossible. Any reconciliation achieved is destroyed as soon as one or more of the views change. The important point here is that these seemingly irreconcilable and diverse classification schemes (views) are simply alternative ways of looking at the same phenomena "business events". Unfortunately, the morass of views make identification of the business events somewhat challenging.

Business Artifacts

Business artifacts include multi-copy forms, checklists, or reports.   As a result we see overly complex and burdensome processes characterized by large numbers of multi-copy forms routed to different functions, each believing it requires its own copy of each form. As the size of the organization grows, so do the number of people handling all the different forms. Eventually, forms management takes on a life of its own, replacing concern for the underlying business events with turf battles over who gets what copy of which form.   In these situations, what must be uncovered is what the artifacts represent. As a general rule, forms are inevitably linked to business events. For example, invoices are inevitably linked to business events such as Purchase Goods From Vendor; Checks to Cash Disbursement, Bills to Customer Buys Goods, and so forth. Unless an organization is careful, it may soon confuse business events with information and decision processes leaving the former largely unmanaged.

Information Processes

A common error is confusing information processes with business events. The relationship between the two is fairly simple—business events trigger information processes.

Information processes come in three flavors: record business event data, maintain reference data, and report useful information. Recording business event data is triggered by the occurrence of events within organizations' business processes like Deliver Goods to Customer, Receive Customer Payment, Call on Customer. Maintaining reference data is triggered by the occurrence of other events that trigger the need to change data about an organization's resources, actors, or locations. For example, Customer Moves triggers the need to update a customer's address; Employee Gets Married triggers the need to update an employee's marital status; or Vendor Changes Product Price triggers the need to update the current cost of something purchased from a vendor.

Decision Processes

Decision processes either trigger information processes or business events. Decision processes break down into three managerial responsibilities: plan, control, and evaluate business processes. Plans are formulated around business processes, business events, and the rules surrounding them. The purpose of control decisions is to trigger business events. For example, the decision to buy a new truck triggers the business event Buy Truck. When decision-makers want to evaluate business processes and events they trigger the reporting information process, then receive useful information. Typically, evaluation decisions lead to subsequent planning and control decisions. For example, a manager evaluates information about machine failures on an assembly line then decides to trigger the event Buy Machine (a control decision). While there is an implicit logic to these decisions, unless the relationship between business, information, and decision processes is kept clear, significant confusion can result. With practice, one can quickly begin to cut through the fog and identify the business events that management wants to plan, control, and/or evaluate. Once the underlying events are identified, then we can begin to build business process models.

REAL Business Process Modelling

REAL Business Process Modelling (BPM) is a formal method of representing the essential characteristics of business processes and events. The title *REAL* is an acronym for Resources, Events, Agents, and Locations which, as we will discuss in this section, collectively describe the essential characteristics of business processes and events. *REAL* BPM builds upon the concepts first proposed by McCarthy (1982) to model event-driven database structures.

This approach is more concerned about what is modeled than how. By this we mean that *REAL* BPM concepts are independent of diagramming techniques. *REAL* BPM is more a philosophy of what is modeled than another modelling technique. It is a way to use familiar modelling tools (e.g. E-R and OO diagrams) to model business processes with an emphasis on identifying and describing the essence of a business process and communicating this essence to business and technical people. It so happens that we will use the basic constructs of E-R diagramming (less the cardinality notation) to illustrate the modelling concepts. However, we must emphasize again that other diagramming techniques can also be used to develop *REAL* BPMs if someone prefers a different modelling tool than we use in this chapter.

Some may suggest that workflow diagrams already model business processes. As we have analyzed workflow diagrams we have found them to provide a tangled picture of business, information, and decision processes. Because they lack a theory of what a business process is, they do not provide a precise definition of a business process. Furthermore, this confusion about the essence of the business process provides little guidance for defining the nature of the supporting information and decision processes. Without a clear differentiation among business, information, and decision processes, reengineering teams struggle to know what workflow activities are critical and how they interrelate. *REAL* BPM simply formalizes the process of identifying and defining business processes, and provides a basis for determining the remaining elements of a business solution.

The heart of *REAL* BPM focuses on answering five questions about each business event. We combine the first two questions for ease of discussion:

> *What happened and when?* The "what" refers to which business event occurred. The "when" describes the order of the events, what time the event started, and sometimes even the time it ended. This is because often it is important to know how long it took to complete an event. For example, when cleaning a

carpet, performing an audit, performing open heart surgery, turning a part on a lathe, or a myriad of other business events, we must know the length of time for the individual events in order to effectively plan, control, and evaluate them.

What roles were played and who/what performed the roles? We must know what roles were performed and who/what performed them. Roles can range from internal responsibilities (e.g., salesperson, cleaning person, supervisor, or inspector) to external roles (e.g., customer or supplier). These roles can be performed by individuals, organizations, or programmable machines (such as robots or computers). Those performing roles are referred to as agents. Events involving the exchange of resources between organizations always involve both internal and external agents, each performing a different role during the execution of the event. For example, the internal role of a salesperson may be performed by a person or a computer terminal that interacts with someone or something playing the external role (customer). Whether the event involves the exchange of resources or not, we must capture data about the roles played and the agents involved. This information is critical to support those planning, controlling, and evaluating business events.

What kinds of resources were involved and how much was used? All business events involve the use of one or more resources. We must also know the type and quantity of resources involved in each event. Identifying and measuring some resources is fairly straightforward, while with others it is not. For example, a sale of groceries (the resource) is easily measured. However, we could also argue that several other resources are involved (e.g., the cash register, bags to package the groceries, and electricity to power the cash register) which are much more difficult to measure. At what point do you stop identifying the type and quantity of resources? It depends on the preferences of those planning, controlling, and evaluating the business events. Regardless of the level of detail, we must have information about the type and quantity of resources involved in each event.

Where did the event occur? Lastly, we must know where events occur. With today's organizations and information technology spread all over the globe, events can occur anywhere and the customer need not be physically present. To the extent that it is important, we should make sure data about the location of an event are captured. Sometimes the location of the event is provided by the location of the agents or resources involved.

However, when the event location cannot be derived from association with the resources or agents, we must explicitly specify the event location.

The important point to emphasize is the impact of recording the essential characteristics of business events, then making them available to information customers across the organization. Once the essential data about the event are recorded, we can support an infinite number of information customer views.

Business Processes and Events

Although the definition of a business event is rather straightforward, starting the process of identifying business events may seem a bit nebulous. The process becomes easier when you divide the business into distinct processes. As we mentioned earlier, in the most generic sense, every organization, regardless of its purpose, goods and services, location, or ownership, has three basic business processes:

- Acquisition/payment process
- Conversion process
- Sales/collections process

Let's take a look at each one in turn.

Acquisition/Payment Process

The acquisition/payment process includes the business events involved in acquiring, paying for, and maintaining the goods and services needed by the organization. The focus is on purchasing only what is needed and can be paid for, receiving only what is ordered, paying for only that which is received, and making sure the resources acquired are available when needed. Organizations acquire a wide variety of goods and services including:

- Human resources (e.g., people's time and skills)
- Financial resources
- Supplies
- Inventories
- Property, plant, and equipment
- New ideas (e.g., research and development)
- Miscellaneous services (e.g., legal, power, telephone, protection, medical, financial, and custodial)

Regardless of the type of goods and services, each causes only minor alterations in the nature of the generic acquisition/payment process. The more common types of acquisition/payment processes are those for human resources (personnel/payroll processing), financial resources, inventories, and fixed assets.

The basic nature of the process, regardless of the type of resource being acquired, has the following types of events:

- Request the good or service
- Select a supplier
- Order the good or service
- Receive the good or service
- Inspect the good or service
- Pay for the good or service

If we think through the events in the process carefully, we will notice some organizations may order the events differently, may use a subset of the events, or may add more detailed events. Nonetheless, the basic nature of the process is fairly stable across organizations and resources.

Conversion Process

The conversion process focuses on developing and executing the most efficient and effective processes for converting goods and services acquired into goods and resources for sale. Conversion processes across, or even within, organizations are very diverse and depend on the type of good or service being produced, the technology and resources utilized, the restrictions of regulators, governments, society, or customers, and the preferences of management. When conversion processes are unique, valuable, and difficult to imitate they create distinctive competence for an organization. Some of the more general types of conversion processes include:

- Assembling
- Growing
- Excavating
- Harvesting
- Basic manufacturing (e.g., metals, woods, and chemicals)
- Finished manufacturing (e.g., tools, instruments, and components)
- Cleaning
- Transporting
- Distributing
- Providing (e.g., power, water, protection, and communication)
- Educating

• Discovering (e.g., research and development)

The diversity of conversion processes makes it difficult to propose a single generalized conversion process. Assembling a toy car is vastly different from defending a client in court or discovering a cure for a crippling disease. Furthermore, any one organization may utilize more than one type of conversion process to generate goods and services for customers. Nonetheless, at the heart of any conversion process is a sequence of business events that serves to convert goods and services acquired into goods and services for customers.

Sales/Collection Process

The sales/collection process includes the sequence of events involved in exchanging goods and services with customers for payment. Essentially, the sales/collection process is the mirror image of the acquisition/payment process. Whenever one organization or individual acquires and pays for goods and services someone else is selling the good or service and receiving payment. Although there is some diversity across the types of goods and services sold, the basic process typically involves the following events:

• Receive an order for goods or services
• Select the good or service to be delivered
• Inspect the good or service to be delivered
• Prepare the good or service for delivery
• Deliver the good or service
• Receive payment for the good or service

As with the acquisition/payment process, some organizations may order the events differently, may use a subset of the events, or may add more detailed events. Regardless, the basic nature of the process remains intact.

Business events and processes are related because a business process is a sequence of business events. Once a business process has been identified, we can begin decomposing the process into a sequence of discrete business events that management wants to plan, control, and evaluate. One frequently asked question is: How far do you go when decomposing business processes into business events?

Decomposing Business Events

The extent to which business processes should be decomposed into business events is fairly simple to determine. Decompose the processes to the level that management wants to plan, control, and evaluate. The appropriate level is one in which a more generalized model would overlook critical events while a more detailed model would include minutiae. Each business process is composed of a series of discrete business events. For example, selling mail-order merchandise might involve the following business events:

- Accept customer order
- Select, inspect, and package merchandise
- Ship merchandise
- Receive customer payment

However, someone may rationally argue that the process really just involves just two events:

- Ship merchandise
- Receive payment

So which is right? The answer depends on the level of detail at which management wants to plan, control, and evaluate the business process. Because of the diversity of management styles, resource availability, and employee talent, differences will exist across enterprises regarding the level at which organizations manage business processes. Instances will exist in which the sequence of events within the same process in two different organization is reversed. For example, some organizations may insist on the following sequence:

- Receive payment
- Ship merchandise

The sequence of events may be a function of the technique for achieving an objective. For example, constructing a building begins with excavation work and laying the foundation. Then the building can be framed, siding put in place, plumbing and electrical systems installed, drywall hung, and so forth until the building is completed. In this case construction techniques and laws of nature determine the event sequence.

Sometimes the sequence of events is dictated by customer preference. Suppose a car dealership operates in four different cities several miles apart. Customers visit the lots and order cars which may be on other lots. Initially, customers are told to drive to the other lot to pick up the car. However, because many customers might be unwilling to drive to the other lot, they cancel their orders. Astute business people will realize something needs to change to stop losing customers. Rather than make the customer pick up the car at another lot, dealers instigate a new business event called "Transport Car." This requires that an employee drive the ordered car to the lot nearest the customer or even to the customer's house. Adding a Transport Car event is management's attempt to meet the customer needs and have the information they want to plan, control, and evaluate the event.

Because of the nature of these three basic business processes (acquisition/payment, conversion, and sales/collection) and their interrelationships, an organization can be accurately characterized as a system that acquires inputs, processes the inputs into outputs, and sells the outputs to customers. This is a helpful characterization because we can begin to model the entire organization, its processes and events, using some rather simple modelling techniques. These models enhance communications among those responsible for solving business problems.

Doing *REAL* Business Process Modelling

As with any modelling effort, developing the model requires significant practice. Because of the managerial focus of this book and chapter we intend to provide an overview for managers rather than a detailed tutorial for developers. Those interested in a detailed description of *REAL* BPM should refer to Denna, et al. (1993). We hope by introducing the steps in developing a model that you see that developing *REAL* BPMs is fairly straightforward. Becoming an expert at *REAL* BPM is far more dependent on business expertise than modelling experience. Unlike other modelling philosophies, the sophistication of the *REAL* BPM modeler is demonstrated by the simplicity, not complexity, of a specific process model.

Developing a *REAL* BPM involves the following steps:

Step 1. Identify business events and represent each with a box. The first task in *REAL* business modelling is to become familiar with the business process and its underlying events. The focus is on identifying the activities management wants to plan, control, and evaluate making sure not to confuse business events with information processes. Figure 2 shows the first step in modelling the business events for a mail order company's sales/collection process. At the heart of identifying business events is differentiating them from information and decision processes. For example, when a Customer Places An Order (a strategically significant business activity management wants to plan, control, and evaluate) it triggers an information process (Record Customer Order) which collects data about the business event to generate useful information (another information process) to support a variety of decision processes

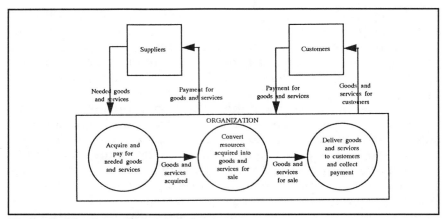

Figure 2: The Organization as a System

(selecting merchandise to purchase, choosing how many people to have answering telephones at various times of the day, or deciding on discounts to give to various customers). Again, the focus is on the business event, leaving the information and decision process modelling to be defined by the resulting *REAL* BPM. Continuing the analysis of the mail order process subsequent events such as Ship Merchandise and Receive Payment would each be identified separate from their related information and decision processes.

Step 2. Identify the general business rules surrounding each event by specifying relationships between each event and its related agents, resources, and locations that serve to complete the description of what happens, when, who is involved, what is involved, and where the event occurs. Again, our theory of business processes suggests that such information models the essential characteristics of the business process. Continuing the mail order process example, completing the description of the Customer Places Order event involves specifying who is involved (Salesperson and Customer), what is involved (Merchandise), and where it occurs (Catalog Center). Ship Merchandise involves Customer, Packer, Carrier, and Shipping Clerk (who in involved?), Packing Material and Package (what is involved?), and the Distribution Center (where it occurs?). The same analysis could be applied to the Receive Payment and any other event management wants to plan, control, and evaluate. In Figure 3 we represent the results of our analysis of the mail order sales/ collection process by connecting the agent, resource, and location boxes to the event boxes with a line. For ease of analysis and validation, the resources and locations are typically placed on the left side of events and the agents are on the right side.

Step 3. Validate the REAL business process model with the business person. Once an initial draft of the *REAL* BPM is completed, the next step is to validate the model's accuracy with business

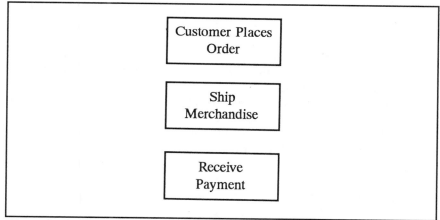

Figure 3: 1st Stage REAL BPM

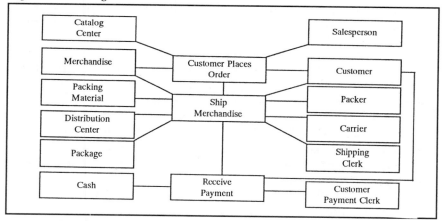

Figure 4: Complete REAL BPM

people. The validation should be performed by those who understand the details and objectives of the business process and events
being modeled and management's objectives concerning planning,
controlling, and evaluating the business process. Validation sessions should result in either the confirmation of the model's accuracy
or modification of the model.

Modifications that might result from validation sessions typically involve decomposing one or more business events into more
detailed business events. For example, in the mail-order sales/
collection example, management may decide the Ship Merchandise
event needs to be decomposed into three events (Inspect Merchandise, Package Merchandise, and Ship Merchandise) as shown in
Figure 4. The choice to decompose to a lower level of detail is
determined by management. The justification for additional decomposition is management's preference about the level of detail it needs

to plan, control, and evaluate the business process. Regardless of the level of abstraction, however, the same modelling concepts are applied.

Only a few simple concepts are required to begin developing fairly precise models of business processes and events. The theory of a business process supporting *REAL* BPMs serves as a template or pattern of business events that can accelerate the conceptualization and development of business processes. Furthermore, as we will see later, it facilitates communicating a businessperson's definition of a business process to others to help coordinate the development of an organization's strategy, structures, measurements, and IT application architecture. Lastly, as is explained in detail in Denna, et al (1993), the *REAL* BPM provides a basis for developing a data model to support event-driven IT applications.

Because of the underlying theory, the complexity of a *REAL* BPM is largely dependent upon the scope of the business process being modeled. The scope can range from a single business event to processes involving dozens of events. However, the essence of the model, no matter how large, rests on identifying and relating an organization's resources, events, agents, and locations. In fact, the *REAL* BPM provides a conceptual basis for developing extended enterprise models that span traditional organization boundaries. Such models are becoming more and more common as organizations develop closer ties with vendors and customers and begin sharing both information and processes common to the organizations.

Regardless of the scope, the fundamental unit of analysis is the business event, because everything revolves around accurately identifying and describing business events. Identifying business events rests upon what management needs to plan, control, and evaluate their business.

REAL BPM: The Foundation for Defining Business Solutions

If BPR is intended to begin with a blank piece of paper, it is important to orchestrate change from a whole systems mindset. Critical to BPR's success is the ability to anticipate ripple effects across systems because when we rethink business processes at the start of a BPR project it is much like dropping a pebble into a placid pond. Quickly, the ripples begin to spread, disturbing the entire body of water.

Given this, another contributor to the high failure rate of BPR projects is the lack of alignment among business solution components. The five solutions components are business processes, structures and stewardships, strategy, measurements, and IT applications architecture. Having defined the nature of business processes and how to model them, it is time to discuss how models of business processes can help align the other business solution components.

Business Processes and Organization Structures and Stewardships

Traditional organization structures are delineated by functional boundaries (e.g. production, accounting, information, systems, marketing, or finance). One of the problems arising from functional boundaries is the business processes to be managed are arbitrarily divided among the various functions creating gaps and overlaps of responsibilities. The alternative is to have a process driven organization structure. Defining the nature of business processes and their specific events automatically defines the stewardships of participants. For example, the *REAL* BPM of the mail order process defined several different stewardships that would typically be scattered across at least three different functions (e.g. Sales/Marketing, Logistics, and Finance). Our experience has shown that if you want to manage a process and make sure it is properly planned, controlled, and evaluated, the process events and all their stewardships must be contained within one organization structure. Otherwise, the process and its supporting systems will eventually become arbitrarily divided among separate functional units with their attendant gaps, overlaps, and handoffs.

Business Processes and Strategy

Defining business processes benefits strategic thinking by providing a precise way to think about what a business does and what it should do in the future. The lack of a clear definition of business processes has been the principal cause of a long-standing disconnect between strategy formulation and implementation. Strategists have been consistently inept at translating strategic objectives into concrete business processes. *REAL* modelling provides the needed know-how for finally making this important connection. It is possible to re-engineer business processes to accomplish strategic objectives.

Strategic thinking provides reciprocal benefit to BPR by furnishing a frame for prioritizing business processes and events. An experience at a large aerospace company shows why this contribution is critical. The company hired consultants to help it re-engineer one of its plants. The effort created a great deal of enthusiasm among managers and workers, and was considered an unmitigated success. When another consulting firm was hired to help the company with its strategy, it was discovered that much of the reengineered work was strategically unimportant.

One approach to strategic thinking, strategic improvising (Perry, Stott, Smallwood, 1993), identifies four categories of business processes:

- Unit of Competitive Advantage (UCA) Processes—the processes and capabilities that create distinctiveness for the business in the marketplace.
- Value-added support processes—processes that facilitates the accomplishment of UCA processes.
- Essential support processes—processes that neither create advantage nor facilitate the processes that create advantage, but must be done if businesses are to continue to operate.
- Nonessential support processes—processes that have lost their usefulness but continue to be done because of tradition.The four categories of business processes can be used to scope BPR initiatives. They suggest what business processes to re-engineer first and interdependently, what processes to re-engineer separately, and what processes to eliminate, not re-engineer.

Business Processes and IT Architecture

Defining the business process also serves as a foundation for developing an IT application architecture that overcomes the weaknesses of the traditional IT architecture. Traditional IT architectures (see Figure 5) are driven by functional boundaries that define various views of the business (e.g. production view, accounting view, or marketing view). Because these views have overlaps and gaps, so do the systems supporting the functions. The resulting IT application architecture can quickly resemble a bowl of spaghetti, replete with redundancies in data and process and with multiple reconciliation points that keep information systems and accounting personnel trapped in low value-added work.

A business event-driven IT application architecture, on the other hand, allows an organization to support any business events and processes with the three technical components illustrated in Figure 6. The Business Event Processor applies business rules while the business event occurs and captures data about the business event at the same time. The data captured by the Business Event Processor is stored in the Business Data Repository. The repository allows all business data to be integrated so that the Reporting Facility can be used by any information customer to generate any type of useful information within the scope of the data stored in the repository. The views of the business can range from financial statements to production schedules to customer analyses and profiles to employee productivity reports. The breadth of information available to information customers is dependent on the number and scope of the business processes included in the repository. Applica-

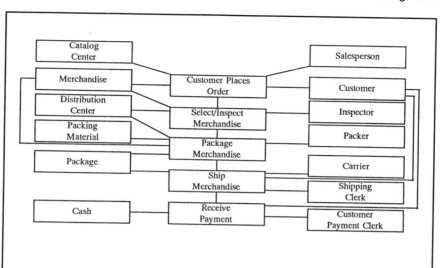

Figure 5: Lower Level REAL BPM

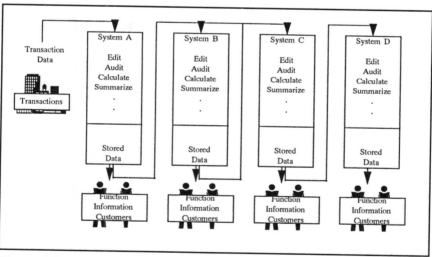

Figure 6: Traditional IT Business Application Architecture

tions in an event-driven architecture are simply collections of recording and reporting rules that govern the capturing and reporting of business data and information. There is no need for any other IT components regardless of the number or type of business processes included in the scope of the business solution domain.

Business Processes and Measurements

Traditional business measurements are typically aligned to functional boundaries, except for accounting information which is typically considered either useless or confusing. Therefore, since each function has only a portion of a business process, the functional systems can only provide partial views of the business processes. Furthermore, because the functionally driven systems have significant gaps and overlaps in terms of stored data and processing, an organization can only get partial, overlapping, or even competing views or measurements. Furthermore, traditional views often do not provide information that enables an organization to manage its business processes.

Focusing on business processes can result in a fundamental shift in the types of measurements an organization uses to plan, control, and evaluate its business processes. For example, rather than look at cost variances, organizations can look at the actual costs of business events over time and recognize trends. The focus on business processes suggests the need for looking at process or cycle times, resource utilization, employee productivity, or resource availability and needs. The event-driven IT application architecture makes such measurements both possible and affordable.

Conclusion: An Agenda for Next-Generation BPR

Recently, we read an article (Cypress, 1994) in which the author, an operations research consultant, created a distinction between first-generation and second-generation business process reengineering. His point was that BPR had reached a plateau. In order to move to a higher level and attack broader and tougher business processes, BPR needed to incorporate more MS/OR (Management Science/Operations Research) thinking. Beyond, the sus-

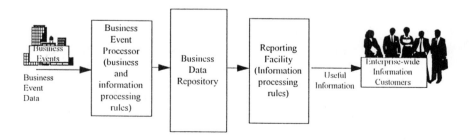

Figure 7: Event-Driven IT Business Application Architecture

piciously self-serving nature of his argument, there are two points to make. First, the link between BPR and MS/OR is a natural one. They are both business solutions that focus on business processes. Second, the author was making exactly the wrong argument for creating the next generation of BPR. Progress is not served by returning to business solution philosophies that failed in the past.

In 1990, reengineering burst onto the scene with an article by Michael Hammer appearing in the *Harvard Business Review*. While BPR has experienced a recent fall from grace, the hope created by BPR remains alive and well. Variations on the original theme are appearing with great rapidity in business periodicals, trade books, and the programs of professional and academic conferences. The agenda for next-generation BPR is being shaped even as we speak, and at least one thing about it is certain: it will be more substantive and less evangelical.

As we stated at the beginning of this chapter, our focus has been on introducing a theory of business processes and their relationship with an organization's structures and stewardships, strategy, measurements, and IT (information technology) application architecture. We also introduce a tool for modelling the essential nature of business processes called *REAL* Business Process Modelling. Our hope is that as the agenda for next-generation BPR is being shaped that the three core ideas presented in this article will be part of it.

First, next-generation BPR must be based on a clearer definition of business processes. Although everyone writing about reengineering constantly refers to business processes lying at the heart of reengineering, little has been offered to precisely define the nature of business processes and how they differ from, and are related to, information and decision processes. Doing so involves separating out business processes from information and decision processes. It also involves the recognition that business processes can be reduced to a series of events.

Second, to facilitate the definition and communication of essential business process characteristics we have introduced a methodology called *REAL* Business Process Modelling. *REAL* BPMs help define the essence of business events, thus ensuring a deeper understanding of specific business processes. They also facilitate communication across organization stakeholders by creating a common understanding of the essence of business processes and events.

Third, we have discussed how *REAL* BPMs provide a foundation for integrated business solutions. For the last 30 years managers have been spectators watching a parade of business solu-

tions affecting processes, strategy, structures and stewardships, information systems, and measurements. Each solution
has provided valuable and important contributions, but their
contribution to business success has been consistently unspec-
tacular. Why have these solutions fallen short? Because there
has been no way to think about them together. When, however,
we adjust our view and see business processes and events as
integrative mechanisms, something profound happens. Sud-
denly, we have a precise way of understanding organizational
behavior. Information system architectures can be built to
reflect the nature of business processes and events. Reengineering
and strategy implementation are one and the same process
because strategies are used to scope BPR projects around the
strategically more important business processes and events.
Organizational structures can be designed around stewardships over specific business processes and events. Finally,
measurements make more sense to businesspeople because
they are directly linked to the performance of specific business
processes and events.

Chaos theorists discuss the sensitive dependence of systems on
initial conditions (Gleick, 1987). Similar principals affect the world
of ideas. A small, but fundamental oversight can wreak havoc over
the life-cycle of an idea. The premise of this chapter is that the BPR
movement made an early, critical error by not insisting on greater
precision about the basic nature of business processes and events.
The contribution we make, while subtle, is unquestionably significant. It provides tremendous leverage because it corrects this early
oversight in BPR's history.

The remaining problem is the damage already inflicted on BPR's
reputation. A recent article, highly critical of BPR, appeared in *The
Economist* (see Editorial, 1994). It concluded: "It is clearly time to
re-engineer the re-engineers." Our remedy is less radical precisely
because it is more focused. All that re-engineers really need is a
conceptual foundation for reengineering. *REAL* BPM provides this
foundation because it offers a more precise definition of business
processes and events, which from our point-of-view is exactly what
the doctor ordered.

References

Cypress, H.A. (February 1994) "Re-engineering," *ORMS Today*.

Denna, E.L., J.O. Cherrington, D.P. Andros, and A. Sawyer-Hollander
(1993), *Event-Driven Business Solutions*, Homewood, IL: Business-One
Irwin.

Denna, E.L., J. Jasperson, K. Fong, and D. Middleman (Forthcoming,
1994) "Modelling Business Processes," *Journal of Information Systems*.

Drucker, P. (1 December 1992) "Be Data Literate—Know What to Know," *The Wall Street Journal.*

Farmer, J.R. (March, 1993) "Reengineering: Achieving Productivity Success," *APICS - The Performance Advantage.*

Gleick, J. (1987), *Chaos: Making a New Science,* New York: Penguin Books.

Hall, G., J. Rosenthal, and J. Wade (November-December, 1993) "How to Make Reengineering Really Work," *Harvard Business Review.*

Hammer, M. (July-August, 1990) "Reengineering Work: Don't Automate, Obliterate," *Harvard Business Review.*

Hammer, M., and J. Champy (1993) *Reengineering the Corporation,* New York: Harper Business.

King, J. (June 13, 1994) "Reengineering Slammed," *Computerworld,* 1, 14.

Ligus, R.C. (Jan, 1993) "Methods to Help Re-engineer Your Company for Improved Agility," *Industrial Engineering.*

McCarthy, W.E. (July, 1982) "The REA Accounting Model: A Generalized Framework for Accounting Systems in a Shared Data Environment," *The Accounting Review.*

McPartlin, J.P. (February 1, 1993) "Just Chasing Rainbows? Critics Brand Much of the Reengineering Clamor as Sheer Marketing Hype," *Information Week.*

Moad, J. (August 1, 1993) "Does Reengineering Really Work?," *Datamation.*

Parker, J. (May 1993) "An ABC Guide to Business Process Reengineering," *Industrial Engineering.*

Perry, L.T., R.G. Stott, and W.N. Smallwood (1993) . *Real-Time Strategy: Improvising Team-Based Planning for a Fast-Changing World,* New York: Wiley.

Stewart, T.A. (August 23, 1993) "Reengineering: The Hot New Managing Tool," *Fortune.*

Value-Based Business Process Reengineering:
An Objective Approach
to Value Added

Valery Kanevsky
Pacific Bell

Thomas J. Housel
Telecom Italia

The purpose of business process reengineering (BPR) is to radically improve company core processes in order to:

1. Increase process capacity
2. Increase, or satisfy, demand for products and services. (Housel, Bell, and Kanevsky, 1994)

Most reported reengineering efforts focus on the first purpose without reference to the second purpose. This may be a result of the current business environment and the demand for cost competitiveness (Bleakley, 1993). Increased process capacity can be translated into a more favorable cost structure by using the extra capacity to produce the same number of "widgets" with fewer employees or more "widgets" with the same number of employees.

For example, Mutual Benefit Life reengineered its processing of insurance applications process and went from 25 days for application processing to as little as four hours. The result of this cycle time improvement was elimination of 100 field office positions.

Using BPR, Ford was able to reduce its accounts payable department from 500 to 125 employees (Hammer, 1991). In this way BPR fits nicely into American corporations current obsession with squeezing as much cost as possible out of operations. While an admirable goal, it is not clear how BPR efforts will ensure cutting the "fat" and not the "meat" out of operations.

Reducing unnecessary operational costs is critical to competitiveness. However, increasing, or statisfying demand for products/services also is critical to competitiveness. And this second purpose of BPR cannot be achieved if BPR efforts inadvertantly destroy value in the end product/service. A clear understanding of both cost and value is required to ensure a successful BPR effort.

Traditional financial approaches use dollars (generated as a result of sales of end products/services) as the only representation of value. Thus, they do not allow disaggregation of value along the value-adding component processes because a market price can be set for most of these interim process outputs. So, these approaches limit objective analysis of the value-producing capabilities of the component processes. Since it is the component processes that will be modified or eliminated in a reengineering effort, it is critical to objectively measure the value they produce, otherwise it will be impossible to know whether the BPR effort has added value (Housel, Morris, and Westland, 1993).

Today, there is no *objective, universal way* to measure the value added by component processes before and after a reengineering effort and, therefore, no way to provide executives with return on investment-based assurances. Objective value allocation among the component processes of a compound process cannot be gotten through existing approaches (e.g., generally accepted accounting practices, activity-based costing, cost of quality, quality function deployment) (Drucker, 1993; Eccles, 1991; Johnson, 1992).

These approaches focus on cost or various subjective assessments of value. No matter how cost is allocated or manipulated, it cannot be a surrogate for value. Likewise, subjective assessments of value cannot be used in return based financial ratios because they do not use comparably objective units of measurement (i.e. dollars).

The promise of business process reengineering (BPR) must be validated by its effect on the "bottom line." It will be taken seriously as a new process improvement framework only when executives can be assured, *a priori*, that it will produce the desired ROI in the reengineered processes, and after the BPR, whether there have been actual improvements. An objective way to measure the value added by component processes must be developed to make this kind of assessment possible. Using an extension of Kolomogorov's Complexity theory, this paper offers a solution to this problem.

Financial measures are the *lingua franca* of business primarily because they are objective, countable, general, and fundamental. Therefore, assessing the success of BPR efforts requires an equally defensible measure of the reengineering's ROI impact. Failing to provide such a measure will relegate BPR to the trash heap of other management fads (Stewart, 1993).

But, the focus of many BPR efforts is to improve the component, or sub-processes within an overall compound process. Many of these component processes do not produce a sellable output: calculating ROI requires a sellable output (for the revenue side of the equation). The problem, then, is to allocate value (e.g., market price) objectively throughout all component processes in a way that return on investment in process (**ROP**) can be calculated for each component affected by the BPR.

The resulting calculation would also provide an objective approach for understanding how value is added throughout the compound process. Even those component processes not directly targeted by a reengineering effort will be affected by it. Therefore, the reengineering analyst needs to understand how the value generating capabilities of all component processes may be affected by the BPR effort.

Value Defined

Value is a nebulous term that is often approached from subjective perspectives. Common definitions of product/service value rely on a direct connection with the customer's perception of value or willingness to pay. This perception can be manifested in the way that products/services meet customer needs through features or functionality, i.e., the customer's perception of *value*. Commonly we cull "precise" information about customer perception of value through, for example, market research, quality function deployment techniques. These approaches often lead to products/services that do not have the anticipated value to the customer, as reflected in their unwillingness to pay for the new or redesigned product/service.

Businesses that rely exclusively on the capriciousness of short term customer perceptions of value are often caught in the losing game of trying to "outguess" the customer. While it is critical to understand what customers perceive as valuable, this understanding may be necessary, but is not sufficient, to predict a product/service's success in the marketplace.

For these reasons, it is necessary to use a more objective measure of value not wholly dependent on customer perceptions. Purchase price is a representation of the value of a product/service a customer is willing to pay for an end product/service at a given point in time regardless of whether the customer might have found exactly the same product for a lower price elsewhere. The advantage of using purchase price is that value can be expressed in the commonly accepted universal unit of value, i.e., money/dollars. The purchase price then becomes an objective way to represent customer perception of value.

The problem is that dollars cannot be used to allocate value to the component processes, for which a price cannot be established. For example, a component process of the order- provisioning cycle for telephone service results in the generation of a service order that defines service features and provides some instructions to an installer. The output of this process, i.e., a service order, has absolutely no value to the end customer. Neither are down stream internal process customers willing to pay a margin over the upstream component process' output cost, and even if they were, the resulting payment would simply be a reallocation of cost.

Therefore, a price for this component process output cannot be objectively established by normal willingness-to-pay pricing criteria. Yet, it is obvious that this component process adds value to the end service because it can be found in the definition of the end product/service. In other words, the end product/service would not be possible without the output of this interim component process.

Given that the customer pays for telephone service, the analyst needs a way to allocate a portion of the total price backward to the component process, based on the value this component contributes to the end service. Because no price can be set for this component process' output, dollars cannot be used to measure the value-added. A way must be found to establish a new universal unit of value that can be used to objectively allocate value (measured in purchase-price dollars) across component processes.

•*A Customer Prespective.* The approach described in this paper ensures that the customer "naive" definition of the product/service's features, functionality, characteristics, which represent the value they are willing to pay for in the end product/service, is preserved in spite of the BPR. On the other hand, this new approach will also provide an objective way of verifying that new value has been added to the product/service when the BPR results in a redefined product/service.

•*An Investor/Analyst Perspective.* Armed with a better understanding of how value is created in a company, the investor, analyst can objectively compare companies within an industry in terms of the value-producing performance of their operations in an objective way. The new approach presented in this paper also will allow them to avoid exclusively cost based methods for assessing operational performance. Instead, it will offer a new performance indicator which will encourage companies to quantify the amount of value-added by each process.

Given the inadequacies of the traditional methods of assessing a company's performance, this approach represents an important new window for investors and analysts to examine the inner workings of an organization in an expanded language of finance. This is particularly important when a merger or acquisition takes place. Because the resulting new company probably will not require redundant functions (e.g., two finance, accounting, purchasing departments) and decisions will be have to be made about which companys' processes produce the best **ROP**.

•*A Company Perspective.* For the company reengineering analyst, this new approach helps determine where to start a BPR effort and how to tell whether the effort has been successful. The decision about where to start the BPR effort will be based, in part, on how the final product is defined in terms of the outputs of each component process. Those component process that do not contribute value to the product/service's final definition are candidates for BPR.

The analyst must also be able to estimate the **ROP** of the BPR effort before beginning as well as calculate any change in **ROP** resulting from the effort. Calculating **ROP** is critical to understanding the effect of a BPR effort on the "bottom line".

An objective understanding of value-added and **ROP** will directly or indirectly benefit customers, analysts, and company reengineers. The problem is that no current approach to process value estimation provides such an objective method.

This paper describes a new objective, countable, general, and fundamental solution to the problem of measuring value-added using an extension of Kolomogorov's Complexity Theory. Complexity theory is a well established, proven framework used extensively in the natural sciences to analyze structure creation in self-organized systems (See Nicolis and Prigogine, 1978; Prigogine, 1980; Prigogine and Stengers, 1984; and Zurek, 1990 for a more indepth discussion of Complexity Theory.)

Kolomogorov Complexity and a Definition of "Value-added"

Businesses are open systems — systems that exchange information, substance, and energy with their environments.[8] As such, businesses have the capability, through their processes, to change the structure of raw material inputs (i.e., substance, energy, information) into final products/services. The structures resulting from these changes (e.g., from nuts and bolts to car doors) can be formally described. Descriptions of the changed structures (process outputs) can be measured using Kolomogorov complexity (K-complexity). The resulting K-complexity of a component process output reflects the amount of change to its inputs.

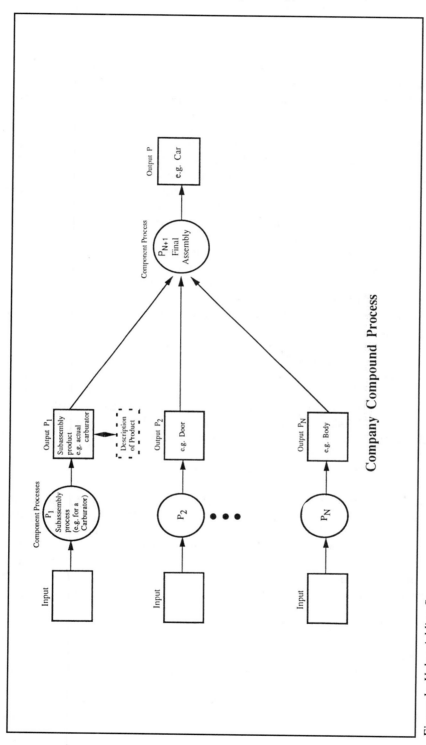

Figure 1: Value-Adding Stream

K-complexity and Value-added

In business, these changes in raw materials are called "value-adding." The value-adding process incrementally changes raw materials into increasingly more "K-complex" structures in the form of interim outputs (e.g., components, subassemblies). In automobile manufacturing, a car begins as a collection of raw materials, which serve as the inputs to subassemblies (e.g., doors, engines, etc.). These are brought together in the final assembly process to produce the "car" (see Figure 1 - Value-Adding Stream). In the telephone business, a customer supplies information about desired service features, name, address. This, with company supplied information about billing, installation, and maintenance (i.e., "raw material" inputs to this service production process), is "sub-assembled" into a service order. The service order provides the billing and installation processes with information to activate service.

These interim outputs of the value-adding component processes can be formally described in terms of their inputs. For the car, the interim outputs (door, engine) can be described in terms of their inputs (nuts, bolts, carburetors, pistons, handles) have been transformed into outputs. The output descriptions can be measured using K-complexity to figure out how much complexity was added, i.e., how much the process's input structure has been changed, by a given process step in the value-adding process. If a direct correspondence between changes in complexity and changes in "value" can be established, K-complexity can be applied to measure value-added changes in product/service production.

Component and Compound Processes

To understand how K-complexity can be used to measure value-added, the value-adding process must break the compound process down into its component processes. Component processes are those interim processes (e.g., sub-assemblies,) whose outputs provide the inputs to other subsequent value-added steps in the production chain. The compound process is the representation of the overall process, including all the component processes (and their outputs) necessary to produce the final product/service.

As the output of each component process makes its relative contribution to the final output product/service, these changes in structure can be measured via K-complexity. The compound process output, then, is the accumulation of all the K-complexities introduced at each step of the value-adding process.

•*Creating formal descriptions.* Having identified the component processes of a compound process, it is possible to formally describe the outputs of these processes in terms of their corresponding inputs. The K-complexity contained in these formal descriptions reflects the changes in structure brought about by the value-adding process. The compound product/service is the total accumulation of the K-complexity manifested in the component process output descriptions. It will be reflected in the formal description of the compound process' final output (i.e., product). Measuring the K-complexity of different output descriptions provides a formal way to quantify the intuitive understanding that an automobile is a more *complex* structure than any of its components.

•*K-complexity and information.* The problem, then, is to specify a unit of K-complexity so that processes and their outputs can be compared in terms of the amount of K-complexity they contain. K-complexity is both a universal measure of changes in the form of matter and a universal property of matter. (Just as weight is a universal measure of gravity's influence on matter, it is also a universal property of matter itself.) Once these changes are formally described, their information content can be derived quantitatively. Creation of K-complexity (and the equivalent information) can be viewed as the universal activity of people. K-complexity (amount of information contained in the product of their activity) itself can be seen as the universal product of their activity.

With K-complexity/information as the universal product, all processes, and the products they produce, are comparable. This kind of comparison permits executives to determine the comparative value of each process across a company as well as between companies. This approach allows a new way of setting process performance goals based on objective benchmarking of **all processes, including component processes,** regardless of industry.

If the relationship between K-complexity/information and value can be rigorously established, there will be an objective method for measuring value added. To do this, K-complexity must be defined and unambiguously connected to the value-adding phenomena.

A Formal Definition of K-complexity

There are three basic concepts from Complexity theory that are necessary to define K-complexity:

1. Finite alphabet
2. Language, i.e., the set of all finite words that can be created with this alphabet
3. "Universal computer" that can accept any word as a program and with output as a word of the same language.

These three concepts provide the requirements for developing formal descriptions of process outputs in terms that allow the amount of information contained in each to be objectively calculated. They are also necessary to ensure that equivalent units of information are used in the formal descriptions of process outputs. This permits comparisons of process outputs to be calculated in equivalent information units.

The length of the descriptions of the same process output can vary. This would create a problem in comparing descriptions in terms of the amount of information they contain. This problem of comparability can be resolved by requiring that the process output descriptions be the shortest length possible that would allow a precise reproduction of the output. This parsimony rule presumes the three defining concepts of Complexity theory.

This theory provides a critical contribution to the **ROP** approach: the requirement of using the shortest description of a process output in terms of its input, which is a reflection of the concept that complexity is conditional upon the available "building blocks" to create this formal description.

Historically, the definition of complexity was formulated for a finite string of letters, i.e., the corresponding word, written in a finite alphabet. For example, in a binary alphabet (i.e., 0,1), a "word" would be a string of 0's and 1's such as: 0000011. Complexity was defined as the length of the shortest computer program that reproduced the original string. For example, a finite binary string such as 010101010101010101 0101010101010101010101could be programmed as:

- print 0101010101010101010101010101010101010101, or
- print 01, twenty times.

It is obvious that the second is a shorter program than the first. To make this definition consistent it was assumed that the program was created for the "universal computer" (e.g., "Turing machine") (see Chatin, 1966; Kolomogorov, 1965; and Solomonoff, 1964 for a more detailed explanation of the use of a "universal computer" in Complexity theory.)

Extending this approach to a business context results in:

Definition 1. **The conditional K-complexity of the output (product) of a process, given its inputs, is the length of the shortest description necessary to reproduce the process's output in terms of its inputs.**

Conditional K-complexity

The length of the shortest description is dependent upon the formal "vocabulary" used. The more powerful or comprehensive the vocabulary used, the shorter would be the shortest description. An example of this phenomenon in human languages is the use of acronyms to shorten texts. The acronyms are more comprehensive because they represent a summary of larger segments of texts.

The description of a product can be shorter or longer depending on the formal vocabulary "building blocks" (i.e., inputs) used to describe it. This implies that the complexity of a product is conditional upon the level of aggregation of the process' inputs. For example, the description of a car in terms of inputs such as doors, engines, transmissions, bodies, etc. would be much shorter than the car described in terms of position of nuts, bolts, pistons, sheet metal, welds, etc.

This simplified explanation of conditional K-complexity shows that the definition of K-complexity depends on the language used to describe the inputs and outputs of the process in focus, as well as the method of description. The BPR analyst's job is to help establish the shortest description of process outputs using the appropriate vocabulary.

An example of how the language used depends on conditional K-complexity is drawn from automobile manufacturing (which most readers have an implicit understanding of at an aggregate level) to illustrate the point. At each point in the car assembly process, value is added as the output of one component process serves as the input of the next higher level component process output. Oversimplifying a bit, nuts, bolts, sheet metal etc. are transformed by component processes to become engines, doors, transmissions, etc. and finally, the engines, doors, etc. are assembled to become a car. To calculate the K-complexity of the car in terms of the "raw materials," it is necessary to accumulate the conditional K-complexities at each step in the value-adding process between the raw materials and final assembly.

The "value-adding" process is nothing more than accumulating conditional K-complexities across the component processes given the definition of the final product. Since conditional complexity can be objectively calculated this approach provides a way to quantify the intuitive notion of value-adding.

A Calculus for K-complexity in Business Processes

The ROP approach is designed to measure value creation for processes with predetermined outputs (**PPO**). For example, in the telephone service provisioning process, the output of a sales contact is a service order that represents the result of negotiating potential features with the customer. Flexible manufacturing systems are another example of software applications that predetermine what, how, and when component processes will be executed in the manufacturing process to produce a given set of outputs.

Outputs of these processes can be described in a common formal language. There also are processes whose outputs are not predetermined, e.g., creative processes such as strategic planning, product/service design, as well as art or science. In the future, the ROP approach will be extended to creative processes that have no predetermined output.

There is a natural correspondence between the set of the **PPOs** and the set of their formal descriptions {**D**}:

$$\{PPO\} <\!\!-\!\!-\!\!-\!\!> \{D\}$$

This correspondence can be extended further to the set of computer programs that are realizations of **D** written in a universal computer language. For example, an assembly line process can be first described in terms of the evolution of raw materials to finished product through the value-adding process. Second, this description can be translated into a computer program that serves as a model of the original process.

Thus, all **PPOs** can be ultimately translated into a universal formal common language (e.g., computer language). This approach is analogous to the common formal language used in accounting and finance. Accounting and finance have formal languages that allow comparisons across business domains in terms of common categories such as time and money.

Still, in practice it is possible to use domain specific descriptions. For example, in the documentation of a car assembly line it is possible to extract descriptions of component products (e.g., engine, transmission, etc.) produced by the corresponding component processes. With these formal descriptions, it is possible to calculate the conditional complexities of each large subassembly (i.e., component products) in terms of its immediate preceding components.

V and V_m Defined

The outputs of information processes can be viewed as texts written in a formal language. It has been proven that the K-complexity of a text is nearly equivalent to the Shannon amount of information in the text: A unit of K-complexity is identical with a Shannon unit of information. (For a detailed description of the logic and mathematical reasoning of this relationship see Cover and Thomas, 1991.) Therefore, amount of information will be used as a substitute for complexity in what follows.

We will define the internal performance of a process, i.e., **V(P)**, given its input, as the amount of information, i.e., **I(P)**, it produces per dollar of process cost, i.e., **C(P)**, over a given period of time. This can be expressed as

$$V = I/C \qquad (1)$$

Since, all companies' products/services can be measured in terms of their complexity, companies can be compared in terms of their efficiency in producing complexity during a given time period.

The ROP approach can be extended to market driven (i.e., external) definitions of performance. $V_m(P)$ represents the market price of a unit of complexity/information and changes simultaneously with the market price of a product/service. Price was selected as the most objective determination of market value given that it can be fixed at one point in time.

$$V_m (P)= M(P)/I(P) \qquad (2)$$

*Where **M** (P) is the market price of the output of a **compound process** P and **I** (P) is the amount of information in the output, given the process input, over a designated period.*

The same formula (2) can be applied to component processes when **M** is allocated along the outputs of the component processes. The problem is to establish an objective way to allocate the market price or value using a method that is consistent with an ROI approach. This can be done in the following way. Let P_i represent an arbitrary component process (i= 1,...,n; where n is the number of component processes) of the compound process **P**. Then $M(P_i)$ is calculated as (i.e., allocation formula):

$$M(P_i) = (I_i/I)M \qquad (3)$$

*Where **M** (P_i) is proportional to the information contributed by P_i (i.e., I_i) to the compound process output (i.e., **I**).*

This formula solves the value allocation problem because $M(P_i)$ represents allocation of value in proportion to the information (i.e., universal product of all processes) produced.

Calculating ROP. **ROP** shows the decision maker how much return can be expected per dollar of investment in *any* process (i.e., component and compound processes). The relationship between **V**, V_m, and **ROP** for any process is as follows:

$$ROP = V \times V_m = (I/C) \times (M/I) = M/C \qquad (4)$$

*Where **M** is proportional to the market price or value of the end product, with the coefficient equal to the ratio between the information produced by the given component process and the total information produced. For compound processes that produce the end product/service, **ROP** is equivalent to **ROI**.*

Calculating **ROP** and V_m for components is possible only after the corresponding amounts of information (**I**) for each component within a compound (that produces a sellable product/service) have been determined. Using formula (3), $Vm(P_i)$ is calculated:

$$V_m(P_i) = M(P_i)/I_i = ((I_i/I)M)/I_i = M/I \qquad (5)$$

As the formula shows, the price per unit of information does not depend on a given component process. The customer pays for the output of the compound process in the form of a final product. This product is represented by a fixed amount of information distributed throughout the components included in the product's definition. The customer is paying the same price for each unit of information, regardless of which component process produces it.

It follows that:

$$ROP(P_i) = \text{Constant} \times V(P_i)$$

Where the **Constant = M/I.**

Therefore, the application of **ROP** for a given compound process can be reduced to the calculation of **V** for all the components of that compound. So, **V** is the crucial measure in making comparisons of the value producing capabilities of the various components of a compound process. This conclusion is also consistent with operational managers intuitive belief that the key to adding value lies in an understanding of processes.

ROP allows decision makers to predict value creation, or "value-adding" throughout the production process, not just on the results of the compound process. As such, this approach allows them to make more precise investment allocations in the operations of a company based on a market-dependent estimator, or V_m, and a market-independent estimator, or **V**.

In this context, creation of K-complexity is a metaphor of the same sort as "making money." Measures of productivity become the amount of K-complexity produced per dollar of cost. Measures of profitability can be represented as the price per unit of K-complexity. Indexes of productivity based on **ROP** can be used as new indicators of company, industry, and an economy's performance.

Calculating V, V_m and ROP: An Example

The following example will help explain how **ROP** might be applied in a telephone company provisioning context. Some calculations of amount of information produced by component processes have been supplied to simplify the example.

Assume that the basic telephone provisioning compound process (i.e., **P**) is defined as billing (i.e., P_1), installation (i.e., P_2) and sales (i.e., $P_{3)}$ component processes. Assume that a **ROP** has provided the K-complexity calculations for the billing and installation. The K-complexity for billing is 10 bits per hour (i.e., I_1) and 4 bits per hour (i.e., I_2) for installation. Thus, the numerator of **V** is provided for two of the componet processes.

For the purposes of this example, the sales process was selected for explicit calculation of I_3. The sales component process reduces the initial uncertainty through the creation of information by the customer answering several questions. Assume that, in the simplest case, the sales process (whose output is a new service order) consists of two sub-component processes: selecting number of lines and selecting features for each line. Assume that there is a customer order with only two kinds of features and line assignment:

1. call forwarding   YES NO
2. call waiting   YES NO
3. number of lines.   1 - 2

If all possible service configurations are equally likely, the initial uncertainty in an order is equal to the log of the number of all possible service configurations. If the customer only wants one line it would be four possible configurations: YES,YES; YES,NO; NO,YES; and NO,NO. If the customer selected two lines, the number of configurations would be 4x4 or 16 possible configurations. The total number of possible configurations would be $4 + 4^2 = 20$. The amount of information necessary to reduce the initial uncertainty is equal to log(base 2) of 20 which is approximately 4 bits. If a service representative is can process 10 new orders per hour then I_3 = 10 x 4 bits = 40 bits/hour.

Assume that the cost is approximately $30 per hour for each of the three components (i.e., $C_1=C_2=C_3$ = *$30 per hour*), and that the average price of a new service order is $25. Cost for each component process may be obtained by any of the existing methods, e.g., generally accepted accounting practices, activity-based costing. The purpose of this chapter is to describe how to obtain a new measure of value — not cost. With the amount of K-complexity or information and cost for each component, it is an easy task to calculate the compound process output **V** and **V$_m$** and **ROP** as follows:

$$V(P) = I_1 + I_2 + I_3/(C_1 + C_2 + C_3) = 54/90 = .6 \text{ bits/dollar}$$

{$V(P)$ = [10 bits] + [4bits] + [40bits]/[\$30]+[\$30]+[\$30] = 54/90
=.6bits/dollar}

$$V_m(P) = M/I = \$25 \times 10/54 = \$4.62 \text{ per bit}$$

$$ROP(P) = V \times V_m = .6 \times 4.62 = 2..77$$

With the **I**s and end service price established, it is possible to calculate **V$_m$** for **P$_1$**, **P$_2$**, and **P$_3$** by calcuating the the **M**s for each component. These are calculated as in the explanation of **M** allocation for formula **(3)**. It follows that, for **P$_1$**, **M** is \$4.63 per order, for **P$_2$**, **M** is \$1.85 per order, and for **P$_3$**, **M** is \$18.52 per order which totals the market price of \$25.

The calculation of the component **ROP**s becomes a simple task once price, cost, and amount of information are known. For example the **ROP** for **(P$_1$)** is **(10/30) x (\$4.63/10) = .152**.

For a better understanding of what component processes need the most performance tuning and which ones provide the most value, compare the relative value of the component processes within the compound provisioning process by comparing **V** for all the components. For example, **V(P$_3$) = 1.33 bits/dollar** and **V(P$_2$) = .133 bits/dollar**. In targeting a BPR, two options for raising the **V(P)** would be to eliminate installation or drastically reduce the cost of installation. (While the current example is hypothetical, we have used the **ROP** approach for a number of **BPR** projects within the company. This approach is required for all new **BPR** projects within our Division.)

The Importance of Product Definition in the ROP Approach

The BPR analyst must define the final product in terms of a minimal extension of the customer's "naive" understanding of the product's features and characteristics. For example, the customer's naive definition of telephone service may include only features such as call forwarding, call waiting. He/she would not include telephone switch programming explicitly. However, this programming is necessary to deliver the expected service features. So the analyst must set the product definition boundary in such a way that it extends the minimal customer definition to include those component process outputs which cannot be eliminated given the current or near term technology.

This minimal extension of the naive product definition serves several purposes:

A. It serves as the criteria for establishing which components will be included in the analysis and therefore considered value-adding for purposes of calculating **ROP**,

B. All other component processes should be evaluated in terms of how they may contribute to future value through new product development or customer services or should be considered overhead cost and candidates for elimination or significant change,

C. It ensures preservation of the minimal defining product features which the customer expects to receive.

There are significant implications of using a narrow (customer naive definition of product) versus a broader definition of final product in focusing a BPR effort. A narrow definition will result in viewing any component process, whose output is not explicitly reflected in the final product definition, as overhead which is not contributing to the value-adding process. This approach to product definition motivates the BPR team to eliminate or significantly curtail the activities of the "non-value-adding" components. This in turn leads to the possible reduction or elimination of components which ensure product quality or customer service.

For example, in providing basic telephone service, the customer's naive definition of service might include only the features which he/she ordered (e.g., call forwarding, call waiting). The fact that the installer normally shows the customer how to use the features properly and that a technician ensures that the switch is correctly programmed would not be included in the customer's definition of the final product. However, without these activities the customer would receive less service instruction and potentially lower quality telephone service.

With a broad definition of the final product, the threat is that every component will be included. If all current components were included, BPR efforts would be severely restricted since the final product requires them in its definition. This would inhibit a company's enthusiasm and creativity in seeking process improvements of the magnitude promised by BPR.

A potential resolution to this dilemma is to examine each component beyond those required to meet the narrow product definition to determine which could be excluded from the final product definition while maintaining a necessary level of quality or customer service. This approach would help focus the BPR effort to ensure that the optimum product definition was maintained. In this way, the product definition becomes the critical tie-breaker in BPR decision making. With the final product definition fixed by this method, the value produced by each necessary component will sum to the total represented in the final product definition. This approach also points out the need to ensure that this final product definition will not be changed by BPR efforts otherwise the product's "value" might be reduced.

ROP and Activity-Based Costing (ABC)

Applying ABC to a process will not help the decision maker understand the relationship of cost to value produced in component processes. For example, assume that an ABC of a telephone service provisioning process revealed that 20% of the cost was due to poor quality. After the process was reengineered, the cost of poor quality was essentially eliminated. This was because the service representatives were provided with a new information system that helped ensure mistakes were not made on orders. Yet, the number of orders processed (i.e., information processed) per time period increased only slightly because the new process was more time consuming than the original. Without **ROP**, the result that the cost of poor quality improvement was significant might lead the decision maker to conclude incorrectly that reengineering was successful.

This example points to the need to capture change in process value creation (i.e., information/complexity creation), not just change in cost, to determine if BPR efforts are successful. **ROP** is designed to "take the temperature" of the process. The precision of ABC is useful in establishing the true costs of the component and compound process outputs. Traditional company measures of process performance, such as cycle time and error rate, are required for "tuning" the component processes. **ROP** will help the decision maker decide whether the tuning had the desired effect .

Need for Business Process Auditing

Business process audits, using the ROP method, must be conducted periodically to audit the performance of major company processes as well as the company itself. "We need new measurements— call them a 'business audit' — to give us effective business control" (Drucker, 1993). **ROP** forms the basis of a new approach to auditing: business process auditing (BPA) that will offer a new method for, and set of supporting tools to, evaluate company performance.

The need for new "tools" to measure a company's capacity for value creation has been widely acknowledged. "For the first time big institutional investors, including some very large pension funds, are working on such ideas and tools to measure the business performance of the companies in which they invest" (Drucker, 1993).

With BPA process tracking tools, the process auditor develops a model of major component and compound processes. This model reveals interdependencies and input/output rates. The processes and outputs are described in terms that allow **ROP** analysis (Kanevsky and Housel, in press).

BPA will supplement existing internal and/or external auditing practices when the goal of the audit is to examine the performance of major company *processes*. Given the difficulties that current auditing practices have in providing a true picture of company performance, BPA may provide an "insurance policy" for auditors as well as very useful information about the efficiency of a client's internal operations which could be used in Annual Reports to help analysts and investors better understand the viability of the firm.

V As A Benchmarking Index For Overall Company Performance

A **BPA** yeilds the data necessary to benchmark companies in terms of their processes. The **V** of an **ROP** analysis can be used as an index of the overall performance of a company's processes. A company level **V** would give executives, as well as analysts, a way to compare the performance of a company's operations to other companies within an industry. This would provide an invariant (with respect to the nature of the company product) index for objective benchmarking based on the common product of all companies: **complexity**. Comparisons among companies can be made as well as comparisons of a single company's internal processes over time by routinely auditing business processes and, once the data gathering procedures can be automated, **V** would be available on a real-time basis.

ROP can be applied at the company level by treating the major compound processes as components of the overall company "process" or **P**. Averaging the **V** values across all the company's processes, following a generalization of formula (**1**) extended to the necessary number of components, provides the total **V** value for the company's process performance. (For an example of how to partition a company's processes prior to calculation of the overall company **V**, see Appendix C.)

Conclusion

ROP is an objective way to measure value based on the understanding that business processes are just another variety of natural processes, all of which can be characterized in terms of K-complexity creation. **ROP** offers a new organizing principle based on value creation that will supplement or replace existing approaches to measuring company performance. As such, **ROP** may hasten a paradigm shift to the use of the K-complexity as the basis for evaluation of value creation in business.

The call for value creation resonates well in the 90's. Executives realize that manipulating assets will not be enough to ensure survival. Investors and customers expect companies to create value.

> The 1990s are shaping up as the 'value' decade. Value comes not just from identifying business needs (the demand side), but also from managing the supply side of the equation. Efficient technical resources become a key component of value. Universally, companies are reexamining and reengineering themselves to provide demonstrable value in the 1990s. (Rogow, 1993, p.2)

We need the results of **ROP**: **V** and V_m, to decide which company processes really are adding value. Until we measure value creation throughout **all** company processes, we will not make the process adjustments necessary to ensure successful value-based business process reengineering.

Appendix: Case Study Example

To provide a means to convey the myriad benefits derived from BPA, data has been extracted from a BPA effort at a Local Exchange Carrier (telecommunications company). Examples are provided for each step of the methodology.

Problem Statement

What is the value added of an intelligent information system to the front-end service negotiation component process of this telephone company? The intelligent information system was designed with two phases of delivery separated by four months. Prototypes had been developed which were used for the extrapolation of feature benefits of the two delivery phases of the intelligent information system. For the purposes of this case study the two phases of the intelligent information system will be designated as Future Method of Operation 1 and 2, or FMO1 and FMO2.

As in all BPR efforts two significant questions needed to be answered:

> Where and how much investment should be made in a company's processes resulting in a significant increase in return on investment (ROI) in the process' final consumable product/service

(i.e., product/service purchased by the consumer)?

How does one measure the return on investment in process (ROP) from this intelligent front-end system on a particular component process (in this case, order provisioning front end), especially if it does not produce a saleable output?

BPA Effort Breakdown

1. Identify the compound and component processes. The area selected for examination was the service order provisioning compound process. The compound process was divided into two large component processes (with their attendant sub-component processes): the service negotiation process, and the downstream provisioning component process. The effort to describe and gain concurrence on the processes required four two hour meetings with process subject matters experts and their management.

The definition of the major component process outputs, as well as, the final service product had been well defined by prior work of quality improvement teams.

2. Create the shortest description possible (K complexity) of each component process using the same language. As previously described, it is necessary to develop an informational description for the final consumable product/service. In this case it was agreed that a service order represented a good informational description of the consumable product. Figure 2 shows a partial example of a service order which is used as a representation of the final product.

The unit of measurement (shortest description possible in terms of K complexity) depends upon the level of accuracy desired. The level of accuracy often will determine the effort required to collect and analyze the data. The selection of the unit of measure must be consistent with the structure of the system whose performance it is designed to gauge.

It this case it was determined that there were four levels of accuracy (for the given sample period) in the hierarchy of measurement units:

1. number of valid orders per dollar of cost
2. number of valid order lines per dollar of cost
3. number of valid order entries per dollar of cost
4. amount of information (bit/byte) provided per dollar of cost

While amount of information (bit/byte) represented the most accurate unit of measure (it captures all activities associated with the compound provisioning process those that produce or fail to produce information), it was determined to be prohibitive to manually collect the necessary information.

Initially, the number of valid order entries was agreed upon to be the most practical unit of measure for the desired level of accuracy. However, it was found that one line could represent several sub-component processes. Later it was found that one entry could represent two sub-component processes, therefore fractional entries were used (see figure 3) as the best level of accuracy for practical measurement.

The number of valid order entries per dollar of cost encompasses performance measures such as error rate, cycle time, customer responsiveness (e.g. time on the phone, number of calls to and from a customer), and time from order completion to provisioning. This unit of measure provided a single cumulative indicator of overall performance.

The following is an example of a telephone service order. Each line is represented by a sequential number starting with 1 and ending with 23. Each line contains a process language *word* or *words*. The order would be incomplete without every entry and therefore it represents a reasonably complete product description. The various lines were generated by the sub-component processes of the service negotiation component process.

As in this case, it is not always necessary to *invent* a new process language. While an individual needs to be trained in the service order language (process language) to understand the entries, the language itself already existed and was commonly understood throughout the entire component process. Gaining consensus on this step of the methodology proved to be the most difficult step of the methodology

---

```
1 XXX XXX XXX/ 835/ LZ152/12182W/ 128J6B/NMKAKFDJI
2 /N/71838355    | BRE | 1001 | C |
3 ZDC/ FEEA(ATTLTB)
4 CTX/ IDPD99
5 ESSC/ CSVM
6 ACNA/ G
7 CCON
8 DDI
9 BS
     .

     .
22 /SCC/ 300.00
23 /DDT/NC
```

The above are examples of valid service order entries. Each line contains order entries or process language *word* (e.g., in line 1: 835, LZ152; and in line 23: DDT, NC).

Figure 2- Example of Service Order as Product Description (only a portion of the service order is shown)

and required a number of meetings over a five week period.

3. Count the number of process language "words" in the component output description. A print out of the service order was obtained for each order examined in the process. The number of entries per order was manually counted and associated with the appropriate component process. In this case historical data (service orders) were used to derive the necessary information for BPA baseline calculations.

After the intelligent front end prototype was developed it was possible to project the increase in valid entries produced within the designated time period. The amount of time (in minutes) necessary for the inclusion of the language "words" into the product description (service order) was collected in the same effort. (Time will be used in Step 6—Calculate the total cost to produce the output for each component.)

In Figure 3, P1. P2, etc. represent the component processes associated with the service provisioning component process. There is no attempt to show operational order to the processes under examination since several occurred in parallel.

4. Designate a time period long enough to capture a representative sample of the company's final products or services created by the compound process. The sample size collected should insure that there is an appropriate representation of all possible final products output by the compound process analyzed. The sample should contain at least ten representations (sales) of each type of final product produced by the compound process.

In the case of this effort one month was needed to collect a large enough sample size to represent six major product lines produced by the service negotiating process. Data was collected separately for processes P3 and P4, but it was determined that P3 and P4 should be represented as one sub-component process.

5. Sum the total amount of K complexity ("words") produced by each component during the designated time period. This step is needed to provide the Is (defined as valid order entries, Entry in this example) used in calculating V1. Approximately 15 minutes per day was needed to tally the number of "words" produced by each component process over a large number of orders. A spreadsheet was used to keep track of the number of "words" and the process sums. While it is recommended to accomplish this step with the help of automated methods, in this case, the numbers were counted manually and entered on a spreadsheet.

Totals were calculated for the service negotiating process using all orders sampled over the one month period. Calculations were made on the PMO environment, as well as, two FMO environments. Enabling technology supporting the FMO environments was logi-

	Order	
Process	**Entry**	**Time**
P1	6	15
P2	29	45
P3&P4	11	40
P5	78.5	45
Total	124.5	145

Figure 3 Service Order with Component Process Language "Words"Tabulated

cally and operationally placed in process P5.

6. Calculate the total cost to produce the output for each component. Cost is calculated using generally accepted accounting practices or any other acceptable costing method. In this case cost (C) was calculated using time duration's and loaded salaries for each process. It was found that P3&P4 (as one process) was the most expensive process, followed by P2, P1, and P5 respectively. Figure 4 illustrates this step of the ROP methodology

The cost of the enabling technology supporting the FMO environments was not amortized over all of process P5. Capital equipment amortization schedules vary from industry to industry. In the telecommunications industry the scheduled periods have traditionally been very long. Given that the cost of the new system was relatively minimal (under $15 million) and the long amortization period, the primary concern was labor costs.

In all cases personnel supporting all processes had union representation, but this did not present a major problem because the data collected was defined in an objective manner.

7. Compute the ROP for each component process. The internal performance of a process is defined as V, given its input, as the amount of information I, it produces per dollar of process cost C, over a given period of time. Vm, the purchase price per unit of information is equal to The purchase price, M, divided by the total

	Order	
Process	**Time**	**$**
P1	15	3.75
P2	45	23.25
P3&P4	40	12.80
P5	45	18.60
Total	145	58.40

Figure 4 Service Order With Cost Calculations

amount of information contained in the final product description. These formulas are expressed as:

$$V = I/C \text{ and } Vm = M/I$$

ROP then is $V \times Vm$, and in this case example, $V1 \times Vm1 = ROP1$ for the service negotiation component process.

Appendix: Conclusions

The rate and cost at which input data was transformed into information was clearly identified for each component process. This allows one to objectively rate the value creating performance of the entire process as well as each component process.

In this case study, the environment FMO1 was able move all the value created by process P1 to process P5 without compromising the product's definition. (This is particularly important in regulated industries where given product definitions must be maintained, regardless of reengineering processes, to ensure quality and to meet regulatory standards.) This improvement eliminated the need for process P1 resulting in a 38% overall performance improvement for the service negotiation component process. The improvement was due to the fact that the cost of P1 had been eliminated while the amount of information produced by the component process in the given sample time period had increased.

The environment FMO2 was able move all value creation (transformation of input data into information) from processes P1 and P2 to process P5. Thereby, eliminating the need for both processes P1 and P2. This resulted in a 75% overall performance improvement for the service negotiation component process due, once again to lower costs as well as greater value creation.

It is interesting to note that in the FMO environment process P5 was able to produce all the value creation in the PMO sub-component processes P1, P2 and P5 and remained the least expensive process. Equally important, is the fact that the return on investment in reengineering the PMO environment with enabling technology could be effectively approximated prior to any capital expenditure. In this manner Return on Process (ROP) can be used as a leading internal economic indicator.

ROP, as a leading economic indicator, can be used to measure and justify reengineering investments, including the associated enabling technology. The project implementation can be evaluated and measured in a real time manner (in this case study, daily) based on the increase in process performance. For example, the FMO2 environment showed a substantial improvement over both the PMO and the FMO1 environments. The investment to implement the

FMO2 environment is justified using an objective measurement and should be the obvious goal.

As the actual implementation progresses, the success of the reengineering effort can also be objectively measured using the calculations for the internal performance of a process V1. Also, there is no additional work necessary to measure the process performance once the procedures for calculating V1 have been established.

Since the measurement of value creation is objective and observable all participants in the reengineering process (management, subject maker experts, supervisors, craft personnel, etc.) can "see" which processes produce the most value and which processes no longer produce value. This makes BPA an effective tool to gain consensus for cultural change associated with a reengineering effort.

In this case BPA provided precise measurement of process value creation which was clearly communicated to all process participants. This let the participants know how each contributed to the value of the product. Knowing they could contribute to product value, the process participants focused on value creation and substantially improved their individual contributions. This resulted in an overall compound process performance improvement.

BPA demonstrated an additional benefit connected to BPR creating a "demand pull" for the new environment. If an organization has a clear sense of its future environment and it is widely shared, individuals are able to find their own roles within the organization

This case demonstrates the viability of Business Process Auditing. It is a practical method for developing an objective measurement of process performance based on units of information and process costs. As made evident by this case study BPA is: a reliable planning guide for management, a leading internal economic indicator, an auditing tool for investment, and a performance improvement measurement tool for ongoing process enhancement projects.

References

Bleakley, F. (July 6, 1993). Many Companies Try Management Fads, Only to See Them Flop. *The Wall Street Journal* , B 2.

Chaitin, G. J. (Vol. 13 1966). On the Length of Programs for Computing Binary Sequences. *Journal of Association of Computing Machines* , 547-569.

Cover, T. M. & Thomas, J. A. (1991). *Elements of Information Theory* . New York: John Wiley & Sons, Inc.

Davenport, T. (1993) *Process Innovation: Reengineering Work* . Cambridge, Ma: Harvard Business School Press, Inc.

Drucker, P. (April 13, 1993). We Need to Measure, Not Count. *The Wall Street Journal* , A14.

Eccles, R. (January-February 1991). The Performance Measurement Manifesto. *Harvard Business Review*, 131-137.

Hammer, M. (July-August, 1990). Reengineering Work: Don't Automate, Obliterate. *Harvard Business Review* , 104-112.

Housel , T. , Bell, A., & Kanevsky, V. (1994, January-February). Calculating the Value of Reengineering at Pacific Bell. *Planning Review,* 40-43,55.

Housel, T., Morris, C., and Westland, C. (April-May 1993). Business Process Reengineering at Pacific Bell. *Planning Review* , 28-33.

Johnson, H. (1992). *Relevance Regained: From Top-Down Control to Bottom-Up Empowerment* . New York: The Free Press Inc.

Kaplan, R. and Norton, D. *(January-February* 1992). The Balanced Scorecard - Measures That Drive Performance. *Harvard Business Review,* 71-79.

Kolomogorov, A. N. (Vol. 1,1965). Three Approaches to the Quantitative Definition of Information. *Problems of Information Transmission* , 4-7.

Nicolis, G. & Prigogine, I. (1978). *Self-Organizations in Nonequilibirium Systems* . New York: Wiley Interscience

Prigogine, I. (1980). *From Being to Becoming* . New York: Freeman Inc.

Prigogine, I. & Stengers, I. (1984). *Order Out of Chaos* . Chicago: Bantam Books Inc.

Solomonoff, R. J. (Vol. 7 1964). A Formal Theory of Inductive Inference. *Information Construction* , 224-254.

Stewart, T. (August 23, 1993). Reengineering: The Hot New Managing Tool. *Fortune,* 41- 48.

Rogow, B. (Spring 1993). Putting the 'T' Back Into IT: Developing the IT Management Agenda for the Mid-1990s. *SIM Executive* , 2.

Zurek, W. (1990). *Complexity, Entropy, and the Physics of Information.* Redwood City, California: Addison-Wesley Publishing Company .

Chapter 15

Lessons Learned from Business Engineering Within the Amsterdam Municipal Police Force:
The Applicability of
Dynamic Modelling

J.W. van Meel
P.W.G. Bots
H.G. Sol
Delft University of Technology

The *Amsterdam Municipal Police Force* is facing serious problems. In the Netherlands, crime is becoming a problem of major importance. Within the last fifty years, crime rates have actually been multiplied by ten (Department of Justice, 1985). From recent governmental research, it appears that every inhabitant of Amsterdam of 15 years or older has a 50% chance annually to fall victim to one or more criminal offenses (Department of Home Affairs, 1991). Thus, Amsterdam has one of the highest crime rates amongst European cities. Note however, that in Holland 'criminal offence' covers anything from bicycle thefts to acts of violence. Regardless of this mitigation, the Amsterdam Municipal Police has an arduous task. A large-scale reorganization process, initiated in the late eighties, to improve the performance of the Amsterdam Police Force, is still ongoing today. Information technology is regarded as one of the building blocks of the reorganization process.

Within the force, numerous plans have been formulated for restructuring the current business and information processes of the force. To judge their effectiveness, their impact on the performance of the force must be established. However, actually experimenting with police departments can be expensive and full of risk. Since the last reorganization was effectuated only recently, the force's management is reluctant in announcing additional changes. The business processes and the information processes themselves are rather complex and unpredictable: most activities are carried out on a basis of experience and professionalism, and are coordinated through mutual adjustment. Few work procedures are formalized. Combined, these reasons make the restructuring of the Amsterdam Police Force a fuzzy, 'soft' problem: complex, difficult to tackle, with both technical and social components. According to the force's management, crime fighting is not a problem of the police alone: it is becoming a problem of major societal importance. This has created a special interest in cooperation with universities and other scientific institutions. In particular, the School of Systems Engineering and Policy Analysis has been asked to investigate the possibilities and impossibilities of changing and restructuring police work.

The first observation that can be made is that the Amsterdam Municipal Police Force is not the only organization in the midst of a large and complex restructuring process (see e.g. Hammer and Champy, 1993; Davenport, 1993 for examples). Many organizations need to transform their business more frequently than they used to do to survive. Business processes of these organizations are becoming more and more information intensive, and yet they are seldom designed with the possibilities of new information technology in mind. It could be fruitful to transform technology and user environment in an integral way instead of what is usually done: holding one constant and changing the other. Such integral design of both organizational structures and processes and information systems is called 'business engineering' (BE) here.

Consider for instance the example of the problematic accounts payable process of the Ford Motor Company as given in (Hammer 1990). A classical information systems consultant would have started off with an analysis of existing processes and structures and would have sold Ford a solution in which the various information systems of the purchasing departments, material control, and accounts payable would have been fine tuned, for instance by introducing standard data definitions for document handling or by defining consistency rules for data integrity checks. A classical management consultant would have started off by organizing a working conference with representatives of all departments involved. Then he would have sold Ford a solution in which the work flows of the various department would have been fine tuned for instance by introducing new work procedures and job definitions, or by institutionalizing a periodical interdepartmental meeting to facilitate interdepartmental communication. A business engineer would have tried to combine the best of both worlds, using information technology to transform existing business processes, for instance, by introducing a corporate database to reduce interdepartmental coordination, herewith creating new work procedures and opening opportunities for a better monitoring of the accounts payable process by cross-functional management information.

BE can have a great effect on the functioning of an organization as a whole (Hammer, 1990; Kaplan and Muirdock, 1991; Gulden and Reck , 1992). Mostly within short time frames, complex design decisions must be made. For a successful BE effort, the personnel, financial, and information policies of an organization need to be aligned (Gulden and Reck, 1992; Guha, 1993; Ligus, 1993). Radical breakthroughs in organizational performance are reported, but the reasons for these drastic improvements are seldom explained. Most of the existing literature is primarily normative, only fragmentary descriptions of engineering are provided and used as anecdotal evidence of the prescriptions being offered (Craig and Yetton, 1994). In fact, BE is not without risks (Hall et al. 1993; Hammer and Champy, 1993) and should be carefully managed and planned (Heygate, 1992). What is needed in fact is a 'good-and-sound' design methodology for guiding a BE-effort (Davenport, 1993). Such a methodology is a means to ensure a minimum level of discipline, to facilitate structuring, planning and monitoring, to codify experience and ideas and is a perquisite for the development of automated support for design efforts (Simsion, 1994). In Meel (1994) and Meel et al. (1994) it is however shown that BE has received little theoretical and methodological support until now.

In this chapter, the possibilities of dynamic modelling for theoretical and methodological support for BE is discussed. First, a general overview of the dynamic modelling approach is given. This is followed by a more detailed account of a case study with dynamic modelling within the Amsterdam Municipal Police Force. The dynamic modelling approach used during this study is analyzed in terms of a way of thinking, controlling, working, modelling and supporting. Subsequently, the 'fits' between the different ways are discussed to show the consistency and coherence of the approach used. Finally, conclusions are drawn and implications are given for further research.

Background: Dynamic Modelling

Dynamic modelling is a structured approach to analyze and diagnose organizational problems using dynamic models. Dynamic models are formal, executable and yet comprehensible representations of the primary business processes of an organization. They can incorporate different levels of abstraction, represent parallel sequences of activities and have an explicit time dimension. Discrete event workbenches enhanced by animation features are used to construct such models. Within the approach, the dynamic model is used as a substitute for dynamic and complex reality. A dynamic model of the current situation is used to analyze the business processes of an organization. 'Soft' qualitative problems can then be supported by 'hard' quantitative figures. Possible solutions can be translated in terms of the dynamic model of the current situation. Afterwards, the experimental outcomes of the model for the various solutions can be compared with the outcomes of the model for the current situation. In this way, the effectiveness of the various solutions can be evaluated without the need to implement them in the complex reality. Finally, 'hard' experimental results are combined with 'soft' insights gained during the modelling process in a number of conclusions and recommendations, preferably supported by a migration path. Both the modelling process and its results are used for structuring a critical debate with respect to dynamic change. Thus dynamic modelling is not a 'hard' scientific instrument 'pur sang', but also an instrument for learning and structuring in organizational change processes.

A dynamic modelling project is carried out in a number of steps. A summary of these steps is given in table 1. A linear representation format is used to make the summary easy to understand. In a real design project though, tasks and subtasks cannot be delineated as sharply. In an actual design effort, work will be carried out simultaneously at different levels of detail (Checkland 81). During the execution of the task 'problem formulation', ideas for improvements of the current situation come to mind, which can be used for the task 'solution finding'. During the execution of the task 'model specification', it is necessary to define clearly what is meant by some concepts, thereby sharpening the results of the task 'problem conceptualization'.

In practice, various iterations and cycles are possible. The task sequences represented in this chapter should therefore only be seen as a way to structure the dynamic modelling effort, not as a set of normative and universal guidelines. The dynamic modelling approach shares with other methodologies that it needs to be tailored to a specific approach for each project to meet the needs of a particular organization effectively (Simsion 94). Depending on the assignment and the amount of re-usable material, specific tasks of the methodology should be given explicit attention or should be left out.

If, for instance, the organization is in the middle of a reorganization and has just started on specifying its own strategy, structure

Tasks and subtasks	Product
Problem formulation formulate project assignment scan organizational environment scan organizational history scan current organization identify problems & problem clusters define problem domain	Problem domain description with references to the names of the critical, problematic, business processes
Problem conceptualization identify object classes define object classes define task structures describe representation schemes	Description of the critical, problematic business process in terms of object definitions and task structures
Model specification specify output variables specify model reductions specify model structure specify input data specify animation specify initial treatment	Machine executable dynamic model of the primary business processes of the problem domain
Model checking check model correctness check structural correspondence check replicative correspondence	Correct dynamic model with a close correspondence to the problem domain in reality
Solution finding generate potential alternatives model implementation alternatives evaluate importance alternatives evaluate effectiveness alternatives evaluate cost/benefits alternatives	Effective directions for change together with an estimation of their costs and benefits
Solution implementation formulate conclusions formulate recommendations formulate migration path present project results elaborate recommendations implement changes freeze new situation	Better functioning of the organization in terms of solved problems

Table 1: Summary of the Approach

and processes, then explicit attention should be paid to the tasks 'problem formulation' and 'problem conceptualization' (see e.g. the second case study within the Criminal Investigation Department as described in Meel (1994). If the organization has already made explicit decisions with respect of strategy, structure and processes, and just needs to have a justification for certain critical decisions (see e.g. the studies described in Streng (1993) on the introduction of

EDI), then explicit attention should be paid to the tasks 'model specification' and 'model checking'. If the organization already has well established strategies, structures and processes but is uncertain about how to improve them, then explicit attention should be paid to the tasks 'solution finding' and 'solution implementation' (see e.g. the case study as described in the next section).

The approach and contingencies as described here were used and refined in a number of research projects (Sol 1992a, 1992b), for example in designing inter-organizational information systems for international rail transport of cargo (Wierda, 1991), in the development of an information system for treasury management and in house banking (Motshagen, 1991), in evaluating the effects of introducing new information technology into administrative organizations (Dur , 1992), in the application of mobile data communication in fleet management information systems (Schrijver, 1993), in supporting investment decisions on application of Electronic Data Interchange in the port of Rotterdam (Streng, 1993), in designing computer support for distributed workplaces for a large insurance firm (Eijck, 1993), in evaluating different coordination mechanisms for the Department of Unemployment Benefits of the Dutch Ministry of the Interior (Vreede et al., 1993), in evaluating the handling of neurology patients by the Neurology polyclinic and supporting departments at an academic hospital (Vreede, 1993), and in supporting the realization of an effective baggage handling system at Schiphol airport (Babeliowsky et al., 1994).

Each of these cases focused strongly on modelling of complex organizational processes to evaluate the effects of introducing information technology into organizations in advance. These results have made clear that dynamic modelling can be of value for supporting business engineering in real life problem situations. The problem, however, is that all these studies were primarily focused on the modelling aspects of the approach, i.e. the development of modelling formalisms and automated modelling support. For these reasons, an explorative case study within the Amsterdam Municipal Police Force was carried out to get a better understanding of the value of the current dynamic modelling approach for business engineering and to elaborate the theoretical and methodological aspects of this approach in more detail. In fact, the definitions given in this section and the summary of table 1 is a result of this effort, see also (Meel 94).

The Case of the Municipal Police Force

The explorative case study within the police force is used here as an example description of the application of dynamic modelling in a real life context. As stated in the introduction, crime is becoming a societal problem of major importance in the Netherlands. A large scale reorganization was set in motion to improve the performance of the Dutch police forces in the late eighties which is still going on today.

Problem formulation

Within the force, lots of ideas do exist to improve the force's performance. Strategic reports contain discussions about topics such as 'innovation', 'prevention', 'the police as an enterprise', and 'the police manager as entrepreneur.' Keywords in the current situation are 'decentralisation', 'management by objectives', 'project work' and 'information technology'. At the operational level, so called 'neighbourhood teams' are created: small, decentralized units responsible for general police work in small geographical areas. This implies that the teams have to deal with all matters in their neighbourhood themselves, from the first call for service by the public to handing someone over to the public prosecutor. Within the neighbourhood teams, 'management by objectives' was introduced. The top management of the force annually defines 'force objectives': problem areas on which the activities of the force must be focused. Based on these objectives, the neighbourhood teams must set up a number of 'project plans', in which the teams define how they expect to reach these objectives. Projects are meant to open up opportunities for more preventive action, and should become the main activity of each neighbourhood team.

Information technology is regarded as one of the essential building blocks of the change process. The Amsterdam police force has developed a multi-user transaction processing system to facilitate the paper work within neighbourhood teams. This system is organized around a central database, which can be used at a remote level. The force's former central registration and information department is no longer needed. In the past, a management reporting tool has been created to provide figures about incidents and crime rates of a neighbourhood as whole. This reporting tool has a lot of shortcomings. It has no interface to the force's central transaction processing system, so it must be fed with data manually. Since it is not very motivating to input the same data twice, the reporting system contains a lot of inaccurate and outdated information. However, the main problem is that the system can deal with 'traditional' police data concerning incidents and accidents, but hardly with data concerning projects. No information can be generated about individual projects. According to the users, the reporting tool did not fit in the project-oriented neighbourhood teams any more.

This problem with relevant, correct and accurate management information for neighbourhood teams was the immediate cause for the Amsterdam Municipal Police Force to authorize a first study. The assignment was to investigate the possibilities of management information systems to support project work. Information and management, however, are not aims in themselves but should contribute to a better functioning of the primary business processes. The primary business process of the neighbourhood teams should therefore be the starting point of the investigation. Dynamic modelling was used to gain insight in these processes.

Problem conceptualization

The first step of the case study was to describe in broad terms the problem domain under study. The daily activities of the neighbourhood teams were looked upon from a conceptual level.

The Amsterdam Municipal Police Force has twenty-four neighbourhood teams, each consisting of sixty to eighty officers. Each team has the same organizational structure: each neighbourhood team has its own chief, assisted by a staff officer, and consists of eight crews of six to eight officers and one chief. Crews work in shifts and have their own schedule, defining starts and ends of the crew shifts. There are two types of shifts: during the 'assistance shift', a crew is responsible for car patrol and answering questions from the public at the desk of the neighbourhood team. During the 'prevention shift', a crew performs tasks like paper work and project activities; these tasks are mostly performed in the office.

Object definitions as described by Bots (1989) were used to document the results of the conceptualization phase, see also Meel (1993, 1994).

Model specification

Based on the results of the conceptualization, a first dynamic simulation model was developed for the activities of one of the neighbourhood teams. With this model, it could be shown that neighbourhood teams spent just 15% of their total daily capacity on project work. The main activities of a neighbourhood team appeared to be car patrol and handling the resulting paper work. Given this observation, it was doubtful whether a new management information system would contribute to a better functioning of the entire organizational chain. The objective of the case study was therefore reformulated from MIS design to looking for ways to increase the time spent on execution of project work. Based on the results of this first prototype dynamic model, a more sophisticated dynamic model was developed for three of the twenty-four neighbourhood teams of the force Meel, 1993, 1994).

The modelled neighbourhood teams consist of a number of crews, each with its own schedule. During a scheduled shift, each police officer is responsible for a specific set of tasks. During car patrol the officers respond to requests for assistance; when on desk duty, an officer helps citizens at the desk of the neighbourhood team; when on office duty, an officer performs administrative tasks, project activities, and other tasks, such as investigation, maintenance and looking after the neighbourhood team dog. Tasks within the model are triggered by work supply. Calls for service are generated by citizens and received by the operator in the communication centre. The operator asks the citizen a few questions to decide whether police action is required. If so, he assigns the call a priority ranging from 1 to 3 and sends it to the operator who communicates with the patrol cars. If no patrol car is available, the communication operator can decide, based on the call's priority, its location, and an additional set of rules, whether it is necessary to interrupt a patrol car, to let the neighbourhood team start a new car patrol team or to ignore the call. The communication operator is therefore able to change the capacity of the number of police officers in the model. After a call has been handled by a car patrol team, it can result in paper work for the neighbourhood team. Other work supply types in the model are project activities, citizens at the desk of the neighbourhood team and 'remainder', which is an aggregation of activities which are too insignificant to be individually incorporated in the model. A work supply generator is used for modelling that piece of the problem situation which influences the amounts of work supply, but which is not direct relevant according to the problem statement.

Data such as inter-arrival times, amounts of paper works, and absence figures were analyzed to be able to simulate the activities of a neighbourhood team. The results of these analyses were added to the model using theoretical and empirical random distributions. Much attention was paid to data related to car patrol as this is the main activity of the neighbourhood teams. For want of aggregated, directly usable information, raw data from the registration system of the communication centre was analyzed. Firstly, the numbers of incoming calls were analyzed for the three neighbourhood teams involved. Per year, per week and per day, these numbers were rather stable, but per hour, they show strong fluctuations, mainly depending on the period of the day. Within the data, seven inter-arrival periods were distinguished with similar characteristics. The inter-arrival time per period was modelled by an exponential distribution.

Other random distributions related to car patrol appeared to depend mainly on the accident type of incoming calls. Accident types were represented by 120 different codes in the registration system of the communication centre. These codes ranged from accidents such as 'traffic accidents' and 'noise disturbance' to more exotic ones like 'ghost driver', 'unleashed pitbull' and 'exhibitionist'. By grouping codes with similar characteristics such as service time, inter-arrival times and definition, the 120 codes were aggregated to 33 code groups. Goodness of fit between these exogenous model data and real data was verified with the Chi-square test and the Kolmochorov-Smirnov test.

Model checking

The dynamic simulation model was first verified to check the correctness of the model, which was validated by means of structural and replicative validation to check the correspondence with the problem area.

Techniques like 'structured walk throughs' (Yourdon, 1978), 'module and integration testing' (Smith and Wood, 1987), and 'tracing of critical model entities (Pegden et al., 1990) were used to verify the correctness of the model. This verification showed a number of minor bugs in the program code which could easily be fixed.

The animation features of SIMAN/Cinema (Pegden et al. 90) were used for the structural validation. In SIMAN/Cinema, graphical animation screens can be defined, representing the internal status of the model. This results in a movie-like animation of the behaviour of the model at run time. An example screen dump of the animation is given in figure 1, showing the business processes of one of the modelled neighbourhood team. The structural validation was carried out with the help of the police officers of the neighbourhood

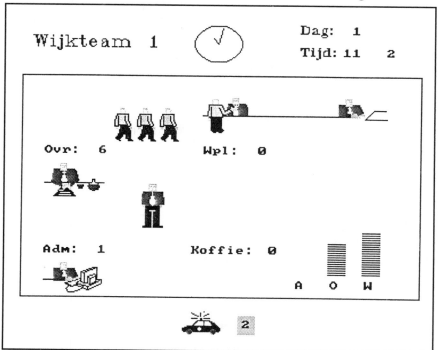

Figure 1: Business Process of a Modelled Neighborhood Team

teams involved. The developed model, and especially the graphical representation of the model, turned out to be very recognizable.

Samples from the time registration system of the neighbourhood teams involved were used for the replicative validation. Discrepancies between model and sample results were tested with the t-test for comparison. Both the structural and the replicative validation indicated an acceptable correspondence between the dynamic model and the problem domain.

Solution finding

Several experiments were carried out with the developed dynamic simulation model. The results were analyzed and discussed with members of the police staff. Based on conversations with police officers, the conclusions of a task group of the police force, and an analysis of the dynamic simulation model, twenty-five potential change alternatives were identified. Among them were alternatives such as the employment of more police officers, the development of faster computer systems, and different procedures for car patrol. After the identification phase, the alternatives were translated in terms of the dynamic simulation model of the problem situation.

Contrary to police expectations, some of the obvious alternatives had no consequences for the time spent on projects. Alternatives such as the introduction of new and faster information technology for paper work, or more rigorous procedures within the communication centre, have no structural effects on the time spent on projects. The optimization of subprocesses does not seem to lead to a better functioning of the police organization. The deployment of more police officers in the model does not lead to a proportional increase in time spent on execution of projects either.

This phenomenon appeared to be caused by detachments to other departments or illness. One third of the police officers of

Alternatives	Time spent on project work
0. Current situation	14.9
1. Handling of requests for assistance by office based teams	+10.7
2. Reducing % time spent on 'remaining' tasks from 19% to 14%	+4.4
3. Reducing % agents absent by illness/leave from 22% to 17%	+5.8
4. Reducing % agents placed in other departments from 7% to 3%	+3.7

Table 2: Alternatives and Their Effects on Project Work

neighbourhood teams is structurally not available for daily operations. Rather than employing more police officers, alternatives should aim at decreasing this structural absence.

The greatest effect is achieved by the radical removal of the division of labour between car patrol and office duties. This implies that car patrol officers are added to the officers doing office work while remaining available for requests for assistance. Between service requests, car patrol officers work in the office. This construction does not automatically result in the expected negative effects such as an increased number of ignored calls or interrupted activities of patrol teams.

Based on the above results, a mix of alternatives is suggested for the three neighbourhood teams examined, see table 2.

Combined, the alternatives lead to an increase in the time spent on execution projects from 15% to 40%. For the total capacity of 156 police officers, this implies up to 40 extra officers available daily for projects for the three neighbourhood teams involved. Extrapolated to the total capacity of the neighbourhood teams of the force, this increase would amount to a saving of 8% on the force's annual budget.

It is interesting to see that the introduction of office based teams, which is in fact a 'radical' break with the past, results in the highest increase in time spent on project work. It is however also interesting to see that the combination of the three other, more 'continuous improvement oriented' alternatives together result in a higher increase than the radical alternative of office based teams individually.

Solution implementation

When the alternatives are to be implemented, project work will become the main activity of neighbourhood teams. However, this change in focus has severe implications. First, the tasks of the neighbourhood team chief need to change. Presently, most of the time of the team chief is taken up by day-to-day operational problems and human resource management. However, when project work becomes a major part of the daily routine, different skills are needed. The team chief must be able to plan projects in advance, to raise funds for the projects of his team within and outside the force, to manage large, time-consuming projects and to evaluate the impact of the projects on the safety in the neighbourhood.

Second, the problems with the current management reporting tool will become more urgent. At the moment, the Amsterdam Municipal Police Force is developing an automated crime analysis system. This expert system can create graphical and tabular representations of the crime rates in a certain geographical area and can analyze trends. However, the management information tools developed by the teams for their own usage are not sophisticated at all.

With the aid of standard software packages, small reporting systems have been developed for answering simple management questions like 'How much personnel capacity is available the coming month?', 'Which projects are currently running and what is their status?', and 'How many incidents have been handled by the neighbourhood team?'. Despite technical and procedural shortcomings, the functionality of the reporting systems seems to be appropriate for the team chiefs and the information is actually being used by them. What is needed, in fact, for the near future are not sophisticated, narrow focused crime analysis systems but flexible reporting tools which can give information about the business processes as a whole.

Project evaluation

The conclusions of the case study were presented to the management and two task forces of the Amsterdam Municipal Police Force. The alternatives given and arguments provided proved to be acceptable. In particular, the low percentage of time spent on project work turned out to be an eye opener. The results showed a gap between the vision of top management and actual daily routines. The alternatives presented were considered as adequate options for improving organizational performance. The fact that the results not only indicated the effective directions, but also the ineffective directions for business engineering, was regarded as one of the major merits of the case study. The presentations formed a basis for a critical discussion about the original reorganization objectives, radical change, continuous improvement, and current business processes. The suggested recommendations are currently being studied.

Reflection

When reflecting on the case study, it can be concluded that the first results are promising. The question whether dynamic modelling can be used for guiding and structuring BE-efforts can not be answered directly. For a proper description of the ideas and assumptions behind this approach, an analytical framework as introduced by Sol (1984) is used. According to this framework, a design approach is characterized by a way of thinking, controlling, working, and modelling. Preferably, these "ways" are supported by a coherent set of automated tools (a designers' environment or workbench). In this section, the analytical framework is used for analyzing the approach used in the case study and relating the results of this analysis to other bodies of literature.

Way of thinking

The way of thinking consists of a delineation of the problem domain and a design theory. In the introduction, the problem domain of Business Engineering is defined as designing organizational and information technical structures in an integral way. The case study's results shows the need of such an perspective. First, the problem of designing an information system can not be solved without looking to related organizational problems also. It is useless to design an expensive and sophisticated project work information system, if only 15% of the total available capacity is spent on project work. Second, changes in the organizational structure should be accompanied with a proper management information system for controlling and evaluating the effects afterwards. Although project work ought to be the main activity of the neighbourhood teams, there are no information systems which can indicate to what extent neighbourhood teams are working on projects.

As a starting point in formulating a design theory, ideas from the area of SocioTechnical Design (STD) seems to be quite appropriate for BE. STD, sometimes also called SocioTechnics, is 'an applied science aimed at improving the quality of work and organization through the adaption or the fundamental redesign of contents and composition of technology and human tasks' (Eijnatten 93). STD is a reaction to the unilateral emphasis placed on technical and human aspects in, respectively, Scientific Management and the School of Human Relations. The origins of STD can be traced back to the pioneering Tavistock studies of the early fifties (Trist and Bamforth 51) and is elaborated into a number of now classical principles and guidelines which are summarized in Cherns (1976; 1987). After the sixties, classic STD was further elaborated into a number of modern variants (Eijnatten, 1993) such as 'participative design' (Emery and Emery, 1974), 'democratic dialogue' (Engelstad and Gustavsen, 1993) and 'organizational renewal' (de Sitter, 1981).

The SocioTechnical Design paradigm distinguishes explicitly between a social and a technical subsystem and advocates a joint optimization of them (Trist et al., 1963). This paradigm can be closely related to the positioning of BE between organization design and information systems design. It is also interesting to notice that the SocioTechnical approach is the only school of thought which has it components both in organization and IS design literature. Further, lots of SocioTechnical design concepts can be found in descriptions of new IT-enabled organizational forms which result from actual BE-efforts, see e.g. (Lewin and Stephens, 1993, Ostroff and Smith, 1992, Stalk et al., 1992).

Four sociotechnical design principles fit with the case results (Meel, 1994):

- in complex and turbulent environments, the organization as a whole needs to be decomposed in a number of parallel operating subunits which are responsible for one complete business process in the chain from supplier to consumer;
- these subunits ought to operate as semi-autonomous teams and must be able to carry out their daily routines quite independently from other subunits;
- management structures should be designed to support general decision making, giving semi-autonomous teams self-control over the budgets, equipment, personnel and information they use;
- management information should not give highly specific information about a limited set of aspects, but ought to give generalized and aggregated information about a business process as a whole.

Together, these four basic principles can be the start of the formulation of a design theory for flexible, information intensive service organizations in complex, hostile environments.

In the approach, the design theory can be used in various ways. In the step 'problem formulation', the design theory can be used to position and interpret the historical transition processes of an organization. In the step 'solution finding', the design theory can be used to generate alternatives related to changes in organizational structure and work flow. In the step 'solution implementation', the design theory can be used to extrapolate the experimental simulation results towards recommendations with respect to control processes.

Way of controlling

The case study is carried out in close cooperation with police officers from various departments. Dynamic models are developed in an incremental way by means of prototyping. The modelling process self is middle-out as opposed to top-down or bottom-up.

A control strategy which seems to fit most with that of the case study is an adaptive strategy (Keen, 1980). This strategy sees a design project as an adaptive process of learning for both consultants and stakeholders. Consultants can learn from the stakeholders about current operations, bottlenecks in current functioning and possible improvements. Stakeholders can learn from consultants about design methodologies, techniques and tools. For effective learning, a close cooperation between stakeholders and consultants is needed.

An incremental model building process implies that a design project must aim at quick delivery of an initial model in order to give stakeholders the opportunity to respond and thus clarify what they really want. The initial model needs to be further developed by means of a number of iterations. At the start of a design project, organizational and informational problems are often fuzzy and ill-structured; final results are seldom very clear. The project plan will be very open-ended at the start of a design project. However, after each completed step, the project plan needs to be adjusted and discussed.

A middle out modelling process can reduce complexity (Jackson, 1983): rather then trying to grasp the complete organization at once, take a single unit or process and start from there.

Way of working

In the case study, the way of working was driven by actual problems in a real world problem situation. Following the problem solving model cycle (Sol 82), based on (Mitroff et al. 74), the following steps were undertaken: 'problem formulation', 'problem conceptualization', 'model specification', 'model correspondence check', 'solution finding' and 'solution implementation'.

A similar problem orientation has been found in several other articles on BE (Davenport and Short, 1990; Davenport, 1993; Fried, 1991; Hammer , 1990; Hammer and Champy, 1993, Harrington, 1991; Kaplan and Muirdock, 1991). A problem solving way of working differs from the traditional steps undertaken in IS design because it focuses not only on information but also on organizational problems. Organization design literature offers far less support for a way of working. (Laboratory) experiments as advocated in some Human Relation literature are not always possible. Diagnostic contingency studies are difficult to relate to real business needs. However, it is interesting to notice that although the way of thinking of the Classical School of Management seems to have become obsolete, their 'scientific' way of working, focusing explicit on real business problems, is currently achieving more recognition (Davenport and Short, 1990). SocioTechnics advocates also a problem oriented way of working (Eijnatten, 1993).

Way of modelling

In the case study, the neighbourhood team's business process proved to be very hard to model. Although some aspects of the force are regulated by law, police officers are professionals and develop their own procedures. Reasons for structuring at the operational level are seldom made explicit and most of them have evolved over time. Police officers use their own 'slang' in order to communicate with each other and it takes some time to understand their language. Most business process are not scheduled, but depend on time and status and are very dynamic.

The vocabulary for describing business processes offered by organization design literature is rather abstract. Relationships between concepts are mostly linear and seldom take interactions into account, see e.g. (Schoonhoven, 1981). Organization design seems to lack a realistic vocabulary for describing functional, material and dynamic relationships. In information systems design, business processes are expressed by means of modelling formalisms such as entity relationship diagrams and data flow diagrams. However these modelling techniques can only represent static aspects. A major exception is formed by the object oriented approaches which model business processes with a number of concurrent interacting objects. However, object oriented modelling techniques focus more on the creation of object oriented program structures than on analyzing and diagnosing business processes. Dynamic models elaborates the object oriented modelling paradigm in a more suitable form for business engineering. In the case study, a special form of dynamic models (task/actor models) has been used (Bots, 1989; Bots, 1992; Dur, 1992).

Automated support

To obtain an executable model for analysis and diagnosis, task/actor models are translated into simulation models. For this, the simulation environment SIMAN/Cinema (Pegden et al. , 1990) was used in the case study. This environment offers a general purpose simulation language and very good real-time animation features. In SIMAN/Cinema, graphical animation screens can be defined, which can represent the internal status of a simulation model. At run time, this results in a movie-like animation of the behaviour of the model.

Organization design literature does not pay much attention to support tools, this in contrast with IS design literature. However, Data Base Management Systems, Data Dictionaries and 4th generation languages can be very useful for implementation, but less for analysis and design. CASE-tools can be very helpful for creating and checking of graphical, static representations of business processes, but are of less help for representing dynamics aspects and experimentations with alternative designs. Discrete event simulation does not have these deficiencies with respect to analysis and design. However, current tools are less sophisticated in the model management area.

Discussion

The results of the preceding section are summarized in figure 2. In order to be able to speak about a consistent and coherent approach, the fit between the different ways is examined and

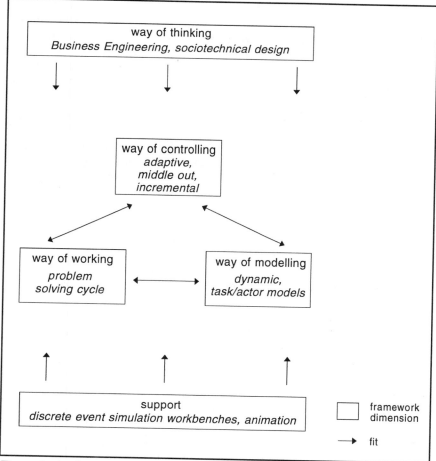

Figure 2: Analyzing the Dynamic Modelling Approach

discussed.

The way of working and the way of modelling show a good fit. The problem solving way of working emphasizes the use of models in a design process. The modelling representation techniques (object class definitions, task structures, animated simulation models) differ in level of abstraction but can be translated into each other in a flexible way. The output of a previous step is input for a successive step. The way of controlling also fits with these ways of working and modelling. The model construction proceeds from low to high complexity, this accounts for middle out control. Multiple iterations of (parts of) the problem solving cycle are needed to construct such models, which fits with the advocated incremental control. The resulting models and model descriptions are recognizable for persons involved in the BE effort which fits with the adaptive control strategy.

The way of thinking is characterized by an engineering perspective (as opposed to an emergent perspective) and is aimed at practical problem solving. This fits with the adaptive and yet controlled problem solving process and the heavy usage of descriptive and prescriptive modelling. The modelling constructs used offer sufficient conceptual freedom to represent both technical and organizational aspects of the problem domain and are 'grounded' in a solid system oriented view of organizations. The way of thinking is also characterized by a socio-technical perspective which is made explicit in a number of design principles. These principles can give guidance for the transformation of the descriptive model into prescriptive models during the solution finding phase. Given a descriptive model, the number of options for changing and combining model objects can be enormous and the number of possible solutions can easily get out of hand. Socio-technical design principles can indicate where to start looking for improvements. Besides design principles, the socio-technical school of thought also advocates a way of working which fits with the general problem solving process, and an adaptive way of controlling which emphasizes a close cooperation between consultants and stakeholders in 'joint optimization'.

Discrete event simulation workbenches and languages effectively support the way of working, modelling and controlling. The adaptive way of controlling emphasizes learning, both for consultants and stakeholders; learning implies experimentation. With respect to field experiments, simulation offers optimal control over experimental conditions. Animation offers possibilities to present understandable models to stakeholders who are mostly not familiar with modelling techniques in general and dynamic modelling techniques in particular. The correspondence of the empirical model with the problem domain at hand can be checked both structurally and replicatively using an animated simulation model. Problems can be analyzed using statistical techniques or by tracing closely animated model behaviour. Solutions can be translated in terms of changes in model parameters and model structure. Simulation methodology itself fits well into the general problem solving cycle. It is also interesting to note that simulation languages such as SIMULA have given an important impulse to the current object oriented approaches. Lots of elegant and sophisticated modelling constructs can be found to represent complex, dynamic entities such as organizations, in simulation languages.

Finally, if looked upon from a researcher's, rather than a practitioner's point of view, the combination of design theories and executable, animated discrete event simulation models can be a very beneficial one. Experimenting with design theories in actual problem settings is often impeded by the high level of abstraction of the theories at hand and seldom feasible. A discrete event simulation model, enhanced by animation, can however, give a concrete form to these design theories. Conversely, simulation makes it possible to test design theories in actual problem situations in an experimental setting. If looked upon from a socio-technical perspective, the application of experimental design techniques for simulation described here can be seen as a structural method for tracing the 'key variances' of a system.

Conclusions and Further Research

Dynamic modelling is a structured approach for the analysis and diagnosis of organizational problems by means of dynamic simulation models. The results of a case study within the Amsterdam Municipal Police Force and the subsequent analysis of the approach used show the applicability of dynamic modelling for BE-efforts. The product of this analysis is a specification of a problem solving approach to BE which uses dynamic simulation models as a substitute for complex reality, together with SocioTechnical principles for organization design, and an adaptive, incremental, and middle-out control strategy.

Further research will focus on elaborating this systematic approach into more detail. New support tools are developed to facilitate the use of such an approach. For example, De Vreede (1993) shows how a group decision room can be used to speed up the dynamic modelling process and enhance stakeholder participation. Meel (1994) shows how support tools for regression based experimental design can lead to an efficient and effective experimenting phase. Combination of the outcomes of all research efforts should result in what could be called an interactive group dynamic modelling approach for BE.

The research reported here indicates that partial theories, tools and techniques from organization and information systems design literature combined with empirical findings from case studies can be forged into a hard core for a systematic approach to solving 'soft' BE problems.

References

Babeliowsky, M.N.F., W.J.R. van der Spek, and H.G. Sol (1994) 'Dynamic modelling of transfer baggage handling at Schiphol airport', Working Paper, School of Systems Engineering and Policy Analysis, University of Technology Delft, The Netherlands

Bots, P.W.G. (1989) An environment to support problem solving, Doctoral Dissertation, University of Technology Delft, Delft, The Netherlands

Bots, P.W.G. (1992) 'Modelling for Organizational Change: From problems to objects to solutions', in: *Proceedings of the Hawaiian International*

Conference on System Sciences, Los Alamitos California: IEEE Computer Society Press, p. 568-578

Checkland, P. (1981) *Systems Thinking, Systems Practice*, Chichester, Wiley

Cherns, A.B. (1976) 'The Principles of Sociotechnical Design', in: *Human Relations*, Vol. 29, No. 8, p. 783-792

Cherns, A.B. (1987) 'Principles of Sociotechnical Design Revisted', in: *Human Relations*, Vol. 40, No. 3, p. 153-162

Craig, J.F., and P.W. Yetton (1994) 'Top down and bottom up management of BPR', in: B. Glasson, I.T. Hawryszkiewycz, B.A. Underwood, and R.A. Weber (ed.), *Proceedings of the IFIP TC8 Open Conference on Business Process Engineering: Information System Opportunities and Challenges*, Gold Coast, Queensland, Australia, 1994, p. 217-226

Davenport, T.H. (1993) *Process Inovation: Reengineering Work through Information Technology*, Masachussetss: Harvard Business School Press

Davenport, T.H. and J.E. Short (1990, Summer) 'The New Industrial Engineering: Information Technology and Business Process Redesign', in: *Sloan Management Review*, Summer, p. 11-27

Department of Home Affairs (1991) *Politiemonitor. Uitkomsten van gestandaardiseerd bevolkingsonderzoek in gemeenten met meer dan 200.000 inwoners*, The Hague, The Netherlands, (in Dutch)

Department of Justice (1985) *Samenleving en Criminaliteit. Een beleidsplan voor de komende jaren*, The Hague, The Netherlands, (in Dutch)

Dur, R.C.J. (1992) Business Reengineering in Information Intensive Organizations, Doctoral Dissertation, University of Technology Delft, Delft, the Netherlands

Eijck, D.T.T. van (1993) 'Designing distributed workplace support: two simulation case studies', in: A. Verbraeck and E. Kerckhoffs, *Proceedings of the European Symposium on Simulation* (ESS'93), Delft, the Netherlands

Eijnatten, F.M. van (1993) The Paradigm that Changed the Work Place. *Annals of STSD*, Assen/Maastricht: Van Gorcum Publishers

Emery, F.E., and M. Emery (1974) *Participative design, Canberra: Centre for Continuing Education*, Australian National University,

Engelstad, P.H., and B. Gustavsen (1993) 'Swedish network development for implementing national work reform strategy', in: *Human Relations*, Vol. 46, No. 2, p. 219-248

Fried, L. (1991, December 2) 'A blueprint for Change', in: *Computerworld*, p. 94-95

Guha, S., W.J. Kettinger, and T.C. Teng (1993, Summer) 'Business Process Reengineering: Building a Comprehensive Methodology', in: *Information Systems Management*, p. 13-22

Gulden, G.K., and R.H. Reck (1992, Spring) 'Combining Quality and Reengineering Efforts for Process Excellence', in: *Information Strategy: The Executive's Journal*, p. 10-16

Hall, G., J. Rosenthal, and J. Wade (1993, Nov-Dec) 'How to Make Re-Engineering Really Work', in: *Harvard Business Review*, p. 119-131

Hammer, M. (1990, Jul-Aug) 'Reengineering Work: Don't Automatie, Obliterate', in: *Harvard Business Review*, p. 104-112

Hammer, M. and J. Champy (1993) *Re-Engineering the Corporation: A Manifesto for Business Revolution*, New York: Harper Business

Harrington, H.J. (1991) *Business Process Improvement: The Break-*

through *Strategy for Total Quality, Productivity and Competitiveness*, New York: Mc-Graw Hill Publishers

Heygate, R., and G. Brebach (1992) 'Rethinking the Corportation', in: *The McKinsey Quarterly*, No. 1, p. 134-147

Jackson, M.A. (1983) *System Development*, Englewood Cliffs: Prentice-Hall

Kaplan, R.B., and L. Muirdock (1991) 'Core Process Redesign', in: *McKinsey Quarterly*, No. 2, p. 444-447

Keen, P.W.G. (1980, Fall) 'Adaptive Design for DSS', in: *Database*, p. 15-25

Lewin, A.Y. and C.U. Stephens (1993) 'Designing Post-Industrial Organizations: Theory and Practice', in: G.P. Huber, W.H. Glick (eds), in: *Organization Change and Redesign: Ideas and Insights for Improving Managerial Performance*, New York: Oxford, University Press

Ligus, R.G. (1993) 'Methods to Help Re-engineer Your Company For Improved Agility', in: *Industrial Engineering*, January 1993, p. 58-59

Meel, J.W. van (1993a) Towards a safer Amsterdam: Dynamic Modelling Supporting Organizational Change, in: J.F. Nunamaker, R.H. Sprague (ed.), *Proceedings of the Twenty-Sixth Annual Hawaii International Conference on System Science* (HICSS), Los Alamitos: IEEE Computer Society Press, p. 438-447

Meel, J.W. van (1994) The Dynamics of Bussiness Reengineering: Reflections on two case studies within the Amsterdam Municipal Police Force, Doctoral Dissertation, University of Technology Delft, Delft, the Netherlands

Meel, J.W. van, P.W.G. Bots, H.G. Sol (1994) 'Towards a research framework for business engineering', in: Proceedings of the IFIP TC8 Conference, Gold Coast, Australia

Mitroff, I.I., F. Betz, L.R. Pondy, and F. Sagasti (1974) 'On Managing Science in the System Age: Two schemas for the Study of Science as a Whole Systems Phenomenon', in: *TIMS Interfaces*, Vol. 4, No. 3, p. 46-58

Motshagen, P.A. (1991) Treasury Management en In-house Banking: Een informatiekundige analyse, Doctoral Dissertation, Delft University of Technology, Delft, the Netherlands, (in Dutch)

Ostroff, F. and D. Smith (1992) 'The Horizontal Organization. Redesigning the corporation', in: *The McKinsey Quarterly*, No. 1, p. 148-167

Pegden, C.D., R.E. Shannon, R.P. Sadowski (1990) *Introduction to Simulation using SIMAN*, McGraw-Hill Inc.

Schoonhoven, C.B. (1981, September) 'Problems with Contingency Theory: Testing Assumptions Hidden Within the Language of Contingency Theory', in: *Administration Science Quarterly*, p. 349-377

Schrijver, P.R. (1993) Supporting Fleet Management by Mobile Communications, Doctoral Dissertation, Delft University of Technology, Delft, the Netherlands

Simsion, G. (1984) 'A methodology for business process re-engineering?', in: B. Glasson, I.T. Hawryszkiewycz, B.A. Underwood, and R.A. Weber (ed.), *Proceedings of the IFIP TC8 Open Conference on Business Process Engineering: Information System Opportunities and Challenges*, Gold Coast, Queensland, Australia, p. 79-88

Sitter, L.U. de (1981) *Op weg naar nieuwe fabrieken en kantoren*, Kluwer, (in Dutch)

Smith, D.J., and K.B. Wood (1987) *Engineering Quality Software: A*

Review of current practices, standards, and guidelines including new methods and development tools, London: Elsevier Applied Science

Sol, H.G. (1982) Simulation in Information Systems Development, Doctoral Dissertation, University of Groningen, The Netherlands

Sol, H.G. (1984) *Expertise rond informatiesysteemontwerp*, Alphen a/d Rijn: Samson Publishers, (in Dutch)

Sol, H.G. (1992a) *Shifting Boundaries in System Engineering and Policy Analysis, School of System Engineering and Policy Analysis*, University of Technology Delft, Delft, the Netherlands

Sol, H.G. (1992b) 'Dynamics in Information Systems', in: H.G. Sol and R.L. Crosslin (ed.), *Dynamic Modelling of Information Systems, II,* Amsterdam: Elsevier Science Publishers (North Holland)

Stalk, G., P. Evans and L.E. Shulman (1992, Mar-Apr) 'Competing on Capabilities: The New Rules of Corporate Strategy', in: *Harvard Business Review*, p. 57-69

Streng, R.J. (1993) Dynamic Modelling to Assess the Value of Electronic Data Interchange, a study in the Rotterdam port community, Doctoral Dissertation, University of Technology Delft, Delft, the Netherlands

Trist, E.L., and K.W. Bamforth (1951) 'Some Social and Psychological Consequences of the Longwall Method of Coal-Getting', in: *Human Relations*, Vol. 4, p. 1-38

Trist, E.L., G.W., Higgin, H. Murray, and A.B. Pollock (1963) *Organizational choice: capabilities of groups at the coal face under changing technologies: the loss, re-discovery and transformation of a work tradition*, London: Tavistock Publications

Yourdon, E. (1978) *Structured Walkthroughs*, New York: Yourdon Press

Verbraeck, A., and G.J. de Vreede (1993) 'Animation as a communication vehicle in simulation studies', in: *Proceedings of the European Simulation Multiconference* (ESM93), Lyon, France

Vreede, G.J. de (1993) 'Improving Coordination within Organizations through information technology. Handling patients and combating organized crime', Contribution to the ICIS Doctoral Consortium, Florida

Vreede, G.J. de, P.W.G. Bots, and A. Verbraeck (1993) 'Simulation as an approach to improve coordination within service organizations. A case study in a Governmental Department', in: Verbraeck, A., and E. Kerckhoffs (ed.), *Proceedings of the European Simulation Symposium* (ESS '93), Delft, the Netherlands

Wierda, F.W. (1991) Developing Interorganizational Information Systems, Doctoral Dissertation, Delft University of Technology, Delft, the Netherlands

Part IV

Implementation

Chapter 16
Strategy Congruence and BPR Rollout
Mitchell and Zmud

Many organizations employ information technology in the redesign of their business processes without understanding the underlying dynamics between the two systems. Business process redesign success (BPR) is, in part, dependent upon the congruence between the BPR and information technology strategies employed. The strategic postures adopted (proactive, reactive or imposed) influence what business units perceive as a need and when that need is acted upon. An ability to meet one's needs is often contingent upon information resource availability and deployment patterns which, in turn, are a function of previously implemented strategies. When BPR information needs cannot be met by the IT infrastructure, an IT gap often results and the project is delayed. This chapter offers some insight into the nature of expected project outcomes given specific BPR and IT infrastructure strategy combinations. Specifically, it examines (1) the congruence among strategies driving BPR projects and IT infrastructure development, (2) the nature of IT-related project delays, and (3) the degree to which the redesign project or the IT infrastructure were altered to facilitate project rollout. The results of an exploratory field study are offered along with cases representative of the 43 redesign projects investigated.

Chapter 17
Assessing Customer Value for Reengineering: Narcissistic Practices and Parameters from the Next Generation
Roth, Julian and Malhotra

This chapter argues that internally focussed process reengineering efforts are narcissistic in nature, and unlikely to succeed because they fail to foster and create lasting customer value. Instead, the focus of reengineering efforts should be on creation of new customer value through strategic integration of customers' processes with the firm's processes such that cross-organizational relationships are leveraged to gain customer intimacy and build competitive capabilities. Next, this chapter critically compares and contrasts the important differences between traditional narcissistic views of customer value creation and the next generation of value integration along relevant customer value issues. These differences are highlighted and illustrated through a case example of the reengineering journey of a $40 million division of a multinational corporation. Finally, four key principles that can be used to span the continuum from narcissistic customer value orientation to engaging in more enlightened customer value creation practices are presented.

Chapter 18
When People "Work Scared": Understanding Attitudes and Gaining Commitment in Business Process Reengineering
Melone

Leaders, process owners, and process team members are faced with managing not only the reality of re-engineering but also attitudes about that reality. To the extent that re-engineering processes can have profound and different consequences for the individual apart from the organization, failure to understand how individuals' attitudes, beliefs, and perceptions develop and are modified is likely to account for at least some of the re-engineering efforts that fail. Clearly, understanding the function served by an individual's attitude about corporate re-engineering, how such attitudes form, and most importantly how they can be influenced by leaders, process owners and process team members constitute a portion of the skill set required for re-engineers. In this chapter, prototypical roles that attitudes play in business process re-engineering are considered. Next, two models of persuasion useful in applied settings are described. The first model focuses on the how messages persuade (process) and the second on what messages persuade (content). With these models as background, a variety of interpersonal and mediated influence strategies relevant in the re-engineering context are described. This chapter concludes with a discussion of the broader implications of attitude and impression management in business process re-engineering.

Chapter 19
Business Process Reengineering, Politics and Management: From Methodologies to Processes
Smith and Willcocks

This chapter addresses how IT-enabled business process reengineering (BPR) can be delivered to organizations. Firstly, it reviews the relevant literature and suggests that BPR activity is too often methods driven. Methods tend to be partial in their approach to issues that need a more holistic perspective. In particular IT-enabled or IT-driven BPR programmes are likely to marginalize attention to human, social and political processes, despite the fact that these may be strong determinants of success or failure. Four case studies - set in aerospace, industrial products manufacturing, pharmaceuticals and health care - are used to pursue these themes. They demonstrate that BPR raises political issues that are inherent, not marginal to BPR activity. An eight-point summary of ways forward, derived from analysing the case studies, is provided for those contemplating BPR activity.

Chapter 20
Public Sector Reengineering: Applying Lessons Learned in the Private Sector to the U.S. Department of Defense
Gulledge, Hill and Sibley

This chapter describes a study that was initiated at the request of the U.S. Department of Defense. The research objective was to develop private sector case studies and identify private sector success factors that are applicable to public sector reengineering efforts. The chapter identifies some basic postulates and prerequiisites for successful implementaiton of reengineering alternatives in both public and private sector organizations. The authors believe that in public sector organizations technology is changing organizational structures and management practices. The size of many public sector organizations and diffuse managerial control make implementation difficult. Recommendations are made for addressing some of the Department of Defense's implementation problems.

Chapter 21
Assessment of the Impact of BPR and Information Technology Use on Team Communication: The Case of ICL Data
Parnisto

Business process reengineering offers methods and tools for improving the way businesses should be organized and run. The benefits of reengineering are achieved by changing the way work is done in organizations. However, changes in activities or business processes may not be enough. In order to make the structural changes permanent, organizations must also change their way of thinking and communicating. Business processes are horizontal chains of activities, which means that employees with different skills from different organizational units must be able to communicate to execute processes. It is assumed in this chapter that changes in communication patterns indicate how people have committed to a new approach. This is especially true in organizations located in information intensive businesses. It is important for managers to be able to assess the impacts of reengineering on employee communication and information exchange. This chapter focuses on identifying key variables in transforming organizations toward team-oriented communication networks and measuring changes in these variables. An analysis tool for this measurement is presented, which captures changes in several key factors of communication and provides valuable information for managers about the progress of reengineering efforts.

Chapter
16

Strategy Congruence and BPR Rollout

Victoria Mitchell
North Carolina State University

Robert W. Zmud
Florida State University

In response to heightened competitive pressures, many companies are employing information technology (IT) in the redesign of their business processes (Rockart and Short, 1989; Hammer, 1990, 1993; Davenport, 1993) without understanding the underlying dynamics between the two systems (Butler, 1988; Weill and Olson, 1989). It is generally recognized that a firm's information technology (IT) infrastructure can facilitate organizational change, particularly when the information needs of the business process are clearly defined (Rockart, 1979; Boynton and Zmud, 1987) and the capabilities of the IT infrastructure fully explored (Ackoff, 1967; Ginzberg, 1981; Moynihan, 1990). Unfortunately, firms engaged in business process redesign (BPR) rarely meet these two conditions. The mismatch between information needs and IT capabilities is reflected in a project failure rate which hovers near 80 percent (Belmonte and Murray, 1993).

Several researchers (Earl, 1988; Madnick, 1991; McDonald, 1991; Grover, Teng and Fiedler, 1993) indicate successful implementation of redesign projects is, in part, dependent upon the BPR and IT strategies employed. A review of the literature suggests BPR success starts in the project conceptualization phase, when a strategic need is recognized (Adler and Shenhar, 1990). The strategic orientations adopted (i.e. proactive or reactive postures) influence what business units perceive as a need and when that need is acted upon (Kotteman and Konsynski, 1984; Ginn and Young, 1992). An ability to meet one's needs is often contingent upon resource availability and deployment patterns which, in turn, are a function of previously implemented strategies (Cleland and King, 1983; Kerzner, 1984). This reasoning has led to the following question: How do various strategic postures affect the rollout of BPR projects?

Prior research indicates planning is the key to success when confronted with new and changing conditions (Hayes and Wheelwright, 1984; Quinn, 1980; MacMillan and Jones, 1986; Porter, 1980, 1985; Mintzberg, 1973, 1988; Hofer, 1975). Ideally, planning for the implementation of a new process and the development of its supporting IT infrastructure takes place concurrently. Mutual consideration of system and process issues facilitates complementary strategies and the congruence necessary to promote organizational effectiveness (Nadler, 1980; Venkatraman, 1989). To approach congruence, managers must assess their internal operations (e.g. IT capabilities), recognizing strengths to be exploited and deficiencies to be overcome (Williamson, 1985). As the BPR project unfolds, demands for new information resources and patterns of deployment emerge. The ability to supply current and emerging needs creates a special challenge for the business unit in transition and the IT infrastructure.

For purposes of this study, BPR is defined as a project, characterized by radical changes in tasks and flows, with prespecified goals, a desired completion date, a series of inter-related activities, an expected level of performance and a limited budget (Pinto and Slevin, 1988). The activities embedded in a business process and their sequencing determine the information resources needed (King, Grover, and Hufnagel, 1989; Sabherwal and King, 1991; Teng, Kettinger and Guha, 1992).

The IT infrastructure embodies a set of components (hardware, software, data and expertise) and linkages (network architecture, sourcing arrangements and policies) that together determine the information resource capabilities available to a business process. When BPR information resource needs exceed the capabilities of the current IT infrastructure, project discontinuities may result which impede rollout. Subsequently, changes to either the intended process design and (or) the IT infrastructure are frequently required to bring the two systems into alignment, thus enabling project completion.

The findings presented in this chapter are based on a two year study of forty-three BPR projects in the health care industry. A multi-phase research design used comprehensive phone interviews, sets of three matched surveys and archival data to collect information regarding the strategies adopted and subsequent project implementation issues. Principal components analysis provided discriminant validity for the BPR and IT strategy constructs, and a cluster analysis identified three basic strategic postures. Hierarchical log-linear models revealed the most likely outcomes associated with different strategy combinations (Mitchell, 1993).

This chapter offers some insight into the nature of expected project outcomes given specific BPR and IT infrastructure strategy combinations. Specifically, the outcomes examined focus on (1) the strategies driving BPR projects and IT infrastructure development, (2) the nature of IT-related project delays, and (3) the degree to which the redesign project or the IT infrastructure were altered to facilitate project rollout. The chapter proceeds as follows. First, a framework and supporting literature are offered for conceptualizing the BPR/IT infrastructure relationship. Next, the results of an exploratory study are discussed, followed by representative cases highlighting the difficulties and changes associated with each strategy combination employed. Finally, management guidelines are offered to assist with the rollout of future BPR projects.

Conceptualizing the BPR/IT Infrastructure Relationship

Several requisite factors for the successful implementation of BPR projects are noted in three complementary bodies of literature, particularly; innovation and technology management (Mohr, 1969; Zaltman, Duncan and Holbek, 1973; Abernathy and Townsend, 1975; Abernathy and Utterback, 1978; Daft and Becker, 1978; Ettlie, Bridges and O'Keefe, 1984; Dewar and Duttan, 1986; Damanpour, 1988; Henderson and Clark, 1990), organizational learning (Cohen and Levinthal, 1990; Leifer, 1988; Huber, 1990), and strategic management (Nadler, 1980; Venkatraman, 1991; Davenport and Short, 1990).

The field of organizational learning provides the concept of absorptive capacity which suggests that a firm's capabilities are a function of its prior knowledge (Cohen and Levinthal, 1990). Tying this concept to the innovation literature provides a basis for understanding evolutionary patterns of organizational change. When the change process is obstructed or delayed, as is the case with incongruent strategies fostering an IT-related project delay, the type of innovation adopted to resolve the delay is a function of the type and degree of knowledge already embedded in the system. The strategic management literature suggests organizations are most effective when their strategies are in alignment (Nadler, 1980; Porter, 1980; Venkatraman, 1991).

The capabilities of an organization are derived from a series of strategic choices over time. Investments in the technology and

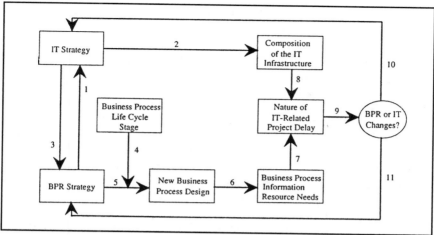

Figure 1: The BPR/IT Infrastructure Relationship

knowledge components of business processes and infrastructures are guided by the strategic orientation adopted. In this regard the organization's absorptive capacity and readiness for change is a function of its strategic history. Drawing from this literature base a more detailed discussion is offered next, along with a conceptual model to provide a common frame of reference in exploring the cases presented later in the chapter.

Considering that the IT infrastructure serves as an input and transformation platform which enables and constrains business process change, IT infrastructure investment decisions should be made in conjunction with a firm's business strategy (Boynton and Zmud, 1987) and vice versa (Lederer and Mendelow, 1986). An inadequate assessment of goals, capabilities and limitations could result in the adoption of incompatible BPR and IT strategies which inhibit the implementation of BPR projects (Earl, 1988; McDonald, 1991; Venkatraman, 1991). Therefore, successful implementation of a BPR project begins in the strategy formulation phase where the context and motivation for the project are identified (Davenport, 1993, p.118).

In general, strategic orientation has been described as a continuum with one pole representing a pattern in a stream of decisions, thus deliberate and the other a pattern in a stream of actions, or emergent (Mintzberg and Waters, 1985). A deliberate strategy is intended, as evidenced by an articulated plan for collective action which identifies the unit's competitive position relative to internal and external factors. An emergent strategy reflects consistency in action without intention, as when an environment imposes a pattern of action on an organization (Mintzberg and Waters, 1985, p. 258).

BPR Strategies

Formed under the umbrella of corporate strategy, a BPR strategy is a plan for implementing, coordinating and controlling the design of an alternative system of artifacts, people and value-added activities. Essentially, the BPR strategy is a plan for implementing, coordinating and controlling business process resources and tasks in a new manner. The orientation of a BPR strategy reflects a business unit's competitive position relative to industry trends and organizational competencies (Porter, 1980; Hayes and Wheelwright, 1984; Williamson, 1985; Johnson and Kaplan, 1987; Marucheck, Panessi and Anderson, 1990; Noori, 1990). In this regard, successful implementation of a BPR strategy is often influenced by the capabilities embedded in its supporting IT infrastructure; thus, the IT infrastructure needs to be considered during BPR strategy formulation. This relationship is depicted by arrow 1 in Figure 1.

Deliberate BPR strategies can be subdivided into proactive or reactive postures. A deliberate proactive BPR strategy anticipates industry trends and installs an innovative process for competitive advantage (Hayes and Wheelwright, 1984; Ruark, 1990; Madnick, 1991; Farmer, 1993). An organization engaging in a deliberate reactive BPR strategy is also aware of industry trends and chooses to adopt a known process developed elsewhere (Hayes and Wheelwright, 1984; Madnick, 1990; Farmer, 1993). Organizations that react slowly to industry trends generally fail to assess their strengths and weaknesses and, thus, are forced to adopt de facto industry standards. This is indicative of firms employing an emergent, albeit imposed, BPR strategy (Mintzberg and Waters, 1985; Ruark, 1990).

IT Infrastructure Strategies

IT infrastructure strategies demonstrate a similar pattern of decisions and actions. The IT infrastructure is a system of artifacts, people and IT-based activities that can facilitate organizational change. Its composition, configuration and capabilities result from a series of IT acquisition and management decisions (depicted by arrow 2 in Figure 1). Essentially, an IT infrastructure strategy is a plan for directing IT resources and guiding the deployment of information resources. Like its BPR counterpart, there are two types of deliberate IT infrastructure strategies. Organizations which take present and possible future BPR needs into consideration during IT strategy formulation (Figure 1, arrow 3), typically conduct a detailed assessment of current IT capabilities, limitations, trends and alternatives, and attempt to put IT resources in place prior to BPR implementation. These decisions are characteristic of a deliberate proactive IT strategy (Earl, 1989; Hammer, 1990; McDonald, 1991;

Venkatraman, 1991; Madnick, 1991; Grover, Teng and Fiedler, 1993; Hammer and Champy, 1993; Davenport, 1993). Organizations employing a deliberate reactive IT strategy often wait until BPR information needs arise before making additional investments in the IT infrastructure. These firms attempt to minimize risk and uncertainty by imitating IT resource patterns used by other organizations in the industry (Madnick, 1991).

Finally, organizations that fail to identify BPR information resource needs prior to BPR implementation are often unaware of IT trends and alternatives (Kotteman and Konsynski, 1984; Boynton and Zmud, 1987; Earl, 1989; Diebold, 1990). Typically laggards in IT infrastructure development, survival for these organizations is often dependent upon their ability to adopt the IT deployment patterns set by their competitors. This mode of adoption often results in serious systems integration problems. Such tendencies reflect the emergence of an imposed IT strategy.

Business Process Development Stage

Another factor which influences BPR/IT infrastructure strategy congruence is the business processes stage of development. Business processes, like products, go through a life cycle. According to Abernathy and Townsend (1975), there are three stages to the process life cycle, beginning with the uncoordinated stage progressing to a segmental stage and finally reaching a systemic state as the process reaches maturity.

When the traditional way of doing work is modified or replaced by a new approach, the new business process is characterized by inefficient utilization of resources and uncoordinated patterns of activity; hence, the term "uncoordinated" (Abernathy and Townsend, 1975). As the process becomes more efficient through standardized tasks and routinized flows, it moves from the uncoordinated to the "segmental" stage. The segmental stage is characterized by highly structured and standardized manual tasks, dedicated automation systems, tightly coupled process flows and the use of process control systems. As the business process becomes institutionalized, it moves into the "systemic" stage of the life cycle. The systemic stage is characterized by the horizontal integration of the business process with other business activities. The relationships among business processes are cemented with formal operating procedures and rigid labor classifications.

Implementation of a redesign strategy can be facilitated or constrained by the life cycle stage a process is in (indicated in Figure 1 by arrow 4). Changes to a process in the fluid, uncoordinated stage are usually easier to make than if an institutionalized process in the systemic stage were being altered. Characteristics of process design in the beginning stages of the life cycle include diverse technologies that are loosely organized and independent of one another. This provides the flexibility needed to produce a wide variety of deliverables under conditions of rapid change. The flow of work is erratic, output rates are unpredictable and much management attention is required, but change is readily accommodated at minimum cost (Abernathy and Townsend, 1975; Abernathy, 1978; Abernathy and Utterback, 1988). As the business process matures, its configuration is altered from one that affords a high degree of independence among its operations and tasks to one with a high degree of integration and balance among its components.

New Business Process Design

Process design decisions tend to be cumulative in nature and persistent in effect (Abernathy, 1978). The strategic orientation adopted early in the design process has profound implications for the evolution of that process (Figure 1, arrow 5). Drawing from the extensive work on manufacturing strategies, one begins to understand the ramifications of early design decisions. The strategy of a business unit consists of a sequence of decisions that, over time, enables a business unit to achieve a desired structure with a set of specific capabilities (Hayes and Wheelwright, 1984). When a firm is competing on product (service) differentiation and rapid response time to environmental changes, a proactive stance would be employed that has high customer contact to quickly identify preferences, with low vertical integration and high resource flexibility for customization. On the other hand, a firm competing on low cost may employ a reactive strategic posture seeking to maintain its competence in standardized and efficient operations (Hayes and Wheelwright, 1984), yet incorporate process changes already tested by its competitors. Firms reluctant to embrace change until industry pressures dictate a course of action emerge with processes dictated by their rivals.

Business Process Information Resource Needs

The types of activities embedded in a business process, their sequencing and reliance on other organizational processes will determine what information resource requirements must be fulfilled to successfully meet the goals of a BPR project (Sabherwal and King, 1991). Information resources refer to an organization's information and information technology (King, Grover and Hufnagel, 1989).

There are several characteristics of information and IT that make them pivotal resources in BPR. The usefulness of information is a function of its accuracy and precision (Table 1). Accuracy refers

Information	Information Technology
Accuracy	Flexibility
Precision	Speed
Timeliness	Performance
Time Horizon	Capacity
Summarization	Connectivity
Completeness	Appropriateness
Reliability	Efficiency
Relevance	Effectiveness

Source: Alter, 1992; Laudon and Laudon, 1993)

Table 1: Distinguishing Attributes of Information Resources

to the degree to which the data portrays what is supposed to be represented. Precision refers to the fineness of detail in the portrayal. Accuracy and precision can be tainted by bias and random error. Bias refers to the systematic inaccuracy attributed to the manner in which data are created, collected, processed, or presented. Random error is introduced as noise or inaccuracy due to inherent variability in whatever is being measured. Timeliness also influences the usefulness of information and its relevance to a particular task. Obviously, information that arrives after making a decision for which it was needed has little value. The reliability of information is affected by its data source, the integrity of the data and security measures. Other criteria for determining usefulness include the level of summarization and completeness of information. Summarization can hide valuable information, while completeness can result in information overload. The quality of information and its value to the firm is highly variable when it's supporting a process undergoing radical change.

Information technology, on the other hand, encompasses the artifacts, skills and IT related activities used to retrieve, process, transform, store and communicate information. IT attributes refer to features of hardware, software, knowledge, procedures, and architectural designs for business process performance. Each IT asset or combination of assets can be described in terms of its appropriateness for a task, level of flexibility, speed and efficiency of execution, performance abilities and effectiveness, processing and storage capacity, and the degree of connectivity provided. The design of a new business process determines what information resources are needed (see Figure 1, arrow 6), by whom, when, where and how in a manner that supports the business goals. It is the IT infrastructure that provides the business process with information resources vital to the project's rollout and continued success.

Hardware	Software	Network
Transmission	Environment	Utilization
Interface	Aplications	Portability
Capacity	Appropriateness	Migration
Storage	Sophistication	Interoperability
Speed	Interface	Connectivity
Input Devices	Efficiency	Typology
Output Devices	Maintenance	Centralized
Processors	Backlog	Distributed
Expertise	Policies	Sources
Technical	Acquisition	Internal Development
Business	Standards	Off the Shelf
Training	Security	Joint Ventures
Consultants	Flexibility	Vendors

Source: Alter, 1992; Laudon and Laudon, 1991; Office of Technology Assessment, 1990)

Table 2: Dimensions of an Infrastructure

Composition of the IT Infrastructure

The capabilities embedded in an IT infrastructure are derived from a combination of components, particularly hardware, software, data, expertise, and their linkages. Component linkages refer to hardware linkages, network configurations, vendors/sourcing arrangements, training and IT policies. To effectively utilize each component, specific knowledge is required about its core design. In addition, knowledge must be obtained regarding the information systems architecture from which the various linkages create synergistic effects (Henderson and Clark, 1990). These two types of knowledge (component and architectural) provide the IT infrastructure with a unique set of characteristics. These characteristics are captured in a number of dimensions used to describe an IT infrastructure (Table 2).

Nature of IT-Related Project Delays

Often BPR information needs cannot be fulfilled by the current IT infrastructure (Figure 1, arrow 7). Information-related difficulties in BPR result when enabling information technologies (ITs) are missing or go unrecognized (McDonald, 1991; Venkatraman, 1991). Enabling ITs are those components and linkages (artifact and human) in the IT infrastructure that can be utilized to bring about business process change (Figure 1, arrow 8). When the IT demands of a business process cannot be met by the current infrastructure, an "IT gap" exists. When confronted with an IT gap, implementation of the new business process is often delayed as a result of hardware difficulties, software acquisition and development challenges, database problems, data acquisition obstacles, or insufficient IT expertise. At the point the project is stalled, successful rollout becomes contingent upon the firm's ability to bridge the IT gap.

BPR/IT Infrastructure Changes

When the transformation of a business process is delayed in this manner, alterations in the new business process design, the IT infrastructure, or both, must often be considered (depicted in Figure 1, arrow 9). Which design (business process or IT infrastructure) to alter is a function of the strategies adopted, organizational resources available (labor, capital and information), core design and architectural knowledge embedded in various processes. Where the knowledge exists for redeploying organizational resources and reconfiguring information flows, the IT infrastructure can be modified to meet BPR needs (Figure 1, arrow 10). An alternative is to modify the business process to accommodate the limitations imposed by the infrastructure (Figure 1, arrow 11). Compatible IT infrastructure and business strategies would minimize the effort, hardship and disruption imposed by organizational change (Venkatraman, 1991) such as BPR.

The framework developed by Henderson and Clark (1990) to illustrate product innovations, particularly component and linkage changes, provides a useful typology for categorizing the nature of BPR and IT infrastructure changes needed to overcome an IT gap (Figure 2). Here, alterations to the IT infrastructure and the intended business process design are categorized according to the degree to

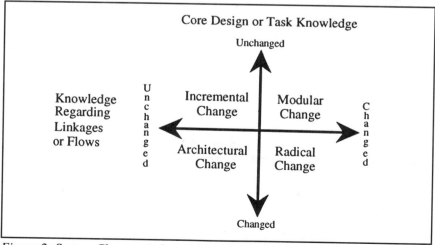

Figure 2: System Changes (adapted from Henderson and Clark, 1990)

which each system's components (or tasks) and linkages (or work flows) are changed.

Each type of change embodies knowledge about the individual components or tasks (i.e. core design concepts) and how the components or tasks are linked together (i.e. architectural knowledge). An incremental change refines and extends the existing design by making minor improvements to components (tasks) embedded in the system, yet linkages (work flows) remain the same. A modular change substitutes an existing component (task) with a new component without changing linkages. An architectural change reconfigures the system by linking components (tasks) in a new way without significantly modifying the core design of each component. A radical change is a new design that uses different components (tasks) and linkages (work flows) than those embedded in the previous process design. The next section illustrates the relationship between strategy congruence and project outcomes.

Strategic Orientations and Project Outcomes

The guiding principle behind many BPR projects in the health care sector involves achieving productivity gains by provisioning services as close to the patient as possible (Metcalf, 1992; Nathan, 1992; Sherer, 1993). To this end, many hospitals are employing IT to collect and disseminate information at the point-of-care, streamline data capture, integrate different forms of information, regulate inputs, track costs and monitor quality of care (Cannavo, 1992; Laughlin, 1992). Yet, antiquated IT infrastructures are often cited as a major obstacle impeding the rollout of BPR projects (Kim and Michelman, 1990; Nash, 1992).

Our study offers some insights toward understanding this paradox. A breakdown of the nature of IT gaps, as well as BPR and IT infrastructure design changes associated with various strategy combinations identified in the study are presented in Table 3. Representative projects for each cell in this table are offered next to illustrate the evolutionary patterns likely to occur with each set of strategies.

Project A:
Proactive BPR Strategy/Reactive IT Infrastructure Strategy

When a deliberate proactive BPR strategy was coupled with a deliberate proactive IT strategy, business units typically assessed the needs, capabilities and limitations of both the intended business process and existing IT infrastructure. Figure 3 illustrates the

Strategic Posture	Proactive IT Strategy	Reactive IT Strategy	Imposed IT Strrategy
Proactive BPR Strategy	Short Delay Architectural BPR Change No IT Change	Short Delay No BPR Change Incremental IT Change	Long delay Modular BPR Change Radical IT Change
Reactive BPR Strategy	Long Delay Radical BPR Change Modular IT Change	Short Delay Incremental BPR Change No IT Change	Long Delay Incremental BPR Change and IT Change
Imposed BPR Strategy	Short Delay Incremental BPR Change No IT Change	Long Delay Architectural BPR Change Radical Change	Long Delay Architectural BPR and IT Changes

Table 3: Strategy Combinations and Impacts on Project Rollout

reciprocal relationship between strategies (a two-way interaction) culminating in complementary systems with a short project delay and process flow modifications. Project A was a $700,000 endeavor spanning 7 hospitals in the same metropolitan area. The BPR effort involved centralizing medical records capture and management in an attempt to reduce storage costs and gain economies of scale across participating facilities. The IT infrastructure was expanded to incorporate a microimaging system which filmed and duplicated records on site, indexed the record for retrieval, then sent a copy of the film to the originating facility and stored the original film off-site for disaster recovery purposes.

The innovative records management process was installed by the consortium in anticipation of industry and IT trends. This strategy combination experienced short IT-related delays (3 months) primarily due to uncertain information requirements, difficulties in standardizing data capture and multiple presentation formats across the participating facilities. To resolve discontinuities between BPR needs and IT capabilities, the business units were able to modify process flows without altering tasks embedded in the reengineered design. The IT infrastructure was not changed, as IT problems were typically resolved through the adoption of standardized screens and policies addressing the utilization of IT resources. The sequencing of business process activities were modified to adhere to new policies and cooperatively exploit IT resources. As a result, the project improved process performance, had a high degree of user satisfaction, came in on time, and was within budget. This suggests a high degree of strategy congruence as IT investments made in anticipation of BPR needs (for an innovative business process) facilitated

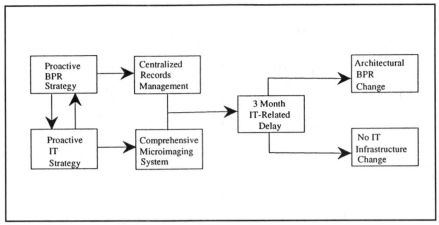

Figure 3: Proactive BPR/Proactive IT Strategies

smooth implementation of the project.

Table 4 summarizes the relationships identified in Project A and subsequent cases. Generally, two-way interactions during the strategy formulation phase of a project minimized IT-related delays and mitigated the need for design changes, thus facilitating strategy congruence. Although two-way strategy interactions often led to high levels of strategy congruence, the particular strategic postures adopted influenced project rollout by enabling or constraining information resource acquisition and deployment. For example, a reactive BPR/proactive IT strategy combination (Project D) had little strategy congruence as the trajectory set forth for the IT infrastructure couldn't support the information needs of the process being imitated. Low levels of congruence were also experienced when either an imposed BPR or IT infrastructure strategy was employed (as in projects C, F, H, I and J).

Project B:
Proactive BPR Strategy/Reactive IT Infrastructure Strategy

Project B was a $72 million dollar undertaking to improve access to health care in rural environments. A deliberate proactive BPR/reactive IT strategy combination was employed in which service delivery was decentralized in anticipation of industry trends and IT investments were made as BPR needs became known. The reengineered process replaced the traditional practice of transporting rural patients to a regional medical center for diagnostic evaluation and treatment, with telemedicine.

Telemedicine is possible through two-way video compression which enables video signals to be transmitted via satellite and

Strategy Combinations	Strategy Interaction	Project Delay	BPR Change Required	IT Change Required	Strategy Congruenece
Proactive BPR and					
Proactive IT	Two-way	3 months	Yes	No	High
Reactive IT	Two-way	3 months	No	Yes	High
Imposed IT	One-way	12 months	Yes	Yes	Low
Reactive BPR and					
Proactive IT	Two-way	9 months	Yes	Yes	Low
Reactive IT	Two-way	1 month	Yes	No	High
Imposed IT	One-way	12 months	Yes	Yes	Low
Imposed BPR and					
Proactive IT	None	4 months	Yes	No	Moderate
Reactive IT	None	12 months	Yes	Yes	Low
Imposed IT	None	6 months	Yes	Yes	Low

Table 4: Strategy Combinations, Project Outcomes and Level of Congruence

dedicated phone lines, then reassembled as images at the receiving site. The IT infrastructure was also equipped with remote-controlled examination cameras with freeze-frame capabilities for radiographics (MRIs, CAT scans, ultrasounds), which could be annotated with an electronic pen, and multiple video monitors for simultaneous viewing (i.e. x-rays and the patient). This manner of interactive consultation is another form of teleconferencing, first introduced in corporate boardrooms a decade ago.

The project experienced one significant delay, lasting 3 months, in which the peripheral devices (electronic stethoscopes and otoscopes) underwent mechanical changes. Tasks and flows embedded in the reengineered process were implemented without modifications, while IT hardware adjustments were made to create the functionality needed to continue project rollout. Facilities employing this strategy-combination typically had high levels of strategy congruence as projects were finished on time, at cost, with a great deal of user satisfaction. Thus, coupling a proactive redesign process with a reactive IT posture appears to reduce the risk of long delays and increase the probability of successful implementation.

Project C:
Proactive BPR Strategy/Imposed IT Infrastructure Strategy

When a deliberate proactive BPR strategy was coupled with an imposed IT strategy, industry trends were recognized but IT trends were ignored. As project C will demonstrate, this approach was low in strategy congruence which increased the likelihood of negative outcomes. In this case an innovative process was installed without first, understanding the IT resources required.

Project C had an initial budget of $20,000 to reengineer the work practices of a coronary care unit. The business unit adopted a managed-care approach in which health services were integrated across functions. This hospital was one of the first facilities to adopt a managed-care approach, yet was reluctant to employ the computerized tools (e.g. electronic records) their competitors had adopted to support similar activities.

After several years had passed, an accrediting body insisted the facility adopt an electronic tracking system for documenting interventions and patient outcomes. Since this occurred after the BPR strategy was formulated, the project was implemented without the input of an IT expert to ensure the necessary IT resources were in place. Consequently, radical hardware, software and network changes were made in an attempt to piece together a system of electronic support. Eventually managed-care tasks had to be altered to compensate for the limitations imposed by the IT infrastructure. BPR rollout was very painful, exceeding budget by $35,000, with many lengthy delays and dissatisfied users.

Project D:
Reactive BPR Strategy/Proactive IT Infrastructure Strategy

IT resources set in place prior to imitating a process developed elsewhere was representative of a deliberate reactive BPR/proactive IT strategy combination and low strategy congruence. As project D illustrates, this approach often results in an inflexible IT infrastructure, unable to meet the information needs of reengineered processes without disrupting other organizational processes.

Project D, funded at $50,000, sought to redesign the staff scheduling process of a major metropolitan hospital. The work process being replaced consisted of decentralized manual scheduling by the nursing units, later aggregated by a scheduling clerk, posted in a central administration ledger and passed back to the nursing units upon approval. Any changes to the schedule were penciled in at the nursing units but were not relayed to central administration. As a result, central administration did not know who worked when, nor what skill mix was available.

Adoption of a centralized scheduling system used by several competitors created a number of problems for this facility. Prior IT infrastructure investments, which provided good support for other organizational processes, did not lend themselves to modification. The automated scheduling package acquired to generate staffing rosters could not access the information in the personnel database. Consequently, the project was delayed 9 months while all of the personnel information was keyed into another, compatible database. In addition, there was considerable dissatisfaction with the new work process due to a number of control issues. Eventually, the intended scheduling process was modified, incorporating part of the old design (manual recording of scheduling changes). Another software program and additional printers were purchased to relay manual staffing changes electronically, in a timely manner, to all parties concerned.

Project E:
Reactive BPR Strategy/Reactive IT Infrastructure Strategy

When a deliberate reactive BPR strategy was coupled with a deliberate reactive IT strategy, a high level of strategy congruence was generally achieved as evidenced by short IT-related project delays. Typically, such delays were resolved through minor BPR changes in order to keep the project moving forward. Such was the case with Project E, a six million dollar endeavor to implement a managed-care approach which had been successful in other facilities across the country. Under the old structure, each functional area had a central supply area from which personnel and technology were dispatched. On average, 20 percent of the staff's time was spent with the patient, 30 percent was devoted to documentation and 50 percent tending to coordination and other activities. By decentralizing services (e.g., placing equipment, supplies and medications in the patient's room), 60 percent of the care-giver's time could be spent with the patient.

In keeping with the new philosophy, work documentation was also desired at the point-of-care. The facility wanted to employ bedside terminals for order/entry, charting and disseminating test results. A consultant was enlisted to help identify information needs and develop the software necessary to support operations. Although the project met its implementation schedule, bedside computer support was delayed because the vendor could not deliver the software as promised. After six months, another vendor was able to provide one portion of the desired software — the order/entry component — but not the other portions. In lieu of electronic bedside charting, paper charts were moved from the central repository (at the nurses station) into each patient's room. This created some unanticipated problems, particularly for physicians, who felt "trapped" in the patient's rooms as they looked for lab results or wrote their notes. Consequently, the intended documentation process was modified. Only the nursing notes were kept at the bedside and the remainder of the patient chart was returned to the nurses station. The modified reengineered process was then accepted by both physicians and nurses.

Project F:
Reactive BPR Strategy/Imposed IT Infrastructure Strategy

Organizations employing this strategy-combination were typically risk averse regarding change, yet low in strategy congruence. In this instance, the organization sought to streamline its order/entry and record keeping operations by employing processes widely used in the industry. In adopting a known process, many of the uncertainties concerning resource acquisition and deployment were removed. Industry standards dictated which IT components and linkages were necessary to achieve the desired functionality.

The primary problem associated with this strategy was a lack of in-house knowledge to facilitate both organizational change and systems integration. Consequently, minor changes to intended tasks and process flows became necessary, which in turn created a need to adjust information flows. Usually, this involved software modifications. Although Project F experienced a 14 month delay (in search of expertise), it came in at budget ($250,000), was readily accepted by its intended users and improved process performance significantly.

Project G:
Imposed BPR Strategy/Proactive IT Infrastructure Strategy

In Project G, the organization made IT investments in anticipation of BPR needs, yet failed to identify a critical process in need of redesign. A moderate level of strategy congruence was achieved in that the initial IT project was very successful in integrating other organizational processes, but did not lend itself to the rollout of this particular BPR project. In an attempt to maintain its competitiveness, the facility automated its information services and implemented a hospital-wide information system based on existing work practices.

With the onset of the nursing shortage in the mid 80's, the facility sought to increase nursing productivity and reduce the costs associated with managing disjointed services and paper flows. Subsequently, industry trends mandated the adoption of decentralized service delivery and documentation at the bedside. Although many nursing functions had received computer support due to prior investments in the IT infrastructure, documentation at the point-of-care was not one of them. There were no funds of the magnitude needed to acquire additional IT resources to support electronic charting. Consequently, manual data capture and paper storage prevailed. Minor BPR adjustments were made as physicians resisted bedside documentation and returned to previous charting practices (again seeking privacy at the nurses station).

Project H:
Imposed BPR Strategy/Reactive IT Infrastructure Strategy

When an imposed BPR strategy was coupled with a reactive IT infrastructure strategy, organizations were confronted with many, difficult implementation issues. "We run this place by the seat of our pants, no goals, no timetables, no plan." This statement, made by the manager of Project H, reflects the ad hoc nature of an imposed BPR/reactive IT approach, and subsequent low level of strategy congruence.

Project H was a $500,000 investment in redesigning the budgeting process of a major metropolitan research hospital. Although the facility utilized a client/server platform for its information needs, the nursing budgets were compiled manually. Each nursing unit would submit expenditure data and budget requests, on paper, to the division director who manually compiled a report that was submitted to the finance office. The chart of accounts used by finance did not lend itself to nursing's spending patterns. Consequently, finance made the budgeting decisions for which nursing was accountable. In its periodic review, the industry's accrediting body suggested the process be changed to better quantify, justify and fund nursing's needs.

In response, the hospital installed a LAN to serve the nursing units. The intent was to provide nursing with the tools to conduct their own financial queries. Although the technology was made available, nursing was reluctant to use it. Had the organization performed an IT assessment beforehand, they would have realized the system's interface was too cumbersome (i.e., too technical and too complicated) for nursing to use. In order to comply with the regulatory mandates, the IT infrastructure underwent radical changes in components and linkages to improve ease-of-use and facilitate interconnectivity among databases. Additional hardware and software was acquired, a new interface written and training provided to assist users with their conversion to the new system. In response to the IT infrastructure changes, architectural BPR changes were made to take advantage of the improvements in information flow. After a 12 month delay in rollout the process was adopted by nursing and considered a major improvement over the previous mode of decision making.

Project I:
Imposed BPR Strategy/Imposed IT Infrastructure Strategy

Business units that were unaware of industry trends and failed to assess their competitive position on a regular basis typically had to adopt a de facto industry process and related IT resources to remain competitive. BPR projects implemented under these circumstances were associated with an imposed BPR/imposed IT strategic orientation and a low level of strategy congruence.

Project I was budgeted at 1 million dollars, over a 5 year period to reengineer patient services. This involved moving from a functional approach (lab, radiology, respiratory therapy, etc., all operating autonomously) to a team approach often used in managed-care. In addition, the facility was converting from a manual paper system of information exchange to a computer-based hospital information system. The project sought improvements in the continuity of care, communication, and better utilization of nursing skills.

Many hospitals had implemented the managed-care model and modified their IT infrastructures to support its information needs. Thus, the process being adopted and its IT support were approaching industry standards, for which specific tasks and flows, as well as IT components and linkages, were readily identified. Under the old system, care was fragmented and the same information was gathered at multiple points of care. That is, identical information was gathered by doctors, nurses, lab technicians, dietary, respiratory therapy, etc., and recorded in their respective charts to be handed off to the next caregiver in that area. Under the new system an interdisciplinary team was assigned to a patient for the duration of their hospital stay. A comprehensive interview conducted at initial contact, generated a patient profile that followed the patient through the system.

As might be expected given the lack of prior preparation for implementing the new work design, policies, training and connectivity issues (particularly information access and dissemination) were initially quite troublesome. For example, team members had difficulty accessing a patient's profile and often had to rely on a verbal network of information exchange. In addition, the dissemination of information was hampered by the absence of standardized forms and procedures.

In order to resolve these difficulties, process flows were altered which, in turn, required significant network adjustments and IT policy modifications. The patient care coordinator became responsible for constructing the patient profile, rather than a secretary. Prior to admission, weekly team meetings were held to identify issues and potential problems. Finally, IT support was altered in that additional network nodes were installed to facilitate information access and policies were rewritten to provide the flexibility needed to support a team approach. Because many other uncertainties had been removed by the adoption of a known process, the project did come in on time despite a six month delay, was close to budget, and increased the efficiency and effectiveness of service delivery.

Guidelines for Managers

The previous discussion offers several insights regarding strategy congruence and project rollout. First, the IT infrastructure's ability to facilitate or constrain the implementation of BPR projects is, in part, dependent upon the combination of BPR and IT infrastructure strategies adopted. Three strategy combinations offered the congruence needed to reduce the risks associated with IT-related project delays and subsequent BPR and IT infrastructure changes.

(1) The deliberate proactive BPR/reactive IT infrastructure combination is likely to experience a short delay due to standardization issues which are readily resolved through minor IT infrastructure adjustments.

(2) When a deliberate reactive BPR strategy is coupled with a deliberate reactive IT strategy, software issues are often encountered which are generally resolved through minor BPR task and work flow adjustments.

(3) Finally, project risks are likely to be minimized when an imposed BPR design is supported by IT investment previously put in place. In such situations, sufficient uncertainty is removed as the organization generally adopts an industry standard. In order to integrate the new process with existing organizational systems, minor BPR adjustments are often needed.

Two strategy combinations appear quite risky, as they are associated with a variety of IT-related problems, long delays, and substantial system changes.

(4) The deliberate reactive BPR/proactive IT infrastructure combination appears to be one of the more risky approaches. This option is likely to experience many diverse IT problems resulting in long delays and radical BPR changes.

(5) Another risky option is the deliberate proactive BPR/ imposed IT strategy-combination. When IT resources are put in

place without anticipating the demands of an innovative BPR project, long delays are encountered and task modifications are likely.

In addition, the study indicates the pattern of IT problems experienced are likely to be resolved through particular BPR and IT infrastructure changes.

(6) Hardware and hardware linkage difficulties frequently result in altered process flows (an architectural change) or task modifications (a modular change), which in turn creates a need for additional training.

(7) Supplier problems (vendors and sourcing arrangements) are likely to be countered with modular BPR changes (task modifications or outsourced operations).

(8) The majority of IT expertise problems lead to radical BPR changes. When people did not know what they were doing, they generally made a mess! Consequently, significant data acquisition, software development, database, network configuration, vendor, sourcing, expertise and policies problems are likely, necessitating alterations to both process tasks and flows.

(9) When policy, data acquisition and software development obstacles arise, they are likely countered by minor (incremental) BPR changes.

(10) Hardware, software, expertise, training and policy problems are likely to be resolved through modular IT changes. When confronted with these deficiencies, organizations typically respond by acquiring or modifying hardware and software, obtain additional expertise from an outside source, and schedule additional training sessions.

(11) Radical IT changes are likely to be made in response to problems with data acquisition, database deficiencies, inadequate network configurations, missing hardware linkages, as well as vendor and sourcing difficulties.

In most cases, foresight offered an opportunity to mobilize resources in an attempt to minimize delays — driving home the need for a thorough assessment of IT strengths and weaknesses, as well as a careful analysis of IT requirements before rolling out a BPR project.

References

Abernathy, W. (1978). *The Productivity Dilemma: Roadblock to Innovation in the Automobile Industry.* Baltimore, Md: The Johns Hopkins University Press.

Abernathy, W. and Townsend, P. (1975). Technology, Productivity and Process Change. *Technological Forecasting and Social Change,* 7: 365-396.

Abernathy, W. and Utterback, J. (1988). Patterns of Industrial Innovation. In *Readings in the Management of Innovation* (Tushman and Moore, eds.). Cambridge, MA: Ballinger Publishing Company.

Ackoff, R. (1967). Management Misinformation Systems, *Management Science,* 14(4): 147-156.

Adler, S. and Shenhar, A. (1990). Adapting Your Technological Base: The Organizational Challenge. *Sloan Management Review,* 32(1): 25-37.

Alter, S. (1992). *Information Systems: A Management Perspective.* Reading, MA: Addison-Wesley Publishing Company.

Belmonte, R. and Murray, R. (1993). Getting Ready for Strategic Change: Surviving Business Process Redesign. *Information Systems Management,* 10(3): 23-29.

Boynton, A. and Zmud, R. (1987). Information Technology Planning in the 1990's: Directions for Practice and Research. *MIS Quarterly,* 11(1): 59-72.

Butler, J. (1988). Theories of Technological Innovation as Useful Tools for Corporate Strategy. *Strategic Management Journal,* 9: 15-29.

Cannavo, M. (1992). Money for Nothing...and Your Chicks for Free. *Computers in Healthcare,* 13(6): 30-31.

Cleland, D. and King, W. (1983). *Project Management Handbook.* New York: Van Norstrand Reinhold Company.

Cohen, W. and Levinthal, D. (1990). Absorptive Capacity: A New Perspective on Learning and Innovation. *Administrative Science Quarterly,* 35: 128-152.

Daft, R. and Becker, S. (1978). *The Innovative Organization: Innovation Adoption in School Organizations.* New York: Elsevier North-Holland, Inc.

Damanpour, F. (1988). Innovation Type, Radicalness and the Adoption Process. *Communication Research,* 15(5): 545-567.

Davenport, T. (1993). *Process Innovation: Reengineering Work Through Information Technology.* Boston, Ma: Harvard Business School Press.

Davenport, T. and Short, J. (1990). The New Industrial Engineering: Information Technology and Business Process Redesign. *Sloan Management Review,* Summer, 11-26.

Dewar, R. and Dutton, J. (1986). The Adoption of Radical and Incremental Innovations: An Empirical Analysis. *Management Science,* 32(11): 1422-1433.

Diebold, J. (1990). How Computers and Communications are Boosting Productivity: An Analysis. *International Journal of Technology Management,* 5(2): 141-152.

Earl, M. (1988). *Information Management: The Strategic Dimension.* Oxford: Clarendon Press.

Earl, M. (1989). *Management Strategies for Information Technology.* New York: Prentice-Hall.

Ettlie, J.; Bridges, W. and O'Keefe, R. (1984). Organization Strategy and Structural Differences for Radical Versus Incremental Innovation. *Management Science,* 30(6): 682-695.

Farmer, J. (March 1993). Re-engineering: Achieving Productivity Success. *APICS - The Performance Advantage*: 38-42.

Ginn, G. and Young, G. (1992). Organizational and Environmental Determinants of Hospital Strategy. *Hospital and Health Services Administration,* 37(3): 291-302.

Ginzberg, A. (1981). Key Recurrent Issues in the MIS Implementation Process. *MIS Quarterly,* 5(2): 47-59.

Grover, V.; Teng, J. and Fiedler, K. (1993). Information Technology Enabled Business Process Redesign, An Integrated Planning Framework. *OMEGA International Journal of Management Science,* 21(4): 433-447.

Hammer, M. (1990). Reengineering Work: Don't Automate, Obliterate. *Harvard Business Review,* July-August: 104-111.

Hammer, M. and Champy, J. (1993). *Reengineering the Corporation.* Harper Collins Publishers, Inc.: New York.

Hayes, R. and Wheelwright, S. (1984). *Restoring Our Competitive Edge.* New York: John Wiley & Sons.

Henderson, R. and Clark, K. (1990). Architectural Innovation: The Reconfiguration of Existing Product Technologies and the Failure of Established Firms. *Administrative Science Quarterly,* 35: 9-30.

Hofer, C. (1975). Toward a Contingency Theory of Business Strategy. *Academy of Management Review,* 18: 784-810.

Huber, G. (1990). A Theory of the Effects of Advanced Information Technologies on Organization Design, Intelligence and Decision Making. *Academy of Management Review,* 15(1): 47-71.

Johnson, T. and Kaplan, R. (1987). *Relevance Lost: The Rise and Fall of Management Accountancy.* Boston: Harvard Business School Press.

Kerlinger, F. (1986). Foundations of Behavioral Research. Fort Worth, TX: Holt, Rinehart and Winston, Inc.

Kerzner, H. (1984). *Project Management: A Systems Approach to Planning, Scheduling and Controlling.* New York: Van Norstrand Reinhold.

Kim, K. and Michelman, J. (1990). An Examination of the Factors for the Strategic Use of Information Systems in the Healthcare Industry. MIS Quarterly, 14(2): 201-215.

King, W., Grover, V. and Hufnagel, E. (1989). Using Information and Information Technology for Sustainable Competitive Advantage: Some Empirical Evidence. *Information and Management,* 17: 87-93.

Kotteman, J. and Konsynski, B. (1984). Information Systems Planning and Development: Strategic Postures and Methodologies. Journal of Management Information Systems, 1(2): 45-63.

Laughlin, M. (1992). Executive Information Systems: Winning the Numbers Game. *Computers in Healthcare,* 13(4): 20-24.

Lederer, A. and Mendelow, A. (1986). Convincing Top Management of the Strategic Potential of Information Systems. *Information and Management,* 10(5): 245-254.

Leifer, R. (1988). Matching Computer-Based Information Systems with Organizational Structures. *MIS Quarterly:* 63-73.

MacMillan, I. and Jones, P. (1986). *Strategy Formulation: Power and Politics.* St. Paul, MN: West Publishing, p. 1-110.

Madnick, S. (1991). The Information Technology Platform. In *The Corporation of the 1990's* (Scott-Morton, ed.). New York: Oxford University Press.

Marucheck, A., Panessi, R. and Anderson, C. (1990). An Exploratory Study of the Manufacturing Strategy Process in Practice. *Journal of Operations Management*, 9(1): 101-123.

McDonald, H. (1991). Business Strategy Development, Alignment, and Redesign. In *The Corporation of the 1990s* (Scott-Morton, ed.). New York: Oxford Press.

Metcalf, K. (1992). The Helper Model: Nine Ways to Make It Work. *Nursing Management*, 23)12): 40-43.

Mintzberg, H. (1973). Strategy Making in Three Modes. *California Management Review*, 16(2): 44-53.

Mintzberg, H. and Waters, J. (1985). Of Strategies, Deliberate and Emergent. *Strategic Management Journal*, v. 6: 257-272.

Mintzberg, H. (1988). Generic Strategies: Toward a Comprehensive Framework. In *Advances in Strategic Management* (Lamb and Shivastava, eds.): 1-67.

Mitchell, V. (1993). An Examination of the Relationship Between Business Process Redesign and IT Infrastructures. Doctoral Dissertation, Florida State University. Tallahassee, Fl.

Mohr, L. (1969). Determinants of Innovation in Organization. *American Political Science Review*, 63 (March): 111-126.

Moynihan, T. (1990). What Chief Executives and Senior Managers Want From Their IT Departments. *MIS Quarterly*, 14(1): 15-26.

Nadler, D. (1988). Concepts for the Management of Organizational Change. In *Readings in the Management of Innovation*, Tushman and Moore (Eds.). Cambridge, MA: Ballinger Publishing Company.

Nash, K. (1992). Users Like DG's MV Upgrades but in No Rush to Buy Them. *Computerworld*, 26(16): 71.

Nathan, J. (1992). Charting a Course to Efficiency. *Healthcare Executive*, 7(2): 37.

Noori, H. (1990). *Managing the Dynamics of New Technology.* Englewood Cliffs: Prentice-Hall.

Pinto, J. and Slevin, D. (1987). Critical Factors in Successful Project Implementation. *IEEE Transactions on Engineering Management*, EM-34(1): 22-27.

Pinto, J. and Slevin, D. (1988). Project Success: Definitions and Measurement Techniques. *Project Management Journal*, 19(1): 67-72.

Porter, M. (1980). *Competitive Strategy: Techniques for Analyzing Industries and Competitors.* New York: Free Press.

Porter, M. (1985). *Competitive Advantage: Creating and Sustaining Superior Performance.* New York: The Free Press

Quinn, J. (1980). Managing Strategic Change. *Sloan Management Review*, 21(4): 3-20.

Rockart, J. (1979). Chief Executives Define Their Own Data Needs. *Harvard Business Review*, March/April.

Rockart, J. and Short, J. (1989). IT in the 1990s: Managing Organizational Interdependence. *Sloan Management Review*, 30(2): 7-17.

Ruark, B. (1990). Reactive Versus Pro-Active Redesign: Organizing for Order or Optimization? *Journal for Quality and Participation,* September: 22-24.

Sabherwal, R. and King, W. (1991). Towards a Theory of the Strategic Use of Information Resources: An Inductive Approach. *Information and Management,* 20(3): 191-212.

Sherer, J. (1993). Putting Patients First: Hospitals Work to Define Patient-Centered Care. *Hospitals,* 67(3): 14-18.

Teng, J.; Kettinger, W. and Guha, S. (1992). Business Process Redesign and Information Architecture: Establishing the Missing Link. *Proceedings of the 1992 International Conference on Information Systems.*

U.S. Congress, Office of Technology Assessment (1990). *Critical Connections: Communication for the Future.* OTA-CIT-407. Washington, DC: U.S. Government Printing Office.

Venkatraman, N. (1989). The Concept of Fit in Strategy Research: Toward Verbal and Statistical Correspondence. *Academy of Management Review,* 5: 423-444.

Venkatraman, N. (1991). IT-Induced Business Reconfiguration. In *The Corporation of the 1990s* (Scott-Morton, ed). New York: Oxford Press.

Weill, P. and Olsen, M. (1989). Managing Investment in Information Technology. *MIS Quarterly,* 13(1): 3-1-7.

Williamson, O. (1985). *The Economic Institutions of Capitalism.* New York: The Free Press.

Zaltman, G.; Duncan, R. and Holbeck, J. (1973). *Innovations and Organizations.* New York: John Wiley and Sons.

Chapter 17

Assessing Customer Value for Reengineering:
Narcissistic Practices and Parameters from the
Next Generation

Aleda V. Roth
University of North Carolina at Chapel Hill

Jerry Julian
Rath and Strong, Inc.

Manoj K. Malhotra
University of South Carolina

Intense competition, deregulation, globalization, and techno-logical advancement are creating new business realities. Virtually no business entity can escape from these structural changes in the marketplace. In order to cope, many organizations are reengineering and innovating their business processes (Davenport 1993). The concept of reengineering business processes has been widely dis-cussed and expounded upon in both the corporate world as well as academia. The seminal article by Hammer (1990) described reengineering as a means of radically altering the way in which business processes have been thought about or practiced over the course of years. The vast majority of reengineering efforts, however, draw upon *internally–oriented* process improvements. In contrast, this chapter emphasizes strategic reengineering, or what we call "customer–value driven reengineering" that uses cross-organizational process integration to create a new class of competitive capabilities. Therefore to maximize value–added to customers, this chapter is more broadly concerned with *externally–focused* process innovations that enhance customer relationships, responsiveness, and intimacy through advanced customer service, cross–organizational alliances and initiatives, and information technology.

Reengineering efforts challenge management to change their views of how work actually gets done. Reengineering initiatives typically take on many interdependent forms – from the management of hierarchical structures that designate organizational responsibilities and reporting relationships, to process structures that characterize dynamic views of value creation. Reengineering pioneers have restructured by flattening their organizations and enhancing coordination through cross–functional work teams (Roth and Marucheck 1994).

Advances in information and telecommunications technologies facilitate and enable entirely new forms of competitive advantage from reengineering. As opposed to merely increasing the levels of automation in order to achieve the desired levels of internal efficiency and effectiveness (Davenport and Short 1990), technological advancement extends the full range of capability development from points of customer contact to cross–organizational integration of supply chain elements. Take for example, telemedicine which gives rural doctors and patients 'virtual' access to urban specialists by fundamentally altering the delivery and practice of medicine. Doctors at Healthnet provide new value to patients hundreds of miles away in real time. Thus affordable access to quality care is enhanced by electronic medium "through a system of telephone lines, big–screen televisions, video cameras, recorders and audio equipment (physicians) can talk to patients, observe their X–rays and blood tests, hear their heart–beats, look inside their ears and examine their eyes" (Wagner 1994).

Such a fundamental shift toward process innovation does more than just identify opportunities for improving the next quarter's bottom line. It can strategically reposition the firm for the long term. Customer–value driven reengineering offers new prescriptions for integrating marketing and operations strategies, thereby providing a significant competitive advantage. The firm can reinvent its portfolio of competitive capabilities in terms of relationships, access, convenience, speed, productivity, cost, and quality (Roth and van der Velde 1992). Importantly, the impetus for radical organizational transformations to achieve large–scale strategic capability and performance improvements stems from the reality that neither business as usual nor continuous improvement are sufficient for competing in an information era.

Customer value–driven reengineering for competitive capability enhancement is seldom simple or intuitive. Managers frequently fail to appreciate the scope and complexity of what it takes to implement such radical interventions in order to create lasting customer value. Arguably, neither will traditional reengineering initiatives, which we characterize as essentially internally–driven and motivated by cost reduction objectives. When we asked one executive why his company's reengineering started with the order fulfillment process, he stated: "We began with the process where it was easiest to identify significant cost reductions." This response typified those of other senior executives. We found that the internal requirements of many firms to approve reengineering projects are based upon short–term financial returns from savings. In contrast, justifying strategic projects based upon the potential for increasing "future" revenue streams is more difficult, especially for companies that have developed mass production–like command and control cultures. In this chapter, we present an alternative view that necessitates gargantuan changes in management mindsets and strategies. The creation of next generation customer value means reengineering processes in order to win new accounts and build customer loyalty.

An Alternative View

We assert that the next generation of value creation must be driven by a keen awareness of customers' business processes and the need to inject the 'voice of the customer' into the organization's culture. Special attention should be given to reengineering customer–facing processes that go beyond providing traditional products and services. Customer facing processes are those that involve direct contacts with customers (e.g., sales, service, logistics, case management, order management, cross–organizational engineering and design, etc.), and/or have interlinking activities and information flows with customers' processes (electronic data interchange (EDI), integrated databases, networking and communications, etc.). Creation of new value through customer process integration, such as by fostering cross–organizational relationships, gaining customer intimacy, and building customers' competitive capabilities, are the key aspects of our alternative viewpoint.

Baxter's Healthcare International I.V. Systems Division provides an excellent example of customer value–driven reengineering (Figure 1). The range of activities that would typically represent a narcissistic approach is also indicated on Figure 1 for comparison. This division of Baxter maps its key business processes against those of its key customers to locate points of customer contact in order to develop an understanding of the structure and flows of information and materials at the organizational interfaces. Effective management of these interfaces is a fundamental aspect of Baxter's cus

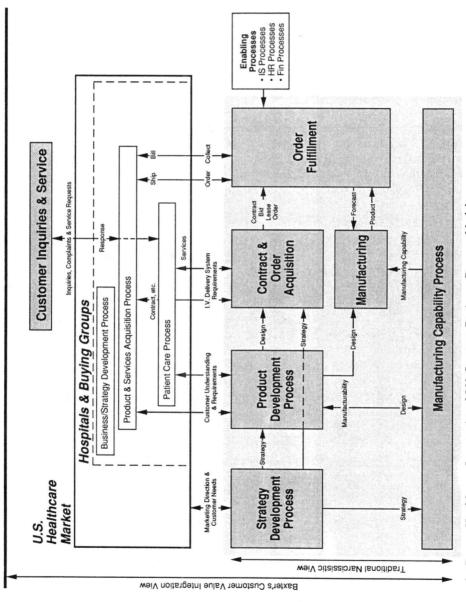

Figure 1: Baxter Healthcare International I.V. Systems Business Process Model

tomer value integration, whereby customer needs are closely related to Baxter's internal strategy formulation and implementation. Take Duke University, for example, where Baxter leveraged the customer intimacy gained from its Value–Link Program. Using this customer–facing process for handling medical/surgical supplies, Baxter created an entirely new source of customer value – managing the hospital's operating room (Fliehman and Auld 1993). Employees from both organizations now work side–by–side. A high level of customer involvement, whether in defining the core products and services or other parameters of the business system, can be a critical issue in the creation of customer value (Davenport and Short 1990, Davidson 1993).

Reengineering for customer value is not limited to service organizations. Executives in leading manufacturing firms claim customer innovations are becoming increasingly vital to success in the 1990s (Roth, Giffi, Shinsato, and Fradette 1993). As it becomes increasingly difficult to sustain leadership in the area of technical competencies, manufacturers' views of their offerings are expanding to combine "tangible" products with "intangible" things; e.g. aesthetically pleasing product features and packaging; information and support services that are fast and reliable; and innovations designed to enhance customers' competitiveness. Northern Telecom's "Win–Win" initiative, for example, focuses upon creating new value by reengineering the customer installation service processes. Much of the wiring work for a new installation of its DMS–100 product, typically performed on the customer's site, has been eliminated or is now performed at the factory. This customer value–driven reengineering effort lessens disruptions to customers, increases quality, and reduces overall costs.

As previously mentioned, these reengineering initiatives are motivated by the globalization of markets, advances in information and telecommunications technologies, and the changing tastes andpreferences of customers in increasingly fragmented markets. Today's customers are more value conscious. Significantly more product information is at their disposal, as is the rich array of product options and features in a given price range. To profit under these new conditions, manufacturers must relentlessly integrate the needs and desires of customers into their own culture and processes.

It is not surprising that many companies have responded to external pressures primarily through internal means: reengineering, restructuring or similarly focused projects to reduce expenses. Unfortunately, as Gouillart and Sturdivant (1994) claim, if competitors fight with the same weapons, then the natural result will be "commoditization" and declining profit margins. Typical reengineering efforts cut headcount in order to provide a quick fix to the bottom line. This hides enormous hidden costs disguised in poor morale and hollowed competencies. "If staffing is reduced without a real improvement in the productivity of the remaining work force, something else will eventually have to give, generally either in the quality or the quantity of the product produced. This is a self–defeating downward spiral to oblivion into which far too many contemporary companies are falling" (Gage 1993, p. 18). For these reasons, it is not surprising that traditional reengineering projects tend to systematically rupture the culture and stifle learning capabilities required to compete. Even Hammer, the reengineering guru, conceded that about 70 percent of reengineering efforts fail to accomplish their goals (Moed 1994).

Leading companies are going beyond simply satisfying the requirements of cost and product quality to generate exceptional value for their customers. Conventional wisdom suggests that winning organizations create intimacy between themselves and their customers. They not only listen to what customers say, but they internalize the voice of the customer and translate customer imperatives into winning strategies (Giffi, Roth, and Seal 1990). Manufacturers can learn a great deal from service organizations in this regard (Heskett, Sasser, and Hart 1990). Consider American Express, which defines service from the customer's point of view and measurers service delivery with the customers in mind. Obviously, senior management of American Express realized that if they could not compete on cost alone, they must find ways to win customer loyalty by integrating or internalizing customer values.

Can such customer value integration offer similar breakthroughs for improving performance in manufacturing organizations? As Vandermerwe states: "The real value for customers today comes not from the core good but from how well it serves their purpose" (1993). New paradigms have been sweeping manufacturing that call for increased cross–functional integration to meet the challenges of creating total customer value (Roth 1994). Unfortunately, the focus of many so–called customer–driven strategies tend to be "narcissistic." The company is centrally concerned with itself and with how satisfied customers are with it (Guaspari 1993).

An alternative view, suggested in this chapter, is to move toward the next generation of customer value added, which we define as one of *customer value integration*. Roth and Van Bennekom (1990) use the "marriage" metaphor to indicate how customer value integration can draw upon the customer's knowledge base to elicit new sales, increase the number of new product and process ideas, and provide dynamic feedback to the firm. Just as self–centeredness can destroy a good "marriage," narcissism has no place in business. "Marriage" relationships with customers must be synergistic and mutually reinforcing. They should stimulate mutual growth and benefit by simultaneously producing opportunities to learn new behaviors and to redesign work processes within and among organizations and their suppliers. It is a competitive necessity for manufacturing firms to break out of their narcissistic mold (Crom 1994).

We evaluate parameters from the next generation of customer value creation and integration by critically comparing and contrasting important customer value parameters. We argue on a conceptual basis the reasons why traditional narcissistic approaches to customer value are likely to fail, while the alternative paradigm of customer value–driven reengineering is more promising. We describe in detail one company's experience in order to illustrate how companies can actually span the continuum from a narcissistic customer orientation to engaging in more enlightened customer value integration practices. Finally, the implications of the alternative view in providing better management planning and control of customer value are discussed.

Customer Value Creation for the Next Generation

To break out of the traditional mold, a new mental model is required. Treacy and Wiersema (1993) present three generic ways to create value for customers: operational excellence, product leadership within the industry, and customer intimacy. Firms must now treat the creation of customer intimacy and value as essential for being a viable competitor, even though they may be more directly involved in providing operational excellence or product leadership within their industry group. Based upon the extant literature and the authors' discussions with executives, most reengineering initiatives seek to gain quantum leaps in competitive capabilities on the first two dimensions: process improvements in metrics of operational excellence (e.g., quality, delivery reliability, flexibility, and cost) or of new product leadership (e.g. speed to market or high R&D content). Few manufacturers have focused reengineering processes to increase customer intimacy. Arguably, manufacturing firms must strive for processes that garner customer intimacy, which is the basis for the next generation. In other words, we believe that by engaging in reengineering efforts which focus solely upon operational excellence or product leadership, companies will miss significant strategic opportunities.

Table 1 highlights the key differences between traditional views of value creation and the next generation of value integration. The differences between these two approaches are highlighted across several key customer value parameters that we believe are important in defining and creating a continuum of customer value. The customer orientation for the "narcissistic" practices is typically more

Value Parameters	Traditional "Narcissism"	Next Generation "Integration"
Basic question to customers	How are we doing?	How are you doing?
Customer orientation?	Does not view customers as extensions of the firm.	Views customer relations as a set of on-going partnerships or a "marriage".
How was customer value defined?	Selected internal functions (e.g., engineering, marketing) provide descriptors of customer value.	Top level customer executives share their own unique objectives and descriptors of what's strategically important to them.
Who should be interviewed?	Next link in value-chain (end-users, purchasing groups, etc.).	Cross-company, cross-functional company and customer employees; non-customers; customers' customers and competitors.
What level of service is to be provided?	Adequate level of service to meet explicit needs.	Match or exceed the desired level of service to meet explicit and implicit strategic needs.
How homogeneous should customer service be?	Customers have uniform preferences across product categories and services within a market segment.	Customers are unique, and may demand or define value differently for different goods and services, regardless of market segment.
Customer communication protocols?	Customers are often faced with ambiguous, ill defined, and confusing communications about the products and customer service policies and practices.	Customers are involved in defining products and customer service policies and practices.
What are the priorities for reengineering processes?	Priorities that have cost reduction opportunity or are internally focussed.	Priorities that strategically optimize value to customers.
Who has the responsibility for customer service?	Customer service function that empowers people within a limited scope of responsibility.	Company-wide integration of service by empowering everyone in the company to meet customer service objectives.
How and when to implement process improvements?	Single shot and ad hoc based upon explicit needs.	Continuous probing and updating based upon market dynamics.

Table 1: Customer Value Parameters and the Next Generation of Value Creation

myopic, inward directed, and less likely to involve the customer. These firms tend to have relatively poor communication with the customers and rarely exceed customer expectations for service. Customers are treated as a homogeneous group, with little attention paid to creating differentiated customer value–added. Consequently, customer process improvements are ad hoc, poorly planned, and driven more by cost reduction opportunities rather than by objectives to maximize customers' capabilities. Such narcissistic practices are unlikely to promote even an acceptable level of customer intimacy as defined by Treacy and Wiersema (1993), or "marriage" relationships as cited by Roth and Van Bennekom (1990). They are doomed to fail or be less competitive over the long run. We hypothesize that narcissism is a major cause of the high failure rate attributed to traditional reengineering.

In contrast, next generation value creation and integration practices must clearly involve the customers in defining their own value (Hauser and Clausing 1988), and must span several links in the value chain. Customer value integration requires differentiation of services and policies across product categories and customers, and the ability to clearly communicate them. At the extreme, the next generation of reengineering is the enabler of mass customization (Davis and Davidson 1991, Pine, Victor and Boynton, 1993). Each customer brings a unique need to the firm, and hence must be valued accordingly. Processes selected for improvement are those that optimize what is strategically important to customers. Everyone is empowered in the company to continuously evaluate, update, and improve these processes. Hence the next generation value firms are more likely to leverage their process dimensions to develop customer intimacy, be reliable and fair, provide or exceed the desired level of service, and consequently build long term relationships with their customers (Parasuraman, Berry, and Zeithaml 1991). Such firms deploy a clear vision for creating customer value, and then listen closely to the voice of the customer in implementing that vision (Keiser and Smith 1993).

All firms cannot excel equally along every customer value parameter shown in Table 1. However, they can move closer to their desired goal by fundamentally changing their orientation toward their customers, and redirecting those components of their processes that now reflect narcissistic tendencies. Even though most firms may not strive to achieve mass customization, or primarily compete on the basis of creating exceptional customer intimacy, they will need to make a transition toward providing customer value in order to be competitive. The key differences between the traditional narcissistic and more enlightened customer value approaches are illustrated through a case example in the next section. We also document how this firm moved closer toward its objective of providing next generation customer value through customer integration.

A Case Against Narcissistic Reengineering

Consider the reengineering journey of a $40 million division of a multinational corporation. The division was motivated to strategically reengineer their processes by a sense of urgency. The CEO mandated stretch sales goals. At the same time, a senior sales executive felt that the division was vulnerable. Close competitors were rapidly adding new services, while division sales revenues were becoming increasingly dependent upon their two largest customers who accounted for 65 percent of sales. Division executives needed to simultaneously broaden market opportunities and strengthen relationships with current customers. The executives wanted a reengineering approach which was consistent with their culture of treating customers as partners. As a result, they embarked upon an experimental journey toward the next generation of customer value. Their primary objectives were to reinvigorate the sales force and to move the organization's culture towards an external focus on customers. At the outset, the division's senior managers specifically sought answers to the following set of strategic questions:

- How can the division's sales be increased?
- How can the sales force be reinvigorated?
- How can the sales force be empowered with the responsibility and authority for meeting and gathering customer expectations?
- How can a sense of ownership for providing excellent customer value be shared throughout the company?

Yet to answer these questions, the senior managers realized that employees required a new mental model. In the past, the company typically took a somewhat "narcissistic" approach to change efforts. They asked customers: "How are we doing?" Now management posed a new model that suggested accepting nothing less than asking: "How are you doing?" Management felt that the new model would be most effective if the sales force and other employees could sit face–to–face with customers and address their concerns, hopes, fears, and expectations. By sensitizing individual employees at all levels of the company to expressed customers needs, management believed that employees could truly learn from the concrete, interactive experiences provided.

How is the division evolving towards the next generation? There were three evolutionary stages in the division's strategic journey. The important aspects of this journey are highlighted in Table 2 along the customer value parameters discussed previously in Table 1. First the groundwork for understanding customer needs and beliefs

Value Parameters	Value Creation Issues	Comments
Basic Questions to Customers	Asked customers in an open-ended fashion what issues they are facing and what is most important to them.	Did not start dialogue with a narcissistic approach that asks customers to evaluate the Division's performance, or how "satisfied" customers were with a specified list of performance criteria.
Customer Orientation?	Wanted stronger ties and partnerships with the largest customers.	A few clients accounted for 65 percent of the sales.
How was customer value defined?	Engaged customers in an open dialogue to determine their value descriptors, and summarized them through thematic analyses of performance on products and services.	A limitation here is that customers may not always know or cannot articulate their latent wants and needs. A more comprehensive effort to map the customers' experiences with their customers' needs is a next step.
Who should be interviewed?	Interviewed current customers to develop seen value descriptors.	Original descriptors were not developed with non-customers.
What level of service is to be provided?	Targets were individually specified by major customers. They outlined a "bronze," "silver," and "gold" level of service, and what metrics were associated with each level of performance.	Customers defined service levels and expectations. While division is dedicated to meeting the "gold" standard, the stretch may not be great enough to produce breakthrough improvements.
How homogenous should customer service be?	A follow-up effort with major customers identified ways for division to mass customize its offerings. Plans are being made for packaging supplies to be offered in different grades for certain product characteristics (e.g., slip resistance, opening and closing forces, etc.)	Customers will be able to choose their particular configuration rather than receiving a specified range of product grades.
Customer communication protocols	Service policies and practices are still in the development stages.	Little change in this area because of transition.
What are the priorities for reengineering processes?	Customer value research drove the selection of two initial processes for improvements.	Focus shifted from internal cost reduction efforts to improving customer value and reducing response times.
Who has the responsibility for customer service?	Business teams of sales personnel, who are business managers, and representatives from finance, production, engineering and other functions are dedicated to specific customers.	The shift has created an unprecedented culture of service orientation with an emphasis on learning and knowledge creation about customers.
How and when to implement improvements?	Established an ongoing system for tracking company's performance around "value descriptors" created by customers' own value research.	Division's improvement efforts will be continuously driven by performance on these descriptors. A current limitation is that these indices are fixed, while other descriptors may become important as industry and customer changes occur.

Table 2: Division's Journey Toward Customer Value Integration

was laid through a set of structured interviews. Next, customer questionnaires and interviews were conducted with the help of the sales force. Third, steps for improvement were determined. Each of these three stages are now described.

Stage 1. Discovering what is strategically important to key customers

What factors win orders? During the first stage, a group of sales people accompanied seasoned facilitators on selected customer visits. The objective was to determine in the customers' own context, the attributes that most influence their buying behaviors and loyalty. Initially, open–ended questioning was used to elicit the key "value descriptors" — those issues and concerns that customers spoke about in their own words as being most important to them. A list of value descriptors was compiled to be later used in more comprehensive interviews of both customers and non–customers (hereafter referred to as target customers) who would later rate the division on these dimensions. A thematic analysis of the initial interview responses produced the following seven key value descriptors for the division's customers:

- "Delivers on Demand"
- "Fast and Flexible"
- "Competitive Prices"
- "Unique Designs that Sell"
- "Is a Member of My Team"
- "Technically Capable"
- "Consistent Quality"

Next a questionnaire was designed to measure these seven value descriptors along with other buying behaviors and demographic information. A broader sample of target customers was selected to respond to the questionnaire. Sales personnel were then trained on administering the questionnaire and participated in role playing exercises in preparation for actual field experiences. Training helped the sales personnel anticipate and prepare for the types of responses they might encounter with target customers in face–to–face meetings.

Stage 2. Face–to–face interviews

In this round of face–to–face interviews with target customers, the sales personnel led discussions while employees from other departments such as accounting, production, engineering, and R&D

observed. Potential customers were asked to rate their primary suppliers for a given product on each of the seven value descriptors previously listed. Less than half (39 percent) of those interviewed considered the division to be their primary supplier. Importantly, both customers and non–customers were asked to rank order the importance of each value descriptor as an "order winner" or "order qualifier" (Hill 1989).

Stage 3. Conclusions and steps for process improvements

The multi–functional employee teams developed cross–organizational linkages and learned first–hand what "value" means to individual customers. More importantly, the customers' own value descriptions provided a direct linkage to the division's processes requiring prioritization for improvement. Management drew several important conclusions:

- New customers other than their current set emerged, each having different sets of needs and concerns. While different customers had different order winning criteria, there was sufficient commonality to segment them afterwards by their shared value descriptors, as opposed to a priori market segmentation.
- Delivery speed is increasingly important to all customer segments. Quick response for the production of samples, the handling of inquiries and problems, and the shipment of orders from production were now "order qualifiers."
- Price is an order sensitive descriptor. Customers were dissatisfied with most suppliers on price but saw this division as especially high in their pricing policies.
- Product design and speed to market were even more critical to maintaining customer loyalty and for maintaining premium prices.
- The excellent product quality that the division was known for in the past no longer gave them a distinct advantage over competitors, and therefore became an "order qualifier."

The conclusions drawn by the interview teams and management during the debriefing and analyses sessions had strategic implications for the division. Their products were being "commoditized" and subjected to pricing problems. Their traditional strengths in providing superior product quality and on–time delivery were jeopardized. This division is not alone in this respect. Roth et al. (1993) reported the closing of the quality and delivery gaps in a broader sample of 1300 manufacturing business units worldwide. This company has, however, distinguished itself in one important new way: employees throughout the company were intimately involved with the interviews and analyses, and subsequently had first–hand knowledge of the issues. Through the division's knowledge creation process, a shared vision emerged along with an understanding of the immediate steps to be taken in order to integrate the newly found customer values.

Employees rallied around internalizing customers' needs and shared a sense of urgency that could not have been created through management edict or benign data from customer satisfaction surveys. The division next began its reengineering journey. It launched "quick response" teams to reduce lead times for two order fulfillment processes: new business and add–on business. Cross–functional teams with members from design, production, engineering, and sales were instituted to make the process of gathering customer needs continuous and to plan orders from design to delivery. New roles for the sales personnel were also created. They became business managers who were to focus on providing complete solutions rather than simply being order takers. Teams with at least one business manager were formed to serve a particular customer segment in both an order fulfillment capacity and in an after–sales service capacity. Because the teams were responsible for after–sales service, they were able to generate real time feedback about products, which, because of the active membership from engineering, production and design, could be used immediately to improve the order fulfillment process.

Customer value integration provided the strategic directions for process reengineering, while the quick response teams provided an innovative approach toward strategy implementation. The teams are well on their way to addressing the four questions originally posed by senior management. First, simply by involving cross–functional teams in the interview process, customer value integration offered a company–wide shared vision and employee ownership of key strategic customer issues. Second, the sales force was reinvigorated by the infusion of responsibility and authority in meeting customer expectations. Third, the sales force now shared their sense of ownership throughout the division. Fourth, the issues centered around increasing sales volume, would be addressed by the quick response teams through a concentrated effort to shore up rapid design and production capabilities, and thereby maintain their premium pricing structure.

Implications for Practice

Most firms exist on a continuum somewhere between narcissistic practices and those associated with the next generation of value creation. The case discussion in the previous section described one firm's progress toward the next generation. Importantly, they have begun the journey – top executives have recognized the challenge and have strategically focused their process reengineering. It is our contention here, as exemplified by the case, that satisfying customers differs from finding ways to create new customer value. *Satisfying customers means meeting explicit requirements, whereas value creation implies going beyond to identify and fulfill real, but often unarticulated customer needs.* Thus, companies aiming to thrive and compete effectively in the 1990's and beyond will be the ones that strive for more than "high" customer satisfaction scores on operational metrics. They will make integration of new customer value the primary driver of their reengineering and process innovation efforts.

It is easy to gravitate toward narcissistic practices, since different parameters of value–added activities from the customers' perspectives may not be synonymous with the firm's perspectives. It is also easier to *a priori* lump customers into market segments based upon demographics and other broad–based criteria than it is to assess and build competitive capabilities aimed at meeting their unique needs. Moreover, in a traditional large corporation, marketing and sales have been relegated to the role of deriving revenues from customers. Yet they are somewhat removed from daily operations and business processes that deliver customer value. This bifurcation of activities isolates the bulk of the company's workforce from customer intimacy, and thereby inhibits the firm's ability to learn and to broaden the scope of value creation.

Merely addressing customer service doesn't provide a guarantee against narcissism. One company gauged its customer satisfaction rating for customer service at 60 percent and saw rapidly increasing costs for customer service. Top management decided that the service process needed to be "reengineered." This approach was narcissistic, and ultimately produced suboptimal results. Had management paid attention to customer value integration, they would have first focused on the product development processes, which are upstream to service. Faulty product designs were a primary source of service failures in this case.

So how can firms strategically reengineer their processes in order to move closer toward the next generation of value integration? Four principles that drive implications for practice are summarized below. Each principle is an integral component of customer value–driven reengineering for growth and renewal.

Principle 1: Reengineering for customer value integration starts with key customers' business strategies .

Customer value integration begins with a clear understanding of the key customers' strategy, mission, and operating objectives. Key customers are the ones who either account for the major portion of the revenues/profits or who are 'up–and–comers' with strategic value to the firm. Reengineering must feed into the strategic capabilities required by these key customers in satisfying their own customers and downstream end–users. Reengineering, while initiated at the top, must help internalize customer values throughout all levels of the organization. The tools for enabling Principle 1 include:

- As illustrated in Figure 1, map your business processes with high level customer processes.
- Focus on the alignment of your business strategies with those of key customers.
- Develop a consensus of strategic directions with customer's CEOs and top management teams consisting of marketing, operations, accounting, purchasing, and finance.

Principle 2: Translate value descriptors into competitive capabilities through process integration.

Start the change process with customer value descriptors – not with internal process improvements. In other words, begin your reengineering by developing a process to link value descriptors to requisite competitive capabilities. Value integration implies an understanding of the total product/service bundle that is important to customers – much of which could neither have been articulated nor predicted in advance. This opens up countless opportunities to derive value from new processes or by adding new features to existing ones. Critical capabilities can only be determined by an external focus—learning about the value chain network of customers and customers' customers. Involving customers in the design and delivery of products and services will generate more uncertainty for the organization (Chase and Tansik 1983). However, managing such uncertainty and learning to use it for competitive advantage are crucial to creating and enhancing customer value.

Reengineering processes through customer value integration evokes external views of the delivered product/service bundle and the processes by which they are created. Traditional reengineering, in contrast, usually begins by an assessment of internal processes and capabilities. Common sense and experience shows that this approach is myopic and may not produce any lasting competitive advantage. Narcissistic approaches to understanding customers also produce "fixed" notions about customer requirements and processes, and fail to account for market dynamics (Argyris and Schon 1978; Roth, Marucheck, Trimble, and Kemp 1994). The tools for enacting Principle 2 are:

- Develop thematic groupings of value descriptors and link them to current capabilities. Assess the competitive gaps between current capabilities and priorities (value descriptors).

- Map the customers' processes from pre–purchase to post–sales against your key processes.
- Highlight areas of customer interface and determine what capabilities are needed to improve the overall value chain "network." "What would the "ideal" processes look like?" is a key question for ongoing dialogue with customers.
- Jointly seek ways to increase revenues and reduce costs over the value chain network.

Principle 3: A "visceral" understanding of the unique needs of customers is required.

The capability to learn and develop cultural sensitivity to customers' unique values is critical to success. A truly internalized understanding by employees is "visceral" and lasting. Sensitivity comes from concrete experiences with customers, where employees and managers have the opportunity for face–to–face interaction and dialogue with customers in the context of their customers' business environment. Side–by–side with customers, employees empathize with customers' pains and priorities as individuals and groups. Note that traditional case management as proposed by Davenport and Nohria (1994), where individual or small teams handle all of the requirements of customers, may in fact actually desensitize over the long run those other employees who are not on the teams. Mechanisms for broader exposure to customers by employees are required because of the changing customer dynamics.

While management must carefully plan for the next generation of customer value, the actual evolution of value descriptors must be collaboratively and iteratively determined. One–time reengineering with little employee participation damages the culture and debilitates organizational learning. This poses formidable barriers to adapt to the inevitable changes in the marketplace. Those processes which either detract from customer–driven capabilities or fail to enhance customer–value must be either eliminated or reengineered. It is worthwhile to invest in those processes that allow the firm to capitalize on customer intimacy and leverage long–term relationships. Customer retention has significant market value (Heskett, Sasser, and Hart 1990). The tools for enacting Principle 3 are:

- Cultivate collaborative customer research and action learning which involves integration of employees with employee counterparts within the customers' organizations. Open–ended dialogue, focusing on "how are you doing" versus "how are we doing," allows employees to empathize and internalize customers values for themselves.

- Develop organizational policies and systems that are designed to keep customers in close contact with as many employees as possible (e.g. customer visits, rotation of activities to customers site, joint task forces, and information and communications technology enablers) and the means to capture employee learning.

Principle 4: Providing customer value is an ongoing process of enactment and information exchange.

The process of providing customer value must be continuously evaluated and adapted in response to dynamic environmental charges. Customer knowledge creation becomes an enactment process (Whyte 1990) of concrete experiences which drive the focus of reengineering. This implies that "double–looped" learning (Argyris and Schon 1978) is essential for accelerated learning, as is the creation of a shared vision of what customers require. The tools for Principle 4 are:

- Take deliberate managerial actions to engage the organization in double-looped learning (Roth et al. 1994).
- Processes that are more horizontally integrated with those of customers are important. The customer is viewed at the beginning, in the middle, and at the end of the integrated processes.
- Use value descriptors as input into building a house of quality (Hauser and Clausing 1988) so that customers' perceptions and needs are translated into product and process designs. Incorporate feedback loops to update the house of quality (Adiano and Roth 1994).

Conclusions

We have argued in this chapter that in order to be successful, reengineering efforts should be externally focussed and strategic, rather than be motivated by objectives that are internally focussed and tactical. Reengineering should not be a mandate for downsizing or for improving those processes that are far removed from the customer and have no obvious impact on increasing customer value. The impetus for customer value-driven reengineering stems from the need to select, grow, and retain target customers. In this sense, integration of customer value must be seen as the dominant philosophy that drives most of the major change efforts in the firm. Internal process developments and innovations that are not directly or indirectly tied in to enhancing customer value are unlikely to succeed in the long run. This also holds true for other firms that compete on the basis of providing product leadership or operational excellence. Externally focused process innovations are more likely to dynamically generate the required set of capabilities and competencies that allow the firm to compete effectively in the marketplace.

There are two major issues that we believe are essential to reengineering for sustainable customer value. First, most firms exist somewhere on the continuum from totally narcissistic practices to the enlightened customer integration approaches shown in Table 1. The transition to the desired end of the spectrum can only come from fundamentally altering the shared views of customer value. The impetus for such a change may come from a more competitive environment and the need to increase market share (as in the case of the division of multinational corporation highlighted in this chapter), or from a need to survive as a business entity. In either case, a paradigm shift toward appreciating customers is essential for successful and lasting change to occur. The trick is to first determine exactly who is a key customer, and second what is strategic to them.

The second issue is centered around recognizing that the process of creating customer value is a dynamic one. Rather than seeking specific service levels at specific points of time, customer value must be perceived as a broader range or window of strategic services that evolve and need to be redefined from time to time. The frequency of re–evaluation would off course be industry specific, since some industries (such as electronics and telecommunications for example) are far more dynamic. Customer value integration should be viewed across the organization as a set of on going process innovations that assists the firm in staying close to its customers.

In conclusion, companies are struggling with how to create value for their customers. While reengineering is not the only tool at management's disposal for creating the next generation of value, it is useful for strategically aligning business processes with competitive capabilities required for effectiveness in the marketplace. Unfortunately, many firms are investing significant resources in traditional reengineering and not getting far. This chapter suggests that "narcissism" is a plausible reason for implementation shortcomings. Importantly, the chapter also provides managerial guidance for customer value–driven reengineering.

When reengineering, one should not throw out common sense and apply the tool mechanistically. It does not always take a radical reengineering effort to effect immediate breakthrough improvement. In fact, focusing on the expense side of the ledger – as opposed to the revenue side – may create the opposite effect. Demoralized, disengaged employees are more likely to continue narcissistic practices, and render the organization incapable of truly internalizing customer needs. As in the case of Baxter, Northern Telecom's win–win initiative, and the case of the multi–national company, it is possible to move away from traditional narcissism toward integrating customer values into the fabric of the organization. Such cross–

organizational integration is ongoing in reengineering and in the continuous improvement that follows. Not only does it provide strategic directions, but it also positions the firm's culture to build processes that maintain closeness to customers.

Acknowledgements:
The authors wish to thank Mr. Bill Anderson, Baxter I.V. Systems Division for his thoughts about reengineering. We also wish to acknowledge Mr. Robert Badelt AVP Business Process Reengineering, Northern Telecom Switching, for his helpful comments. We thank Ms. Barbara Napier and Mr. Steve Crom of Rath and Strong, Inc. for their ideas and for the use of their client's change effort as one of the case examples in this chapter. The authors would also like to credit Mr. John Guaspari of Rath & Strong Inc. for his insights on "customer narcissism" and value.

References

Adiano, C., and A.V. Roth, 1994. "Beyond the House of Quality: Dynamic QFD," *Benchmarking for Quality and Technology Management*, Vol. 1, 25–37.

Argyris, C and D. A. Schon, 1978. *Organizational Learning: A Theory of Action Perspective*. Addison–Wesley Pub., Reading, MA.

Buzzell, R. D. and B. T. Gale, 1990. *The PIMS Principles: Linking Strategy to Performance*, The Free Press. New York.

Chase R. B. and D. A. Tansik. 1983. "The Customer Contact Model for Organization Design," *Management Science*, Vol. 29, No. 9, 1037–1050.

Crom, S., 1994. "Integrating Processes and Learning New Behaviors," *The Total Quality Review*, July/August.

Davidson, W. H., 1993. "Beyond Reengineering: The Three Phases of Business Transformation," *IBM Systems Journal.*, Vol. 32, No. 1, 65–79.

Davis S. and B. Davidson, 1991. *2020 Vision*, Simon & Schuster, New York.

Davenport T and J. Short, 1990. "The New Industrial Engineering: Information Technology and Business Process Redesign." *Sloan Management Review*, Summer, 11–27.

Davenport T. H., and N. Nohria, 1994. "Case Management and the Integration of Labor," *Sloan Management Review*, Vol 35, No. 2, Winter, 11–23.

Fliehman D. G. and D. D. Auld, 1993. *Customer Retention through Quality Leadership*, ASQC Quality Press, Milwaukee, WI.

Gage S.,1993. "The Management of Key Enterprise Processes," *Quality Management*, Spring, 13–18.

Giffi C., A. V. Roth, and G. Seal, 1990. *Competing in World Class Manufacturing: America's 21st Century Challenge*, Business One Irwin, Homewood, IL.

Gouillart F. J. and F. D. Sturdivant, 1994. "Spend a Day in the Life of Your Customer," *Harvard Business Review*, January–February, 116–125.

Guaspari J., 1993. "Are You a Customer Narcissist?", *Leadership Report*, Rath & Strong, Inc.

Hammer, M., 1990. "Reengineering Work: Don't Automate, Obliterate," *Harvard Business Review* , July–August, 104–112.

Hauser J.R., and D. Clausing, 1988. "The House of Quality," *Harvard Business Review*, May–June, 63–73.

Heskett J.L., E. W. Sasser, and C. W. L. Hart, 1990. *Service Breakthroughs*, The Free Press, New York.

Hill T., 1989. *Manufacturing Strategy*, Homewood, IL: Richard D. Irwin.

Keiser T. C., and D. A. Smith., 1993. "Customer–Driven Strategies: Moving from Talk to Action," *Planning Review*, September/October, 25–32.

Miller J. G. and A. V. Roth, 1994. "A Taxonomy of Manufacturing Strategies," *Management Science*, Vol 40, No 3, March, 285–304.

Moad J., 1993. "Does Reengineering Really Work?" *Datamation*, August 1.

Northcraft, G. B. and R. B. Chase, 1985. "Managing Service Demand at the Point of Delivery," *Academy of Management Review*, Vol. 10, No. 1, 66–76.

Parasuraman A., L. L. Berry, and V. Zeithaml, 1991. "Understanding Customer Expectations of Service," *Sloan Management Review*, Vol. 32, No. 3, Spring, 39–48.

Pine, B. J., B. Victor, and A. C. Boynton, 1993. "Making Mass Customization Work," *Harvard Business Review*, Vol. 71, 108-119.

Roth A.V., 1994. "Global Manufacturing Strategies: What It Takes to Win!" Paper presented at the Annual Meeting of the Planning Forum, New York, April.

Roth A. V. and J. G. Miller, 1992. "Success Factors in Manufacturing," *Business Horizons*, Vol. 35, No. 4, 73–81.

Roth A. V. and F. Van Bennekom, 1990. "Closing the Loop through After–Sales Service." *Proceedings of the 1990 Decision Sciences Institute Annual Meeting*, San Diego, CA, November.

Roth A. V., and M. van der Velde, 1991. "Operations as Marketing: A Competitive Service Strategy," *Journal of Operations Management*, Vol. 10, No. 3, 303–328.

Roth A. V., C.A. Giffi, D. Shinsato, and M. Fradette, 1993. "Critical Success Factors for Global Competition," in *Visions in Manufacturing*, Vol. I, Deloitte Touche Tomahsu–UNCC Kenan Flagler Business School Research Reports, Cleveland, OH.

Roth, A. V. and A. Marucheck, 1994. "Global Business Process Reengineering: Lessons from the Pioneers," Academy of Management Annual Meeting, Dallas TX.

Roth, A.V., A. S. Marucheck, A. Kemp, and D. Trimble, 1994. "The Knowledge Factory for Accelerated Learning Practices," *Planning Review*, May/June, 26–33.

Schleisinger L. A. and J. L. Heskett, 1991. "Breaking the Cycle of Failure in Services," *Sloan Management Review*, Spring, 17–28.

Treacy M., and Wiersema F., 1993. "Customer Intimacy and Other Value Disciplines," *Harvard Business Review*, January–February, 84–93.

Vandermerwe S., 1993. *From Tin Soldiers to Russian Dolls – Creating Added Value Through Services*, Butterworth–Heinemann Ltd.

Wagner, B., 1994. "Healing by Long–Distance," *The Herald–Sun*, November 6, p. G1–G2.

Whyte, W. F., 1990. *Social Theory for Action: How Individuals and Organizations Learn to Change*, Sage Publ. Newbury, CA.

When People "Work Scared":
Understanding Attitudes and Gaining Commitment in Business Process Reengineering

Nancy Paule Melone
University of Oregon

When you change processes radically, you have huge ripple effects through your organization. Once you change how work is done, you change what people's jobs are, you change how they are measured, how they are managed, how they are paid, what their careers are. ...IS people continue to be notoriously bad at recognizing the human aspects of reengineering.

Michael Hammer
***ComputerWorld*, January 24, 1994**

For the most part, research and writing on managing change processes and implementation have focused on the organization as the primary unit of consideration. While this body of literature lends considerable insight into the roles that macro constructs such as corporate vision, politics, context, and larger organizational processes play in understanding why organizational change efforts succeed or fail, it provides very limited insight into understanding change processes within individuals and even less into how to manage them. Yet, in corporate reengineering efforts, individuals often play key roles as leaders, process owners, members of process teams or more likely as implementers of the redesigned processes. Their attitudes about reengineering, commitment to these efforts and in some cases their roles as communicators can make the difference between success and failure.

That individuals might find reengineering and related notions associated with the "horizonal organization" intimidating, threatening, or scary should come as no surprise (Byrne, 1993; Hammer, 1990). Certainly, a person responsible for reengineering should expect this. A job is central to one's life as a source of income, psychic rewards and social relationships (Christiansen, 1992). The redesign of work processes changes people's jobs, how they are evaluated, rewarded, managed; in some cases it may even result in termination of the employment relationship. Corporate reengineering efforts are further complicated because, unlike earlier management innovations, redesigned business processes can have an impact on the jobs of managers, engineers, and other professionals as easily as those of hourly workers, historically the more typical targets of such "innovations." Some have gone so far as to call reengineering nothing more than a euphemism for downsizing (Byrne, 1994). Reengineering is not necessarily synonymous with downsizing. Unfortunately, when such events occur roughly simultaneously with reengineering efforts as they have recently, human beings have difficulty distinguishing one from the other. Furthermore, casual comments from well-intentioned sources responsible for reengineering efforts can be interpreted by individuals with disastrous consequences. The phrase, "tradition counts for nothing" (Hammer & Champy, 1993, p. 49), may be interpreted by employees as either an opportunity for positive change or an excuse to disregard loyal and dedicated service.

Leaders, process owners, and process team members are faced with managing not only the reality of reengineering but also attitudes about that reality. To the extent that reengineering processes can have profound and different consequences for the individual apart from the organization, failure to understand how individuals' attitudes, beliefs, and perceptions develop and are modified is likely to account for at least some of the estimated 75% of the reengineering efforts that fail (Maglitta, 1994). Clearly, understanding the function served by an individual's attitude about corporate reengineering, how such attitudes form, and most importantly how they can be influenced by leaders, process owners and process team members constitutes a portion of the skill set required for re-engineers.

The chapter is organized in the following way. First, we ask and answer the basic questions of why attitudes matter in reengineering and more specifically why management should focus attention on understanding and managing them. Second, we consider the functions that attitudes play in helping an individual process information about the world. In reengineering efforts, identification of an attitude's function for the individual provides insight into how and why the person holds particular views. This element of information is vital in determining if there are basic misunderstandings that should be addressed by management before process reengineering is initiated. Next, we consider two models of persuasion that are most relevant for the current context. The first of these is the elaboration likelihood model (ELM; Petty & Cacioppo, 1986), which describes the two primary routes, the central route and the peripheral route, through which persuasive messages are processed by individuals. The second model, the appropriateness-consistency-effectiveness (ACE) model (Reardon, 1981, 1987, 1991), describes which messages are likely to be persuasive. Consideration of these two models offers insight into the content of messages most likely to persuade (ACE) and the processes by which such messages persuade or fail to persuade. These two models form a useful background for the following section, which describes interpersonal and mediated influence strategies. Finally, we reflect on the broader implications of managing attitudes and impressions during the course of corporate reengineering.

Why Are Attitudes Important in Process Reengineering?

Reengineering business processes is complex enough without delving into what people think about it. Hence, it is logical for the re-engineer to ask why he or she should care about people's attitudes about corporate reengineering.

There are several answers to that question. The most concise answer is because an individual's attitude has a significant influence on his or her perception of the world, processing of information about the world, and behaviors in the world (Melone, 1990; Pratkanis & Greenwald, 1989). Pratkanis (1988) provides additional elaboration (i.e., attitude correspondence effects) on how positive or negative attitudes influence people's understanding of their world. We consider five of his eleven attitude-correspondence notions that are most applicable to reengineering and incorporate some examples showing how these notions might relate in practice.

First, an individual's attitudes influence his interpretations and attributions about the reasons underlying management actions. In this sense, an individual's attitude could determine whether he or she sees management's motivation for reengineering as necessary to remain in business, to serve the customer better, or to eliminate middle managers and other employees. Second, attitudes influence a person's reconstruction of past events. A generally positive attitude toward reengineering can prompt more positive recollections of earlier reengineering efforts even if considerable difficulties were encountered during those projects. Third, an individual's attitudes influence the evaluation of other social stimuli surrounding reengineering. For example, if an individual's attitude toward the company is positive, then that individual will tend to view the goals of corporate reengineering positively and as being consistent with his or her own goals. Fourth, an individual's attitudes influence expectations for and evaluations of the results of management actions. Translated into the present context, if reengineering is considered to be "good" (i.e., attitudes are generally positive), then it is more likely to be seen as having "good" effects, such as empowering employees by giving them the authority to make their own decisions, rather than having "bad" effects, such as dumping more work on employees without increasing their compensation. Fifth, an individual's attitudes influence that person's predictions of future events. This attribute of attitudes is critical for both current and future reengineering efforts. Essentially it implies that if people want reengineering to succeed, they tend to think that it will. Table 1 provides a summary of these points.

The Function of Attitudes in Reengineering

A person's attitude about reengineering can serve various psychological needs for that individual. At the most basic level, attitudes are evaluative responses to attitude objects (McGuire, 1969). Attitude objects can be things, events, institutions, people, or other distinguishable aspects of a person's world (Ajzen, 1989). Attitudes are

---

Attitudes influence:

- interpretations and attributions about management's reasons for re-engineering;

- the recollection and reconstructs of past events associated with re-engineering or other management actions;

- the evaluation of other social stimuli surrounding re-engineering;

- expectations for outcomes or results of re-engineering; and

- predictions of future re-engineering efforts.

Table 1: Ways Positive (or Negative) Attitudes Influence Perceptions of Reengineering (adapted from Pratkanis, 1988)

evaluative (i.e., positive or negative, favorable or unfavorable, good or bad). Contemplated change of corporate processes is likely to be something about which most employees form an attitudinal evaluation, regardless of how much knowledge they have of the proposed process change. While reengineering efforts often emphasize discarding the past, management's record with employees in the past will likely determine the initial support given to a reengineering effort. Knowing both the nature of these attitudes (e.g., favorable, neutral, unfavorable) and the functions that they serve in helping the individual negotiate his or her workplace (e.g., ego defensive) is the first step in designing strategies to manage individual fears and to build broad-based support for process change.

Understanding the needs that attitudes serve can suggest why people hold certain attitudes and how we might manage them or change them in the course of reengineering. Five functions of attitudes for individuals have been identified: knowledge, utility, social adjustment, ego defense, and value expression (Perloff, 1993). Although these functions are discussed individually, attitudes can serve multiple functions. Similarly, an astute manager can identify ways in which attitudes could serve both the needs of the individual and the reengineering effort. A summary of attitude functions discussed in more detail below appears in Table 2.

- A **knowledge function** - helps people make sense of and negotiate the workplace, particularly when events are ambiguous or hard to forecast as in re-engineering;

- A **utility function** - guides behavior that is instrumental in achieving a desired goal (e.g., a secure job) or avoiding a negative outcome (e.g., obsolete skills);

- A **social-adjustment function** - helps people accommodate to new reference groups or to cement relationships with people who are important to them;

- An **ego-defense function** - allows people to avoid confronting weaknesses in themselves or aspects of the world that they fear or dislike;

- A **value-expression function** - functions as a mechanism by which people express their core values.

Table 2: Summary of Functions Attitudes Serve for the Individual in Corporate Reengineering (adapted from Perloff, 1993)

A Knowledge Function

Attitudes can function as knowledge structures that help people make sense of and negotiate their world. Such functions of attitudes are likely when people are confronted with ambiguous or unforecastable events which they try to understand. Corporate reengineering can be such an event. While the information stored in these structures is not necessarily objective or accurate, this attitude function might predominate in process team members and affected employees when old processes are being discarded and new ones are being considered, when these efforts encounter delays or setbacks, or when whole jobs are eliminated as a result of task aggregation and "bad things happen to good people." In short, an attitude is likely to serve as a repository of what the person knows or thinks he or she knows about reengineering and its consequences.

A Utility Function

Attitudes function as instruments by which people acquire rewards and avoid penalties. Individuals may adopt a positive attitude toward an unattractive, difficult or complex task (e.g., serve as a process owner for sales and fulfillment) that when accomplished will provide something that the individual desires (e.g., reduced costs and increased customer and employee satisfaction for an area that one manages, greater job security). In adopting a positive attitude, the individual is able to approach the task in a more enthusiastic or optimistic way and do the work that must be done. The individual's attitude can guide behavior, and that behavior can move the individual closer to the desired goal (e.g., reducing costs and increasing satisfaction).

A Social-Adjustment Function

Attitudes function to help people adjust to new reference groups or to solidify relationships with people who are important to them (e.g., management, fellow employees, family, friends). Although attitude consistency would seem logical and maybe even rational, such consistency is not a requirement when attitudes function to help the person adjust socially. The attitude that an individual projects to two different groups may be inconsistent. For example, a manager may express a negative attitude about reengineering to his or her staff or cohorts but a positive one to superiors or lower level employees.

An Ego-Defense Function

Attitudes can function to allow people to hide from weaknesses in themselves or aspects of the world that they do not like or that they fear. For example, individuals can adopt attitudes of superiority or arrogance which paradoxically may be rooted in feelings of inferiority. Individuals may devalue technology because they feel controlled by rather than in control of such systems. Similarly, managers can evaluate their contributions to be more significant than they really are or than the contributions of hourly workers, older employees, people of color, or individuals without college degrees. Such behavior can stem from fear, problems with self esteem or some other deep-seated personality attribute. When reengineering tampers with a job that has made an individual's career or a skill that defines the individual in a personal way, the surfacing of attitudes that serve an ego-defense function are possible and indeed probable.

A Value-Expression Function

Attitudes are mechanisms by which people express their core values. For example, some assembly line employees may adopt negative attitudes about reengineering because they do not want decision-making responsibility to become a part of their jobs. They may draw a distinction between physical and cognitive labor, believing that managers are paid to make decisions and assume responsibility. An employee may want a job that although physically demanding allows time to think his or her own thoughts (e.g., the best place to fish after work, the layout of a garden, the details of a daughter's wedding, where the family will vacation, the impending birth of a grandchild). Such a view may express a central value that the job is not where this employee wants to self actualize, and that he or she feels that the firm pays for physical labor but not for private thoughts.

Models of Persuasion

Beyond identifying an attitude's function, to be an effective change agent one must understand how attitudes can be influenced to become consistent with organizational objectives. In some ways, we can think of the design of persuasive strategies as analogous to the construction of a sentence. Nouns (attitude functions) and verbs (models or theories of persuasion) are combined in special ways to form sentences (influence strategies). In this section, we discuss models of persuasion.

There are a number of (theory-based) views of how individuals form attitudes about their world and then change them. Among them are cognitive dissonance theory (Festinger, 1957), information integration models (Fishbein, 1967a, 1967b; Anderson, 1971), the theory of reasoned action (Ajzen & Fishbein, 1975), social judgment theory (Sherif & Hovland, 1961), the elaboration likelihood (ELM) model (Petty & Cacioppo, 1986), and the appropriateness-consistency-effectiveness (ACE) Model (Reardon, 1981, 1987, 1991). Not all of these theories are easy to apply in practice. From among the list, we have selected two models that are more easily applied to real-world contexts of reengineering. The two models are the ELM and the ACE models. The ELM is a model of how persuasive messages are processed, whereas ACE is a model of what messages are likely to be persuasive. Readers interested in the theories listed previously but not described below are urged to consult the (classic) references cited.

The Elaboration Likelihood Model (ELM)

ELM is a basic framework for understanding the effectiveness of exposures to persuasive communications. It assumes that an employee is motivated to hold attitudes that are "correct" in some subjective sense (i.e., "beneficial for the physical or psychological well-being of the person," Petty & Cacioppo, 1986, p. 6). The model is based on the notion that under some conditions, an employee will vary the extent to which he or she is likely to engage in issue-relevant thinking ("elaboration") about a persuasive message. When the employee is both motivated and has the ability to process issue-relevant arguments, elaboration likelihood is said to be high. When elaboration likelihood is high, the employee typically allocates considerable cognitive resources to activities such as attending to the message, recalling message-relevant information from memory or locating it in external sources, scrutinizing and elaborating upon the arguments embodied in the message, making inferences about the validity of the arguments, and finally forming an attitude (evaluation) toward the position advocated in the message. This effortful processing is associated with the "central route" to persuasion and attitude changes that are likely to: (1) to persist over time, (2) to reflect actual behavior, and (3) to be resistant to counterpersuasion. On the other hand, when an employee lacks motivation to expend much cognitive energy processing a persuasive message or is incapable of processing the message because of distractions or lack of critical knowledge, then elaboration likelihood is low and peripheral cues (e.g., attractiveness of the person conveying the message) become more relevant as determinants of persuasion. Persuasive messages processed via this "peripheral route" are likely to result in attitude changes that are short lived, unrelated to actual behaviors, and highly susceptible to counterattitudinal messages.

The model assumes that the amount and nature of issue elaboration and scrutiny in which people can or are willing to engage varies as a function of factors associated with the individual and the situation. These factors include the employee's involvement with the issue, multiple message sources who represent multiple or diverse views on the issue, and the individual's need for cognition (O'Keefe, 1990). For example, as reengineering topics become more personally relevant to an individual, his or her motivation for thoughtful consideration of the pro and con arguments related to reengineering increases. Similarly, multiple sources of information about reengineering representing different arguments increase issue elaboration and scrutiny. Hence, if one wishes to increase thoughtful consideration of reengineering issues, then one should invite to the discussion two or three employees with differing views. Such a tactic is consistent with the suggestion that process teams consist of "insiders" and "outsiders" to bring about better process designs (see Hammer & Champy, 1993). On the other hand, it is dangerous to engage confederates in a "set up." If argument sources are perceived as having collaborated or as representing the same view, issue elaboration and scrutiny are reduced. Finally, employees can have varying needs for cognition. Those with low needs for cognition tend to be more influenced by peripheral cues than those with high needs for cognition. Conversely, employees with high needs for cognition are more influenced by the quality of the arguments than people with low needs for cognition.

Factors such as prior knowledge about a topic can influence an employee's ability to engage in issue elaboration or argument scrutiny. Hence, the more one knows about a topic, the more he or she is able to elaborate on the issues, the greater the influence argument strength will have on persuasion and the less influential peripheral cues will become. As might be expected, an employee with extensive prior knowledge opposing (favoring) reengineering can generate better arguments against (favoring) it and, compared to employees with less knowledge, is less likely to be persuaded by those favoring (opposing) it. However, employees with extensive prior knowledge opposing (supporting) reengineering are more likely to be persuaded by the strength (i.e., quality) of arguments favoring (opposing) reengineering (as compared to those with less knowledge). Managers should assess both the level of knowledge employees have about the general topic of reengineering and their current attitudes about it. Depending on the extent of knowledge and the nature of attitudes (e.g., favorable or unfavorable), various influence strategies may be required to gain compliance with requests made as a result of process redesign.

Central routes to persuasion. When the likelihood of elaboration is high, then the degree to which the employee is persuaded to adopt the communicator's position will be determined by the predominant attitude direction (supportive or nonsupportive) held by employee who is the target of the persuasive message. If thoughts about the message are mostly favorable, then the target employee is likely to be persuaded. If they are mostly negative, then it is not likely that the individual's mind will be changed by the persuasive message. So, the critical question is what influences the direction of elaboration?

Two factors seem to influence the valence of elaboration: proattitudinal versus counterattitudinal messages and message strength. The term "proattitudinal" means that the message being advocated by a communicator (reengineering will help the company lower costs) is similar to the position already held by the individual who is the target of the message (reengineering is a good idea). Conversely, "counterattitudinal" indicates that the message advocated by the communicator (reengineering will reduce the bureaucracy by eliminating management layers) is not one that the employee who is the target of the message is inclined to support (reengineering is not a good idea). When the message advocates a proattitudinal position, the employee will tend to be favorable toward the position advocated by the communicator. In contrast, when the message advocated by the communicator is counterattitudinal, the target of the message will tend not to support the position advocated. Clearly, no one would ever be persuaded if this were always true. The fact that people are persuaded suggests that something else must be involved — that something else is the strength or quality of argumentation. ELM argues that when an individual is involved in the issue and elaboration likelihood is high, the quality of the message's arguments will influence the direction of the elaboration and the persuasiveness of the message. Unfortunately, the research does not indicate how to construct strong arguments, which is the motivation for reviewing the ACE model.

Peripheral routes to persuasion. According to ELM, when employees exhibit low levels of elaboration, persuasion will not be the result of scrutiny of arguments but will instead depend on the application of simple heuristics. These heuristics are triggered by peripheral cues or surface features of the communication situations such as the perceived credibility of the communicator, how well the receiver likes the communicator, the attractiveness of the communicator, and the reactions of other people (O'Keefe, 1990). In general, the lower the employee's involvement in issue elaboration, the more likely he or shee will be persuaded by a communicator who appears credible and likeable and will exhibit a position similar to one that is supported by others.

Appropriateness-Consistency-Effectiveness (ACE) Model

The attractiveness of the ACE model for use in applied settings is its simplicity. ACE assumes that when employees are motivated and able to reason they evaluate the persuasive message according to three criteria: message appropriateness, message consistency, and message effectiveness. Appropriateness is the degree to which the issue is sanctioned by important others or whether it is reasonable according to some set of rules or laws operative in such a situation or in a similar situation. An appropriateness appeal in the reengineering context might be, "Every firm in our industry is looking for opportunities to simplify processes. If we don't re-engineer, managers and hourly workers alike are likely to be out of jobs — and looking for jobs at the firms that took reengineering seriously." Consistency is the degree to which a persuasive message advocates something that an employee believes a person with a similar background to himself or herself would do or think or is similar to something that he or she has done or thought in the past. A consistency appeal in the reengineering context might be, "Crystal, you are a person who is open to new ideas but who is not fooled by fads. You would be an excellent person to serve as a member of the process team responsible for reengineering the new product development process." Effectiveness refers to the degree to which the idea or action advocated leads to something that the person wants. An effectiveness appeal related to reengineering might be, "If we re-organize ourselves as self-managed teams, then we will have more control over how the work is done." Reardon has identified several situations in which people are likely to be influenced by specific appeal types. People who are sensitive to peer pressure (e.g., high self monitors) and are in a public forum are likely to be persuaded using appropriateness and consistency appeals. In situations that are highly formal or where authority lines are clearly articulated, even non-conformists are likely to be persuaded by appropriateness and consistency appeals. Otherwise, effectiveness appeals are likely to work best with non-conformists. In essence the effective persuader must determine which of these appeals carries the most weight for the individual who is the target of the appeal, since it is likely that appeals may lead to conflicting positions. Given knowledge of the situation, the ACE model provides a simple way to categorize persuasive appeals in ways that can be used to determine which appeals are likely to succeed.

Influence Strategies

Mechanisms for bringing about change in individuals and for gaining compliance can be categorized as interpersonal or mediated. Although each of these general approaches is discussed, emphasis is placed on interpersonal strategies, which we believe will be the strategies used most extensively by re-engineers.

Interpersonal Strategies

Cialdini (1993) has articulated several strategies of influence which can be used in situations where individuals publicly or privately resist business process re-design. These strategies can be used in gaining initial compliance by individuals to requests triggered by reengineering. The influence strategies include reciprocity, consistency, social proof, liking, authority, and scarcity. While these six strategies vary in terms of their social acceptance, all are known to be effective in persuading individuals to comply with requests. The descriptions provided here are of necessity brief, and the reader is encouraged to consult Cialdini (1993) for a more complete treatment.

Reciprocity. The norm of reciprocity is perhaps the most powerful and broadly accepted of the basic norms shared by humans. We learn the reciprocity rule as children and are sanctioned by society to the extent that we violate it. Briefly, reciprocity involves giving a favor or token to someone with the cultural expectation that it will be returned. Such future obligation facilitates long-term relationships that are extremely functional for individuals, organizations, and society. The reciprocity rule can be successfully applied to gain the cooperation of a co-worker when he or she is asked to participate in process re-design. The power of the rule is substantial because: (1) it has been shown to supersede other rules that typically determine compliance; (2) even an unwanted favor (e.g., a sample taste of sausage at the grocery store) can influence a person to comply (buy the sausage even though they don't like sausage); and (3) to rid themselves of favor-induced indebtedness, people will often give substantially more than they get just to transfer the debt to the other person. What is perhaps most applicable to the reengineering context is that people can get other people to reciprocate concessions much in the same way that they reciprocate favors. A well used technique called rejection-then-retreat involves making a major request first which is rejected, and then a smaller one which is accepted. This smaller request looks like a concession (i.e., a gift) from the requester, and so the other person feels obligated to honor this smaller request. People on whom this technique is used experience increased likelihood of compliance and will agree to comply with requests beyond that being currently made. This technique can be socially beneficial to both individuals and organizations.

Commitment and consistency. People are motivated to appear consistent in what they say and what they do. Aside from the value that society places on consistency, it reduces the amount of information processing required when similar situations are encountered. Using the commitment-and-consistency rule to gain cooperation in process redesign, the re-engineer might try to get an individual to assume a position or make a commitment that is consistent with the behavior that the reengineer will later request of the individual. For example, the reengineer might ask, "Do you think that we could simplify this process a bit?" If the individual responds, "yes," then the re-engineer might ask if the employee would be willing to help out. Commitments that are public, effortful, and uncoerced are much more effective at gaining cooperation in the future than those that are private, superficial, or coerced.

Social proof. People often look to the behaviors of others in deciding whether to comply with requests. Such behavior has been observed across all age groups and many different activities. A typical strategy is to tell a person that prestigious others have already complied with the request that is about to be asked of them. The strategy of social proof can be applied most effectively beginning with the selection of the first process to be re-designed. People in this group are likely to serve as the social proof for others. A wise choice would involve people who are generally positive about reengineering. The members of this initial group can serve as social proof for subsequent and perhaps less positive groups. In situations that are uncertain or ambiguous, people tend to follow the actions of others and to evaluate them as being correct. When people consider themselves to be very similar to others, they also tend to use social proof to decide if they will cooperate.

Liking. Liking a person tends to increase compliance with that person's requests. Hence, it is best to put individuals who are well liked in positions responsible for directing and leading process redesign efforts. When people are similar to us, praise us, or have repeated interaction with us in positive circumstances, we tend to like them and to comply with their requests. Often this liking produces a desire to associate with the object of liking and an increased likelihood of cooperation with their requests.

Authority. Socialization teaches us to comply with the requests of true authorities. Such compliance is beneficial when authorities have knowledge that can aid us. On the other hand, research has demonstrated that normal people often accept the dictates of authority blindly. According to Cialdini, people who follow authority blindly often do so in response to the trappings of authority such as titles, clothing and, interestingly, the cars that they drive. Furthermore, they are influenced by these surface elements far more than they estimate that they are. Perhaps the most significant element of these findings is that organizations themselves may have conditioned people to respond to the trappings of authority rather than to genuine authority. As a result it may be difficult for those responsible for process redesign (authorities) to distinguish when people are committed to the project and when they are merely acquiescing.

Scarcity. When opportunities, information, time, or things are scarce, we tend to value them more. Deadlines or limits are often signals that the scarcity principle is likely to be in operation. With regard to information, researchers have found that when information access is limited, this stimulates individuals to want it more and to become more positive about its message. A way in which scarcity might be used to gain compliance is by requiring a sign-up (because of legitimate reasons such as limited seating) for presentations on process redesign. Limiting access by requiring sign-up not only facilitates planning, but it also may serve to increase demand and generate a positive evaluation of the process-redesign message.

Mediated Strategies

Most influence strategies related to process redesign are likely to be interpersonal. Nevertheless, some information about business process reengineering is likely to be presented using media such as newsletters, bulletin boards (electronic and otherwise), flyers, computers, kiosks, and maybe even radio or television. According to a summary by Perloff (1993), mediated informational campaigns are likely to succeed (i.e., persuade or result in cooperation) when they (1) are consistent with the messages of other institutional sources (e.g., trade and professional associations, government agencies), (2) do not require the creation of a new attitude that is in conflict with old ones but rather simply require re-directing an existing attitude in a slightly different direction (e.g., attitudes associated with TQM might be re-directed toward reengineering), (3) reinforce messages that are also communicated using other media (i.e., use multiple media to "sell" reengineering), (4) create new opinions rather than change existing ones (i.e., get to people before they have formed opinions), and (5) connect with the individual's needs and values (e.g., the American worker builds quality products). Other tactics that are important and have possible application to informational campaigns related to business process redesign include using a trustworthy communicator, focusing arguments on salient beliefs, promoting self-efficacy, engaging the person's mind, and targeting messages strategically, based on issue involvement (i.e., low issue-involvement people respond to emotional messages, whereas high issue-involvement people respond to rational ones).

Implications for Management

Reengineering can be frightening to people at all levels of an organization. It is not the prospect of a redesigned process per se that frightens people, but rather it is the likelihood that reengineering will redesign their jobs, their lives, and their sense of worth that is scary.

When processes change, jobs change, relationships to others change, and a person's value to himself, his family and his peers may change for better or worse. American management has not traditionally involved employees in major decisions. The concept of "management rights" is well established in corporate governance within the United States. Hence, concepts such as "empowerment" and all that it implies are difficult to grasp and believe, given the historical relationship between labor and management in this country. In earlier times, middle management typically identified strongly with the goals of upper management. Recent efforts to make organizations "lean and mean" have probably changed the attitudes of at least some middle managers. Those who were purged may identify more with the hourly worker than with upper management. Those who remain may suffer their own pain, as survivors often do. Hence, anyone contemplating leading or participating in corporate reengineering efforts must manage both organizational and individual change processes. Firms must persuade employees at all levels that reengineering is not another management fad but has the potential for ensuring the firm and its employees a place in the global economy. To be credible, firms and their managements must honestly represent the objectives of reengineering and the likely positive and negative consequences for employees. Persuasive campaigns must address two issues: a lack of knowledge about reengineering and a lack of trust. Without knowledge, people fear; without trust, people withhold their best efforts.

The notion of managing attitudes and gaining cooperation might conjure up images of manipulation or coercion. Any effort by management to be dishonest, to conceal, to coerce or force people to do something against their will or better judgment cannot succeed for very long. The models and strategies advocated in this chapter are based on assumptions of free choice and ethical management. The models and strategies assume individuals are motivated and have the cognitive means to consider the merits of the positions advocated in the persuasive message—in the instant case, the merits of reengineering. This puts the manager or re-engineer in a somewhat new and perhaps awkward position of influencing without authority and being open with people whose jobs will be changed by the reengineering efforts. Most of us did not study these indirect methods of influence in business school. Unfortunately, authoritarian strategies do not work very well in modern organizations. As any parent will confess, neither do they work with today's teenagers who are tomorrow's employees. The problems facing firms today require radical new management approaches. The chapter has argued that it is important for managers to understand the role attitudes play in successful reengineering efforts. We acknowledge that in some cases it may be necessary to assume a more active role in managing

- Review management's historical relationship with employee groups who are the targets of re-engineering;

  If the relationship is negative, resolve the points of conflict and distrust. DO NOT proceed with re-engineering until these issues are resolved.

  Proceed if the relationship is generally positive.

- Assess employees' level of re-engineering knowledge and their attitudes toward it (i.e., favorable, neutral, unfavorable);

  If critical knowledge is lacking, provide background to employees;

  If attitudes are favorable, proceed with re-engineering and continuously monitor attitudes. Respond accordingly (see below);

  If attitudes are unfavorable or neutral, determine if the re-engineering effort is "personally relevant" to the employees (i.e., Who is likely to engage in issue-relevant thinking about the re-engineering and who is not?);

    If relevance is high, then appeal to elements central to the argument (argument strength and quality). Use multiple communicators with somewhat divergent perspectives;

    If relevance is low, appeal to elements peripheral to the argument (attractiveness, credibility, or likability of the communicator);

- Continuously monitor attitudes.

Table 3: Guidelines for Managing Attitudes in Re-engineering Efforts

attitudes during process re-design. Table 3 summarizes the basics of the approach suggested in this chapter.

Social influence and compliance gaining is a reciprocal activity. While we have focused primarily on influencing those who are the objects of process redesign efforts, such "objects" should and do influence the leaders of business process redesign. As Reardon notes, persuasion is done with people, not to them (1990).

At the organizational level, there is a great deal of emphasis in the management literature on "impression management." For a short time, a firm may succeed in managing impressions that are not generally consistent with the facts. The same can be said for attitudes. The attitudes that people are being urged to adopt and the requests with which they are asked to comply must ultimately be supported by the facts surrounding process redesign. Management attempts to persuade people to adopt attitude positions that do not reflect reality, though possible in the short run, are not sustainable in the long run. Today's manager must possess the skill set to bring about voluntary change in individuals through persuasion and influence rather than through the traditional management tools of authority and formal power. This chapter provides a glimpse into why this is essential in business process reengineering, what is required, and some ways to accomplish it.

References

Ajzen, I. (1989). Attitude structure and behavior. In A.R. Pratkanis, S.T. Breckler, and A.G. Greenwald (Eds.), *Attitude structure and function* (pp. 241-274). Hillsdale, NJ: Erlbaum.

Ajzen, I. & Fishbein, M. (1975). *Understanding attitudes and predicting social behavior*, Englewood Cliffs, NJ: Prentice-Hall.

Anderson, N.H. (1971). Integration theory and attitude change. *Psychological Review*, 78, 171-206.

Byrne, J.A. (1993, December 20). Horizontal organizations: It's about managing across, not up and down, *Business Week*, pp. 76-81.

Byrne, J.A. (1994, May 9). The pain of downsizing: What it's really like to live through the struggle to remake a company. *Business Week*, pp. 60-69.

Christiansen, D. (1992, October). Spectral lines: Challenges to management. *IEEE Spectrum*, pp. 21.

Cialdini, R.B. (1993). *Influence: Science and practice* (3rd edition), New York, NY: HarperCollins

Festinger, L. (1957). *The theory of cognitive dissonance*. Stanford, CA: Stanford University Press.

Fishbein, M. (1967a). A behavioral theory approach to the relations between beliefs about an object and the attitude toward the object. In M. Fishbein (Ed.), *Readings in attitude theory and measurement* (pp. 389-400). New York: Wiley.

Fishbein, M. (1967b). A consideration of beliefs, and their role in attitude measurement. In M. Fishbein (Ed.), *Readings in attitude theory and measurement* (pp. 257-266). New York: Wiley.

Hammer, M. (1990, July-August). Reengineering work: Don't automate, obliterate. *Harvard Business Review*, pp. 104-112.

Hammer, M. & Champy, J. (1993). *Reengineering the corporation: A manifesto for business revolution*. New York City, NY: HarperCollins.

Maglitta, J. (1994, January 24). In depth: One on one — Michael Hammer, *ComputerWorld*, pp. 84-86.

McGuire, W.J. (1969). The nature of attitudes and attitude change. In G. Lindzey and E. Aronson (Eds.), *The handbook of social psychology* (pp. 136-314), 2nd ed., Vol. 3. Reading, MA: Addison-Wesley.

Melone, N.P. (1990). A theoretical assessment of the user-satisfaction construct in information systems research, *Management Science*, 36:1, 76-91.

O'Keefe, D.J. (1990). *Persuasion: Theory and research*. Newbury Park, CA: Sage.

Perloff, R.M. (1993). *The dynamics of persuasion.* Hillsdale, NJ: Erlbaum.

Petty, R.E. & Cacioppo, J.T. (1986). *Communication and persuasion: Central and peripheral routes to attitude change* (Springer Series in Social Psychology), New York City, NY: Springer-Verlag.

Pratkanis, A.R. (1988). The cognitive representation of attitudes. In A.R. Pratkanis, S.T. Breckler, and A.G. Greenwald (Eds.), *Attitude structure and function* (pp. 71-98). Hillsdale, NJ: Erlbaum.

Pratkanis, A.R. & Greenwald, A.G. (1989). A socio-cognitive model of attitude structure and function. In L. Berkowitz (Ed.), *Advances in experimental social psychology, 22.* New York City, NY: Academic Press.

Reardon, K.K. (1981). *Persuasion: Theory and context.* Beverly Hills, CA: Sage.

Reardon, K.K. (1987). *Interpersonal communication: Where minds meet.* Belmont, CA: Wadsworth.

Reardon, K.K. (1991). *Persuasion in practice.* Newbury Park, CA: Sage.

Sherif, M. & Hovland, C.I. (1961). *Social judgment: Assimilation and contrast effects in communication and attitude change.* New Haven, CT: Yale University Press.

Chapter 19

Business Process Reengineering, Politics and Management:
From Methodologies to Processes

Gill Smith
Olm Systems

Leslie Willcocks
Templeton College

Business Process Reengineering (BPR) is being widely adopted by organizations in the 1990s, though a variety of different terms are in use to describe BPR activities, including for example process innovation (Davenport, 1993), business process redesign (Short and Venkatraman, 1992), business reengineering (Spurr et al, 1993) and combinations of such terms. In The United States a 1993 Deloitte and Touche survey found the average Chief Information Officer involved in 4.4 reengineering projects (Moad, 1993). In the United Kingdom a 1992 survey of Times Top 100 companies found nearly two-thirds claiming to have adopted process innovation (Haughton, 1992). Such figures probably reflect survey weighting towards big corporations. For example a more random-based British survey found only 27% of all respondents were undergoing or had completed BPR programmes, but almost all with BPR activity were large companies (Preece and Edwards 1993). However, all surveys showed increasing BPR activity into 1994, reflected also in the size of fees collected by various management consultancy firms. As one example, William Stoddard of Andersen Consulting estimated his firm's worldwide income from BPR as some $700 million in 1992/3 (Thackray, 1993).

However what bears analysis is why, despite a veritable growth industry in advice and prescription, BPR so often fails to live up to expectations. Famously, Hammer and Champy (1993) estimated a 50-70% failure rate for reengineering. If this reflects their own focus on radical breakthrough, and therefore high risk projects, nevertheless other surveys show reengineering projects consistently falling short of their expected benefits. As one example only, a 1993 North American survey showed significant corporate disappointment on BPR projects whether objectives related to improvements in customer service, process timeliness, quality, reduced cost, competitiveness, new/improved technology, or sales/revenue impacts (Moad, 1993).

In this chapter we look to investigate empirically, through case studies, why BPR activities can so often disappoint, and what learning points there might be for conducting BPR activities more effectively. We will find that the difficulties stem both from what is new, but also what is not so new, about business process reengineering. Briefly, the focus on process makes reengineering multidisciplinary and cross-functional and implies cultural change; the focus on transforming performance leads to radical, and so high risk approaches to transforming the organization often being adopted; and the concern for IT-enabled or IT-driven BPR brings in a technology dimension that always add further risk of failure to any major project (Stringer, 1992; Willcocks and Griffith, 1995). What is not new about BPR is that it necessarily involves change management across a number of functions and across time periods of two to four years. While the recipes for success for managing change are well rehearsed in the literature, it is also the case that the human and organizational, including political and cultural issues in change are frequently underplayed, even neglected, in practice especially where Information Technology (IT) is heavily implicated in the change process, as in the four cases investigated below. All too often budgetary and time constraints, together with a concern for technical issues lead to a focus away from the softer, behavioural factors that are in fact often strong determinants of long-term success or failure (Walton, 1989; Willcocks and Mason, 1987).

We argue that this is precisely the major trip-wire experienced in BPR, including in the case studies we detail below. To pursue this theme the chapter first assesses the many different approaches to operationalising BPR. We then present four researched case studies set in the aerospace electronics industry, a specialised industrial products manufacturer, a pharmaceuticals multinational and a health care organization. Through these we investigate the complexities, difficulties and successes experienced by participants when attempting to make BPR work. The findings from the case studies are then reviewed and summarised, from which ways forward on BPR are developed and detailed. One major conclusion is that politics breed in times of BPR, and unless the political dimensions are managed explicitly, what BPR activities produce will continue to disappoint many stakeholder expectations and objectives, not least those of senior management.

Reviewing BPR: Concepts, Issues and Research

For the purposes of this chapter, BPR can be described as a means of facilitating significant, even fundamental, change in the way an organization operates. A key element is a focus on process, usefully defined by Davenport (1993) as a structured, measured set of activities designed to produce a specified output for a particular customer or market. The BPR activity described in the literature varies in the scale and type of change contemplated (Jones, 1994). A useful distinction for our purposes can be made between process improvement - an incremental, bottom-up, narrow change to an existing process achieved within a function over a short time period, and process innovation a radical, clean slate, top-down, broad, cross-functional change in how an organization operates (Davenport, 1993).

This dichotomy can be further developed into a typology that represents increasing radicalism, moving from single process redesign, through multiple process redesign, single major business model change to multiple integrated business model changes, including developing business network processes extending into customers, suppliers and strategic allies (Heygate, 1993; Short and Venkatraman, 1992). The type of process being reengineered can also be classified into core (central to business functioning and relating directly to external customers); support (the back-office of core processes); business network (those extending beyond organizational boundaries); and management (those by which firms plan, organize and control resources) - see Earl and Khan (1993). Of the case studies detailed below three represent single or multiple process redesign, while the fourth involves a major business model change with elements of developing business network processes. The case studies also focus variously on the different types of processes identified above.

Central to BPR practice is a holistic approach to strategy, structure, process, people and technology. Hence, despite the origins of the term in commercial and academic circles promoting or focusing on IT-based BPR, the "ownership" of BPR is held by a wide

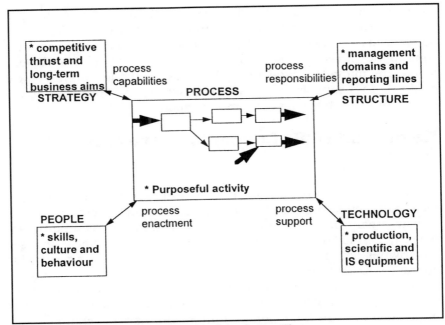

Figure 1: Central Role of Process in Stimulating Change

community of business disciplines. Whereas there is evidence that IT can act as an "agent of change" (Hammer, 1990; Keen, 1991), there is also a case for framing the issues in a wider "systems view" (Beer, 1975), for considering why people get stuck in out-dated management practices (Goldratt and Cox, 1989) and for analysing corporate culture (Kanter, 1989). Figure 1 represents a theoretical framework to indicate the multidisciplinary approach and the central role of process thinking in transforming organizations through BPR.

Emerging Issues

However, a prime question raised by the multidisciplinary holism at the heart of BPR study and practice, is whether there are robust methodologies and tools available to facilitate the outcomes required from BPR activities. Many consultants and their companies have developed and promote their own methodologies, as represented for example by Barrett, (1994); Davenport and Short, (1990); Hammer and Champy, 1993; and Klein (1994). There is a large literature on methodologies for developing the enabling role of IT in BPR (see for example Couger, Flynn and Hellyer, 1994; Davenport, 1993; I/S Analyzer, 1993; Spurr et al., 1993). Methodologies and tools are recommended from diverse business disciplines such as industrial engineering (Davenport and Short, 1990; Watts, 1993), software development (Born, 1993; Farhoodi, 1993), operational research and systems analysis (Morris and Brandon, 1993; Wang, 1994)), organizational behaviour and change management (Belmonte and Murray, 1993; Buday, 1992; Earl and Khan, 1994), and the quality movement (Harrington, 1991; Johannson et al., 1993). The conclusion must be that there are many approaches, methodologies and tools more or less useful, but that bringing together the offerings from such diverse fields has so far proved difficult, and adds up to an immaturity and a lack of integratedness on the methodological front (Earl and Khan, 1994; Klein, 1994).

This can have several significant ramifications that then feed into less than successful BPR activity. One relates to methods-driven approaches generally, whether adopted for business planning, Information Systems (IS) strategy formulation and implementation or for BPR planning and activities. A range of commentators point to the rigour and structure that methods can bring, but also to a number of downsides relative to other approaches (see for example Earl, 1993; Mintzberg, 1994; Peters, 1987). The structured approach must be continuously related to business objectives, but goals can become easily displaced into serving the method, the mistaken assumption being that in itself this will engender an overall success-ful outcome. Often the adoption of methods, together with external consultants is a sign of an immaturity in the organization's ability to manage change projects. Instead of developing more exploratory, learning-based approaches to develop capability, managements may delegate responsibility; once again methods, driven by external stakeholders, can become self-justificatory ends in themselves. Methods-driven approaches can also encourage inflexibility and one-off, "initiative" approaches, and push out the learning and incrementalism and attention to social and political processes identified as vital where new and radical change is being undertaken (Craig and Yetton, 1994; Davenport and Stoddard, 1994).

Secondly, the methodologies adopted are often partial, and handle some aspects of what should be a holistic approach better than others. There are dangers in managing BPR from predomi-nantly Information Engineering, Systems Analysis, or Behaviourist conceptual and methodological positions, for example. Such partial approaches are not least the case where IT is heavily implicated in BPR, as in the case histories we will examine below. Frequently IT-based change activities have utilised methodologies that focus on information flows and processes, and are based on systems analysis techniques, but in such a way as to marginalize human, social and political processes and issues (Clegg et al. 1994; Mason and Willcocks, 1994; Walsham, 1993) . Such predilections often flow into how the increasing number of IT-enabled, or IT-driven BPR projects are handled. Indeed, what emerges from the BPR literature itself is the frequency with which failure is related, amongst other reasons, to mismanagement of human, social and political issues and processes (for examples only see Belmonte and Murray, 1993; Moad, 1993; Thackray, 1993).

We have already suggested ways in which such neglect can occur. However, given our theme, it is worth pointing out that such predilections are encouraged by several seminal—and influential—works on BPR, not least those of Hammer (1990) and Hammer and Champy (1993). Putting aside the persuasive rhetoric and the cultural and symbolic resonances ably analysed by Grint (1993) and Jones, (1994), Hammer and Champy in fact promote a hard approach to managing the complex, softer issues necessarily inherent in BPR activities. It is not that the softer issues are ignored. However there is a violence inherent in the approach— "On this journey we.... shoot the dissenters" (Mike Hammer, quoted in *Forbes* magazine, Summer, 1993, p. 71) - that can be dysfunctional. Moreover, as Strassmann (1993) points out, this violence derives from an essentially mechanistic, almost 17th. century view of how organizations function and can be changed; if the clock is broken, replace it with a new one. In this respect the use of the word reengineering in their work is not accidental, but symptomatic of a world view that rides over a number of concepts commonly associated with BPR such as empowerment, teamwork, participation, and long-term commitment, and the complexities inherent in managing continuity and change.

Other authors have already suggested more revisionist approaches to the all-or-nothing philosophy. Thus Heygate (1993) suggests that a feature of successful redesign programs is focus - that is moderation in the selection of activities and processes to redesign, but immoderate ambition about improving those selected. Davenport (1993b) and Davenport and Stoddard (1994) also point to a revisionist alternative that allows reengineering and quality to exist in tandem, applying the radical approach only where it is absolutely necessary, and being happy with ten percent improvements elsewhere. Davenport (1993b) also suggests that such an approach is the only way to employ the reengineering concept and preserve employee loyalty and commitment, and to successfully enlist employee ideas for better processes.

Research Methodology

These issues will be further investigated through the four case studies detailed below. In themselves the cases do not represent testimonials to the success of BPR in general, or of particular methods and techniques. Nor do they claim quantum leaps in improvement in productivity, service or quality. However they do represent academically researched cases that provide some counterpoint to the many under-researched cases found in the literature, all too often prematurely declared by interested stakeholders as examples of success.

All the cases chosen had a strong IT-enabling aspect to the BPR activity being investigated. This was partly to reflect, and enable the investigation of, the strong correlation posited in the literature between BPR 'newness'/ effectiveness and the development of appropriate information systems. This selection also enabled us to examine the degree to which IS can have a leadership role in BPR, and at what point this may need to be relinquished, as suggested for example by Davenport and Stoddard (1994). Thirdly it allowed us to investigate, in two cases at least, the degree to which BPR can develop out of ostensibly systems development projects, or may degenerate into systems development projects when there is a lack of senior management involvement, political opposition, or where IS professionals are left to deliver technology, not BPR.

The research adopted a range of qualitative techniques to investigate and construct the case histories. One element was regular participant observation in the events as they occurred. A second was semi-structured interviews, each of between one and one and a half hours in length, with stakeholders from different levels in the organization and with different roles in the BPR process being undertaken. The objective here was to achieve at least a triangulation of viewpoints on events as they developed. A third element was to focus on the process of change over periods ranging from one to three years, rather than take an aprocessual snapshot of events at a particular moment in time. A fourth element was to utilise detailed internal documentation available in the organizations studied in order to enrich the accounts and explanations arrived at. To avoid the ahistorical, aprocessual and contextual character of much research on organizational change (see Pettigrew, 1985; Willcocks, 1994), data gathering techniques were also focused on organizational history and context, as well as the content, process, and emergent outcomes of change.

From the research experiences and from reviewing the extensive literature on BPR and change management, we developed the following framework for analyzing events in the case histories. Outcomes seemed to relate to five significant factors:

- pressure to act
- locus of support
- levers for change (intervention points from which to initiate activity)
- themes (focal messages in the rhetoric of change)
- approach (types of technique, degree of participation)

For the purposes of this chapter general prescriptions and ways forward arising from the cases are discussed at the end of each case, and in a general discussion section at the end of the chapter.

Case A—An Aerospace Electronics Manufacturer

Background

This case is set in the 1991-93 period. The company was a multinational operating mainly in the United States and United Kingdom civil and defense aerospace industries. In 1991 turnover and profits were £431.3 million and £60.7 million respectively. As at 1991 market recession had hit the manufacturing division, but because customers were trying to prolong the active life of engine components and instrumentation, the repairs business was more or less holding its own. However, if the recession were to cause shrinkage in the airline industry, or if it stimulated operators to take more of their repair business in-house, then the effects would soon be felt. There were also worrying long-term trends. As components become more sophisticated, there are less of them and they last longer between failures. There is also a growing tendency in all industries to replace rather than repair electronic components. In practice the following two years saw worsening financial results, with reduced turnover and profit in both 1992 (£390m. and £48.5m), and 1993 (£393m. and £40.5m.).

During 1991, in the repairs division, two strategies were talked of at middle management level: diversification into other forms of repair, or building partnerships with the airlines, based on outsourcing their entire maintenance operation. These strategies were actively debated, both by those who termed themselves "old style" managers, who had been in the business most of their working lives, but were able to see that times had changed, and by "new style" managers, who were equally immersed in the avionics industry but had developed different ways of thinking, based on managerial challenges they had encountered.

Given their roles in subsequent BPR activity, some feel for middle management characteristics is useful. One had been an active shop steward and was seen as having defected to management. His confrontations with management issues in different roles were a formative influence, and he was particularly keen to show that his job change was beneficial to staff, by enabling him to champion their interests during the introduction of new technology. Another middle manager had recently completed an MBA, and though a quiet individual and somewhat marginalised in the hierarchy, he was seen as a resource for new ideas. Two other managers had been moved sideways from mainstream engineering jobs, one into reliability (which monitored and researched component defects) and one into the quality section. The Reliability department was fighting its corner, since it was widely perceived as a soft option, where people wrote a lot of reports and potentially caused trouble by ascribing faults to design or manufacturing (rather than customer usage). Quality personnel were involved in another fight: to bridge the gap between what the engineers did in repairing components and what the releasing officers did in certifying the work done against the original order. There were grey areas about working to order versus putting right everything that was wrong, and certification affected the warranty process and subsequent claims.

Despite the degree of interest in strategic and operational issues at middle management level, there appeared to be an almost total absence of debate higher up the organization. The Commercial Director (in charge of finance and order processing staff) and the Works Director (in charge of the repair workshops) were seen around the factory and talked to staff, but the talk was confined to day-to-day matters. The Managing Director was rarely seen and was widely held to be an indifferent communicator. Senior management were seen as somewhat paralysed by having to play the "numbers game" dictated by the holding company. Differences of opinion were assumed to exist. As one example, on one occasion the company had prepared a bid to run the repair operations of a major airline. However, the bid team had been recalled by a high level telephone call, as they sat in the customer's office preparing to make the presentation.

The division was split across sites in the United Kingdom and The United States, and these had different views of the repairs process due to their different customer bases, management styles and practices. On the whole, the US was regarded the more progressive, with clear ideas of how to improve customer service by changing processes and introducing Information Systems. However, the United Kingdom staff regarded them as mavericks; moreover funding was controlled from the United Kingdom.

At the time the project began, in 1992, there was therefore a mood of some anxiety and frustration at middle management level. The project was not particularly ambitious: the replacement of current order-processing systems. These were ageing, and had duplicate data entry, together with manual interfaces to financial systems and a mix of incompatible hardware. A new technical architecture was needed, which provided integrated operations and financial systems and promoted standard working practices in the North American and British divisions.

Reengineering The Repairs Division

The British IS department had spent two years investigating solutions before deciding to purchase a suite of financial systems, but also commission a bespoke repairs module that could be possibly be marketed to other avionics companies. The IS department had evaluated manufacturing packages, but the repairs business is complex in that units are taken in and worked on rather than being produced in a manufacturing process. There are also complications where a set of, say, ten units is stripped down to make good, say, five units. Part-tracking is difficult in this situation and is exacerbated where "rush" orders borrow parts from other work-in-progress or from a customer's private stock held on the premises.

Since this was a more ambitious project than previously attempted, and was seen as very visible in both The United States and the United Kingdom, as well as to the holding company, it was widely felt vital that it be seen to be managed professionally. The project was sponsored by the Commercial Director, who controlled the order processing staff. However he had little experience of IS, and deferred control to the British IS manager (the American IS group was very small, concerned mainly with end-user support).

The IS manager was essentially a technician who believed in a rational, positivist approach to systems development (though espousing no particular structured development methodology). He was most comfortable when solving specific problems (for example a project on the use of bar-coding to track units and components). However, he had available to him a self-styled hybrid manager who was doing an MBA and was interested in both IS methodologies and organizational development. This manager had worked for the company previously, left to become a salesman in an international engineering firm, and been promoted back by the Works Director. He was thus seen as having both wider experience and influence with management, as well as being a creative person, and his appointment as project manager was widely supported.

The project manager decided to involve management in the project through the formal structure of the PRINCE project management methodology, and to create user buy-in by fronting the project with a 30-day interactive survey of system requirements. For this, the IS supplier was asked to provide two staff to demonstrate the financial package, and two staff to create and demonstrate a prototype of the potential repairs system. Thirty in-house staff were co-opted onto the survey phases, with half-day workshops running throughout in which staff reviewed different functional areas and worked with different combinations of colleagues and people from other units. The project manager had produced a "business model", consisting of a series of entity-relationship (E-R) models for various functional areas, which he expected would guide the work and would be confirmed and/or amended in the form of a final business requirement specification.

The IS supplier was a major international vendor of technology, business applications and consultancy. Its staff were used to building systems using structured methodologies but were prepared to work interactively with users as long as the 30-day repairs prototype was seen only as an aid to specification. The two staff assigned to this work were a strategic analyst (to act as facilitator) and a technical analyst/designer (to build the prototype).

The project was launched with a presentation, during which the facilitator described how work processes could be studied in order to improve them and design possible IS support. It was apparent that people responded positively to various things that were said:

- the idea of a creative task: to challenge the status quo and come up with better ways to run the repair business
- the suggestion that IS had potential to be used in the repair shops, as an operational tool, rather than just in the office for processing orders
- the demonstration of prototyping tools as a means for users to try out ideas (obviating the need to hand power over to the IS department at the specification stage)

Encouraged by the positive responses, the facilitator led a series of sessions where users drew process charts, assessed current performance and areas for improvement, commented on how roles and procedures had evolved and imagined better ways of working. It was difficult to elicit process measures (e.g. order turnaround, stock turns, repair time, % rework, warranty claims) since people tended to only look at their own area or work. However, an Order Management process was defined, mapping the progress of a job through various stages where commercial, engineering, finance, technical, reliability and office staff all provided input. Opportunities to simplify, add value and agree working practices between the US and UK were also discussed.

During the course of the survey, it was found that not only was the project manager's E-R model unsuitable as the basis of a prototype, but it was restricted in its view of how elements of work could be integrated into a more meaningful process. The main problem was the functional bias common to structured methodologies, which isolates "do-able" items of development as the expense of the "big picture". An alternative documentation was therefore invented, which used process diagrams, backed by comments about the kind of capabilities which would assist more integrated methods of working. The pre-existing work flows and tracking points are shown in Figure 2.

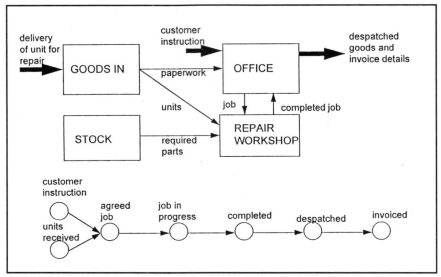

Figure 2: Case A Flows and Tracking

E-R models were re-drawn, but kept in the "technical" folder, since they were of little interest to most users. The project manager was disappointed that his business model had not been confirmed, and the IS manager was uncomfortable with the emphasis on describing a new working environment. He asked for a list of system functions which could form the basis of contractual negotiations with the supplier.

A series of final presentations were made to share the findings. The main recommendations were threefold. Firstly, empower the repair shops through IS, enabling them to see orders coming and plan accordingly, talk to the customer direct and make better use of engineering data. Secondly use IS to connect the four centres of activity (see Figure 2). Thirdly, use IS to track milestones in activity, and produce information feedback to stimulate improved performance. There was a mood of determination to tackle the challenges, exemplified by the remark of the Quality Manager: "There's no point in changing the systems if we don't change the organization as well". The final presentation was to the Managing Director, who listened to the arguments for change and agreed to place the project under the Works Director instead of the Commercial Director, because of the new emphasis on bringing the repair workshops into the "team" which serviced the customer. He remarked that he thought it would be difficult to implement. The facilitator then prepared a separate proposal for Change Management, in order to link the technical project with other activities such as further process analysis/ redesign, education and training.

This part of the project finished in June 1993. Thereafter, senior managers from the avionics company and the IS supplier spent several months in contractual negotiations. These were overseen by the Commercial Director. The Works Director made no attempt to take up his role on the project. The facilitator and the hybrid manager both left their respective organizations and the IS manager took charge of the project. Although work then started on the repairs module, it then proceeded to be built using a conventional structured methodology with little role for the users and little opportunity to develop the innovative approaches envisaged at the outset.

Analysis of Findings

The most positive aspects of the project were:

- the change levers (in this case the opportunity to use IT in the repair shops)
- the themes (challenging the status quo, streamlining the core processes, adding value to the customer),
- the approach (process analysis, prototypes).

In terms of the pressure to act, staff and middle managers were prepared to put their energies into determining a new direction. They were anxious about the recession, frustrated by the working environment, and resentful of the domination by the Commercial Director and finance staff. Even the office staff, (who might lose power when the repair shop had access to customer data), welcomed the opportunity to expand their roles away from form-filling and towards better customer service. The weak point was locus of support. The project was set up by the IT department, and though the user task force gained a substantial influence during the initial study, power transferred back to the Commercial Director during the protracted negotiations for the contract. Given that the IS department had already spent two years evaluating options, spirits were dampened by the further delay. The departure of the project manager and facilitator lessened the chance of recapturing the spirit of change.

A further factor affecting pressure to act and locus of support was the equivocal position of senior management, who seemed to be trapped in a defensive position by the holding company. Their reluctance to discuss strategy with their own middle managers was compounded by the apparent apathy with which they responded to the survey.

In summary, a promising start to the change initiative was hijacked by focusing on the need for a tighter specification (technical bias) and control of the contract (asserted by the Commercial Director). The IS manager was then able to revert to the technical project with which he felt more comfortable. Middle managers were likely to comply with this since the earlier attempts to be innovative had resulted in substantial delays and could offer little resistance to the managerial politics inherent in the situation. "Better something than nothing" was a resigned response to the delivery of systems by the IS department.

Case B—Specialised Industrial Products Manufacturer

Background

Despite the recessionary climate and rising competition, the company —a multinational —showed rising turnover and profits in the 1991-93 period, culminating in a 1993 profit of £21 million on sales of £152 million. In 1992, concerned to remain competitive, senior management in the manufacturing division identified that the bid process for major (2-5 years) contracts was a drain on time and resources. The bid process started whenever dialogue with the customer about a potential contract took place. However, the formal process was triggered by a request for a proposal. There were then only four weeks to get the bid out, of which two weeks were spent in pulling together the final version, and management clearance. This put pressure on engineering to get a technical specification out as quickly as possible, so that costing could review it in comparison with similar past projects, and request changes in the technical approach where component costs or cash flow were problematic. The process was complicated by other iterations, for example if the Reliability department rejected proposed designs or materials on safety criteria, or when Engineering revised the specification for their own reasons.

When asked about outcomes, managers said they could report on tenders won and lost, but were much less sure about efficiency and the quality of decision-making (whether they won the right contracts on the right terms and turned them into profitable business). As in case A, the IS department initiated a project. Rather than proposing a new system, they invited senior/middle managers from various units in the commercial and engineering parts of the division to a two-part workshop, for which they provided an outside facilitator. The IS manager emphasised the need to take a new look at the problem, and he and the facilitator discussed the potential of BPR to challenge assumptions and reframe the issues. The company was at that time struggling with a major bid, on which much of the next few years' work depended. The IS manager said he would not be able to attend the workshop due to prior commitments but would send a member of his staff.

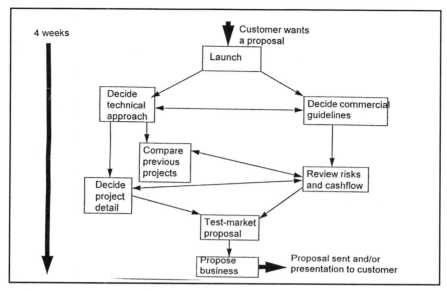

Figure 3 - Case B: The Bid Process

Reviewing The Bid Process: A No/Go Decision

In the first session of the workshop, a bid manager described the process (see Figure 3), and representatives of engineering, costing, reliability and manufacturing commented on their roles.

The facilitator asked how the commercial guidelines for the bid were set, how the merits of technical solutions were evaluated, how customer views on potential options were sought and how the final form of the bid was approved. There was some reluctance to talk about process in these terms, but it was stated that senior management "kept an eye on things" and that the bid manager facilitated teamwork by acting as a go-between for the various parties. It was rare for the senior management to spell out the commercial guidelines or for the team to meet formally. The technical specification and projected costs could go backwards and forwards several times (to accommodate any change in either of them); the bid was sometimes revised drastically at a late stage if management were not happy; and the project manager had to exercise considerable skill and effort in resolving issues.

At the second workshop, the facilitator fed back an analysis of the process (see Figure 4), and suggested that the key areas to address were better direction of the process and better group working. IT could be used to help in both areas, in the first by building up profiles of technical options from past contracts (with projected profits), and in the second by offering shared access to an

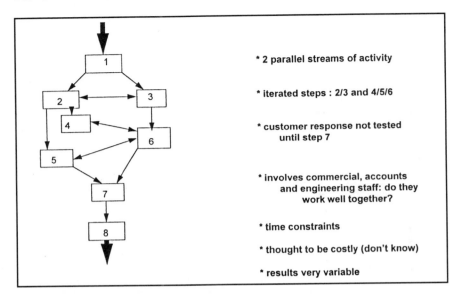

Figure 4 - Analysis of the Bid Process

electronic version of the bid, so everyone could see what changed. There was also the option to share the bid electronically with the company's customers, since they were increasingly interested in joint working on contracts.

The response was hostile. The managers said they did not have time to experiment with the process. Furthermore the big bid they were concerned about on the previous occasion had now been won and their attention had moved on. When pressed to describe what they had been expecting from the workshop, they seemed to want a proposal for a ready-made IS solution to their problems. Moreover, they felt that the type of system which they needed was not a process-oriented one, but perhaps a costing tool or something to rationalize the various databases of parts data (e.g. suppliers' parts listings, parts in stock, customers' parts codes and serial numbers).

At the end of the workshop, the facilitator and IS manager who had commissioned the work compared notes. It was disappointing that the managers felt unable or unwilling to adopt a diagnostic approach to the problem. They agreed there was no point in buying yet more "bits of computing", which would only serve to compound the current disorganised state of processes. The organization was not ready to take a process view of its problems.

Analysis of Findings

In terms of our analytical framework case B had a poor progno-sis from the outset. Although there were problems in the bid process, (pressure to act), it was uncomfortable to raise them publicly because of the fear of blame within what was widely described as the "unforgiving" culture of the organization. Besides, the problem had gone away (for the time being) when the latest big contract moved into the design stage.

The locus of support was IS, since the middle/senior managers invited to the workshop declined to accept responsibility. There was some evidence that they were unable to separate their own roles from a more general discussion of the process, so that suggestions for process improvements were seen as personal criticism. This seemed to be a particular issue with senior management, whose positions reflected their success at working within the status quo; in practice middle managers seemed more able to detach themselves from "the system" and analyse its strengths and weaknesses. There was also evidence of a "heroic management" culture, in which battling against the odds is more acceptable than acknowledging the problem and sharing it with staff (let alone outsiders). Only one manager (who was newly appointed from outside) showed any inclination to analyse the situation, but his contributions to the discussion were curtailed when none else joined in.

There were therefore few levers for change and the suggested "themes" (to explore ways of developing better direction and coordination of the bid process) were deflected by proposing solutions (buying a costing tool or database of parts data). This kind of IS usage would probably not act as a catalyst for change. Finally, the approach of analysing pressure points in the process, collecting process measures and talking about people's roles was so uncomfortable that it led old rivals (commercial and engineering) to unite against what became perceived as a common threat.

In summary, senior management did not want to change the way they worked and regarded IS as a commodity to be purchased rather than an opportunity to innovate. The IS manager resisted pressure to throw technology at the problem, but remained in the background and did not confront the senior managers with his views about the underlying causes of the problem. There emerged little political momentum in favour of reengineering the bid process.

Case C—A Multinational Pharmaceuticals Company

Background

This case relates to the period 1992-93. It is set in a multinational, North American pharmaceuticals company whose financial results showed a rising trend on an already healthy 1991 base of $4.98 billion in revenue, and some $350 million in net earnings.

Senior management in the clinical trials division had been considering how best to manage the support of centres participating in a trial. This was closely linked with collection of clinical data, and also preparation of drug submissions to the Regulatory authorities (see Figure 5). The three activities were managed separately and it was difficult to answer questions about the overall success of a trial. Had it been chosen well? Designed well? Run well? Resulted in significant clinical findings? Resulted in good relations and publicity for the drug within the medical industry? Supported the progress of a drug to market? These were particularly important questions, not least because the answers could help to speed the all-important time to market for a new drug.

The Clinical Trials Division: Suitable Case For Treatment?

Once again the IS department took the first step by commissioning a short study of the system needed to support centres participating in a trial. The IS manager had created his own small system for recording data about centres and tracking the paperwork sent to and from them, based on current manual forms. It now needed replacing and he was anxious to get on with the task. However, he wanted user input, to address some of the shortcomings of his original design, and he was not averse to gaining the approbation of the Medical Director, since this would facilitate the approval of resources. He worked closely with an external consultant commissioned to undertake the study, turning the findings into presentation-quality materials and checking out process models with the users. The consultant had little access to the users, but was involved in meetings with the Medical Director.

A process analysis was performed by the consultant deriving diagrams from current documentation, discussing these with the IS manager, and airing them with the Medical Director to check balance and focus. The results showed how tightly the three areas of the clinical trials process were coupled (see Figure 5).

The various unit managers registered interest. They had experienced difficulties in hand-offs at various parts of the cycle. Furthermore the Quality Manager who had been trying to create a framework for defining working practices decided to use process diagrams as the basis for future work. The Medical Director was particularly interested in the "big picture" afforded by the diagrams and suggested that arrangements be made to extend the process analysis, perhaps using the consultant to coach and provide quality assurance to staff as they performed the investigation.

In this case, the participants were not threatened by any specific problems and were attracted (as scientists) to an exploratory tech-

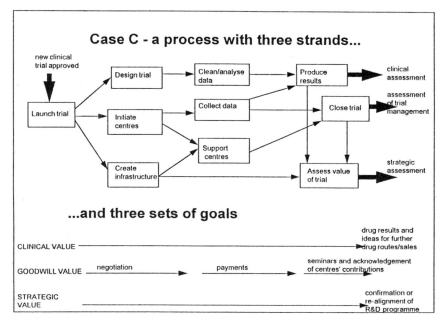

Figure 5 - Case C: Analysing the Existing Process

nique like process analysis. They found process diagrams easy to understand and use. They were accustomed to statistical analysis (used in preparing the drug submission) and could see the possibilities of applying these skills in analysing process measures. A process view could also help to identify and possibly facilitate some well known organizational constraints and structural rigidities. It also gained the Medical Director's approval, offering as it did a way to demonstrate the contribution that his division was making to the corporation. However, the IS manager was anxious that users did not get "carried away" with a new initiative and delay the development of his system. He said he was also doubtful about the Medical Director's commitment, since he had a reputation for picking up on new ideas and then losing interest.

After a number of further months delay, by the end of 1993 it seemed likely that the division would develop process analysis as a management tool at some point, but no respondents felt they were likely to move quickly as an organization into any kind of radical redesign programme.

Analysis of Findings

In this case the prognosis for further development through BPR was fairly positive. The locus of support shifted from the IS department to the Medical Director, and the lever for change was a desire to integrate the strands of work in the division and prove its contribution. Both the themes and the approach were enthusiastically received. The response to charting processes and examining areas for improvement/redesign were succinctly described in one respondent's remark that: "Exploration is what we're good at", indicating a receptive culture for BPR activity.

However there was a noticeable lack of pressure to act. The IS manager had gained sufficient insight into the processes to provide his system for managing the centres. Without his prompting, it was likely that the Medical Director would forget his intention to widen the initiative and use a process approach to encourage ongoing improvement.

In summary, the department could be described as protected from financial pressure, and laissez faire in its approach. User staff were articulate, interested and willing, but the "cozy" atmosphere and the absence of a champion for new approaches meant that process improvement or innovation were unlikely to be seriously adopted. However, if the Medical Director found himself having to justify the work of the department in more detail, or if the market conditions changed, it may well be that senior managers would take a more serious view of setting stretch targets and analysing performance, and some form of BPR would be regarded by the power brokers as a viable option.

Case D—A Health Care Organization

Background

This case is set in the 1990-94 period in a major acute hospital in the United Kingdom National Health Service (NHS). From the mid-1980s the NHS was the subject of radical management and organizational reforms prompted by central government. One major feature was the introduction of general managers, and private sector management practice, into hierarchically-based administrative structures replete with occupational and professional groupings. Relatedly a Resource Management initiative sought to introduce mechanisms to identify and improve performance in this area. Government also increased pressures to control NHS spending, and sought to develop an internal market in health care. This involved devolution of responsibility for service delivery and increased competition amongst service providers, for example hospitals. These reforms came together in the implementation of a purchaser-provider split across the NHS, accompanied by radical changes in the basis of allocation of finance to purchasers. Henceforth cash-constrained purchasers would seek the most cost-effective health care whether from NHS or private sector providers.

An Organization Under Pressure: Implementing BPR

The National Health Service reforms made sound financial performance a critical issue for hospitals, such as the one under study. Here a number of critical success factors were identified for operating in the new NHS environment. Financial net income had to be maximized. This made efficiency in resource management, together with accurate costing and activity information crucial. At the same time hospital reputation, standards of care and staff morale had to be maintained, a broad case-mix was necessary for teaching hospital purposes, and there needed to be timely and detailed clinical and audit information to maintain and improve clinical performance.

Earlier top-down reforms of the structure, breaking hierarchically-based administration into clinical directorates, only partially worked. It was recognised that a bottom-up approach was needed. The response in late 1990 was to begin a pilot BPR project, facilitated by external consultants. A lead clinician was identified in each of six pilot areas, for example radiology and cardiac services. Each clinician then led a multi-disciplinary team to identify the core clinical processes in its own area. In each case there were identified up to 20 processes with a definable start and finish, and for which resources - own and bought-in - could be defined and measured. The pilot study proved successful and BPR concepts, together with the pilot way of working, were then applied to the whole hospital.

The essence of the changes were described by a leading clinician as "a move from separate, vertical hierarchies for doctors, nurses and managers toward a more horizontally-orientated multi-disciplinary team culture". The main elements were: describing hospital work in process terms; producing an organizational structure enabling management of those processes and related resources; and developing IS supportive of the new arrangements. Using process analysis, and an incremental bottom-up approach, nearly 70 Service Delivery Units (SDU) or service areas were identified.

An example of a Service Delivery Unit is shown in Figure 7. Though no rigid model was developed, typically each SDU became responsible for delivering a defined set of services to patients or other SDUs, and consumed resources that it owned or bought in from other units. Typically a senior clinician and nursing manager would lead a Service Delivery Unit and develop and manage its service plan. SDUs became responsible for delivering services and managing their own resources. SDUs were grouped into Service Centres of related medical specialties or support services, each with, typically, a clinical consultant chairman and full-time service manager. These would be responsible for interfacing with senior hospital manage-

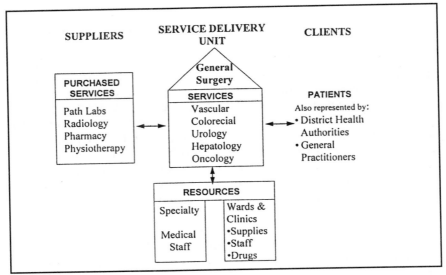

Figure 6 - Example Of A Service Delivery Unit

ment. Service Centre chairmen would meet senior management monthly as the hospital strategy and policy board, Service Centre managers and senior management fortnightly as the hospital operational board. Essentially the approach pushed down responsibility and accountability to the SDU level, and gave professional staff, such as clinicians and senior nursing staff, critical roles in management.

Information and IS would provide vital underpinning to the new organizational arrangements. In the period under study existing IT-based systems were widely adjudged inadequate even for previous ways of working. An Information Strategy Steering Committee of senior managers, clinicians and IT specialists involved a wide range of hospital staff in a number of task groups for developing ways forward. Early on it was commonly recognised that not only eliciting the information requirements, but also developing and implementing the information systems needed would have to be an incremental and highly participative process. Some reasons for this are suggested by the following comment:

> *"We're finding the hospital a very complex place in which to develop information systems. We're taking an evolutionary approach, and supporting the process changes. Even in low level jobs, there are major differences in the way one secretary does the same job to another one. The technical problems are small; it's defining what's needed and getting the agreement and buy-in that's taking the time."* (IT Consultant).

Moreover, systems had to be developed to meet not just clinician needs but also underpin Service Delivery Unit operations, budgeting and management, together with meeting higher level hospital requirements. A range of interest groups pulled in several different directions at once, not least clinicians with considerable power:

> "The hospital will demand data from me in my management role, but if they insist on a data collection through a system unfriendly to us at the operational end —in how we do our jobs - then they will get data but it will not be accurate. These sorts of issues mean that we (doctors) need to be fully involved in the management of implementation." (Senior Clinician).

Clearly, it was not just the complexity of the environment and the difficulties in identifying information requirements that led to an evolutionary, bottom-up approach, but also the political dimensions inherent in the situation.

Throughout 1991-92 a new hospital information system was prototyped based on client server architecture and open systems. Different Service Delivery Units would share the same data held on a patient data server, essentially a hospital wide database of data collected mostly by the SDUs. The database would hold all details relating to patients treated at the hospital. This data could be used in different ways in a range of activities, including contract and case-mix management, financial management, SDU work and for clinical support. Additionally Service Delivery Units would develop their 'private' information needed exclusively to support their own activities. Both the common and 'private' data would be available through new user-friendly clinical workstations; these would be linked to the patient data server, and also to each other where required.

By 1993 the new process-based structure was in place and working. On the whole, clinicians were positive about running their own service groups. Operationally the new arrangements were held to be more efficient, despite rising pressure, financial constraint, and unprecedented demand in terms of patient numbers. Forward planning had also become more accurate. Throughout 1993-4 the information systems were being rolled out slowly. Politically and culturally this approach was acknowledged as a wise one, for example the following comment from a nursing manager in Trauma Services:

> "The way that the IT-systems are lagging behind is quite positive. In devolved management, unless you have got a team used to and wanting to work together and take responsibility you can have all the IT systems you like but it's not going to work. This way we also are becoming much more clear about the systems and information we really need".

Even so a number of respondents suggested that implementation plans were not being well communicated even to immediately affected stakeholders. Also many nurses still remained cautious to skeptical about the usefulness of information systems in their work. Additionally, in the more advanced implementations in the Critical Care Service Delivery Units, there were potential problems arising as a result of lack of experience within the SDUs of rolling out information systems. Funding issues were also being raised—in particular about getting enough terminals and operators for data entry, and getting sufficient IT support staff. There was also emerging a shortage of time and resources—human and financial - to support the IT/IS training required in each Service Delivery Unit. A senior clinician summarized the implementation problems in the following way:

> *"End-games are difficult in the NHS. Government or the Department of Health, for example, move the goal posts, staff move on, outside support in the form of consultants and software suppliers starts working then funding runs out. You also get political opposition, given the range of professional groups and stakeholders. In information systems there are many interests to look after. Not only must it be a patient-centred system that also produces management information; critically it needs to be a user-centred system as well."* (Member of Information Strategy Steering Committee).

Analysis of Findings

The case provides an example of a fairly successful, but as yet incomplete, application of some fundamental BPR concepts in a public sector organization. Pressure to act was high and came from radical reforms imposed externally by Government. However it was clear that little could be achieved unless the diverse professional and occupational groupings of which the hospital staff comprised actively supported change. One part of the resulting approach was to devolve responsibility and management functions to professional and occupational groups. Another was to reorganize along process lines, and involve the relevant stakeholders closely in analysis and process design. The pilot studies enabled basic problems to be addressed, established workable alternatives, and also released the energy needed for change. The careful use of consultants also provided levers for change; methods were not imposed, but rather both BPR and IS consultants facilitated incremental learning both by themselves and key stakeholders.

Information systems could have been a major hurdle to delivering the new arrangements. However the political and human issues surrounding IS development and implementation were well understood, and explicitly managed through adoption of an incremental, prototyping, user-led approach, rolling out the information systems an SDU at a time and carefully eliciting the different information requirements and IT/IS demands of each service unit.

However the case does demonstrate the long time period it requires to roll out an effective BPR program within a large organization such as an acute National Health Service hospital. Though begun in 1991, the BPR activity in question was likely to continue into 1995/6, especially where delivering information systems to service units was concerned. This raises the question of whether there is a Catch-22 in BPR: effective large-scale BPR may take many years to implement, but can organizations wait that long for the effects to come through, and can energy, attention and resources continue to be focused sufficiently to maintain momentum?

Discussion: The Politics of BPR

The case studies were analysed through a five factor framework that proved useful in highlighting significant issues in BPR programs. A summary of our findings is provided in Figure 7. In addition to the points made earlier in analysing each case, what is interesting throughout the case studies is the different degrees to which political momentum was maintained for BPR. In case A, there was considerable pressure to act, but arising mainly from staff and middle managers. The change lever involved using IT in the workshops. There emerged little support for BPR, however, partly because it was initiated from the IS department, and partly because momentum was lost quickly once the hybrid manager and external facilitator left the scene, while power was being transferred to the Commercial Director.

Case B had a poor prognosis from the outset, in terms of the five change factors. Although there were problems in the bid process, it was uncomfortable to raise them publicly because of fear of blame. Besides, the problem had gone away (for the time being) when the contract moved into the design stage. The locus of support was IT, since the middle/senior managers invited to the workshop declined to accept responsibility. Themes of better direction and coordination of the bid process were therefore deflected by suggestions of buying a costing tool or database of parts data. This kind of IT usage would not act as a catalyst for change. Finally, the approach of analysing pressure points in the process, collecting process measures and talking about people's roles proved so uncomfortable that it led old rivals (commercial and engineering) to unite against the common threat.

Compared to this, case C had great potential. The locus of support shifted from the IT department to the Medical Director, and

CASE AND SECTOR FOCUS	A Aerospace	B Industrial Products	C Pharmaceuticals	D Health Care
Pressure to Act	Avionics sector under threat. Business not good at working together. IS already spent 2 years on evaluations	More pressure not to change. Current contract passed the bid stage.	Need to replace clinical trial management system	Government imposed reforms. Pressure to measure and improve performance. Development of internal market in health care. Budgeting pressures.
Locus of support	Initially an IS project. Survey led to grass roots enthusiasm. Ownership by IS and commercial director when negotiations stalled.	IS invited senior management to discuss options. Managers did not want to pick up the responsibility	Medical director an 'ideas' person, but easily distracted. IS manager didn't want project getting out of control.	Through management, clinical and nursing groups - grown over time. Senior clinician supported the process of change.
Levers for change	Middle managers' desire to change organization e.g. use IS to empower repair workshops.	An improved bid process could cut down on 'fire-fighting' and improve targeting and winning of appropriate business.	Managers and staff interested in investigation, and experienced in stats. Process analysis a framework to address issues.	Careful use of Consultants; methods not imposed; mutual incremental learning facilitated. Need to respond to external pressures.
Themes	More integrative/co-operative working. Track milestones, measure results. Improve service and costs.	Better team work on the process. Improved direction on commercial guidelines. IS to help with technical options; teamwork.	What is a successful trial? What value does it create? What contribution is the Division making?	Improved measurement and control. Devolved responsibility, empowerment of service staff. IS in a support role.
Approach	Challenge status quo before IS introduction. Analyze processes and discuss change to the organization.	Preliminary analysis of bid process indicated areas for further investigation ... 'no, we'd rather buy some more technology'.	Plant process analysis ideas at staff level, and opportunities at Medical Director level. Leave to incubate.	Bottom-up getting clinicians involved. Use of consultants to develop incremental learning. Representative steering committees. Service delivery staff made responsible for changes.

Figure 7 - Five Factor Analysis of the Case Studies

the lever for change was a desire to integrate the strands of work in the division and prove its contribution. Both the themes and the approach were enthusiastically received: "Exploration is what we're good at". The only weakness in this case was the lack of pressure to act. The IT manager had gained sufficient insight into the processes to provide his system for managing the centres. Without his prompting, it is likely that the Medical Director would forget his intention to use a process approach to encourage ongoing improvement.

Case D represents BPR on a more ambitious scale than in the other three cases. There was clear and demanding external pressure to act. The locus of support was throughout management, clinical and nursing echelons, but this had to be grown over time through the incremental, participative approach adopted. BPR provided a mode of addressing fundamental and intractable problems that previous attempts had failed to resolve. A strong point favouring the new BPR activity was that much had been learned from past experiences in the organization about how NOT to introduce large-scale change and information systems into the organization. What proved particularly important was the choice to relegate the development and implementation of IS to a support role - after processes had been reengineered, and while the working arrangements were being refined. This enabled better elicitation of information requirements, and meant that the BPR program did not become captured by, and subordinated to, technical considerations. The approach adopted involved all salient stakeholders and tended, in terms of Figure 1, to be suitably multi-disciplinary and holistic in its operationalization.

All the cases indicate the importance of our earlier statements in terms of needing to take a holistic, multidisciplinary approach, avoiding a methods-driven approach, not allowing technical considerations and agendas to subvert business and organizational objectives, and paying critical attention to the human, social, cultural and political issues invariably bound up with any major change process. However it is worth highlighting that respondents deeming BPR as relatively successful all regarded management of politics as an important part in that success. This is not to say that effective management of politics can in itself turn a poor BPR program into an effective one; for example, if the wrong processes are being focused on, little performance gain will accrue to the organization whatever the expertise in managing the change. However, it is to say that expertise in the management of politics of change can help to turn the potential of a BPR program into a reality. How, then, can the politics of BPR be managed?

Developing A Politics Track

Drawing upon the experiences in the case histories, a first step is to accept as part of the brief of managing BPR, that a politics, or 'shadow' track is needed to monitor and shape throughout the program the political momentum for and against change options. In other words the politics of change programs are dynamic and need to be explicitly managed. Such management clearly occurred in Case D, but was much less prevalent in the other, less successful cases. An explanation might be that the large size of the BPR program, together with the organizational learning on relative failure on previous change projects made the need to manage the politics more obvious than in the other cases. Case D also raises the question: Who should manage the politics track? In this case senior clinicians who were important power brokers in the organization were involved together with general managers. But an important principle seemed to be the diffusion and sharing of power throughout the organization in order to effect change. This can be contrasted with cases A, B, and C, where political management largely stayed within the IS department, resulting in little real political momentum for change. The cases also support to some degree the difficulty of sustaining BPR where political management is top-down or primarily consultant-led.

A second step is to regularly carry out a power audit. This involves analysing the prevailing political and cultural configuration of the organization. Who is in the dominant coalition and what are the sources of their influence? What are the power bases of lower-level participants? Who is likely to support or resist BPR, to what degree, and what difference will it make? Where there be different responses to different change content, or processes by which change is managed? The main thrust here is to gain a sense of the political feasibility of different approaches to BPR-based change.

A third step is to continuously maintain political momentum behind the BPR program by mobilising power, gaining power where necessary and dealing with countervailing power. An overview of the influence management process is suggested by Mayes and Allen (1977) and is outlined here. Political goals need to be formulated and an ends-means analysis carried out i.e. what do wish to achieve and how do we go about achieving it. Targets to be influenced are then identified and incentives desired by the targets can be determined. Implementation involves mobilizing these incentives and monitoring the results. The management of politics and culture must continue throughout the BPR program. In organizational settings like those covered in our case studies, a political approach is rarely just a matter of accumulating enough power at the beginning to do whatever you like thereafter. Tactics for mobilizing and gaining power are widely rehearsed in the literature and will not be discussed in detail here (see for example Keen, 1981; Schein, 1985).   Managing politics in the context of BPR programs involves addressing at least three major issues: resistance to change; the danger of the change process running out of control; and relatedly, how to maintain influence over the political dynamics of change. It is necessary to stress that implementing BPR must be seen in the context of objectives wider than the limited goal of gaining acceptance for a specific process innovation or related IT-based system. Modifications to the content of change may be necessary in the face of politico-cultural problems.

Techniques for reducing resistance to change are most apparent in our health care organization study. Some general principles include: making visible any organizational dissatisfaction with the present; addressing people's attention to the consequences of not carrying out change; building in reasons and rewards for people supporting the transition and the new; developing an appropriate degree, level and type of participation for different affected parties; giving people time and opportunity to disengage from the present state. Adequate planning and resources are needed to see the transition through. Beckhard and Harris (1977) suggest the need to develop and communicate clear images of the future to organizational members. Nadler and Tichy (1981) suggest establishing multiple and consistent leverage points, that is, aimed not just at individuals but also at social relations, task and structural changes. Handling the power dynamics of BPR-based change means ensuring leaders and key groups maintain active support for change, that a culture and climate of success is created, but also that enough stability remains, and the pace of change is judged so that the change remains acceptable to involved parties.

A contingency approach is required, that is retaining a flexible orientation, and building opportunities to modify reengineering content and process where it emerges as deficient. Contingency also means adopting a change strategy appropriate to the organizational circumstances in which those responsible for BPR find themselves. The problem with much of the prescriptive literature on BPR-related change is that it tends to suggest that one change management model will suit every organization or sets of circumstances (see for example Hammer, 1990, discussed above). However a "closed" strategy—top-down imposed with little consultation—might be appropriate where the benefits of participation are low, or there is widespread agreement and support for BPR, or the promoters of BPR are all-powerful, or where the level of disagreement and hostility about the changes are so high that participation is perceived to have little purpose. On the other hand a more 'open' strategy might be more relevant where there is underlying support for BPR, a large number of parties will be affected, there are differing views on how BPR can be achieved, power is widely distributed, and where stakeholder involvement will provide vital information for the BPR program.

Ways Forward: Summary

The case studies reveal the following guidelines for those contemplating BPR activity:

- There must be a strategic thrust, a vision of the future, a determination to change things...even a challenge to the survival of the organization or unit in question;
- The intervention must be owned by the organization or unit (even if outside consultants are used): it must have active senior management support and buy-in from a critical mass of middle management;
- The people involved in the process must undertake their own voyage of discovery, must be convinced of the possibilities and participate in the innovation; a *closed* change strategy constrains these possibilities;
- IT must not be seen as the reason for the process redesign: it is often one of the enabling factors, but the reason for change must be a business one;
- BPR can rarely be led by IT departments, or by IT professionals alone; a holistic approach is best enabled by a multi-functional set of people driving the change;
- Methods and external consultant recipes should not be drivers, only facilitators of change.
- Transforming an organization, or one of its sub-units, can take years rather than months, and the various components (strategy, structure, process, people and technology) must be coordinated under a change management programme which clearly projects the purpose and progress of the various phases.
- The politics of BPR have to be explicitly managed over the lifetime of the program.

Conclusions

The case studies re-emphasize that business process re-engineering, even on a small scale, can be fraught with difficulty. The problems stem from the multidisciplinary, cross-functional ambition at the centre of BPR. The focus on process in BPR serves to redirect attention, channel dissatisfaction with the status quo, and can be a powerful lever for change. However, while this focus can stimulate radical change, it also raises complex implementation issues that become even more intractable when IT is implicated in any significant way.

This puts change management at the core of BPR activity. The case study findings on this issue are reinforced by 1994-5 survey findings showing major political and cultural barriers to BPR, and at the same time insufficient early attention given to managing such barriers (Willcocks, 1995). In particular, a focus on and search for methodologies to deliver BPR tends to side-track in practice, dealing with, rather than marginalizing human, social and political issues. As with culture and excellence in the 1980s, the rhetoric of BPR may also serve the purpose of disguising BPR initiatives as essentially political events in organizations. However, as our case studies show, relying heavily on the rhetoric, and an emphasis on the new will be a less sustainable way forward than adopting some well-known, even old-fashioned, practices for the management of change. In particular, in BPR programs, as in any major change project, the politics track needs to be planned for and followed, or managers will find their way there by chance, unexpectedly, and invariably under less favourable circumstances.

References

Barrett, J. (1994, Spring). Process visualization: Getting the vision right is key. *Information Systems Management*, 14-23.

Beckhard, R. and Harris, R. (1977). *Organizational Transitions*. New York: Addison-Wesley.

Beer, S. (1975). *Platform for Change*. Chichester: John Wiley and Sons.

Belmonte, R. and Murray, R. (1993, Summer). Getting ready for strategic change: Surviving Business Process Redesign. *Information Systems Management*, 23-29.

Born, G. (1993). APACHE: A pictorial CASE tool for business process reengineering. In. *Software Assistance For Business Re-Engineering*. Spurr, K., Layzell, P., Jennison, L. and Richards, N. (eds.) Chichester: John Wiley and Sons.

Buday, R. (1992). Forging a new culture at Capital Holding's Direct Response Group. *Insights Quarterly*, 4, 38-49.

Clegg, C., Waterson, P. and Carey, N. (1994, June). Computer supported collaborative working: Lessons from elsewhere. *Journal of Information Technology*, 9,2, 72-86.

Couger, J., Flynn, P. and Hellyer, D. (1994, Spring). Enhancing the creativity of reengineering. *Information Systems Management*, 24-29.

Craig, J. and Yetton, P. (1994). The dual and strategic role of IT: A critique of business process reengineering. Working Paper 94-002 Australian Graduate School of Management, Kensington: University of New South Wales.

Davenport, H. (1993). *Process Innovation: Reengineering Work Through Information Technology*. Boston: Harvard Business Press.

Davenport, H. (1993b, Fall). Book review of Reengineering The Corporation. *Sloan Management Review*, 103-104.

Davenport, T. and Short, J. (1990, Summer), The new industrial engineering: Information Technology and business process redesign. *Sloan Management Review* 31, 4, 11-27

Davenport, T. and Stoddard, D. (1994). Reengineering: Business change of mythic proportions? *MIS Quarterly,* 18, 2, 121-127.

Earl, M. (1993, March). Experiences in strategic information systems planning. *MIS Quarterly,* 17, 1, 1-24.

Earl, M. and Khan, B. (1994, Spring). How new is business process redesign? *European Management Journal* , 12, 1, 20-30.

Farhoodi, F. (1993). CADDIE: An advanced tool for organisational design and process modelling. In. *Software Assistance For Business Re-Engineering.* Spurr, K., Layzell, P., Jennison, L. and Richards, N. (eds.) Chichester: John Wiley and Sons.

Goldratt, E. and Cox, J. (1989). *The Goal.* London: Gower.

Grint, K. (1993) Reengineering history: An analysis of business process reengineering. *Management Research Paper* 93/20, Oxford: Templeton College.

Haughton, E. (1992, July). Business process reengineering: Moving the corporate goalposts. *Computer Weekly,* July 30th., 20-23.

Hammer, M (1990, July/August), Don't automate - obliterate. *Harvard Business Review,* 104-112.

Hammer, M and Champy, J (1993) *Reengineering the Corporation: A Manifesto for Business Revolution,* London: Nicholas Brearley Publishing

Harrington, H. (1991). Business Process Improvement. London: McGraw Hill. Heygate, R. (1993, Spring). Immoderate redesign. *The McKinsey Quarterly,* 1, 73-87.

I/S Analyzer (1993, August). The role of IT in business reengineering. *I/S Analyzer,* 31, 8, 1-16.

Johannson, H., McHugh, P., Pendlebury, A., and Wheeler, W. (1993). *Business Process Reengineering: Breakpoint Strategies for Market Dominance.* Chichester: John Wiley.

Jones, M. (1994,) Don't emancipate, exaggerate: Rhetoric, 'reality' and reengineering. *Proceedings of the IFIP WG.82 Conference,* Ann Arbor, Michigan. August 13-15th.

Kanter, R. (1989). *When Giants Learn to Dance: Mastering the Challenge of Strategy, Management and Careers in the 1990s,* New York: Simon and Schuster.

Kaplan, R. and Murdock, L. (1991, Summer). Rethinking the corporation: Core process redesign. *The McKinsey Quarterly,* 2, 27-43.

Keen, P. (1981, January). Information systems and organizational change. *Communications of the ACM,* 24, 1, 24-33.

Keen, P. (1991). *Shaping the Future: Business Design Through Information Technology.* Boston: Harvard Business School Press.

Klein, M. (1994, Spring). Reengineering methodologies and tools. *Information Systems Management,* 31-35.

Mason, D. and Willcocks, L. (1994). *Systems Analysis, Systems Design.* Henley: Alfred Waller Publications.

Mayes, B. and Allen, R. (1977). Toward a definition of organizational politics. *Academy of Management Review,* 2, 88-102.

Mintzberg, H. (1994, January-February). The fall and rise of strategic planning. *Harvard Business Review,* 107-114.

Moad, J. (1993, August). Does reengineering really work? *Datamation* August 1st., 22-28.

Morris and Brandon (1993). *Reengineering Your Business.* London:

McGraw Hill.

Nadler, D. and Tichy, N. (1981). *Organization Development in Health Care Organizations*, Margulies, N. and Adams, J. (eds). New York: Addison-Wesley.

Peters, T. (1987). *Thriving on Chaos*. New York: Harper and Row.

Pettigrew, A. (1985). *The Awakening Giant: Continuity and Change in ICI*. Oxford: Blackwell and Sons.

Preece, I. and Edwards, C. (1993). A Survey of BPR Activity in the United Kingdom. Unpublished Research Paper. Cranfield: Cranfield University Business School.

Schein, E. (1985, February) Organizational realities - the politics of change. *Training and Development Journal*, 20-28.

Short, J. and Venkatraman, N. (1992, Fall). Beyond Business Process Redesign: Redefining Baxter's business network. *Sloan Management Review*, 7-21.

Spurr, K., Layzell, P., Jennison, L. and Richards, N. (1993). *Software Assistance For Business Re-Engineering*. Chichester: John Wiley and Sons.

Strassmann, P. (1993). Achieving Superior Corporate Performance With IT. Seminar presentation for Business Intelligence, London, November 18th.

Stringer, J. (1992). Risks in large projects. In *Operational Research Tutorial Papers* ed. Mortimer, M.. London: Operational Research Society.

Thackray, J. (1993, June). Fads, fixes and fictions. *Management Today*, 41-43.

Walsham, G. (1993). *Interpreting Information Systems in Organizations*. Chichester: Wiley and Sons.

Walton, R. (1989). *Up And Running*. Boston: Harvard Business Press.

Wang, S. (1994, Spring). OO modeling of business processes: Object-oriented systems analysis. *Information Systems Management*, 36-43.

Watts, J. (1993). A practical approach to redesigning and implementing business processes. In. *Software Assistance For Business Re-Engineering*. Spurr, K., Layzell, P., Jennison, L. and Richards, N. (eds.) Chichester: John Wiley and Sons.

Willcocks, L. (1994). *Information Management: Evaluation of Information Systems Investments*. London: Chapman and Hall.

Willcocks, L. (1995). Implementing Business Reengineering: Current U.K. Practice and Experience. Oxford Institute of Information Management Research and Discussion Paper. Oxford: Templeton College, (forthcoming).

Willcocks, L. and Griffiths, C. (1995, Spring). Predicting the risk of failure in major Information Technology projects. *Technological Forecasting and Social Change*, (forthcoming).

Willcocks, L. and Mason, D. (1987). Computerising Work: People, Systems Design and Workplace Relations. London: Paradigm.

Public Sector Reengineering:
Applying Lessons Learned in the Private Sector to the
U.S. Department of Defense[1]

Thomas R. Gulledge
George Mason University

David H. Hill
David H. Hill, Inc.

Edgar H. Sibley
George Mason University

According to a recent General Accounting Office Report, the U.S. Department of Defense (DoD) spends about $9.2 billion annually to acquire, operate, and maintain automated information systems. Each dollar saved in supporting this infrastructure may be transferred to military force sustainability, an extremely important issue during a period of declining budgets. It is generally accepted that many inefficiencies exist in the management of information by the DoD. Hence, in 1989 the Corporate Information Management (CIM) initiative was established with the following objectives:

1. Ensure the standardization, quality, and consistency of data from the Department's multiple management information systems,
2. Identify and implement management efficiencies throughout the information system life-cycle, and
3. Eliminate duplicate development and maintenance of multiple

information systems designed for the same requirement.

Impending budget reductions resulted in a redefining of these ambitious objectives for CIM:

> CIM seeks to help DoD over the long-term (1) implement new or improved business methods through the use of modern technology—for example, how it pays its civilian employees or manages its $100 billion inventory should be of interest to executives who are implementing process improvement initiatives.

After providing some background material and definitions, the DoD experience is described. We describe the problems at three management levels (i.e., high-level, mid-level, and low-level), and then summarize our major findings. We provide our recommendations, followed by our conclusions. Finally, we provide the details of two of the case studies on which our conclusions and recommendations are based.

Source and Background of the Problem

This chapter is based on our readings, interviews with public and private sector managers, and notes, primarily during the Spring of 1993. We were searching for new ideas, strategies, and tools to effect Functional Process Improvement implementation throughout the Department of Defense. The sponsor's desire for such a study is based on the observation that implementation, in general, has not been successful, especially when accompanied by personnel reductions.

In our review of the Corporate Information Management (CIM) initiative we see both successes and failures. It is easy to analyze failures from a position of 20/20 hindsight. However, it is important to examine them so that we can learn from them. The processes of technological innovation, business process reengineering, and continuous process improvement are prevalent in the private sector; and it is unlikely that government could or should insulate itself from the new management culture that evolves from them. In fact, it is this new management view of efficiency and response to the needs of the customer that drives "reinventing government."[2] Within the DoD, additional factors are contributing to the desire to implement improvement methodologies. A changing mission, combined with a change in public policy, creates pressure to downsize. Functional Process Improvement provides a way to increase effectiveness even as resources decline. Every dollar saved through process innovation is a dollar that potentially could be applied to the DoD's primary mission.

We believe that process innovation should be pursued by all public sector managers. We make suggestions in this document about how to proceed in the DoD, but we also suggest a cautious approach. There are basic postulates and prerequisites that must be satisfied preparatory to a process innovation exercise. These are introduced in the summary of our findings. In order to avoid misunderstanding first we introduce some definitions and terminology.

Basic Terminology

We chose the term "business process innovation," because it encompasses all aspects of the DoD's problem; i.e.,

> Radical process change initiatives have been called various names — e.g., business process redesign and business reengineering. For several reasons, we prefer the term business process innovation. Reengineering is only part of what is necessary in the radical change of processes; it refers specifically to the design of the new process. The term process innovation encompasses the envisioning of new work strategies, the actual process design activity, and the implementation of the change in all its complex technological, human, and organizational dimensions [Davenport (1993), p. 2].

Within the DoD, business reengineering has gained much attention, while business process innovation has received less. Process innovation includes all aspects of the change process, including implementation. That is, the change process includes problem recognition and identification, planning and enterprise modeling, process mapping and core process identification, high-level business case development, and implementation planning. The implementation plan also includes a human resource plan. It is also important to note that implementation includes the development of information systems and the establishment of performance/cost measurement systems.

Continuous process improvement is a management process, the purpose of which is to effect increased performance over time. The business reengineering component of process innovation results in radical process redesign and the potential for discrete and large increases in performance. The distinctions between these concepts are noted in Figure 1.

To monitor improvement during and after implementation, a performance/cost measurement system must be designed and implemented. Our concept of a performance/cost measurement

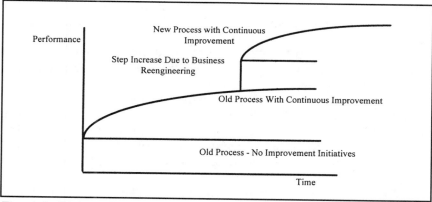

Performance

New Process with Continuous Improvement

Step Increase Due to Business Reengineering

Old Process With Continuous Improvement

Old Process - No Improvement Initiatives

Time

Figure 1: Business Reengineering and Continuous Improvement

system is modeled after the CAM-i Cost Management System (Berliner and Brimson, 1988). This is the system that is advocated in the CIM process improvement methodology. It focuses on

1. Continual improvement in eliminating non-value-added activities,
2. Activity accounting,
3. Externally driven targets, including target costs, and
4. Improved traceability of costs to management reporting objectives.

The establishment of such a system shifts the emphasis from cost accounting to cost and performance management.

There is a distinct difference between performance measures and performance measurement systems. Performance measures are established prior to designing a performance measurement system. The performance measurement system is developed to collect, organize, and display the measured performance data.

The Department of Defense Experience

The DoD approach to process improvement under the CIM initiative is summarized in three documents:

1. Functional Process Improvement (1993),
2. Corporate Information Management: Process Improvement Methodology for DoD Functional Managers (1993).
3. Corporate Information Management: Functional Economic Analysis Guidebook (1993).

The first is a policy document. The other two are technique and tool oriented. All three documents encourage management of processes. They should also persuade that Functional Economic Analysis should be used to establish the framework for performance/cost measurement systems. While much analytical activity has been generated as a result, there have been few successful implementations. Our interviews indicate why.

The primary problem derives from the lack of commitment and involvement at the highest levels of the DoD. Process improvement studies were viewed as analytical hurdles that must be cleared in order to obtain funds for information technology. The reasons are deeply embedded in the organizational culture and values of the DoD.

The managerial problem is better understood by considering Figure 2. This postulates two types of processes in the modern corporation:

1. Processes that convert material to product, and
2. Processes that convert data to information.

There are general management concerns that become the parameters directly influencing both types of processes. The most pervasive is public policy. Other high-level concerns include:

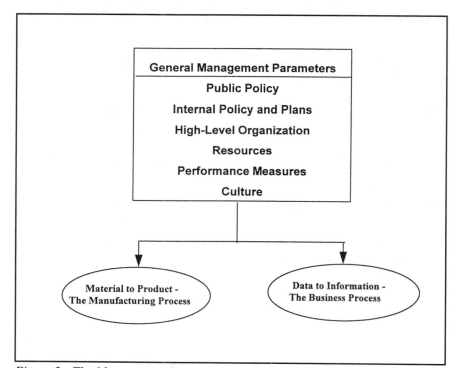

Figure 2: The Management Process

1. Internal policy and plans,
2. High-level organization,
3. Resources, both external and internal,
4. Performance measures, and
5. Culture.

The early focus of CIM was on the way that the functional managers should change the business processes, ignoring the general management activities and the parameters that indirectly influence the business processes. Though this is the CIM reality, this was never the intent of the original Executive Level Group who recommended the CIM initiative. For successful business process innovation there must be more attention to general management activities and the parameters that bind the business process.

We hypothesize two levels in the original Executive Level Group model (see Figure 3.): the senior executive level and the business process level. Early CIM implementations, as discussed above, focused on the lower levels, because of pressures to reduce costs by elimination of duplicate information systems. The consequence was a reduction of emphasis on the upper level of the model, which should have been of prime concern. The lesson from the private sector is that without a high-level managerial commitment to process innovation, failure is almost certain.

A second key point relates to the behavioral aspects of process innovation. The distinction between business reengineering and business process innovation is that the latter encompasses the implementation of the change in all its complex technological, human, and organizational dimensions. Within the DoD, technological aspects have received much more attention than human and organizational dimensions. Two major areas of concern were identified through our research.

1. Even the best constructed plans for improvement fail unless the human resource component is addressed. In many private sector implementations, employees are protected or re-deployed. The current environment in the DoD calls for major reductions in personnel. During the Spring of 1993 the number was projected to be somewhere between 200,000 and 300,000 Civilian Personnel. Hence plans for improvement are being implemented in an environment where it is impossible to re-deploy all displaced employees. This makes it imperative to prepare a human resource plan, combined with tools that provide appropriate managerial incentives for its implementation. This concern is also mirrored in the success factors of the private sector during downsizing: Managers and employees must believe that their

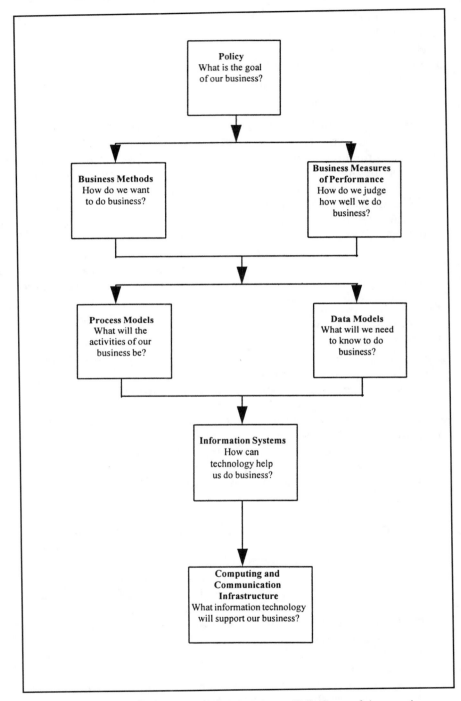

Figure 3: Executive Level Group Model (Source: U.S. General Accounting Office (1992)

interests are protected.

2. Our interviews also uncovered implementation impediments imposed by external organizations, especially the US Congress and the Office of Personnel Management. We hypothesize that these externally imposed rules and regulations impede process innovation, especially with respect to personnel issues. However, we do not understand the extent of these restrictions. It appears that many impediments are self-imposed through Office of the Secretary of Defense and Service interpretations of external regulations and are used as an excuse for not acting. This issue requires investigation.

From these initial considerations, we have found it instructive to focus on three implementation levels:

1. The high level—The Office of the Secretary of Defense, the Congress, and other government agencies,
2. The mid level —The interaction between the Director of Defense Information and the functional process managers, and
3. The low level—The interactions among the functional process managers, the line managers, and the employees.

A number of problems are classifiable at each level. Our intent is to "chunk" and "segment" general truisms within each and explaining how they are necessary for successful business process innovation.

High-Level Management Problems

During our interviewing process the following areas of concern were identified. We have not ranked them in order of importance, and we do not consider them complete.

The DoD Culture and the Reward System

There is a strong belief that the DoD culture and reward system is an impediment to process improvement implementation. Management compensation (in both the DoD and private sectors) is often a function of the number of employees who report to the manager. Thus a manager's status (i.e., level within the organization) may be diminished by the elimination of people that can be a consequence of functional process improvement. In one of our interviews the question was asked: What motivates the manager to reduce the workforce and increase efficiency? The difficulty in answering centers around the fact that the people who should increase efficiency are the ones who are likely to lose, either due to a reduction in the number of people who report to them (potential grade drop) or in the elimination of their own position. For example, it was noted that managers will often go through the motions without being committed to the process innovation vision. When this behavior occurs, top management must rejuvenate the management team and obtain the appropriate commitment. There is no other route to success.

This problem is also faced in many private sector organizations. Managerial status (power) and compensation are often directly related to the number of people reporting to a manager. This type of reward system causes opposition to downsizing. From an efficiency point of view the ultimate objective of every manager should be to eliminate non-value-added activities. Thus, if a manager reduces the number of reporting employees from 500 to 400, his or her future compensation should be more, not less. If personnel reductions threaten the employee and the supervisor, how can we motivate people to downsize efficiently? Consequently, how do we motivate people to participate actively in business process innovation and continuous process improvement?

The Relationship Between the Office of the Secretary of Defense (OSD) and the Services

A second difficult issue relates to the decentralized DoD management structure and the relationships among the OSD, the Services, and Defense Agencies. The OSD is often frustrated because there is insufficient management control to effect implementation throughout the Services. The OSD "has no institutional staying power," though the Services do. In the Services, "the faces change over the years, but they have continuity." Even the best plans may not be implemented. CIM guidance views the DoD as a business with budget centers, but the functional managers generally lack the institutionalized power over the Services to implement the plans.

There is a belief that this control problem was institutionalized by the 1981 Carlucci initiatives that called for centralized guidance and decentralized management (policy enforcement). One comment we heard was: "we need an Undersecretary for Change." The Services should be educated in change management so they will want to enforce policy decisions made at the OSD level. Layers of "underhead"[3] must be eliminated.

Management Incentives

There is a general belief that even if a properly designed performance/cost measurement system were in place, DoD managers would not have the incentives to act on the information provided by the system. The best designed system will fail if the information it provides is ignored. As long as managers do not see its value, information will not be used. The performance/cost measurement system must be designed and supported by the process manager. We are not advocating a system to replace the PPBS. We are advocating additional visibility that the PPBS does not provide; i.e., a tracing of performance and cost to process activities. These performance measures will help the manager monitor the organization's progress through time. Hence, the issue is: How does the DoD provide incentives that will encourage managers to design, develop, and use performance/cost measurement systems that have been successfully implemented in the private sector?

Private Sector Experiences

Throughout our interviews, it was generally acknowledged that much could be learned from benchmarking the private sector. However, there was a recognition that the DoD is unique in its improvement implementations. While it is difficult to draw general conclusions from case studies of different private sector organizations, we have found the experiences of Aetna Life and Casualty and Digital Equipment Corporation (DEC) to be relevant to the DoD experience. These case studies are attached as Appendices A and B.

Our interviews with Aetna and DEC indicate two different approaches to reengineering. The Aetna experience was top down in the sense that it was driven by a Chairman with a vision that included reengineering. The reengineering group from Aetna stated that successful reengineering requires high-level support and the Chairman must want reengineering more than anything in the world. At DEC the need for reengineering was identified by lower levels of the organization within the corporate finance function. After successes in the financial area, reengineering was initiated within other organizational processes with top management support. Our primary finding at both organizations is relevant to the DoD. Reengineering is likely to fail without commitment and continuous involvement from the highest levels of management. As indicated in our findings, we did not detect such a commitment from the highest levels of the DoD.

The case studies also indicate that the impetus to reengineer is usually associated with a real or perceived external threat. In the case of Aetna and DEC the threat was deteriorating profitability and market share. While the DoD is experiencing significant budget reductions, top management apparently does not yet view reengineering as mechanism for addressing this threat.

There are two related problems faced by the private sector:

simplification and downsizing. Efficient firms have simplified as they grew, unlike the DoD. In the cases of Federal Express and Wal-Mart, simplification provided the competitive edge that led to their growth. The DoD apparently cannot point to examples of effective streamlining even when downsizing. This points to a major issue, and a major challenge for the DoD. Business process innovation and continuous process improvement must be initiated in organizations that are experiencing downsizing. Aetna Life & Casualty, Inc. provides one example of an organization experiencing both, yet they did not terminate employees as a result of reengineering. The downsizing was distinctly separate from the reengineering, and at the time of our interview all employees who were displaced by reengineering were re-deployed. However, Aetna has not ruled out the elimination of personnel in future reengineering efforts.

Our discussions with Aetna led to the conclusion that while process innovation and downsizing can occur simultaneously, it is better to keep them separate. Employee involvement is a prerequisite to success. It will be less than enthusiastic if termination of employment is the reward. That is, it will be very difficult to obtain employee support for process reengineering if jobs are being eliminated unless measures are taken to help them obtain employment elsewhere. Downsizing of the DoD is ordained; continued employment cannot be promised.

There are successful implementations accompanied by downsizing, but few have been identified. One such success was the Ford Motor Company example that was discussed by Hammer (1990). While Ford was contracting, the employees that participated in the process innovation were promised re-deployment. Private sector successes in declining markets need to be studied, especially those that involve employee separations.

Mid-Level Management Problems

Mid-level issues were hardly addressed. However, a problem often mentioned during our interviews was the relatively low level of the Director of Defense Information in the DoD organization chart. Functional process improvement implementation appears to have been impeded because the DDI was unable to exert pressure higher in the organization.

We have not interviewed anyone who wants to eliminate the Director of Defense Information, and there is general agreement that its role as a "change manager" is needed. However, the primary focus of the Director of Defense Information should be on the process of management, with a secondary focus only on information technology and systems.

Low-Level Management Problems

Much of our early interviewing was spent addressing low-level management problems. Our initial hypothesis was that they are the primary impediments to successful functional process improvement implementations. There are many low-level management problems and hence many are impediments to change, but even if all of these are addressed, improvement efforts will probably fail without change in culture and values plus commitment and involvement from top management.

Low-level problems are associated with the line manager/civilian personnel interface. Process innovation calls for the radical reengineering of work, investments in information technology, efficiency gains, and cost reductions, which usually implies personnel reductions. New federal government personnel policies must be designed to facilitate process innovation methodologies.

Director of Defense Information and Office of the Assistant Secretary of Defense Efforts

In general, we found that neither the Director of Defense Information nor the Office of the Assistant Secretary of Defense (FM&P) was aware of several initiatives underway by the other. We uncovered many tools designed to deal with civilian personnel reductions that could easily be integrated into business process improvement initiatives and the development of the functional economic analysis package. However, most of the tools are not designed to deal with process innovation and radical change. For example, improvement guidelines for personnel under development in the Work Force Quality and Productivity Division of the Defense Civilian Personnel Center are excellent for continuous process improvement, but may not be applicable in a radical reengineering environment. The Office of the Director of Defense Information has proposed a strategy for redesigning business processes, but implementation guidelines for personnel have not been provided by the Office of the Assistant Secretary of Defense (FM&P). If the guidelines were better known, employees would know their options.

New and Creative Human Resource Ideas

An issue for future study concerns the development of personnel reduction tools that can be applied during process innovation. Many of the existing Office of the Assistant Secretary of

Defense (FM&P) tools may be directly transferable to this environment, but new and creative ideas are needed. DoD should benchmark its human resource initiatives against private sector reductions and the experiences of other public sector organizations; e.g., The US Postal Service and the Internal Revenue Service.

The Individual Employee

Successful implementation requires an environment where employees feel their interests are protected. The effects of downsizing on human resources should be anticipated and planned. During the interviewing process, this factor emerged as the most important low-level issue. The interests of the employees must be protected.

The following issue must be addressed. How do we create an environment where employees feel that their interests are protected? This is a challenge in the private sector, but it is even more of a problem in the DoD, where re-deployment is generally not an option.

Summary of Findings

The findings summarized here are discussed in more detail later. While many of them are understood by both private and public sector managers, they have not been uniformly adopted by functional managers in implementing the DoD's CIM initiative. The evidence is that managers focus attention on the technical aspects of process innovation while not placing sufficient emphasis on business methods.

The findings are separated into two groups: first prerequisites that should be completed prior to initiating a process innovation project; and second conditions necessary for successful process innovation.

Prerequisites for Process Innovation

1. There should be a clear understanding of the direction the organization is taking. There must be a plan based on a vision that emphasizes the needs of the customer.
2. Business process innovation might call for reorganization. This reorganization could be extensive (e.g., the complete organization) or minor (e.g., reorganization to establish process ownership). Where this is the case, reorganization should take place in advance of process innovation in order to establish accountability and responsibility for the effort.

3. The resources available for executing the process innovation effort

must be decided before the effort begins. Resources, of course, include capital and qualified personnel.

4. Prior to process innovation, management should establish performance metrics that apply to the baseline "as-is" process; these should also apply to the alternative "to-be" process. Without such metrics, it is impossible to determine the ultimate success or failure of the innovation effort.

Critical Success Factors

1. There must be a commitment to process innovation from senior management. Without this, functional managers might not give proper attention to the initiation and implementation of business process reengineering.
2. There must be employee involvement at all stages of the reengineering effort.
3. While it may be impossible to guarantee employment, there must be some indication that the organization will make every effort to protect the interest of the employees; i.e., reengineering is more successful when displaced employees are re-deployed. Managers must also be assured that their status will not diminish if they successfully reengineer their processes. There may be rare counter examples, but management participation is more enthusiastic if status is not diminished. Reengineering and downsizing can be initiated simultaneously, however, reengineering is more successful when displaced employees are re-deployed.
4. There should be a high-level understanding of both the "as-is" and "to-be" business processes prior to initiating any detailed process modeling, data modeling, or activity-based costing. Process modeling and economic analysis must support the high-level study. There should be a mutual agreement between top management and the process management on the acceptance of the high-level study prior to a decision to implement.
5. There must be some facility for prototyping new ideas. Reengineering by definition calls for radical process redesign. Regardless of the techniques and technologies used, it is imperative that radically changed processes are tested to see if they work as planned.

We believe that the above prerequisites and factors are relevant to both private and public sector reengineering endeavors.

Relationship Between Downsizing and Process Innovation

Downsizing is a reduction in the resources employed. There are many scenarios that can lead to downsizing, but two particularly relevant here are:

1. Decreasing revenues, and
2. Demand for increased efficiency.

While downsizing and process innovation may occur simultaneously, they are distinctly different. Downsizing does not usually focus on process improvement. Hopefully, personnel reductions made possible by process innovation are attained through normal attrition, but this is not always possible. This poses a dilemma for which we provide one solution in the next Section.

Strategies for Attacking the Implementation Problem

There is a new focus on reinventing government, competition, and private sector reengineering. Information technology has changed forever our approach to managing transactions oriented business processes. Even though the public sector might lag the private, government cannot insulate itself from new ways of doing business. Hence, the problem is how to shorten the adoption lag.

The Business Advisory Board

Consideration should be given to the creation of a new position entitled the Undersecretary for Change advised by a Defense Management Board that would address process management issues and problems. The board should be comprised of business executives and government managers (including DoD managers). The board must be permanent, keenly aware of the differences in public and private sector organizations, and should solicit the support of the Senior Executive Service and General Officers to ensure influence over the bureaucracy. The board should be bipartisan.

The business advisory board should devise strategies to identify, involve, and inform key Congressional and external agencies. Successes should be widely disseminated. Implementations should be attempted in all government agencies, not just the DoD.

Management Education and Training

The education and training needs of the DoD are large, spanning the services and Office of the Secretary of Defense. Executive training on reinventing government should be a top priority. Training on change management, process innovation, continuous process improvement, activity accounting, performance/cost measurement, and performance budgeting are also needed. Such training is particularly effective when delivered by private and public sector executives in the form of case studies of both successes and failures.

Obtaining a Successful Functional Process Improvement Implementation

As an initial step, the DoD should form a "tiger team" to demonstrate a success with at least one major business process. A tiger team is a group of the best and brightest line and staff employees that are assembled to work on a particular process innovation problem. The merits of tiger teams were discussed in our interviews. Several conclusions were reached. In most organizations, top management is reluctant to place the complete organization in turmoil by implementing radical change through all parts of the organization at once. However, they may be willing to take a tiger team approach to one part of the organization. If success results, then the process innovation approach may be attempted in other parts of the organization. On the other hand, a success in one area is not necessarily translatable to another. While often true, this can be a rationale for ignoring a good example.

Since the Assistant Secretary of Defense (Command, Control, Communications, and Intelligence) is responsible for the CIM initiative, then perhaps a process under his direct control should be considered. It is probably easier to obtain top-management commitment there than in other parts of the DoD, and hence, success is more likely.

Should a tiger team attempt a "private sector" process innovation initiative within the DoD? If the organization has an eminent cash flow problem, then more stringent short-term actions are indicated. A longer-term approach calls for a well-crafted plan for the tiger team to follow. Resource reductions required in the DoD are of a magnitude that suggests a long-term approach, even though downsizing is to be achieved quickly.

One possible process innovation strategy is to re-deploy workers who would be displaced to more secure positions. This encourages employee involvement during process innovation and insulates these employees from the downsizing taking place elsewhere in the organization. This enhances the probability of success by resolving the dilemma described in the previous section.

The tiger team should rely upon comparative analysis and benchmarking. The DoD might have the ambition to "leap frog" the competition, but may be content to merely emulate private sector organizations. A failure of the CIM initiative was an absence of benchmarked goals. A reasonable beginning for a process innovation experiment would be:

1. An historical legal review of externally imposed rules and regulations, and
2. Private sector benchmarking.

A common ingredient of successful business method change is a set of goals that are not only ambitious, but damn near ridiculous. This forces a zero-based approach to problem solving.

The DoD's time horizon is driven by the election cycle. There are two 18-month time lines, driven by the Congressional and Presidential elections. These argue for a demonstration project. The Office of Personnel Management has indicated renewed interest in such projects.[4]

Summary and Conclusions

This paper, which summarizes our views on reengineering within the DoD, is influenced by interviews with managers at all levels. Issues and problems that affect functional process improvement implementation are identified. Problems and issues are categorized at three levels.

We have also identified some basic postulates and prerequisites for successful business process innovation. We believe that public sector organizations inevitably must address many of the same problems currently being addressed by the private sector where technology is changing forever organizational structures and management practices. These same changes will permeate the public sector. The DoD should anticipate them by renewing its efforts in process innovation by building on the CIM initiative.

Our major contributions relate more to the similarities of the public and private sector reengineering efforts than to the differences. In our case studies and other interviews we noted many similar technical problems; i.e., legacy systems and data, outdated systems and telecommunication infrastructure, etc. We encountered inefficient business processes and inconsistent business rules in both public and private organizations. Surprisingly, we encountered many bureaucratic behavioral problems in both. However, there are differences.

The size of many public organizations and diffuse managerial control make implementation very difficult in public organizations. We are convinced that process innovation cannot occur without top management commitment and close involvement. We have not seen a strong top management commitment in the DoD, and without this, managerial culture and values will not change. Also, private sector successes are usually led by line management with support from staff units. We think the same must be true for successes in the DoD, but given the complex relationship between the Office of the Secretary of Defense and the Services, such a relationship is difficult to solidify.

Also general management elements that are parameters for change must be present. Given they are, several key processes should be selected for change. Innovation should begin with these processes, perhaps as Office of Personnel Management special projects with promises of employee re-deployment. Once success is demonstrated, additional processes should be reevaluated and selected for innovation.

Appendix A
Aetna Life & Casualty Case Study
May 21, 1993

Participants from Aetna Life & Casualty

Ms. Sue Leroux, Mr. Matt Robertson, Ms. Geraldine (Beanie) Weaver

Background of the Participants from Aetna

Sue Leroux is Manager, Reengineering Communications, Corporate Effectiveness; she is currently consulting on all of Aetna's reengineering projects. Beanie Weaver is a member of Aetna's Reengineering group and has participated in seven major reengineering efforts. She is responsible for high-level business modeling. Matt Robertson is in Business Consulting; he focuses on the details of the internal implementation process.

Key Points

In Order To Be Successful, There Must Be High-Level Support in the Organization

The impetus for reengineering in Aetna is clearly associated with Mr. Ron Compton, the CEO. In Ms. Weaver's words, "successful reengineering requires high-level support, and the chairman must want reengineering more than anything in the world."

At first, Aetna divided reengineering into Big R and Small r. This distinction was related to the size of the reengineering effort. Small r is sponsored by the reengineering group, but Big R is always sponsored by the chairman of the organization. In either case the reengineering was, and still is, always driven by the business side of the organization with support from the "information technology partners." The Big R and Small r distinction is no longer made as the chairman supports all of the reengineering projects.

Downsizing Is Perceived Distinctly Different From Reengineering

Aetna has been through downsizing and reengineering, and has had simultaneous efforts in both areas. So far Aetna has lost many more people to downsizing than to reengineering. The workers would often ask: "Are you coming to eliminate our jobs?" The response was: "We will probably change what you do, but we can't tell you whether or not we will eliminate your job."

Legacy Systems Are Often Used (Incorrectly) as an Excuse

It was noted that the DoD is hampered in its reengineering efforts by a multitude of legacy systems. The Aetna participants agreed that legacy systems are an encumbrance but that is never a reason for not tackling a project. They noted that reengineering allowed them to quit using legacy systems as an excuse for not moving forward!

A Good Understanding of the As-Is Process Is Essential

Too often the claim is made that the old process is unimportant, especially if reengineering is to be applied with some radical change. This is wrong. First, unless the affected unit is fully aware of the reasons for change they will resent if not subvert it. Second, the unit needs to help the reengineering team understand the process (otherwise some part may be ignored or incorrectly specified). But primarily, change requires buy-in by the people affected and that is developed by working with them to understand their work.

Time Line for Introducing Reengineering at Aetna

Initial Efforts to Apply Economics to Redesign and Reengineering

Many of the early steps were in place as early as 1988. Mr. Compton Became President of Aetna in 1990 and CEO in January of 1992 No one knows if Mr. Compton envisioned the amount of reengineering that has occurred since he came to office in 1990, but it is generally believed that he had a clear vision about how the organization should function, even though many of his employees were unaware of his vision. The strategic vision involves being quick, flexible, and right. He revealed the plan to management gradually over time.

Through the Aetna Institute, which Compton uses as his change agent, he introduced the Aetna Management Process, a decision-making and problem solving tool which everyone is expected to use (it's the infrastructure of the business plan), and the notion of competency-based performance development.

In 1990, the company reorganized into 16 business units, eliminating its traditional divisional structure. The idea was to create a multi-niche company with a customer focus. As one participant from Aetna said, "We define customer processes first and business processes second." The move to business units helped to reduce bureaucracy and established accountability. Prior to the reorganization, most managers had little concern for the customer, much less ever talked to the customer. Management acted as though the objective was to enlarge the size of the organization. Mr. Compton required each business unit to benchmark and become one of the top-three or "best-of-breed." Otherwise, the unit knew that on some pre-negotiated date their funding would be eliminated.

Aetna Reengineering Effort Announced in October of 1990

At the same time Mr. Compton announced reorganization he also introduced reengineering and launched a massive management education process. Although management was not specifically aware of it, Mr. Compton's previous changes (i.e., Aetna Management Process and competencies) was an attempt to change the management culture prior to reengineering.

Reengineering Is Currently Progressing to Cultural Change

Now, after three years of reengineering, Aetna is continuing to make necessary cultural changes by changing incentives: compensation, status, perks, etc. This is the major focus of Aetna Human Resources in 1993. Internal auditing is beginning to monitor that the savings promised as a result of the reengineering process are being realized.

Downsizing, Reengineering, and the Aetna Environment

Reengineering has had major impact in Aetna; e.g., in the property-casualty claim area the number of field offices is being reduced from 65 to 22. The elimination of the people was accomplished "in a prudent and informed manner." Consolidation into regional service centers was the catalyst. The employees and the managers did not like the downsizing, but they understood why: 1.) improve service and 2.) reduce costs. Though many have left from all levels, attempts are always made to re-deploy good people who become redundant. "We have eliminated at lower levels, but we are also eliminating mid-level management." The resulting company is getting flatter.

The prime reason for reengineering was to become one of the top-three (per the concept of General Electric) or to get-out-of-the-business. Thus Aetna initiated reengineering efforts over a number of processes, from corporate wide (acquisition) to new business ventures. Aetna follows a type of Critical Success Factor approach, but the personnel feel that this is not describing a success in Rockart's sense, but more a critical failure factor; as Ms. Leroux said, "We fail if we don't do it." Strategic Business Units (SBUs) are normally autonomous, being associated with particular lines of business (e.g., homeowners, auto, etc.), but there are some that cross over lines (e.g., purchasing and acquisition, or property/ casualty and claims, which are bundled). Some of the problems of integrating business plans (for new initiatives) were, like other organizations, impeded by the use of legacy systems with little or no capability to cross business lines. However, this was not allowed to stop progress.

Although Mr. Compton allowed a specified time for each unit to meet the Best of Breed challenge, each business unit negotiated their own time-table within reason. He takes a keen interest in progress, but is very busy. He has direct control, but empowers and then checks on results. However, he does not allow anyone to subvert the process. Only one SBU has been terminated. It had been struggling for some time and was finally eliminated due to lack of progress and low probability of reaching the challenge. The pilot had been constructed with participation from four business units. No one (or everyone) was at first accountable; little was accomplished in the first year. No operational decisions had been made. Jobs were assigned on a day-to-day basis. A new leader was then appointed. She decided that a new start may prove successful. She informed the sponsors and they recommitted to the project. It did not reengineer.

Process and Method Used in Aetna Reengineering

Reengineering started with SBUs that "were sure to be a clear-cut winners." The team worked with managers who called for help; some even asked though their business was apparently bloom-ing. Some volunteered due to a potential dramatic change in the market (e.g., though the return on group life and health insurance was significant, the health area was becoming a national issue—this was therefore seen as an activity taken to ensure survival, not for success).

Aetna's core reengineering group reports through corporate strategies to the CEO. They lead the effort in performing the high level process assessment; a plan that is presented to top management for debate and approval. It addresses many issues, including:

1. What are the benefits to Aetna?
2. What are our competitors doing?
3. What do our customers want?
4. What are the potential savings?
5. What are the technology implications?

The high level process design team, in addition to members of the reengineering staff, also includes a group of people from within the organization being studied, making up a reengineering team of about 15. "We always go for the best and the brightest. About 60% are from primary and related businesses. The other 40% are comprised of the core reengineering team, information technology types, risk takers, and radical thinkers. We try to avoid top-heavy teams because they tend to delegate the work. We also search for people who can be implementation team leaders later."

The high-level process assessment uses a DEC tool (Top Mapping). This is a paper-based tool used for understanding how the work is actually performed. It allows the team to understand the current processes "right down to the bottlenecks."

The first phase of process redesign lasts approximately 4 months and costs approximately $100,000. The first two weeks are devoted to planning. This starts with three days in pre-study of the business unit and organizing the team, followed by two days of business education for the new participants and one week of logistics and general planning on who-visits-where.

At this point, the team goes on the road, traveling around the country, talking to field organizations, agents and the customer. The group visits field offices for one to two days each. A good team of 3 to 5 people from the total group can obtain an understanding of the process from the clients in about 1.5 hours. "We actually go to the customer and ask what they think. Most analysts would agree that this is unusual." The part of the staff that travels may be on the road for weeks at a time, however, they meet every Friday to discuss the week's findings and prepare for the next week.

The phase ends with a two-to-three week redesign of the high level process. This was termed, by Ms. Leroux "the business model at 30,000 ft." The team is charged to "invest in their own new business. Build it from scratch using what you've learned." The costs and benefits of the redesigned process are not collected in detail (indeed, there is no attempt at ABC until implementation), however, the team attempts to collect as much data as possible at the early phases to support later analyses. The plan is then presented to management for discussion and buy-in. The business now "owns" the implementation.

The post-reengineering implementation phase then starts. Mr. Robertson is brought in as a consultant to use a computer-based tool. It begins with a reorganization that relates to process flows and moves away from functional silos. It moves on into increasingly more detailed work flows. At the point it drives down to individual work groups it involves computer-assisted methods. It is very operational and takes a long time.

A baseline model is established, followed by a redesign. Mr. Robertson noted that this approach disagreed with that advocated by many consultants (e.g., Mike Hammer), but it is an approach that has worked well for Aetna. "At implementation, concentrate on the fundamental process and having it correct. Technology is an enabler, not a driver." Tools, such as IDEF, are not used during the assessment phase. In fact, detailed process and data modeling are only attempted during implementation, where Texas Instrument's IEF and Coopers and Lybrand's SPARKS are used. Thus Aetna uses the James Martin approach tailored to their needs. There is some cost analysis in the early stages, but detailed activity-based costing is not used at this time.

Conclusions

Proactive Participation of Top-Level Management Is Crucial to the Effort

The Aetna participants all agreed that Mr. Compton is a key person, and if he leaves the organization, there could be some changes with some managers or employees attempting to slow the process. However, the team feels that there will never be a return to the old ways. In fact, there are even some Aetna employees that believe the reengineering program should be more aggressive.

Mr. Compton learned his skills in a command and control environment but, in general, he empowers the reengineering team and then "gets out of the way." For example, there was one business unit that was "going through the motions," but it was clear to Mr. Compton that they were not achieving the reengineering vision. Mr. Compton continually prods the effort and has renewed the commitment.

The Reengineering Group Hopes to Put Itself Out of a Job.

If they continue to be successful over the next few years, the reengineering group feels that they will no longer be needed as a corporate entity. The consequence of success is an understanding of the need for continuous change and reengineering. Thus the job of monitoring and keeping ahead of the competition should disappear into the infrastructure, no longer needing to be a CEO initiative.

Appendix B
Digital Equipment Corporation Case Study
June 15, 1993

Participants from the Digital Equipment Corporation

Mr. John Fisher

Background of Participant from DEC

About eight years ago, Mr. John Fisher was DEC Corporate Comptroller and an Assistant to the President. During that time Mr. Fisher was associated with the first reengineering efforts at DEC. In the interim, he resigned from DEC but later returned and is now the Dean of the DEC Finance Institute and Senior Corporate Finance Manager.

Key Points

Although management issues were the primary focus, the discussion had a substantially information systems and "information" bias, possibly because of DEC's business. Thus much was about information flows and how to improve stove-piped systems to provide better information to internal clients, as well as providing for better information flows throughout DEC. This is not at odds with the material discovered elsewhere, but it is a distinctly different bias towards a methodology and design based on data rather than functionality. Some of Mr. Fisher's discussion was also derived from his work at DEC for external customers.

After initial successes, there will be high level support for reengineering. Mr. Fisher was, of course, initially in a powerful position. However, he said that the reengineering program was initiated by lower-level executives with no CEO involvement. After initial successes were reported to upper management, they gave full support to the concept.

Downsizing Is Different From Reengineering

DEC did not reorganize prior to reengineering. Mr. Fisher felt that reorganizing around business processes prior to reengineering is often not possible, though it may be desirable. "We have 100 years of stovepipes," and the fundamental question is: "How do we integrate the processes across the functional stovepipes? We must look at common systems and see how to make them much better."

Legacy Systems Are a Major Problem

As an example, DEC has one client with 58 plants, 18 warehouses, 300 sales offices, and it is using 1950's style management techniques. "How can you change this situation? What are the new roles of the key people in running the business? What are key programs that will move the organization in the appropriate direction?"

A Good Understanding of the As-Is Process Is Not Essential

DEC management "did not spend a lot of time in assessing the current situation, because we knew that things were a mess." They asked: How do we want to run this company? "We focused on a customer dimension, but we also wanted information on many additional dimensions. We located an operating manager who was willing to support a pilot reengineering project and identified a spin doctor to publicize the win."

There Is a Need for a New "Corporate Vision" of Information Flow

The initial situation at DEC was common to most firms that initiate reengineering: "We were against the wall; we needed to do business a very different way." The most important ingredient is a corporate vision. Someone must ask: At 50,000 feet, how should a 21st century organization flow information? Then corporate culture and values must be changed. "Culture eats change for lunch." After this, management must establish principles for achieving the vision; e.g., "collect data at the source and don't move it unless it is needed" and "make data available to everyone at the same time."

Publicize the Successes

For DEC, there were major changes and managing them was extremely difficult. They had to establish programs that led to early wins (some were throw-aways; implemented to show people the value of the concepts). "White papers don't solve problems; people follow models. There are two problems to be faced: enemies and apathy." When people see successful models, they are more likely to change. This is when demand pull occurs.

Time Line for Introducing Reengineering at DEC

Initial Efforts to Perform Reengineering

Eight years ago, an effort was started to integrate all financial systems and establish a centralized database. The central repository is termed a "data warehouse." The financial reengineering was characterized by the establishment of a "data-to-information bridge."

Major Progress in the Last Decade

Over the last decade DEC has downsized 40,000 positions, including a reduction from 7,600 to 4000 people in finance during an 18 month period.

Downsizing, Reengineering and the DEC Environment

Many organizations are just beginning to face up to the need for a major change. This awareness is being driven by companies realizing that if they do not reengineer, they may not be in business several years from now. Mr. Fisher believes that 40-60% reduction in organizational size will not be uncommon. This is partly because we now have the information technology tools that allow firms to operate better, faster, and cheaper.

Reorganization occurred as a consequence of reengineering, and not vice versa. For example, accounting and other management information systems were in multiple locations throughout the organization, including 76 general ledger systems and 29 accounts payable systems. "We identified five managers and convinced them that they could get better service by sharing." Not much time was spent in analyzing the as-is situation. "The savings were obvious; we just looked for better and cheaper ways of doing things." Even though DEC did not reorganize prior to reengineering, reorganization occurred as the reengineering proceeded. "We now have five shared resource centers. We changed most of the people at the top, and then we identified ways that we could reorganize. The early wins allowed all of this to happen."

Many of the people who initiated reengineering at DEC have moved to other tasks, but the ideas and culture have survived. Some processes just can't be changed quickly. The situation at DEC, however, was not one of choice. "Our profit went away; we changed our CEO, and we had a business model that was not sustainable. We literally fired people. We had 'tree-huggers' who were holding on to the old ways. Senior people were fired, and we moved to a reward system that assigned accountability to the links in the supply chain." Mr. Fisher noted that they were just not far enough into the change process to provide a thorough assessment of the new reward system. Also, he stated that they were not yet giving bonuses or additional compensation for improving the value chain.

Examples of Success

Mr. Fisher provided two mini-cases as examples. The Finance Data reengineering effort started when it became obvious that managers often had different versions of corporate financial data. The problem was a gap between the data and the systems that needed to access them. Thus the data was not transformable into information. The CEO finally said: "Fix it." It was difficult to have executive meetings. To correct this, a centralized data warehouse concept was implemented. The ultimate indicator of its success was when the CEO refused to accept corporate data as evidence in a meeting unless it was obtained from the warehouse. We went from supply-push to demand-pull overnight. Everyone wanted our information. The transition was, however, painful, and many jobs were eliminated. The overall effort has been going on for about ten years.

DEC has reengineered their complete product supply chain. The 18-36 month life-cycle begins with development of the needs and flows (for both hardware and software); it continues through production and marketing to warehousing, with one of its major goals as inventory reduction.

Critical Success Factors

Mr. Fisher felt that DEC is always assessing Critical Success Factors that will ensure that they remain best in class. We focus on profit, quality, time-to-market, customer satisfaction, etc. "We view DEC as a chain where each component is a link. The customer sees the end of the chain." DEC examines each link and tries to identify value-added links. Non-value-added links are eliminated.

Cultural Aspects of Prototyping as a Tool

When asked how people were empowered for cultural change, Mr. Fisher said: "Our objective was to go from the data entry to the data user directly, eliminating all of the intermediate data massagers, transcribers, etc. The operating people did not know what they needed in terms of information. We put all of the data in the warehouse, and then we created tools called workbenches." These workbenches are process and data information systems that focus on particular functions; e.g., marketing workbench, production workbench, etc. We constructed prototype workbenches and gave them to the managers. They allow the user or an MIS consultant to develop a trial system. Each manager approves and improves the workbench, and every managerial generation does the same. This helped in the transition from a supply-push to a demand-pull data environment. "When you go from supply-push to demand-pull, you can feel the tide change." Once the tide has shifted (i.e., managers become empowered for cultural change), then it becomes a problem of managing the change process. "How de we manage the process that gets us from the as-is to the to-be?"

The Role of the CEO

Mr. Fisher noted that the meetings with all of the briefing charts are not always effective in making the point about where the organization should go. "Sometimes you need to take the CEO to dinner, and you must efficiently choose your terms and use the proper spin. Its lonely when you have a vision and you don't believe that anyone else knows what you are talking about." Mr. Fisher's advice to the DoD is: DoD needs some marketers.

There was a focus on the need for the reengineering team to encourage top management to proceed. "Top management's role is to say yes or no. You must nurture the top person; you have to ghost-write and nurture the investment so that the top person will champion the idea. You may have to write the CEO's speech. You have to understand the limits of the CEO, and you must feed the CEO with the necessary information to keep the project moving. This is the way to champion your ideas. A bright person supporting a good top person can use the top person to achieve the reengineering goals."

Resistance to Change

Mr. Fisher noted that the biggest resistance to change is fear. The challenge is to turn fear into excitement. "The people who understand the vision are more valuable to the organization and society. Turn the adrenaline of fear into the adrenaline of excitement." Another key factor is the realization that change involves giving up something. At DEC people were opposed to change at first, but then they accepted the change. "I have even seen parties celebrating the end of the old ways." "Once everyone accepts the fact that change is inevitable, it becomes a problem of managing the bucking bronco. You don't know where the bronco is going, but you know that sooner or later it will come back to the barn for oats."

Process and Method Used in DEC Reengineering

Get people who have the "big perspective" on a particular area in a room with ONE sheet of clean paper and pose one question: How do we want the information to flow in the organization? In DEC, such a vision takes four people two weeks. And these people are not to do anything else while this effort is being accomplished. Next the question, to be answered using only ONE new piece of paper, is: What principles are required to implement this vision? The major challenge is then: How can your current system be made to operate five times better?

In conclusion, "The real issue is how you induce fundamental change in a political service oriented environment. Select a space where there are enlightened people, and dedicate your best people to the effort." After the first success is obtained, the focus shifts to marketing. "You need 'spin' after you get success. What are the events that must be choreographed to move from where we are now to where we want to go?"

Endnotes

[1]This work was sponsored by the Office of the Deputy Assistant Secretary of Defense for Information Management. The sponsor was Ms. Mary Howard Smith. At the time this work was initiated, the sponsoring office was the Office of the Director of Defense Information (DDI). Since many of the items discussed require historical context, we have retained the more familiar DDI terminology.

[2]We use the term "reinventing government" to call attention to the general ideas that were presented by Osborne and Gaebler (1992). However, we are not wedded to their specific ideas. We view it from an internal DoD perspective; i.e., efficiently meeting the needs of the customer while responding to the budgetary realities of a changing world situation.

[3]Underhead is a term that describes mid-level non-value-added management. These are managers who don't add value to the customer in any appreciable way.

[4]This renewed interest in innovative projects was expressed by Mr. Paul

Thompson, Chief of the Innovations Development Staff of the U.S. Office of Personnel Management. The comments were made at the 16 April 1993 initial meeting of the DoD Task Force for Expanding Innovative Civilian Personnel Management Practices.

References

Berliner, Callie and James A. Brimson. (1988) *Cost Management for Today's Advanced Manufacturing: The CAM-I Conceptual Design*. Boston: Harvard Business School Press.

Bowlin, Samuel. (April, 1991) *Challenges Facing Defense's Corporate Information Management Initiative, Statement Before the Subcommittee on Readiness*, Committee on Armed Services, U.S. House of Representatives, GAO/T-IMTEC-91-10. Washington: U.S. General Accounting Office.

Corporate Information Management: Functional Economic Analysis Guidebook. (1993) Washington, DC: Director of Defense Information.

Corporate Information Management: Process Improvement Methodology for DoD Functional Managers, Second Edition. (1993). Washington, DC: Director of Defense Information.

Davenport, Thomas H. (1993) *Process Innovation: Reengineering Work Through Information Technology*. Boston: Harvard Business School Press.

Functional Process Improvement, DoD 8020.1-M (Revised). (January, 1993). Washington, DC: Director of Defense Information.

Hammer, Michael. (July-August, 1990). Reengineering Work: Don't Automate, Obliterate. *Harvard Business Review*, 104-112.

Johnson, Kirk. (March 1, 1992). *The New Marching Orders at Aetna*. New York Times.

Osborne, David and Ted Gaebler. (1992). *Reinventing Government*. Reading, MA: Addison-Wesley.

U.S. General Accounting Office. (September, 1992) *Corporate Information Management Must Overcome Major Problems*, GAO/IMTEC-92-77. Washington, DC: U.S. General Accounting Office.

U.S. General Accounting Office. (April, 1994). *Stronger Support Needed for Corporate Information Management Initiative To Succeed*, GAO/AIMD/NSIAD-94-101. Washington, DC: U.S. General Accounting Office.

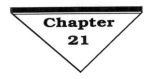

Chapter 21

Assessment of the Impacts of BPR and Information Technology Use on Team Communication:

The Case of ICL Data

Juha Parnisto
*Turku School of Economics
and Business Administration*

A real transformation towards an information society is happening and this process will effect on every organization's activities. As Peter Drucker says: "The information-based organization requires far more specialists overall than the command-and-control companies we are accustomed to. Moreover, the specialists are found in operations, not at corporate headquarters" (Drucker 1988). The new organization emerges as a dynamic network, which consists of experts and communication channels, and the connections will increasingly cross organizational boundaries (Miles and Snow 1986; Yarnell and Peterson 1993). These visions are common in management literature.

However, management literature also emphasizes the increasing complexity of the business environment. Changes in market structures, increasing speed of product development, new emerging businesses and innovative use of technology form a complicated and turbulent environment. Customers simultaneously demand both first-class service and low prices. In this situation, flexibility and the ability to adapt to changing customer preferences become the critical sources of competitive advantage. These properties must be included in organizational structures and processes.

Distributed work groups, teams, provide a good basis for operation in complex environments (Drucker 1988). The basic purpose of team organizations is the effective sharing of knowledge and expertise. According to Huber, organizations are becoming more and more dependent on the problem-solving capabilities of teams (Huber 1984). Teams enable effective management and control of complicated business processes and new ways to organize things. For employees, teams provide a forum where they can effectively get information, resources, and the support required in their work.

The interplay between information technology and organizational form is receiving growing attention. The trend towards team organizations is supported by information technology (Rockart and Short 1989). New technologies, like work flow management and communication support tools offer many new possibilities for teamwork. As a result of emerging network structures and modern information technology, teams are becoming organizationally and geographically distributed. Different people from different functional units and different locations are working together. This does not necessarily mean that the traditional hierarchical organization is disappearing; the functionally divided organization has its own advantages (Jacques 1990). The control and allocation of resources are perhaps easier to manage in traditional companies. But the team as an organizational unit has greater abilities to concentrate on managing and performing cross-functional business processes.

In this chapter, we discuss building a competitive organization through business process reengineering. Our aim is to try to understand how team organizations support the effective performance of business processes. Team communication and communication technology have an important role to play as a part of this support. We also present a model, which helps us to identify some important determinants and elements of team-based reengineering and evaluate the success of the change process. This model should offer a guideline to business managers. It helps them to identify some critical factors concerning business process reengineering, teams and information technology. These factors have a major impact on managing structural change efforts. The model also offers possibilities to generate hypotheses for further research. The purpose of this chapter is not to construct any BPR methods, because management literature is already filled with such methods; neither does the chapter describe any particularly successful BPR project. The aim is to discuss measuring or assessing the impacts of BPR in organizations. The findings of this study are based on a case study, which implies that they are guiding and suggestive in nature rather than exact and highly generalizable.

The evolving relationship between information technology and the business domain is discussed in the next section. Some background theories concerning organization development and information technology use in organizations are then briefly introduced. The actual research model is presented in the section entitled A Model of team communication. The analysis tool for measuring communication and information technology use in teams is also introduced in this section. The use of the model in the case company and some implications of the study are discussed in the final sections.

Background: BPR in the Alignment of Business and Information Technology

Strategic alignment

Information technology (IT) has many links to business process reengineering (BPR). Hammer (1990) suggested that information technology has often been used to automate existing processes, but the enabling effect of IT has not been recognized. IT is only one of several enablers of business change, but the effects of these enablers should be identified in an early phase of the reengineering effort (Davenport 1993).

BPR aims to achieve strategic outcomes. This means that the ultimate objective is improved competitiveness (Reponen 1993). Combining business and IT domains has been a difficult problem in many organizations (Earl 1993; Galliers 1987). Several frameworks have been developed to help managers align these domains. The strategic alignment model by Venkatraman (1991) focuses on strategic fit between the competitive environment (external domain) and organizational structures, business processes, and the human resource skills required to achieve organizational competencies (internal domain). This strategic fit is important to the IT domain as well. The external domain explicates the company's competitive position in relation to competitors and the internal domain comprises activities and skills within the internal information systems function.

Functional integration occurs at two levels. At the first level is the integration of business strategy and IT strategy, that is the capability of IT functionality to both shape and support business strategy; at the second level is the integration of organizational infrastructure and processes, including the IT infrastructure and processes (Henderson and Venkatraman 1993). The purpose is to achieve a strategic fit between business needs and the IT services.

The model of strategic alignment firmly connects business processes to business strategy. This is an important link that has perhaps not been sufficiently emphasized in some BPR models. In addition to creating competitive advantage, strategic planning must also support the sustenance of competitive abilities. Organizations must be able to change radically when necessary. Flexibility and renewal are prerequisites of survival (Waterman 1988). The basis for business competition never ceases to evolve. In the future, the decoupling of product and process life cycles will probably be one of the key creators of competitive advantage (Pine 1993). The importance of individual products decreases as the same processes can be used to develop, produce, market and deliver many products. Process flexibility can be achieved through BPR.

BPR as organizational change

In the previous chapter we discussed aligning information technology and business processes. This alignment can be achieved through BPR. In this section we first define BPR, then draw attention to a number of important factors affecting BPR planning and implementation. These include the scope and nature of the change, the information intensity of business processes, and the management of organizational interdependencies. Questions concerning actual BPR methods will also be raised.

To understand the concept of business process reengineering we must first define it. A business process is "a specific ordering of work activities across time and place, with a beginning, an end, and clearly identified inputs and outputs: a structure for action" (Davenport 1993). A process also has a customer or customers who use its output. The customer may be internal or external to the organization.

Defining BPR is a more difficult problem. BPR is understood here as a radical change process that is supposed to improve competitiveness significantly. Information technology and information resource management have a central role in implementing BPR. Grover et al. have analyzed several definitions of BPR and identified the following common features (Grover, Teng and Fiedler 1993):

• BPR involves the radical redesign of business processes,
• BPR typically employs information technology as an enabler,
• BPR attempts to achieve organizational level strategic outcomes, and
• BPR efforts tend to be interfunctional.

On the basis of these features we could define BPR as a methodology for the redesign of business processes in order to achieve strategic outcomes. It is important to understand the nature of BPR as organizational change.

The scope and organizational level of reengineering efforts may vary (Davenport 1993). Continuous improvement means proceeding slowly in small steps towards improved effectiveness. It is sometimes characterized as a bottom-up process, which means that the initiatives and suggestions for improvement usually come from operative level employees. Information about improvements may be gathered systematically by using total quality management systems. The starting point of the change is usually an existing process. Some parts of that process are considered to be redundant or non-value-adding. Changes are then aimed at eliminating these problems.

BPR is more radical in nature. Initiatives start from a clean slate, rather than from existing processes. The role of management is very critical. It is by no means insignificant in a continuous improvement approach, but BPR really must be managed effectively. BPR usually requires many more resources (at least in the short term) than continuous improvement, because the planning phase tends to be more complicated and achieving employee commitment to change is more difficult. Business process reengineering emphasizes innovativeness and creative thinking. Old and established operational models often restrict our thinking and inhibit the occurrence of new ideas. Only minor benefits and improvements can be achieved if these models and habits are not questioned. Major benefits, which BPR might produce, include increasing productivity 100 %, or cutting cycle time in half. Objectives like these require entirely new thinking and often the application of technology in a new way. According to Hammer and Champy, BPR must be based on the total redesign of existing processes. "Nothing is taken for granted" (Hammer and Champy 1993). A radical approach is certainly required, but can we really start BPR from the beginning, with a "clean sheet" as Hammer and Champy suggest? Existing structures and routines may certainly be described as organizational ballast, but they also form an important source of experience and knowledge. The real challenge is to get people to think in a new way and then find new ways to organize work. Flattening organizations or cutting bureaucracies are not objectives of BPR, but its results.

Venkatraman (1994) suggests that the benefits of IT are marginal if it is only used to support existing activities. The benefits are substantially increased if corresponding changes are also made in organizational characteristics.

Porter and Millar (1985) suggested that the information intensity of products and services has important effects on information technology use in organizations. Information is used to customize products on the basis of individual customer needs (Pine 1993). Information is also used as a value-adding element in the product. Many new products and services are completely based on information.

The information intensity of structures and processes is also increasing. Organizational structures of coordination and cooperation are becoming more complex, which emphasizes the need for effective information management. Information intensive core processes provide competitive advantage in many industries. Information and communication technology enable the direct distribution of many products and services. But it may also lower obstacles to market penetration. Many small companies have used information technology to compete successfully against big manufacturers, because the technology has provided the potential for product customization.

Rockart and Short (1989) claim that information technology provides a new approach to managing organizational interdependence: the focus of planning is not on optimizing operations within functional departments, but on optimizing business processes, which tend to be cross-functional. Companies usually have highly specialized functional units (e.g. manufacturing, sales, purchasing). However, these units are also interlinked by the value chain. What happens in one function affects another. Interdependencies also exist at an interorganizational level: companies rely on other companies to supply products or services. Effective information sharing and cooperation are required to manage organizational interdependencies, and information technology is a major factor that enables the management of information flows between units. However, the use of IT alone is not usually sufficient. Structural solutions are also required. Teamwork is one way to coordinate interdependent activities among separate units.

A Model of Team Communication

The Nature of Team Organizations

Many traditional hierarchical organizations have emphasized efficiency ahead of effectiveness. Hierarchical structures may lead to ineffective processes and overlapping work procedures. Too much attention is paid to vertical processes (reporting and control), while horizontal activity chains are neglected. BPR emphasizes these horizontal processes. One way to manage these processes is to use teams. The term team refers to a group of people, who have complementary skills and knowledge, and who control and perform a process (Katzenbach and Smith 1993).

The members of the team do not necessarily meet each other at all. They use information systems to communicate. The term information system here includes traditional technologies like telephone and fax, as well as more sophisticated applications like electronic mail, group decision support systems, work flow applications etc.

Teams may of course have meetings (face-to-face communication has many advantages). Electronic communication media are, however, used more and more often in routine work procedures.

The nature of groups and group processes has been examined intensively in social psychology. Kurt Lewin was one of the most influential researchers in this area. His Field Theory suggests that the group is an important and independent research object (Worchel, Wood and Simpson 1990). Many other researchers have continued Lewin's work. In information systems literature, the research has mainly focused on group decision support systems. However, the development of new communication technology has brought about a need to rethink the concept of work group. Groups do not have to meet physically in the same place. Communication may also be asynchronous, which means that messages to other group members can be sent at any time. They will receive them when they, for example, read their e-mail messages. The effects of these new forms of communication on organizations and teamwork have yet to be thoroughly examined.

Business processes are cross-functional and require cooperation between organizational units. Different skills and knowledge must be brought together in order to manage processes. A chain of people is required to control a process and this chain is called a team. If we want to change the way organizations operate, we must also take into account the structures behind the operational activities. Structuration theory suggests that social action is capable not only of reproducing existing social structure, but also of producing new structure (Giddens 1979). This means that the way people act changes their values and norms (structures) but these structures also influence the activities. This has important consequences for teamwork.

Teams as Networks of Social Relationships

Organizations or organizational subunits (work groups) can be analyzed as social networks. A social network is a set of nodes (e.g. persons, organizations) linked by a set of social relationships of a specific type (Krackhardt and Hanson 1993). This perspective also applies to organizations at several levels of analysis —individuals, groups, subunits of organizations, and entire organizations.

The network theory was originated by social researchers in the 1930s. According to Nohria (1992), social network perspective has only recently expanded to include organization researchers. This perspective has attracted more attention as researchers have noticed that small informal organizations are very flexible and effective, especially in complicated business environments. The increased information processing capacity of organizations and continuing specialization of employees and experts has also emphasized the significance of horizontal connections. Network theory offers possibilities for new perspectives on organizing, management, information management and communication.

Network analysis is commonly used in the field of sociology for modeling social relationships and structures (Segars and Grover 1994). It is also an effective method for modeling patterns of organizational communication (Fulk and Boyd 1991), providing several methods for network model construction and analysis. The focus is on relationships or links between one or more persons, objects or other entities. Through various operationalisations, network analysis can be used to identify and measure a variety of network features.

The network perspective enables researcher to focus on relationships between organizational actors. According to Ibarra (1992), two kinds of network structures exist in organizations: prescribed and emergent networks. Prescribed networks are composed of a set of formally specified relationships between superiors and subordinates and among functionally differentiated groups that must interact to accomplish an organizationally defined task. Emergent networks involve informal, discretionary patterns of interaction where the content of the relationship may be work-related, social, or a combination of both. Ibarra views teams as prescribed networks. She wants to draw a distinction between formal task-oriented relationships and mainly social relationships, and then compare the networks of relationships to identify differences and similarities. She also suggests that informal organizational structures have significant effect on action and performance. Segars and Grover (1994) claim that a particularly strong feature of network analysis is its focus on emergent communication networks. Network analysis is able to capture the communication pattern of network members, and their perception of what the pattern should be. If members think that communication patterns are poor or their opinions are very different, then communication processes are a likely area for redesign efforts.

Formal organization charts do not capture the complex network of relationships that exist in an organization. Informal or emergent networks are very important for productivity and learning in organizations (Tapscott and Caston 1993; Nohria 1992). Social networks may cross organizational boundaries. For example, customers or vendors are often connected to organizational processes and this means that they are also included in social networks. Burt and Minor (1983) suggest that the behavior and action of organizational actors can be understood by identifying their network position and role. Centrally positioned actors have more power and possibilities to influence other actors, although this perspective is not dominant in this study. The focus is rather on communication patterns and information exchange in networks. Special interest lies in a communication and groupware technology use.

The analysis of social networks may be based on formal, mathematical network analysis (e.g. Rogers and Kincaid 1981, Burt and Minor 1983, Ibarra 1992), or more qualitatively oriented analysis (Contractor and Eisenberg 1990). The problem inherent in the quantitative approach is that it includes only some identifiable variables in the analysis. It also requires a large sample and, most importantly, the dynamic nature of the network is not included in the model.

The best approach is perhaps to combine both quantitative and qualitative research approaches (Fitzgerald 1991). Quantitative methods provide ways to analyze and compare the communication patterns in social networks. They enable a robust and strict analysis and produce results that are easier to generalize in a scientific sense. However, qualitative methods are required to understand the context in which networks emerge and act (Markus and Robey 1988; Kling 1987). Simply describing networks in quantitative terms does not capture the rich organizational reality. Conditions in organizations sometimes change rapidly and a qualitative analysis is therefore required to ensure that quantitative analysis measures the right things.

Rogers and Kincaid (1981) emphasize the significance of the relationships between actors as the unit of analysis. The relationships describe information exchange patterns, and the actual research variables are attributes of these relationships (e.g. information intensity or technology use). The nature of cause-effect relationships between different variables is very complex. The variables of interest in communication are depicted in figure 1.

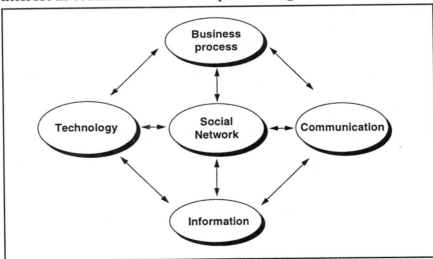

Figure 1. The research framework

Model components

Process characteristics

The business process that a work group performs, constitutes the basis for analysis. Several researchers (McGrath 1984; Kutsko and Smith 1991) term this variable a task, but the concept of business process seems to extend the perspective of analysis. A task is a narrow series of activities, whereas teams usually perform large business processes, because these processes are so complicated that individual persons are not capable of managing all the information and actions needed. Business processes contain several tasks.

The complexity and nature of the business process have a significant impact on group communication and information processing. At least the following properties of the business process should be analyzed:

- nature of the process (horizontal business process, management process),
- scope of the process (intrafunctional, cross-functional, inter-organizational),
- duration of the process, and
- standardization of the process.

Management processes (e.g. reporting, objective setting) are vertical processes between supervisors and their subordinates. These processes are also important for organizational effectiveness because reporting, meetings, and planning are time consuming and often include redundant activities.

Intrafunctional processes are often quite efficient. If the process is performed entirely within a single functional unit, participants in communication concerning the process tend to have similar backgrounds and models of behavior. They form a tightly coupled social network. Cross-functional processes are more difficult to perform since the linkages between participants are looser. They have different tasks and methods of action. Processes crossing organizational boundaries are perhaps the most complicated if we think of the amount and complexity of communication involved. The participants may have different and conflicting objectives, which leads to fragmented communication patterns. On the other hand, organizations tend to pay more attention to interorganizational processes. The effectiveness of these processes may be at a higher level than that of some internal processes. For example, relationships with customers and vendors are often standardized and carefully managed.

Processes having a clear life cycle (e.g. projects, product deliveries) are perhaps more manageable and usually more standardized than continuing processes (e.g. product development, organization development). Highly standardized processes require less information sharing and coordinating activities, because everyone involved knows what to do and when.

Information. Information refers to the meaning human actors assign to items or collections of data (Zmud 1990). Information is gathered from various internal and external sources and it guides the setting of objectives, performing tasks, and assessing the extent to which objectives are met. The characteristics of information affect communication procedures and communication media selection. The complexity of information is usually based on two concepts: uncertainty and equivocality. Uncertainty refers to the absence of information or the difference between the information needed and that available in a certain situation. Communication is a way to receive information and therefore reduce uncertainty (Daft and Lengel 1986). Equivocality means that human actors perceive and interpret information in multiple and conflicting ways (Weick 1979; Daft, Lengel and Trevino 1987). Equivocality arises when individuals have different approaches and mental models, and negotiations are required to reach understanding of a situation or solution.

Some business processes include a lot of information processing. Contemporary information systems are able to process huge amounts of simple data. The processing and exchange of complicated information usually requires a lot of information interpretation. This results in a need for intensive communication and effective information management tools.

Information richness theory claims that if the complexity of information is low, electronic channels (e.g. electronic mail) are effective information exchange media. The term complexity covers both the degree of uncertainty and the degree of equivocality in this study. If information richness or complexity is high, face-to-face communication is a better alternative, because people use more contextual expressions (e.g. gestures, tone of voice). Information richness theory has been criticized by several researchers (Markus 1990; El-Shinnawy and Markus 1992). It seems that media richness is not sufficient as the sole determinant of the ability to handle equivocality. Several other factors must be assessed in order to examine how human actors process and interpret information and why certain communication media are used.

Communication. The communication process itself is an important part of group work. The frequency of communication and the different communication channels used have implications for communication effectiveness e.g. the amount of interpretation required. The process has drawn growing attention as traditional linear models of communication have turned out to be insufficient. Shannon and Weaver (1949) presented their model of linear communication, which was originally constructed for electronic communication but was also adopted by organization researchers. The communication process was described as a process between information source and destination; the media used was also included in the model, message interpretation was not. Rogers and Kincaid (1981) introduced a convergency model of communication: human communication is a cyclical process that aims to achieve shared interpretations and mutual understanding. Collective action is possible only if the interpretation and understanding of information reaches the level of shared interpretation and mutual understanding.

The social influence model of communication (Fulk, Schmitz and Steinfield 1990; Fulk 1992) emphasizes situational factors and cognitive processes in communication. Perceptions are used for rationalizing and giving meaning to behavior; they may also arise from a prior history of social interaction. This theory comes close to structuration theory, which is discussed in the next section. Both theories assume that human actors perceive things differently in different situations. A deep understanding of contextual factors, work processes related to communication, and communication media characteristics is a prerequisite for analyzing computer supported communication effectiveness.

Technology. The characteristics of the technology used (specially information technology) in supporting the process of communication should be analyzed. Groupware technology offers different tools for communication support (e.g. e-mail, bulletin boards, work flow management). More traditional communication channels (telephone, fax and meetings) are often used together with computer-based information systems.

Poole and DeSanctis (1990) have identified several features of technology that might influence group interaction (the list below is somewhat modified, the original list of features concerning group decision support systems):

- face-to-face versus dispersed group support (if the group works as a dispersed unit, a groupware system may be the only communication channel available),
- level of sophistication of the groupware system,
- degree of structure (how well the system supports group activities),
- degree of member control over the system (group members can directly control some groupware systems, while others may require a facilitator e.g. electronic conferencing may require assistance from technical personnel),
- asynchronous versus synchronous support (if members meet asynchronously, the system must regulate their interaction, while in synchronous work members regulate their interactions directly).

The analysis of the characteristics of technology implies accepting the concept of technological imperative, i.e. viewing technology as an exogenous force (Markus and Robey 1988). It has a great deal of effects (or even determines) the behavior of organizational agents, behavior that is the result of external forces. Leavitt and Whisler (1958), for example, described the effects of computerization on managerial work and Simon (1977) suggested that technology would centralize decision making in organizations. The relationship between technology and organizations or human action is seen as one-sided and causal (certain changes occur because of the development of technology).

Contractor and Eisenberg (1990) criticize this approach. Technology should be assessed as a tool that has dynamic characteristics. Communication technology is not simply a carrier of users' information and intentions. Technology is a tool with varying capabilities: it is used define problems, develop solutions and change environments (Dhar and Olson 1989). Groupware technology is a good example of this, because different people with different intentions use it to coordinate and perform mutual activities. In the typology of Markus and Robey (1988) this could be called organizational imperative. It suggests that there are always several different technological options from which an organization can choose. Designers and systems analysts make rational choices and organizations are able to control the effects and consequences of technology. According to technological imperative, technology is an independent variable, but organizational imperative views technology as a dependent variable. Organizations determine how technology is used and developed.

Contractor and Eisenberg (1990) suggest that both media characteristics and the dynamic nature of these characteristics should be recognized. This emergent imperative suggests that the cause-effect relationships of technology use and organizational activities and structures are quite complicated. The behavior of organizational systems cannot be predicted a priori because the preferences, values, skills and abilities of human actors change over time. The consequences of technology use emerge unpredictably from complex social interactions. The reciprocal relationships among objectives, technology and action should be the basis for understanding and research, not just some specified attributes of these elements.

Social Networks as Dynamic Systems

According to structuration theory, structure and action in organizations are not separate elements. They are connected to each other through modalities. Structures are images of relationships (for example power relationships) perceived by organizational actors. Structures have a significant impact on the way people act and behave; they both enable and restrict action. The influence is not one-sided. Action also affects structures, which are either reproduced or changed by the behavior and acts of people; it may also stimulate new structures. This approach can be useful in BPR efforts. Understanding structures and action and their significance to organizational processes is essential for real improvements.

Adaptive structuration theory (AST) attempts to evaluate the structural changes that technology causes in organizations (DeSanctis and Poole 1991). AST is a move from object-centered research towards social-actor-centered research (Gopal, Bostrom and Chin 1993). The research object is not technology itself (hardware or programs), rather its use in different social and organizational contexts. According to Poole and DeSanctis, group outcomes reflect the manner in which groups appropriate the structures of the technology and the context of its use (Poole and DeSanctis 1990). The focus is not on identifying and modeling causal relationships but rather on analyzing how groups use information technology. Social technologies place group members in unfamiliar cognitive ground (Poole and DeSanctis 1989). Technology provides tools for information management, and the nature and processes of communication are changed along with the use of the technology. Social processes and structures are produced and reproduced. The use of technology becomes an adjustment process, one of adaptation. A group can adapt technology in many different ways and the adaptation process usually has some emergent features that cannot be foreseen. For example, users of an information system may not use some of the system's tools or features at all, but on the other hand they often invent new ways to apply some parts of the system.   By using technology users also change the purpose of the technology. This process of change and adaptation is called appropriation. In the appropriation process, the group fits structures to its own use through the structuration process.

AST emphasizes organizational contexts. Groups adapt situations and contexts through the adaptation process. Exogenous variables like task, resources, previous experiences etc. affect this process. Group members use resources (e.g. technological resources) in order to be able to act purposefully in a certain situation or context. The adaptation process may be explicit (group analyzes context and makes a plan for action) or implicit (group reactively adapts to situations). In group support systems the adaptation process takes place through the use and sharing of information and models of action. The appropriation of technology includes learning to use those rules and resources that the group support system enables. For example, the use of electronic bulletin boards enables the effective and almost real-time communication of a distributed team. This also increases the efficiency of team members and may give technical experts much more influence than they would otherwise have. The use of technology emphasizes the skills and knowledge of team members and decreases the significance of formal structures.

Structuration theory offers a good basis for understanding the behavior of people and groups in organizations (Walsham 1993). AST is represented very briefly in this chapter. It is discussed in a more detailed form by, for example, Poole and DeSanctis (1989), and has mainly been applied in the research of group decision support systems. But the foundations of the theory are not tightly connected to any specific technology; we may therefore apply it to other forms of technology as well. AST tends to construct models of the effects of technology and tasks on group decision making. In our model, task is replaced with process. Decision making is only one dimension of group work. Teamwork also involves coordinating and collaborative tasks like planning, management processes, reporting etc.

Structuration theory suggests that the interaction between elements of the model is quite complicated. It is difficult to identify strict cause-effect relationships; the elements rather bind together in a process of mutual interaction. It is natural that the relationships between elements change over time. Social networks are not stable, but rather change as people's values and intentions change (McGrath 1991). This dynamic process of change is depicted in figure 2. Social networks are open systems that gather information and influences from their environment and react to changes. Management may cause significant changes in the structure and action of networks by setting objectives and performance measures. The previous knowledge and experiences of network members also affect the structures of network; organizational culture forms a further contextual factor.

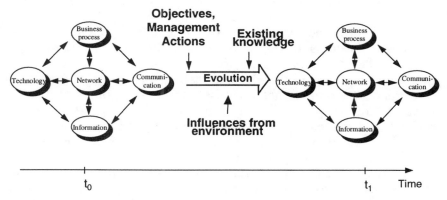

Figure 2. The dynamics of social networks

Some organization cultures support open communication or encourage risk taking in all actions, while others prefer formal communication channels and avoid risks.

Communication Profile as an Analysis Tool

In order to understand and assess action and communication in social networks, an analysis tool termed the communication profile was constructed for this study (the structure of the profile is described in figure 4). It is based on a contextual approach, which means that the researcher must first examine the organizational context; this context prescribes how human actors behave in different situations. Another requisite factor for the tool is that it must enable analysis over time. If we want to understand the structuration of communication technology, the development of communication patterns and technology use should be analyzed over a long period.

A communication profile can be constructed using interviews or questionnaires. Interviews were used in this study because the profile tool was in the construction phase and researcher wanted to make sure that the questions were relevant.

The first step in constructing a communication profile is environmental analysis. The complexity of the environment in which the team is working has important consequences for teamwork (Larson and LaFasto 1989). The team members may also perceive the external environment in different ways, which then causes different interpretations and even conflicts within the team. Research by Coleman (1986) provides evidence that the failure of the team to perform a given task is usually attributed to factors outside the team itself. The culture and basic strategy of the organization must also be analyzed. Interviews with some key members of the team are perhaps the best method in this phase, since it is essential to capture the working atmosphere and objectives of the team. This enables the calibration of the tool for subsequent phases and makes interpretation of the results easier.

Second step is to analyze the factors depicted in the team communication model. The complexity and structure of the business process are important determinants of communication requirements. The resources allocated to the team are also a key factor. Limited use of resources like time, management support, equipment etc. causes unnecessary delays and lack of commitment. The allocation of resources is mainly a managerial task. Larson and LaFasto (1989) emphasize the significance of tangible and structured support as a creator of a collaborative climate in teamwork. It is useful to divide a process into phases or subprocesses, especially if the composition of the team changes between different phases.

The complexity of the process can be assessed using several measures, e.g. resource intensity (costs, skills required to perform the process), or cycle time of the process. The purpose of process analysis in communication profile construction is not necessarily to assess the effectiveness of the process; this is usually included in the BPR methodology. The purpose is to assess the perceived complexity of the process, because complexity has important consequences for communication and information intensity.

The third phase in constructing the communication profile of a group is to identify different linkages in the network. Several quantitative measures are available. The size of the network is naturally a very basic variable. Connectedness measures the degree to which a unit is linked to other units (the unit of analysis may be the individual, a group, or the whole system). Connectedness is indexed as the actual number of links between the focal individual and the other members of the network, divided by the number of possible links (the number of individuals in the network minus one). Integration is the degree to which the units linked to the focal unit are linked to each other. Integration is measured as the number of indirect links between the focal individual and the members of his/her personal communication network, divided by the possible number of such links. Diversity is the degree to which the units linked to the focal unit are heterogeneous in some variable. Openness is the degree to which a unit exchanges information with its environment. All these measures are quantitatively calculated on the basis of interview or questionnaire data. Methods of network analysis are discussed in more detail elsewhere (e.g. Rogers and Kincaid 1981; Burt and Minor 1983). The quantitative analysis is able to describe some elements of the social network, but these can be complemented with qualitative analysis.

The communication process itself needs to be analyzed. The frequency and nature of communication procedures in the group implies the degree of collaboration and group coupling. The complexity and amount of information exchanged in the communication process also affect the use of communication technology. Information complexity can be assessed by analyzing the degree of equivocality and uncertainty through various operationalizations (El-Shinnawy and Markus 1992). Equivocality can be assessed by analyzing how much negotiation is included in the process, how much explanation and clarification is required in order to achieve mutual understanding. Uncertainty refers to accuracy, objectivity, and the quantitative nature of information (i.e. how much numerical information is processed).

One of the core questions in this study is how teams use groupware technology. It can be analyzed by examining the technology the team is using, how often it is used and for what purposes. The

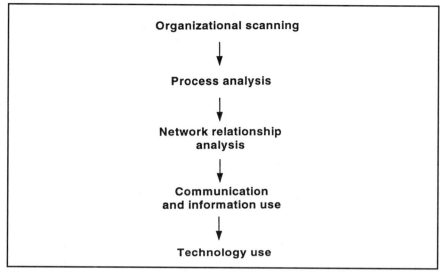

Figure 3. The construction of a communication profile

properties of technology have important effects on group productivity (Dennis, George, Jessup, Nunamaker and Vogel, 1988). Structuration theory helps us to understand how a group's technology use develops during task performance.

The actual communication profile is a graphical representation of information gathered in the construction phase (figure 4). The answers to questions concerning the different components of the model are scaled using the Likert five-point scale.

The communication profile offers information about different components of the research framework (network structure, technology use, communication patterns, information use and business process). The profile can be used to analyze the strengths and weaknesses of a single work group concerning its components. The profile may provide valuable indications to a team leader about ineffective communication or insufficient technology use. The profile also enables comparisons between different work groups.

Case ICL Data

Case organization

ICL Finland is part of the multinational ICL corporation (International Computers Limited). The head office is located in England. The corporation's main products are microcomputers and software products. ICL focuses primarily on selling information systems to big companies in Europe, although the expanding markets in the Far

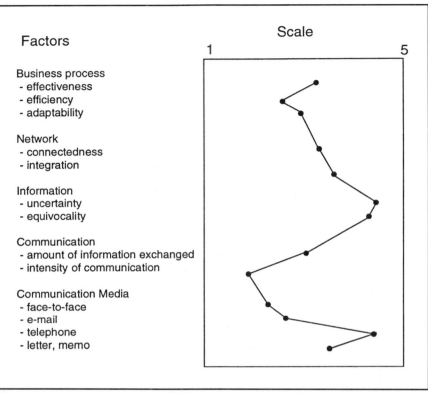

Figure 4. The structure of a communication profile

East are a major growth area. ICL also has some operations in the USA. Fujitsu is ICL is most important partner in Japan, and a major shareholder. In Finland, ICL is the market leader in the information technology industry with a market share of around 20 %.

ICL Finland consists of two separate companies: ICL Personal Systems manufactures hardware (e.g. work stations, servers, monitors), ICL Data is more oriented to software production and marketing activities. ICL TeamSales, which is the actual case organization, is part of ICL Data. It is a quite independent sales company, which sells groupware products, computer hardware and offers consulting services. Other parts of ICL Data include technical service and maintenance units and a software company called Softia.

Competition in the information technology industry is rather intensive. Selling software is a little more profitable, but on the other hand ICL cannot sell at the same volume as major American software manufacturers. The only way to survive in competition against companies like IBM, Digital, or Microsoft is to invest heavily in customer service.

Redesign of the sales process

ICL Data started the evaluation of its business processes by defining the strategic competence areas required to act in the information technology market. ICL defined its strategic mission as follows:

Our purpose is to sell teamware products, hardware and services profitably to large and middle-sized organizations.

ICL sees its own role as a systems integrator. This requires the ability to plan and deliver large scale information systems, which include work stations, network servers and software. ICL has strongly focused on developing so-called teamware products, which include technical solutions for group communication and effective information management in organizations. Teamware consists of both software and hardware products. Teamware systems are sold and delivered to customers mainly as large projects. These projects involve many different activities such as negotiations with the customer organization, customer requirements analysis, system planning, system installation and system maintenance.

The managers of ICL Data perceived that the products of the company were competitive and met customer requirements well. However, some internal processes required development.

ICL decided to improve customer service activities significantly by redesigning sales processes. ICL used a BPR method called ProcessWise. It is developed and used widely in different business units of ICL Corporation. The method consists of six phases:

1. Definition of objectives
2. Identification and priorization of processes
3. Description of critical processes
4. Innovative redesign of processes
5. Assessment of effects
6. Implementation

First, critical success factors of sales activities were defined. These included time spent on the sales process, skills required, customer satisfaction and costs. The objectives of the BPR effort were defined on the basis of these factors. For example, costs should not exceed a certain proportion of sales or time spent on actual sales activities should be increased to a certain level. Each objective was explicitly connected to corporate strategy, i.e. strategic fit was achieved.

The sales process was divided into several subprocesses, which were then prioritized and the current level of performance was compared with objectives. Linkages to other processes (marketing, delivery, management) were also assessed. The subprocesses identified were:

- definition of customer needs,
- configuration of the system,
- offer preparation,
- negotiations about price and terms of delivery,
- order from warehouse, and
- delivery arrangements.

Each subprocess was depicted using graphical representation tools (the ProcessWise method includes computer supported tools for depicting processes). The graphs revealed some communication problems in the corporation. Technical experts were usually not involved in the early phases of the sales process (customer requirements analysis). Experts could have told customers about different solutions at the beginning of the process.

A lot of information exchange takes place between the sales process and some other processes (marketing, internal order-delivery, financial reporting). For example, information created in the marketing process (product descriptions, price lists, technical specifications) is used in the sales process. This information was not easily available, because the links between processes were *weak*. Information exchange was occasional and communication channels between technical planning personnel and salespersons were not standardized. Technical information becomes obsolete very quickly in high-tech organizations like ICL. Access to updated information concerning both customer information and technical matters is thus critical.

Feedback gathering from customers was not effective enough. Only formal customer complaints were dealt with at meetings. However, customers were supplying feedback about project success and product functionality. The problem was that salespersons did not report this feedback. They reacted to feedback at a personal level and used informal channels to correct errors and guide the process. The problem is that organizational learning is not achieved because customer feedback is not shared effectively. One of the managers of ICL Data estimated that 80 % of customer feedback is not captured at organizational level. This is a major obstacle to the systematic improvement of activities.

The results of the organizational scanning (first part of the communication profile construction, see figure 3) also confirmed the existence of these problems. A number of other problems were also detected (insufficient communication between geographically distributed units and problems in the order-delivery chain).

Based on these findings, ICL decided to initiate a BPR project. New, redesigned processes were depicted so that connections between processes were emphasized. A new sales support system called SalesLog was developed. It is a team application that enables the effective sharing of customer related information. All customer linkages are registered into a shared data base. Management also receives accurate information about sales projects. SalesLog further works as an organizational memory. Previous information about a specific customer is always important when a new project is about to begin.

A new office concept called *service center* or *piazza* was also introduced. This describes an office that has a wide, open space in the middle, the use of which is considered to improve teamwork and communication significantly. Managers have desks in the middle of the service center. They can follow most sales activities without separate reporting, and support operative level actions effectively. Salesmen can go to the service center from their own rooms when they need support from management or other employees. The rooms next to the service center are mainly negotiation rooms and shared workrooms, which are available for private discussions and negotiations.

The service center helps to create an open and supportive work environment. The employees also feel that management has committed itself to their work and is able to support them. Removing walls from offices makes the change visible and is of primary importance. If the way people think needs to be changed, very visible things must be done; people will otherwise soon return to previous working habits.

Team organization

ICL has been applying a team approach to organization development for some time. They have developed tools for group communication and applied these tools in internal activities. Previous experiences have encouraged the management of ICL Data to extend the use of teams further.

ICL Data consists of several functional units. Sales focuses on actual sales activities. Sales staff makes offers, negotiate with customers and coordinate projects. Technical experts mainly offer technical planning services. Network planning and system implementation in large projects require many special skills. Technical support offers maintenance and installation services. The structure of ICL Data is depicted in figure 5.

A team is formed when a customer contacts ICL. The structure and activities of the team are not standardized, they appear and change emergently as the process proceeds. A salesperson usually

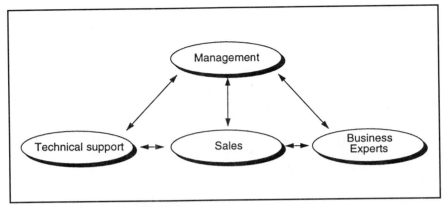

Figure 5. The structure of ICL Data

makes a preliminary customer needs analysis. If technical assistance is required, the salesperson contacts technical experts or the technical support department. Sometimes a product manager (the person responsible for a certain product or product group) is also involved. The size of a sales team typically varies from three to ten people. If the customer wants special changes in software products, systems designers from Softia also become involved.

Team communication in sales teams

The communication profiles of several teams were constructed in the study. Communication in two sales teams is analyzed in this chapter. Both teams delivered an information system, which consisted of TeamOffice groupware system, work stations and network servers. The financial value of the delivered system was about the same in both cases. The customer organizations (large Finnish industrial companies) were also quite similar. Both had bought information system products from ICL before. The major difference is that the first team worked before the BPR effort, and the second after the change.

Team A. Sales team A consisted of 12 people (sales manager, two salespersons, product manager, two technical experts, two technicians, sales secretary, and three representatives of the customer organization). The team worked in three phases: In the first phase, the customer organization contacted ICL Data and asked for an offer concerning the information system. A series of negotiations followed between salespersons and customer representatives (CEO and Manager of the Information Systems Department). Based on customer requirements, the sales staff made a preliminary offer for the system.

Further negotiations concerning price and the system's technical properties followed in the second phase. Technical experts and the product manager participated in the process, as well as the accounting manager of the customer organization. Technical details were discussed and the experts discovered that some components should be added to the intended system, if it were to be possible to connect the new system to the customer's existing systems. This caused further negotiations and a lot of planning and design work was done by the experts. Finally, an agreement was reached and the system was delivered.

The third phase was the installation of the system, a job for technicians from the technical support unit. Technical experts worked as project managers. This whole process from first contact to system implementation took about eight months.

The communication profile of the team was constructed by interviewing all team members. They were asked to answer questions related to three major process measurements: effectiveness, efficiency and adaptability (Harrington 1991). These items were operationalized on a more specific level. The respondents answered several questions related to these three items using the Likert five-point scale.

The degrees of connection and integration of the team were calculated using formal network analysis. Team connectedness was calculated by analyzing how many direct connections each specific team member had to other members. The number of all connections was divided by the number of possible connections. The number of direct links in the team was 36 while possible links numbered 66; connectedness was $36/66=0.55$. Network integration refers to the number of indirect (in this case two-step links) between a specific team member and the members of his/her personal communication network. The degree of network integration is interesting because it is often negatively related to new information acquisition (Rogers and Kincaid 1981). If members are well linked to each other, there is a higher frequency of information exchange among them; they are more likely to possess the same information and so any given message is more likely to be redundant. The degree of integration of the first team was 0.62. Both degrees of connectedness and integration were scaled on a five-point scale, so that they could be presented in the same graph with other factors.

Information complexity was assessed using two measures: uncertainty and equivocality. The operationalization of these factors is discussed by El-Shinnawy and Markus (1992).

Communication intensity in each linkage between team members refers actually to the number of messages exchanged. The amount of information exchanged in each connection was also assessed, again on a five-point scale. Finally, the media (face-to-face communication, e-mail, telephone call, letter or memo) used in each

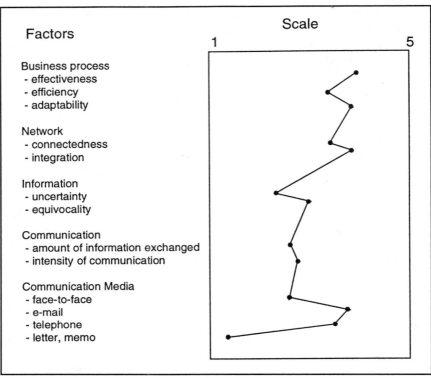

Figure 6. Communication profile of Team A

connection and the frequency of use as well as information content were identified. The communication profile was then constructed (figure 6). A numerical presentation of the results is also included in table 1.

Factor	Team A	Team B
Process effectiveness	3,6	4,1
Process efficiency	2,7	3,1
Process adaptability	3,4	3,8
Network connectedness	2,2	2,8
Average network integration	2,5	1,9
Information uncertainty	1,9	1,5
Information equivocality	2,4	2,6
Amount of information exchanged	2,0	2,5
Intensity of connections	2,1	2,7
Face-to-face communication	2,0	2,4
E-mail messages	3,1	3,9
Telephone	2,7	2,5
Letter, memo	1,3	1,2

Table 1. Factor values of communication profile

Team B. Sales team B consisted of 9 persons (sales manager, salesperson, two technical experts, two technicians, product manager, and two customer representatives). The sales manager and product manager were actually the same person as in team A. The customer representatives in this team were a Chief Information Officer and system designer. The team's task was to deliver a TeamOffice system to a large manufacturing company. The system also included some hardware products.

The first phase was a little easier to accomplish, because technical experts were involved from the beginning and customer requirements were defined on a very exact level at the beginning of the project. The negotiation and installation phase were quite similar to the first case.

Network connectedness in team B was 0.45 and the average integration 0.22. The whole process took about six months. The communication profile and interview results are presented in table 1 and figure 7.

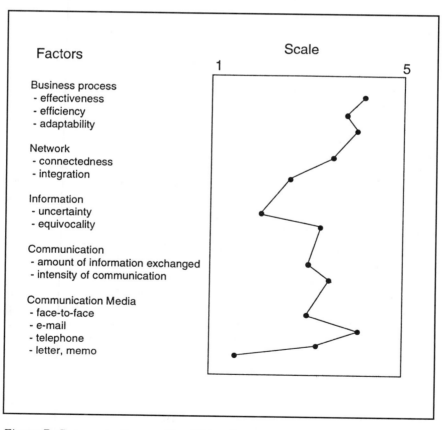

Figure 7. Communication profile of Team B

The impacts of BPR in the case company

The communication profiles of the two sales teams indicate a number of important changes in the sales process as a result of the BPR effort. The activities performed in the process did not change significantly, but it seems that information exchange increased in the second team. Improvements were achieved in process effectiveness, process efficiency and process adaptability. However, these improvements were not as significant as management had expected. Customer members of team B did not perceive higher process effectiveness than team A customer members. Only ICL employees thought that process effectiveness had improved. Improvements were achieved in process efficiency and process adaptability. Customer members in team B acknowledged the team's ability to meet changing expectations and listen to customer opinions. Team A customer members felt that ICL employees had more influence over the team's work than customers.

Communication structures in team B were quite different to those of team A. Team B communication was based on direct links between team members. Almost all team members had direct links to several other members. In team A, salespersons and sales manager had direct contacts to almost all team members, while technicians or customers had only a few direct contacts. The average network integration in team B was lower, which implies that there were fewer indirect connections in the team.

Information uncertainty was lower in team B, mainly because of improved coordination. Direct links enabled more effective coordination. The uncertainty decreased even though the intensity of communication and amount of information exchanged increased. Information equivocality increased, which is probably a natural consequence of the increased information exchange. Team B members received more information than team A members. This also suggests that more interpretation is required.

Face-to-face communication between sales staff was much more common, mainly due to the service center. Technical experts and salespersons also communicated much more on a face-to-face basis. The number of meetings with customers or technicians remained at the same level as before. The use of e-mail was much more common in team B. The customer organization did not have an e-mail system in either case, which means that e-mail was used only between ICL team members. E-mail was by far the most important internal communication channel for ICL. The telephone and meetings were the main communication channels with customers. Letters or memos were not used very much: only formal contracts and some technical specifications were presented in paper form.

It seems that the BPR effort in ICL was quite successful, but not a complete victory. The main objective of the BPR was to increase communication and information sharing between team members, which would then improve sales process effectiveness. The communication profiles of teams A and B indicate that communication was increased. The sales process in both cases was quite similar, and it is therefore justified to say that the BPR project caused at least part of the increase. However, the increase in sales process effectiveness was not satisfactory. One reason for this might be the fact that team B members were interviewed right after the BPR project had been completed. They had not adopted new working methods yet. Employees were not quite sure what kind of information should be shared by the SalesLog system. At first they did not feel comfortable in service centers, because they did not have their own rooms any more. The increased communication and improved efficiency of the sales process are signs of success. ICL will just have to maintain the achieved level of performance and hope to improve it further. The real benefits of BPR will appear when the implications of change have spread to the whole organization.

Implications

Implications for management

The case study reveals some important factors concerning the implementation and impact of BPR on organizations. Managers should be prepared to meet with both expected and unexpected results. Employees often react unexpectedly to radical changes. The effects of technology are not always anticipated, or even desirable. The groupware technology used in the case organization was familiar to staff there. In fact, their job is to sell same technology to their customers; still they found it difficult to apply the technology in new circumstances. This also supports the conclusion that using a completely new technology as an enabler of BPR involves risks. Organizations adopt new technology quite slowly, and if working procedures are changed at the same time, the possibilities of success are endangered. Consistency and continuous guidance are required. If managers do not explicitly present objectives and reasons concerning the BPR effort, it will probably fail.

The ICL case also emphasizes the significance of measurement. Information about business processes and the level of performance should be gathered before any BPR is initiated. Organizations should be able to understand their current situation before any changes are made. This will make it easier to set BPR objectives. Communication is a good indicator of change in organizations like ICL Data, because the business processes are information intensive and require a lot of communication and information exchange. A communication profile is able to capture changes in information flows and communication procedures related to business processes. These indicate how people adopt technology and new ways to act. This also implies that the communication profile could be used to measure the diffusion of a specific technology in organizations.

Implications for future research

BPR seems to be increasing in favor as a management tool to reorganize corporations. A lot has been written about the necessity of BPR impact measurement, and indeed some measurement instruments have been developed, but they have mainly focused on optimizing process cycle time, or process costs. It is suggested here that this perspective is inadequate, if we are to understand the large scale impacts of BPR. These impacts are not easy to identify in advance. They appear as people act and adopt new rules and regulations. It is suggested that the appropriation processes related to major organizational changes determine whether changes succeed or fail. If this is the case we need effective tools to detect these appropriation processes.

The social network approach was adopted in this study. It provided a useful perspective on organizations for several reasons: it furnishes us with an opportunity to examine behavioral patterns on several organizational levels. In the case study, this was mainly a group level, but it would be easy to expand the study to individual or organizational levels. Network analysis also offers standardized methods to analyze groups as social networks. It was possible to analyze the use of several different communication media. The use of e-mail, face-to-face communication, telephone and written material as communication channels was measured in the case organization. Many previous studies have focused on the use of a specific tool or system or comparisons between two media. Changes in network structures also indicate important changes in technology use. Network analysis can be used to increase our understanding of emerging patterns of technology use and adoption. The network approach seems to be especially suitable for examining the impacts of groupware technology.

The emergence of complicated social theories is a challenge to organization and information systems research. It seems that traditional cause-effect models that have been widely used to explain organizational behavior are not sufficient. For example, structuration theory suggests that human action emerges from complicated interactions. These theories seem to offer increased understanding about organizational changes and human behavior in change situations. However, these theories need to be operationalized. The instrument introduced here, namely the communication profile, is an attempt to apply these theories in practice. Although the instrument is still under construction and it has not yet been properly validated, it offers some potential for understanding the nature of changes in business processes and how well technology is able to support these changes. Further development of organizational theories related to communication technology and the development of similar instruments is a major task for researchers.

Conclusions

The development of communication technology and especially of groupware technology means that we must also develop new theories and tools for assessing the impacts of these technologies. This is particularly important since new technologies are considered to be key enablers of organizational change. A lot has been written about BPR and its relationship to technology, but we still know rather little about its impacts and consequences. Many case studies has been presented describing what to do, and how, in order to achieve top performance. The nature of BPR as a strategic change was discussed in the opening sections of this chapter. BPR implies profound changes in the way people do their work. It should not occur just at the level of organizational processes or activities. It should also happen in people's ideas.

Work groups or teams as organizational units were also discussed. Teams are often effective, because people with different skills and ideas are brought together. Teams also tend to be cross-functional, just as business processes are cross-functional. Teams were analyzed as social networks, an approach which aims to identify important changes in communication patterns. The team communication model presented in this chapter aims to identify some determinants of BPR success. The assessment of BPR impacts is based on five model components: business process, social network, technology, communication and information. These components and their development over time can be assessed by using the communication profile tool. The use of this tool in assessing the impacts of BPR in a case organization was described: the tool captured several changes in communication patterns and process characteristics. The management of the case organization received important information about the success of BPR and was able to detect new opportunities for improvement.

Management faces several challenges in BPR efforts. Employees seem to change their attitudes and values quite slowly, which emphasizes management's role in all phases of BPR. The change should be made visible. Changes in the physical working environment may establish commitment effectively. Technology is an important source of change, but not sufficient alone.

References

Burt, R. S. & Minor, M. J. (1983) *Applied Network Analysis. A Methodological Introduction.* Beverly Hills, CA: Sage Publishing Company.

Coleman, J. S. (1986) Social Theory, Social Research, and a Theory of Action. *American Journal of Sociology,* Vol. 91, No. 6, 1309-1335.

Contractor, N. S. & Eisenberg, E. M. (1990) Communication Networks and New Media in Organizations. In J. Fulk & C. Steinfield (eds.) *Organizations and Communication Technology,* 143-172, Newbury Park, CA: Sage Publishing Company.

Daft, R. L., Lengel, R. H. & Trevino, L. K. (1987) Message Equivocality, Media Selection, and Manager Performance: Implications for Information Systems. *MIS Quarterly,* Vol. 11, No. 3, 355-368. Daft, R. L. & Lengel, R. H. (1986) Organizational information requirements, media richness and structural design. *Management Science,* Vol. 32, No. 5, 554-571.

Davenport, T. H. (1993) *Process Innovation.* Boston, MA: Harvard Business School Press.

Dennis, A. R., George, J. F., Jessup, L. M., Nunamaker, J. F. Jr. & Vogel, D. (1988) Information Technology to Support Electronic Meetings. *MIS Quarterly,* Vol. 12, No. 4, 591-624.

DeSanctis, G. & Poole, M. S. (1991) Understanding the Differences in Collaborative System Use through Appropriation Analysis. *Proceedings of the Twenty-Fourth Annual Hawaii International Conference on System Sciences,* Vol. 3, 547-553.

Dhar, V. & Olson, M. H. (1989) Assumptions underlying systems that support work group collaboration. In M. H. Olson (ed.) *Technological Support for Work Group Collaboration,* 33-50, Hillsdale, NJ: Lawrence Erlbaum Associates.

Drucker, P. F. (1988) The Coming of the New Organization. *Harvard Business Review,* Vol. 66, No. 1, 45-53.

Earl, M. J. (1993) Experiences in Strategic Information Systems Planning. *MIS Quarterly,* Vol. 17, No. 1, 1-24.

El-Shinnawy, M. M. & Markus, M. L. (1992) Media Richness Theory and New Electronic Communication Media: A Study of Voice Mail and Electronic Mail. *Proceedings of the 13th International Conference on Information Systems,* 91-105.

Fitzgerald, G. (1991) Validating New Information Systems Techniques: A Retrospective Analysis. In H.-E. Nissen, H. K. Klein & R. Hirschheim (eds.) *Information Systems Research: Contemporary Approaches & Emergent Traditions,* 657-672, Amsterdam, Holland: North-Holland.

Fulk, J. (1992) Social Construction of Communication Technology. *Academy of Management Journal,* Vol. 36, No. 5, 921-950.

Fulk, J. & Boyd, B. (1991) Emerging Theories of Communication in Organizations. *Journal of Management,* Vol. 17, No. 2, 407-446.

Fulk, J., Schmitz, J. & Steinfield, C. (1990) A Social Model of Technology Use. In J. Fulk & C. Steinfield (eds.) *Organizations and Communication Technology,* 117-140, Newbury Park, CA: Sage Publishing Company.

Galliers, R. D. (1987) Information Systems Planning in the United Kingdom and Australia - a Comparison of Current Practice. *Oxford Surveys in Information Technology,* Vol. 4, 223-255.

Giddens, A. (1979) *Central Problems in Social Theory.* London: Macmillan Press Ltd.

Gopal, A., Bostrom, R. P. & Chin, W. W. (1993) Applying Adaptive Structuration Theory to Investigate the Process of Group Support Systems Use. *Journal of Management Information Systems*, Vol. 9, No. 3, 45-70.

Grover, V., Teng, J. T. C. & Fiedler, K. D. (1993) Information Technology Enabled Business Process Redesign: An Integrated Planning Framework. *Omega*, Vol. 21, No. 4, 433-447.

Hammer, M. & Champy, J. (1993) *Re-engineering the Corporation. A Manifesto for Business Revolution.* New York: Harper Business.

Hammer, M. (1990) Reengineering Work: Don't Automate, Obliterate. *Harvard Business Review*, Vol. 68, No. 4, July-August 1990, 104-112.

Harrington, H. J. (1991) *Business Process Improvement.* New York: McGraw-Hill.

Henderson, J. C. & Venkatraman, N. (1993) Strategic alignment: Leveraging information technology for transforming organizations. *IBM Systems Journal*, Vol. 32, No. 1, 4-16.

Huber, G. P. (1984) The nature and design of post-industrial organizations. *Management Science*, Vol. 30, No. 8, 928-951.

Ibarra, Herminia (1992) Structural Alignments, Individual Strategies, and Managerial Action: Elements Toward a Network Theory of Getting Things Done. In N. Nohria & R. G. Eccles (eds.) *Networks and Organizations,* 165-188, Boston, MA: Harvard Business School Press.

Jacques, E. (1990) In Praise of Hierarchy. *Harvard Business Review,* January - February 1990.

Katzenbach, J. R. & Smith, D. K. (1993) *The Wisdom of Teams: Creating the High-Performance Organization.* Boston, MA: Harvard Business School Press.

Kling, R. (1987) Defining the Boundaries of Computing across Complex Organizations. In R. J. Boland & R. A. Hirschheim (eds.) *Critical Issues in Information Systems Research,* 307-362, Chichester, Great Britain: Wiley.

Krackhardt, D. & Hanson, J. R. (1993) Informal Networks: The Company Behind the Chart. *Harvard Business Review,* Vol. 71, No. 4, 104-111.

Kutsko, J. & Smith, J. Y. (1991) Effectiveness measures for distributed teams using electronic meeting technology: the Larson/LaFasto instrument. *Proceedings of the Twenty-Fourth Annual Hawaii International Conference on System Sciences*, Vol. 4, 458-470.

Larson, C. E. & LaFasto, F. M. J. (1989) *Teamwork. What must go right/ What can go wrong.* Newbury Park, CA: Sage Publications.

Leavitt, H. J. & Whisler, T. L. (1958) Management in the 1980s. Harvard Business Review, November-December 1958, 41-48.

Markus, M. L. (1990) Toward a Critical Mass Theory of Interactive Media. In J. Fulk & C. Steinfield (eds.) *Organizations and Communication Technology,* 194-218, Newbury Park, CA: Sage Publishing Company.

Markus, M. L. & Robey, D. (1988) Information Technology and Organizational Change: Causal Structure in Theory and Research. *Management Science,* Vol. 34, No. 5, 583-598.

McGrath, J. E. (1991) Time, Interaction, and Performance. *Small Group Research*, Vol. 22, No. 2, 147-174.

McGrath, J. E. (1984) *Groups: Interaction and Performance.* Englewood Cliffs, New Jersey: Prentice-Hall.

Miles, R. E. & Snow, C. C. (1986) Organizations: New Concepts for New Forms. *California Management Review*, Vol. 28, No. 3, 62-73.

Nohria, N. (1992) Is a Network Perspective a Useful Way of Studying

Organizations? In N. Nohria & R. G. Eccles (eds.) *Networks and Organizations*, 1-22, Boston, MA: Harvard Business School Press.

Pine, B. J. (1993) *Mass Customization.* Boston, MA: Harvard Business School Press.

Poole, M. S. & DeSanctis, G. (1990) Understanding the use of group decision support systems. In J. Fulk & C. Steinfield (eds.) *Organizations and Communication Technology*, 173-191, Newbury Park, CA: Sage Publishing Company.

Poole, M. S. & DeSanctis, G. (1989) Use of Group Decision Support Systems as an Appropriation Process. In: *Proceedings of the Twenty-Second Annual Hawaii International Conference on System Sciences*, Vol. 4, 149-157.

Porter, M. E. & Millar, V. E. (1985) How Information Technology Gives You Competitive Advantage. *Harvard Business Review,* Vol. 63, No. 4, 149-160.

Reponen, T. (1993) Information Management Strategy - an Evolutionary Process. *Scandinavian Journal of Management*, Vol. 9, No. 3, 189-209.

Rockart, J. F. & Short, J. E. (1989) IT in the 1990s: Managing Organizational Interdependence. *Sloan Management Review*, Vol. 30, No. 2, 7-18.

Rogers, E. M. & Kincaid, D. L. (1981) *Communication Networks. Toward a Paradigm for Research.* New York: The Free Press.

Segars, A. H. & Grover, V. (1994) Communications Architecture: Towards a More robust Understanding of Information Flows and Emergent Patterns of Communication in Organizations. *European Journal of Information Systems*, Vol. 3, No. 2, 87-100.

Shannon, C. E. & Weaver, W. (1949) *Mathematical Theory of Communication.* Urbana IL: University of Illinois Press.

Simon, H. A. (1977) *The New Science of Management Decision.* New York: Prentice-Hall.

Tapscott, D. & Caston, A. (1993) Paradigm Shift. The New Promise of Information Technology. New York: McGraw-Hill.

Venkatraman, N. (1994) IT-Enabled Business Transformation: From Automation to Business Scope Redefinition. *Sloan Management Review*, Vol. 35, No. 2, 73-87

Venkatraman, N. (1991) IT-Induced Business Reconfiguration. In M. S. Scott Morton (ed.) *The Corporation of the 1990s. Information Technology and Organizational Transformation*, 122-158, New York: Oxford University Press.

Walsham, G. (1993) *Interpreting Information Systems in Organizations.* Chichester: Wiley.

Waterman, R. H. (1988) *The Renewal Factor.* London: Bantam Press.

Weick, K. E. (1979) *The Social Psychology of Organizing.* New York: Addison-Wesley.

Worchel, S., Wood, W. & Simpson, Jeffry A. (1992) *Group Process and Productivity.* Newbury Park, CA: Sage Publishing Company.

Yarnell, D. A. & Peterson, M. F. (1993) Networking in the Mid-1990s. *Journal of Management Development*, Vol. 12, No. 5, 60-71.

Zmud, R. W. (1990) Opportunities for Strategic Information Manipulation Through New Information Technology. In J. Fulk & C. Steinfield (eds.) *Organizations and Communication Technology*, 95-116, Newbury Park, CA: Sage Publishing Company.

Part 5

The Information Systems Function

Chapter 22
**Business Process Reengineering and the Role of the
Information Systems Professional**
Markus and Robey

Most definitions of business process reengineering accord a prominent role to information systems and technology. Consequently, it would seem to follow that information systems professionals have an important role to play in business process reengineering. But the authors find that information systems professionals are often left out in the early stages of reengineering projects. Why is this so? In this chapter, it is argued that information systems professionals often fail to participate effectively in reengineering projects and are often perceived to resist making necessary changes in their own work practices. Similar behavior has been observed of staff specialists in a wide variety of disciplines. It is observed that the core reengineering principle of cross-functional integration should apply, not only to the line functional areas affected by a reengineering project (e.g., sales and manufacturing), but also to the staff functions whose expertise is used in reengineering a process (e.g., information systems, human resources, accounting, etc.). Reengineering requires "joint optimization" of different organizational design elements and that this in turn requires different techniques, behaviors, and skills on the part of information systems specialists. In particular, the authors discuss the role of the information systems specialist as a consultant and partner to line managers and other staff specialists.

Chapter 23
Reengineering the IS Function: A Managerial Perspective
Smith, McKeen and Nelson

The objective of this chapter is to provide a managerial perspective on how to go about reengineering a functional area of an enterprise. To this end, the managers of information systems (IS) functions within twenty different organizations in the United

States and Canada were asked to challenge the status quo and come up with a set of recommendations that would achieve dramatic improvements in the performance of their function. Although the managers seemed to have a difficult time looking inward and reexamining themselves, their experience with the process of reengineering yielded a set of guidelines for other managers, regardless of which function they represent, to consider when attempting a similar endeavor.

Chapter 24
Toward Reengineering Information Systems Development Process
Sabherwal

Information systems (ISs) can be used to fundamentally transform, or reengineer, the very nature of an organization's business processes. Several chapters in this book examine the issues surrounding such use of ISs for business process reengineering. By contrast, this chapter focuses on one kind of business processes which seems to be in need for reengineering, namely the IS development (ISD) process itself. It identifies six myths, or basic assumptions, about ISD processes which are well-entrenched but need to be questioned. Based on some primary case studies, suggestions are offered for accomplishing ISD process reengineering by reducing the influence of these six myths. Specifically, it is suggested that the value of emotions, conflict, user ownership, flexibility, creativity, and redundancy should be recognized during the ISD process, and more careful attention should be given to the potential problems. Some implcations for future research are also examined.

Chapter 25
Surviving Business Process Redesign: The Impact on IS
Zeibig

Today, companies are buffeted by a sea of change unrivaled in depth and pace. With businesses of every shape and size designing, or inventing, new ways of doing work, especially ways that leverage information technology (IT), many Information Systems (IS) organizations are reeling from the impacts of corporate reengineering. The new process structures that are being developed can be characterized along four dimensions: process flow, team-work, knowledge-work, and information resources. The reengineering spectrum is comprised of three major types of improvement initiatives that represent challenges for traditional IS roles and responsibilities. The most significant reengineering initiatives frequently represent five major impacts on today's IS organization. Specifically, they:

- generate demands for a broad-based complex of integrated IT capabilities;
- tax existing IT infrastructure services and capacities;
- strain even the most productive IT delivery process;
- require new skills and experience-levels among IS resources; and
- raise new questions of priority and resource allocation for the IT management process.

To survive, let alone prosper, in this complex and dynamic environment, IS organizations must understand the significant impacts that reengineering initiatives can generate and must develop specific strategies for managing them. This chapter explores these themes as a framework for management in preparing for corporate reengineering.

Business Process Reengineering and the Role of the Information Systems Professional

M. Lynne Markus
The Claremont Graduate School

Daniel Robey
Florida International University

New ideas, like business process reengineering (BPR), raise numerous points of disagreement over philosophy and technique. One of these is the appropriate role of information systems (IS) professionals in the BPR process (Bashein, Markus & Riley, 1993; IT Management Programme, 1993; Krass, 1991; 1992). Although there is no consensus about precisely what this role should be, almost everyone agrees that IS professionals have an important role to play in BPR projects—everyone, that is, except line managers and external BPR consultants.

For example, when the California State affiliate of the American Automobile Association (CSAA) began to reengineer its customer service processes, the internal IS department was initially left out. CSAA relied on outside consultants for advice about information technology (IT) because its internal IS department had an extremely poor track record in delivering systems on time. IS managers were able to turn the situation around and earn themselves a place in CSAA's subsequent reengineering projects, but the process was painful (Moad, 1993).

Unfortunately, this is not an isolated story. Exclusion and expulsion of IS specialists from BPR projects is a recurrent theme in the trade literature on BPR and in the experience of BPR consultants. Why might this occur? What does it mean? And what can be done about it? In this chapter, we explore these questions through an examination of themes in the emerging literature and lore of BPR, in comparison to academic and practical perspectives on the role of staff specialists in sociotechnical change.

Background

Experts on BPR efforts generally concur that IS specialists have an important role to play, although there is little agreement about what this role should be. While some might claim that the CIO is a legitimate sponsor, champion, and leader of BPR efforts, others recommend that IS be involved in a more circumscribed way, limited perhaps to identifying BPR opportunities, researching enabling information technologies, and supporting BPR efforts though systems modification or new application development (cf., Davenport, 1993a; IT Management Programme, 1993). For example, a study by Deloitte & Touche of 430 reengineering projects (cited in Krass, 1992) concludes that BPR projects are best led by the head of the organization that "owns" the process, and that projects led by CIOs tend to flounder.

In general, reengineering experts advise internal IS specialists who identify needs and opportunities for reengineering to ally themselves with a partner from the line management ranks, since line managers make more effective champions and sponsors of BPR projects. But this advice still assumes that internal IS departments have an important, even essential, role to play in reengineering, since almost all BPR projects have IT implications (Davenport, 1993a). Thus, descriptions of best practices in "how to do" reengineering hardly prepare us for stories like that of CSAA (see Appendix), in which the line managers deliberately excluded IS specialists from the BPR effort.

The CSAA case would cause little concern if it were an isolated incident, particularly since there was such an obvious explanation for line managers' lack of confidence in their internal IS shop. But ongoing research by one of the authors suggests that similar cases may be quite common. Furthermore, this research suggests that the root causes of IS exclusion from BPR efforts may be far more complex than simple performance failures in core IS processes such as application development. A brief summary of the research and some preliminary findings follows.

IS Specialists—Excluded and Expelled

The research study was funded by the Advanced Practices Council of SIM International[1] to identify ways to accelerate the transformation of business processes associated with the introduction of new information technologies. In the first phase of the study, interviews were conducted with over 50 successful consultants who specialized in BPR, IT, or organizational change. (See Bashein, Markus & Riley, 1994, for a description of the research methodology.) In the second phase, retrospective and prospective cases studies of BPR projects were conducted.

Among the topics covered in the interviews with consultants was the appropriate role of IS specialists in BPR projects. The results were fascinating. Consultant after consultant told us that "it happened" that internal IS specialists were occasionally left out of BPR projects altogether or else were involved "too late," sometimes with unfortunate consequences for the quality of the reengineered process. For instance, one consultant admitted that he and his colleagues had not spent enough time working with his client's internal IS staff; consequently, the reengineered process "probably" did not take enough advantage of emerging information technologies. Unlike many of the consultants interviewed, he shouldered full responsibility for failure to work effectively with inhouse IS personnel. He confessed that the consulting team and the internal IS specialists had had numerous fights over what systems changes were or were not technologically feasible, the priorities for application development or modification, and the timeframe for the changes. After numerous unpleasant interactions with the IS specialists, he had avoided further contact with them whenever possible. Discussions with other parties revealed that the IS specialists may have been disgruntled that they had not been asked to lead the BPR effort; they frequently expressed the opinion that the organization was not getting value from the fees paid to the consultants, despite the fact that the project had obviously yielded radical improvements on numerous performance indicators.

Other consultants attributed responsibility for excluding IS specialists from BPR projects to line managers in the client organizations. The consultants claimed[2] that client organization managers hold very poor opinions of their inhouse IS staffs. They implied that the line managers were justified in these opinions; they cited numerous reasons to support them. Among the charges leveled against IS professionals involved in BPR projects are the following:

1) IS specialists do not understand the business, and they cannot describe technological issues in business terms;

2) IS specialists do not see the value in change proposals that do not involve systems; in particular, they react poorly to suggestions by the human resources experts who focus on the people side of organizational improvement;
3) IS specialists try to turn reengineering projects into system development projects;
4) IS specialists are so preoccupied with the limitations of current applications and infrastructure and the difficulties of changing them that they inappropriately reject innovative proposals made by managers, workers, or consultants; and
5) IS specialists cannot produce modifications or new systems in the time required by client company management.

For their part, client managers sometimes described having excluded IS specialists from the earliest BPR discussions. Most often, they described the exclusion as oversight—not understanding soon enough that the proposed changes had systems implications. However, the consequences of their oversight could not be overlooked; in some cases, they had to settle for less than optimal information technology support, because they had not got expert input early enough in the design process.

More interesting even than these instances of IS exclusion were a few cases involving IS expulsion. On this score, external IS consultants appear to be as much at risk as internal IS specialists. In one organization, an external consultant hired for his firm's reengineering prowess proceeded to employ a highly structured system development methodology that emphasized requirements definition over radical process improvements. He persisted in this course despite frequent warnings from the client that his approach was unacceptable. Eventually, his engagement was terminated, and the project continued without him and his staff. If such an extreme technical orientation can exist in a consulting firm that specializes in business reengineering, we suspect that it is even more common when internal IS specialists lead BPR projects.

In short, the picture that emerges from these findings is one in which IS specialists, both internal and external, more than occasionally engage in a set of behaviors that have the potential to compromise the success of BPR projects. Among these behaviors are:

- overemphasis on technical issues central to the IS specialty, to the detriment of issues central to other improvement specialties —like human resources management or BPR—and to the business as a whole;
- failure to collaborate effectively with other participants both internal or external to the organization;
- unwillingness to abandon the role of leader or expert for a role of

co-participant or facilitator;

- conscious or unconscious attempts to sabotage BPR efforts, perhaps out of resentment at having been passed over for leadership or excluded early on; and
- conservatism—reluctance to embrace, or active rejection of, proposals for radical change—perhaps due to attachment to the existing technological regime or fear of the effort required to make changes.

This picture is not a pretty one. And it is not unique to IS professionals in the context of BPR.

Staff Specialists as Resistant to Change

Table 1 summarizes the conclusions from both classic and contemporary literature about staff specialists of several varieties: industrial and manufacturing engineers—especially those concerned with advanced manufacturing technologies, operations and general management consultants, human resource managers, organizational development consultants, accounting and finance specialists, and IS professionals. The themes in this diverse literature are extraordinarily consistent despite differences in the nature of the professional specialty being discussed. And the themes are the same as those that emerged from the research on IS involvement in BPR projects, described above.

The conclusion one takes away from this literature is that the very people who think of themselves as agents of change may act as inhibitors to change because of the way in which they ply their trades. By remaining rooted in their functional specialties— whatever these specialties are—internal or external specialists do not approach change in the integrated, holistic fashion that successful change management requires (Kanter, 1983). When this happens, they often fail to achieve improved organizational functioning and performance.

Functional Approaches to Cross-Functional Change?

The irony of organizational improvement specialists taking a narrow functional approach to change is particularly acute in BPR. The hallmark of BPR is its cross-functional approach to organizational change. BPR focuses on business processes, which are generally defined as the sets of activities involved in achieving a defined business outcome (Davenport, 1993a; Davenport & Short, 1990); the business processes of greatest interest to BPR specialists are so large[3] that they cut across major organizational and functional

AUTHOR	SOURCE	THEMES
Paul Lawrence	(1969, January-February; originally published in 1954). How to deal with resistance to change. Harvard Business Review, 4-12, 176.	resistance is created by the blind spots and attitudes of staff specialists, resulting from their preoccupation with the technical aspects of new ideas; use of participation by staff specialists is a new psychological gimmick for getting other people to think they want to do what they are told; staff specialists get into trouble by expecting people to resist change
Robert H. Schaffer	(1966, June). Maximizing the impact of industrial engineering. American Management Association Management Bulletin #82. (1976, Autumn). Advice to internal and external consultants: Expand your client's capacity to use your help. Advanced Management Journal. (1983, November). Improving quality from within: The role of the internal consultant. Productivity, 4, 11.	industrial engineers should help line managers accomplish improvement rather than working independently as technical experts; consultants can contribute more by designing projects that expand the client's capacity to absorb and use technical help than by designing state-of-the-art projects; former managers who become internal consultants need to make the transition from decision-manger to advisor
Wickham Skinner	(1974, May-June). The focused factory. Harvard Business Review, 113-121.	manufacturing structures incongruent with corporate strategy occur because professionals in different fields such as quality control, personnel, labor relations, engineering, inventory management, materials handling, systems design, etc., attempt to achive goals which, though valid and traditional in their fields, are not congruent with goals of other areas; the problem is growing, due to increased professionalism

Table 1: Some Themes in the Literature on the Role of Staff Professionals in SocioTechnical Change

Peter Block	(1981). Flawless consulting: A guide to getting your expertise used. San Diego, CA: Pfeiffer & Co. (1993). Stewardship: Choosing service over self-interest. San Francisco, CA: Berrett-Koehler Publishers.	internal or external consultants can work with line managers in one of three ways: in an expert role, in a pair-of-hands role, or in a collaborative role, and only the third role is really effective; strong, top-focused staff functions (information system, finance, human resource management) inhibit organizational change, and decentralizing staff services alone does not solve the problem
Albert Cherns	(1987, first published 1976). Principles of sociotechnical design revisited. Human Relations, 40, 3, 153-162.	organizations can adapt to their environments by adding new roles or modifying old ones; adding new roles by hiring specialists and experts is the mechanical response, whereas training existing workers to enlarge their repertoire is more organic; experts add to the problem of organizational integration by increasing line-staff confusion of authority and by acquiring regulatory functions that can become dysfunctional
John Child and colleagues	(1987). Technological innovation and organizational conservatism. In J. M. Pennings and A. Buitendam (Eds.), New technology as organizational innovation: The development and diffusion of microelectronics (pp. 87-115). Cambridge, MA: Ballinger.	staff specialists such as engineers assume significant roles as organizers of work; where their theories have been shaped by long-established principles (e.g., Taylorism), their influence on organizations and work tends to be of a conservative nature, thus retarding change; when several professional staff groups are involved, they may compete among themselves for the attention of top management
M.L. Markus and N. Bjørn-Andersen	(1987, June). Power over users: Its exercise by systems professionals. Communications of the ACM, 30, 6, 498-504.	IS professionals can exert power over users in specific development projects and through IS management policy decisions

Table 1: (Continued)

Richard Beckhard	(1988). The executive management of transformational change. In R.H. Kilmann, T.J. Cover, and Associates (Eds.), Corporate transformation: revitalizing organizations for a competitive world (pp. 89-101). San Francisco, CA: Jossey-Bass.	heads of staff must move away from the position of being the "experts" to a position of being supporters, facilitators, and leaders in long-range thinking
John Alic	(1990). Who designs work? Organizing production in an age of high technology. Technology in Society, 12, 301-317.	managers have abdicated the design of work to technical experts; work design in the US is dominated by the industrial engineering paradigm, directly descending from Taylor; this approach really analyzes work, rather than designs it, since design is much more difficult, so work is not really designed, but evolves incrementally; socio-technical systems approaches are an improvement, but still suffer from the same failings as industrial engineering: an oversimplified view of technology
Carol Beatty	(1992, Summer). Implementing advanced manufacturing technologies: Rules of the road. Sloan Management Review, 49-60.	new technology champions play three roles: pathfinder or visionary, problem-solver, and implementor (a political role); the "rationally" educated engineers who make up the majority of new technology champions have great difficulty adopting the implementor role
H.A. Smith and J.D. McKeen	(1993). Re-engineering the corporation: Where does I.S. fit in? Proceedings of the Twenty-Sixth Annual Hawaii International Conference on Systems Sciences, Vol. III, 120-126.	IS participation in reengineering efforts is essential, but a very different approach on the part of IS specialists is required; reengineering is not simply another systems project; IS staff must rise above their traditional procedural and analytic thinking

Table 1: (Continued)

boundaries, e.g., engineering, manufacturing, sales, customer service, etc. In addition, proponents of reengineering claim that their redesigns involve simultaneous changes in multiple aspects of the organization. At a minimum, BPR experts say, reengineering efforts should alter the business process, information and information systems, and people aspects of organizations, such as jobs and rewards. More radical reengineering designs may also involve modifications to business strategy, organizational structure, organizational demographics, management systems (such as cost accounting), IT infrastructure, and so forth.

In other words, BPR efforts cut across organizational functions horizontally, and they require contributions from various improvement specialties, including strategists, accountants, human resource management and organizational development specialists, operations researchers, information systems professionals, and so forth. Thus, it would be supremely ironic if each organizational improvement specialty redefined BPR from its own vantage point and systematically discounted the contributions of other specialties. Yet, ironic as it is, this seems to be the case.

For instance, it has frequently been observed that the approach to reengineering described by Hammer and Champy (1993) pays only lip service to the people aspects of change. In his review of Hammer and Champy's book, Davenport (1993b) observes that it may not be necessary to "obliterate" (Hammer, 1990) the social system in order to bring about radical improvement through process and IT change. Radical improvement may still be achievable, if the change is designed so that it is consistent with key elements of organizational culture. And the probability of success with such "culturally-consistent innovations" is likely to be much higher than the 70% failure rate that Hammer often cites. Thus, it is perhaps not too much of an overstatement to say that Hammer's approach to BPR subordinates the people dimension of organization to the process and technology dimensions, since it requires jobs and culture to fill the roles accorded to them once the process and the supporting information technologies have been designed.

The same sort of criticism has been leveled against traditional system-building practices (Markus & Keil, 1994) and at BPR efforts that are conceptualized as a "front-end" to the system development life cycle (Johnson, 1992). Markus and Keil (1994), for example, have described traditional system building as a process in which the developer starts with a design for what the information system will do. Often the developer does not get involved in details of job redesign, which may be left to line managers to work out or delegated to another staff specialist group. If job design is explicitly addressed, it is often approached as a problem of figuring out how to partition the tasks left over after automation, rather than as a question of sorting out to people the tasks that people do well and to the computer the tasks that it does well (Mumford & Weir, 1979). Conversely, redesigning the business process before considering systems implications can lead to process designs that cannot be implemented or that do not take full advantage of IT capabilities (Davenport, 1993a).

An equally dangerous approach is to redesign processes without regard for business strategy (Johnson, 1992; Hall, Rosenthal & Wade, 1993). This can result in improvements that do not "drop to the bottomline" or in changes that reduce cost but that decrease customer satisfaction or employee quality of working life.

In short, the design problem in BPR differs from that found in more traditional approaches to organizational improvement. In general, traditional approaches to organizational improvement are aligned with different functional specialties. In each specialty, the goal is seen as one of maximizing the performance criterion of greatest interest to practitioners of the specialty. Strategists focus on market share; human resource managers and organizational development specialists focus on quality of work life; accountants focus on cost; industrial engineers focus on efficiency; IS specialists focus on data quality, and so forth. Each attempts to maximize its most important criterion, on the assumption that this will make the greatest contribution to overall organizational performance, blissfully ignorant of those all-too-common situations where improvements on one indicator involve degradations on another. For instance, increases in throughput may decrease cost but increase worker stress.

Joint Optimization in BPR Design

Sociotechnical systems theorists (e.g., Cherns, 1987) have long recognized the need for changes in the way work systems are designed. The traditional design strategy employed by industrial engineers in manufacturing plants, for example, is to design the assembly line for maximum throughput and then to determine what kinds of jobs are required to run the line. This approach maximizes one performance criterion—throughput —while perhaps also considering a few additional performance criteria (e.g., labor cost) as "constraints," at the expense of social system criteria, such as job quality. Instead, sociotechnical systems theorists have argued, work system designers should adopt the principle of "joint optimization," in which the sociotechnical system is designed to achieve both technical and social system goals simultaneously. Applied to information systems, the concept of joint optimization refers to the "strategic triangle" of business strategy, IT strategy, and organization strategy (Walton, 1989). Applied to BPR, the principle of joint optimization implies that strategy, process, jobs, management structures and systems, information and information technology should all be co-designed (Johnson, 1992).

The principle of joint-optimization, while conceptually quite simple, is very difficult to achieve in practice. In the first place, design itself is a difficult skill to teach and learn. Design involves synthetic reasoning that is much more difficult to "program" than is analysis. Consequently, while we have many methodologies for job and business process analysis (cf. Harrington, 1991; Rummler & Brache, 1990), we have almost no methodologies for job and process design (Alic, 1990).

Secondly, it is hard to structure a design process in which two or more quite different dimensions are considered simultaneously and given equal weight. Most sociotechnical systems design approaches do not address this problem well. For instance, the traditional sociotechnical systems approach (cf. Cummings & Markus, 1979; Taylor & Felten, 1993) starts with an analysis of unit processes and variances in the technical system. The technical system analysis is followed by a description of social system needs and the roles that are required to cope with the production variances. This approach does not consider (as BPR experts would advocate) the possibility of a completely different role system performing a completely different technological process for accomplishing the same task.

An alternative sociotechnical systems approach (Mumford & Weir, 1979) provides more scope for radically different social systems by creating two separate design teams—one for the technical system, one for the social system—that operate in parallel. Once the teams have independently enumerated social and technical alternatives, the teams meet jointly to match them up. Alternatives that do not "match" are rejected, and the matched pairs are ranked. While this approach avoids some of the limitations of the traditional technical-system-first approach, it ignores potential synergies between the social and technical realms. Thus, the designers who use it might have a tendency to overlook social system designs that are only possible given a radically new technology. (This is precisely the sort of synergy that most BPR advocates are attempting to capture.)

Recursive-Sequential Design Process

Given the difficulty of operationalizing jointly-optimized design, even the very best sociotechnical designers seem to have adopted a design approach that is predominantly sequential, but employs some recursion. In this approach, one design dimension implicitly dominates the others. The dominant dimension usually reflects the designer's primary expertise or specialty; individual designers do not usually vary the dominant dimension on different design projects. The dominant dimension is designed first, becoming the "fixed" or center point around which all other elements are designed; the other dimensions are tailored to match it. Recursion comes in when the form of the dominant element is designed or selected. Here, the best designers consider non-dominant elements as constraints on the form of the dominant member.

The recursive-sequential design approach is certainly an improvement over designs in which a single criterion is optimized. However, it still falls short of the joint optimization ideal. More importantly (since the ideal may be impossible to realize in practice), the recursive-sequential design approach opens the door to conflicts of philosophy and technique among organizational improvement specialists who adopt *different dominant dimensions* as the starting point for design.

For example, in the area of manufacturing work systems, the usual point of departure in design is a proposed advanced manufacturing technology, such as CAD/CAM, robotics, or MRP II. Even among those researchers who are most attuned to the human element in work systems, there is a tendency to pose the design question in terms of what the technology requires in the way of a supportive human system. Tornatzky and Fleisher (1990, chap. 9), for instance, advise implementors to understand characteristics of the technological innovation that has been selected for implementation (step 1), and then (step 4) to redesign the organization, (step 5) modify human resource policies, (step 6) redesign jobs, and (step 7) install the innovation and integrate it with the existing technical system. Similarly, Majchrzak (1991) focuses on the organizational design elements that "need to be in place" for successful implementation of different computerized technologies.

Because these researchers are extremely sensitive to the systemic nature of technology implementation and organizational change, they approach the design problem recursively. That is, they implicitly or explicitly select for implementation in the first place only those technologies they judge the existing social system has the capacity to absorb. But it remains an open question whether they would have arrived at the same sociotechnical design if they had selected the human system, rather than the technical system, as the dominant dimension for design. Thus, their specialty may bring them into conflict with other specialists who adopt a different starting point and thus possibly create different sociotechnical designs. For instance, a labor relations specialist who wishes not to disturb the terms of a current union agreement might not select the same advanced manufacturing technology and might prefer a very different sociotechnical solution.

In general, human resource managers and organizational development specialists tend to adopt a different point of departure for sociotechnical design than do specialists in advanced manufacturing technology and IS. When "people" specialists attend to technology, they tend to inquire how the technology can be adapted to human and social system needs, rather than the other way around. For example, in a book devoted to a strategy for revitalizing manufacturing organizations (so that the interventions of Tornatzky and Fleischer and Majchrzak would also be appropriate), Beer, Eisenstat, and Spector (1990) focus almost exclusively on the human side of change. While changes to information systems, formal structures and policies "can certainly help ensure the success of the revitalization effort" (pp. 94-95, passim), this topic receives no further mention in their book. Again, the purpose of our analysis is not to disparage an obviously sensible and successful approach to change, but rather to show how strongly it reflects the functional specialty of its authors.

Clearly, neither of these approaches to the improvement of manufacturing organizations is the only possible successful approach, and neither is obviously superior to the other in every situation. But where are the frameworks for deciding when one of these approaches might be preferable to the other? And should not all improvement specialists be conversant with, and respectful of, the potential contributions of the others, so that the client organization adopts the best approach to change?

One of the implications of this line of argument is that BPR can be a very different intervention depending on who is leading it. The BPR of operations researcher Harold Cypress (1994) looks very different from that of IS specialist James Senn (1991). Cypress would clearly weigh process changes more highly than IS changes; the opposite would be true for Senn. This difference in orientation can help to explain the conflicts that we have described above among the different staff specialist groups who participate in reengineering projects.

All proponents of reengineering observe that successful business process redesign requires members of a design team to let go of their "narrow" functional orientations. But what they usually have in mind, we believe, is that *others*, e.g., process worker representatives from sales, manufacturing, etc., should drop *their* narrow functional orientations. By contrast, we argue that reengineering also requires the *staff specialists* working on these projects to adopt a cross-functional perspective vis-a-vis the expertise of other improvement specialists. Thus, IS specialists (as well as others like operations researchers) must learn to understand how BPR differs from system-development-as-usual, to work effectively with external or internal BPR consultants as co-participants rather than as leaders, and to incorporate lessons from non-IS approaches (e.g., organizational development) to bringing about organizational improvement.

And yet, our analysis shows that this is hard for IS and other staff specialists to do. In the words of the IS manager at CSAA:

It was easy for [IS professionals] to understand that the business had to change ... It was harder for them to understand that they had to change. (Moad, 1993)

Apparently, change is as hard for change agents as it is for change targets.

Implications for the IS Professional

In this chapter, we have claimed that IS professionals in organizations (as well as external consultants) are strongly influenced by the typical preoccupations of their functional specialty, and that this orientation frequently prevents IS professionals from working effectively with other change agents on BPR projects. Our analysis suggests that IS professionals almost certainly lack the resources, attitudes and skills to lead BPR projects; they may also often lack the motivation and ability to collaborate effectively as participants in BPR projects (Davenport & Stoddard, 1994; Smith & McKeen, 1993).

As more and more IS professionals adopt roles in BPR projects, it seems appropriate to rethink the nature of their role in terms of the consultant-client relationship. An interesting classification of consultants' roles vis-a-vis their clients has been provided by Block (1981). Consultants (external or internal organizational performance improvement specialists) can act as experts, as extra "pairs of hands," or as collaborators with their clients. Drawing the distinctions among these roles helps us understand the different kinds of contributions that improvement specialists can make.

Expert Role

In the expert role, according to Block, the client plays a passive role and holds the consultant responsible for results. Not only is the consultant expected (by the client and by him- or herself) to produce the solution, the consultant is also expected to diagnose the problem. Typically, such problems are already diagnosed to some degree (possibly wrongly), because the client has called in an expert in one particular area of performance improvement.

For IS specialists, the expert role is a familiar one. Charged with such tasks as automating a manual operation, or converting an application from one generation of hardware to another, IS specialists have become good experts. In fact, many IS professionals view their primary mission to be the application of IT to eliminate inefficiencies in relatively circumscribed processes. Debugging faulty code represents perhaps the extreme case of a circumscribed problem domain. Somewhat larger areas, like office automation, also seem to call for IS specialists to act as technical experts.

The consultant who adopts Block's "expert role" does not collaborate well with others and serves the needs of the client by working independently. The main problem faced by IS specialists who adopt the expert role in BPR projects is that few cross-functional business processes lend themselves to solutions that involve only IS technical expertise. Redesigning business processes effectively requires the coordinated efforts of specialists in various functional areas. When experts won't work together well and even fight with each other, the client suffers. Not surprisingly, a frequent solution is to expel the offending consultants.

Pair-of-hands Role

Block's second role makes the IS specialist available to the client as an extra pair of hands, providing additional resources to solve problems that might otherwise go unaddressed, because the client lacks time or specialized knowledge. Here, the client plays the active role, while the consultant passively follows directions, completing the tasks that the client has assigned. The assumption is that the client understands the problem well enough to guide the consultant effectively, and that the services provided by the consultant only add real value when specialized knowledge is applied.

Within the IS domain, IS specialists adopt the pair-of-hands role in "user-led" system design. When systems specialists view their role as building a system to the users' specifications, they abdicate to clients all the important sociotechnical design decisions. This role allows clients to dictate the terms of IT application and the goals to be addressed. Since clients are often unwilling to fund IS projects that benefit other parts of the organization, we frequently find examples of systems that reinforce, rather than break down, the organization's functional "stovepipes;" often the systems designed this way just "pave the cowpaths" (Hammer 1990; Hammer & Champy, 1993).

As should be clear, the pair-of-hands role is virtually the opposite of that of the expert. However, it comes no closer than the expert role in serving the needs of the organizations engaged in business process reengineering. Most clients lack both the broad knowledge of the whole business process and the sociotechnical system design skill to make all the important decisions on BPR projects. Consequently, effective BPR requires IS professionals to adopt a much more collaborative role.

KNOWLEDGE OR SKILL	DESCRIPTION
Knowledge of the Business	familiarity with the industry, the firm's business strategy, and its key people, activities, technologies, etc.
Communication Skills	ability to listen effectively to clients and others; to describe technologies in business terms
Consulting Skills	ability to enter into a collaborative relationship with clients, workers, and non-IS staff specialists; to help other participants diagnose and solve business problems
Change Management Skills	ability to diagnose resistance and to deal effectively with it through creative system designs, implementation efforts, and healthy relationships with clients and users
Organizational Systems Integration	ability to integrate information systems development and implementation projects with other dimensions of the organization and with other change initiatives
Knowledge of Individual and Organizational Learning	understanding of how people and organizations learn from their experiences, particularly those involving technology and information; ability to design good "learning laboratories"
Knowledge of Non-IS Approaches to Organizational Improvement	familiarity with non-IS approaches to organizational improvement, such as cost control and management systems, human resources management and organization development; understanding of the strengths and weaknesses of each; rules for determining when each approach might be superior to the others and how these approaches can be used in combination
Knowledge of BPR and Sociotechnical Systems Concepts, Methodologies and Design Principles	ability to identify, describe, document and analyze business process; ability to set appropriate boundaries around change efforts so that the problem of "suboptimization" can be avoided; understanding of "joint optimization;" skill in applying the principle of "minimum critical specification" in sociotechnical systems designs

Table 2: Knowledge and Skill Requirements for IS Specialists in BPR Projects

Collaborative Role

In what Block calls the collaborative role, consultants work with clients, actively applying their knowledge and skill to *help* clients diagnose and solve problems. Rather than separating out and distributing the roles of expertise, direction, and effort to either the client or the consultant, collaboration involves both parties sharing the responsibility for performance improvement. Communications between the partners is intense and bi-directional; conflicts are resolved in a constructive fashion. The outcome of a collaborative relationship between client and consultant is a more thorough understanding by both parties of the problem being addressed and the solution being designed. This understanding forms the basis for future collaborations and future improvement efforts.

Performance in a collaborative role requires that IS professionals develop new skills in order to become effective agents of business process change. In Table 2, we identify some of the specific new skills that we believe IS professionals must acquire. These skills reflect the spirit of collaboration rather than technical expertise. Because IS participation in BPR projects involves relationships with clients and other improvement specialists, collaborative skills and knowledge are more likely than narrowly applied specialist knowledge to produce success in BPR.

The collaborative role is appropriate in all domains of traditional IS practice from system development to data center operations and end-user support. However, we believe it is particularly suited to IS involvement in BPR projects. And the collaborative role of the IS specialist should not be restricted to relationships with the managers who fund or lead BPR efforts, but rather should be extended to all members of BPR design teams, especially other organizational improvement specialists.

Conclusion—A New Spirit of Partnership

For IS to adopt the collaborative consulting role on BPR projects is for IS to enter into partnership. The word partnership is overused in business discourse, and its meaning has been diluted as a result. While we do not know of a more accurate term than partner to describe the spirit of the truly collaborative relationships that IS specialists must create in BPR projects, we have found a metaphor that may restore the force of its meaning. In nautical usage, according to Webster, a partner is one of the reinforcing timbers used to support the mast and to strengthen the point where the mast joins the deck of a ship. In this function, the partner is a hidden source of strength for the much more visible sails.

On a successful voyage, captain, crew and ship all work together; a failure of any component is a failure of the whole. The question is not whether any single component is needed but rather what its role should be. Similarly, in BPR projects, it is clear that IS is only one component in the overall sociotechnical design. And its essential role is to operate in harmony with all the others. For this to happen, we believe, IS specialists must enter into collaborative partnerships with clients, workers, and other organizational improvement specialists. These partnerships are the hidden source of strength in successful BPR projects.

Appendix
IS Involvement in Business Process Reengineering—A Case Study[4]

For IS organizations that have consistently failed to deliver the right applications on time, simply being thought of as an effective reengineering participant takes change. One case in point is the San Francisco-based California State Automobile Association. Top management at the northern California affiliate of the American Automobile Association (AAA) decided to embrace BPR two years ago in response to several problems, including declining service ratings and productivity.

Managers at the 300-person CSAA IS organization, however, quickly found that they were on the outside looking in. IS wasn't included on the team chosen to redesign the firm's key business processes such as customer service. Instead, for IT input, CSAA was relying on consultants.

In order to get a glimpse of the future, IS managers at CSAA were literally forced to snatch after-hours peaks of the charts in the deserted meeting rooms where the reengineering team had earlier been doing its work.

What they saw shocked them. What the reengineers had in mind was a customer service process that would allow a single person to answer questions and handle claims and other transactions pertaining to practically any CSAA product, such as auto insurance, homeowners insurance or travel services. That would require a whole new set of applications based on shared relational databases, all due within one year. And they would have to replace CSAA's existing set of mainframe-based applications.

IS managers at CSAA quickly realized their organization wasn't ready for business process reengineering. Not only was the information architecture unprepared, but IS was widely regarded as a problem rather than a business partner. New application projects frequently missed their target dates by a wide margin. Projects typically took from three to five years, recalls CSAA manager of business systems planning David Carlson. And the backlog of projects stretched out seven years.

So newly arrived CIO Greg Smith decided to reengineer CSAA's IS shop to get into shape for reengineering. He formed a committee of top company executives to oversee the effort. The committee included CSAA's president, two executive vice presidents and a general manager. Smith also created four teams to look at key elements of IS: data infrastructure, management leadership practices, application renewal and support for BPR.

That led to a number of changes. For one thing, he introduced project management methodologies and decreed that everyone would be judged on delivering applications on time. IS also began redirecting resources away from projects that weren't considered critical and toward projects that supported reengineering.

Those changes ruffled feathers both inside and outside IS, says Carlson. Business executives had to realize that maintenance on some legacy applications that was once routinely approved would no longer be funded. And IS workers who had maintained those applications had to accept new roles. Many also had to accept 14-hour work days as they struggled to reengineer IS.

As a result, says Carlson, IS has started to be included in reengineering at CSAA. The phalanx of reengineering consultants—which at one time numbered 120—is being reduced, he adds. Moreover, IS is beginning to upgrade the information architecture, introducing client/server and other new technologies.

But this progress has not come without a price. Unwilling or unable to cope with the changes, many long-term IS workers have left the company. "It was easy for them to understand that the business had to change," says Carlson. "It was harder for them to understand that they had to change."

Endnotes

[1]   Founded in 1968, the Society for Information Management (SIM) is the premier professional organization for senior information systems executives with significant leadership responsibilities in major corporations, government entities, and non-profit groups. SIM's mission is to provide international leadership and education in the successful management and use of information technology to achieve business objectives. The Advanced Practices Council (APC) is a special membership program of SIM, comprising chief information officers from major companies representing a variety of industries. The APC supports high quality research in applied and business-focused topics. The subject areas are particularly relevant to the successful management and use of information technology to achieve business objectives.

[2]   This description clearly understates the consultants' responsibility for excluding the IS specialists. They cannot have been ignorant of it, so they

must have given at least tacit approval. Few clients would have insisted on leaving their IS personnel out, if the external consultants had explicitly counseled against it.

    [3]   Reengineering experts claim that even large organizations have only about 4 to about 20 key business processes (Davenport, 1993a; Cypress, 1994).

    [4]   Source: Jeff Moad, Does reengineering really work? Reprinted from *Datamation*, August 1, 1993, page 24. Copyright 1993 by Cahners Publishing Company. Reprinted with permission.

References

Alic, J. (1990). Who designs work? Organizing production in an age of high technology. *Technology in Society*, 12, 301-317.

Bashein, B. J., Markus, M. L., & Riley, P. (1993, October). *Business process reengineering: Roles for information technologies and information systems professionals*. Working paper, Programs in Information Science, The Claremont Graduate School.

Bashein, B. J., Markus, M. L. & Riley, P. (1994). Business reengineering: Preconditions for BPR success, and how to prevent failure. *Information Systems Management*, 11, 2, 7-13.

Beer, M., Eisenstat, R. A., & Spector, B. (1990). *The critical path to corporate renewal*. Boston, MA: Harvard Business School Press.

Block, P. (1981). *Flawless consulting: A guide to getting your expertise used*. San Diego, CA: Pfeiffer.

Cherns, A. B. (1987). Principles of sociotechnical design revisited. *Human Relations*, 40, 153-162.

Cummings, T. G., and Markus, M. L. (1979). A socio-technical systems view of organizations. In C. L. Cooper (Ed.), *Behavioral problems in organizations* (pp. 59-77). Englewood Cliffs, NJ: Prentice-Hall, pp. 59-77.

Cypress, H. L. (1994, February). Reengineering. *OR/MS Today*, pp. 18, 29.

Davenport, T. H. (1993a). *Process innovation: Reengineering work through information technology*. Boston, MA: Harvard Business School Press.

Davenport, T. H. (1993b, Fall). Review of Reengineering the Corporation. *Sloan Management Review*, 103-104.

Davenport, T. H., & Short, J. E. (1990). The new industrial engineering: Information technology and business process redesign. *Sloan Management Review*, 31, 4, 11-27.

Davenport, T. H., & Stoddard, D. B. (1994). Reengineering: Business change of mythical proportions? *MIS Quarterly*, 18, 121-127.

Hall, G., Rosenthal, J., & Wade, J. (1993). How to make reengineering really work. *Harvard Business Review*, 73, 6, 119-131.

Hammer, M. (1990). Reengineering work: Don't automate, obliterate. *Harvard Business Review*, 70, 4, 104-112.

Hammer, M., & Champy, J. (1993). *Reengineering the corporation: A manifesto for business revolution*. New York, NY: HarperBusiness.

Harrington, H. J. (1991). *Business process improvement: The breakthrough strategy for total quality, productivity, and competitiveness*. New

York, NY: McGraw-Hill Publishers.

The IT Management Programme. (1993, November). *The role of IS in business process reengineering.* (Available from Centre for Management Research, Park House, Wick Road, Edgham, Surrey, England TW20 0HW)

Johnson, T. H. (1992). *Whole-brain re-engineering.* (Available from Tenex Consulting, Cambridge, MA)

Kanter, R. M. (1993). *The change masters: Innovation and entrepreneurship in the american corporation.* New York, NY: Simon and Schuster, Inc.

Krass, P. (1991, March 25). Building a better mouse trap. *Information Week*, pp. 24-28.

Krass, P. (1992, May 5). The role of the CIO: A delicate balance. *Information Week.*

Majchrzak, A. (1991). Management of technological and organizational change. In G. Salvendy (Ed.), *Handbook of industrial engineering* (2nd ed.) (pp. 767-797). New York, NY: John Wiley and Sons.

Markus, M. L. & Keil, M. (1994, Summer). If we build it they will come: Designing systems that users want to use. *Sloan Management Review*, 11-25.

Moad, J. (1993, August). Does reengineering really work? *Datamation*, pp. 22-24, 28.

Mumford, E., & Weir, M. (1979). *Computer systems in work design -- The ETHICS method.* New York, NY: Wiley.

Rummler, G., & Brache, A. (1990). *Improving performance: How to manage the white space on the organization chart.* San Francisco, CA: Jossey-Bass.

Senn, J. (1991, March-April). Reshaping business processes through reengineering. *SIM Network*, pp. 4-6.

Smith, H. A., & McKeen, J. D. (1993). Re-engineering the corporation: Where does I.S. fit in? *Proceedings of the Twenty-Sixth Annual Hawaii International Conference on System Sciences, Vol. III*, 120-126.

Taylor, J. C., & Felten, D. F. (1993). *Performance by design: Sociotechnical systems in North America.* Englewood Cliffs, NJ: Prentice Hall.

Tornatzky, L. & Fleischer, M. (1990). *The processes of technological innovation.* Lexington, MA: Lexington Publishing.

Walton, R. E. (1989). *Up and running: Integrating information technology and the organization.* Boston, MA: Harvard Business School Press.

Reengineering the
IS Function:
A Managerial Perspective

Heather A. Smith
James D. McKeen
Queen's University

R. Ryan Nelson
University of Virginia

In the face of intense competition and other economic pressures, organizations of all sizes and sectors are attempting to survive by reducing cycle time, eliminating levels of hierarchy, empowering employees, and forming alliances with suppliers, customers, and even competitors. In this quest to *reengineer* the enterprise, functional areas such as marketing, finance, and information systems are being driven to reexamine what they are doing and to determine whether there's a better or simpler way of accomplishing the same objectives. The goal of these efforts is to achieve dramatic improvements in organizational performance that will result in savings in cost and time, higher quality products, and better customer service —in short, in a more effective organization.

Information technology and the people who manage, develop, and operate systems that use IT have been labelled as "crucial enablers," capable of facilitating dramatic improvements in cost, quality, service and speed. But as many organizations are finding out, the "crucial enablers" may need to be reengineered themselves. This chapter addresses this issue by reporting the results of two focus groups held with information systems (IS) managers in Canada and the United States. Within each focus group, participants were asked to propose ways in which the IS function could be reengineered. A total of twenty–two specific recommendations were made suggesting that the IS function in many organizations has a lot of room for improvement.

In the process of conducting both focus groups it was evident that, although IS managers had little problem coming up with ways to streamline processes and reduce costs, they did have a difficult time when asked to "think outside the box" and look beyond traditional solutions. We believe that this difficulty will be shared by all functional area managers as they attempt to reengineer their own business areas (Dejong, 1994). Therefore, we suspect that many of the guidelines gleaned from this study of IS managers will be useful to management in general, regardless of their functional area.

The chapter is organized into four sections. First, we discuss the impetus for the study and describe the approach we took to find out more about this relatively unstructured process. Next, we begin to report the findings of our study by addressing the realities of reengineering as discovered by managers from our focus groups, representing twenty different organizations. The third section of this chapter presents a set of guidelines for management, illustrated by the experiences of our group of practitioners. Finally, a few concluding remarks are made at the end of the chapter.

Background

It is understood that information technology (IT) plays an important role in enabling and supporting reengineering (Cyprus, 1994; Davenport, 1993; Hammer and Champy, 1993; *IS Analyzer*, 1993; Osborne and Gaebler, 1992; Schnitt, 1993). In addition, the valuable role that systems analysts play in process analysis and redesign has also been acknowledged (Davenport and Short, 1990; Freiser, 1992; Roby, 1992). But what of the design of the information systems (IS) function itself? Is it effective? Are all its parts really necessary? For many years, users and business executives have been asking these questions of IS management, but, for the most part, have received very few answers. However, in today's challenging and competitive marketplace, even IS is not immune from the reengineering undercurrent. As some IS managers have found out, those who do not take a proactive stance toward reengineering may end up losing control of their own destiny. It is not difficult these days to find organizations where the IS function was "outsourced" when an external competitor demonstrated that it could do the same job for less money.

Can IS reengineer itself to achieve the dramatic changes in its own operations that companies are coming to expect? To address this issue, we convened two separate focus groups of senior IS managers. One group included participants from ten leading Canadian firms representing five industry sectors: retail, manufacturing, banking, communications, and insurance. The second focus group involved twenty–two IS practitioners from ten large U.S. organizations representing seven industry sectors: manufacturing, chemical, communications, insurance, higher education, healthcare, and the federal government. The format for both focus groups was a moderated roundtable discussion. Each session lasted approximately two hours while allowing ample time for each participant to contribute to the discussion. First, each participant was asked to address the ways that he or she might reengineer the IS function in their organization. In order to force participants to challenge their own assumptions about the work of IS, we chose a "stretch" objective for this reengineering exercise which would encourage them to look beyond traditional solutions. We asked each participant: "What would your functional area do if faced with a 20% budget cut this year?" While a cut of this magnitude was designed to simulate a crisis within which reengineering could be fostered, we cautioned participants that reengineering requires two other prerequisites:

- a bold vision of what their function should be/do, and
- discontinuous thinking that recognizes and consciously breaks away from the outdated rules and fundamental assumptions that underlie functional activities.

The stretch exercise was then followed by a brainstorming session in which participants were asked to come up with a list of practical suggestions for how to go about reengineering a functional area. The results of these two exercises are described below.

The Reality of Reengineering

For both focus groups, the results of our reengineering exercise were mixed. It was harder for our managers to look inward than it is for most IS professionals to look at other functions in their organization. Furthermore, the reengineering process is not nearly as straightforward as management consultants would have us believe. The process was complicated by the fact that, overall, our participants were proud of what they had achieved within their organizations and found it hard to believe that any magic answer could be found that would lead to the desired result.

Their difficulty illustrates the first reality about reengineering: reengineering is *not* magic. It requires a lot of hard work and causes considerable organizational disruption. The exercise also drove home a practical point that it is hard to be objective about one's own area. The tendency is to protect and support, rather than challenge. While this does not invalidate the reengineering process, it underlines the serious problems facing anyone who attempts such an endeavor.

A second reality of reengineering is that it is difficult to break away from traditional solutions. Although we had set our target in financial terms, participants were cautioned against excessive attention to cost reduction alone because it results in trade-offs that are usually unacceptable to stakeholders (Davenport & Short, 1990). However, when confronted with a cost-reduction objective, most of the participants proceeded to address ways to reduce costs, rather than take the more roundabout route of identifying a vision and challenging their own assumptions about work. Thus, reengineering seems to be counter-intuitive to traditional management techniques.

Some of the participants also had trouble identifying the fundamental assumptions that underlie IS activities (i.e., the third reality of reengineering). Very few questioned the work they were doing or considered the value particular activities added to their organization. This illustrates yet another fact about reengineering. Some managers considered self-reflection to be part of an ongoing and continuous process of improvement, not a one-time-only activity. Effective managers, they believed, were always questioning the assumptions on which their work was based. But other participants disagreed. Particularly in organizations where costs were completely charged back to users, there was a tendency to accept high overheads or administrative functions because these costs are buried in the chargebacks. By implication if certain aspects of their work can be challenged, then managers haven't been doing their jobs effectively. In other words, reengineering is threatening and makes even the best managers distinctly uncomfortable.

The fourth reality is the realization that reengineering is not an approach for the fainthearted. According to Tellier (1994), you "cannot expect to create change through tentative, half-hearted and timid measures." In order for reengineering to work, you require bold implementation. Maglitta (1994) offers the following words of advice: expect resistance, keep focused, don't fear conflict, and get ready for blood, sweat, tears— and long days!

A final reality of reengineering is that it requires three distinct approaches as depicted in Figure 1. Each approach requires a different focus, involves a different level of management, and attempts change in a different manner.

Enterprise Reengineering focuses on the organization as a

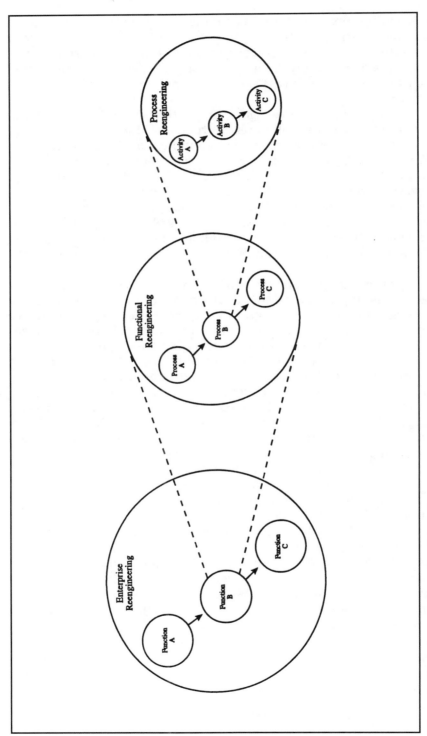

Figure 1: Three Approaches to Reengineering

whole. This approach takes a corporate–wide viewpoint and is concerned with how functions will be integrated. In addition, organizations sometimes will need to extend their analysis beyond their "corporate walls" to include functions contained within external entities such as suppliers and customers (Treacy and Michaud, 1992).

Functional Reengineering views a functional area as a "business within a business." Therefore, in the case of IS, the focus is on establishing a vision for the IS function and deciding what "business" IS should be in, given the needs of its customers. An additional objective includes determining where the boundaries for a functional area should be drawn and if the analysis will need to extend to include other areas within the organization.

Process Reengineering concentrates on making processes more efficient. Here, the emphasis is on process simplification and streamlining activities to make them run smoother, reduce paperwork, improve quality, and improve response time. It also attempts to re–establish "natural entities" by linking related processes and activities regardless of their geographic or organizational location.

Our managers surmised that, *theoretically*, effective reengineering involves taking each approach in turn. For example, top management should initiate the reengineering process by examining the organization as a whole, eliminating (or possibly outsourcing) entire functional areas if necessary. Next, functional area managers should reexamine such fundamental issues as vision and scope from an area perspective. Finally, managers responsible for specific processes should be asked to focus on activities within their purview. Therefore, it seems imperative that organizations always begin with enterprise reengineering and only proceed to the next level after finishing with the first; i.e., streamlining processes first makes little sense because those same processes may be eliminated during enterprise or functional reengineering.

In *practice*, however, our managers concluded that waiting for the enterprise to be reengineered before starting their own efforts would be "suicidal." Wait to reengineer and you may end up not having anything to reengineer! For this reason and because our focus was on reengineering the IS function, we have limited our analysis to functional reengineering and process reengineering. Enterprise reengineering, while no less important, was considered beyond the scope of our study.

Guidelines for Management

In spite of the difficulties presented by this exercise, our participants came up with a number of practical suggestions for managers wishing to reengineer their functional area (see Table 1). While it is expected that some of these strategies could lead to considerable cost savings, they are not quick fixes. While the payoffs can be high, the stakes are high as well. These strategies are meant as a guide to stimulate and direct the reengineering process. They are not a substitute for the insight and experience of management. Guidelines will be presented under the following headings: a) functional reengineering, and b) process reengineering.

While the twelve guidelines contained within the functional reengineering section focus more on macro issues such as vision, boundary setting, and management structure, the ten process reengineering gidelines represent the fundamental activities performed by the IS function such as planning, development, operations, and support.

A: Functional Reengineering

Build a Clear Vision of Your Functional Area. The first step in the reengineering process is to delineate a vision for the functional area as a whole. This process starts at the enterprise level where key questions about what the area should be doing are addressed (Morris and Brandon, 1993). It continues within the function itself as senior managers clarify a coherent vision for their area.

How important is this vision? Consider two different visions of IS that are current in the industry:

Vision #1. IS should *be responsive to* users' needs through building, promoting, and effectively using an IT infrastructure.

Vision #2. IS should *contribute to* the business' profitability and service goals through building, promoting and effectively using a responsive IT infrastructure.

The differences between a *reactive* vision (#1) and a *proactive* vision (#2) are substantial. If these visions are effectively implemented in two independent organizations, they will result in two markedly different approaches to IT delivery. Properly articulated, a vision can be a powerful message to all IS personnel about how business is to be conducted. Sadly, many functional area "visions" have deteriorated into meaningless, toothless mission statements full of platitudinous statements that cannot be effectively imple-

Functional Reengineering
· *Build a clear vision of your functional area.*
· *Map strengths onto this vision.*
· *Decide what business you are in.*
· *Use outsourcing effectively.*
· *Welcome comparisons.*
· *Get tough with sacred cows.*
· *Look for embedded assumptions.*
· *Remove artificial barriers to productivity.*
· *Eliminate fixers.*
· *Empower staff - eliminate vertical handoffs.*
· *Value long-term staff.*
· *Reintegrate natural entities - eliminate horizontal handoffs.*
Process Reengineering
· *Benchmark development.*
· *Invest wisely in technology.*
· *Adopt a single application system image.*
· *Facilitate parallel development.*
· *Reuse existing software.*
· *Benchmark operations.*
· *Evaluate procurement practices.*
· *Maximize equipment utilization.*
· *Reflect true costs in chargeback.*
· *Standardize platforms.*

Table 1: Reengineering Guidelines for Management

mented.

Implicit in the reengineering process is an "apolitical" or "egoless" approach to redesigning a functional area. The crisis precipitating the reengineering process is critical to this step. Only if the entire function is threatened will managers start thinking as a team and stop protecting their roles. One participant told how some of his group of IS specialists served much the same function as another group of specialists in another part of the organization. He remarked that he and the other manager involved would never have had the motivation to merge the two groups, resulting in a 20% staff reduction, without the serious economic recession that has brought the existence of his entire company into question.

Map Strengths onto this Vision. With the overall vision as a guide, the management team needs to identify area strengths and core competencies and how they contribute to this vision. Strengths that do not complement it should be challenged. It is unfortunate, but true, that many managers have bought into specialized visions for a particular aspect of their area that do little, if anything, to further the vision for the area as a whole. For example, an IS function may have a very strong data modelling group but this may only have a tangential impact on the overall goals of the IS area. In assessing strengths, management must be brutally honest and willing to break away from prevailing industry thinking. What is the point of a group of highly paid, highly trained specialists who may do excellent work but who have a vision of IS that is substantially different from that of the overall IS function?

Decide What Business You Are In. The primary focus of most IS functions appears to be development and support activities. For example, in one company 2,000 of their 4,000 employees are classified as "developers." Therefore, within this area, companies should question where the boundaries of its IS function should be drawn. Some companies include business analysts within each user department. Others consolidate all their analysts within the IS function. Arguments can be advanced for each method, but the key question is—is the IS function in the business of providing technology and technological advice? or is it in the business of providing business systems solutions to business problems? If it is in the business of providing technological advice, then many business analytical functions can be shifted to business groups. In the view of one participant from a U.S. government agency, "We want to be viewed just like a utility ... we lay the cable right to their (the user's) front door and let them develop their own solutions."

Use Outsourcing Effectively. The activities of IS vary widely by company, but our managers felt that organizations should consider eliminating activities if they are both straightforward and not central to the main business of IS. They suggested outsourcing (i.e., hiring an outside company) for most data entry activities. Furthermore, small– to medium–sized organizations should seriously consider outsourcing operations as well. Newer approaches to operations have led to considerable savings in this area, but only if companies are large enough to take advantage of the economies of scale that are available. All companies should take advantage of outsourcing services that can be shared, such as communications, while shopping for a third party organization that can offer subscribers the benefits of bulk purchasing.

Once core IS activities have been determined, management should selectively use outsourcing to handle staffing peaks and to supplement staff where specialized skills are required. While development is a basic IS function, outsourcing can be effectively used in this area to reduce staff overheads and numbers of permanent staff. When staff with specialized knowledge are required, savings can be realized by recognizing the lack of competency in a particular area and supplementing it temporarily from the outside, rather than trying to hire expensive specialists.

Welcome Comparisons. Most functions within organizations can be benchmarked against other comparable functions. These comparisons may occur with direct competitors or may be found in entirely different industries. The key is to identify the "best of breed" for a given function. This process of comparison challenges management to review its goals, its performance, and its measurement techniques. This review, in and of itself, is beneficial. Comparison, by identifying areas of strength and weakness, motivates as well as focuses the reengineering effort.

Previously, many IS managers have reacted protectively when users announce an external IS provider would be able to provide the same service for less money. Typically, IS managers will begin to list all the benefits they provide that the external provider does not. From a reengineering perspective, this is missing the boat. As Michael Hammer (1990) notes, it was only when Ford saw how its competitor Mazda handled its accounting paperwork, that it realized what could really be done in automating its accounting function.

One of our participants described how a benchmarking study revealed that his IS function was more expensive than of any of its competitors, by an order of magnitude. But when he informed his managers of this fact the first thing they did was argue with the numbers, missing the cold reality that "even if the numbers were off by 50% they were in trouble." Another participant told of a user who was being charged six times the amount of money by her in–house IS function than it would have cost to go to an outside provider. No amount of internal benefits is worth this much. True comparisons with other service providers force IS managers to face realities in their own organizations. These comparisons can also be a learning experience if IS managers use these facts to force change on their own organizations. In fact, part of the reengineering process should be a close look at how competitors and other companies operate their IS functions.

Get Tough with Sacred Cows. Another area in which management must be strong and clearly focused is in addressing "sacred cows." You will know you've hit upon one of these when others react in horror at the thought of questioning its purpose. A large number of administrative overheads often fall within this category. Sacred cows are the never–stated (and therefore never challenged) implicitly held organizational beliefs. It was not until one organization challenged the organizational truism "we service what we sell" that they were able to outsource service to a separate company allowing them to concentrate more effectively on their product design and marketing.

With respect to IS, organizations that charge all their costs back to groups of "captive" users are particularly susceptible in this area. This is because there is little motivation to challenge these activities. For example, project control reporting could easily be a "sacred cow" in many organizations. Many developers spend a significant amount of their time each week reporting on the work they've done. Much of what they're reporting may not benefit the user or the project in any way, but may be designed for the sole benefit of justifying the existence of the IS function.

Another "sacred cow" may be the amount of time spent on training staff. While project control and staff training may be desirable in themselves, how much is necessary and how and when it is required may be very appropriate questions. Too often, IS management tends to take a broadbrush approach with such issues, instead of using a more finely tuned approach that delivers the necessary amounts only when needed. Other "sacred cows" that our participants came up with include authorizations, requisitions, invoices, "just–in–case" inventory, control by bottleneck, and the view that all vendors are the enemy.

Look for Embedded Assumptions. Embedded assumptions, unlike sacred cows, can be challenged without significant acrimony. It is just that they go unnoticed and therefore unchallenged. As a result, management must root out these buried assumptions by digging deeper into the detail during the reengineering process.

Many assumptions about IS work may be embedded in other activities and not immediately apparent. This is why it is important to challenge and explore every aspect of IT delivery. For example, one of our participants told of how certain forms of history collection were discovered only when the chargeback mechanism was challenged. When the details were explored, it was determined that months of history data were saved for users on online storage. When consulted, users stated that they rarely, if ever, needed to access this data and that online storage was unnecessary. Cheaper means of history storage resulted in savings for both the users and IS. This anecdote underlines the importance of getting into enough detail to really understand what is occurring. It is all very well to say that history collection is essential, but to question what is being done, how it is being done, and how much of it is being done, truly challenges assumptions about this process.

Remove Artificial Barriers to Productivity. While methods and controls can be an important component of productivity, many may actually be lowering productivity by what they are measuring. As Goldratt and Cox (1984) point out in *The Goal*, certain accounting measures of productivity that have been well accepted in manufacturing firms, can actually decrease throughput and increase inventories, resulting in poor bottom–line performance. These are "artificial" barriers because they are created by management and are not an innate part of the basic process.

In addition to functionally separating systems into pieces, IS has also created artificial barriers to productivity through the use of complex system development life cycles and project control techniques. An example of this could be two traditional IS measurements of performance—schedule and budget. Many IS managers have worked long and hard to ensure that all projects are completed on time and on budget. Yet users still express dissatisfaction with systems developed in this way. A closer look at how these measures are implemented reveals why. IS managers often cut functional pieces out of systems that look like they are not going to meet their target schedules and budgets. The result is systems that do not meet users' needs. If all that is being measured is how much got done in a particular time or budget, what is the real value of these measurements? When reengineering IS, managers should pay careful attention to the bottom–line goals of their organization and use only those measures that actually contribute to these goals.

Eliminate Fixers. Many organizations have staff devoted to fixing things that go wrong. This is particularly true in operations where "expediters" are used to ensure that operational errors are fixed quickly. To ensconce the task of expediting into the organizational structure is to formally acknowledge failure!

Typically, some systems encounter significantly more problems than others. The mistake is to assign someone the task of continually attending to these problems without addressing the root causes. This not only fails to solve the problems permanently but lends legitimacy to the process of continual bandaging.

Our managers recommended a careful analysis of these problems. Efforts to correct their causes should result in the elimination of fixers on staff. Similar studies should be made in any part of IS that feels it is necessary to employ fixers.

Empower Staff – Eliminate Vertical Handoffs. Bureaucracy and management structure can prevent staff from doing their jobs most productively. If staff have to consult with management before making most decisions, or if staff are kept waiting while senior managers make decisions, they are not being productive. Many organizations have found that creating a culture of "do it yourself" where staff have the ability to make decisions without management approval have substantially improved productivity (Kelleher, 1993; Smith & McKeen, 1992).

Value Long Term Staff. One manager suggested that the reason why the Japanese are more productive than North Americans is that their employees stay with them much longer. IS staff are highly mobile and every time a staff member leaves, he or she takes with them, not only technical skills, but accumulated and valuable knowledge of business practices, systems, and procedures. He has calculated that the turnover in his area costs the company millions of dollars in retraining and lost knowledge. If IS management can retain its staff longer then it may reap significant benefits from the intangibles that long term staff bring to the job. Another company stated that being viewed as the "employer of choice" is one of three major goals for the IS function.

Reintegrate Natural Entities – Eliminate Horizontal Handoffs. Previously, functional groups were created to handle different pieces of a customer's needs or a product's development. Unfortunately many of these have added little to a company's overall product or service. In many cases, they actually decreased productivity and service because work had to be handed off between organizational units, thus increasing the likelihood of error. The elimination of such handoffs and the reintegration of natural entities such as a "customer" or a "product" are the main goals of reengineering (Huff, 1992; Moad, 1993a). This is why many companies are rapidly moving to put functional pieces back together either organizationally or through the use of a computer system that enables a composite view of an entity. One manager representing a major insurance company described that when his company consolidated a host of separate IS units into one they were able to downsize from 5,800 to 4,000 employees. It was estimated that the elimination of duplication accounted for approximately 900 of those jobs.

In IS, the natural entity is the system. In the past twenty years, systems development has become increasingly fragmented as maintenance and development were separated; analysis and programming were separated; and numerous pieces of the development effort were farmed out to specialist groups, such as security, system audit, quality assurance, data administration, development centers, operations analysis, system testing and the like. Each of these groups has created handoffs by developing their own standards, bureau-cracy, and paperwork. The elimination of as many of these handoffs in systems development as possible is probably the biggest single activity that managers can undertake to reengineer IS.

B: Process Reengineering

Benchmark Development. A common goal is to develop systems faster, with higher quality, at lower cost, and with fewer people. Therefore, ongoing improvement of these capabilities is not only desirable but requisite when faced with the thought of inter-organizational comparison (Moad, 1993b). The following represent a sampling of possible benchmarks for applications development:

- speed of development; e.g., project cycle time (a.k.a. "time to market");
- cost of development; e.g., development cost per function point;
- development productivity; e.g., function points per person–month; and
- quality measurements; e.g., number of defects per function point.

Invest Wisely in Technology. Current development tools such as computer–aided software engineering (CASE) and fourth–genera-tion languages can promote productivity but they are not a panacea for systems development productivity problems (Loh and Nelson, 1989). Overlaying CASE technology on existing development prac-tices is analogous to developing an information system on top of existing business practices (a.k.a. "paving the cowpaths"). Similarly, it is not always appropriate to invest in the newest technology for systems solutions. Often, proven technology is more cost–effective to implement. New technology may be more appealing for IS staff, but, unless the benefits are obvious for the business, it doesn't make sense to use it.

Adopt a Single Application System Image. With more and more users being required to use multiple systems, many organiza-tions have found that it saves both developer and user time to adopt a single system image; i.e., a standardized look and functionality for all systems. This simplifies the development effort in many areas. Screen designs are easier and common data elements are used across systems. In addition, access to systems is standardized and function keys are the same. A single system image also promotes shared program modules. The benefits of this approach continue after implementation since users need less time to learn the system.

Facilitate Parallel Development. The key to maximizing performance in supercomputers is to have multiple, high–speed processors operating in parallel. The key to developing *complex* applications quickly is to have multiple, high–speed teams operating in parallel (Martin, 1991).

Reuse Existing Software. The fastest application development generally occurs when applications are created from pre-existing designs or building blocks. Perhaps the most important change in software development that CASE tools will bring is the building of systems from reusable parts. There is a direct analogy with CAD/CAM systems used in engineering today. In mature engineering, almost everything is built from existing parts. As Michael Hammer points out, "[reengineering] absolutely requires heavy reuse of existing software." (Moad, 1993a, p.24).

Reuse of existing software also includes packaged software. Unfortunately, many IS staff and users consider that packaged software is always undesirable since they could do a better job. As a result, many hours are spent modifying packages that are bought or developing systems for which packages are readily available. One of our managers noted that this attitude was "crippling" IS productivity. Many hours have been spent developing "gold–plated" solutions to business problems instead of considering whether the missing functionality in packages is truly necessary.

Benchmark Operations. Many advances in operations management in the past few years have led to substantial efficiencies in computer operations (Cole *et al*, 1993). At present, the average operations department spends about 60% of its budget on equipment and 40% on people. The most efficient operations departments spend about 80% on equipment and 20% on people (McKeen and Smith, 1993). There is currently substantial expertise available in streamlining operations and it is reasonable for IS managers to aim for this 80/20 balance in their operations. The ultimate objective of a cost–effective operations department should be no people. IS functions should invest in the proven technology available in this area to achieve this goal.

When one of our managers decided to benchmark his utility costs (including data center, communications, and printing–related costs) against what it would cost to outsource these activities to IBM he encountered some fear and self–doubt from his utilities manager. The result of this comparison process was that in one year's time they were able to get their utility costs below IBM's proposal by $10 million and they forecast that they will be $50 million cheaper than IBM by next year. Needless to say, they will continue the benchmarking process not only in the utilities area but throughout the IS function.

Evaluate Procurement Practices. A participant representing a major chemical firm pointed out that organizations need to pay careful attention to procurement practices. The larger and more decentralized the organization, the higher the likelihood of finding inefficient procurement practices. In fact, as a result of a recent consolidation, this particular firm saved several hundred million dollars, reducing their expenditures by roughly 50% by leveraging their buying power. This particular manager stated, "With our culture the vendors liked us because we were an easy mark! They had a strategy of 'divide and conquer' ... selling to the individual pieces of our company all over the world."

Maximize Equipment Utilization. With effective capacity planning, an organization can save a considerable amount by operating its mainframes and DASD storage at close to 100% utilization. Whereas this used to be an impossible target, improved operating systems have meant that organizations can expect more from their equipment. Upgrades should be carefully planned so that the organization utilizes all available machine power before a larger machine is purchased, without running out of capacity.

One of our participant organizations planned to reduce costs by 40% over a three–year period. To achieve this goal they have reduced their number of data centers around the world from over 200 to 125 in the preceding year and plan on reducing the number to 25 in the near future. The manager representing this company described this approach as "focusing your reengineering efforts on the supply side."

Reflect True Costs in Chargeback. While this would seem to be axiomatic, in many organizations the true costs of a system cannot be accurately determined because chargeback mechanisms are sometimes adjusted for a number of reasons. Where this is the case, it is very difficult to identify problem areas in operational systems because comparisons are impossible to make. This problem is exacerbated where comparisons with outside suppliers are being made. Charging algorithms should be a true reflection of the costs of doing business and always reflect system usage accurately.

Standardize Platforms. One of the largest expense factors for many operations groups is the requirement that it operate from numerous software platforms. One manager noted that he was managing four data base packages and had to have fifteen people to maintain them. Our managers recommended that IS select a standardized software platform from which all systems should operate. This platform should provide options but limit the amount of infrastructure required to maintain it. Systems which use non-standard platforms should have a "sunset" clause to ensure they are migrated onto this platform within a reasonable time frame.

Conclusions

On their own, each of the guidelines listed above might be classified as merely being "good management practices". However, the guidelines can also be logically grouped at a higher level into such categories as core competencies, measurement issues, cost structures, and elimination of buffers for functional reengineering, and automation, standardization, flexibility, and measurement for the process reengineering guidelines. Furthermore, when viewed collectively, these same guidelines become a means for achieving *dramatic* improvements in performance at either the functional or process level. In addition to a new philosophical approach, reengineering requires knowing what levers to push and when to push them.

In concluding our reengineering exercise, one of our managers commented that, if they were going to survive, his function needed to be "run like a business." To this end, he suggested that they commit to three goals: being viewed as the vendor of choice by their *customers* (formerly known as users); being viewed as the employer of choice by their employees; and being able to show a return on their investment. In addition, this manager went one step further by establishing four specific objectives for his functional area:

- increase customer satisfaction level by 50% within two years;
- increase employee satisfaction level by 50% within two years;
- operate as a break–even profit and loss business; and
- become price competitive with the marketplace within two years.

In order to achieve these goals, this particular organization will be forced to *reengineer* its IS function. More specifically, as suggested within this chapter, it will be forced to restructure the functional area to focus on its core competencies; rethink the work that the area does; and ensure that all work is done as efficiently as possible.

Indeed, based on our experience, the reengineering exercise encourages functional area managers to use their analytical skills and approach their own function with the same objectivity as they approach other functions in the organization. If management can rise to the occasion and overcome some of the more difficult conceptual (e.g., discontinuous thinking) and political problems inherent in reengineering, we believe that they and their customers will be pleasantly surprised with the results.

References

Cole, C. C., Clark, M. L. & Nemec, C. (1993, May–June). Reengineering information systems at Cincinnati Milacron. *Planning Review*, 22–23.

Cyprus, H. L. (1994, February). Reengineering. *OR/MS Today*, Vol. 21, No. 1, 18–29.

Davenport, T. H. (1993). *Process Innovation: Reengineering Work Through Information Technology*. Boston, MA: Harvard Business School Press.

Davenport, T. & Short, J. (1990, Summer). The new industrial engineering: information technology and business process redesign. *Sloan Management Review*, 11–27.

Dejong, J. (1993, February). Smart Marketing. *Computerworld*, 113–119.

Freiser, T. J. (1992, Fall). The right start for business reengineering. *Information Strategy: The Executive's Journal*, 26–30.

Goldratt, E. M. & Cox, J. (1984). *The Goal: Excellence in Manufacturing*. Croton–on–Hudson, NY: North River Press.

Hammer, M. & Champy, J. (1993). *Reengineering the Corporation: A Manifesto for Business Revolution*. New York: Harper Business.

Hammer, M. (1990, July–August). Reengineering work: Don't automate, obliterate. *Harvard Business Review*, 104–112.

Huff, S. (1992, Winter). Reengineering the Business. *Western Business Quarterly*.

IS Analyzer. (1993, August). The role of IT in business reengineering.

Kelleher, J. (1993, September 13). The reincarnated organization. *Computerworld – Premier 100*, 23–26.

Loh, M. & Nelson, R. R. (1989, July 1). Reaping CASE harvests. *Datamation*, 31–34.

Maglitta, J. (1994, January). Glass Act. *Computerworld*. 80–88.

Martin, J. (1991). *Rapid Application Development*. New York: Macmillan Publishing Co.

McKeen J. D. & Smith, H. A. (1993, January 5–8). Linking IT investment with IT usage. *Proceedings of the 26th HICSS*. Maui, HI, 620–629.

Moad, J. (1993a, August 1). Does reengineering really work? *Datamation*. 22–28.

Moad, J. (1993b, November 1). New Rules, New Ratings as IS Reengineers. *Datamation*. 85–87.

Morris, D. & Brandon, J. (1993). *Re–Engineering Your Business*. New York: McGraw–Hill.

Osborne, D. E. & Gaebler, T. (1992). *Reinventing Government: How the Entrepreneurial Spirit is Transforming the Public Sector*. Addison–Wesley Publishing Co.

Roby, C. (1992, August). Reengineering will only work if IS shares the development technologies with users: Give everyone keys to the asylum. *Information Week*, 60.

Schnitt, D. L. (1993, January). Reengineering the organization using information technology. *Journal of Systems Management*, 14.

Smith, H. & McKeen, J. D. (1992). Computerization and management: A study of conflict and change. *Information and Management*, 53–64.

Tellier, P. (1994, February 25). It's Time to Reengineer the Public Service. *The Globe and Mail*, Toronto, Canada, A27.

Treacy, M. E. & Michaud, J. M. (1992, Spring). Channel partnerships: Cooperating to compete. *CSC Insights*, 16–20.

Chapter
24

Toward Reengineering the Information Systems Development Process

Rajiv Sabherwal
Florida International University

Numerous case examples demonstrate that information technology (IT) can be used for business process reengineering (Davenport, 1993; Hammer, 1990; Hall, Rosenthal, and Wade, 1993) or business process redesign (Davenport and Short, 1990; Teng, Grover, and Fiedler, 1994). Information systems (ISs) can fundamentally transform the very nature of an organization's business processes. Of course, the use of ISs for business process reengineering is no easy task, and several chapters in this book examine the various issues and opportunities surrounding it. This chapter differs somewhat in that it focuses on one kind of business processes which seems to be in need for reengineering, namely the processes of developing ISs themselves. Several recent articles (Beath and Orlikowski, forthcoming; Hirschheim and Klein, 1994; Levine and Rossmoore, 1993; Westell and Newman, 1993) have questioned the firmly-held assumptions underlying the traditional IS development process and suggested ways of modifying this process. In fact, Rockart and Hofman (1992) have argued that:

> Given the dramatic change in what the IS department must deliver to the organization, it is not surprising that how it is delivered must be changed dramatically as well (p. 25).

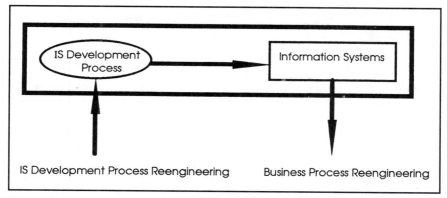

Figure 1: Reengineering and Information Systems

The use of ISs to enable business process reengineering is indicated in Figure 1 by arrow A. Moreover, as shown by arrow B, the ISs depend on a number of activities, such as project approval, analysis and design, coding, implementation, testing, and so, which comprise the IS development (ISD) process. These activities, and the overall ISD process, may themselves need to be reengineered, as shown using arrow C. This chapter focuses on arrow C, arguing that it may be necessary to reengineer the ISD process and providing some specific suggestions for this ISD process reengineering.

The next section of this chapter uses the IS literature to assess the current nature of the ISD process and argue for the need to reengineer it. This is followed by a description of six specific changes which may facilitate ISD process reengineering. Finally, in the discussion section, some implications for research and practice are examined followed by some concluding remarks.

The Information Systems Development Process

A number of activities are needed to produce ISs, including project approval, design, development, implementation, testing, training, and so on (Sabherwal and Robey, 1993). Like other business processes, the ISD process, which these activities comprise, has customers that may be either internal or external to the organization. This process often crosses organizational boundaries, because it usually takes place across organizational units, such as the various user departments and IS. The ISD process evidently seems to fit the definition of a business process:

"a set of logically related tasks performed to achieve a defined business outcome" (Davenport and Short, 1990; p. 12).

Limitations of the Traditional Information Systems Development Process

Despite the progress in IT and the accumulation of knowledge in the field of information systems, the ISD process continues to encounter numerous problems. Common problems include unrealistic user expectations, absence of an overall IS plan, top management's lack of IT knowledge, priority resetting, uncertainty involved in IT decisions, technology mania, incompatible ISs, and poor communication between users and IS (Doll and Ahmed, 1983; Lederer and Mendelow, 1990; Lyytinen, 1987; Vitale, Ives, and Beath, 1986).

These problems in the ISD process frequently lead to delays and cost-overruns. In some projects, labeled as "runaway IT projects" (Keil and Mixon, 1994), these cost-overruns may be quite enormous. Process problems may also cause problems in the ISs (i.e., IS products), including difficulty in using the system, awkward user-interface, slow and unreliable system, bugs or errors, irrelevant data, the system being too complex, and so on. In some cases, these problems may lead to the system being a failure, and sometimes they may cause the IS project to be abandoned midway (Ewusi-Mensah and Przasnyski, 1991).

That a number of problems are commonly encountered when using the traditional ISD process may be due several apparent limitations of this process, some of which have been identified by some IS researchers (Hirschheim and Klein, 1994; Robey and Markus, 1984; Westell and Newman, 1993). Some specific tactics have been suggested for addressing some of the problems faced in the traditional ISD process (Doll and Ahmed, 1983; Lederer and Mendelow, 1990). By and large, these suggestions involve improvements but use the same fundamental approach. More recently, the basic assumptions that underlie the traditional ISD process have been questioned, and the need for radical changes has been highlighted (Beath and Orlikowski, forthcoming; Hirschhemim and Klein, 1994; Westell and Newman, 1993). These two types of modifications in the ISD process represent ISD process refinement and ISD process reengineering, respectively, as discussed below.

ISD Process Refinement and ISD Process Reengineering

Figure 2 depicts the nature of change associated with ISs. The degree of innovativeness could be either incremental (i.e., minor adjustment or refinement) or radical (i.e., requiring a fundamental shift in norms, practices, relationships, etc.) The target of change could be either the ISD process or business processes. As shown in

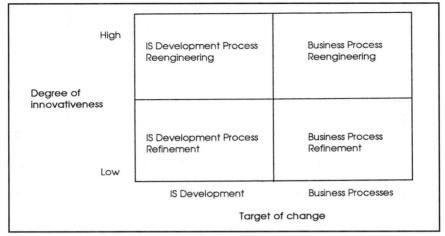

Figure 2: Refining and Reengineering the IS Development Process

Figure 2, combining these two dimensions results in the four cells, namely ISD process refinement (Cell I), business process refinement (Cell II), ISD process reengineering (Cell III), and business process reengineering (Cell IV). It may be noted that the primary focus of this chapter is on Cell III while most of the other chapters in this book focus on Cell IV.

The suggestions that are commonly made to address the widespread IS problems represent relatively minor, "fine-tuning" changes, or variations (Orlikowski, 1993), which fit in the "ISD process refinement" cell (Cell I) in Figure 2. For example, the objective of IS developers often is to identify system specifications completely before proceeding to the next stage, even in cases where users lack IT knowledge. Moreover, to address the problem of unrealistic user expectations, early user involvement is commonly recommended. It is implicitly assumed that if the users are involved early in an ISD process, they would have more realistic expectations about the eventual system. However, because at the start of the process the users' knowledge of IT and its potential contribution is less than their knowledge during the later stages, no amount of user involvement during the early stages can produce realistic expectation.

Instead, in the above situation the system specifications should be kept flexible so that they may be modified as the users acquire greater knowledge about IS. This represents "ISD process reengineering" (Cell III) because it questions a key unarticulated assumption — "we should finish one job before starting the next" — and causes a fundamental shift in the nature of the ISD process. In addition, several other unarticulated assumptions, or myths, such as "we should all get along because disagreement is bad," "we should delineate the responsibilities precisely without any overlaps," and so on, seem to govern the ISD process. ISD process reengineering involves breaking away from such old myths about how we organize and conduct this process. The following comment on business process reengineering is relevant for ISD process reengineering as well.

> At the heart of reengineering is the notion of discontinuous thinking - of recognizing and breaking away from the outdated rules and fundamental assumptions that underlie operations.... We cannot achieve breakthroughs in performance by cutting fat or automating existing processes. Rather, we must challenge old assumptions and shed the old rules that made the business under perform in the first place (Hammer, 1990; p. 107).

For ISD process reengineering, not only should the need for it be recognized by some senior IS executives, but the other IS professionals also need to be convinced. This may not be easy. Pastore and Hildebrand (1994) thus describe the situation faced by Rebecca Dawley, vice president and director of business information services at Federated Mutual Insurance Company:

> Dawley wants to step back, rethink the services her department offers, and find a new strategy that works better.

> Dawley's department is in the early stages of service redefinition, and she knows that one of her first jobs will be to convince her staff that things need to change. "They are aware of the custom complaints, but we often get caught in a loop trying the same things over again whenever there's a problem," she notes, "We need more self-contemplation." The hurdles here include an ingrained bias against outside ideas and aversion to rocking the boat in this close-knit organization (p. 74).

The need for reengineering the ISD process has been clearly articulated by Rockart and Hofman (1992), who consider it to be an important instance of business process redesign:

> "The key business process of the IS organization is the system development process. Changing the way systems are delivered, therefore, is a major "business process redesign." IS often helps other functions redesign their business practices, placing special emphasis on helping them to meet future as well as current needs and to redesign the associated roles, processes, and structures. If the cobbler's children are not to be without shoes, the same thinking must be brought to bear on the redesign of the systems development process" (p. 30).

Possible Steps for Reengineering the ISD Process

ISD process reengineering is a "critical reformulation" (Hirschheim and Klein, 1994), and it therefore involves two broad steps:

(1) assumption analysis, which identified the basic building blocks of a methodology and reveals the dependence of their validity on the acceptance of underlying philosophical principles; and (2) the proposal of improvements for overcoming the limitations inherent in the assumptions (Hirschheim and Klein, 1994; p. 99).

Following these two steps, I identify six myths, or basic assumptions about ISD processes which have been well-entrenched but need to be questioned if we are to effectively reengineer the ISD process. Based on a review of the literature and evidence from some primary case studies, I offer some suggestions for each of these six myths to reduce their influence and accomplish ISD process reengineering. In making these suggestions, I question the traditionally exclusive focus on a process attribute, and argue for the inclusion of attributes which have received minimal attention so far, and some of which (for example, conflict and redundancy) are actually considered harmful in all circumstances. The six myths and the suggestions for ISD process reengineering are summarized in Table 1, and discussed in detail below.

1. From Exclusive Focus on Rationality to Recognizing the Value of Emotions.   The ISD process is based on logic and reasoning. This seems understandable, especially given the logical and non-emotional nature of the primary tool of IS professionals — the computer.   However, IS professionals sometimes carry their logical stance to such an extent that they completely disregard feelings, emotions, and any behavior which seems unreasonable.

More recently, however, there has been some recognition of the importance of emotions in organizations. According to Duck (1993), if an organization denies certain kind of emotions, managers may isolate themselves from their own emotional lives and may also ignore the ideas, solutions, and new perspectives that other people can provide. Westell and Newman (1993) have also examined the role of one kind of emotion, stress, in two IS development processes. They conclude:

our work suggests that stress is a normal, natural part of system development and that resistance in many circumstances may

From focusing exclusively on	To recognizing the value of	Key references
Rationality	Emotions	Davenport (1994); Duck (1993); Levine and Rossmore (1993); Westell and Newman (1993).
Cooperation	Conflict	Goss et al. (1993); Hirschheim and Newman (1991); Levine and Rossmoore (1993); Markus (1984); Schein (1993); Stokes (1990).
Involvement	Ownership	Hirschheim and Newman (1991); Levine and Rossmoore (1993); Robey and Markus (1984); Westell and Newman (1993).
Closure	Flexibility and creativity	Davenport (1994); Goss et al. (1993); Hammer (1990); Schein (1993); Swanson (1988); Tyre and Orlikowski (1994).
Efficiency	Redundancy	Hirschheim and Klein (1994); Mumford (1981, 1983); Nonaka (1994); Tyre and Orlikowski (1994).
Opportunities	Problems	Janis (1972); Lyytinen (1987); Mason and Mitroff (1981); Schein (1993).

Table 1: Goals of IS Development Process Reengineering

represent an emotionally-based response to the anxieties and uncertainties of the development process, not a calculated act of defiance. Stress is not uniformly a bad thing.... the main conclusion of our paper is that theories of information system development need to be enlarged to accommodate emotional factors. We have concentrated on negative emotions here ... though ... positive feelings, such as elation, can exert an equally potent influence on behavior" (Westell and Newman, 1993; p. 144).

Another excellent example of the role which emotions can play in the ISD process has been described by Duck (1993). The organization was undergoing a large and complex computer conversion which was making huge demands on the IS department. Instead of denying these demands and the enormous stress they were causing, the project director decided to acknowledge how difficult the conversion was. He got some T-shirts made for the team members. On the front of these T-shirts were the words, "Yes, it's hard," and on the back, "But we can do it." In addition, he scheduled weekly meetings with the team and their primary users. These meetings were very emotional and useful:

For the first 15 minutes ... people would go on and on with the usual gripes that come up at a difficult time. As a group, they could acknowledge just how horrible all this really was — but only for 15 minutes. Then for the next 15 minutes, the meeting became a brag session, where people would showcase all the little victories — the things that had worked, ways they had delighted their customers, problems they had turned into successes. The one rule was that everyone had to participate at least once every week in both the griping and the bragging (Duck, 1993; p. 114).

These sessions created tremendous camaraderie among the team members over the ten-month duration of the project. One woman in particular illustrated the importance of emotions in ISD. When the sessions began, she did not want to participate feeling that she did not need "an emotional crutch." However, the supervisor told her that she should still participate. As the sessions progressed, she found that they changed her feelings toward her colleagues and also made her more willing to seek help. The effects of this emotional approach was also evident on the other team members:

The team came to realize that the conversion program hard for everyone. Moreover, from listening to the complaints, they began to give each other ideas about ways to handle tough situations. They told each other of the little victories, they began to feel like they were part of a winning team. When the project was over, they felt even better about themselves and their organization than they had at the beginning (Duck, 1993; p. 114).

2. From Exclusive Focus on Cooperation to Recognizing the Value of Conflict.

Focus on cooperation and agreement is reflected in such popular statements as "let's ensure the cooperation of all the involved parties" and "before we proceed with system development, let's all agree on the information requirements." This emphasis on cooperation causes people to keep their concerns private. Participants hesitate to disagree, and withhold disconfirming evidence (Schein, 1993), as reflected in the following example:

> ... there was a tacit collusion among the management group to refrain from surfacing the disagreements an lack of clarity in order to appear to be a "team player." ... the COO and two of the three EVPs on the Executive Task Force reported directly to the CEO. ... Significant differences among the three were uncovered in our confidential interviews. including whether the global system should be regionalized or centralized and whether Operations or Marketing should control products and profit centers. These disagreements were never publicly surfaced in the appropriate organizational forums" (Levine and Rossmoore, 1993; p. 68).

However, in Japan, conflict is an integral part of management, and is legitimized in the form of waigaya sessions, which can be called by any employee and in which the participants talk openly and without inhibitions (Goss, Pascale, and Athos, 1993). If an organization has a culture where conflict and disagreements are considered acceptable and normal, conflict can be very useful (Markus, 1984).

> When you extend participation to those really accountable for critical resources, or who hold entrenched positions, or who have been burned by past change attempts, you guarantee conflicts. But as the group faces and handles difficult issues, there is a shift in how they relate to contention. Participants learn to disagree without being disagreeable" (Goss et al., 1993; p. 106).

Thus, conflict is not a behavior that must be eradicated, as is sometimes implicitly or explicitly believed by IS professionals.

> ... if team members argue and disagree that does not mean that

they are not a team. Many systems professionals often become upset when disagreements occur, believing that a good team should always be characterized by harmony. However, quite the opposite is true. Arguing is a necessary part of the life cycle of productive teams. Because conflict is inevitable, it must be managed rather than avoided" (Stokes, 1990; pp. 38-39).

In fact, if users and designers are open and willing to learn from each other, conflict between them can be constructive and valuable (Hirschheim and Newman, 1991). One large company followed an interesting approach when developing an information system linking it to its dealers. It deliberately involved dealers who were likely to resist the system in the requirements analysis process so that they could incorporate different perspectives and also find out if they could address these dealers' concerns effectively. Since they were able to do, it helped them win further support from the dealers. If they had not been able to address some of the concerns, they would have made the necessary changes, and that would have been helpful as well.

3. From Exclusive Focus on Involvement to Recognizing the Value of Ownership. IS researchers and practitioners have greatly emphasized the need to involve users in the IS development process. Such user involvement has been supported using rational as well as political arguments (Franz and Robey, 1984). Often, the user involvement is only a ritual (Robey and Markus, 1984), as illustrated by the following comment by a system analyst:

"I had one person, one female, who had been with the company 10 years at that time, and she was the top person. Boy did she resist! Took a long time to win her over ... I kept asking her advice ... I had already figured it out but I wanted her to do it ... You have to work on these people, butter them up ... You are actually sometimes designing it yourself but let them think they did it" (Hirschheim and Newman, 1991; p. 42).

Despite the ritual of user involvement, IS professionals try to exercise control over the ISD process while users play a passive role. However, at the end of the process, users are expected to be responsible for the system. Beath and Orlikowski (forthcoming) have described this contradiction, which they found specifically in the case of Information Engineering methodology, as follows:

"This contradiction leaves both users and analysts in an untenable position: users submissive during the development process are expected to take charge at the end, while analysts in-charge throughout the process are expected to yield to the users at implementation" (p. 25).

In some cases, the issue of ownership even at the end of the ISD process may be a difficult one, especially if the system is very successful so that all the involved parties (including users and IS) want to take credit, or if it is a complete failure, so that no one wants to be blamed for it. The following example illustrates the battle for ownership of successful systems:

> In a large manufacturing company, the engineering group used a manual system to acquire design data. Top management decided to replace it with one using electronic links and micro-computers for data acquisition and display. However, the responsibility and control of the new system were not made adequately clear. When the project proved to be a big success, a power struggle ensued between the engineering and MIS groups. The engineering group felt that it should control the system since it had been acquiring and using the data before automation. On the other hand, the MIS people wanted control on the grounds that the system utilized their tools and expertise (Grover et al., 1988; p. 152).

The likelihood of successful ISD may be much greater if instead of concentrating on user involvement, due recognition is given to their ownership of the system. The users should be made to feel that they own the system and will therefore be responsible for its success or failure. Naturally, this will cause them to participate in ISD, even though there may be some problems due to their tendency to depend on IS professionals. In one of the case studies described by Westell and Newman (1993), involving the development of an on-line cata-logue for a large research library, a group of a systems analyst and 10 librarians was formed to design the system. Despite some problems, the development progressed successfully, with a sense of ownership among the librarians:

> The attachment of the librarians to "their system" was striking ... When all the pieces start coming together and you see it coming alive then of course for everybody they get very emotional about it ... they started to cry. They were very attached to it (Westell and Newman, 1993; p. 139).

A similar focus on "user ownership" was also present during the development of one large system I studied recently. The comments by two key players in the ISD process illustrate this emphasis on user ownership.

> IS Director: "It is their (users') system, why wouldn't we take their inputs into consideration?... Of course, we did ... !"

Director of user department: "I honestly started believing now that it is not my programmers' system anymore — they have done enough of my stuff and it is MY system! And I never thought I would come to that point."

4. From Exclusive Focus on Closure to Recognizing the Value of Flexibility and Creativity. The focus on closure is quite evident in the traditional system development lifecycle (SDLC), which is characterized by "sign-offs" and unidirectional flow (Swanson, 1988). It creates a desire to "complete" the specification of information requirements before proceeding to logical design, "complete" the logical design before moving to physical design, and so on (Sabherwal and Robey, 1993). The following criticism of traditional business processes is applicable to SDLC as well:

> ... our business processes and structures are outmoded and obsolete: our work structures and processes have not kept pace with the changes in technology, demographics, and business objectives. For the most part, we have organized work as a sequence of separate tasks and employed complex mechanisms to track its progress (Hammer, 1990; p. 107).

In the traditional system development processes, in an attempt to finish requirements analysis, the users are commonly asked to identify the information they require from the system when they have little understanding of what the system can do. The following comment by a user is illustrative:

> we didn't have an altogether ... realistic idea about an on-line system and what it could do for us and what it couldn't ... We were asked to make decisions with background we didn't have (Newman and Noble, 1990; p. 100).

Another example is from the development of an information system at a large organization, which used an external vendor (let's call it vendor X) to perform the information requirements analysis. After the vendor developed a set of information requirements, the client organization began to select a vendor for the development of the system. One of the vendors (say vendor Y), which was technologically and otherwise quite capable, was rejected primarily because it wanted to redo the information requirements analysis. This went again the notion of "closure" and another vendor (say vendor Z), which was willing to start from the information requirements prepared by vendor X, was selected. Later, vendor Z had numerous problems because it did not understand the information requirements very well, and consequently it ended up taking slightly more time than the amount of time vendor Y had proposed to take, including the time taken for redoing the requirements analysis.

A similar desire to complete a task and move to another, without revisiting that task at any later time, has been encountered in other cases as well:

> At SCC ... formal procedures explicitly dictated that the CASE tools be defined at the beginning of the project and then held stable. Even after the projects were complete, there were few opportunities to revisit questions about the technology and its mode of use (Tyre and Orlikowski, 1994; p. 113).

However, due to the rapid change in information technology as well as the dynamic nature of organizational and environmental factors, it is essential to adopt a more flexible approach in system development.

> Today we hear that the problem is no longer the management of change but the management of "surprise" (Schein, 1993; p. 85).

> All information doesn't have to be common; an element of flexibility and disorder is desirable" (Davenport, 1994; p. 122).

To some extent, prototyping methodology may enable greater flexibility and creativity in the ISD process, at least as compared to traditional SDLC. However, it is also necessary for IS managers and top managers involved in ISD to be more flexible and creative in their overall attitude, regardless of the specific methodology employed.

In a large decentralized organization, the IS manager of this organization tried to obtain funding for a major IS project. Until then, a top-management steering committee had decided on the funding for all IS projects. This steering committee rejected the project proposal. If the IS manager had taken the rejection of the project proposal as final, as would be commonly done, the project would have been terminated. Instead, the IS manager tried a creative approach to overcome this rejection. He directly approached the heads of some large departments and asked them for funding, describing to them several benefits from the proposed system. He was able to get some parts of the project funded from some of these individuals, and over time received support from some other departments as well. The role of the steering committee at this organization has diminished considerably following the successful development of this system. Thus, the questioning of a previous decision, which seemed irrevocable, by the IS manager led to the reengineering of the

ISD process (project approval as well as other activities involved in this process) at this organization.

5. From Exclusive Focus on Efficiency to Recognizing the Value of Redundancy. Efficiency in the ISD process is indubitably desirable. Often, however, too much emphasis is placed on efficiency, causing a reduction in creativity, as reflected in the following comment by some mangers in a case study by Tyre and Orlikowski (1994):

> We push ourselves too hard. And the problem is that as a result we don't have time to learn how to do something new, or develop new tools (p. 106).

The emphasis on efficiency leads many people to consider redundancy as undesirable, requiring unnecessary duplication. However, introducing redundancy can provide several benefits, as identified by Nonaka (1994). It can help enhance creativity by incorporating seemingly unnecessary perspectives of individuals who lack knowledge of the area and are therefore not constrained by the traditional beliefs in that field of knowledge. It also promotes interaction among organizational members, helps build greater mutual trust between them, and reduces incidents of cheating (due to the greater likelihood of being caught during a redundant activity). It can also reduce the domination of the organization by a few individuals, as information is more widely available in the organization.

Redundancy in the ISD process may be attained through rotation of employees across different groups (including user departments and various components of the IS area). Another, and potentially more effective, way of achieving redundancy in ISD processes involves overlapping, parallel activities to achieve the same task. For example, in an IS planning meeting, if all the key participants (including top managers, users, and IS personnel) participate in the same meeting, it is possible that the comments by one group may inhibit, or otherwise influence, the creativity of the other participants. If, on the other hand, three separate meetings are held in parallel, for the key top managers, for users, and for IS personnel respectively, and the agenda of each meeting is the development of the IS plan, each group would independently come up with some useful ideas.

When these three meetings are followed up by a fourth meeting where the outputs of the three individual meetings serve as a starting point (preferably without identifying the group that produced it), the IS plans are more likely to reflect the true opinions of each group. Of course, such an approach, and any other approach involving redundancy, may be considered wasteful of time and resources, but its benefits, in terms of better plans and fewer implementation problems, are likely to more than make up for the additional resource requirement.

Mumford's (1981, 1983) ETHICS approach for ISD is an excellent example of an approach that explicitly incorporates redundancy in the process. Hirschheim and Klein (1994) characterize this approach as follows:

> The most prominent feature by which ETHICS distinguishes itself from the other methodologies is that it advocates pluralist or dialectical inquiry. It insists on setting out technical and social criteria and solutions separately from each other... ETHICS assigns the role of proposing technical solutions to one part of the design group and social solutions to the other part of the design group, i.e., the users. It is in keeping with the spirit of ETHICS to assign these two lines of enquiry to separate teams that then report back to the design group for the purpose of ranking and synthesizing the relatively best solution (p. 95).

6. From Exclusive Focus on Opportunities to Recognizing the Value of Problems. Considerable attention has traditionally been given in the IS literature to approaches which may be used to identify opportunities for using IT beneficially and even "strategically" (Bergeron, Buteau, and Raymond, 1991; Rackoff, Wiseman, and Ulrich, 1985). However, there has been little advice on the kind of techniques that may be used to identify the potential obstacles even though the ISD process continues to face numerous problems (Lyytinen, 1987). Moreover, the desire to "sell the system may cause a tendency to withhold information about potential problems. The emphasis on agreement and being a "team player" can also lead to a groupthink phenomenon (Janis, 1972), wherein the participants individually, and the group as a whole, underestimate the problems that may be encountered and consequently overestimate the likelihood of success. A "devil's advocate" approach may be invaluable on such occasions (Mason and Mitroff, 1981).

An interesting approach was used to address this problem during the development of a large information system. A senior user executive and the company's CIO were the champions of this system. In meetings with the top management, the senior user executive would reaffirm his belief that the system was essential for successful business operations. The CIO would then provide a realistic evaluation of the progress and point out that several hidden obstacles might lie ahead. Even though the specific problems were not identified in advance, this company did recognize the importance of problems.

Unfortunately, in many companies, although individuals who

identify opportunities are justifiably rewarded, those who identify problems that may potentially arise in ISD processes are penalized. The following comment therefore seems appropriate for ISD processes:

> We need consistent rewards not only for correct responses but also for detecting errors so that they can be corrected. Rewards for error detection are often lacking (Schein, 1993; p. 87)

The tendency to ignore problems may to some extent be because individuals who make important IS decisions are often later responsible for evaluating the success or failure of those decisions. This may be avoided through separation of responsibilities, for example by excluding individuals who initially approve an ISD project from the group that evaluates project progress later, or by keeping individuals who decide on project funding distinct from those who personally participate in system development. Moreover, the hesitation to identify problems can also be reduced by making the penalties for failure less severe so that individuals are not afraid of being fired or getting demoted for supporting an ISD project which eventually failed.

Discussion

Arguing that the traditional ISD processes encounter frequent and numerous problems, are often delayed and over budget, and also sometimes lead to failed systems, this chapter has stressed the need for reengineering the ISD process.   Six common myths about traditional ISD processes have been questioned and a number of suggestions have been provided for reducing their influence and achieving ISD process reengineering.

IS practitioners who are dissatisfied with current ISD processes in their organizations may find these suggestions useful in making radical changes in ISD processes. Possible ways include facilitating the participants' expression of their emotions instead of expecting them to be kept hidden, the introduction of conflicting viewpoints, through an approach such as the "devil's advocate" (Mason and Mitroff, 1981), incorporating redundancy, using an approach such as ETHICS (Mumford, 1981, 1983), intentionally introducing problematic situations, or "organizational breakdowns" (Goss et al., 1993), and rewarding those who help identify potential problems. In addition, two suggestions, promoting ownership rather than only involvement, and emphasizing creativity and flexibility, reiterate similar suggestions made previously by IS researchers but present them more emphatically and place them in the context of ISD process reengineering.

In initiating ISD process reengineering, IS practitioners may find it useful to view reengineering along two dimensions: breadth and depth (Hall et al., 1993). Breadth of ISD process reengineering represents how many, and which of the activities comprising ISD processes—such as planning, project approval, development, implementation, and so on—are being reengineered. Depth of ISD process reengineering represents how many, and which, aspects of the activities)—such as roles and responsibilities, incentives, measures, values, skills, structures, and so on— are being reengineered. In some organizations, ISD process reengineering may be narrow but deep, implying that only one or two of the activities are being reengineered but most or all aspects of them are being transformed. On the other hand, in some organizations ISD process reengineering may be broad, implying that several activities comprising the ISD process are being reengineered, but shallow, implying that only one or two aspects of these activities are being reengineered.

The six steps to achieving ISD process reengineering may support each other. For example, redundancy may enable better recognition of potential problems, and creativity in ISD may be enhanced by a shift from opportunities to problems. Moreover, conflict has been argued to be a major force behind creativity.

> Almost all significant norm-breaking opinions or behavior in social systems are synonymous with conflict.... Conflict jump-starts the creative process" (Goss et al., 1993; p. 106).

The six broad steps suggested here should not be considered cumulatively exhaustive because several additional steps may also contribute to ISD process reengineering. Future research should identify such other steps. Critical case studies of ISD processes that do not follow the traditional patterns should be helpful in doing so. In addition future research should also directly assess the value of the steps identified here. For example, do ISD processes in which there is considerable conflict produce better or worse systems? Moreover, if they sometimes produce better systems, what are those circumstances? And under what circumstances do they produce worse systems? Future research examining these questions should help identify the circumstances in which the reengineered ISD processes may be most needed.

To summarize, this chapter has argued that while ISs can certainly be used to reengineer business processes, it is also important to recognize that ISD processes encounter numerous problems and often produce outcomes that are below desired levels. Therefore, following what we, as members of the IS community, preach to others, we should also seriously consider reengineering the ISD process itself. This chapter has identified six steps which may prove useful in ISD process reengineering. At the very least, it is hoped that this chapter would lead to greater recognition of the need for ISD process reengineering and stimulate further research in this important area.

Endnotes

[1] The order of these six steps in this chapter is based only on clarity considerations, and does not suggest any specific temporal order in performing these steps.

[2] This differs from the approach proposed by Rackoff, Wiseman, and Ulrich (1985), because in their approach the various meetings are held sequentially and not in parallel. Consequently, one group's deliberations would be affected by the conclusions reached by the previous group(s).

References

Beath, C.M. (1991), "Supporting the Information Technology Champion," *MIS Quarterly,* 15(3), 355-372.

Beath, C.M., and W.J. Orlikowski (forthcoming), 'The Contradictory Structure of Systems Development Methodologies Deconstructing the IS-User Relationship in Information Reengineering," *Information Systems Research.*

Bergeron, F., C. Buteau, and L. Raymond (1991), "Identification of Strategic Information Systems Opportunities: Applying and Comparing Two Methodologies," *MIS Quarterly,* 15(1), 89—104.

Davenport, T. (1993), *Process Innovation: Reengineering Work through Information Technology,* Harvard Business School Press.

Davenport, T. (1994), "Saving IT's Soul: Human-Centered Information Management," *Harvard Business Review,* March-April, 119-131.

Davenport, T., and J. Short (1990), 'The New Industrial Engineering: Information Technology and Business Process Redesign," *Sloan Management Review,* Summer, 11-27.

Doll, W.J., and M.U. Ahmed (1983), "Diagnosing and Testing the Credibility Syndrome," *MIS Quarterly,* 7(1), 21-32.

Duck, J.D. (1993), "Managing Change: The Art of Balancing," Harvard Business Review, November-December, 109-118.

Ewusi-Mensah, K., and Z.H. Przasnyski (1991), "On Information Systems Project Abandonment: An Exploratory Study of Organizational Practices," *MIS Quarterly,* 15(1), 67-88.

Franz, C.R., and D. Robey (1984), "An Investigation of User-Led System Design: Rational and Political Perspectives," *Communications of the ACM,* 27, 1202-1209.

Goss, T., R. Pascale, and A. Athos (1993), "The Reinvention Roller Coaster: Risking the Present for a Powerful Future," *Harvard Business*

Review, November-December, 97-108.

Grover, V., A.L. Lederer, and R. Sabherwal (1988),"Recognizing the politics of MIS," *Information and Management,* 145-156.

Hall, G., J. Rosenthal, and J. Wade, (1993), "How to Make Reengineering Really Work," *Harvard Business Review,* November-December, 119-131.

Hammer, M. (1990), "Reengineering Work: Don't Automate, Obliterate," *Harvard Business Review,* July-August, 104-112.

Hirschheim, R., and H.K. Klein (1994), "Realizing Emancipatory Principles in Information Systems Development: The Case for ETHICS," *MIS Quarterly,* 18(1), 83-109.

Hirschheim, R., and M. Newman (1991), "Symbolism and Information Systems Development: Myth, Metaphor, and Magic," *Information Systems Research,* 2(1), 29-62.

Janis, I.L. (1972), *Victims of Groupthink,* Boston, MA: Houghton Mifflin.

Keil, M., and R. Mixon (1994) "Understanding Runaway IT Projects: Preliminary Results from a Program of Research Based on Escalation Theory," *Proceedings of the Twenty-Seventh Annual Hawaii International Conference on System Sciences,* IEEE Computer Society Press.

Lederer, A.L., and A.L. Mendelow (1990) "The Impact of the Environment on the Management of Information Systems," *Information Systems Research,* 1(2), 205-222.

Levine, H.G., and D. Rossmoore (1993), "Diagnosing the Human Threats to Information Technology Implementation: A Missing Factor in Systems Analysis Illustrated in a Case Study," *Journal of MIS,* 10(2), 55-73.

Lyytinen, K. "Different Perspectives on Information Systems: Problems and Solutions," *ACM Computing Surveys,* 19(1), 1987, pp. 5-46.

Markus, M.L., *Systems in Organizations — Bugs and Features,* Pitman Publishing, Inc, Marshfield, MA, 1984.

Mason, R., and I. Mitroff (1981) *Challenging Strategic Planning Assumptions,* John Wiley and Sons, New York.

Mumford, E. (1981) "Participative Systems Design: Structure and Method," *Systems, Objectives, Solutions,* January, 5-19.

Mumford, E. (1983) *Designing Human Systems: The ETHICS Method,* Manchester Business School, Manchester, UK.

Newman, M., and F. Noble (1990), "User Involvement as an Interaction Process: A Case Study," *Information Systems Research,* 1(1), 89-113.

Nonaka, I. (1994), "A Dynamic Theory of Organizational Knowledge Creation," *Organization Science,* 5(1), 14-37.

Orlikowski, W.J. (1993), "CASE Tools as Organizational Change: Investigating Incremental and Radical Changes in Systems Development," *MIS Quarterly,* 17(3), 309-340.

Pastore, R., and C. Hildebrand (1994), "Redefining Moments," *CIO,* May 15, 74-84.

Rackoff, N., C. Wiseman, and W.A. Ulrich (1985), "Information Systems for Competitive Advantage: Implementation of a Planning Process," *MIS Quarterly,* 9, 4, 285-294.

Robey, D., and M.L. Markus (1984), "Rituals in Information System Design," *MIS Quarterly,* 8(1), 5-15.

Rockart, J.F., and J.D. Hofman (1992), "Systems Delivery: Evolving New Strategies," *Sloan Management Review,* Summer, 21-31.

Sabherwal, R., and D. Robey (1993), "An Empirical Taxonomy of

Implementation Processes Based on Sequences of Events in Information System Development," *Organization Science*, 4(4), 548-56.

Schein, E.H. (1993), "How Can Organizations Learn Faster? The Challenge of Entering the Green Room," *Sloan Management Review*, Winter, 85-92.

Stokes, S.L., Jr. (1990), "Building Effective Project Teams," *Journal of Information Systems Management*, Summer, 38-45.

Swanson, E.B. (1988), Information System Implementation: Bridging the Gap between Design and Utilization, Irwin, Homewood, IL.

Teng, J.T.C., V., Grover and K.D. Fiedler (1994), "Re-designing Business Processes Using Information Technology," *Long Range Planning*, 27(1), 95-106.

Tyre, M.J., and W.J. Orlikowski "Windows of Opportunity: Temporal Patterns of Technology Adaptation in Organizations," *Organization Science*, 5(1), 98-118.

Vitale, M.R., B. Ives, and C.M. Beath (1986) "Linking Information Technology and Corporate Strategy: An Organizational View," *Proceedings of the Seventh International Conference on Information Systems*, San Diego, CA, 265-276.

Westell, D., and M. Newman (1993), "The Behavioral Dynamics of Information System Development: A Stress Perspective," *Accounting, Management, and Information Technologies*, 3(2), 121-148.

Chapter 25

Surviving Business Process Redesign:
The Impacts on IS

Robert Zeibig
Nolan, Norton & Co.

Today, companies are buffeted by a sea of change unrivaled in depth and pace. Tidal waves of "insurmountable opportunity" are crashing onto our organizations. Time-to-market is critical. Customer satisfaction is paramount. Quality must be world-class. Smaller is nimbler.

The rules have all changed. New management precepts espouse mass customization, cross-functional integration, employee empowerment, and self-managed work-teams. While it may seem that

Organizations are being driven to improve

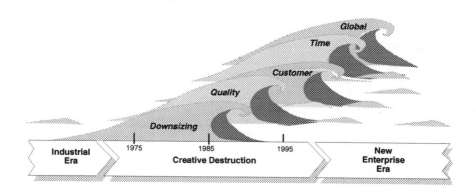

these buzz-phrases spewed out of some paper-shredder jammed into reverse, the fact remains that they represent concepts about how organizations work that are dramatically different than those around which most large organizations have been built. The sea-change occurring in virtually every large organization today reflects a drive, sometimes a mad scramble, to shed those old concepts, and learn a new slate of tricks. It has been broadly labeled "reengineering." With businesses of every shape and size designing, or inventing, new ways of doing work, especially ways that leverage information technology (IT), many Information Systems (IS) organizations today are reeling from the impacts of reengineering.

Three Types of Reengineering

Reengineering is a common, yet often misunderstood term used to describe a wide range of improvement initiatives being conducted within public and private sector organizations. These initiatives have varying objectives, from incremental improvements in functional areas of the business to the wholesale rethinking of the entire entity - its mission, its goals, its reason for being. Such divergent objectives cannot be undertaken with a single, one-size fits all approach. It is useful to view the reengineering spectrum as being comprised of three major types of improvement initiatives, as shown below.

These three types of initiatives can be described briefly:

• Type I - Functional Improvement: reducing costs and/or improving cost-effectiveness through incremental change and streamlining, typically within a business function or department.

Three types of reengineering

Type I	Type II	Type III
Functional Improvement	**Process Innovation**	**Business Innovation**
• Department/functional orientation	• Cross functional participation (including customers)	• Cross-enterprise participation -customers -suppliers -consumers
• Focus on reducing unnecessary tasks and streamlining workflow	• Focus on redesigning workflow, technology, and people components of processes	• Focus on re-defining the business mission and vision
• Incremental improvement in productivity	• Order of magnitude improvement in process performance	• Dramatic change in -products -services -channels -markets

- Type II - Process Innovation: achieving order-of-magnitude im-provements in time, cost, and/or quality in the performance of a business process by redesigning activities, sequences, controls, and resources, typically across organizational (functional) bound-aries.
- Type III - Business Innovation: fundamental competitive and strategic repositioning of the organization through definition and redesign of mission and vision, products/services, distribution channels, markets, customers and consumers, as well as the corresponding redesign of core business processes and structures.

These designations are intended to help in communicating and defining the degree of change and the corresponding level of effort associated with various types of reengineering initiatives. None of the types is inherently superior to any other, despite frequent implications (or exhortations) in today's trade press that radical change is better than incremental. This is part of corporate management's challenge: determining what type or scale of change is needed for the organization's well-being and when to apply it. Many companies today are applying a combination of approaches in order to balance the flow of investments and returns.

The Nature of Reengineering Impacts

The redesign of traditional work structures represents the most obviously visible (and written-about) set of changes. This is not surprising, since reengineering disciplines are built on the founda-tion of process improvements developed for physical processes in manufacturing environments. These techniques have proven appli-cable to other, non-physical processes such as order fulfillment or procurement. Although applicable, it should be noted that experi-ence has shown that human processes are not as tractable as physical processes—it's easier to rearrange and streamline physical components of an assembly line than human beings in a complex, information-intensive process.

The new process structures that are being developed can be characterized in a number of ways:

- *Process flow* is streamlined by reducing capacity bottlenecks, increasing the number of parallel paths that can be executed simultaneously, minimizing redundancies, and imbedding con-trols in the transaction flow. For example, Amica Insurance has significantly reduced the elapsed time to process an automobile glass damage claim by eliminating process steps, restructuring approval requirements, and using technology to directly connect the flow of information among themselves, customers and suppliers such as repair facilities. The resulting work flow expedites customer repairs without the usual "paperwork" hassle, thereby improving customer satisfaction and retention.

- Many new process designs depend for their success on heightened degrees of *teamwork*, indicating the need for stronger communications and interpersonal skills. Although perhaps not quite as obvious, new cultural values may also be defined that reflect the organization's new direction and goals. These changes typically come with increased communications requirements, particularly team-oriented, horizontal communications that cut across the organizational hierarchy[1]. Royal Dutch KLM, a major European airline, adopted a design for the maintenance of Boeing 747 aircraft based on 'self-steering teams'[2]. They found this to be the most effective approach to integrating the multiple disciplines required to maintain a complex aircraft, eliminating the "oversteering" that had developed with layers of management, and improving both productivity and the quality of results to their customers.

- Further, at the individual level, workers in reengineered processes are frequently expected to perform their tasks more autonomously, using more information, and applying greater skill —*knowledge work*. This is an element of the breakdown of the functional hierarchy: deploying controls and decision-making closer to the actual transaction and thereby eliminating management layers. To meet the requirements of empowerment, workers are being expected to bring higher degrees of knowledge and skill to their tasks. In addition to keeping up with the ever-increasing knowledge requirements within their respective specializations—disciplines such as engineering, accounting, or marketing—workers in reengineered processes are typically expected to also contribute a broader, cross-functional understanding of how the organization works as well as knowledge of activities up- and down-stream of the business process in which they work. Quality-driven analytical and problem-solving skills along with "soft" skills such as negotiation and team management are also becoming expected. These changes are evident in Fairfax County's Human Services organization, which is structuring cross-agency and cross-program information into knowledge-based support systems to enable County case workers to better meet the multiple needs of their clients— whether they are for relatively simple needs such as enrollment in a day-care center, or for much more complex needs such as food stamp entitlement according to all appropriate regulation[3].

- Since decisions frequently become more complex as a result of process compression through reengineering, *i* are richer. Decisions that had been made in piece-meal, step-wise fashion, are now expected to be made by a single, "empowered" individual. Decision-making, therefore, demands greater information from a broader

variety of sources in a time-sensitive manner. Optimizing information availability for decision-making is a critical enabler of empowerment and teamwork. In addition, requirements for "meta-
information" or information about the process and its performance
also increase to ensure proper work-flow coordination, to allow
real-time adjustment, and to enable management accountability
for results. Many organizations have implemented improved
processes that adapt in real-time to changing workload requirements based on current performance and demand trends.

Each of these factors is present to some degree in every
successful reengineering effort.

The design challenges that face the business and IT designer
must in some fashion yield an integration of these factors. Collectively, they challenge many of our assumptions about information
technology and the traditional role of the Information Systems
organization.

Reengineering Impacts and Information Technology

Clearly, new applications of information technology are a potential outcome of a redesign. Generic examples of innovative IT

The playing field for the future will be created by harnessing knowledge, teamwork and process

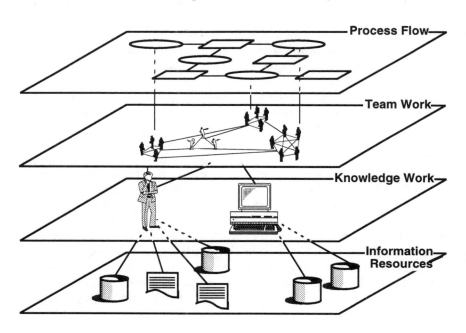

applications along process lines have been identified and described. While not every successful reengineering effort must incorporate information technology, the fact remains that most do because of the technology's potential to change what and how things are done.

If an enterprise can be said to have a shape and structure, that is, a certain arrangement of resources, processes, and relationships with its environment that uniquely describes the organization at a point in time–a *business architecture*–then it is clear that a typical outcome of any significant reengineering initiative is a change in that shape and structure. The well-known case of American Hospital Supply demonstrates an extension of that company's order fulfillment process into the supplies acquisition processes of its customers, almost like an amoebae's pseudopod. This has the effects of redefining the traditional boundaries of the process so that they now extend outside the enterprise proper. It also represents an extension of the process' geographical implementation since customers must be tied in electronically, and a redefinition of the roles and responsibilities of the resources involved in the execution of the process. These now well-known changes reflect not just changes in the competitive strategy adopted by an organization, but also changes to the shape and structure of an enterprise, and indeed, an industry. Which is what the strategic use of information technology is about.

Historically, most institutional IT applications have been built to match the needs of the functional departments they supported. It should be no surprise that the *cross-functional* and *cross-enterprise* business process orientation required by reengineering highlights the inadequacies of these legacy systems. These inadequacies include:

- lack of or inappropriate functionality to support the needs of the process;
- conflicting definitions of information and data elements;
- inability to provide information responsively; and
- incompatibility of the technologies involved.

For example, most organizations have by now experienced the frustration of multiple customer databases, each with name and address information that cannot be kept in synchronization because the databases belong to different departments and are used for different purposes. Reengineering means addressing each and all of these shortcomings to yield net improvement.

As noted above, today's new "knowledge workers" must be able to work with a higher degree of autonomy, which may or may not be accompanied by a higher degree of ambiguity. They must also be able to communicate efficiently and effectively with co-workers. Communication here means not just transferring data, but rather sharing information and, more subtly, building shared knowledge. As individuals become increasingly empowered to take responsibility for customer satisfaction and other enterprise goals, they must evaluate and make decisions on more complex issues. The opportunities for IT to support information needs, knowledge, communication, and learning also become more varied and potentially yield more complex configurations. Knowledge-based systems, peer-to-peer networking, groupware, just-in-time training, and other capabilities designed to support individuals and teams are representatives of potential IT demands from a reengineering effort. To deploy many of these capabilities, new "retail" technologies are frequently called for, whose specifications and justification ultimately lie in the hands of the consumer. As the proliferation of choices continues, the challenge for integration grows apace.

Finally, the broader definitions associated with *information* as opposed to *data*, as typically used in reengineering initiatives, reflect both the emerging capabilities of information technology, and a set of disciplines and resources within the organization that may not have historically been associated with IS. Services such as on-line document management, abstracting of external information sources, video broadcasting of management meetings and public announcements, and secured network access from remote mobile locations, are all examples of capabilities that are beginning to be considered part of an organization's infrastructure. Although these services will in the future likely be built around IT components, they have historically been offered through organizational units other than IS, such as the corporate library, the records management division, the facilities engineering group, or the marketing department.

The Role for Information Systems Organizations

Since many reengineering initiatives today are launched by executive management, one of the first impacts frequently felt by IS organizations is a request to assist in the reengineering activity. The most common role is that of technology specialist, helping the business community determine what technologies are now or will soon become available, what competitors are doing with technology, and what infrastructure implications might arise. IS may also be asked to lead or facilitate the reengineering effort itself. Since many IS organizations readily perceive improvement opportunities within the business—in part because IS' enterprise-wide mission enables a cross-functional viewpoint—IS has frequently undertaken an advocacy role. Sponsorship must come from those charged with achieving the improvements desired; however, IS may provide a leadership role in organizing the effort, supplying skills and experience in process analysis, group problem-solving, change management, and the use of automated tools. In any event, IS' knowledge of the current IT environment—data structures, system capabilities and capacities, application functionality and interface characteristics—is vital to gaining full leverage from existing and potential uses of IT in the future design.

When preparing for reengineering, most organizations face a series of questions about how to best resource the effort. Some establish internal process reengineering teams to lead or facilitate reengineering projects. Others choose to hire outside consultants to do the reengineering and implementation. Frequently, there is some combination of the two, utilizing outside resources initially to provide a leverage base of in-depth experience for reengineering teams to draw on. For many, at issue is the degree to which the organization perceives itself as making a long-term commitment to reengineering. Broader and longer-term commitments to reengineering will support the investment required to build and sustain skilled internal resources. On the other hand, some organizations lack confidence in their own abilities, particularly given the visibility of reengineering "failures" at ostensibly capable organizations.

In addition to resourcing, there is a frequently a question about ownership of the implementation once a design has been developed. There are two models that seem to be predominant today. The first model calls for the people who created the new design to live with it through to successful implementation. This model frequently makes use of outside consulting services in the design stage. The second model emphasizes the development of a core competency represented by individuals with specialized reengineering skills and experience. As a group, these individuals may be positioned as a separate staff function outside IS, while others are within IS. The group is typically composed primarily of senior analysts. These individuals usually conduct the initial design portion of the work and turn it over to other staff functions, such as IS and Human Resources, for implementation. They may proceed from one area of the business to another, or they may support multiple user design teams simultaneously.

Of the three types of reengineering, Type I Functional Improvements are essentially analogous to the "systems projects" that comprise the backlog of work in many Information Systems organizations. Most application development methodologies in use today emphasize the need to understand the business process that the IT capabilities to be built must support. The major difference is that the driver of change is the need for improvement in the performance of the process, which may or may not indicate the need for new IT capabilities. This suggests that Type I reengineering should serve as the driver for IT maintenance activities other than those for repair, especially since IT maintenance consumes over half of the IS resources in many organizations today.

Reengineering Types II and III represent the greatest potential degree of impact from IT capabilities, and at the same time, the greatest potential challenge to most businesses and their IS organizations. These types of reengineering initiatives frequently represent five major impacts on today's IS organization. Specifically, they:

- generate demands for a broad-based complex of integrated *IT capabilities*;
- tax existing *IT infrastructure* services and capacities;
- strain even the most productive *IT delivery process*;
- require new skills and experience-levels among *IS resources*; and
- raise new questions of priority and resource allocation for the *IT management process*.

Reengineering Impacts on IT Capabilities

Efforts were undertaken by IS organizations in many companies during the mid-1980s to develop "information architectures" that would eliminate or minimize problems of information integrity and availability by describing all the significant data elements in an organization and correlating them with the business functions of that organization. Once completed, the resulting information architecture could then be used as a blueprint for developing IT capabilities more efficiently and effectively. Unfortunately, most of those efforts suffered from a goal-orientation that exclusively emphasized the development of IT systems, thereby generating massive amounts of documentation to enable coding applications, but generally ignoring the other challenges imbedded in changing how the business worked through automation. In addition, those early efforts and many current application development methodologies demonstrate a lack of understanding that the future state (shape and structure) of the organization will likely be quite different from the current one.

Disassembling the business architecture into its elemental building blocks—Type III reengineering of products, customers, markets, processes, resources, and controls—and reassembling it based on a vision for the future is both a management challenge and a creative one. Type II reengineering, focusing on processes, resources and controls, is the same, on a lesser scale. The results of either may add or eliminate entire segments of business functionality, or shift them from one organizational unit or geographical location to another. For example, an insurance company found that providing the customer with a final deal price for a product, on-the-spot and at the customer's location, was a competitive imperative. The luxury of lengthy back-office review and approval cycles at the home office could no longer be tolerated. The functionality had to be moved out into the field, with decisions made at the hands of the salesperson, and the entire transaction had to be handled on an "event" basis rather than being batched for later processing.

This relatively common example can be partially viewed as a set of changes at the transaction level. This might mean, for example, new processing logic operating on a lap-top personal computer that transmits data periodically to home office for "final" disposition. However, the redesign of these non-physical processes, frequently labeled "white collar," "knowledge-worker," or "administrative" processes, typically involves defining new roles and responsibilities for workers in the process. In many cases, this means new skills, different types or levels of experience, and correspondingly different career path opportunities. Further, particularly across multiple departments, fewer workers may be needed in the new process design.

There are three major challenges:

1. Articulating the future shape and structure of the business based on a desired future state (vision);
2. Identifying what future role might be played by any of the multitude of information technologies currently available or envisioned to be available within the planning window; and
3. Crafting an appropriate set of interim states or evolutionary platforms by translating the difference between the future state and the realities of today into a cohesive program of actions that match and enable the evolution of the business.

Note that these are not linear, but rather iterative. For example, a vision of the future of the business might be altered based on emerging IT capabilities, or on recognition of certain realities of today's world that must be overcome. This means that a fourth challenge is implementing monitoring and adjustment mechanisms to guide the evolution.

Reengineering Impacts on IT Infrastructure

As the set of shared IT services that support the organization— enterprise networks, central processing facilities, and increasingly, shared databases are examples— the IT infrastructure often must bear considerable impact as the result of a reengineering initiative.

Capacity implications are perhaps the most obvious. As an example, few data networks today are designed to carry the tremendous volumes of data associated with static or moving images, which may be required by multi-media applications imbedded in a new process design. Even today's large central processing sites may not be equipped to provide all of the repository services required in a data warehouse environment. A large, multi-modal transportation company found that the impacts of a new process design would more than double its already significant capacity projections for data center and network requirements — within 12 months.

Perhaps more dangerous than projections of average capacity requirements, capacity "spikes," or temporary demand surges, may occur that were not anticipated in the initial design. Further, the increased business urgency and criticality resulting from reengineering frequently demands adherence to higher performance standards for availability, reliability and throughput from the IT infrastructure. This will be especially true if external participants, such as customers or vendors, are integrated into elements of the new design, as was the case at American Hospital Supply.

Beyond these capacity issues, the services provided to the organization by the basic functionality of the infrastructure — telecommunications, data storage and retrieval, transaction processing, etc. — may also undergo a redefinition. Some of these redefinitions are relatively natural expansions of services already provided. An example would be the provision of an integrated data communications network instead of several autonomous networks. Although there may be some organizational tension over who owns and manages the resulting network, for the most part, data communications services fall within the province of the IS organization(s) and can ultimately be resolved on the basis of the commonalty of disciplines. Although this frequently raises the issues of compliance with technical standards and compatibility of infrastructure components, the business pressures associated with reengineering typically mean that technical standards are forced to yield in order to achieve business results. The contentions of technology purists notwithstanding, these issues readily fall to logic and pragmatism. The role of IS here is not to keep the faith vis a vis a particular technology standard or vendor offering, but rather to ensure that the trade-offs made to achieve business ends are fully informed.

Reengineering initiatives reshape not only core business processes, but they also reach into the infrastructure underpinnings and resource management processes of most organizations as well. The definition of information as "data plus context" is likely to drive a second, ripple-effect wave of reengineering of resource management processes such as "information management". This may be especially true in organizations where IS has mostly been concerned with the data and/or the technology. A few organizations, in efforts to embrace this new, broader definition of information management, have begun integrating missions and operations of previously disparate groups. A leading pharmaceutical company, for example, seeking to shorten the cycle time of its products from research and development through FDA approval and into production, has integrated the corporate library and the records management functions within the IS organization. The efforts are intended to focus internal and external information resources so that they may be brought to bear as efficiently and effectively as possible on critical aspects of the product development process. This has resulted in redefinitions of specific services and sub-processes such as external literature searching and research, collection development, and internal document management.

Reengineering Impacts on the IT Delivery Process

Along with the demands for new applications from a corporate reengineering initiative come heightened expectations by the business community. Given the pronounced benefits-orientation of reengineering, delivery of new IT functionality is demanded in terms of days and weeks, not months and years. In the days when IT was merely a support resource, balancing the corporate accounts or posting the day's transactions for the next day's processing, it was not untenable to think otherwise. But in today's environment, where the processing *is* the transaction or the transaction doesn't occur, the corporate top line and bottom line are both on the line. Time is, in fact, pretty close to the same thing as money. Businesses can no longer afford to wait four years for the "new system" to come on-line. Like virtually every other business process, IT delivery must also be geared for speed (and, of course, quality and productivity).

Typically, this means that the IT delivery process itself must change from the traditional, methodical life-cycle composed of back-room work to a much more fluid, interactive, build-as-you-go process that leans heavily on newer development technologies, user ownership and teamwork.

Leading IS organizations have more than doubled their "throughput" capabilities while at the same time significantly increasing business unit and top management "customer satisfaction" by applying reengineering principles to their own operations. A frequently successful tactic is to apply the 80/20 rule, seeking to re-scope the commitment so that 80 percent of the original benefits can be achieved with significantly less resources. Of course, the benefits orientation also means that there is potentially much higher visibil-

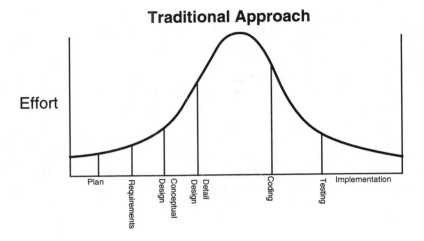

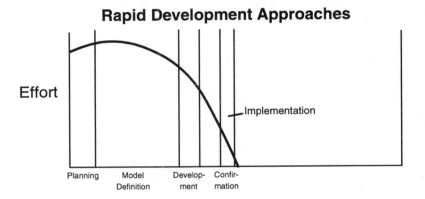

ity to these development efforts. Success is defined not in terms of application code tested and delivered, but rather in terms of measures such as "average time from customer order to shipment received" or "percent of increase in customer satisfaction with service responsiveness." Here lie the seeds of further culture change as IS disciplines and professionals become more intimately entwined with the organization's business practices and goals.

Reengineering Impacts on IS Resources

The prospect of all-new, state-of-the-art technologies developed in a joint user-centered process may seem attractive, but may also be thoroughly daunting. This is especially true if the organization's past history has defined punishable failure as anything less than intergalactic success. These same considerations are also true of the rest of the IS value chain. Systems deployment and integration, maintenance and enhancement activities, and production operations all face potentially similar circumstances as the tidal wave of new requirements and expectations begins to break.

In many cases, the new technologies identified through reengineering and the new IT development processes both require technical, managerial and organizational skills that are in short supply. Few IS organizations have the capacity to keep abreast of all the technical and technological developments taking place in today's environment. Beyond the technology skills, orchestrating the potentially numerous projects that must all be related if success is to be achieved requires broader managerial skills, including program management, scenario planning and change management. Interpersonal skills such as group facilitation, negotiation, and confrontation management are also frequently required. Few of these skills were included in the typical job descriptions of the IS professional over the last decade. Further, many organizations have become so deeply mired in simply maintaining and enhancing antiquated legacy systems that even traditional managerial and organizational skills have atrophied as well.

This shortage of sufficient skills and experience levels represents a significant challenge for many IS organizations faced with the impacts of reengineering. The lack of qualified resources to accommodate these impacts frequently generates discussion of alternative sourcing approaches at senior management levels. "Outsourcing" is a popular term applied to what is actually a variety of different approaches to meeting these business imperatives. Outsourcing approaches may include emphasizing the use of third-party software packages for new applications, turning over data center operations to a vendor organization, shifting applications development to contractors, or establishing a long-term strategic relationship with a particular vendor or group of vendors to jointly build the envisaged future design.

In any event, these discussions invariably cause turbulence within the IS organization as individuals begin to wonder about their future. IS can best be prepared by understanding, in depth, its own capabilities and capacities, and by recognizing that virtually no organization can do everything itself. This is not an admission of failure, but rather an expression of priority. As company after company refocuses on its core competencies, so too must IS reexamine and reaffirm what it must do well in order to maximize the value it contributes to the health and success of the organization.

It is also a reflection of today's realities that the discipline of IT— of coaxing value from silicon and electricity, of structuring the logic of complex tasks, and of harnessing information resources for shared organizational benefit—is virtually as much a part of the "user" community as it is a part of IS. Linked departmental spreadsheets, compound documents with mail/merge lists, shared calendars and contacts databases are all examples of the lexicon of today's "user" of information technology. Formal and informal "departmental IS" groups serve to demarcate the shifting boundaries, but they also highlight new concerns. For example, a research chemist at a multinational chemicals organization has been supporting the departmental IT initiatives of the research and development group—where he had previously been assigned—for the past year and a half. Recently, he has begun wondering whether he is now on the "computer" career path or the "chemistry" career path. He estimates that in another six months or a year it will be a moot question, since he will have become so distanced from the discipline in which he was trained academically as to make it virtually impossible for him to return.

This phenomenon represents both a challenge and a resource to organizations that are embarking on reengineering, but one that needs to be dealt with consciously if it is to turn out as a "win-win" in the long run.

Reengineering Impacts on the IT Management Process

Reengineering impacts typically require resources - people, time, capital - to be invested for both near-term gain and the longer-term future of the organization. And there's a sense of urgency and commitment that must be sustained to enable the cultural and organizational changes to occur. Thus, reengineering implementation initiatives typically receive very high priority from line and executive management. Benefits, both near-term and long-term, are the drivers of this urgency and priority.

Today, benefits are defined in more complex terms than the traditional return-on-investment (ROI) financial analysis[4]. Process performance, customer satisfaction and organizational learning all count as benefit measures in addition to direct bottom-line contribution. The importance of clear benefits criteria lies in the need to establish relative priorities. Only with consistent, objective goals and metrics can management evaluate the tradeoffs of costs, risks and benefits associated with the opportunities that arise from reengineering. Management's emphasis on a benefits-based approach is imperative because the projects required to implement a new design are also likely to be cross-functional and multi-disciplinary. Clearly articulated benefits serve in part as a motivational force—a "carrot" leading the organization forward. They also serve as the yardstick by which progress (or the lack thereof) can be measured and accountabilities matched with rewards.

In the heat of the moment, with a spanking new business or process design and projections of untold benefits begging to be harvested, it is possible to overlook the fact that most of the organization's resources are likely to already be committed to some purpose. With the average IS backlog running from one to two years, the potentially massive developmental and infrastructure requirements from a reengineering effort force the question of priorities and resource allocations. Of course, reengineering benefits are brighter and shinier than the ones reflected in the backlog, but the fact remains that the backlog represents commitments that have been made.

Some organizations have used the existing commitments as reasonable justification for contracting outside resources to build and implement the new future design. Unfortunately, without sufficient involvement, internal resources may be left poorly positioned to support the organization going forward. Other organizations have reasoned that the new order has higher priority simply because it is the new order, without which the organization may fail. Indeed, some of the opportunities identified through the design activities may already be on the organization's approved "priority" list for development. Many reengineering efforts in fact start as automation projects since users may easily see opportunities for process improvement through automation. Frequently, however, the approved projects reflect more narrow, functional requirements than the broader scope implied by reengineering. Certainly, the possibility exists that some outstanding commitments may need to be modified and that segments of the business community will perhaps once again be disappointed with delayed delivery of IT capabilities.

Clear benefits definitions, a well-oiled management process and open channels of communication throughout the organization are required for the delicate balancing act of priority alignment and resource allocation. The IT management process must operate with a high degree of consistency, regularity and participation in order to ensure appropriate dynamic balancing of business priorities and resource allocation, as well as to ensure that performance improvements are continuously occurring. Several leading IS organizations have begun applying the concepts of the "balanced scorecard" to managing information technology in alignment with the organization's overall scorecard. One leading financial services organization is using the company's critical success factors and performance measures in an evaluation process for new IT opportunities that integrates other evaluation criteria such as implementation risk and life cycle cash flows.

Benefits-oriented approaches, while appealingly simple in nature, can be very powerful mechanisms, and frequently serve to highlight the need for cross-functional perspective. Particularly with regard to the IS organization, which is constantly seeking and under pressure to define productivity measures, a benefits-orientation raises the level of dialogue beyond the coding sheet. This is advantageous to the organization overall, but, like any other reengineering effort, may face resistance from entrenched factions. A clear understanding of the IT (not IS) process is required to understand process performance and contributions to core business process performance.

The Role for IS: "Leading from Behind"

Reengineering initiatives raise new questions of priority and resource allocation, strain even the most productive IT delivery processes, tax existing IT infrastructure capabilities, and challenge traditional IS roles and responsibilities. To survive, let alone prosper, in this complex and dynamic environment, IS organizations must develop specific strategies for managing the significant impacts that reengineering initiatives can generate:

- **IT capabilities** deployed to support a new business and/or process design should reflect a "plug and play" modularity within the context of a target enterprise-wide framework or architecture. This means operating with a design principle for IT capabilities that ensures the ability to quickly and easily add new capabilities. It also means establishing clear reference points in the IT architecture by identifying application functionality, data and information structures, and interfaces based on the business architecture as envisaged for the future of the organization. Finally, the migration path should identify a series of "checkpoint" states or platforms that represent interim targets where progress can be reevaluated and end-goals confirmed.
- The **IT infrastructure** should be designed and valued based on its service contributions to IT capabilities and business objectives. Service definitions, service levels and expectations, capacities and constraints must be clearly delineated, as well as appropriate explicit and de facto standards, sourcing arrangements, and monitoring processes.
- The **IT delivery process** should be geared for rapid development and deployment of IT capabilities. Technological advances such as pseudotyping, rapid prototyping, object orientation and client/ server approaches should be added to the IS toolkit, while strategies that enable the user community to "do for itself" should be enacted. A cold-hearted pragmatism should be applied to "make

versus buy" decisions and vendor relationships should be strengthened as valuable resources. In addition, the 80/20 rule should not be forgotten.

- **IS resources** should be marshaled to reflect significant breadth and depth in interpersonal, managerial and business skills as well as advanced technical skills. Sourcing strategies should be viewed as opportunities to provide leverage for the organization in accomplishing what needs to be done. Capabilities within the user community should not be underestimated.
- The **IT management process** must in fact be an element of the organization's business management process. A broad, but clear definition of benefits and an orientation towards their achievement are the most powerful lever for clarifying the priority and resource allocation issues that inevitably arise.

For the most part, these strategies fall, to one degree or another, within the auspices of the IS organization itself. The examples cited above, however, indicate that current best practice is built on a shared level of understanding and commitment among senior management, the business community, and IS. Ensuring that this is in place is therefore a first step. Aside from this prerequisite, there is no implied precedence in the strategies suggested. Leading organizations appear to be moving on all fronts, although with priorities and pace specific to their needs.

Whether the business is just beginning to think about reengineering or is already actively engaged, IS organizations have a critical role to play. IS has much to offer reengineering efforts: awareness of advanced technologies, knowledge of what is already in place, skills and experience in analytic techniques, and a charter that encompasses the entire organization. "Leading from behind" means that although reengineering must be driven by the business community to achieve business imperatives, IS' experience and role in the organization indicate an advocacy position should be adopted. This means dialog with senior management and business leadership, translating the messages of reengineering into what it means for them and for the organization. It means circulating articles, attending conferences, talking to other companies about what they're doing, how they're doing it, and what they're achieving. It means building consensus and commitment, ensuring that all constituencies are represented and viewpoints heard. And, it means contributing substantively to accomplishing the organization's goals, not just developing applications or operating a network.

While the preparation for reengineering is not prohibitively difficult, it does require commitment, leadership and flexibility. Without this kind of preparation, IS organizations will find themselves scrambling frantically to accommodate reengineering impacts. Thus, instead of being viewed as opportunities to significantly improve business performance, these challenges will be viewed as threats to IS' well-being.

The IS organization has a critical role to play in the redesign effort to ensure successful reengineering. However, it is IS' responsibility to shape and adapt this role, which can offer significant benefits and opportunities for future growth and success.

Endnotes

[1] R. L. Nolan, A. J. Pollock, and J. P. Ware, "Toward the Design of Network Organizations", Stage by Stage, Nolan, Norton & Co., Volume 9, Number 1, pp. 1-12

[2] D. Meyer, "Integrating Business and IT Planning", 1992 Nolan, Norton & Co. Symposium

[3] R. Terdiman, "BPR Case Study: Fairfax County, Virginia", IS Research Note, GartnerGroup, July 28, 1992

[4] Robert S. Kaplan and David P. Norton, "The Balanced Scorecard - Measures That Drive Performance, *Harvard Business Review*, January-February 1992, pp. 71-79

Author Biographies

BOOK EDITORS

Varun Grover is an Associate Professor of Information Systems in the Management Science Department at the University of South Carolina. He holds a B.Tech. in Electrical Engineering from the Indian Institute of Technology, New Delhi, an MBA from SIUC, and a Ph.D. degree in MIS from the University of Pittsburgh. Dr. Grover has published extensively in the information systems field, with over 50 publications in refereed journals.   His current areas of interest are business reengineering, strategic information systems, telecommunications and inter-organizational systems, and organizational impacts of information technologies. His work has appeared in journals such as MIS Quarterly, JMIS, Communications of the ACM, Decision Sciences, IEEE Transactions, California Management Review, Information and Management, Database, Omega, Interfaces, Long Range Planning, Information Systems Management, Journal of Systems Management and numerous others. He is currently co-editing a Special Issue of JMIS on Business Process Reengineering. Dr. Grover is the recipient of the Outstanding Achievement Award from the Decision Sciences Institute. He is currently on the Editorial Review Board of the Journal of Information Technology Management, the Journal of Management Systems and the Journal of Market Focused Management and is an active referee for 12 other journals. He has also consulted with numerous organizations and is a member of TIMS, DSI and AIS.

William J. Kettinger is Director of the Center of Information Management and Technology Research at the University of South Carolina. Dr. Kettinger is also an Assistant Professor of MIS within the College of Business Administration where he teaches in the Masters of International Business Studies (MIBS) program.   Dr. Kettinger has served as the college's Director of Information Systems and Assistant Dean.   He has over 15 years of international consulting experience with such companies as IBM, NCR, AT&T, Phillips and numerous university and governmental organizations. He has been the principal investigator on several million dollars worth of research grants and contracts. Recently, Kettinger has been involved in a long term project with AT&T GIS to investigate the process management marketplace and to outline a BPR software product and services strategy. His current research focuses on business process management, IS quality, strategic intelligence, marketing and customer-based IT, and electronic commerce. He is currently busy co-editing a Special Issue of the Journal of Management Information Systems on Business Process Reengineering. He has published extensively in such academic journals as MIS Quarterly, Decision Sciences, JMIS, Public Administrative Review, JSIS, DataBase, and Information & Management and in such practitioner journals as Journal of Information Systems Management and Journal of Systems Management. He received his Ph.D. and an M.S. in Information Systems from the University of South Carolina and an M.P.A. from the University of Massachusetts at Amherst. He is a member of the Society for Information Management (SIM), TIMS and DSI.

CHAPTER AUTHORS

Daniel S. Appleton, chairman and founder of D. Appleton Company, Inc., is an executive consultant, author, and internationally recognized lecturer on organizational strategy. Prior to establishing D. Appleton Company in 1979, Mr. Appleton was director of Strategic Business Planning for Borg-Warner, director of Management Systems for the six world-wide divisions of Byron Jackson, manager of Business Systems Development for Litton Ship Systems, a case officer in the CIA, and an operations research analyst in the Office of the Secretary of Defense. He received an M.B.A. from American University and a B.A. from the University of California at Berkeley. Mr. Appleton has authored two books, PROBE: Principles of Business Engineering, and Corporate Information Management Process Improvement Methodology for DoD Functional Managers and published over 40 articles on high-involvement change, business automation, and information asset management. Mr. Appleton has been key in the creation and operation of numerous high-tech programs such as: ICAM, CALS, CIM, and PDES, Inc., which focus on the modernization of complex organizations, In addition, Mr. Appleton consults to numerous Fortune 500 firms, including Digital Equipment, EDS, GTE, and American Airlines. He received a commendation from the Office of the Secretary of Defense for his work on CALS and CIM, and a Visioneering Award from the Society of Manufacturing Engineers.

Perakath C. Benjamin received a Bachelor's degree in Mechanical Engineering from the Birla Institute of Technology and Science (India) in 1981, graduating with honors. Dr. Benjamin worked as a management executive at the Indian subsidiary of Robert Bosch Gmbh, Germany, supervising production planning and control functions from 1983 to 1987. He joined Texas A&M University in the fall of 1987 as a Ph.D. student in Industrial Engineering. While at Texas A&M, Dr. Benjamin was involved with several research and development projects at the Knowledge Based Systems Laboratory. His work there included developing intelligent environments for simulation modeling, developing knowledge representation benchmarks, and applying Artificial Intelligence to the design and analysis of manufacturing systems. After receiving his Ph.D in May 1991, Dr. Benjamin joined the Texas A&M faculty as a Visiting Assistant Professor. Dr. Benjamin is Vice President of Innovation and Engineering, at Knowledge Based Systems, Inc. He was the project manager on a National Science Foundation research project which resulted in the development of the commercial simulation model design tool, PRoSim™. Dr. Benjamin is responsible for managing and directing research and development projects in the areas of systems simulation, cost analysis methods, manufacturing systems design and analysis, qualitative reasoning methods, manufacturing systems analysis and design, and knowledge acquisition techniques.

Pieter W.G. Bots is associate professor at the School of Systems Engineering, Policy Analysis and Management of Delft University of Technology, the Netherlands. He has a Master's degree in Computer Science from the University of Leiden and a Ph.D. in Information Systems from Delft University of Technology. His main research interest lies in the analysis and design of processes and supporting information systems in both public and private organizations. He has published in Decision Support Systems, The Journal of MIS and in numerous proceedings of international conferences on information systems, in particular decision support systems and office systems.

Bruce E. Caraway received his Bachelor of Science and Master of Science degrees in Industrial Engineering from Texas A&M University in 1990 and 1994, respectively. While working on his degrees, he worked for the Department of Engineering on the INFAC project conducted at Bell Helicopter Textron, Inc. He performed a system analysis of Bell's precision gear manufacturing facility using the IDEF activity and information modeling methods, identified problems, and proposed possible solutions. Mr. Caraway joined Knowledge Based Systems, Inc. in January of 1993 as a Systems Analyst. Mr. Caraway is currently working on a project at Tinker Air Force Base which seeks to baseline and identify process improvements on the E-3 AWACS Programmed Depot Maintenance (PDM) line using IDEF methodologies. He is also working on the development of a simulation and shop floor control system for the E-3 PDM line.

Paul Cule is currently a doctoral student in the CIS Department in the College of Business Administration at Georgia State University. Prior to joining the program at Georgia State he spent 33 years in industry, 18 of them in management, in Britain, Canada and the United States. His experience spans manufacturing, marketing, software development and planning and strategy development. As part of his strategy development role he did extensive research on the future of the information technology industry. His current research interests are in future modes of software development and the sociological impacts of information systems in organizations. He has an MBA from Emory University.

Tom Davenport is the Curtis Mathes Fellowship Professor and Director of the Information Systems Management Program at the University of Texas, Austin. He is also a Research Fellow at Ernst & Young's Center for Business Innovation, where he was previously a partner and Director of Research; he also directed research at CSC Index and McKinsey & Company. Davenport wrote the first article on reengineering and the first book—*Process Innovation: Reengineering Work through Information Technology* (Harvard Business School Press, 1993). His articles have appeared in the *Harvard Business Review, Sloan Management Review*, and many other publications. He has a Ph.D. from Harvard in organizational behavior and has taught at the Harvard Business School, the University of Chicago, and Boston University. He is also a frequent speaker to senior executives in firms and at conferences on information and process management topics.

Jesus A. Ponce de Leon is an Assistant Professor of Strategy and Technology Management in the Department of Management of Southern Illinois University. He is a graduate of Indiana University at Bloomington and teaches strategy and technology. His research interests are international strategic management, reengineering, total quality management, and high tech industries. Dr. Ponce de Leon is active in consulting projects with American and Mexican firms.

Eric L. Denna is the Warnick/Deloitte & Touche Faculty Fellow at Brigham Young University's (BYU) Marriott School of Management. He the author of several books and articles on alternative IT application architectures, data modeling, artificial intelligence, and business process modeling. His book Event-Driven Business Solutions introduces an alternative IT application architecture to support BPR efforts.

Kirk Dean Fiedler is an Assistant Professor of MIS at the University of South Carolina, School of Business Administration. He received a B.A. from Wittenberg University, a M.B.A. and a M.S. in Information Systems and Systems Science from the University of Louisville before completing his Ph.D. in MIS at the University of Pittsburgh. His work experience includes several years at Arthur Young & Company and he has earned a C.P.A. certificaiton. Currently, his research interests involve the investigaiton of technology assimilation and business process redesign and he has published this research in various journals including MIS Quarterly, California Management Review, Long Range Planning and Omega; the International Journal of Management Science. He is a member of the Academy of Management, American Institute of Certified Public Accountants, Decision Sciences Institute, and Institute of Management Sciences.

Bob Galliers is Chairman of Warwick Business School in the University of Warwick, England. He is Lucas Professor of Business Systems Engineering, and prior to taking up the Chairmanship of the Business School, he headed its Doctoral Programme in Information Systems and its Information Systems Research Unit. Previously, he was

Foundation Professor and Head of the School of Information Systems at Curtin University, Perth Western Australia and a Consultant for Lancaster University's Management Systems consultancy company - ISCOL Ltd. He has consulted and published widely on aspects of Information Systems Strategy, Business Innovation and Change. Included in his publications are four books and numerous articles in such journals as Communications of the ACM, European Journal of Information Systems, Information Systems Journal, International Journal of Information Management and Journal of Information Technology. He is editor-in-chief of the Journal of Strategic Information Systems. His most recent book, co-authored by Bernadette Baker, is entitled Strategic Information Management: Challenges and Strategies in Managing Information Systems, published by Butterworth Heinemann in 1994, and he is currently working on a further text entitled Building Bridges: Strategies for Information Systems, Business Innovation and Change, to be published in 1995.

Subashish Guha is a Senior Product Manager at the Integrated Client Server Systems division of AT&T GIS Corp. He is also a Ph.D. candidate in MIS from the College of Business Administration at the University of South Carolina. His current research interests are in the areas of Business Process Innovation, TQM and QFD, Product Planning and Strategic Marketing. He has authored articles in such journals as MIS Quarterly and Journal of Information Systems Management and several international proceedings.

Thomas Gulledge is Professor of Public Policy and Operations Research at George Mason University and Director of the Policy Analysis Center within the Institute of Public Policy. He lectures in the areas of Engineering Management, Economic Systems, and Systems Engineering Economics. He is a member of Corporate Information Management (CIM) group that is currently funded by the Defense Information Systems Agency (DISA) and the Office of the Deputy Assistant Secretary of Defense (Information Management). He is also the principal investigator for the U.S. Advanced Research Projects Agency Funded Continuous Acquisition and Life-Cycle Support Shared Resource Center and co-principal investigator for the DISA sponsored Defense Enterprise Integration Services Contract. Professor Gulledge's research has been supported in the past by several agencies, including the Office of Naval Research and the Air Force Office of Scientific Research. He maintains research links with several federally funded research and development centers, including the Institute for Defense Analyses and the MITRE Corporation.

David H. Hill, who joined General Motors in 1944 at the AC-Sphinx Sparking Plug Company in England as a tool and die making apprentice, has had a variety of assignments with GM. Most recently, he was Executive in Charge, Corporate Informaiton Management, responsible for the application of information technology worldwide. Previously, Hill was president of Motors Trading Corporation. He recently served as chairman of the advisory committee on information management to the Department of Defense, for which he was awarded the Distinguished Public Service Medal.

Tom Housel is an internationally recognized scholar in the areas of business process reengineering and the strategic applications of information and telecommunications technology. He has published widely in this area as well as in international accounting journals. He joined Telecom Italia as the Research Director for the Centro Studi San Salvador for a two year period ending in 1995. The center's focus is research on modern telematic and informatic applications such as multimedia, personal digital assistants, virtual reality, desktop videoconferencing from a consumer behavior and future market adoption perspective. He was Chief Process Engineer for Pacific Bell from 1991 to 1994 where he was responsible for helping to guide the company through its many reengineering initiatives. Prior to joining Pacific Bell he served for nine years as an adjunct professor and associate director for two research centers (Center for Operations Management and Center for Telecommunications Management) at the

University of Southern California business school.

Tim Huckvale is a Principal Consultant at Praxis, the Software Engineering Company of Touche Ross Management Consultants. He has twenty-five years' experience in the computer industry, including software development, project and line management. He now specialises in process modelling and workflow analysis and has worked with clients in the pharmaceutical, insurance, financial and transport industries to model, analyse, design and improve their business processes. He contributes to the development of STRIM, Praxis' own.

'Jon (Sean) Jasperson is a Ph.D. student at Florida State University. He holds a bachelor's degree in accounting and a Masters in Information Systems from BYU.

Jerry Julian earned his Bachelor's degree in Industrial Engineering from the School of Engineering & Applied Science at Columbia University. He also received an M.B.A. in General Management from the Kenan-Flagler Business School at the University of North Carolina in Chapel Hill.   Mr. Julian is Certified in Production & Inventory Management (CPIM) by the American Production and Inventory Control Society (APICS). He has worked with organizations to improve performance by focusing on business process improvement efforts that deliver both short- and long-term operating results. He has particular expertise in the strategic application of information technology as an enabler of organization change, improved resource productivity, and market responsiveness. His work spans a number of industries including telecommunications, steel distribution, airline maintenance, electronic equipment manufacturing, and gas and electric utilities. Prior to joining Rath & Strong, Mr. Julian worked as a senior consultant for a large systems integration consulting firm. In this role, he helped clients to formulate information strategies, design hardware and software architectures, and implement information systems based on a range of technologies from large mainframe solutions to workstation-based solutions.

Valery Kanevsky is an internationally recognized authority on complexity theory and its applications to business process reengineering and the stock market. He has published extensively on the applications of complexity theory, mathematical modelling to solve a wide variety of scientific and practical problems. He won the Soviet Union's Olympics of Math competition twice. He joined Pacific Bell in 1992 and serves as its lead member of technical staff for statistical and mathematical problem solving. Since joining Pacific Bell, he has (with Tom Housel) applied his expertise to developing the breakthrough return on investment in process methodology to quantify the value added by large reengineering interventions which utilize information technology (i.e., expert systems, databases, employee performance management and evaluation systems). He has also solved a number of company problems (e.g., data network queuing, service office sizing, maintenance repair person scheduling, predicting network breakdowns) that required the building and implementation of formal mathematical models. Prior to joining Pacific Bell, Dr. Kanevsky was an adjunct professor at San Jose State University and a full professor at several prestigious Russian universities.

Mathew J. Klempa is a consultant in the application of computer information systems. He previously has taught at the University of Southern California and the California State University.   He holds a B.S. in Mathematics/Economics from Allegheny College, M.S. degree in Management Science, M.B.A. degree in International Business, and Ph.D. degree in Business Administration from the University of Southern California.   His doctoral majors were Decision Support Systems and Corporate Policy and Strategy. He was formerly a corporate planning officer for a major bank holding company, systems analyst at IBM and operations research analyst at McDonnell-Douglas. His professional affiliations include the Information Resources Management Association, DIGIT - Diffusion Interest Group in Information Technology, Academy of Management, INFORMS, and the Decision Sciences Institute. His research interests include business process reengineering; business process change; organization impacts of information technology; the interaction among information technology and organizational structures, control mechanisms, culture, learning, work processes, and performance; information technology diffusion; and cognitive and individual differences in DSS use. E-mail: mklempa@delphi.com.

Manoj K. Malhotra is an Assistant Professor of Management Science at the University of South Carolina, Columbia. He earned his Ph.D., M.A., and M.S. from The Ohio State University, and B'Tech from I.I.T. Kanpur, India. His teaching and research interests include production planning and control in multistage production systems, shop floor control, service sector scheduling, business process reengineering, and manufacturing/operations strategy. He has published several papers on these and related issues in Decision Sciences, European Journal of Operational Research, International Journal of Production Research, OMEGA, and Production and Operations Management Journal. Dr. Malhotra is a member of The Institute of Management Science (TIMS), the Decision Sciences Institute (DSI), Production and Operations Management Society (POMS), and American Production and Inventory Control Society (APICS).

Donald A. Marchand is professor of information management and strategy at IMD— International Institute for Management Development—in Lausanne Switzerland. Professor Marchand's research interests focus on the strategic role of information management in enterprise transformation and business process redesign, building core and distinctive competencies in I/T, strategic intent benchmarking and performance measurement of IS in the business. He is the author of four books and over 80 articles, book chapters, cases, monographs and reports on information management strategies in business and government. From July, 1987 to June, 1994, Professor Marchand was Dean of the School of Information Studies at Syracuse University. In his earlier career, he founded and directed the Institute for Information Management, Technology and Policy in the College of Business Administration at the University of South Carolina where he taught the IS management course in the Master's in International Business Program.

M. Lynne Markus (B.S. Industrial Engineering, University of Pittsburgh; Ph.D. Organizational Behavior, Case Western Reserve University) is Professor of Information Science, the Peter F. Drucker Graduate Management Center at The Claremont Graduate School, and Consultant to The RAND Corporation. Her research focuses on the role of information technology in organizational performance and change. She also specializes in the implementation of information systems, electronic communication media, and group support technologies. Prior to joining the faculty at CGS, Dr. Markus taught at the John E. Anderson Graduate School of Management at UCLA and the Alfred P. Sloan School of Management at MIT and consulted with Arthur D. Little, Inc. Dr. Markus is the author of Systems in Organizations: Bugs and Features and has contributed articles to Organization Science, The Information Society, Information Technology and People, Management Science, Communication Research, Communications of the ACM, ACM Transactions on Information Systems, Management Information Systems Quarterly, and Interfaces. She is currently a member of the editorial boards of Information Systems Research, The Journal of Strategic Information Systems and Organization Science. Markus is The Drucker Center's 1994-95 Deloitte & Touche Research Fellow. In 1992 and 1994, Markus served as Visiting Scientist at the Nanyang Technological University in Singapore. Dr. Markus has recently completed a contract from the Advanced Practices Council of the Society for Information Management to study effective change management practices in reengineering projects. In prior years, Markus was awarded research grants and contracts from the National Science Foundation and the Office of Technology Assessment (US Congress). Markus consults on issues of organizational redesign, information systems implementation, and the management of information technology.

Richard J. Mayer received his Bachelor of Science in Mathematics/Physics from Purdue University in 1974, and received a Master of Science in Industrial Engineering from Purdue University in 1977. In 1988, Dr. Mayer received a Ph.D. in Industrial Engineering from Texas A&M University. Until 1984, Dr. Mayer was Project Manager, Integrated Computer Aided Manufacturing (ICAM), for the Manufacturing Technology Division, Wright-Patterson AFB, OH. From the years 1984 to 1989, Dr. Mayer was Project Manager and Principal Investigator on thirty-nine funded research efforts in the Knowledge Based Systems Laboratory and he has been Assistant Professor and Director at the Laboratory since 1989. He founded Knowledge Based Systems, Inc. in 1988 and has received funding for applications in engineering design assistance, systems analysis, and concurrent engineering methods and tools. His areas of expertise include large scale information integration of logistical engineering and manufacturing information, artificial intelligence (AI) application to manufacturing, knowledge engineering tool and method development, AI application to design and engineering, AI application to defense-related embedded software, and AI applications to agriculture.

James D. McKeen is an Associate Professor at the School of Business, Queen's University at Kingston, Canada and the Director of the Queen's Research Consortium for Management of Technology. He received his Ph.D in Business Administration from the University of Minnesota in 1981. Dr. McKeen serves as the MIS area editor for the Canadian Journal of Administrative Sciences and as a feature columnist for Ernst & Young's IT Management Issues. His research interests include methods of user participation, the design and implementation of application systems, and strategies for selecting application systems in organizations. Most recently, he is involved in a large program of research to determine the value of information technology. Dr. McKeen's research has been published in many journals including the MIS Quarterly, the Journal of Systems and Software, Information and Management, Communications of the ACM, Computers and Education, OMEGA, Canadian Journal of Administrative Sciences, Strategic Information Technology Management: Perspectives on Organizational Growth and Competitive Advantage, and Database. He is currently co–authoring a book on IT management issues with Heather Smith.

Arlyn J. Melcher is Professor and Chair of the Management Department at Southern Illinois University. He was Professor of Administrative Sciences at Kent State University from 1961 to 1989. His publications include four books on organizational theory, articles on leadership, organization analysis, strategy formulation, and theory building methodology and current projects include books on continuous improvement developing a typology of production systems and on organizational systems. Dr. Melcher is a consultant on organizational design and strategy formulation for large organizations.

Nancy Paule Melone is Associate Professor of Management in the Charles H. Lundquist School of Business at the University of Oregon. She received an MBA and Ph.D. in Management Information Systems (MIS) from the Carlson School of Management at the University of Minnesota, where she was affiliated also with the Center for Human Learning in the Psychology Department. She holds graduate degrees from the University of Iowa in Information Science and in Industrial and Labor Relations. Her industrial experience includes strategy and research positions at Honeywell and at First Bank System's First Computer Corporation and First Bank Minneapolis. Dr. Melone's research is interdisciplinary, spanning such areas as attitudes and behaviors toward technology, group and individual decision processes in mediated and nonmediated environments, decision authority and information flows in high-risk, high-reliability organizations and more recently professionalism in software engineering. Her work has appeared in such journals as Management Science, Organization Science, Organizational Behavior and Human Decision Processes, Journal of Systems and Software, Systems Objectives and Solutions, and Journal of Health and Social Behavior. She currently serves on the editorial board of Technology Studies, a multi-disciplinary journal with open peer commentaries.

R. Ryan Nelson is an Associate Professor and the Director of the Center for the Management of Information Technology (CMIT) at the McIntire School of Commerce of the University of Virginia. He received his Ph.D. in business administration from the University of Georgia in 1985 and spent five years on the faculty of the University of Houston before joining UVa. His research has been published in such journals as the MIS Quarterly, Journal of Management Information Systems, Information & Management, International Information Systems, Data Base, and Datamation. In addition, Dr. Nelson recently edited a book entitled End–User Computing: Concepts, Issues & Applications, which was published by John Wiley & Sons.

Victoria L. Mitchell received a PhD in Management Information Systems from Florida State University in 1993. Prior to that time she spent 10 years in the health care industry as a registered nurse and health services consultant. She is currently an assistant professor at North Carolina State University investigating IT infrastructure issues related to business process redesign.

Margaret O'Hara is a doctoral candidate in the Department of Management at the University of Georiga. Her area of specialization is management information systems. Prior to entering the Ph.D. program, she was director of MIS for a regional transportation firm in the Southeast. Her research interests include the relationship between information technology and organizational change; organization development and transformation; and new/emerging technologies, specifically client/server computing. Her dissertation focuses on the relationship between managerial intentions and capabilities in selecting and implementing new information technology. She has presented lectures on the use of information technology for competitive advantage and and has received a grant from the OD Network to study the use of Group Support Systems in organization development efforts.

Michael K. Painter received a Bachelor's degree in Mechanical Engineering from Utah State University in 1985. Mr. Painter has over seven years of increasingly responsible experience as a leader, manager, and creator of United States Air Force (USAF) advanced technology development and technology application activities. He has won national recognition as an expert in systems integration. He is skilled in technology planning and implementation, product development, and innovative problem solving. Mr. Painter is currently a Senior Systems Analyst at Knowledge Based Systems, Inc.

Juha Parnisto is a researcher and doctoral student at Turku School of Economics and Business Administration, which awarded him an M.Sc. in economics (information systems science) in 1992. He also studies at a graduate school, Turku Centre for Computer Science. His main professional interests are in research into organizational design and change, group systems, and the effectiveness of information technology use. He is currently working on a project with ICL, a major European software manufacturer, the aim of which is to develop methods for effective group technology adoption for large organizations.

Lee Tom Perry is a Professor of Strategy and Organizational Behavior at BYU's Marriott School of Management. He holds a Ph.D. in Adminstrative Sciences from Yale University and has been a member of the faculty of the Krannert School of Management, Purdue University and the College of Business Administration, The Pennsylvania State University. He has written extensively about organizational decline, mergers and acquisitions, radical product innovation, and competitive business strategies.

Arun Rai is an Assistant Professor of Management Information Systems in the Department of Management and a faculty associate for the Pontikes Center for the

Management of Information at Southern Illinois University at Carbondale. His primary research interests include implementation of advanced information technologies, business process reengineering, software engineering, and intelligent support systems. He is currently leading a major reengineering project at the enterprise level for a fund-raising organization.

Daniel Robey is Professor of Information Systems at Florida International University. He earned his doctorate in 1973 from Kent State University and has served on the faculties of The University of Pittsburgh, Marquette University, Gannon University, and the Copenhagen School of Economics and Business Administration. Professor Robey's research deals with the consequences of information systems in organizations and the processes of system development and implementation. This research includes empirical examinations of information systems development work and of the effects of a wide range of technologies on organizational structure and patterns of work. It also includes the development of theoretical approaches to explaining the development and consequences of information technology in organizations.

Aleda V. Roth is an Associate Professor at Kenan-Flagler Business School of the University of North Carolina at Chapel Hill. She holds a doctorate degree in operations management from The Ohio State University, as well as a master's degree in biostatistics from the University of North Carolina at Chapel Hill. Dr. Roth has acted as a consultant to numerous large companies including Baxter International, Glaxo, Smith & Nephew, Northern Telecom, Johnson and Johnson, Bank of Boston, Raytheon, General Electric, Deloitte-Touche, IBM, Bank Administration Institute, John Hancock, Black & Decker, Duke University Medical Center, and other Federal State and private agencies. Dr. Roth is a member of the prestigious U.S. Quality Council-II and the Quality Management Center of the Conference Board. She also serves on the Board of Directors of the Operations Management Association, and is an Associate Editor of the Journal of Operations Management and Decision Sciences. At UNC, she is the principal investigator of the Cato Center's Global Business Process Reengineering Project and the Knowledge Factory Research. Dr. Roth's current research interests reside in the empirical and theoretical development of competitive capabilities, core competencies, and contextual factors associated with operations strategy. Her research addresses strategic operations decisions, including those on total quality management, business process reengineering, knowledge workers, information and process technology development, and their linkages to superior performance and organizational learning. She has written books on world class manufacturing, banking, and health care, and her published articles have appeared in Management Science, Journal of Operations Management, Journal of Production and Operations Management, International Journal of Technology Management, Benchmarking for Quality and Technology Management, Business Horizons, Decision Sciences, International Journal of Operations and Production Management, IEEE Engineering Management Review, Operations Management Review, and others.

Rajiv Sabherwal is an Associate Professor in the Department of Decision Sciences and Information Systems at Florida International University. He earned a Ph.D. in Information Systems from the University of Pittsburgh in 1989 and a Post Graduate Diploma in Management from Indian Institute of Management, Calcutta, in 1983. Dr. Sabherwal has authored numerous articles, which have appeared in Decision Sciences, European Journal of Information Systems, Information and Management, Journal of High Technology Management Research, Journal of Information Systems, Journal of Strategic Information Systems, Organization Science, and other journals. His research interests include strategic utilization of information technology, information systems planning and decision making, behavioral aspects of information systems development, and global information systems.

Edgar H. Sibley is university professor and eminent scholar in the Department of Information and Software Systems Engineering and The Institute for Public Policy at

George Mason University in Fairfax, Virginia. He has been very active in all areas of large scale information systems design, especially matters dependent on database management, data modeling, and economic issues. He has recently been working on the problems and methods in reengineering and otherwise improving the business processes in industry and the DoD. This has recently been extended into some DoD and industrial enterprise efforts, such as the CALS Shared Resource Center activities and the textile industry. Over 100 of his articles have been published and for the past five years, he has been a consultant at the Institute for Defense Analyses. He has also acted as an expert witness for three law firms and is working with the Argonne National Laboratory and the Batelle Memorial Institute.

Gill Smith is currently an executive with OLM Systems, with the role of coordinating for clients the range of management and information systems skills needed to deliver strategic projects. She is also Editor of Management Issues in Social Care. Previously she was a strategy and IS consultant with Oracle UK, dealing with clients in a variety of industries including banking, pharmaceuticals, local government, manufacturing and the National Health Service. She maintains an interest in the human aspects of computer-based systems, and uses both analytical and creative approaches to explore what organizations wish to achieve from their use of information-based technologies. She has published a number of papers on strategy and information systems.

Heather A. Smith is a Research Associate at the School of Business, Queen's University. She has an M.A. from Queen's University and has worked in and researched business and non–profit organizations for twenty years. Her interests include: the impact of information technology on organizations, identification of best management practices, and effective management of information technology. Currently, she is co–facilitator of Queen's Management Forums, and is conducting a large research program to develop organizational benchmarks that will enable improved analysis of productivity in the service sector. In addition, she is Executive Director of Performers for Literacy, a national charity, director of WATAP Films, and founding director of the Malignant Hyperthermia Association. Ms. Smith has published articles in The Journal of Information Technology Management, The Canadian Journal of Administrative Sciences, Information & Management, Canadian Data Systems, and Strategic Information Technology Management: Perspectives on Organizational Growth and Competitive Advantage.

Henk G. Sol is chaired professor of Systems Engineering at the Delft University of Technology. He is dean of the School of Systems Engineering, Policy Analysis and Management and responsible for the design and implementation of the curriculum and the research programme. He organized numerous international conferences and workshops and gave a great many invited presentations. He is a member of the editorial board of various journals in the field. He chairs the IFIP Working Group W.G. 8.3 'Decision Support Systems'. He is member of IFIP TC 8, W.G. 8.1, 8.2, 8.4 and various other professional organizations. He received the IFIP Outstanding Service Award as well as the IFIP Silver Core. He has acted as a management consultant for a large range of national and international organizations since 1972. He is chairman/ member of the Board of Directors of several companies. At the moment, his research interests lie mainly in designing information-intensive, innovative organizations.

Michael Stanford worked on this chapter while he was a research associate working on the Manufacturing 2000 research project at the International Institute for Management Development (IMD) in Lausanne, Switzerland. During his three years on the project, he developed case studies on a number of topical management issues, including: the challenges of aligning strategy, organizational structures and core competencies with changing market demands; identifying and aligning distinctive copetencies according to market discontinuities; implementing dramatic cultural change; sustaining a far-reaching organizational and cultural change program; and creating a distinctive competence is supply chain management. One of the cases, "CarnaudMetalbox: The Sutton Factory-Sustaining Success", won the 1993 European Foundation for Management Development Case Writing Award in the category Innovations in Organizational Structures and Processes. Prior to joining IMD, Michael completed his MBA at the University of Western Ontario, and worked as a sales and marketing manager in the retail industry.

James T.C. Teng is Associate Professor of MIS in the Management Science Department of the College of Business Administration at the University of South Carolina. Dr. Teng has also held teaching and research positions at several universities including most recently, the University of Pittsburgh. He has written extensively on numerous IS subjects and recently has focused his research attention on the business process redesign where he has published on this topic in such journals as California Management Review, Omega, Long-Planning, and IEEE Transactions in Engineering Management. He has a Ph.D. in MIS for the University of Minnesota.

Jeroen W. van Meel is research associate of the School of Systems Engineering, Policy Analysis and Management of Delft University of Technology, the Netherlands. He received a Master's Degree in Computer Science from Delft University of Technology. His Ph.D. thesis investigates the possibilities of 'dynamic modelling' to support Business Engineering. He has acted as a free-lance management consultant since 1988. His current research focuses on the possibilities of combining 'hard' system techniques like simulation and experimental design with 'soft' system methodologies like qualitative analysis and action research. He has published in proceedings of international conferences on information systems, simulation, and business engineering.

Richard Watson is an Associate Professor and Graduate Coordinator in the Department of Management at the University of Georgia. He received his Ph.D. in MIS from the University of Minnesota in 1987. His academic honors include a Fulbright Award (1984-87). Prior to joining the University of Georgia in 1989, he was Principal Lecturer and Head of Information Systems at the School of Business, Edith Cowan University, Perth, Western Australia. His publications include articles in MIS Quarterly, Communications of the ACM, and Decision Support Systems. He edited Computer Augmented Teamwork: A Guided Tour with Robert Bostrom and Susan Kinney and is currently writing Data Management: An Organizational Perspective. He has had research grants to investigate Group Support Systems, and was recently invited to be an associate editor of MIS Quarterly. He is investigating how the journal can use the Internet. He coordinates a research project involving scholars in Singapore and Finland, and has given invited seminars on all continents except Antarctica.

Leslie Willcocks is Fellow in Information Management at Templeton College, University Lecturer in Management Studies at Oxford University, and Editor of the Journal of Information Technology. He worked for ten years in accountancy, management consultancy and training, for Touche Ross and several smaller firms. Co-authored publications include Computerising Work (Paradigm, 1987); Systems Analysis, Systems Design (Alfred Waller, 1994), Information Management (Chapman and Hall, 1994) and The Business Guide to IT Outsourcing (Business Intelligence, 1994). He has published numerous academic papers, on the above themes and on IS evaluation and human and organizational issues. Additionally he has been consultant, and produced a number of research reports, for major corporations and government.

Robert Zeibig is a Principal in Nolan, Norton & Co., an information technology firm of KPMG Peat Marwick. He is located in the Boston, Massachusetts headquarters office. His work is focused on business transformation and strategies that enhance organizational performance through information technology. Mr. Zeibig has been involved with the technical, managerial, and strategic aspects of information technology for over nineteen years in industry and as a consultant. He has consulted to senior management in leading organizations in the manufacturing, telecommunications, retail, and financial services industries, as well as in the public sector. His clients include Xerox, American Airlines, The Travelers, IBM, Merrill Lynch, and Dow Chemical. Mr. Zeibig publishes and speaks frequently on issues of business transformation through reengineering and information technology.

Robert Zmud is Professor and Thomas L. Williams, Jr., Eminent Scholar in Management Information Systems in the Information and Management Science Department at the College of Business, Florida State University. He is Editor-in-Chief of MIS Quarterly and the Associate Editor on several leading journals. His current research interests focus on the impact of information technology in facilitating a variety of organizational behaviors and on organizational efforts involved with planning, managing, and diffusing information technology. Both his PhD (University of Arizone) and his S.M. (MIT) are in management.

Index